Clermont, B

The Professed Cook

ISBN: 978-1-948837-06-4

This classic reprint was produced from digital files in the Google Books digital collection, which may be found at http://www.books.google.com. The artwork used on the cover is from Wikimedia Commons and remains in the public domain. Omissions and/or errors in this book are due to either the physical condition of the original book or due to the scanning process by Google or its agents.

This edition of B. Clermont's **The Professed Cook** was originally translated from *Les Soupers de la Cour* and published in 1769 (London).

Townsends
PO Box 415, Pierceton, IN 46562
www.Townsends.us

THE PROFESSED COOK:

Or the MODERN ART of
Cookery, Paſtry, and *Confectionary,*

Made PLAIN and EASY.

Conſiſting of the moſt approved Methods in the
FRENCH as well as ENGLISH COOKERY.

In which the French Names of all the different Diſhes are given and explained, whereby every Bill of Fare becomes intelligible and familiar.

CONTAINING

I. Of Soups, Gravy, Cullis and Broths
II. Of Sauces
III. The different Ways of Dreſſing Beef, Veal, Mutton, Pork, Lamb, &c.
IV. Of Firſt Courſe Diſhes
V. Of Dreſſing Poultry
VI. Of Veniſon
VII. Of Game of all Sorts
VIII. Of Ragouts, Collops and Fries
IX. Of Dreſſing all Kinds of Fiſh
X. Of Paſtry of different Kinds
XI. Of Entremets, or Laſt Courſe Diſhes
XII. Of Omelets
XIII. Paſtes of different Sorts
XIV. Dried Conſerves
XV. Cakes, Wafers and Biſcuits
XVI. Of Almonds and Piſtachias made in different Ways
XVII. Marmalades
XVIII. Jellies
XIX. Liquid and Dried Sweetmeats
XX. Syrups and Brandy Fruits
XXI. Ices, Ice Creams and Ice Fruits
XXII. Ratafias, and other Cordials, &c. &c.

Tranſlated from *Les Soupers de la Cour*; with the Addition of the beſt Receipts which have ever appear'd in the *French* Language.

And adapted to the *London Markets* by the EDITOR, who has been many Years Clerk of the Kitchen in ſome of the firſt Families in this Kingdom.

THE SECOND EDITION.

LONDON:
Printed for R. DAVIS, in *Piccadilly*; and T. CASLON, oppoſite *Stationers-Hall.* MDCCLXIX.

THE TRANSLATOR's APOLOGY.

THIS Book, whose Translation I here presume to offer to the Public in general, is the last Production upon French *Cookery*, printed in Paris, by the King's Privilege granted for a certain Term of Years, intitled, *Les Soupers de la Cour*. I shall not pretend to make any further Apology for the Title of *Supper*, than that the French are, in general, more elegant in their Suppers than Dinners. I had it brought over for my own Help and Instruction, as a Clerk of the Kitchen; and as I found it of great Use, I thought that a Translation would be both agreeable and useful to many Gentlemen and Ladies, and others; as it contains the far greater Number of the most approved and newest Receipts in Cookery, Pastry, and Confectionary of the present Time and Practice: and as Bills of Fare are mostly made in French, I also thought it very necessary and of particular great Use, to retain all the French Names and Appellations, giving at the same Time a literal Translation, or the Meaning from whence derived; by which I hope to be allowed the Expreſſion of reconciling the Engliſh *Maitre d'Hotel* to the French Cook. Although it may (with Propriety) be ſaid that great Numbers of thoſe Receipts were known by the ſame Names Years ago, I am very ſenſible of the Truth thereof; but I am alſo, that the Performing is very different, and of much better and genteeler Taſte, than is to be found in any Books treating on Cookery, &c. having examined many prior to this, as *La Cuiſine Royale*, *Le Maitre d'Hotel Cuiſinier*, and *Les dons de Comus*; of which this Book may be called the *Eſſence*, with Improvements. Gentlemen and Ladies are liable to Deception, in ſeeing their Bills of Fare, not caring to inquire into the particular Merit of every Diſh, which often takes its Name from the Inventor, or the Perſon of Conſequence whoſe Palate it pleaſed firſt, and under a pompous Name often proves frivolous in the Execution. By referring to the different Kinds of Meat propoſed, every body may eaſily find out any particular Diſh, or what may be moſt agreeable to furniſh their Tables with. It is more particularly uſeful to Engliſh Cooks, Houſe-keepers, and every one employed in providing and making Bills of Fare, who have not had Opportunity of being acquainted with French *Cookery*. When Dinners or Suppers are to be dreſſed by Cooks hired for the Time, they are moſtly allowed to make the Bill of Fare: this Book will greatly aſſiſt the Houſe-ſervant, how to provide the proper Neceſſaries for the Execution of it; the Maſter will find what Proviſions are to be allowed, and the Servants will receive great Aſſiſtance for the Performance of their Duty in each Station:

APOLOGY.

Station: Clerks of the Kitchen, whose Duty it is to make Bills of Fare, and to provide accordingly, will also find it of very great Use; as, by this Means, Concord and Unanimity will reign between Cook and Provider, which, if either is deficient in his Business, often creates disagreeable Altercations to Masters and Mistresses, by Changes and other Inconveniences more to be attended to. I have myself, as well as many others, been Witness of the Diffidence of English Cooks, in looking at Bills of Fare, of which they had probably executed the whole several Times, only under different Denominations. This has been my greatest Inducement, to retain all French Names as in the Original, and to render their Meanings in English as concisely as I was able; although many which go by certain Appellations, which cannot be rendered in English with any tolerable Interpretation (at least by me), being mostly adopted from proper Names, or Titles; they soon will become familiar to every common Understanding, being mostly adopted in the English Language already, at least in Terms of Cookery and Millinery, &c. The French Cook (how far this may please him) will lose nothing by the Perusal, as very few are thoroughly acquainted with the whole, and will help the Memory to great Advantage: there is still Room in Abundance for those who have Understanding, and Inclination for Improvement. To the Complete *Cookery*, the Author has also added Confectionary; in which I have been more particularly exact, as knowing it to be very much wanted amongst English Servants. Ladies who delight in the *profitable* Amuse-

APOLOGY.

ment of making their own Sweet-meats, and House-keepers, whose Business it is to do in most Families in England, will find it of very great Utility, not only for the Number of different Receipts, but the particular Methods of preparing the Sugar, by which they will save the Trouble and Expence of renewing their Summer's Work in Winter, as the Sugar being prepared according to the Method laid down in this Book, will keep the Sweet-meats of any Kind in their proper Colours and Goodness for Years.

This Book was published in four small Volumes. I thought it too full of Words and Repetitions, and that the Sense of the Author could be explained, without all the *Volubility* of the French Language, which I have (as much as I was capable) supplied with the *Expressiveness* of the English; at the same Time doing all the Justice in my Power to the Original, not forgetting the Public, (my only Aim to please), as presuming it for the better in a Work of this Kind. For that Reason I have passed over few Receipts of no Consequence, and have taken a few Liberties with the Original; but that only, where Self-conviction, Remarks, and good Intelligences have prevailed, since my first Inclination to a Translation; and made References, by way of Abridgment, by which I was enabled to reduce the Work about one-fourth. The Author thought engraved Tables of Bills of Fare unnecessary, but gave few without; and I do further presume to say, that either are absolutely needless, as a fertile Imagination, and a

LARDER

APOLOGY.

LARDER provided accordingly, is the only Rule that can be given for furnishing a Table properly, considering the Company, and the Size of the Dishes which are to be used: I have upon that same (I hope) reasonable Supposition left them out: every Body can judge that the Book contains the whole, without being particularly picked out.

I beg the Candour of the Public will excuse the Incorrectness of the Language and Diction, as it is not a Book of Erudition for the Library of the great. My Inabilites, and Situation in Life, as an actual Servant, will, I trust, plead my Apology, and hope for my Presumption, as a Foreigner, that it will be found easy to all common Understandings, for whose peculiar Service it is intended. And for a very *obvious* Reason, I wish I could flatter myself (as the Author begins his Advertisement), that this Work would excite the Curiosity of many People.

N. B. As I could not follow the Original, in giving the different Productions according to each Season in the London Markets, as every Country produces many Articles peculiar to itself, and considering the Difference of Climates, which either forward or retard Numbers of Articles for this very Purpose; not relying absolutely on my own Knowledge, in regard to each Article, while in full Season, I applied to three Tradesmen, all eminent in their Profession, one for *Fish*, one for *Poultries* in general, and one for the Productions of *Gardening*, to which Gentlemen I am particularly thankful for their ready Compliance, equally for myself, as for all that may hereafter make Use of this Translation, as a *Guide* to Market.

The whole is here annexed together, and *Poultries* in general again by itself, in Vol. II. under roast Articles; that the Produce of each Season for Roast, may be more readily found out; few Observations will be found in the Progress of the Work, to each different Sort of Aliments, contained in it, with Notes and Remarks by the Translator, according as they occurred, necessary by way of Explanation. Should I have the Happiness of meeting with the Approbation of the Public, the Sense of my Friends, and all Persons versed in English Cookery, shall be noticed with that particular Regard I owe to this Country.

ERRATA.

IN THE CONTENTS.

Cooling Broth	*ib.*	read	4
A Family Cullis	8	read	9
Queen Cullis meager	13	read	12
Olio, or Turine of different Manners	14	read	13

IN THE BOOK.

Page 25. *Line* 28. Lazagne Soop Description, rectified in Italian Paste Article, Vol. II.
    70.   22. *before* Fillet *delete* a.
    192.   8. *for* Timbals *read* Tumbals.
In several Pages, for Leafs *read* Leaves.

THE AUTHOR's ADVERTISEMENT.

I AM perſuaded that this Work will excite the Curioſity of many People, more particularly Cooks, who take Delight in the *Art* of *Cookery* and its Improvements; it is thoſe in whoſe Approbation I ſhall glory. I ſcorn little Artiſts of ſmall Knowledge, and more confined Notions, whoſe Pretenſion to merit affects to deſpiſe all Sorts of Works proper for their Inſtruction. Some are even ſo ridiculous, that they would be very much aſhamed, were they ſeen looking in a Book which treats of their Art; they would think it a Diſhonour to be thought to have had recourſe to a printed Book of any Inſtructions. Don't they perceive that they ſhew abſurd Preſumption, and an invincible Obſtacle to their Improvement, or a Narrowneſs of Underſtanding which demonſtrates their Incapacity?

Shall we ſee a Phyſician, a Lawyer, an Architect, &c. aſhamed to conſult Works which treat of their Profeſſion? Did any ever think that Reading would hurt their Reputation, or undervalue their Underſtanding? The *Art of Cookery* has (like all others) its Rules and Principles: if Practice has Advantages, Theory has equally its own; it is only the Union of both which can perfect, and both may almoſt equally be taught in Books. Either the Workman has Capacity, Taſte, and a fertile Imagination,

ADVERTISEMENT.

gination, or may be unprovided of all. This laſt will never work with Succeſs, as it is only Length of Practice which can form him, incapable of himſelf. Theory is neceſſary; then he cannot do better than to follow thoſe Inſtructions laid down (as a Repoſitory) in Books of Approbation. Reading is no leſs neceſſary to the firſt to attain to Perfection, as it will furniſh him with Ideas and Combinations, which without would never occur to his Thoughts. I know of what Importance a quick Apprehenſion, and (if I may be allowed the Expreſſion) that Dexterity of *handy Work* ſo neceſſary in the Laboratory of a thorough Artiſt. It is not to be learned in Books, nor to be attained without a deal of Practice; but when once poſſeſſed of good Notions, nothing is more eaſy than to follow and improve the Proceedings laid down in good Books; it is then above all, as has been ſaid of other Arts, that Theory is anticipated by Practice, and the Way to each other is extremely ſhort and eaſy. It is to be wiſhed (undoubtedly) that Artiſts ſhould be more verſed in the Theory, than they commonly are; of what great Uſe it would be to be thoroughly acquainted with the different Qualities of thoſe Aliments they are to prepare. If they had examined and ſtudied the Nature of the different Flavours, their Differences often difficult to find, and the Reſult of their Mixtures; then the Hand, guided with Prudence, would often regulate their Differences with more Equality, and would form Combinations more prudent and ſucceſsful, would give to all Preparations more Harmony and Propriety, Taſte and Health would equally participate abundantly.

There

ADVERTISEMENT.

There are other Works, wherein to find sufficient Instructions, which are necessary for ancient Cookery; but I rely upon this to show the Improvements and Progress which have been made in the *Art* of *Cookery* in our Days. Some excelling Artists have happily invented new Dishes, of which, it is to be feared, the Composition would have remained unknown to great Numbers, although their Merit ought to be preserved. I do not doubt, but several will here find the Work of their own Invention; but I am certain they will not envy in others, so necessary a Knowledge to the Art they profess: they will instruct through my Organs, and the principal Honour will reflect on them; it will be by this Means, that our Tables will abound with more Variety, Taste, and Gentility: the Satisfaction will be to them, if the Work I now publish, will induce Men of Parts to follow their Steps; and I shall have the Pleasure to attain the End I propose. In my Application to this reformed Cookery, I could not but take notice of the old, as being its Foundation; they are too near allied to each other to be separated. The same Reason has induced me to join to *Cookery*, that of *Pastry* and *Confectionary*. They are of mutual Help to each other, as the first cannot do without the second, nor properly both without the last; as great Numbers of Dishes belong to Confectionary, which would be impracticable to such as should be unacquainted with the Principles and Practice of that Art.

Instructions upon the different Productions which Nature affords in regard to Aliments, in the four Seasons of the Year, divided into four Parts.

DU PRINTEMS. OF SPRING.

THE Spring is the first and most promising Season of the Year, although the most confined in its Productions, in regard to Poultry, Fruits, and Gardenings; it comprehends March, April, and May. The London Markets are constantly well supplied with Butcher's-meat, through the whole Year. I shall take no further Notice of these Articles, than that London has the Advantage of *Paris*, in the Articles of Veal and Lamb, which are to be had in London all the Year; an Advantage to Entertainments, which the French have not. To render this in the easiest Manner I am able, I shall take particular Notice of Monthly Productions of each Kind, under their different Sorts, and give the Preference to *Fish*, in the Course of the four Seasons. *March* produces, Salmon, Cod, Haddocks, Whitings, Smelts, Carps, Tench, Perch, Pike, Eels, Gudgeons, Lobsters, Crabs, Craw-fish, potted Lampreys, pickled Sturgeon, Salt-fish, Oysters, John-dorey, by chance, fresh Sturgeon, and Turbots, the same with Plaice, Flounders, Herrings, Mussels, and Cockles at Times. *April* continues much the same, with the Addition of Soals, Scate, Turbots, the latter End, Mackerels, Trouts, fresh Sturgeon, pretty common, Thames Salmon, (commonly called Crimp-Salmon). *May*, Thames Salmon, plenty, Turbots, and Uxbridge Trouts, Scate, Maids, Soals, red and gray Mullets, Mackerels, Flounders, Smelts, from the Beginning of the Month; Eels, Lobsters, Prawns, Craw-fish, and fresh Sturgeon at Times. *Poultry:* The beginning of this Season produces Ducklings, Turkey-polts, green Geese, wild and tame Pigeons, and Squabs ditto, Quails, wild Rabbits, Guinea Fowls, Pea-Fowls, Capons, Pullets with Eggs, Pullards, Spring-fowls, Chickens, Bustards, Cock's-combs, fat Livers, Eggs, and Stones, Turky Pinions, Leverets, Plover's Eggs. N. B. That this Month also produces wild Ducks, Easterlings, Widgeons, Teals, Dunbirds, but all going out of Season. *In fruits and*

PRODUCTIONS of the SEASONS.

Garden-stuff: Fruits remaining the begining of this Season, are Golden Pippin, Nonpareil Apples, Pearmain ditto, Chesnuts, Medlers, dried Apples, St. Germain Pears, and Winter Chaumontelle Royal, Lemons and Oranges, Stone Pippins, for Kitchen Use, Savoys, Sprouts, white and red Cabbages, Carrots, Parsneps, Potatoes, small Lettuces, white Endives, Sellery, large and small Onions, Cardoons, Asparagus, almost all the Year between natural and forced; all Sorts of sweet Herbs, either green or dried, Sage, Horse-radish all the Year, Bed-mushrooms much the same, Water-cresses, Beet-roots, small Salleting, Spanish Onions, Sorrel, Charvil, Leeks, Spinages, Jerusalem Artichokes, Parsley, and Parsley-roots, all the Year, except the Winter is extremely severe; many forced Articles of Gardening are produced in this Season, as Cucumbers, Peas, Beans, &c. I shall take no further Notice of these Things, as the Purchase of them is very high, and the Things are of small Value in regard to their Goodness. Pomegranate to be had in this Season. *April,* golden Pippins, Nonpareils continue good; also Winter Bon-chretien, and Colmar Pear, China and Seville Oranges, the Kentish-stone Pippins, and Non-such Apples for Kitchen-use, and much the same Sorts of Garden-stuffs, with white and purple Brocoli, Asparagus, and young Radishes, green Plants, small Salleting; all Sorts of green, sweet, and cooling Herbs. *May,* most of the Winter-greens scarce, but produces fresh Provisions, both for Desserts and Cookery; as first, towards the End, early Duke Cherries, Scarlet and Wood-strawberries, and for Kitchen-use, green Peas, Kidney-beans, young Plants, Colliflowers, Sellery, Carrots, both young and old, the last mostly called Sand-carrots, Spinages, Lettuces, natural Asparagus, green Gooseberries, Apricocks for Tarts, young Artichokes, and many other Articles, according as the Season is favourable. The French Author here gives the different Sorts of Wines, which are the most esteemed, although not absolutely consistent with this List; I shall here give the same, as it may be useful to some People in many Instances, Wine, is of all Season, the Soul of good Entertainments, when used with Moderation; the best *Burgundy Wines* are those of Chambertin, de Nuis, Pomart, Beaune, Chassaigne, Sauvigny, Voujaux, L'hermitage, la Côte-rôtie, and several other Sorts which are not reckoned of the best Wines; those of *Champagne* are those of Reims, le blans de Sillery, le Pierry, l'Auvillieres; there are also other very good Sorts of Wines, as the Vin du Rhin, de Moselle, de Grave, de Bourdeaux, le St. Peré de Languedoc, le Bouru d'Harbois, d'Harbois, & d'Arty; les Vins de Liqueurs, viz. *Sweet-wines*, are le Muscat, le Frontignan, le St. Laurent, le Condrieux, le Darbois, and several other Sorts as well of their own Growth, as imported from other Countries.

DE L'ETE. OF SUMMER.

THIS Season comprehends June, July and August. *June* produces of *Fish*, Thames Salmon, Turbots, plenty, Trouts, Mackerels, Soals, red Mullets at times, and fresh Sturgeon the same, Scate, Maids, Flounders, Eels, Lobsters, Crabs, Prawns, Craw-fish, and some times John-doreys, with Brills, and Hallibot. *July* continues much the same. *August*, Thames Salmon, Turbots, only the beginning of the Month, and then often indifferent; Trouts are out of Season the latter End of this Month, Soals are good, Scate, Brills, Maids, Plaice, Carps, Tenches, Prawns, and Craw-fish. In *Poultry*, dry puled Geese and Ducks, wild Rabbits, wild Pigeons, Fowls, Chickens, dry puled Turkeys, tame Pigeons, Giblets, Wheat-ears, large Fowls, and middling Chickens, Quails, Guinea-Fowls, Chickens, and Leverets. Of *Fruits* and *Garden-stuffs*, Strawberries of all Sorts in full Perfection, and early Duke-cherries, Currants, both white and red, Melons, Peas and Beans of all Sorts, Colliflowers, young Turnips, all Sorts of Roots, Herbs, and Salleting. Also, *July*, with the Addition of the Masculine Apricocks, both for Desserts, Tarts, and Preserves, Hautboys, and all the early Sorts of Cherries, Melons, and Cucumbers plenty, Artichokes, Caroline Strawberries, Finochio Duke Cherries. *August* continues some Time much the same, with the Addition of black and white Heart Cherries, Peaches, and Nectarines, Hautboys, late scarlet and wood Strawberries, ripe Goosberries, and Currants of all Sorts, some early Sorts of Plums; this is the Season when Confectionary replenishes its Store for the Winter with dried or liquid Preserves, Marmalades, Cake, Paste, Syrup, &c. The Kitchen is supplied abundantly with all Sorts of Roots and Greens, of which a Recapitulation would be both tedious and useless.

DE L'AUTUMNE. OF AUTUMN.

THIS Season comprehends September, October, November; and gives us the greatest Varieties of any for good and great Entertainments, in regard to Game and Venison of all Sorts. In *Fish*, *September* produces Cod, small Whitings, Smelts, Haddocks,

PRODUCTIONS of the SEASONS.

Haddocks, Soals, Brills, Scate, Maids, Flounders, Eels, Crabs, Prawns, Herrings, Craw-fish, John-dorey, and Turbots at Times, Carps, Tench, Perch and Pikes. *October* continues much the same, with very good Craw-fish, Gudgeons, Carps, Eels, Lobsters, and Salmon, the latter End of this Month; also Brawn coming into Seafon, and fold by the Fishmongers. *November*, Salmon plenty, Crimp-Cod, and Whitings, Haddocks, Smelts, Soals, Brills, Scate, and Flounders, Plaice, with the same Productions as the last; *only* Lobsters, often deficient in this Month; pickled Sturgeon, Oysters, Mussels, and Cockles at Times. Of Butchers-meat, Pigs, and Pork in full Seafon. In *Poultry*, the beginning of this Seafon, tame Ducks, large Fowls, middling ditto, Quails, Partridges, Land and Water Reals, Hares, Rabbits, Pigeons. *October*, Geese in Perfection, Giblets, Pheafants, Turkeys, Wood-cocks, the latter End, wild Ducks, Teals, Easterlings, Widgeons, Plovers coming into Seafon, Snipes, Larks, Wood-pigeons, and tame Rabbits, Dunbirds. In *Fruits*, &c. the beginning continues much as the last Seafon, with late Dukes-cherries, Peaches, Nectarines, Figs plenty, Sweet-water Grapes, red and white Currants, green Gages, Plums, and St. Catherine ditto, with other Sorts of inferior Quality, Mulberries, Walnuts, Filberds, Arline Plums, red Currants, Morella-Cherries, for Tarts and Preferves; Field-mushrooms best for pickling; Garden-greens of all Sorts, pretty plentiful, fresh Cardoons, and Potatoes; feveral Sorts of Apples for Tarts, and other Kitchen-ufes. *October* continues much the same, with Nectarines, latter Catherine Peaches, good for raw eating, ſtewing, and baking, &c. and the Newington Nectarines, Grapes of all Sorts, Bergamotte-pears, Burée, and Creffant ditto, golden Pippins coming in good, Medlers, Mulberries, Walnuts, Imperatrice Plums, Chefnuts, English Truffles coming in, and continue for about four Months; the Kitchen is ſtill well ſupplied with common Roots and Greens, red Beetroots, good for Sallet, with Spanish Onions, Sellery in Perfection for all Uses; Cardoons, Cloreri, Brocoli, Endives, Lettuces, young Spinages. *November*, Grapes, Burée-pears, Creffant, and St. Germain, Colmar and Bon-chretien-pears, golden Pippins, Nonpareil Apples, and all other Sorts for Kitchen-ufe, Love-apples, good to mix with *fumé* Sauce, and much the same Roots and Greens, as the Month before.

PRODUCTIONS *of the* SEASONS.

DE L'HYVER. OF WINTER.

This Seaſon comprehends December, January, and February. The Produce of *Fiſh* in *December*, are Salmon, Crimp-Cod, Scate, Haddocks, Whitings, Smelts, Soals, Brills, Plaice, Flounders, Crabs, Craw-fiſh, Carp, Perch, Eels, Gudgeons, Turbots, by chance, pickled Sturgeon. And *January* much the ſame, with potted Lampreys, Salt-fiſh, Barrel Cod, freſh Sturgeon, John-dorey at times, Oyſters of all Sorts, Muſſels, Cockles, Perch, Turbots, by chance. *February* continues much the ſame, except that Cod, Haddocks, and Whitings are going out of Seaſon, and Plaice and Flounders are but indifferent; of *Poultry*, Cock-turkeys, Hen dito, large wild Rabbits, Larks, Snipes, Wood-cocks, Plovers, Buſtard, Capon, Pullards, middling Fowls, Chickens, Quails, *Hares, Pheaſants, Partridges*. N. B. Dry pulled Geeſe and Ducks are almoſt out of Seaſon about January. The Garden furniſhes us ſtill moſt part of this Seaſon, with golden Pippins, Nonpareils and Pearmain-apples, Medlers, dried Apples, Cheſnuts, St. Germain and Winter Chaumontelle-Royal-pears, Colmar-pears, golden Rennets, and ruſſet Apples for Kitchen-uſe, with Savoy-ſprouts, red Cabbages, *Borcole*, Carrots, Parſneps, Potatoes, Endives, the French *Choux Rave*, commonly called Turnip-cabbages, Sellery, Onions, Cardoons, and much the ſame Sorts of Roots and Greens, as ſet forth at the beginning of the Spring-ſeaſon; all Sorts of *Purée*, and Italian Paſte are very uſeful at this time, for Soups, as the Herbs are rather ſcarce and of very little Flavour; all Sorts of Butcher's-meat is good, with Pork and Pigs in full Seaſon; alſo ſeveral Sorts of Roots, although very little uſed in England, as Corſioners, Skirrets, Saffafix-roots for Kitchen-uſe, with Kentiſh-ſtone Pippins, and ſmall Salleting, and all Sorts of ſweet and cooling Herbs coming into Seaſon, at the latter End.

CONTENTS

OF THE

FIRST VOLUME.

	Page
BOUILLONS de mitonage, ou bouillons générales. Of soaking or general broth, gravy, and cullis	1
——— *pour les potages & sauces.* Broth for soops and sauces	ibid.
Bouillon à la hâte. Broth made in haste	2
——— *au bain-marie.* Broth made with one pot boiling in another	ib.
Consommé. Jelly Broth	ib.
Roumeftec. Jelly broth of all fragments	3
Bouillon rafraichiſſant. Cooling broth	ib.
Autre bouillon rafraichiſſant. Another cooling broth	4
Bouillon printanier. Spring broth	ib.
——— *pour adoucir l'acreté du sang.* Broth to sweeten the sharpness of the blood	ib.
Eau de poulet. Chicken water	5
Panade de blans de poularde. Panado of breast of fowl.	ib.
——— *de gruau.* Grits panado.	ib.
——— *à la Bourgogne.* Burgundy panado	ib.
Jus de veau. Veal gravy	6
—— *de Bœuf.* Beef gravy	ib.
Coulis général. General cullis	ib.
——— *de ce que l'on veut.* Cullis of what you please	7
——— *d'écrevisses.* Craw-fish cullis	ib.
——— *à la reine.* Queen's cullis	8
——— *de jambon.* Ham cullis	ib.

Vol. I. a *Coulis*

CONTENTS.

	Page
Coulis bourgeois. A family cullis	8
—— *blanc à la bourgeoise.* White family cullis	9
—— *de fèves de marais.* Cullis of garden beans	ib.
—— *de lentilles.* Lentils cullis	ib.
—— *de pois.* Peas cullis	10
—— *de marons.* Chesnut cullis	ib.
Des bouillons, jus et coulis maigre. Of meager broth, gravies, and cullis	ib.
Bouillon maigre pour les potages de la table. Meager broth for soops	11
—— *de poisson.* Fish broth	ib.
Jus maigre. Meager gravy	ib.
Coulis maigre. Meagre cullis	12
—— *d'oignons en maigre.* Onion cullis meager	ib.
—— *maigre à la reine.* Queen cullis meager	13
—— *maigre de navet.* Turnip cullis meager	ib.
—— *de pois maigre.* Meager peas cullis	ib.
Ouille de différentes façons. Olio, or turine of different manners	14
Potage à la fom-bonne en gras & en maigre. Soop of all sorts of herbs with meat or without	ib.
—— *de ris à la pluche verte en gras ou maigre.* A rice soop of both sorts, pale green	15
—— *de chapon au ris.* A capon or fowl rice soop	ib.
—— *à la Conty en gras ou maigre.* Soop Conty, meat or fish	ib.
—— *de biberot au fromage.* Cheese soop of both sorts	16
—— *glacé de toutes sortes de viande.* Glazed soop of all sorts of meat	ib.
—— *de vermicel en gras & en maigre.* Vermicelly soop, with meat or fish	17
Soupe bourgeoise. A family soop	ib.
Potage au marons. Chesnut soop	ib.
—— *d'issus d'aigneau au coulis à la reine.* Lamb's head soop, and all purtenances, with queen cullis	18
—— *à la Chartre.* Chartre soop	ib.
Bisque de cailles. A quail turine soop	ib.
Potage de toutes sortes de legumes. Soop of all sorts of herbs	19
—— *aux choux.* Cabbage soop	ib.
—— *Julienne gras & maigre.* Soop Julienne with meat or fish	20
—— *de différente purée.* Soops of different porridge	ib
—— *de semouille.* Italian paste soop	ib

Potag

CONTENTS.

	Page
Potage à la Dauphine. Dauphine foop	20
———— *de gibier.* Game foop	21
———— *de toutes fortes de croutes.* Soop of all forts of cruft	ib.
———— *à la Parme.* Parma foop	22
———— *à l'Autriche.* Auftrian foop	ib.
Garbure. A turine with different forts of meat	ib.
Potage à la madelonette. A common innocent foop	23
———— *de macarony.* Macarony foop	ib.
———— *à la moufquetaire.* Soop for a good ftomach	ib.
———— *à la marquife.* An epicure's foop	ib.
———— *à la Rhinoceros.* Pigeon foop called Rhinoceros, from an Indian bird	24
———— *de navets à l'Italienne.* Turnip foop Italian fafhion, meat or fifh.	ib.
Ouille au bain-marie. Hufpot of all forts of meat	ib.
Potage à la Creffy. Soop Creffy	25
———— *de Lazagne.* Lazagne foop	ib.
Soupe maigre de differentes façons. Meager foops of different forts	ib.
Potage maigre d'ecreviffe au ris. Meager craw-fifh and rice foops	26
———— *maigre à la purée verte.* Meager peas porridge foop	ib.
———— *maigre à la purée de lentilles.* Lentil foop meager	ib.
———— *maigre de ris à la reine.* Rice foop maigre à la reine	27
———— *de lait de plufieurs façons.* Milk foop of different forts	ib.
Ouille au citrouille. Pompkin foop	28
Bifque maigre aux écreviffes. Meager craw-fifh turine	ib.
Potage maigre de moules. Muffels foop meager	29
Ouille maigre de plufieurs façons. Olio, or turine of different forts	ib.
Potage de croutes en maigre de plufieurs façons. Meager cruft foop of different forts	ib.
———— *de lait d'amande.* Almond milk foop	30
———— *d'orge mondé.* Peeled barley foop	ib.

Des Sauces. ib,

Of Sauces.

Sauce nompareille. Nonparel fauce	31
———— *à la Nivernoife.* Nivernois fauce	ib.
———— *petite Italienne.* A little Italian fauce	ib.

a 2 Sauce

CONTENTS.

	Page
Sauce *Italienne blanche.* White Italian sauce	32
—— *au celadon.* Sea-green sauce	ib.
—— *au coloris.* A lively-colour sauce	ib.
—— *au consommé.* Jelly broth sauce	33
—— *à la Saxe.* Saxon sauce	ib.
—— *à la liaison.* Sauce of a thick consistence	ib.
—— *à l'ozeille.* Sorrel sauce	34
—— *à la mariette.* Common sauce	ib.
—— *au cerfeuille.* Charvil sauce	ib.
—— *au persil.* Parsley sauce	ib.
—— *à la civette.* Small herb; sauce civet	35
—— *à la Garonne.* Gascoon sauce	ib.
—— *au fenouil.* Fennel sauce	ib.
—— *a l'amiral.* Admiral's sauce	ib.
—— *Royale.* Royal sauce	36
—— *à la Flamande.* Flemish sauce	ib.
—— *à la hâte.* Sauce in a hurry	ib.
—— *à l'aigneau.* Lamb sauce	ib.
—— *à l'avare.* The miser's sauce	37
—— *au verjus.* Verjuice sauce, or poor man's sauce	ib.
—— *au pauvre homme.* Another poor mans sauce	ib.
—— *douce.* Sweet sauce	ib.
—— *au fumèt.* Sauce made with game	ib.
—— *ravigotte.* Relishing sauce	38
—— *ravigotte froide.* The same cold	ib.
—— *à la Madeleine.* A common simple sauce	ib.
—— *à l'aspic.* Sharp sauce aspick	ib.
—— *à la gendarme.* Military sauce	39
—— *à la belle-vue.* A well-looking sauce	ib.
—— *à la morue.* Skate sauce or cod	ib.
—— *à la Polonoise.* A Polish sauce	40
—— *au foye.* Liver sauce, or sauce of liver	ib.
—— *blanche.* White sauce	ib.
—— *à l'Espagnole.* Spanish sauce	ib.
—— *Robert.* Robert sauce	41
—— *à la moutarde.* Mustard sauce	ib.
—— *à la carpe.* Carp sauce	ib.
—— *à l'anguille.* Eel sauce	42
—— *à la Bechamel.* Begamel sauce	ib.
—— *au maquereau.* Mackerel sauce	ib.
—— *remoulade.* Horse-radish or mustard sauce	ib.
—— *poivrade.* Sharp sauce	43

CONTENTS.

	Page
Sauce *au fenouil.* Another fennel sauce	43
—— *hachée.* Minced sauce	ib.
—— *au bain-marie*	44
—— *au porc frais.* Fresh pork sauce	ib.
—— *à la nonette.* Nun's sauce	ib.
—— *verte.* Green sauce	45
—— *verte d'une autre façon.* Another green sauce	ib.
—— *piquante.* Sharp or relishing sauce	ib.
—— *au bleu celeste.* A sky-blue sauce	46
—— *au pontife.* Pontiff sauce	ib.
—— *à la nichon.* The house-wife's sauce	ib.
—— *au reverend, gras ou maigre.* The parson's sauce	ib.
—— *à la Milanoise.* Milan sauce	47
—— *à l'orange.* Orange sauce	ib.
—— *au canard.* Sauce for ducks	ib.
—— *à l'echalotte.* Shallot sauce	ib.
Une autre sauce au persil. Another parsley sauce	48
Sauce au bled verd. Green wheat sauce	ib.
—— *à la reine.* Queen's sauce	ib.
—— *d'acide.* Acid sauce	49
—— *à la becasse.* Wood-cock sauce	ib.
—— *au trufes.* Truffles sauce	ib.
—— *maigre de plusieurs façons.* Meager sauces of different sorts	ib.
—— *general.* General sauce	50
—— *au beure noir.* Burnt butter sauce	ib.
—— *simple.* Simple sauce	ib.

CHAPITRE PREMIER. *Du Bœuf.* 51

CHAPTER FIRST. Of Beef.

Langue de bœuf au gros sel. Fresh tongue in a plain way	ib.
Langues de bœufs en caisses. Sham beefs tongues	52
Langue de bœufs à la remoulade. Beefs tongue with a relishing sauce	ib.
—— *de bœuf en ragout.* Beef tongue ragout	53
—— *de bœuf grillée.* Broiled beef's tongue	ib.
Langues fumées. Smoked tongues	ib.

CONTENTS.

	Page
Langues de bœuf fourées. Smoked tongues of another fashion	54
Langue de bœuf à la broche. Beef's tongue roasted	ib.
—— *de bœuf à la braise.* Beef's tongue brazed	ib.
—— *de bœuf en crepine.* Beef's tongue in cowl veal, or other	55
—— *de bœuf à la St. Menehoult.* A brazed tongue broiled	ib.
—— *de bœuf au gratin*	56
Paté & tourte de langue de bœuf. Beef's tongue pye, with raised puff-paste	ib.
Langue de bœuf au Parmesan. Beef's tongue and Parmesan cheese	ib.
Cervelle de bœuf. Ox's brains	57
Palais de bœuf à la St. Menoult. Beef's palates St. Menoult	ib.
—— *de bœuf à la poulette.* Fricassee of palates	ib.
—— *de bœuf à l'Angloise.* Beef's palates English fashion	58
—— *de bœuf au petit lard.* Beef's palates with pickled pork	ib.
—— *de bœuf au Parmesan.* Beef's palates and Parmesan	ib.
—— *de bœuf en filet*	ib.
—— *de bœuf en timbale.* Beef's palates in moulds of any sorts	ib.
—— *de bœuf à la brochette.* Beef's palates broiled on small skewers	59
—— *de bœuf en menus droits.* Beef palates cut in fillets or minced	ib.
—— *de bœuf à la mariette.* Beef palates in a common way	60
—— *de bœuf à la Provençale.* Beef's palates Provence fashion	ib.
—— *de bœuf au Parmesan aux oignons.* Beef's palates with Parmesan and onions	ib.
—— *de bœuf au gratin*	61
—— *de bœuf à l'escalope.* Collop of beef palates	ib.
—— *de bœuf à la marmotte.* Beef's palates country fashion	ib.
—— *de bœuf à la ravigotte.* Beef's palates with a relishing sauce	62
—— *de bœuf de plusieurs façons.* Beef's palates of different fashions	ib.
Queue de bœuf au choux. Beef's tail and cabbage	ib.
—— *de bœuf aux lentilles.* Beef's tail and lentils	63
—— *de bœuf en pâté chaud.* Beef's rump pie	ib.

Queue

CONTENTS.

	Page
Queue de bœuf de plusieurs façons. Beef's rump of different fashions	*ib.*
Gras double à la Robert. Tripes sauce Robert	64
—— *double au verjus.* Tripes verjuice sauce	*ib.*
—— *double de plusieurs façons.* Tripes of different fashions	*ib.*
Rognon de bœuf à la moutarde. Beef's kidney and mustard sauce	65
Rognons de bœuf à la môde	*ib.*
Rognon de bœuf en filets. Kidney minced	*ib.*
Rognons de bœuf en pâté chaud. Hot kidneys pie	*ib.*
Rognon de bœuf à la bourgeoise. Kidney family way	66
Tetine de vache au verjus. Cow's udder and verjuice sauce	*ib.*
Usage de la graisse de bœuf & moüelle. The way to use beef's suet and marrow	*ib.*
Tranches de bœuf à la bourgeoise. Beef steaks family way	67
Tranches de bœuf à la Camargot. Beef steaks, by the name of a famous dancer	*ib.*
Tranches de bœuf à la royale. Beef steaks, court fashion	*ib.*
—— *de bœuf à la servante.* Beef steaks to eat hot or cold, family fashion	68
—— *de bœuf au caramel.* Beef steaks glazed or fricandeau	*ib.*
Canellons de bœuf. Beef forced meat in form of a pudding	*ib.*
Andouillettes de tranches de bœuf. Beef puddings or sausages	69
Bœuf de desserte à la Sainte Menehoult. Cold beef marinaded	*ib.*
—— *de desserte à la bourgeoise*	*ib.*
—— *de desserte en papillotte.* Cold beef broiled in paper	70
Culotte de bœuf à la Mantouë. Rump of beef, Mantouë fashion	*ib.*
—— *de bœuf fumée.* Beef's rump smoked	71
—— *à l'ecarlate sans salpêtre.* Scarlet beef without saltpetre	*ib.*
—— *de bœuf à la Gascogne.* Rump of beef Gascogny fashion	72
—— *de bœuf dans son jus.* Rump of beef in its own gravy	*ib.*
—— *de bœuf diversifié.* Rump of beef diversified	*ib.*
—— *de bœuf au vin de Champagne.* Rump of beef boiled in white wine	73
—— *de bœuf à la royale.* Rump of beef court fashion	*ib.*
—— *de bœuf à la Sainte Menehoult*	*ib.*
Aloyau au demy sel. Chump of beef half salted	74
Filets d'aloyau de toutes façons. Fillets of beef of all sorts	*ib.*
Aloyau au four. Sirloin baked in the oven	*ib.*

Aloyau

CONTENTS.

	Page
Aloyau en ragout. Small sirloin ragout	75
—— *à la Dauphine.* Sirloin Dauphine fashion	ib.
Filet d'aloyau en crepine. Fillet of beef in cowl	ib.
—— *d'aloyau aux fines herbes.* Fillet of beef and sweet herbs	76
—— *d'aloyau aux oignons en crépine.* Fillet of beef and onions in cowl	ib.
—— *de bœuf à l'intendante.* Fillet of beef à la commissary	ib.
—— *de bœuf aux anchois.* Fillet of beef and anchovies	77
—— *de boeuf à l'amiral.* Fillet of beef, admiral fashion	ib.
—— *de boeuf glassé.* Fillet of beef and jelly	ib.
Filets de boeuf grillés. Fillets of beef broiled	78
Filet de boeuf à la Nivernois. Fillet of beef Nivernois sauce	ib.
—— *de boeuf à l'Italienne.* Fillet of beef Italian sauce	ib.
—— *de boeuf à la gendarme.* Fillet of beef gendarme fashion	79
Poitrine de boeuf à la monarque. Brisket of beef, monarch fashion	ib.
—— *de boeuf à la St. Menehoult.* Brisket of beef broiled, St. Menehoult	ib.
Tendrons de boeuf de plusieurs façons. Beef gristle of different fashions	80
Côte ou carbonade de boeuf au four. A rib of beef in the oven	81
—— *de boeuf à la remoulade.* A rib of beef with mustard or horse-radish sauce	ib.
—— *de boeuf à l'Angloise.* Rib of beef English fashion	ib.
Côtes de boeuf à la Hollandoise. Ribs of beef Dutch fashion	82
Oreilles de boeuf. Beef's ears	ib.

CHAPITRE SECOND. Du Veau,   ib.

CHAPTER SECOND. Of Veal.

Tête de veau à la bourgeoise. Calve's head family way	83
—— *de veau farcie.* Calve's head stuffed	ib.
—— *de veau à la poivrade.* Calve's head with a sharp sauce	84
—— *de veau au verd-galant.* Calve's head fried with parsley	ib.
—— *de veau en crépine.* Calve's head in cowl	ib.

Tête

CONTENTS.

	Page
Tête de veau à la sauce au porc frais. Calve's head with fresh pork sauce	85
—— *de veau à la Sainte Meneboult.* Calve's head St. Meneboult	ib.
—— *de veau marinée,* Calve's head marinaded	ib.
Oreilles de veau frites. Calve's ears fried	ib.
—— *de veau en menus droits.* Calve's ears shredded	86
—— *de veau au gratin*	ib.
—— *de veau au pontife.* Calve's ears pontiff sauce	ib.
—— *de veau à la Martine.* Calve's ears house-wife fashion	ib.
Panache de veau. Calve's ears broiled	ib.
Oreille de veau au fromage. Calve's ears and cheese	87
—— *de veau à l'Italienne.* Calve's ears Italian sauce	ib.
—— *de veau à la Sainte Meneboult*	ib.
Cervelles de veau à la crême. Calve's brains cream sauce	ib.
—— *de veau aux petit oignons.* Calve's brains and small onions	88
—— *de veau aux ecrevisses.* Calve's brains and crawfish	ib.
—— *de veau au soleil.* Calve's brains fried crisp	ib.
—— *de veau à la Gascogne.* Calve's brains Gascoon fashion	ib.
—— *de veau au reveil.* Calve's brains mustard sauce	89
—— *de veau à differentes sauces.* Brains of different fashion and sauces	ib.
Yeux de veau de differentes façons. Calve's eyes of different fashions	ib.
Langue de veau, Calve's tongue	ib.
Fraises de veau au naturel. Calve's caldron in a plain way	ib.
—— *de veau au soleil.* Caldron fried of a fine clear colour	90
—— *de veau à la Provençale.* Caldron Provence fashion	ib.
Crepinettes de fraises de veau, Caldron dressed olive fashion	ib.
Baignets de fraises de veau, Caldron fried, small fritters	ib.
Fraises de veau en crepine. Caldron in veal cowl	91
Tourtes aux zephirs de fraise de veau, Calve's caldron pie	ib.
Foye de veau à la bâte. Calve's liver in a hurry	ib.
—— *de veau à la rocambole.* Calve's liver with green shallots or chibbol	ib.
—— *de veau à la broche* Roasted	92
—— *de veau en bâtereaux.* Calve's liver haslets	ib.
—— *de veau à la braise.* Calve's liver brazed	ib.
Saucisses de foye de veau. Calve's liver sausages	93

Rognons

CONTENTS.

	Page
Rognons de veau de plusieurs façons. Veal kidney of different fashions	93
Pieds de veau de plusieurs façons. Calve's feet of different fashions	ib.
—— *de veau farcis.* Calve's feet with forced meat	ib.
Pied de veau au citron. Calve's feet lemon sauce	94
Ris de veau de plusieurs façons. Sweet breads of different fashions	ib.
—— *de veau à la Duchesse.* Calve's sweet bread à la Duchess	ib.
—— *de veau au pontife.* Sweet breads pontiff sauce	95
—— *de veau en hérisson.* Sweet breads as hedge-hogs	ib.
Rissolle à la choisy. Fried forced-meat	ib.
Queuës de veau aux choux. Calve's tails and cabbages	96
—— *de veau diversifiées.* Calve's tails of different fashions	ib.
Amourettes de plusieurs façons. Lamb's fry, and others of different fashions	97
Tendrons de veau au petit pois. Veal gristles and green peas	ib.
Tendrons de veau printaniers. Veal gristles spring sauce	98
Tendrons de veau frits. Veal gristles fried	ib.
—— *de veau à la poulette.* Veal gristles fricassee	99
—— *de veau aux legumes.* Gristles with any sorts of greens	ib.
—— *de veau en fricandeau.* Gristle or breast of veal larded fricandeau	ib.
Poitrine de veau à l'Italienne. Breast of veal Italian fashion	100
—— *de veau frite.* Breast of veal fried	ib.
—— *de veau en surprise.* Breast of veal masked, or wonder, &c.	ib.
Oreilles de veau farcies à la quenelles. Calve's ears stuffed	101
Poitrine de veau marinée. Breast of veal marinaded	ib.
—— *de veau farcie en ragout.* Breast of veal stuffed ragout	ib.
—— *de veau au court bouillon.* Breast of veal in its own sauce	ib.
—— *de veau au pontife.* Breast of veal pontiff sauce	102
—— *de veau en crepine.* Breast of veal in cowl	ib.
—— *de veau à la Romaine.* Breast of veal Roman fashion	ib.
Cotelettes de veau à la mariée. Veal cutlets, bride fashion	ib.
—— *de veau grillées.* Veal cutlets broiled	103
—— *de veau en ragout.* Veal cutlets ragout	ib.
—— *de veau en papillottes.* Veal cutlets in paper	ib.

Cotelettes

CONTENTS.

	Page
Cotelettes de veau marinées. Veal cutlets marinaded	103
—— *de veau composées.* Veal cutlets composed or shammed	104
—— *de veau en fricandeau.* Veal cutlets fricandeaux	ib.
—— *de veau aux fines herbes.* Veal cutlets and sweet herbs	ib.
—— *de veau aux petits pois.* Veal cutlets and green peas	105
—— *de veau au cruchon.* Veal cutlets in crust	ib.
—— *de veau à la poële.* Veal cutlets half fried	ib.
—— *de veau à l' Italienne.* Veal cutlets Italian sauce	ib.
—— *de veau en crepine.* Veal cutlets in cowl	ib.
—— *de veau diversifiées.* Veal cutlets of different manners	106
Carré de veau glassé ou piqué à la broche. Neck of veal glazed, larded, or roasted	ib.
—— *de veau à la servante.* Neck of veal stewed	ib.
—— *de veau à la poivrade.* Neck of veal and sharp sauce	ib.
—— *de veau au monarque.* Neck of veal monarch fashion	107
—— *de veau en crepine.* Neck of veal in cowl	ib.
—— *de veau en surprise.* Neck of veal stuffed	ib.
Cuisseau de veau aux epinards. Leg or knuckle of veal and spinage	108
—— *de veau à la crême.* Leg of veal white sauce	ib.
—— *de veau à la daube.* Leg of veal dobed or à la mode	ib.
Quartier de veau au chevreuil. Leg of veal cut venison fashion	109
—— *de veau au caramel.* The same cut as above, glazed	ib.
Epaule de veau. Shoulder of veal	ib.
Blanquette de veau. Roasted veal with white sauce	ib.
Grenadins de veau aux anchois. Small fricandeaux anchovy sauce	ib.
Rissolettes de veau. Veal collop	110
Paupiettes de veau. Veal olives	ib.
Brezolles de veau. Veal brazed, a different collop	ib.
Poupeton. Meat-pudding	111
Marbrée. Marbled, coloured, &c.	ib.
Grenade. A grenado	112

Grenade

CONTENTS.

	Page
Grenade en daube. Grenado dobed	113
Favorites. Different olives	ib.
Venetienne de veau. Broiled veal Venetian fashion	114
——— au jambon	ib.
——— à la moële. Venetian with marrow	ib.
——— au vin de Champagne	115
Fricandeaux aux legumes. Fricandeau with garden greens	ib.
Noix de veau au pontife. Knuckle of veal pontiff sauce	ib.
——— de veau à Saint Cloud. The same, St. Cloud fashion	ib.
——— de veau glassée. Fillet of veal glazed	116
Rouëlle de veau à la daube. Small fillet of veal stewed	ib.
——— de veau à la cendre	ib.
Andouillettes au céleri. Sham sausages with sellery	ib.
Filets mignons	117
——— de veau à la Conty. Fillets of veal Conty fashion	ib.
Timbale à la Romaine	ib.
Veau à la folette. Without art	118
Gateau de Mai. A spring cake	ib.
Pain à la Flamande. A Flemish loaf	ib.
Crepinettes de Godiveau	119
Gateau de veau en crepine. Veal cake in cowl	ib.
Veau à la villageoise. Veal peasant fashion	ib.
Bagatelles de veau. Trifles of veal.	120
Filets de coulis à la Bechamel. Fillets of cullis meat Bechamel	ib.

CHAPITRE TROISIEME. Du mouton. ib.

CHAPTER THIRD. Of mutton.

La queuë de mouton de differentes façons. Sheep's rumps of different fashions	ib.
Langues de mouton. Sheep's tongues	ib.
——— de mouton à la Provençale. Sheep's rumps Provence fashion	121
——— de mouton glaceés. Sheep's tongues as fricandeau	ib.
Langue de mouton à la royale. Sheep's tongue royal fashion	ib.
Langues de mouton aux oignons en crepine. Sheep's tongues with onions in cowl	122
Langue de mouton en papillottes. Sheep's tongues in paper	ib.

Langue

CONTENTS.

	Page
Langue de mouton au Parmesan. Sheep's tongues and Parmesan cheese	122
Langues de mouton en surprise. Sheep's tongues masked or shammed	123
——— *de mouton à la liason.* Sheep's tongues ragout	ib.
——— *de mouton à la Dauphine.* Sheep's tongues Dauphin fashion	124
——— *de mouton à la bourgeoise.* Sheep's tongues plain family fashion	ib.
——— *de mouton en tourte.* Sheep's tongues pie	ib.
Canelons de langue de mouton. Sheep's tongue fried in paste	125
Pieds de mouton de differentes façons. Sheep's trotters of different fashions	ib.
——— *de mouton à la belle-vuë.* Sheep's trotters	ib.
Pied de mouton en canon. Sheep's trotters fried in paste	126
Pieds de mouton à la Sainte Menehoult. Sheep's trotters fried or broiled	ib.
——— *de mouton à l'aspic*	ib.
——— *de mouton à la ravigotte.* They are served with the sauce so called	127
Carré de mouton au reverend. Neck of mutton larded with ham and anchovy	ib.
——— *de mouton en fricandeau*	ib.
——— *de mouton sans façons, viz.* plain	128
——— *de mouton en crepine,* in cowl	ib.
——— *de mouton à l'echalottes.* With sweet herbs	ib.
——— *de mouton au jambon*	ib.
——— *de mouton à la mode*	ib.
——— *de mouton à la jardiniere, ou à la capucine.* So called from the greens, &c.	ib.
Cotelettes de mouton sans malice. Mutton steaks without art, a plain way	ib.
——— *de mouton de plusieurs façons.* Mutton steaks of different way	ib.
——— *de mouton au fenouil;* fennel.	ib.
——— *de mouton à la cendre.* Mutton chops stewed slowly	129
——— *de mouton en herisson.* Mutton chops masqueraded	ib.
——— *de mouton à l'amoureux*	ib.
——— *de mouton en crepine.* Mutton steaks in cowl	130

CONTENTS.

	Page
Cotelettes de mouton en crepine d'une autre façon. Another way	130
—— *de mouton en surtout.* Mutton steaks masked, or disguised	ib.
—— *de mouton à la Chartreuse.* Mutton steaks, called after the above, frier fashion.	ib.
—— *de mouton frites.* Mutton steaks fried	131
—— *de mouton à la Villeroy*	ib.
—— *de mouton à la servante*	ib.
—— *de mouton à l'Allemande.* German fashion	ib.
—— *de mouton à la Dauphine*	132
Bresolles de mouton. Mutton collop	ib.
—— *de mouton à la poële.* Mutton collop another way	ib.
—— *de mouton à la Périgord*	ib.
—— *de mouton aux concombres.* Mutton collop with stewed cucumbers	133
Mouton à la bechamel aux onions	ib.
Hatereau de mouton. Mutton olive fried, brazed, or roasted	ib.
Filets de mouton marinés	ib.
—— *de mouton à la coquette*	134
—— *de mouton glassés aux concombres*	ib.
—— *de mouton en canellon*	ib.
Fricandeau de mouton	ib.
Cascalopes de mouton au vin de Champagne. Mutton collops and white wine	135
Rouëlles de mouton aux oignons	ib.
Poitrine de mouton de plusieurs façons. Breast of mutton different ways	ib.
Epaule de mouton à l'eau. Shoulder of mutton	ib.
—— *de mouton à la Parme.* Shoulder of mutton Parma fashion	136
—— *de mouton au four.* Shoulder of mutton baked in the oven	ib.
—— *de mouton à la Sainte Menehoult.* Shoulder of mutton broiled	ib.
Sauçissons d'epaule de mouton. Sausages or coloured shoulder	ib.
Epaule de mouton à la bonne femme. The good housewife	137
—— *de mouton en timbale*	ib.
—— *de mouton au sang*	ib.

Selle

CONTENTS.

	Page
Selle de mouton à la Sainte Meneboult. Saddle or loin of mutton broiled	138
—— *de mouton en canapé.* Matted	ib.
Rôt de bif de mouton	ib.
—— *de bif glassé*, glazed	139
Gigot de mouton au chou-fleur. Leg of mutton and colliflower	ib.
—— *de mouton au vin de Champagne*	ib.
—— *de mouton en filets farcis*	ib.
Grenadins de mouton. Small fricandeau of mutton	ib.
Gigot de mouton à la mode	ib.
—— *de mouton à la Houlan*	140
—— *de mouton à la Gascogne*	ib.
—— *de mouton à l'Italienne*	ib.
—— *de mouton à l'eau*	ib.
—— *de mouton à l'Espagnole.* Leg of mutton Spanish fashion	ib.
Mortadelles de mouton. See the receipt	141
Gigot de mouton en venaison	ib.
—— *de mouton à la servante*	ib.
—— *de mouton à la Modène*	ib.
—— *de mouton au militaire*	ib.
—— *de mouton aux légumes*	142
—— *de mouton au bacha*	ib.
—— *de mouton à la St. Geran*	ib.
—— *de mouton en salade*	ib.

CHAPITRE QUATRIEME. Du cochon. 143

CHAPTER FOURTH. Of hogs and pigs.

De la connoissance & dissection du cochon. How to chuse hogs meat, and to cut it up	ib.
Cochon de lait rôti. Suckling pig roasted	144
—— *de lait en galantine.* Coloured pig	ib.
—— *de lait au Moine blanc.* Pigs white Monks fashion	145
—— *de lait au pere Douillet.* Pig in jelly	ib.
Roulades de cochon de lait. Large olives	146
Cochon de lait à la Bechamel. Pig Bechamel sauce	ib.
Paupiettes de cochon de lait. Olives of suckling pig	147
Cochon de lait en timbale. Suckling pig in mould	ib.

CONTENTS.

	Page
Hure de cochon en sanglier. Hog's head as wild boar	148
Ballon de cochon. Made round, the form of a foot-ball	ib.
Usage du sang de cochon & autres. The use of hog's blood and others	149
Petit salé. Pickled pork	ib.
Echinée à la poivrade. Chine of pork poivrade sauce	ib.
Le lard, comment le faire. How to make bacon for kitchen use	150
Queuës de cochon de plusieurs façons. Pig's tails of different fashions	ib.
Pieds de cochon à la St. Menehoult. Pig's feet brazed and broiled	ib.
Oreilles & panache de cochon de plusieurs façons. Pig's ears of different fashions.	151
Boudins de cochon. Black puddings	ib.
———— *de Saint Germain*	ib.
———— *fins.* Fine, delicate, better than the former	152
———— *blancs.* White puddings	ib.
———— *blancs communs.* Common white puddings	ib.
———— *de foyes de merlans.* Puddings of whitings livers	153
———— *de foyes gras.* Puddings of fat livers	ib.
———— *d'ecrevisses.* Craw-fish puddings	154
———— *de faisand.* Of pheasant	ib.
———— *de lapins.* Of rabbits	ib.
Cervelats fumés. Large sausages smoked	155
———— *de plusieurs façons.* Of different sorts	ib.
Saucisses de cochon. Common pork sausages.	ib.
———— *en crepinettes.* In cowl	156
———— *de veau en crepinettes.* Of veal meat	ib.
———— *aux trufes.* With truffles.	ib.
———— *de plusieurs façons.* Of different sorts	ib.
———— *de Champagne.* With Champaign wine	157
Timbale de boudin. A mould so called, filled with black pudding preparation	ib.
———— *à la mariniere.* Sailor fashion	ib.
———— *à la Saint Cloud*	158
———— *à la Sainte Menehoult.* Sausages broiled	ib.
———— *aux fines herbes.* With sweet herbs	159
———— *au gratin*	ib.
———— *en ragout ou purée.* Sausages as ragout, or with any sorts of porridge	160
Andouilles de cochon. Chitterlings or large sausages	ib.

Andouilles

CONTENTS.

	Page
Andouilles de bœuf. Beef chitterlings	161
———— *de veau.* Chitterlings of veal	ib.
———— *de Rouen*	ib.
———— *à l'Angloise.* English fashion	162
———— *de gibier.* Chitterlings made of game	ib.
———— *à la Béchamel.* White chitterlings	ib.
———— *de poisson.* Of fish	163
———— *à la Flamande.* Flemish fashion	ib.
Andouillettes de veau au Parmesan. Small chitterlings with Parmesan cheese	ib.
Saucissons de sanglier. A thick short sausage made of wild boar meat	164
———— *au brodequin.* Made square between boards, rachtied	ib.
Façon de faire les jambons. How to make hams	165
Jambon de Mayence. Hams Mayence fashion	ib.
———— *en gelée.* Ham in jelly	166
———— *au naturel.* Ham dressed the common way	ib.
———— *roti.* Ham roasted	167
———— *à la braise.* Ham braized	ib.
Rôties de jambon. Toasted bread and ham with eggs	ib.
Filets de porc frais. Fillets of fresh pork	168
Cotelettes de porc frais. Fresh pork steaks	ib.
Langues fourées de porc. Pork's tongs stuffed	ib.

CHAPTER FIFTH. *De l'Aigneau.* Of Lamb. 169

Tête d'aigneau à la pluche verte. Lamb's head of a pale green sauce	ib.
———— *d'aigneau à la Mordienne.* Lamb's head after the name of the inventor	170
———— *d'aigneau de plusieurs façons.* Lamb's head of different manners	ib.
———— *d'aigneau au pontife.* The same another way	ib.
———— *d'aigneau à la Condé.* Lamb's head Condé fashion	171
Issu d'aigneau de plusieurs façons. Lamb's head with all its appurtenances of different manners	ib.
Epaule d'aigneau à la Dauphine. Shoulder of lamb Dauphine fashion	172
Epaule d'aigneau à la voisine. Neighbour fashion	172
Quartier d'aigneau en crepine. Quarter of lamb in cowl	ib.
Rot de bif d'aigneau au monarque	173
Quartier d'aigneau aux fines herbes. Quarter of lamb with sweet herbs	174
———— *d'aigneau à la Reine.* Quarter of lamb with white sauce	ib.
Queuës d'aigneau au soleil. Lamb's rumps fried, &c.	ib.

CONTENTS.

	Page
Quartier d'aigneau en saucissons. Quarter of lamb as thick saufages or chitterling	175
Carré d'aigneau à la belle-vuë. Necks of lamb looking agreeable, &c. &c.	ib.
Du chevreau ou cabrit. Of kid.	176

DES GROSSES ENTREES EN TERRINES & AU-
TRES. Of large, firſt-courſe diſhes, tureen and others — ib.
Terrines à la Flamande. Tureen Flemiſh faſhion — ib.
Terrine à l'Angloiſe. Engliſh faſhion — ib.
———— *de ce que l'on veut.* Tureen of what you pleaſe — 177
———— *de bécaſſes.* Of woodcocks — ib.
———— *de perdrix.* Tureen of partridges — 178
Terrines de queuës de mouton, & ailerons au coulis & ragout de marons. Tureen of ſheep's rumps, and poultry pinions with cheſnut cullis and ragout — ib.
Terrine de volailles. Tureen of poultries — 179
———— *au monarque* — ib.
———— *de lapreaux.* Tureen of rabbits — 180
———— *de macreuſes au jambon.* Tureen of wild or ſea ducks with ham — ib.
———— *de poiſſon.* Tureen of fiſh — 181
———— *à la neuvaine.* Tureen as you pleaſe, or any how ib.
———— *de ſaumon.* Tureen of freſh ſalmon — 182
———— *de ſaumon aux écreviſſes.* With craw-fiſh — ib.
Caſſerole au ris — 183
Different hochepot. Hotchpotch of different ſorts — ib.
Salamalec. A fancy diſh, or tureen — 184
Financiere. Meaning a rich expenſive diſh — ib.
Chartreuſe. After the name of thoſe friars — 185
Marbrée. Marbled, coloured — ib.
Corbillon. Intermixed like a baſket — 186
Matelotte royale — 187
Matelottes de ce que l'on veut. Matlot of what you like — ib.
Pruſſienne. Matlot Pruſſian faſhion — 188
Matelotte au general. Fit for a general — ib.
———— *aux oignons d'Hollande.* With large Dutch or Spaniſh oinions — 189
Gateau de viande de ce que l'on veut. Meat cake of what ſorts you pleaſe — ib.
———— *à l'Eſpagnole.* Cake Spaniſh faſhion — ib.
Compoſition de panade pour toutes ſortes de viandes. How to make a proper batter to uſe with all ſorts of roaſting meat — 190

CHAPTER SIXTH. *De la volaille.* Of poultry. ib.
Poulets en fricaſſee. Fricaſſee of chicken — ib.

Fricaſſés

CONTENTS.

	Page
Fricassée de poulets à la fermiere. Fricassée farmer fashion or in haste	191
Differentes fricassees de poulets. Chicken fricassee of different manners	ib.
Poulets à la giblottes de plusieurs façons. Jumbals of chickens of different manners	192
——— *à l'etuvée.* Chickens stewed or matlot	ib.
——— *à la cavaliere.* Meaning without art or ceremony	193
——— *mignons aux ecrévisses.* Small chickens with craw-fish	ib.
——— *à la perle.* Chickens in the form of pearl	194
——— *au vin de Champagne.* Chickens with white wine sauce	ib.
——— *au pontife.* Chickens pontiff sauce	195
——— *à la folette.* Wanton, fantask, &c.	ib.
——— *à la belle-vuë*	196
——— *à la mariée.* Chickens, bride fashion	ib.
——— *à l'Italienne.* Chickens Italian fashion	ib.
——— *à l'aspic*	197
Filets de poulets à la Béchamel pannée. Fillets of chickens Bechamel sauce with bread crums	ib.
——— *soufflés à la Béchamel.* Fillets puffed Bechamel sauce	198
Fleurons à la brunette. Flourish in form of petit paté	ib.
Poulets à la bricoliere	199
Petit poussins aux pavies. Small chickens, and preserved nectarines	199
Fricassée de poulets à la Bourdois. Fricassée of chickens, after the name of the Author	200
DES COULEURS QUE L'ON SE SERT A LA CUISINE. Of colours used in cookery	ib.
Poulets historiés. Chickens garnished, embellished, &c.	201
Culottes de poulets aux petits oignons	202
Poulets aux ecrevisses. Chickens with, or as craw-fish	ib.
——— *à la broche avec ragoût de légumes.* Roasted chickens with stewed greens	203
——— *à la broche à differentes sauces.* Roasted chickens with different sauces	ib.
——— *à l'excellence,* excellency	ib.
——— *à la jardiniere.* From the garden-greens which make the same	204
——— *à la bonne amie.* Chickens without art	ib.
——— *en papillottes.* Chickens in paper	205
——— *à la Dauphine.* Chickens Dauphine fashion	ib.
——— *en saucissons.* Chickens as large sausages	206
——— *à l'amiral.* Chickens admiral fashion	ib.
——— *à la Tartare.* Chickens Tartary fashion	207
——— *entre deux plats.* Chickens done between two dishes	ib.
——— *marinés.* Chickens marinaded	208

CONTENTS.

	Page
Poulets à la Sainte Menehoult. Chickens broiled	ib.
Fricandeaux de poulets à l'Espagnole. Spanish fashion	209
Poulets au verd-pré. Meadow-green	ib.
——— *à la cardinal*	ib.
Matelotte de poulets à la broche. Matlot of chickens roasted	210
——— *de poulets à l'anguille.* With eel	ib.
——— *de poulets cuits.* Of roasted chickens	211
Grenadins de poulets	ib.
Poulets aux trufes. Chickens with truffles	ib.
——— *à la Saint Cloud.* Chickens St. Cloud fashion	212
——— *à la liaison aux petits œufs composés.* Chickens liason sauce, and small eggs shammed	ib.
——— *à la villageoise* Chickens country fashion	213
——— *au gratin*	ib.
——— *en surtout.* Chickens masqueraded	ib.
——— *à la reine*	214
——— *au céladon*	ib.
——— *en caisses.* Chickens in paper cases	215
——— *au roumestec.* Cullis made of fragments	ib.
Cuisses de poulets à différentes sauces & ragoûts. Legs of chickens with different sauces and ragouts	216
Poulets à la duchesse	ib.
——— *aux petits pois.* With green peas	ib.
——— *au Parmesan.* With Parmesan cheese	217
——— *au blanc-mangé*	ib.
——— *au verjus.* With verjuice grapes or others	218
——— *au Sultan.* Chickens, Turkish fashion	ib.
——— *à la favorite*	ib.
——— *en salade*	219
——— *mignons aux pistaches.* With pistachio-nuts	ib.
Matelotte des poulets aux racines. Matlot of chickens with roots	220
Poulets glacés. Chickens glazed	ib.
——— *à la paysanne.* Chickens country-wife fashion	221
——— *en gelée; appellés au pere douillet.* Chickens in jelly; called a fribble, codling, &c.	ib.
——— *à l'Indienne*	222
——— *à la marmotte*	ib.

CHAPTER SEVENTH. *Du dindon.* Of Turkey, ib.

Dindon à la broche à différents ragoûts. Roasted turkey with different ragouts	ib.
——— *farci d'oignons & petit lard.* Turkey stuffed with onions and pickled pork	223
——— *au pere douillet*	ib.

Dindon

CONTENTS.

	Page
Dindon en galantine. Turkey coloured	224
—— *à la daube.* Turkey dobed	ib.
Daube de dindon fouré. Turkey dobed another way	225
Dindon au court bouillon. Turkey in its own gravy	ib.
—— *farci de trufes à l'Espagnole.* Turkey stuffed with truffles, Spanish fashion	ib.
—— *en timbale.* Timbale, a mould made in the form of a kettle-drum	226
—— *à l'ecarlate.* Turkey scarlet colour	ib.
—— *à la Mayence.* Turkey Mayence fashion	227
—— *à la poële.* So called for being done with very little liquid	ib.
Dindon farci de marons & saucisses. Turkey roasted, stuffed with sausages and chesnuts	227
Salmi de dindon. Turkey hashed	228
Cuisses de dindon à la Provençale, &c.	ib.
Ailes & cuisses de dindon glacées. Wings and legs of turkey glazed	229
Filets de dindon de plusieurs façons. Fillets of turkey different ways	ib.
Cuisses de dindon en surprise. Sham legs of turkey	230
Pates de dindons à la Sainte Menehoult. Stumps of turkeys, Sainte Menehoult; fried or broiled	ib.
DU PIGEONS. Of pigeons	231
Fricassée de pigeons à la poulette. White fricassee of pigeons	ib.
—— *de pigeons aux petits pois.* With green peas	ib.
—— *de pigeons à la paysanne.* Country fashion	232
Pigeons en surtout. Pigeons masqueraded, &c.	ib.
—— *au soleil*, transparent like the sun	ib.
—— *fourés aux pistaches.* Stuffed pigeons and pistachio-nuts	233
—— *au court bouillon*	ib.
—— *glacés aux legumes.* Glazed and served with stewed greens	ib.
—— *à la Périgord au gratin*	ib.
—— *au cingara*	234
—— *à la broche à differentes sauces & ragoûts.* Roasted pigeons with different sauces and ragout	ib.
—— *au basilic.*	235
—— *en hochepot à l'Espagnole.* Hotchpotch of pigeons, Spanish fashion	ib.
—— *en crépine au pontife.* Pigeons in cowl pontiff sauce	236
—— *aux écrevisses.* The same with craw-fish cullis	ib.
—— *en surprise à la Ravigotte.* Pigeons masked, with Ravigotte sauce	ib.
—— *aux trufes*	237
DES CANARDS, CANETONS, OYES, & OISONS. Of ducks and ducklings, geese and goslings	ib.
Duck and green peas	ib.

Canetons

CONTENTS.

	Page
Canetons roulés. Duckling rolled	238
———— *en hatereau.* Roasted on small skewers called hatereau	ib.
———— *de Roüen à la broche.* Rouen duckling roasted	ib.
Canetons à l'Italienne. Italian fashion	239
———— *en fricandeaux*	ib.
———— *à la purée verte.* With green peas porridge	ib.
Canard en timbale	240
———— *à la Romaine*	ib.
———— *à la Nivernoise.* Duck with sauce Nivernoise	ib.
———— *à la daube.* Duck dobed	ib.
———— *aux navets.* Duck with turnips	ib.
Grenadins de canard à la royale. Small fricandeau of duck	241
Filets de canard de plusieurs façons. Duck hashed of different ways	ib.
Oyes & oisons de plusieurs façons. Geese and goslings of different manners	242
Cuisses & ailes d'oyes, comment les conserver. How to preserve legs and wings of geese	ib.
Oye à la daube. Dobed goose	ib.
DES POULARDES & CHAPONS. Of fowls and capons	243
Poularde au gros sel. Fowl plain boiled	ib.
———— *au court bouillon.* A fowl in its own gravy	ib.
———— *au reveil. Reveil,* quick sharp sauce to the palate	244
———— *à la royale.* Fowl court fashion	ib.
———— *à la servante*	ib.
———— *au duc,* from the title duke	245
———— *à la reine*	ib.
———— *en saucisse.* Done in the form of a large sausage	246
———— *frite.* A fowl fried	ib.
———— *en cingara.* With slices of ham	ib.
———— *à la Sainte Menehoult*	247
———— *à la Tartare*	ib.
———— *au point du jour,* from the various colours	ib.
———— *aux trufes.* A fowl with truffles	248
Fricandeau d'une poularde. Fricandeau of a whole fowl	249
Poularde etuvée. Stewed fowl	ib.
———— *au sang.* Fowl stuffed with black pudding preparation	250
Filets de poularde à la poulette. Fillets of fowl fricassee	ib.
Poularde glacée. Fowl glazed	ib.
———— *en crepine.* Done in cowl	251
———— *en galantine.* Fowl in cake or marbled	ib.
———— *à la Silvie*	ib.
———— *à la financiere*	ib.
Cuisses de poularde accompagnées; meaning with other things. Legs of fowls garnished	252
Filets de poularde soufflée à la Béchamel. Fillets of fowl with a raised Bechamel sauce	ib.

CONTENTS.

	Page
Poularde au miroir. A looking-glass, a very clear jelly	253
Cuisses de poularde à l'eventail. The shape of a fan	ib.
——— *de poulardes au quadril*	254
Rissolles à la Béchamel. A fry of poultry with Bechamel sauce	255
Poularde en hochepot. Hotchpotch of fowl	ib.
——— *en hérisson.* Fowl as a hedge-hog	ib.
——— *au fumé*	256
——— *en chipoulate.* A tureen, or fowl matlot	ib.
Cuisses de poularde aux trufes. Legs of fowl and truffles	257
——— *de poularde au prince*	ib.
——— *de poulardes à la gendarme.* Military fashion	ib.
Poires de poulardes aux trufes. Legs of fowls in the form of pears	258
Cuisses de poulardes en gelée. Legs of fowls done in jelly	ib.
Culottes de poulardes à l'Italienne	ib.
Quenelles de poularde. Forced meat balls	259
Cuisses de poulardes bachique. From Bacchus	ib.
Ailerons de poulardes ou dindons de differentes façons. Pinions of fowls or turkeys of different manners	ib.
——— *composés.* Shammed pinions	260
Terrine d'ailerons aux marons. Tureen with chesnuts	ib.
Crêtes en fricassées au blanc. Cock's-combs white fricassee	ib.
Des foyes gras. Of fat livers	261
DE LA VENAISON OU VIANDE NOIR. Of venison, or brown meat	262
Du sanglier ou cochon sauvage. Of wild boars or wild hogs	ib.
Sanglier à la daube. Leg of a wild boar dobed	ib.
Hure de sanglier à la braise. Boar's-head brazed	263
Sanglier à la poivrade. Roasted, and served with a sharp sauce	ib.
——— *en petit salé.* Pickled	ib.
Boudin de sanglier. Black puddings of wild boar	264
Du marcassin. Of the suckling wild boar	ib.
— *cerf, biche, daim, chevreuil, & faon.* Of deer, hind, buck, doe, kid, and fawn	ib.
DU GIBIER EN GENERAL. Of game and wild fowls	265
Lapreaux en cailles. Rabbits roasted as quails	ib.
——— *au pontife.* Rabbits pontiff sauce	ib.
Lapreaux à l'escalope. Rabbit collop	266
——— *en galantine.* In cake or marbled	ib.
Lièvre en terrine à la daube. Tureen of hare dobed	268
——— *au sang.* Hare with its own blood	269
Roulades de lièvre. Coloured hare	ib.
Filets de levreaux à l'escalope. Collop of leveret	270
Gateau de lièvre. Hare cake	ib.
Cotelettes de levreau. Cutlets of leveret	ib.
Lièvre en civet. Hare stewed	271
Levreau au chevreuil. Leveret, kid fashion	ib.

CONTENTS.

	Page
Lièvre à la Polonoise. Hare Polish fashion	272
—— *en haricot*	ib.
Levreaux en crepine, & gratin	ib.
Filets de levreau aux legumes. Fillets of hare with stewed greens	273
Boudins de levreaux. Black puddings made of hare or leveret	ib.
Filets de levreaux aux anchois. Fillets with anchovies	ib.
Levreaux à la minute. Quick in a moment	274
Des ramereaux. Of wood-pigeons	ib.
Ramereaux à l'Allemande. German fashion	ib.
—— *aux fenouil.* With fennel sauce	275
Bécasses, Bécassines, & Bécaux à la broche à differentes sauces. Wood-cocks, snipes of both kinds, roasted with different sauces	ib.
Salmie de bécasses	ib.
—— *de bécasses à la Sainte Menehoult*	276
Becassines à la duchesse	ib.
Bécaux à la Perigord	277
—— *au salmie de Provence.* Snipes salmie, Provence fashion	ib.
Filets de bécasses au jus de canard. Fillets of wood-cocks with duck gravy	ib.
Bécasses & bécassines aux trufes, & aux olives. Wood-cocks and snipes with truffles and olive ragout	278
Des alouettes. Of larks	ib.
Alouettes en cerises. Larks in the form of cherries	279
Des pluviers, vaneaux, & grives. Of plovers, lapwings, and thrushes	ib.
Pluvier à la Perigord. Plover with truffles	ib.
Cailles à la Flamande. Quails Flemish fashion	280
Cailles au laurier. Quails with laurel	280
—— *en ragoût,* ditto *en matelotte, au gratin, &c.*	281
Des perdreaux & perdrix. Of partridges young and old	ib.
Perdreaux à la broche à differentes sauces & ragoûts. Roasted partridges with different sauces and ragout	ib.
—— *à la Madelaine*	ib.
—— *grillés aux fines herbes.* Boiled with sweet herbs	282
—— *à la Provençale, au pontife*	ib.
—— *au consommé.* With rich cullis sauce	ib.
—— *à la Perigord*	ib.
—— *à la Dauphine*	283
Perdrix à la Villeroi, from the title	284
—— *en aspic*	ib.
Perdreaux à la Mandui. After the name of the maker	285
Achis à la Turque. Hash Turkish fashion	ib.
Perdrix à la daube Sicilienne. Partridges dobed Sicily fashion	ib.

CONTENTS

OF THE SECOND VOLUME.

CHAPITRE HUITIEME.
CHAPTER EIGHTH.

Des Ragoûts & Rissolles.

Of Ragouts, Collops or Fries.

	Page
RAGOUT *de salpiquon.* Forced-meat ragout	289
Ragoût de salpiquon à farcir, prepared for stuffing any thing	290
——— *de salpiquon à l'arlequine*	ib.
——— *de foyes gras.* Of fat livers	ib.
——— *de crêtes.* Of cock's-combs	291
——— *de jambon.* Of ham	ib.
——— *de petits oeufs & rognons de coq.* Ragout of small eggs and cock's-kidneys	ib.
——— *de ris de veau.* Of calves sweet-breads	292
——— *mêlés de trufes & d'huîtres.* Ragout of truffles and oysters	ib.
Ragoûts à l'Angloise. English fashion	293
Ragoût d'écrevisses. Of craw-fish	ib.
——— *de laitances.* Of carp-roes	ib.
——— *de moules.* Of mussels	294
——— *d'huîtres de plusieurs façons.* Of oysters of different manners	ib.
——— *de morilles.* Of morels	295

Vol. II.   b   *Ragoût*

CONTENTS.

	Page
Ragoût de champignons. Of mushrooms	295
—— de concombres. Of cucumbers	296
—— de pois. Of green peas	ib.
—— de verjus. Of verjuice-grapes, or others	297
—— de trufes. Of truffles	ib.
—— d'asperges en petits pois. Asparagus as green peas	ib.
—— de petits oignons. Of small round onions	298
—— de racines. Of roots	ib.
—— de navets. Of turnips	ib.
—— de chicorée. Of endives or any sorts of lettuces	ib.
—— d'ozeille. Of sorrel	299
—— d'Epinars. Of spinages	ib.
—— de cardons d'espagne. Of Spanish cardoons	ib.
—— de pistaches. Of pistachio-nuts	300
—— de cerneaux. Of green walnuts	ib.
—— de choux. Of cabbage	ib.
—— d'haricots verd. Of kidney-beans	ib.
Rissolles à la Béchamel. White collops	301
—— à la Choisy	ib.
—— de palais de bœuf. Of beef-palates	302
—— de gibier. Of game	ib.
—— de différentes farces. Of different forced-meats	ib.
—— à la présidente.	303
—— à la Provençale	ib.

DU ROTI, & DE LA FAÇON DE PRÉPARER. ib.

OF ROAST, AND HOW TO PREPARE EACH KIND.

Du Printems. Of the Spring	304
De l'Eté. Of Summer	ib.
— *l'Automne.* Of Autumn.	ib.
— *l'Hyver.* Of Winter	305
— *la preparation de toutes sortes de rotis.* Of the preparation of all sorts of roast	ib.
Des oiseaux de riviere. Of fresh-water fowls	306
— *oiseaux que l'on sert avec de rôties dessous.* Of the kind of birds which are served with a toast under	ib.
Du poisson d'eau douce, & de mer. Of fresh and sea water fish	307

CONTENTS.

	Page
Des glaces & braises maigres. Of meager glazes and brazes	307
Farce de poisson. Fish forced-meat	308
—— *maigre sans poisson.* Farce without fish	ib.

DU POISSON. OF FISH ... ib.

Carpe au court-bouillon, & au bleu. Stewed carp, blue sauce	ib.
—— *à la Bourgogne.* With red wine	309
—— *à la financiere*	ib.
—— *farcie à la gendarme.* Military fashion	310
—— *grillée à la farce.* Carp stuffed and broiled	ib.
—— *frite.* Fried carp	311
—— *à l'étuvée.* Stewed	ib.
Etuvée de carpe à la Chartreuse	ib.
Carpe en matelotte	312
—— *en matelotte à la mariniere*	ib.
—— *à la Jacobine*	313
—— *aux fines herbes.* With sweet-herbs	ib.
—— *farcie.* Stuffed	ib.
—— *à la Dauphine*	314
—— *au monarque.* Monarch	ib.
—— *à la Polonoise.* Polish fashion	ib.
—— *à la broche.* roasted	315
—— *en hachis.* Hashed	ib.
—— *en redingotte.* Masked	ib.
—— *en écusson.* In the form of a scutcheon	316
—— *au prince.* From the richness of the preparation	ib.
Filets de carpes de plusieurs façons. Carp-filets of different manners	317
Du brochet. Of pike	ib.
Brochet à la poulette. Pike white fricassee	ib.
—— *frit.* Fried	318
—— *à l'Italienne à la broche.* Roasted Italian fashion	ib.
—— *en dauphin.* In the form of the dolphin fish	ib.
—— *à la mariée.* Bride-fashion	ib.
—— *au gros sel.* In a plain way	319
—— *à la broche en gras & en maigre.* Roasted pike with meat-sauce or meager	ib.
—— *à la Simone.* Country-wife fashion	ib.
—— *en grenadins.* As small fricandeau	320
—— *en étuvée.* Stewed as matlotte	ib.

b 2   Brochet

CONTENTS.

	Page
Brochet au vin de Champagne. With white wine	320
——— à la *Provençale*	321
——— à la *duchesse*	ib.
——— *moitié au bleu, moitié frit*; half stewed and half fried	ib.
——— à l'*Allemande*. German fashion	322
——— à l'*Espagnole*. Spanish fashion	ib.
——— à l'*arlequine*. Of various colours	ib.
De l'anguille. Of eels	323
Anguille en fricassée de poulets. As chicken-fricassée	ib.
——— à la *Nivernoise*	ib.
——— à la *broche diversifiée*; roasted, to different sauces	ib.
——— *glacée*. Eel glazed, or as fricandeau	324
——— à la *Chartreuse*. From an order of Friars so called	ib.
——— à la *sainte Menehoult*	325
——— *au brodequin*. Racktied	ib.
Façon de conserver les anguilles, ou autres poissons. How to preserve eels, or any kind of fishes	ib.
Anguille frite. Fried eel	326
——— à l'*étuvée*. Stewed or matlotte	ib.
——— à la *Choisi*	ib.
——— *en canapé*. Matted, or any other kind of fish	327
Andouillettes d'anguilles. Sausages or chitterlings of eels	ib.
Anguille à la Napolitaine. Naples fashion	328
——— à l'*aspic*. With a sharp sauce	ib.
De la lamproie. Of lampreys	ib.
Etuvée de lamproie. Stewed lamprey	329
Lamproie grillé à remoulade	ib.
——— à l'*Italienne*. Italian fashion	ib.
——— à la *Burgogne*. With Burgundy or any other red wine	330
De la perche. Of perches	ib.
Perche au beurre. Perches with butter sauce	ib.
——— à la *Tartare*. Tartary fashion	ib.
Perches à différentes sauces & ragoûts	331
——— à l'*Angloise*. English fashion	ib.
Mattelotte de perche à l'eau	ib.
Perches au vin de Champagne. With white wine	332
——— *frites*. Fried	ib.
Des tenches. Of tenches	ib.
Tenches à la poulette. As a chicken-fricassée	ib.
Tenche au pontife. With pontiff-sauce	333

Tenches

CONTENTS.

	Page
Tenches en ragoûts	333
——— *à la bonne-femme.* The good house-wife's fashion	ib.
——— *à la ravigotte*	334
——— *au monarque.* Monarch	ib.
——— *de plusieurs façons.* Of different manners	ib.
——— *à l'Italienne.* Italian fashion	335
De la truite. Of trouts	ib.
Truite aux fines herbes. With sweet-herbs	ib.
——— *à l'Allemande.* German fashion	336
——— *au bleu.* Of fine blue colour	ib.
Truites à la Chartreuse	337
Truite à la Perigord. With truffles	ib.
——— *glacée.* Glazed as a fricandeau	ib.
Filets de truites de différentes façons. Fillets of different manners	338
Truites au four. Done in the oven	ib.
Filets de truites au vin de Champagne. With white wine	ib.
Du barbillon, goujon, & grenouilles. Of the barbel-fish, gudgeon, and frogs	339
— *barbillon.* Of the barbel-fish	ib.
Des grenouilles. Of frogs	ib.
— *goujons.* Of gudgeons	340
Matelottes de goujons	ib.
Du saumon. Of salmon	ib.
Saumon au court-bouillon. In its own sauce	ib.
——— *aux écrevisses en gras & en maigre.* Salmon with craw-fish, gras or meager	ib.
——— *accompagné,* viz. garnished with other things	341
——— *aux fines herbes.* With sweet-herbs	ib.
——— *en fricandeaux*	342
——— *à la bonne-femme.* The good house-wife's fashion	ib.
——— *frit.* Fried salmon	ib.
Filets de saumon à l'Italienne	343
Saumon en hatelet. As haslets	ib.
Hure de saumon à différentes sauces & ragoûts. Joul of salmon with different sauces or ragouts	ib.
Darde de saumon à la Choisi	344
Caisses de saumon fumé. Cases of smoked salmon	ib.
Saumon salé à la Hollandoise. Dried salmon Dutch fashion	ib.
Salade de saumon salé & autres façons. Sallad of dried salmon, and other manners	345
De l'esturgeon. Of sturgeon	ib.

CONTENTS.

	Page
Esturgeon au court-bouillon	345
——— *à differentes sauces en gras et en maigre.* Sturgeon with different sauces, gras or meager	ib.
——— *à la broche en gras & en maigre.* Sturgeon roasted, gras or meager	346
——— *à la Mayence*	ib.
——— *à la bonne-femme.* The good house-wife	347
——— *grillé.* broiled	ib.
——— *à la sainte Menehoult en gras & en maigre*	ib.
——— *à l'Angloise.* English fashion	348
——— *à la Provençale*	ib.
——— *à la hâte.* Sturgeon in haste	ib.
——— *Grenadins d'esturgeon.* Small fricandeau of sturgeon	349
Esturgeon à la cendre. On Ashes, or brazed very slowly	ib.
Du turbot & turbotin. Of large and small turbots	ib.
Turbot au court-bouillon. Meant as plain boiled as others	350
Turbotins aux fines herbes. With sweet-herbs	ib.
Filets de turbot de differentes façons	ib.
Turbotin à la sainte Menehoult. Small turbot broiled	351
Turbotins au Parmesan. Small turbots with Parmesan cheese	ib.
Turbot au pontife. With pontiff-sauce	ib.
——— *glacée.* Glazed	352
——— *au citron*	ib.
——— *à la financiere*	ib.
——— *à la Hollandoise.* Dutch fashion	353
Des carlets, plies, et halibotte. Of flounders, plaice, and hallibut	ib.
Carlets au citron. Flounders lemon-sauce	354
De la sole. Of soals	ib.
Soles au suprême, viz. excelling, &c.	ib.
——— *au pontife.* With pontiff-sauce	355
——— *de plusieurs façons.* Of different ways	ib.
——— *aux fines herbes.* With sweet-herbs	ib.
——— *au four.* Baked in the oven	356
——— *en batereaux.* Olives, either fried or roasted	ib.
——— *en fricandeaux*	ib.
Filets de soles à la Béchamel	357
——— *de soles au verjus.* Verjuice-sauce	ib.
De l'alose. Shad-fish	ib.
De la vive. Of the fish called weaver	358

CONTENTS.

	Page
Vives de differentes façons. See foals of different ways, and numbers of others	358
Des merlans, et surmulets. Of whitings and mullets	359
Merlans à la sauce à la morue	ib.
———— *en batereaux*	360
Quenelles de merlans	ib.
Merlans à la moutarde. With mustard-sauce	ib.
———— *au pontife.* With pontiff-sauce	ib.
Filets de merlans à differentes sauces	ib.
Eperlans à la sainte Menehoult. Smelts broiled	361
———— *en surtout.* Masked	ib.
———— *au fenouil.* Smelts with fennel-sauce	ib.
Matelottes, ou eperlans aux fines herbes	ib.
Du maquereaux. Of mackerels	362
Maquereaux à la maître d' hôtel	ib.
———— *aux fines herbes.* With sweet-herbs	ib.
———— *à la Flamande.* Flemish fashion	363
———— *au court-bouillon*	ib.
———— *à l' Italienne.* Italian fashion	ib.
———— *en fricandeaux*	ib.
———— *frit.* Fried mackerels	364
———— *à la Nivernoise*	ib.
Filets de maquereaux au jus d'orange. Orange-sauce	ib.
Caisses de maquereaux aux trufes. Broiled in paper-cases, with a truffles farce	ib.
Maquereaux aux écrevisses. With craw-fish sauce	365
———— *en cailles;* as quails	ib.
Des harengs & sardines. Of herrings and pilchards	ib.
Harengs frais à la moutarde. Fresh herrings, mustard-sauce	366
———— *frais marinés*	ib.
———— *frais sauce au capers.* Fresh herrings with caper-sauce	ib.
———— *frais au fenouil.* With fennel-sauce	ib.
———— *frais à la sainte Menehoult*	ib.
Harengs frais aux fines herbes	367
———— *frais en matelotte*	ib.
Sardines grillées. Pilchards broiled	ib.
Harengs sors & salés à la sainté Menehoult. Dried and pickled herrings broiled	ib.
Rouget aux capre. Roaches caper-sauce	ib.

CONTENTS.

	Page
DU CABILIOT, DE LA MORUE, & MERLUCHE	368

Merluche à differentes sauces. Dried cod, or stock-fish — *ib.*
Hure de cabiliot aux huitres. Cod's head, oyster-sauce — *ib.*
Morûe fraiche aux fines herbes. Codling, with sweet-herbs — 369
—— *ou merluche à la Flamande.* Flemish fashion — *ib.*
—— *à la capucine* — *ib.*
—— *à la jardiniere* — 370
—— *à la maître d' hotel* — *ib.*
—— *à la moutarde* — *ib.*
—— *au beurre noir.* With burnt butter — *ib.*
De la raie. Of scate — 371
Raie à differentes sauces. Scate to different sauces — *ib.*
—— *au beurre noir.* With burnt butter — *ib.*
—— *marinée.* Scate marinaded — 372
—— *grillée.* Broiled — *ib.*
—— *aux fines herbes à la Jacobine* — *ib.*
—— *en matelotte au Parmesan.* As matlot and Parmesan cheese — *ib.*
—— *au vin de Champagne.* Wine-sauce — 373

DE LA PATISSERIE. OF PASTRY *ib.*

Pâte brisée. Puff-paste — 374
—— *feuillettée.* Rich puff-paste — *ib.*
—— *feuillettée à l' huile.* The same with oil — *ib.*
—— *à la graisse de boeuf.* Paste with beef-suet — *ib.*
—— *à demi-feuilletage.* Not so rich — 375
—— *à baignet.* Friture-paste, or batter — *ib.*
—— *croquante.* Paste for crokants — *ib.*
—— *à la royale.* Royal paste — *ib.*
—— *à la reine.* Queen-paste — 376
—— *à l' Espagnole.* Paste Spanish fashion — *ib.*
—— *à canellon* — *ib.*
—— *au ris.* Rice-paste — *ib.*
—— *au beurre d' écrevisses.* With craw-fish butter — 377
—— *au sucre.* Sugar-paste — *ib.*
—— *au fromage.* Cheese-paste — *ib.*
—— *à la duchesse* — *ib.*
—— *d' amande.* Almond-paste — *ib.*
—— *à échaudée.* Choudy-paste — 378
—— *à brioche* — 379

CONTENTS.

                Page

Pâte de flan, dariole, & de ce que l'on veut. Paste proper for large and small custards — — — *ib.*
—— *à la Flamande.* Flemish fashion —— 380

DE PATES, OF PIES.

Pâté de boeuf. Beef-pie —— —— *ib.*
—— *de veau.* Veal-pie —— —— 381
—— *de mouton melé.* Mutton-pie mixed — —— *ib.*
—— *de cochon de lait.* Of suckling pig —— *ib.*
—— *de jambon.* Ham-pie —— —— 382
—— *de venaison.* Venison-pie, or pasty —— *ib.*
—— *de poulardes, dindons, & autres volailles.* Pies of all kinds of poultries, and wild fowls — — *ib.*
Pâté d'Amiens en pâte fine. Fine paste —— 383
— *d'Amiens en pâte bise.* The same in common paste *ib.*
— *de perdrix.* Partridge-pie —— —— 384
— *à la Choisi* — — *ib.*
— *de pluviers, becasses, et becassines.* Plovers, woodcocks, and snipes pie — — *ib.*
— *de pigeons, ortolans, cailles, alouettes, &c. &c.* Pigeon-pie, quails, and all sorts of small birds, fit for eating 385
— *de Perigueux.* A town in Perigord famous for those pies, commonly called *Perigord pies* — *ib.*
— *de lièvres & de lapins.* Of hares and rabbits 386
— *de faisand.* Of pheasant —— —— *ib.*
— *d'esturgeon.* Sturgeon-pie — — *ib.*
— *de macreuse.* A wild fowl — — *ib.*
— *de truite.* Of trouts, a cold dish —— 387
— *de soles.* Of soals —— *ib.*
— *de saumon.* Of salmon —— —— *ib.*

DES TOURTES, PATES CHAUDS, ET PETITES PATISSERIES.   388

Of pastry for first course, and small for second, hot or cold.

Tourtes d'ailerons. Of pinions of poultries —— *ib.*
—— *de becasses.* Of wood-cocks — — *ib.*
Tourte aux cailleteaux. Of young quails — — *ib.*
—— *de filets de levrauts.* Of fillets of leverets — 389
—— *de foies gras.* Of fat livers — *ib.*
Tourtes de langues de boeuf, veau, & mouton. Puff-paste pies of beef, veal, and sheep's tongues — — *ib.*

                Tourte

CONTENTS.

	Page
Tourte de lapreaux. Of rabbits	390
—— *de pigeons.* Of pigeons	ib.
—— *de perdreaux.* Of young partridges	ib.
—— *de godiveaux.* A raw forced-meat	391
—— *de tendrons de veau.* Of veal-gristles	ib.
—— *de saucisse accompagnée.* Of sausages garnished with other things	392
—— *à la Condé*	ib.
—— *de lasaques.* A dumpling paste-pie	ib.
—— *de viandes blanches.* Of white meats	393
—— *de filets de mouton à la Robert.* Of fillets of mutton with onions	ib.
—— *en puits*	ib.
—— *de cannetons au vin de Champagne.* Of ducklings	394
—— *au zephir*	ib.
—— *de lapin au zephir.* Of rabbit	ib.
—— *de macaroni au zephir*	395
—— *d'œufs.* Of eggs	ib.
—— *de soles.* Of soals	ib.
—— *de moules & d'huitres.* Of oysters and mussels	396
—— *de cabilliot.* Of cod, &c. &c.	ib.
Tourtes d'esturgeons, tourte d'anguilles, de brochet & carpes	ib.
Des petits pâtés de godiveaux	ib.
Petit pâté en saucisses. In the form of sausages	397
Petits pâtés à la reine. Queen-pates from the sauce ditto	ib.
—— *pâtés au pontife*	398

DES TOURTES & AUTRES PATTISSERIES D'ENTREMETS 399

Of tarts and other second-course Pastry.

Tourte de cerises froide. Cold cherry tart	ib.
—— *de framboises.* Of rasberries	400
—— *de fraises à la glace.* Of strawberries and iced cream	ib.
—— *d'abricots.* Of apricocks	ib.
—— *de franchipane.* Italian, after Frangipani, a proper name	401
—— *à la moële.* Of marrow	ib.
—— *d'amande.* Of almonds	ib.
—— *de verjus.* Of verjuice-grapes or any others	ib.
—— *de muscat.* Of muscado, or sweet grapes	ib.
—— *de pistache.* Of pistachio-nuts	402

Tourte

CONTENTS.

	Page
Tourte à la Chantilli	402
—— *de pommes.* Of apples	ib.
—— *de poires.* Of pears	ib.
—— *de prunes.* Of plums	403
—— *d'épinards.* Of spinages	ib.
—— *de groseilles vertes.* Of green gooseberries	ib.
—— *de chocolat, & tourte de caffé.* Of chocolate and coffee	ib.
—— *à la paysanne.* Common, or country-fashion	404
—— *de trufes à la glace.* Of truffles iced	ib.
—— *d'entremets de ce que l'on veut.* Second-course pastry of any kind of fruits or jelly	ib.
Petites jaloufie	405
Tartelettes à la crême. Custard in paste	ib.
——— *de massepains.* Tartlets of sugar-paste	ib.
Rissolles d'entremets de ce que l'on veut. Fritures for second-course of any kind	406
Soufflets. A raised puff-cake	ib.
Croquantes à la d'Estrées	ib.
——— *en caramel.* Burnt sugar crokant	407
——— *de pâte d'amandes.* Of almond-paste	ib.
Nœuds d'epées, Sword-knots	408
Massepains de fleurs. Sugar or almond paste, cut in flowers	ib.
Paniers de vendange	409
Petites rossettes. Small knots	ib.
——— *corbeilles de massepains à la glace.* Small buckets of sugar-paste, with ice-cream	ib.
Gâteaux à la madeleine, Common small cakes.	410
——— *de la neige.* Whipt cream, like snow	ib.
——— *de Niauffles* } where made	ib.
——— *de Bourneville* }	411
Biscuit de Turin, ou gateau de Savoy. Savoy cake	ib.
Bonnet de Turquie à la glace Turk's cap, with ice-cream	ib.
——— *de Turquie en surprise.* Sham Turk's cap	412
Gateaux en turbans	ib.
Biscotins. Small biscuits	ib.
Gâteaux en feuillage	413
——— *à la Polonoise.* Polish fashion cake.	ib.
——— *au Sultan*	ib.
——— *d'amandes.* Almond-cake	ib.
——— *à la Bechamel*	414
——— *de Compiegne*	ib.
——— *au ris.* Rice-cake	ib.

Gâteaux

CONTENTS.

	Page
Gateaux de piſtache. Of piſtachio-nuts	415
——— *de verjus.* Of verjuice-grapes preſerved	ib.
——— *à la Dauphine*	ib.
Ramequins. Cheeſe-cakes	ib.
——— *vole-au-vent.* Light to fly with the wind	416
——— *à la Toulouſe.* A city in France	ib.
Timbals. A mould ſo called, for being in the ſhape of a kettle-drum	ib.
Petits choux. A ſmall ſort of choudee	ib.
Biſcuit au clinquant. Beautified with tinſel. Tinſel-cake	417
Talmouſes. Cheeſe-cakes of a different kind from ramequin	ib.
——— *de Saint Denis*	ib.
Flancs. A large cuſtard	ib.
Darioles. A mould ſo called	418
Feuillantine. A cream-cake	ib.
Echaudés au ſel. Dumpling-paſte	ib.
Puits d'amour. From moulds to cut paſte ſo called	419
Gobelets à la moële. Marrow-tumblers	ib.
Differentes entremets de biſcuits. Different ſecond or laſt courſe diſhes of biſcuit-paſte	ib.
Genoiſes. Olive-fritures	ib.
Canellons. In the form of a cane or ſmall gun	420

DES ENTREMETS DE CREME, LEGUMES, & AUTRES, EN GRAS & EN MAIGRE. ib.

OF LAST COURSE DISHES, OF CREAMS, GARDENINGS, AND OTHERS, GRAS OR MEAGER.

Crême legere. Light cream	ib.
——— *au chapelet.* From the border made in the form of beads	ib.
——— *en quadrille.* Four ſquares, or partition of four colours	421
——— *à la croix de Malthe.* Malta croſs	ib.
——— *à la ſultane*	ib.
——— *à l'abbeſſe*	422
——— *à la mariée.* Bride-cream	ib.
——— *frite.* Fried cream	ib.
Autre crême frite. Another fried cream	423
Crême de chocolat	ib.
——— *de caffé*	ib.

Crême

CONTENTS.

	Page
Créme d' herbages de ce que l'on veut. With garden-herbs of what kind you please	ib.
—— *veloutée.* Velveted, soft, rich, &c.	424
—— *brûlée.* Burnt cream	ib.
—— *de vermicel ou de ris.* With vermicelly or rice	ib.
—— *à la Strasbourg.* The inventor's name	425
—— *à la Dauphine*	ib.
—— *au gratin*	ib.
—— *au caramel*	ib.
—— *meringuée.* Whites of eggs froughted, called a *meringue*	426
Autre créme meringuée. Squirted cream	ib.
Créme soufflée. Raised or puff cream	ib.
—— *à la reine.* Queen's cream	427
—— *d'œufs à l'eau.* Eggs and water cream	ib.
—— *au blanc-mangé*	ib.
—— *d'écrevisses.* Craw-fish cream	ib.
—— *bachique*	428
—— *à la Bourgogne.* Burgundy-cream	ib.
—— *de ris au bouillon.* Rice-cream boiled in broth	ib.
—— *à la duchesse.*	429
—— *à la nourrice.* Nurse-fashion, or nurse-cream	ib.
Baignets Italiens. Fritures Italian fashion	ib.
—— *à l'Angloise.* English fashion	430
—— *en surtout.* Masked	ib.
—— *d'amandes.* Of almonds	ib.
—— *soufflés de pâte.* Raised paste fritures	431
—— *de pain à chanter.* Wafer-baignets	ib.
—— *de blanc-mangé*	ib.
—— *de pommes en piédesteaux.* Apple-fritures on pedestals	ib.
—— *de pommes en surprise.* Masked, &c.	432
—— *à la mariée.* Bride-fritures	ib.
—— *de pêches & d'abricots.* Of peaches and apricocks	ib.
—— *à la créme.* Cream-fritures	ib.
—— *de fraises.* Of strawberries	433
—— *de sureau, & de vigne.* Of elder-flowers, and vine-leaves	ib.
—— *à l'Espagnole.* Spanish fashion, or orange-fritures	ib.
—— *de ramequins*	ib.
—— *à la dauphine*	434
—— *à la fermiere.* Farmer, or house-wife fashion	ib.
—— *à la nonnette.* Nuns fritures	ib.
—— *en caisses.* In paper-cases	ib.
—— *de plusieurs façons.* Of different sorts	435

CONTENTS.

	Page
Rôtie (toast) à la minime	435
—— à la Genoise. Italian toast	ib.
—— à l' infante. Spanish fashion	436
—— au mortier. Pounded toast	ib.
—— de Bretagne. Brittany toast	ib.
—— de foies gras. Fat liver toast	ib.
—— de rognons de veau. Veal-kidney toast	437
—— au jambon. Ham-toast	ib.
—— de foies de raies, & autres Of scate-livers, and others	ib.
—— à l' Allemande. German fashion	438
—— de légumes. Of garden-greens, &c.	ib.
—— en rochers. Rock, to look like biscuits so called	ib.
—— soufflées. Puffed or raised	439
Pommes en farbalat. Apples festooned	ib.
—— en colimaçon. In the shape of snails	ib.
—— en surprise. Masked apples	440
—— farcies. Stuffed apples	ib.
—— glacées. In jelly, or glazed	ib.
Pain de jambon à la Mayence. Ham roll, or cold loaf	441
—— en surprise	ib.
—— de morilles & de champaignons. Morels or mushroom-loaf	ib.
—— à l' Espagnole. Spanish	442
—— à la crême	ib.
—— à la duchesse	ib.
Fondues en caisses. Melted cheese in paper-cases	443
Caufres à la Flamande. Flemish gawfers	ib.
Laitances de carpes à la Hollandoise. Carp-roes, Dutch fashion	444
—— de carpes à la bellevue. Agreeable, well-looking	ib.
—— de carpes à l' Angloise. English fashion	445
—— de carpes frites. Carp-roes fried	ib.
Timbals d'anchois. From the moulds so called	ib.
Anchois au basilic. Anchovies with basil	ib.
—— au Parmesan. With Parmesan-cheese	446
Oreilles de lièvres & de lapins de plusieurs façons. Hares and rabbits ears, to different sauces	ib.
Gelée de viande. Meat-jelly	ib.
—— de blanc-mangé	447.
CONTINUATION DE PETITS PLATS D'ENTREMETS. Small last-course dishes continued.	ib.
Huîtres frites. Broiled oysters	ib.

Huîtres

CONTENTS.

	Page
Huitres en ragout	448
———— *sautées.* Jumped, or done in a hurry	ib.
———— *à l' Espagnole.* Spanish fashion, or sauce	ib.
———— *à l' etuvée.* Stewed oysters	ib.
———— *en coquilles.* Scollop oysters	449
———— *en surtout*	ib.
Ecrevisses au court-bouillon. Craw-fish plain boiled	ib.
———— *à la poulette, ou à la Bechamel.* Craw-fish fricassée, or Bechamel-sauce	450
———— *farcies.* Stuffed craw-fish	ib.
———— *à la Flamande.* Flemish fashion	ib.
———— *à l' Italienne*	ib.
———— *au trufes.* With truffles	451
———— *à la sainte Menehoult*	ib.
———— *aux fines herbes.* Craw-fish stewed with sweet-herbs	452
———— *à la broche*	ib.
———— *à la hâte.* Quickly done	ib.
———— *au monarque*	453
Fromage d' écrevisses. Craw-fish cheese	ib.

BEURRE D' ECREVISSES. CRAW-FISH BUTTER 454

OMELETTES. OF OMELETS. — ib.

Omelette à la gendarme. Military	455
———— *au basilic en baignets.* With sweet basil	ib.
———— *soufflée.* Raised, &c. &c.	ib.
———— *à la farce.* With a ragout of stewed greens	ib.
———— *à la crême de ris.* With cream, and rice-flour	456
———— *aux amandes*	ib.
———— *d' anchois, ou de harengs sorets.* With anchovies, or red herrings	ib.
———— *aux oignons*	457
———— *à la dauphine*	ib.
———— *à la crême,* &c.	ib.
———— *au Parmesan.* With Parmesan-cheese, &c.	458
———— *en neige.* Snow-balls of eggs	ib.
Oeufs à la dauphine	459
——— *au caffé.* Coffee-eggs, or with coffee	ib.
——— *à l'eau au caramel.* Eggs with water caramel	460
——— *brouillées à la Provençale.* Mashed eggs, Provençale fashion	ib.

Oeufs

CONTENTS.

	Page
Oeufs au gratin au Parmesan	461
—— *au prevôt*, as sheriff, or judge-advocate, &c. &c.	ib.
—— *à l' étuvée.* Stewed	ib.
Des oeufs frits, & des oeufs pochés, à ce que l' on veut. Of fried and poached eggs, to any sauce or ragout	462
Oeufs à la tripe ou à la crême. Eggs fricassee	ib.
—— *en filets à la moutarde*	463
—— *à la tripe au petit pois.* With stewed pease	ib.
—— *à la tripe au concombres.* With stewed cucumbers	ib.
—— *farcies au concombres.* Stuffed with a cucumber-ragout	ib.
—— *à la farce.* Hard boiled	ib.
—— *à la Flamande.* Flemish fashion	464
—— *à la môde*	465
—— *glacés.* Glazed	ib.
—— *au pere Simon.* Father Simon, or Gaffar any thing	ib.
—— *au coulis de légumes.* With a cullis or garden-stuff porridge	466
—— *à la vestale.* Virgin, from being white, unsoiled, &c.	ib.
—— *aux épinars.* With spinages	467
—— *à l' eau.* With water	468
—— *en surprise au basilic.* Sham eggs, with basil	ib.
—— *au point-du-jour.* The dawn of day, taken from the colour of	ib.
—— *en crépine, a ce que l' ont veut.* Eggs in cowl to what you please	469
—— *au céladon.* Sea-green	470
Façon de faire les petits oeufs pour garnir. How to make small eggs or little bullets for garnishing	474
Bouillie. Pap or thick milk	ib.
Du ris & greuau au lait. Rice milk and gruel	ib.
Ris au caramel. Glazed with sugar-caramel	475
Des petits pois. Of green or young pease	ib.
Petits pois dans leur suc. Green-pease in their own juice	ib.
—— *pois au lard.* With bacon, or pickled pork	ib.
—— *pois à l' Angloise.* English fashion	476
—— *pois à la crême.* Stewed pease, or fricassee	ib.
—— *sans parchemin*, or *pois goulus*	ib.
Pois secs. Of dried pease	477
Féves de marais à la crême. Garden-beans, cream-sauce	ib.
Haricots verds. Green kidney-beans	ib.
—— *verds en salade.* Green kidney-beans sallad	ib.
—— *verds au coulis.* With cullis-sauce, or as a ragout	478

Haricots

CONTENTS.

	Page
Haricots verds frits. Fried	478
———— *verds à la Flamande.* Flemish fashion	ib.
———— *verds pour confire & sécher.* How to keep dried or preserved green kidney-beans	479
———— *blancs à la poulette.* White kidney or Roman beans fricassée	ib.
———— *blancs en salade.* The same as a sallad	480
———— *blancs à l' oignon.* With onions	ib.
Lentilles fricassées. Fricassée of lentils	ib.
Choux brocolis. Brocoli, white or green	481
———— *rave*	ib.
———— *rouge.* Red cabbages	ib.
———— *farcis.* Cabbage stuffed	482
———— *à la Flamande.* Cabbages Flemish fashion	ib.
———— *à la Saint Cloud*; either the name of the place, or the inventor	ib.
———— *à la marechal.* Field-general of an army, &c.	483
———— *à la Lyonnoise.* From Lyon, a city in France	ib.
Des oignons, ail, persil, ciboules, echalottes, & rocamboles. Of onions, garlick, parsley, chibbol, shallots, and rocamboles	484
Oignons à l'Italienne. Italian fashion	ib.
———— *aux oeufs de carpes.* Stewed with carp-roes	485
Des navets, ravioles, raves, poireaux, carotes, & panais. Of turnips, turnip-radishes, common radishes, leeks, carrots, and parsneps	ib.
Navets en cardons. Turnips as cardoons	ib.
Ravioles & raves de plusieurs façons. Radishes different ways	486
Des carotes, panais, racines de persil, de plusieurs façons. Carrots, parsneps, and parsley-roots, of different fashions	ib.
Poireaux & celleris. Leeks and cellery	ib.
Epinars à la crême. Spinage with cream	487
———— *en tabatieres.* In snuff-boxes	ib.
———— *à la bonne femme.* The good house-wife	488
Du pourpier. Of purslain	ib.
Des cardes de plusieurs façons. Cardoons of different manners	489
De l'oseille, laitues, & chicorées. Of sorrel, lettuces of different sorts, and endives	ib.
Laitues de plusieurs façons. Different ways of dressing lettuces	ib.
Choux-fleurs. Colliflowers	490
———— *fleurs à la reine.* Colliflower, Queen's-sauce	ib.
———— *fleurs au jus.* With gravy, &c.	491

CONTENTS.

	Page
Concombres à la poulette. Cucumbers fricassee, or white sauce	491
——— *farcis.* Stuffed cucumbers	ib.
Melons, comment les confire. How to preserve melons for cookery	492
——— *en baignets.* Melon-friture	ib.
Des chervis, salsifix, & taupinambours. Or skirret, salsifix or white beet-root, and potatoes	493
Des fines herbes. Of sweet-herbs	ib.
Du houblon. Of hops	ib.
Des artichauts. Of artichokes, dried or preserved	ib.
Artichauts à la sauce blanche. With white sauce	494
——— *frits.* Fried artichokes	ib.
——— *à la glace, ou en crysteaux.* From looking-glass, or cut glasses	ib.
——— *à la Barigoult*	495
——— *au prevôt*	ib.
A la marinière	496
Artichauts aux trufes. With truffles-farce	ib.
——— *à la brie*	497
——— *à la Saint Cloud*	ib.
——— *au pere Bernard.* Father or gaffar Bernard, &c.	498
——— *en accolade.* Glued or soldered together	ib.
——— *à la Mayence.* With Westphalia ham-sauce or slices	499
Des trufes. Of truffles	500
Trufes au court-bouillon. This is commonly meant for plain boiled, &c.	ib.
Trufes en puits. Truffles gored and stuffed	501
——— *à la poele.*	ib.
Asperges en batons. Asparagus plain boiled	502
Des morilles, mousserons, & champignons	ib.
Morilles à la Provençale	503
——— *au prince, & à la créme*	ib.
——— *au lard.* With bacon	504
Mousserons ou champignons de plusieurs façons. Champignons or mushrooms, different ways, being both dressed alike	ib.
Champignons en canellons. Mushrooms fried in paste	ib.
——— *à la St. Menehoult.* Broiled mushrooms	505
——— *au pere Douillet*	ib.
DE L'OFFICE OF CONFECTIONARY.	506
Des différentes cuissons de sucre. Of different degrees of preparing sugar	507

D4

CONTENTS.

	Page
De la façon de clarifier le sucre. The method to clarify sugar	507
Premiere couisson du sucre, qui est le petit lissé. First degree of refining sugar, called small *lissé*, sleeked, &c. —	508
Cuissons au grand perlé, à la petite & la grande queue de cochon, au soufflé, & à la petite plume. Third, fourth, fifth, sixth, seventh, and eighth degrees of refining	ib.
La grande plume. A large feather, ninth degree	509
Le petit boulet. A small ball or bullet, tenth degree	ib.
Le caramel. Burnt sugar, thirteenth degree	510
DE PATES DE TOUTES SORTES DE FRUITS —	ib.

PASTE OF ALL SORTS OF FRUITS.

Pâte de cerises. Cherry-paste	ib.
—— *de groseilles.* Of goosberries and currants	511
—— *d'amandes vertes, & abricots verds.* Paste of green almonds, and green apricocks	ib.
—— *de violettes.* Violet-paste	512
—— *d'abricots murs.* Paste of ripe apricocks	ib.
—— *de pêches.* Peach-paste	ib.
—— *de raisin muscat.* Paste muscadine-grapes	513
—— *de verjus.* Of verjuice-grapes	ib.
—— *de coigns.* Quince-paste	ib.
—— *de marons.* Chesnut-paste	514
—— *de citrons.* Lemon or citron paste	ib.
—— *de pommes.* Of apples	515
Observation sur les pâtes des fruits. Observation on fruit-pastes	ib.
DES PATES DE PASTILLAGES.	ib.

OF PASTIL-PASTES.

Pâte de pastillage de chocolat. Pastil-paste of chocolate	ib.
Pastillage de réglisse. Licorice	516
—— *de violettes.* Violet-pastils	ib.
—— *de fleurs d'orange.* Of orange-flowers, and lemons	ib.
—— *de caffé.* Coffee-pastils	517
—— *de canelle.* Of cinnamon and cloves	ib.
—— *d'epine-vinette.* Barberry-pastil	ib.
DES SABLES D'OFFICE ET DES COULEURS	518

OF THE SANDS AND COLOURS USED IN CONFECTIONARY.

De la couleur rouge. Of red colour, how to make it	ib.
—————— *bleue.* Of bleu colour	ib.
—————— *jaune.* Of the yellow colour	ib.
—————— *verte.* Of green colour	519
Maniere de faire les sables. How to make the sands	ib.
DES CANDI. OF CANDIED SUGAR	ib.
Candi de fleurs d'orange. Orange-flower candied	520
—————— *canelle.* Candied cinnamon	ib.
—————— *jonquilles.* Of jonquils	ib.

CONTENTS.

	Page
Sucre candi en pierre. Rock candied sugar	520
Candi de violettes. Of violets	521
DES CLAREQUETS. Of clear transparent paste	ib.
Clarequets de pommes. Clear apple-paste	ib.
———— *de verjus.* Of verjuice-juices	522
———— *de coigns.* Of quinces	ib.
———— *de poires.* Clear pear-paste	ib.
———— *de prunes.* Of plums	523
———— *de fleurs d'orange.* Of orange-flowers	ib.
———— *de violettes.* Violet clear paste	ib.
———— *de muscat.* Of muscadine-grapes	524
DES CONSERVES. Of dried conserves	ib.
Conserve de fleurs d'orange, & autres. Of orange-flower water	525
———— *safran.* Saffron-conserve	ib.
———— *d'avelines.* Conserves of filberds	ib.
———— *d'amandes au jus de citron.* Almond-conserves with lemon-juice and cedar	526
———— *d'oranges douces, bigarades, & citrons.* Conserve of China, and Seville oranges and lemons	ib.
———— *blanche de citron.* White lemon-conserve	ib.
———— *de muscat.* Conserve of muscadine-grapes	527
———— *de grenade.* Of pomegranate	ib.
———— *de guimauve.* Of marsh-mallows	ib.
———— *d'abricots.* Of apricocks	ib.
———— *de cerises.* Of cherries, &c.	528
———— *de groseilles.* Of red currants	ib.
DES COMPOTES DE POMMES ET DE POIRES. Compotes, or stewed apples and pears	529
Compôte bourgeoise. Common family-way	ib.
———— *de gelée blanche.* Compote of white jelly	530
———— *à la cloche.* Bell or cap fashion, black caps	ib.
———— *de pommes farcie.* Stuffed apples	ib.
———— *grillées.* Broiled or fried	531
———— *de pommes en gelée rouge.* Red jelly	ib.
———— *d'autres pommes.* Of other sorts of apples	ib.
———— *de poires d'été, d'automne, & d'hyver.* Compotes of summer pears, autumn, and winter	ib.
———— *de poires à cuire.* Compote of baking apples	532
———— *rouge.* Red pear-compote	ib.
DES COMPOTES DE COIGNS, DE PECHES, ET ABRICOTS. Compotes of quinces, peaches, and apricocks	533
———— *de coigns.* Of quinces	ib.
———— *de coigns en gelée vermeille.* A lively colour jelly	ib.
———— *d'abricots vertes.* Of green apricocks	ib.

Compôte

CONTENTS.

	Page
Compôte d'amandes vertes. Of green almonds	534
——— *d'abricots mûrs.* Of ripe apricocks	ib.
——— *de pêches.* Of peaches	ib.
——— *grillée de pêche.* Roasted or broiled peaches	535

DES COMPOTES DE VERJUS, DE MUSCAT, DE PRUNES & MARONS — ib.
Compotes of verjuice and muscadine-grapes, plums and chesnuts.

De verjus et muscat	ib.
Compôte de prunes. Of plums	536
——— *de marons.* Of chesnuts	ib.

DES COMPOTES D'ORANGES & CITRONS. 537
Compotes of oranges and lemons

Compôte d'oranges douces. Of sweet or China oranges	ib.
——— *de zestes.* Of bits of rinds of the same	ib.
——— *de tailladins.* Cut in pieces, quarters more or less	538

DES COMPOTES DE CERISES, GROSEILLES FRAMBOISES, & FRAISES. ib.
Compotes of cherries, goosberries, rasberries, and strawberries.

Compôte de cerises. Of cherries	ib.
——— *de groseilles.* Of goosberries, meant for ripe ones	539
——— *de groseilles vertes.* Of green goosberries	ib.
——— *de framboises.* Of rasberries	ib.

DES GATEAUX. Of cakes — 540

Gâteaux de fleurs d'orange. Of green orange-flowers	ib.
——— *de violettes & de jasmins.* Of violets and jessamines	ib.

DES GRILLAGES. Of broilings 541

Grillage de bigarade. Of Seville orange-chips	ib.
——— *de citrons.* Of lemons	ib.
——— *d'amandes.* Of almonds	ib.
——— *de pistache.* Of pistachio-nuts	542

DES GAUFRES, CORNETS, & AUTRES PATES ib.
Of gaufers, wafers, and other pastes

Des gaufres. Of gaufers	ib.
Gaufres au caffé. With coffee	543
Des gimbelettes. Of jumbals or buns	ib.
Pâte de vin d'Espagne. Spanish wine paste	544
——— *pour des petits ronds.* Paste for small hoops or rings, &c.	ib.

DES MOUSSELINES & MERINGUES ib.
Coloured pastry diversified.

Des meringues. Whites of eggs batter	545

CONTENTS.

	Page
DES MASSEPINS & MACARONS	545
Sweet paste of different fashions.	
Massepins, eatable or sugar-paste	ib.
———— à la reine	ib.
———— *vole au vent.* Meaning very light to fly in the air	546
———— *de cerises.* Of cherries, and others	ib.
Macarons en canellon. Longways, macaroni-biscuits	547
———— *au liquide.* With cream or marmalade	ib.
DES BISCUITS. OF BISCUITS	548
Biscuit à la cuillere. Spoon-biscuits	ib.
——— *de fruits confits.* Of preserved fruits	ib.
——— *à la fleur d'orange.* Orange-flower biscuits, &c.	549
Biscuits d'amandes. Almond-biscuits	ib.
——— *de chocolat*	ib.
——— *à la glace.* Iced biscuits	550
Biscuit de pistache. Pistachio-nuts biscuits	ib.
DES OUVRAGES D'AMANDES, ET DE PIS-TACHES	ib.
OF THE DIFFERENT PAEPARATIONS OF ALMONDS AND PISTACHIO-NUTS.	
Amandes à la praline. Dried, preserved, or burnt almonds	ib.
——— *à la praline rouge.* Red colour	551
——— *soufflés.* Blowed or raised, and others	ib.
Pralines blanches. Sugar-almonds, white	ib.
Amandes à l'Angloise. English fashion	552
Pistache au caramel	ib.
DES MARMELADES. OF MARMALADES	553
Marmalade de Pommes & de poires. Of apples and pears	ib.
———— *d'orange.* Orange-marmalade, &c.	ib.
———— *d'abricots.* Apricock-marmalade &c.	554
———— *de fleur d'orange.* Orange-flower marmalade	ib.
———— *de cerises.* Cherry-marmalade	ib.
———— *d'amandes & d'abricots verts.* Of green almonds and apricocks	555
DES GELEES. OF JELLIES	ib.
Gelée de pommes. Jelly of apples	ib.
——— *de muscat.* Muscadine-grapes jelly	556
——— *de grenades.* Of pomegranate, &c.	ib.
——— *de cerises.* Of cherries, &c.	557
——— *de groseilles d'une autre façon.* Another method of making currant-jelly	ib.
——— *de coigns.* Quince-jelly	ib.
——— *de groseilles vertes.* Of green goosberries	558

CONTENTS.

	Page
DES CONFITURES AU LIQUIDE OF LIQUID SWEETMEATS.	558
Confiture d'abricots. Liquid apricock sweetmeats	ib.
———— *d'abricots d'une autre façon*	559
———— *de groseilles.* Of goosberries or currants	ib.
———— *de cerises.* Of liquid cherries	560
———— *de mûres.* Of mulberries	ib.
———— *de pêches ou pavis.* Of peaches or nectarines	561
———— *d'epine vinette.* Of barberries	ib.
———— *de verjus.* Of verjuice-grapes	ib.
———— *de coigns.* Of liquid quinces	562
Confitures d'orange, citron, cedras, bergamottes, & bigarrades Liquid sweetmeats of China and Seville oranges, citron, lemon, and bergamotte pears	ib. ib.
———— *de grosses noix.* Of walnuts	563
———— *de prunes.* Of plums	ib.
DES CONFITURES AU SEC. Of dried sweetmeats.	564
Confiture de cerises au sec en bouquets, &c. &c. Dried preserved cherries in nosegays or bunches, &c.	ib.
———— *de prunes, & pommes tapées.* Of plums, and dried or baked apples	565
DES SIROPS. Syrup d'orgeat and others	ib.
Sirop de capillaire. Maiden-hair syrup	566
———— *de mûres.* Mulberry-syrup, and others	567
Autre sirop de ce que l'on veut. Syrups of whatever you please	ib.
DES FRUITS A L'EAU-DE-VIE. Of brandy-fruits.	568
Pêche à l'eau-de-vie. Peaches in brandy	ib.
Poires à l'eau-de-vie. Pears preserved in brandy	ib.
Prunes à l'eau-de-vie. Plums in brandy	569
Cerises à l'eau-de-vie. Cherries in brandy	ib.
Amandes vertes & abricots verts à l'eau-de-vie. Green almonds and green apricocks in brandy	570
Oranges douces à l'eau-de-vie. Sweet or China oranges	ib.
DES MOUSSES. Of froughted or whipt creams.	ib.
Mousse à la créme. Whipt cream	571
———— *de caffé*	ib.
DES GLACES. Of ices	572
Glace à la créme. Cream-ice	ib.
———— *de fruits,* fruit-ices; *de cerises,* of cherries, &c. &c.	573
———— *de violettes, de jasmin, & de fleurs d'orange.* Ices of violets, jessamines, and orange-flowers	ib.
———— *de citron,* lemon-ice; *de grenade,* pomegranate	574
———— *de bigarades, & d'oranges douces.* Of China and Seville oranges	ib.

CONTENTS

	Page
Glace de canelle. Cinnamon-ice	574
——— *de roses & jonquilles.* Of roses and jonquils	ib.
——— *de pavis, de pêches, & d'abricots.* Ices of nectarines, peaches, and apricocks	575
——— *de coriandre, d'anis, et de genievre.* Ices of coriander-seeds, anise, and juniper-berries	ib.
DES FRUITS GLACES. Of iced fruits.	ib.
DES FROMAGES GLACES. Iced cheeses.	576
Fromage à la crême glacé. Iced cream-cheese	ib.
——— *de marmelade glacé.* Of marmalade of any sorts	ib.
——— *à la Chantilly glacé*	577
——— *de beurre glacé.* As iced butter	ib.
DES EAUX RAFRAICHISSANTES SANS ETRE A LA GLACE. Of cooling liquors, without icing	578
Eau rafraîchissante d'orgeat. Orgeat-waters	ib.
Eau rafraîchissante de fenouil, & de cerfeuil. Cooling waters of fennel, and of charvil	ib.
Lemonade	579
Lait de pistache, & d'amande Almond and pistachio milk	ib.
Pâte d'orgeat. Orgeat-paste	ib.
DES FROMAGES A LA CREME	580
Of fresh cream-cheese.	
Fromage à la crême bourgeoise. A plain family-way	ib.
——— *à la crême de marmelade*	ib.
DES CRESMES D'OFFICE	581
Of creams as part of confectionary.	
Crême fouettée. Whipt cream	ib.
——— *au blanc d'œufs.* With whites of eggs	ib.
DES RATAFIATS. Of sweet drams or cordials	582
Ratafiat de noyaux. Of kernels	ib.
——— *de citron.* Of lemon-peel	ib.
——— *de genievre.* Of juniper-berries	ib.
——— *de muscat, &c.* Of muscadine-grapes and others	583
——— *d'anis.* Of aniseeds and apricocks	ib.
——— *de noix.* Of walnuts	584
——— *de fleurs d'orange*	ib.
——— *de cerises.* Of cherries, &c.	ib.
Du caffé. Of coffee	585
DU CHOCOLAT. OF CHOCOLATE	ib.
DES OUVRAGES DE DIVERSES FACONS	586
Of various sorts of works.	
Des amandes vertes. Of green almonds	ib.
— *fraises.* Of strawberries	ib.
— *fraises au caramel*	587
— *marons.* Of chesnuts, &c.	ib.
— *diablotens.* From *diable,* small or young devils	ib.
— *cerises en surtout.* Coated cherries	588

THE ART OF
MODERN COOKERY
DISPLAYED.

Tranflated from the FRENCH.

Bouillons de Mitonage, ou Bouillons Général.

Of Soaking or General Broth, Gravy and Cullis.

THIS is made of a Rump or Piece of Brifket, or fhort Ribs of Beef, which is moft convenient; the Meat ferves for a large Difh: this is the French *Bouilli*, or the Piece *Tremblante*; and is commonly eat plain, with a little Salt over, and fome of the Broth, with a little fine chopped Parfley, or any Sauce which is moft agreeable; when the Pot is well fkimmed, put in it Roots and Herbs, at Difcretion; the Broth ferves to make your Gravies, Cullis and Brazes, and for common Soops, adding to it what Herbs or Roots you pleafe.

Bouillons pour les Potages & Sauces.

Broth for Soops and Sauces.

ACCORDING to the Quantity wanted, put in your Pot large Slices of Beef, of Leg and Knuckle of Veal, of Neck or Loin of Mutton, and a Fowl, (an old one is very good for this Purpofe); take particular Care to fkim it very well, then add Roots and Herbs as you think proper, as Leeks, Carrots, Parfneps, a Head of Sellery, Parfley-Roots, and large Onions, ftuck with few Cloves, a little Parfley and Thyme tied together; you may boil in this Broth what Meat you propofe to ferve serve in the Soop, such as Fowls, Pigeons, Partridges, &c.; take particular Care that the Broth be very clear and well tasted, not too much of the Herbs or Roots; it serves you to simmer your Soops, being coloured and strengthened with a little Gravy or Cullis; and also to make the Liquid of Sauces.

Bouillon à la hâte.

Broth made in haste.

CUT small Slices of Fillet of Veal, lean Meat of Beef, Carrots, Sellery, sliced Onions, a Couple of middling Turnips, one Head of Clove; garnish the Bottom of a Stew-pan with few Slices of Lard; then put in the Meat and Roots; soak it on a middling Fire, until the Meat begins to catch at the Bottom of the Pan; then pour some boiling Water on it, and let it boil smartly about half an Hour, or more; add Salt, skim it, and sift it clear for Use.

N. B. I use the Words Slices of Lard, for Shortness, of larding Bacon; and it is to be understood as of Bacon prepared for Kitchen Use.

Bouillon au Bain-Marie.

Broth made with one Pot boiling in another.

PUT an earthen Pot into a large one with boiling Water; cut Slices of Beef, Fillet of Veal, half a Fowl or Capon skinned, a large Onion stuck with one or two Cloves, few Bits of Roots; boil it in that Manner for five or six Hours, taking care to supply the first Pot with boiling Water pretty often, and some of the first Broth in the Broth Pot; skim it very clean, sift it in a Lawn Sieve; it ought to be strong enough to cool to the Consistence of a Jelly.

N. B. The French use this Method with earthen Vessels, which are not common in England, that will stand the Fire for this Purpose; but Copper ones will answer the same with Care.

Consomme.

Consommé.
Jelly Broth.

PUT in your Pot or Stew-pan Slices of Beef, of Veal Fillet, a Fowl, one or two Partridges, according to the Quantity required; put it on the Fire without Liquid until it catches a little; and turn the Meat now and then, to give it a proper Colour; then add some good clear boiling Broth, and scalded Roots, as Carrots, Turnips, Parsneps, Parsley-Roots, Sellery, large Onions, two or three Cloves, a small Bit of Nutmeg, whole Pepper; boil it on a slow Fire about four or five Hours with Attention, and add few Cloves of Garlick or Shallots, a small Nosegay, or Bunch of Parsley and Thyme tied together; when it is of a good Colour, sift it; it serves for Sauces, and to add Strength to your Soops, particularly those made of Herbs or Italian Paste.

N. B. I am very sensible that many People (more particulary in England) have an Aversion to the Taste or Smell of Garlick; I nevertheless presume to say, that its Effects are very good when used with Moderation, and will make either hot or cold Dishes very agreeable, as Experience will shew. Taste must direct, which no Cookery can be good without.

Roumestec.
Jelly Broth of all Fragments.

WHEN you work for a great Entertainment, you may make a good *Consommé* very cheap, by gathering all Kinds of Parings and Trimmings, as Legs, Pinions, and Bones of Poultries, and of such Game as you employ; also Parings of Butcher's Meat; put all together in a Stew-pan as the last; soak it some Time; then add some small Broth, or boiling Water, one or two Glasses of white Wine, a good Quantity of Parsley, Chibbol, two Laurel Leaves and Thyme, a little sweet Basil, few Cloves of Garlick, two or three Heads of Spice Cloves, and whole Pepper; boil this slowly as the former, skim and sift it for Use: it will serve to add Strength to all Sorts of made Dishes and Sauces. The Name of *Roumestec* is given this *Consommé*, when made mostly of Game.

Bouillon Rafraichissant. Cooling Broth

THE Herbs, Fruits, or Seeds, Flowers or Roots, which are employed for cooling Broth, are, Purflain, Lettuces, Charvil, Leeks, Borage, Burnet, Sorrel, Garden and wild Endives, Buglofs, Hop-tops, Gofs Lettuces, young Nettles, Cucumbers, Tips of Elder, Dandelion, Liver-wort, Fumitory, Beet-Roots, &c. Wash and chop what Quantity is proper, and according to Order, and boil a short Time in thin Veal or Chicken Broth; sift, and keep it in a cool Place; warm it for Use without boiling.

Autre Bouillon Rafraichissant.
Another Cooling Broth.

TAKE a Calve's Liver, cut out the Gall, and all the Flesh round it; then cut it in thin Slices, and boil it in a Quart of Water till it is reduced to half; then add a little Charvil, Watercresses, wild Endives, and Burnet, all coarsely chopped; boil it few Minutes, and sift it for Use.

Bouillon Printanier.   Spring Broth.

PUT a Crust of Bread, and a good Bit of Butter in a small Soop-pot, or Stew-pan, with two or three Handfuls of Herbs, as Beet, Sorrel, Charvil, Lettuces, Leeks, Purflain, all well washed and coarsely chopped; boil in a Quart of Water till reduced to half; sift it for Use.

Bouillon pour adoucir l'Acreté du Sang.
Broth to sweeten the Sharpness of the Blood.

SLICE half a Pound of Veal, boil it in three Pints of Water, with five or six Craw-fish pounded alive; add to it white Endives, a small Handful of Charvil, and as much Purflain, three or four Lettuces, all coarsely chopped; reduce the Liquid to half, and strain it through a Cloth or Stamine, without skimming it.

Eau de Poulet.   Chicken Water.

BOIL a well-drawn Chicken in three Pints of River Water; put in the Body one Ounce and a half of the cold Seeds, first pounded in a Mortar; boil it till reduced to a Quart, then sift it: you make also another Chicken Water, where you add half an Ounce of Rice, as much Pearl Barley, the Bigness of a Walnut of Sugar, for those that like it sweeter. The four greater cold Seeds are Water Melons, Cucumbers, Gourds, and Melons; the four lesser, Succory, Endives, Lettuces, and Purslain.

Panade de Blans de Poularde.
Panado of Breast of Fowl.

BOIL a Bit of Crum in some good Broth, add to it a Couple of Breast of Fowl roasted, and pounded very fine; sift all together in a Cloth, with strong pressing; put Broth according to the Consistence you would have it.

Panade de Grueau.   Grits Panado.

WASH two Ounces of fresh Grits in warm Water several Times, and boil it in a Quart of Water, till the Liquid is reduced to about a Pint; then sift it as the former, and add a Spoonful of white Wine and a Bit of Sugar to it; boil it a Moment before using.

Panade à la la Bourgogne.
Burgundy Panado.

BOIL two or three Ounces of Rice very tender in thin Broth, first well washed, then sift it as the last; it ought not to be very thin nor thick; then add one Yolk of Egg beat up, to thicken it on the Fire without boiling: this is called making a *Liason*: a Panado is also made with Bread Crums instead of Rice, and finished in the same Manner.

N. B. As the word *Liason* will often be repeated hereafter, it is to be understood in the Sense of Cookery, as conglutinating the different Liquids together, with which it is mixed, and always to be done without boiling.

Jus de Veau. Veal Gravy.

GARNISH the Bottom of the Stew-pan with thin Bits of Lard, then few Bits or Slices of Ham, Slices of Veal Fillet, sliced Onions, Carrots, Parsneps, Sellery, few Cloves upon the Meat, a Spoonful of Broth; soak it on the Fire in this Manner till it catches to the Pan, and the Veal throws its Gravy; then add a proper Quantity of thin Broth, and simmer it on a slow Fire, till the Meat is thoroughly done; you may put a little Thyme and Mushrooms; skim and sift it clear.

Jus de Bœuf. Beef Gravy.

ACCORDING to the Quantity wanted, cut Slices of lean Beef, which you put in a Stew-pan upon sliced Onions, and Roots of all Sorts fit for Broth, few Bits of Lard, or other fat Meat, two Spoonfuls of fat Broth; soak this on a slow Fire about half an Hour, turning the whole two or three Times; let it catch to a proper Colour, then add thin Broth as directed for *Mitonage*, and finish it as the former: always observe, that in all Gravies you must put a little Fat, and to take it off the Fire, when you add the Broth; after it is properly coloured, your own Judgement must guide you for the Colour, which is done by the catching with proper Care, not to give it a burnt Taste.

Coulis Général. General Cullis.

GARNISH the Bottom of your Stew-pan with Slices of Veal Fillet, Bits of Ham, according to the Quantity and Goodness required; and upon the Meat two Carrots cut in large Bits, one Parsnep the same, one or two Onions stuck with Cloves, a Spoonful of fat Broth; soak it on a slow Fire, until the Meat gives its Juice,

Juice, then on a stronger Fire, until it forms a fine brown *Caramel*, viz. a Glaze at Bottom, and round the Stew-pan; then take all out except the *Caramel*; put the Pan on the Fire again, with a good Bit of Butter worked with Flour, and stir it continually with a Spoon, until it is of a fine yellowish Colour; take proper care the Fire is not too violent, to give it a burnt Taste; then add as much Broth and Gravy as will keep it of a proper Colour and Consistence, meaning not very thick nor clear; then put the Meat back again, and simmer it a long while, skim it often; when the Meat is thoroughly done, take it out with a Skimmer, and sift the Cullis in a Lawn Sieve, or a sifting Cloth, without expressing.

Coulis de ce que l'on veut.

Cullis of what you please.

THIS is made with any Sorts of Meats, Parings and Trimmings of Poultries, Game, &c. as Pinions, Necks, Stumps, and few Slices of Veal with it; and finished as the last.

Coulis D'Ecrevisses.

Craw-fish Cullis.

THE first Preparation of this *Coulis* is the same as the general Cullis; when the Glaze is formed in the Stew-pan, add Broth according to the Quantity required, trim the Tails off of half a hundred of Craw-fish, pound the Inside of the Bodies, and dry the Carcases on the Fire, or in the Oven, to pound with the rest; sift the Cullis through a Sieve, and put some in the Mortar with the Craw-fish; when properly pounded, sift all together in a Lawn Sieve, or a Cloth Strainer with Expression: this Cullis will serve in whatever you think proper; the Tails serve to garnish Soop or Ragout: Meager Cullis is done the same, using Meager Broth, Carps, or any other Kind of Fishes.

The ART *of*

N. B. The French use three different Names to signify much the same Thing, viz. *Coulis,* *Consommé,* and *Restaurant.* The first is the thinnest and clearest, and is often made with a little Flour, Butter, and Broth, for the sake of giving a proper Colour to any Sauce, excepting those Coulis made of Roots or Seeds, which I have distinguished by the Name of *Porridges* and *Purée*; the second is stronger of Meat, and is for the Purpose of adding Goodness and Strength, to whatever it is mixed with; the last is for the same Purpose, and made as rich in Taste and Flavour, as Meat, Poultry, and Game, and proper Seasoning can make it, from which it has the Name of *Restorative.* This is the true Foundation of Cookery, and wherein every one ought to be as perfect as possible.

Coulis à la Reine.
Queen's Cullis.

PREPARE a Stew-pan for this as all others, with Slices of Fillet of Veal, few Bits of Ham and Roots; soak it on a slow Fire without letting it catch at Bottom; then put some Broth of a natural Colour; you may also put half of an old Fowl, or a whole one, to give it more Strength; simmer it as all former Cullis; pound one or two Breasts of Fowls or Chickens, with half a Handful of sweet Almonds scalded, few hard Yolks of Eggs, Bread Crums soaked in Broth; mix all together in the Mortar, and strain it in a Stamine, rubbing it hard with a wooden Spoon; you may add a little Cream to give it a finer white: this is often used, and ought always to be warm as the *Liason* without boiling, and the same with every Thing where Eggs are Part of the Composition.

Coulis de Jambon.
Ham Cullis.

THIS is done with Slices of Veal Fillet, and Ham sufficient to give it a pretty strong Taste of, and all Sorts of Roots; give it the same Colour as the general Cullis; then add Broth without Salt, a Glass of white Wine, a Nosegay of Thyme and Parsley, half a Laurel Leaf, one Clove of Garlick, few Mushrooms, Chibbol or Shallot; finish as usual.

Coulis

Coulis Bourgeois. A Family Cullis.

TAKE a Bit of Butter rolled in Flour, ſtir it in your Stew-pan till the Flour takes a fine yellow Colour; then add ſmall Broth, a little Gravy, a Glaſs of white Wine, a Noſegay of Parſley, Thyme, Laurel, ſweet Baſil, two Cloves, a little Nutmeg, or Mace, few Muſhrooms, whole Pepper and Salt; boil for an Hour on a ſlow Fire; ſift it in a Lawn Sieve, well ſkimmed from Fat: this Cullis is made either with Meat or Fiſh Broth, according as you pleaſe.

Coulis Blans à la Bourgeoiſe.

White Family Cullis.

POUND about a Dozen of Coriander Seeds with half a Dozen of bitter Almonds ſcalded, and mix it with Bread Crums ſoaked in good Broth, and Broth ſufficient to make it to what Conſiſtence you pleaſe; ſift it in a Lawn Sieve, and add four raw Yolks of Eggs, beat up with Cream; make the *Liaſon* without boiling.

Coulis de Féves de Marais. Cullis of Garden Beans.

SCALD the Beans, to peel the Huſks off, then boil them in Broth to a Maſh with Parſley, few green Shallots, a little Winter-ſavory; then ſift them to Marmalade, and mix it with middling Meat Cullis: it ought to be of a pale green Colour, well ſeaſoned, and not too thick, as all thoſe Cullis thicken greatly in cooling.

Coulis de Lentilles. Lentils Cullis.

MAKE a Meat-gravy as before, with Veal and Ham, Onions, Parſley, Chibbol, two Cloves, and Winter-ſavory; ſoak it till it catches; then add Broth, and ſimmer it till the Meat is done; then your Lentils being well boiled in Broth, and pounded, ſift them, and put the Porridge in the Stew-pan, and boil a Moment;

ment; then take the Meat out, and sift your Cullis in a Stamine; it is a very well tasted Cullis: don't make it too thick.

Coulis de Pois.   Peas Cullis.

GREEN Peas Cullis is made by boiling the Peas in good Broth, with a Nosegay of Parsley, Chibbol, a little Winter-savory; sift them in Porridge with the Broth of the Boiling; dried Peas are equally boiled in Broth, and sifted into a Porridge; and mixt in a Cullis, such as you have for the former; to make it green, add Juice of pounded Spinnage.

Coulis de Marons.   Chesnut Cullis.

PREPARE your Stew-pan with sliced Veal and Ham as before; peel the first Husk off your Chesnuts, and roast them until you can peel off the second; boil in Broth to a Marmalade; take the Meat out of your *Consommé*, and add the Chesnuts, boil a short Time, and sift all together: if you would have it pretty thick, put less Broth to keep it of a thicker Consistence.

As more Repetition would become tedious, I shall only say, that, with a small Notion of Cookery, Cullis of any Roots, or Seeds, are mostly made upon the same Principles, such as Carrots, Turnips, white Beans, &c. which are all very useful for Soops, particularly in Winter, when Herbs are scarce, and of very little Taste.

Des Bouillons, Jus, & Coulis Maigre.

Of Meager Broth, Gravies, and Cullis.

FOR the common or soaking Broth, wash a proper Quantity of dried Peas in several warm Water; then boil them in Water with few large Onions, sliced Carrots, Parsneps, few Heads of Cloves, whole Pepper, a little Salt; boil this together till the Peas are thoroughly

Modern COOKERY *Displayed.*

roughly done; then take it off the Fire, and sift it through a Sieve with Expression; the Liquor being much reduced, mix it with Meager Cullis, and sift again through a Strainer: this will serve you for the same Purpose, as the first directed, to simmer your Soops and Sauces, adding Butter and Herbs as you like.

Bouillon Maigre pour les Potages de la Table.

Meager Broth for Soops.

SCALD all Sorts of Roots, as Onions, Parsley-roots, Carrots, Parsneps, half a Savoy, Turnips, Leeks, Sellery; boil all together in Peas Broth, as directed above; put it into a clean Bag, called a *Mixionette*, with a small Quantity of long Pepper, Ginger, Cinnamon, Cloves, Coriander, Mace, a Clove of Garlick, Shallots, Winter-savory; boil till the Greens are done; and to give it a good Colour, make a brown Gravy with sliced Onions, and other Roots, and Butter; when it yields a proper Colour as in all Cullis, salt it according to Taste, mix it together; it will serve you to make what Soops you please.

Bouillon de Poisson. Fish Broth.

TAKE what Fish you think proper, as Pikes, Eels, Carps, &c. cut in Slices, and put them in your Stew-pan with a little Butter, sliced Onions, a Nosegay of Parsley, Thyme, Bay-leaf, Basil, a Clove of Garlick, Carrots, Parsneps; soak it until it forms a slight Glaze in the Bottom; add to it of the former Broth, and boil on a slow Fire for about an Hour; sift it clear: It will serve for Soops and Sauces.

Jus Maigre. ' Meager Gravy.

MELT a proper Quantity of good Butter, and fry sliced Onions in it with such other Roots as are used for Gravies; soak it some Time on a slow Fire, then

then on a stronger to bring it to a proper Gravy Colour; then add some of the common Broth, and a little Parsley, half a Clove of Garlick, half a Laurel Leaf, three Cloves, whole Pepper and Salt; boil slowly for about an Hour, then sift it as usual for Gravies.

Coulis Maigre. Meager Cullis.

TAKE what Fish you think proper; the best and most common is Carps; cut in large Pieces, and put in your Stew-pan with a little Butter, sliced Onions, and other Roots; soak it a while on a slow Fire, then a stronger, until it forms a *Caramel*, then put half Broth and half Gravy; fry some Flour with good Butter, and add it to your Cullis, also a Bit of Garlick, a Leaf of Laurel, a Gill of white Wine, a Couple of Slices of Lemon first peeled, and Mushrooms; boil half an Hour on a slow Fire; skim it well before you sift it: if you desire a simple Cullis, make a *Caramel* with Flour and Butter; when it is of a good Colour, add Broth and Onion Gravy sufficient to colour it; add some Mushrooms, Parsley, Garlick, Thyme, sweet Basil, a Glass of white Wine; boil for an Hour on a slow Fire, and sift it.

Coulis d'Oignons en Maigre. Onion Cullis Meager.

SLICE many Onions, and set them on a brisk Fire, with Butter, till it catches; add two Spoonfuls of Flour, which you stir continually till it is well coloured; then put Broth, a Glass of white Wine, two Heads of Cloves, a Bay-leaf, Thyme, Basil; boil it for an Hour, skim it well, and salt it according to Taste.

Coulis Maigre à la Reine. Queen Cullis Meager.

CUT a Carp in large Slices, and Onions, soak it with good Butter on a slow Fire; when the Carp is ready to catch, put some Broth of a natural Colour, and boil

boil on a flow Fire; foak fome Crums of Bread in Cream; and pound a Dozen of fweet Almonds, with half as many hard Yolks of Eggs, and few Fillets of boiled Fifh; fift your Extract of Carp, mix all together, and fift it again; it muft never boil after when you ufe it.

Chefnut Cullis is made after the fame Manner as the former, only the Difference of Meat Broth or without.

Coulis Maigre de Navet. Turnip Cullis Meager.

PEEL and cut as many Turnips, each in four or five Pieces, as you require of Cullis; if you would have it of a brown Colour, fry them fome time in Butter; if for a natural Colour, boil them without frying in common Broth to a Marmalade, the fame if coloured; then mix this with Fifh Gravy and Cullis, and fift it in a Stamine as all thick Cullis: it ferves for Soops or any Ufes.

Lentil Cullis is made after the former Direction, only obferving the Difference of Broth, &c.

Coulis de Poi Maigre. Meager Peas Cullis.

BOIL green Peas in Fifh Broth and Butter, a Nofegay of Parfley, Chibbol, Winter-favory; when well done, pound them, and fift with the Broth of their boiling, and add a little Gravy.

White Beans Cullis is made after the fame Direction; all Roots, Seeds, and Herbs may be done after the fame Manner, to the Confiftence of a Cullis.

Ouille de differentes Façons.

Olio, or Turine of different Manners.

BOIL in a Broth Pot, a Fowl, one Partridge, a fmall Leg of Mutton, five or fix Pound of large Slices of Beef, a Knuckle of Veal; foak all this together without

out Broth for some Time, turning the Meat to give it a brown Colour as for Gravies; then put small Broth, or boiling Water, and let it boil slowly about six or seven Hours; when it has boiled about an Hour, add all Sorts of Roots, as done in Soop Broth, and a *Mimonette*, as directed in Meager Broth, page. 11. This Broth ought to be of a fine brown clear Colour; it serves for all Sorts of Turine, which are only distinguished by the different Sorts of Roots, or Greens, which are served with; and also for Craw-fish or Rice; simmer Crusts or toasted Bread a long while with some of this Broth, then put it in the Turine, and garnish it with any Sorts of Garden Stuff: all kind of Soop may be served in Turine, with or without Meat.

Potage à la som-bonne en Gras & en Maigre.

Soop of all Sorts of Herbs with Meat or without.

SCALD all Sorts of Roots, as Onions, Carrots, Turnips, Sellery, Leeks, two Cloves of Garlick; boil this together about a Quarter of an Hour; then drain, and put them in a Soop-pot, with a proper Quantity of very good Broth, and about a Pint of dried Peas tied loose in a Cloth; boil slowly until the Peas are done tender, which mash, and sift as Peas Cullis with the Broth, and simmer in a small Soop-pot, with small Leaves of young Lettuces, Sorrel, Charvil, half a Carrot and Parsneps cut small; add a little Gravy, to colour and strengthen it; let the Roots and Greens be done very tender; simmer the Bread with some of the same Broth; pour it first in the Dish, and garnish it round with the Fillets of Carrots and Parsneps, intermixed with some of the Greens; prepare it after the same Manner, for Meager using Butter and Fish Broth, Cullis and Gravy.

Potage de Ris à la Pluche Verte, en Gras, ou Maigre.

A Rice Soop of both Sorts, pale Green.

WASH half a Pound of Rice, more or less, in warm Water several Times; if for *Gras*, boil it in Meat Broth, and a little melted Lard; if for *Meager*, with said Broth and Butter; stir it often, that it may not clog at the Bottom of the Pan; when it is very tender, pour it in the Soop Dish, with a proper Quantity of very good Broth, a little Gravy to colour it; and melt a good Bit of Butter rolled in Flour, a small Quantity of fine chopped Parsley, first scalded, three or four Spoonfuls of Broth, two Yolks of Eggs to make a *Liason*, without boiling, and pour this in the Dish upon the Rice.

Potage de Chapon au Ris.   A Capon or Fowl Rice Soop.

TRUSS the Capon or Pullard, as for boiling, viz. Legs inside, and leave the Pinions; boil it in a small Soop-pot with about half a Pound of Rice; boil flowly till the Rice is quite tender, without skimming the Fat off; add Gravy sufficient to colour and strengthen it, and a little Salt, or serve without Gravy, the Fowl in the middle: a Fowl is also served, being boiled with few Slices of Beef, Veal, Mutton, and Roots, the Broth sifted; simmer the Bread with some of this Broth, with or without Herbs; serve the Fowl in the Soop Dish: all Sorts of boiled Poultries are done enough, when they feel tender under the Finger; this is called Soop *Santé au naturel*, viz. plain.

Potage à la Conty, en Gras ou Maigre.

Soop Conty, Meat or Fish.

SLICE large Onions, according to the Quantity required, and simmer them in Butter till they are thoroughly done, and simmer some fried Bread in very good Broth of either Sort; when ready to serve, mix a Couple of pounded Anchovies with the Onions, and pour the Broth and Bread in the Dish, and the Onions upon it; you may also sift the Onions as a Cullis, either for Soop, or other Uses.

Potage de Bibcrot au Fromage.

Cheese Soop of both Sorts.

TAKE about half a Pound of Bread Crums, sifted in a Cullender, and about a Quarter of a Pound of Gruiere Cheese, commonly called *Swiss* Cheese, or Parmesan; simmer this together in a Stew-pan with some good Broth, either Meager or *Gras*, until the Bread and Cheese are well stewed; make a Liason in another Pan with three or four Yolks of Eggs, and as many Spoonfuls of Broth; when ready to serve, mix this last with the first without boiling: this Soop must not be very clear nor thick; this should be made with Broth without Salt, as the Cheese may salt it sufficiently; your Judgment must always guide you for Seasoning.

Potages glacés de toutes Sortes de Viandes.

Glazed Soops of all Sorts of Meat.

USE which Sorts of Meat you please, as Fowl, Chickens, Pigeons, Ducks, Lamb, small Fillet of Veal, Neck of Mutton, Turkey-pinions, or others; each Kind is dressed after the same Manner; which ever you use, lard it, and scald it a Moment in boiling Water; then stew it in good Broth, a Nosegay of sweet Herbs, and simmer the Bread in very good Broth, as usual for other Soops; when the Meat is thoroughly done, serve it in the Dish or Turine; put a Spoonful of Broth in the Stew-pan to gather the Glaze of the Fricandeau, with which you glaze the larded Side being uppermost; garnish the Dish round with Herbs or Roots, as most convenient, and sift some of the Glaze to mix with the Broth to colour it.

Potage

Potage de Vermicel en Gras et en Maigre.

Vermicelly Soop, with Meat or Fish.

FOR a middling Dish, take about a Quarter of a Pound of Vermicelly, which you scald a Moment in boiling Water, then drain it and boil in good Broth, with a little Gravy, and a Bit of Bacon; when boiled tender take out the Bacon, season it with Salt, and skim the Fat off very clean; it must be served of a middling Consistence, if you would make it with Craw-fish Cullis, or any other, you'll only mix it a Moment before you serve.

If it is for Meager scald your Rice as above, and boil it with Fish Broth and Butter, adding a Liason of Yolks of Eggs made with the same Broth and Gravy.

Soupe Bourgeoise.

A Family Soop.

BOIL about three Pounds of Beef in three Pints of Water, and skim it very well, then add three or four Carrots, two Parsneps, few Onions, according to their Bigness, stuck with two Heads of Cloves; put few Leeks, a Lettuce, Sellery, Sorrel; boil all together, and add a small Knuckle of Veal, first scalded; and boil it for about two Hours; serve your Broth and the Knuckle in it.

Potage au Marons.

Chesnut Soop.

PEEL the first Husk of the Chesnuts, then roast them sufficiently to peel off the second, and boil them in Broth and Gravy; when they are done take out the few that remain whole, and mash the others in your Broth, fit to sift it in a Stamine; serve without boiling, and garnish the Dish with the whole ones.

Potage Diffus d'Aigneau au Coulis à la Reine.

Lamb's Head Soop, and all Purtenances, with Queen Cullis.

TAKE a Lamb's Head, &c. well scalded, and paired properly, boil in a small Pot with a Couple of Slices of Lemon, first peeled, a Nosegay of Parsley, Chibbol, two Heads of Cloves, a Laurel Leaf, two Carrots, one Parsnep, two or three Onions, few Slices of Lard, and Salt, boil in Broth and Water on a slow Fire, garnish your Dish with some of the Inside, open the Head and serve it in the middle; mix some Queen Cullis with the Broth, and add it to the Soop.

Potage à la Chartre.

Chartre Soop.

TAKE three or four Sweet Breads, well cleaned in warm Water, and scalded in boiling, put them in your Pot with scalded Coxcomb, a Nosegay of Parsley, green Shallots, two Heads of Cloves, few Mushrooms; stew all with good Broth on a slow Fire, have Crusts of Rolls well soaked in Broth in the Soop Dish, until it catches a little at Bottom; then put upon this the Sweet Breads and Mushrooms, leave it a little on the Fire, and add a sufficient Quantity of Broth.

Bisque de Cailles.

A Quail Turine Soop.

BOIL three or four Quails in good Broth, with few Slices of Lard, and two scalded Sweet Breads, one of Veal, the other of Lamb, in another Stew-pan with a little Butter and Flour, Broth, Gravy, a Spoonful of Cullis, a Nosegay of Parsley, Chibbol, two Heads of Cloves; stew it till well done; when the Quails are also done mix it all together with their Broth first sifted,

and

and very free from Fat; put it on a stronger Fire to bring it to a middling Consistence; add some good Broth and serve all together in a Turine.

Potage de toutes Sortes de Legumes.

Soop of all Sorts of Herbs.

THAT of Turnips is done by cutting as many as you think proper in different Shapes; give them Colour by frying with a little Butter or Broth, then boil it tender in Broth, a little Gravy, mix half this Broth with other, and garnish the Dish with Turnips; that of *Radishes* is made after the same Manner, only scalding the Radishes longer; that of small *Onions*, if round, you colour them as the Turnips; if green, cut them of a proper Length, scald them, and boil in Broth, and garnish your Dish with it; that of *Sellery* or Leeks, and Lettuces, scald them tied together; boil in your Soop-pot, take them out when done, and cut them according to Fancy, to garnish your Dish with.

Asparagus is done by breaking the Tops off, and boiled by themselves, then added to your Soop Broth; observe that the Bread you soak for these Soops be of a good Taste, and only use the Crust, which should be well dried in the Oven or toasted slowly; in those Soops you may serve what Butcher's Meat you please or Poulteries.

Potage aux Choux.

Cabbage Soop.

PUT in your Pot few Pounds of sliced Beef and Ham, let it catch a little, then add weak Broth and all Sorts of Roots, a Cabbage tied, and all scalded; a Bit of Bacon, a Bag, as directed in Page 11: if you would garnish this Soop with any Wild Fowl, boil it in the same Pot, and garnish the Dish with the Cabbage cut in Pieces.

Potage Julienne Gras & Maigre.

Soop Julienne with Meat or Fish.

CUT in small Slices two Carrots, a Parsnep, half a Head of Sellery, Lettuces, Sorrel, and Charvil; boil them in a small Pot with two or three whole Onions, a whole Carrot, Parsneps, a Nosegay of Parsley, Chibbol, two Heads of Cloves, a Laurel Leaf; simmer in good Broth about two Hours, then take out the Nosegay, Onions, and whole Roots: it is done the same for Meager, using the Broth, Onion, Gravy and Butter.

Potage de Différente Purée.

Soops of Different Porridge.

THAT of Lentils is made by boiling them in Broth with few Roots, and a Nosegay as the former, only adding a little Winter Savory; when the Lentils are done sift them, and put as much of the Porridge to your Soop or Broth, as will give it a proper Consistence; that of Turnips, Carrots, Beans, &c. is done the same.

Potage de Semouille.

Italian Paste Soop.

BOIL your Semouill as you do Rice in good Broth, of either Sorts, and add as much Gravy as will give a good Colour; it is a Paste that comes from Italy: you must chuse it by tasting, as it is apt to musty like Vermicelly.

Potage à la Dauphine.

Dauphine Soop.

FEW Slices of Lard in the Bottom of your Stewpan, sliced Ham and Veal, two or three Onions sliced, a Carrot and a Parsnep; soak over the Fire till it catches,

catches, then add weak Broth or boiling Water, and boil it on a flow Fire till the Meat is done; pound the Breast of a roasted Fowl, fix Yolks of hard Eggs, and as many sweet Almonds; sift your Broth, and add enough to your pounded Compound as will sift with a Stamine; soak your Bread in Broth tender; warm your Cullis without boiling, and mix it as much with Broth as gives it a pretty thick Consistence; you may garnish this Soop with a Fowl or Knuckle of Veal, as in all white Soops.

Potage de Gibier.

Game Soop.

CUT in Pieces either a Partridge, or a Pheasant, or a Rabbit, soak it with Slices of Veal, Ham, Onions, Carrots, Parsneps; let it catch a little on a flow Fire, as you do for Gravy; then add some good Broth, according to the Quantity you desire; boil easy till the Meat is done; sift the Broth and put it in your Soop Pot, and stew in it what Herbs you please.

Potage de toutes Sortes de Croutes.

Soop of all Sorts of Crust.

CUT one or two Rolls in two, take out the Crums which you will put in the Soop-dish, soak the Crust in Broth (your common Pot will do) place them upon the Crums, then put to it some Fat Broth over a flow Fire; let the Crums catch at Bottom; take care to refresh the Crust often with Broth; when it is all of a mash Consistence and no Broth to be seen, keep it on Ashes Fire; take particular Care that it does not catch too much, to give it a burnt Taste; when ready to serve, add some good Broth and Gravy with whatever Cullis you please: observe, if you propose a white Soop, you must not brown your Crust, nor let it catch at Bottom.

Potage à la Parme.

Parma Soop.

CUT Slices of Bread in what Shape you please, fry them in Lard of a good Colour, and soak it in good Broth; garnish the Dish with what Herbs you please, when ready to serve, rasp Parmesan Cheese over it.

Potage à l'Autriche.

Austrian Soop.

CUT a large Chicken in Pieces, give it Colour with frying in Butter and sweet Herbs, then boil it in good Broth, then roll it in Crums of Bread and Parmesan Cheese, colour it in the Oven or with a Salamander; garnish the Soop-dish with thin Slices of Bread, upon this some rasped Swiss Cheese or Parmesan, then a Bed of Cabbage with more Slices of Bread; add your Broth and stew it till it catches a little at Bottom; add a little more Cheese upon the Bread; colour it with a Salamander, add a little more Broth, and serve the Chicken on the Top.

Garbure.

A Turine with different Sorts of Meat.

TAKE a good Bit of Ham, Slices of Lard and Beef, two Legs of Goose, let it catch a little, until the Meat has taken Colour; then put Broth, three or four Onions, Carrots, Sellery, a green Cabbage, first scalded in boiling Water; boil it on a slow Fire till the Meat is done; garnish the Bottom of your Dish with Slices of Bread, and soak it with some of the said Broth until it catches; put upon it the Ham and Legs of Goose; add Broth sufficient only to keep it of a thick Substance.

Potage à la Madelonette.

A common innocent Soop.

BOIL either in Water or weak Broth all Sorts of Herbs and Roots, as Onions, Turnips, Cabbage, Leeks, Sellery, Endives, Sorrel, Lettuces, Carrots, altogether; put with it Legs and Pinions of Fowl, Necks, and all Sorts of Giblets; garnish the Dish with Roots and serve altogether.

Potage de Macarony.

Macarony Soop.

BOIL it in good Broth, then lay a Bed of it in the Bottom of your Soop-dish; then one of Parmesan Cheese, and the same over two or three Times, add a little Broth, stew it on a slow Fire, and colour it with a Salamander; then add what Quantity of Broth you think proper.

N. B. I have had this done with mixing good mild Cheshire Cheese, to save Parmesan Cheese; it answered very well.

Potage à la Mousquetaire.

Soop for a good Stomach, viz. Military.

TAKE a Pint of green Peas, a Handful of Sorrel, boil in your Broth and Gravy on a slow Fire, in it a Neck of Mutton, which when done glaze it as a Fricandeau, and serve altogether.

Potage à la Marquise.

An Epicure's Soop. A Delitanti.

TAKE a good large Roll, empty the Crums and fill it with a Ragout of Sweet-bread, Coxcomb, Artichoke Bottom, all well dressed; put this Roll in the

Middle of your Dish with other small Bits of Crums, and soak it with very good Broth; let it catch a little, and mix it with very good Cullis à la Reine and Broth.

Potage à la Rhinoceros.

Pigeon Soop called Rinoceros, from an Indian Bird.

TAKE three Pigeons, without trimming them, truffed for boiling, run a small Scuer through the Head and Neck to keep it bent upwards, scald and boil them in Broth and Veal Gravy, with Herbs and Roots cut small as for a *Julienne*; stew altogether on a slow Fire and season it well; put the Pigeons in your Soop-dish upon the Breast, the Heads above as to appear as swimming.

Potage de Navets à l'Italienne.

Turnip Soop Italian Fashion, Meat or Fish.

CUT Turnips in what Shape you please, colour them with Lard or Butter in a Stew-pan, and two Spoonfuls of Oil, add Slices of Roots as before, and boil it in good Broth and Gravy, either Meat or Fish; garnish the Dish with the Turnips, and give it a Consistence with any Sorts of Porridge.

Ouille au Bain-Marie.

Huspot of all Sorts of Meat.

TAKE an earthen Pot well scalded, put in it four Pound of sliced Beef, one Pound of Loin of Mutton, two Pound of Fillet of Veal, one Partridge, a Fowl, two large Onions with two Heads of Cloves, one Carrot, boil or more properly stew in a Quart of Water; make a Flour and Water Paste to put round the Cover to stop the Steam, make it simmer in another Pot for about seven or eight Hours; take care to supply the first Pot with boiling Water to keep the other in constant stewing,

ing, then sift the Broth in a Sieve, let it settle, then sift it in a Napkin, and serve Meat and Broth together in a Turine.

N. B. I have given this according to the Author, but I shall observe that all Butcher's Meat and Poulteries may be done the same way, and equally good, without an earthen Pot boiling in another, taking proper Care to keep the Steam in it, when it is well skimmed and boiled on a very slow Fire.

Potage à la Cressy.

Soop Cressy.

SCALD all Sorts of Roots, and boil them in short Broth, with Slices of Veal and Ham, a Bit of Butter; when thoroughly done pound altogether in a Mortar; sift it to a Cullis; add as much Broth as necessary for your Quantity of Soop; if for Meager, instead of Veal and Ham, use Carps or Pike, and Meager Broth.

Potage de Lazagne.

Lazagne Soop.

LAzagne is an Italian Paste, which we call in England flat Macarony; wash it well and boil it in Broth like Rice, and very little Salt, then sift it in a Cullender; garnish the Bottom of your Dish with Lazagne, and few Bits of Butter, then Parmesan Cheese or Gruiere, viz. Swifs, then Lazagne and Cheese until the Dish is full enough; the last Bed ought to be Cheese; put it in the Oven or cover it with the Tops of a brazing Pan or Dutch Oven; make it take a good Colour, add some good Broth and serve it.

Soupe Maigre de Differentes Facons.

Meager Soops of Different Sorts.

MAKE a soaking Broth, as directed in Meager Broth; with this Broth you make all Sorts of Soops, it is the different Sorts of Herbs and Roots which

which give it Names; according to the Quantity of Soop you want scald your Herbs and stew it in short Broth and Butter, when done add what Quantity of Broth you please: take care it does not taste too strong of the Herbs: this Soop must be clear and well seasoned for a *Julienne* Meager, cut in small Slices, a Carrot, a Head of Sellery, Charvil, Sorrel, half fryed in Butter, then add them to the Broth and a little Onion Gravy; when the Herbs are done, make use of this Broth to soak your Bread, and garnish your Dish with some of the Roots.

Potage Maigre d'Ecreviffe au Ris.

Meager Craw-fish and Rice Soops.

SOAK a Carp with a little Butter, Carrots, sliced Onions, Parsneps; let it catch very little, then add Broth and simmer till the Fish is done; pound the Bodies of half a hundred of Craw-fish and keep the Tails to garnish your Soop, add some Broth to your pounding to enable you to sift it in a Stamine; the Rice being boiled in Broth and Butter, mix it all together without boiling.

Potage Maigre à la Purée Verte.

Meager Peas Porridge Soop.

BOIL a Quart of green Peas with Parsley, Chibbol, a Bit of Butter, and Broth; when almost done, mash them and sift them in a Stamine, soak your Porridge with good Broth of a middling Substance; with dried Peas, take Spinnage Juice to make it green.

Potage Maigre à la Purée de Lentilles.

Lentil Soop Meager.

RUB the Bottom of your Stew-pan with Butter, and put in it sliced Onions, Carrots, Parsneps, a little
Winter

Winter Savory, a Clove of Garlick, two Heads of Cloves, few Mushrooms, soak on a slow Fire till it catches, then add Broth and boil for half an Hour; your Lentil being well boiled and sifted in a Stamine, sift the Broth and mix the Porridge with it; warm without boiling.

Potage Maigre de Ris à la Reine.

Rice Soop Maiger à la Reine.

HALF Pound of Rice well washed in boiling Water, boil it tender in Broth and Butter; make a Gravy without colouring, with Carp, Onions, Carrots, Parsneps; when it is ready to catch, add Broth and boil it some Time; then sift it, pound a Dozen sweet Almonds with six hard Yolks of Eggs, few Bits of boiled Fish, Crums of Bread soaked in Milk; mix it all together with the Gravy, and sift it in a Stamine; warm it without boiling, and serve this Cullis upon the Rice.

Potage de Lait de Pleusieurs Facons.

Milk Soops of different Sorts.

TO make it in the common Way, boil the Milk with Laurel Leaf, a Bit of Sugar, very little Salt, pour half the Milk in your Dish upon sliced Bread, and keep it on Ashes Fire without boiling; to the remaining Part, add few Yolks of Eggs and mix it well without boiling any more; in boiling the Milk you may also put in it Cinnamon, Coriander, a Bit of Lemon-peel, boil it half and sift it for Use as the preceding; if you would make it with *Onions*, slice a few which you boil in Butter without colouring, then add some boiling Milk and a little Salt, boil for some Time, soak your Bread as the former, and mix it when ready to serve; if you would make it with *Cabbage*, boil it in Peas Broth and a little Butter, and Salt; when it is well
done

done in short Broth, add some boiling Milk, and finish as the preceding.

Ouille au Citrouille.

Pompkin Soop.

CUT your Pompkin in such a Manner as you may join it again handsomely; take out all the Seeds, and half of the Flesh, (which you may do easily with a Table Spoon) then scar the outside in what Design you please; garnish the Scars with froughted Whites of Eggs and Sugar, then put it in a lukewarm Oven; when it is of a good Colour, put it in the Dish you intend to go to Table, and put into a Soop made in this Manner; cut in Dices Bits of the Inside, boil in Water to a Marmalade, then add a Pint of Milk boiled with a Bit of Butter, Sugar, and Salt; when you are ready add six Yolks of Eggs, put dried Crust of Bread in the Pompkin, and pour the Milk upon it, cover it as to appear whole.

Bisque Maigre aux Ecrevisses.

Meager Craw-fish Turine.

MAKE a Craw-fish Cullis, as directed in Page 7 for Craw-fish Soop, take the Tails, which you put in a Stew-pan, with Carp Liver, Artichoak Bottom, first scalded in boiling Water, and a Bit of Butter; soak it awhile, then add some Broth, and boil for half an Hour, soak your Bread and a little Broth in your Turine, until it catches a little at Bottom, then put the Carp Liver, Craw-fish Tails, Artichokes, Mushrooms, and the Broth; boil a short Time, then mix with it as much Craw-fish Cullis as will give it a good Substance.

Potage Maigre de Moules.

Muffel Soop Meager.

FIRST clean your Muffels very well in feveral Waters, and boil until they open, then take them out, and put them in a Stew-pan with fhort Broth, a Bit of Butter, a Nofegay of Parfley, Chibbol, reduce to a fhort Sauce, put a few in the Shells to garnifh your Difh, the reft in a Roll, and foak it in the Difh you are to ferve, a few Crums foaked with Muffel Broth, ftew it till it catches; when ready add to it fome Cullis à la Reine, or the Yolks of fix Eggs, well mixed with Fifh Broth.

Ouille Maigre de Pleufieurs Facons.

Olio, or Turine of different Sorts.

SCALD all Sorts of Roots, as Onions, Carrots, Parfneps, Parfley Roots, Sellery, Turnips, Leeks, boil all together in Peas Broth, and a *Minionette,* as in Page 11; Carp Parings, boil on a flow Fire till the Roots are done; add to it Root Gravy of a good Colour, when done fift it, and it will ferve you for Vermicelly and Parmefan Cheefe, Turine or Rice, or a Julienne, or any other Italian Pafte Soops.

Potage de Croutes en Maigre de Pleufieurs Facons.

Meager Cruft Soop of different Sorts.

CUT in two a large Roll, or two middling ones, take out the Crums and lay them in the Bottom of your Soop Difh, fry the Crufts in Butter, then lay them upon the Crums, and foak with good Fifh Broth, let it catch at Bottom, add Broth as often as neceffary to keep it from burning; when you are ready to ferve, put half Broth and half Onion Gravy, or if you pleafe, a Cullis of Peas, Lentils, or à la Reine, Turnips, or Craw-fifh,

&c.

&c. It takes its Name from the different Cullis you mix with it; you may also make it with Cucumber stewed, Truffles, Mushrooms; according as Conveniency and Fancy directs.

Potage de Lait d'Amande.

Almond Milk Soop.

BOIL in Water a little Cinnamon, Lemon Peel, Coriander, little Salt and Sugar, which Water you mix with Almonds well pounded and sifted several Times in a Stamine, soak your Bread in the Soop Dish with some of the Milk on a slow Fire, then add the rest, and serve as hot as you can.

Potage d'Orge Mondé.

Peeled Barley Soop.

WASH your Barley very well in warm Water, then boil it in good Broth slowly, then add a little Butter, and give it Substance with either Craw-fish Cullis or a little à la Reine.

Des Sauces.

Of Sauces.

N. B. This is where true Taste shews itself, and must meet with Approbation or Condemnation; as all boiled Meat stewed or brazed are to be made relishing, with the Addition of a well-timed good Sauce, and as it is absolutely impossible to direct Quantities so minutely as to agree with different Palates, I shall strongly recommend to all Cooks of either Sex, to keep their Stomach free from strong Liquors, and Noses from Snuffs.

Sauce Nompareille (unequal.)

Nonparel Sauce.

TAKE a Bit of boiled Ham, as much Breast of roasted Fowl, a pickled Cucumber, a hard Yolk of Egg, one Anchovy, a little Parsley, a Head of Shallot chopt as fine as possible; boil a Moment in good Cullis, and use it for Meat or Fish.

Sauce à la Nivernoise.

Nivernois Sauce.

PUT in a small Stew-pan a Couple of Slices of Ham, a Head of Garlick, two Cloves, a Laurel Leaf, sliced Onions, and Roots, let it catch a little, then add Broth, a small Quantity, two Spoonfuls of Cullis, a Spoonful of Taragon Vinegar; stew it for an Hour on the Side of a Stove, then sift it in a Sieve, and serve it for a relishing Sauce.

Sauce Petite Italienne.

A little Italian Sauce.

A Slice of Ham, few Mushrooms, few Shallots, half a Laurel Leaf, a large Spoonful of Oil; simmer all together on a flow Fire, add some rich Cullis, half a Glass of *Champagne*; boil like all Sauces, on a flow Fire for half an Hour, skim it well, and sift it in a Sieve.

N. B. The French often recommend a Glass of Champagne; it may be supplied in England with Lisbon, the Price being considered.

Sauce Italienne Blanche.

White Italian Sauce.

SIMMER on a flow Fire a Spoonful of Oil, chopt Truffles, two Cloves of Garlick, two whole Chibbol, Parsley, half a Leaf of Laurel, two Slices of Lemon, first peel'd, and good Consumee, viz. Jelly Broth, a Glass of white Wine; skim it well and sift it.

Sauce au Celadon.

Sea-green Sauce.

TAKE small Slices of Lard, Ham, Veal, Onions, Carrots, Parsneps, Shallots, and Cloves; let it catch a little, then add a Jill of white Wine and Broth, boil for an Hour on a flow Fire, then sift it, and put in some fine chopt Parsley, some Butter rolled in Flour; boil it to a good Consistence, stirring it often the while for fear it should burn at Bottom; when ready to serve add Lemon Juice sufficient to relish it.

Note. That when you use whole Cloves of Garlick in any Sauces, always take it out before you serve.

Sauce au Coloris.

A lively-colour Sauce.

THIS Sauce serves for all Sorts of white Meat brazed; take Slices of Veal, Ham, Onions, put upon it what Meat you will braze, with a Nosegay of Parsley, Chibbol, Shallots, two or three Heads of Cloves, two Slices of Lemon, half a Leaf of Laurel; cover all with Slices of Lard, soak it, and add to it some good Broth, a Glass of Wine; the Meat being done, sift it in a Hair-sieve, add two Spoonfuls or more of Cullis, skim it free from Fat, boil to the Consistence of a Sauce; add a little Butter and Flour, simmer without boiling, and it is done.

N. B.

N. B. There remains a very good Confumee in the Bottom of all Brazes; let the Fat cool, and take it off with a Spoon, the Confumee will give a very good Taste and Strength to all Sauces, with which you'll chuse to mix it.

Sauce au Consommé.

Jelly Broth Sauce.

TAKE few Slices of Lard, Ham, Beef, an old Partridge, Onions, Carrots, a Parsley Root, half a Head of Sellery, two Turnips, a Nosegay of Parsley, Chibbol, two Heads of Cloves, a Bay-leaf, a little Thyme, and soak it on a slow Fire; when it begins to catch, add Broth as much as you think proper, then stop your Pot very well, and let it simmer for about five Hours, then skim the Fat, and sift it; this Confumee serves for particular Sauces, or to add Strength to all Sorts.

Sauce à la Saxe.

Saxon Sauce.

SLICES of Veal, Ham, Onions, Carrots, Parsneps, soak in a Stew-pan on a slow Fire, let it catch very little, then add Broth, a Glass of white Wine, chopt Mushrooms; simmer for about an Hour, sift it, and add some fine chopt Parsley, few Taragon Leafs, and Mint, first scalded; a Lemon Squeeze when you serve.

Sauce à la Liason.

Sauce of a thick Consistence.

PUT in your Stew-pan few Slices of Veal and Ham, all cut small, a Bit of good Butter, a Nosegay of Parsley, Shallots, two Heads of Cloves, a Laurel Leaf, two of Taragon, a little sweet Basil; soak it according to all such Directions; then add good Broth, and simmer it till the Meat is done; sift it, and when you are ready to use it, add three Yolks of Eggs, well beat with some of the Liquors, grated Nutmeg, little chopt Parsley, Butter, Salt, Pepper, and a good Squeeze of Lemon.

Sauce à l'Ozeille.

Sorrel Sauce.

POUND Sorrel sufficient to draw two Spoonfuls of Juice, sift it, and boil it in Butter, rolled in Flour, Salt, Pepper, Nutmeg, and two Yolks of Eggs, without boiling.

Sauce à la Mariette.

Common Sauce.

SOAK Slices of Veal, Ham, Onions, Parsneps, two Cloves of Garlick, two Heads of Cloves, a few Taragon Leafs; then add Broth, a Glass of white Wine, two Slices of Lemon, simmer it on a slow Fire, skim it well, and sift it; add three green Shallots pounded.

Sauce au Cerfeuil.

Charvil Sauce.

SOAK few Mushrooms in Butter, Parsley, Chibbol, Shallots a few, two Cloves, a Laurel Leaf, a few of Taragon; then add two Spoonfuls of Broth, as much white Wine, some Salt and Pepper, reduce it slowly to a Consistence, sift it without skimming, and add to it some scalded chopt Charvil, warm without boiling.

Sauce au Persil.

Parsley Sauce.

POUND a Handful of Parsley, and put it in a Stewpan in good Cullis, sufficient for the Quantity of Sauce you want; simmer it a Quarter of an Hour, and sift

sift it in a Sieve; then add some Butter rolled in Flour, make a Liason, then add a Lemon Squeeze.

Sauce à la Civette.

Small Herb; Sauce Civet.

MIX some good Consumee with a Glass of white Wine, simmer it a Quarter of an Hour; add to it chopt Civet, a Bit of Butter rolled in Flour, coarse Pepper and Salt, and add a Lemon Squeeze.

Sauce à la Garonne.

Gascoon Sauce.

SLICES of large Onions, boil in two Spoonfuls of Oil a Moment, then add a Nosegay of Parsley, Chibbol, a Laurel Leaf, three of Taragon, sweet Basil, three Cloves of Garlick, three Cloves, few Slices of Lemon, first peeled, two Spoonfuls of Cullis, a little Broth; simmer on a slow Fire for half an Hour, skim it, and sift it for use.

Sauce au Fenouil.

Fennel Sauce.

SOAK four or five sliced Onions in two Spoonfuls of Oil, two of Cullis, and two of white Wine, with two Cloves of Garlick; simmer it an Hour, skim the Fat, and sift it in a Sieve, then add chopt Parsley and Fennel, coarse Pepper and Salt; boil a Moment before using.

Sauce a l'Amiral.

Admiral's Sauce.

CHOP an Anchovy, Capers, seven or eight green Shallots, pass it on the Fire with a little Consumee, a little Salt and Pepper, grated Nutmeg, Butter rolled in Flour; when ready add a Lemon Squeeze, or a Spoonful of Verjuice.

Sauce Royale.

Royal Sauce.

CUT small Slices of Veal, Lard and Ham, scald them and cut a Chicken in two, three or four Shallots, soak it until it is ready to catch, then add a Glass of Champagne, and as much Cullis, a Spoonful of good Oil; simmer it for an Hour and Half, skim it very clean and sift it.

Sauce à la Flamande.

Flemish Sauce.

ONE single Clove of Garlick, one of Cloves, two Slices of peeled Lemon, coarse Pepper and Salt, chopt Parsley, two Spoonfuls of Cullis, a little Broth, a Bit of Butter rolled in Flour; soak for a Quarter of an Hour, then take out the Lemon and Garlick, and serve upon what you please.

Sauce à la hâte.

Sauce in a hurry.

ROLL a Bit of Butter in Flour, put it in a Stew-pan, with some good Consumee, Pepper, and Salt, and add a Lemon Squeeze.

Sauce a l'Aigneau.

Lamb Sauce.

ROLL a Bit of Butter in Crums of Bread, three Shallots chopt, with Parsley, a small Quantity of good Broth, as much white Wine, boil a short Time; when ready, add a Squeeze of Lemon.

Sauce à l'Avare.
The Miser's Sauce, or Poor Man's Sauce.

CHOP five or six green Shallots, and add a little Verjuice or Vinegar, Pepper and Salt, a little Water; warm it and serve in a Sauce Boat.

Sauce au Verjus.
Verjuice Sauce.

POUND green Grapes, and sift it; chop two or three green Shallots, Pepper and Salt, a Spoonful of Oil; serve in a Boat.

Sauce au Pauvre Homme.
Another Poor Man's Sauce.

BOIL half a Lemon sliced in two, Spoonful of Broth, two or three chopt Shallots, Pepper and Salt; take out the Lemon before you send it, or use.

Sauce Douce.
Sweet Sauce.

TWO Glasses of red Wine, one of Vinegar, three Spoonfuls of Cullis, a Bit of Sugar, one sliced Onion, a little Cinnamon, a Laurel Leaf; boil it a Quarter of an Hour, sift it, and serve it in a Boat.

Sauce au Fumet.
Sauce made with Game.

TAKE the Remainder of a Hare or Rabbit roasted after it has served, chop it in small Pieces, put it in a Stew-pan with a Glass of white Wine or red; a little Cullis, Bay Leaf, Thyme, a sliced Onion, a Spoonful

ful of Vinegar, a little Broth, Pepper, and Salt; reduce it to the Confiftence of Sauces, and fift it in a Sieve.

Sauce Ravigotte.

Relifhing Sauce.

CHOP a Clove of Garlick, Charvil, Burnet, Taragon, Garden Creffes, Civet, all in proportion to their Flavour; when well wafhed and fqueezed, infufe it with a little Cullis without boiling; fift it with Expreffion; then add a Bit of Butter, Flour, Pepper and Salt, boil it to a good Confiftence, and add a Lemon Squeeze fufficient to make it relifhing or fmart tafted.

Ravigotte Froide.

The fame Cold.

TAKE half a Head of Sellery, two or three green Shallots, a Clove of Garlick, one Anchovy, few Capers, Taragon, Charvil, Burnet, Garden Creffes, pound it all together; add a little Cullis and fift it; then you will add Muftard, Vinegar, Oil, Pepper, and Salt; mix it well together.

Sauce à la Madeleine.

A common fimple Sauce.

PUT in a Stew-pan few Rafpings of Bread, two Shallots chopt, a Bit of Butter, half a Spoonful of Vinegar, coarfe Pepper and Salt, two Spoonfuls of Confumet; boil a Moment, not too thick.

Sauce à l'Afpic.

Sharp Sauce Afpick.

INFUSE Charvil, Taragon, Burnet, Garden Creffes, a little Mint in a little Cullis for about an Hour; then fift in a Sieve and add to it a Spoonful of Garlick,

lick, Vinegar, Pepper, and Salt; ferve cold in a Sauce Boat.

Sauce à la Gendarme.

Military Sauce.

INFUSE for an Hour in Confumee, a good deal of Parfley, three Cloves of Garlick, upon a very flow Fire; then fift it in a Sieve; then add to the Sauce a boiled pounded Lettuce, three Yolks of Eggs, Butter, Pepper, Salt, and Lemon.

Sauce à la belle-vue.

A well-looking Sauce.

TAKE Beef-Marrow a middling Quantity, Slices of Ham and Fillet of Veal, a common Chicken cut in two; two Onions, one Carrot, half a Parfnep, a Nofegay of Parfley, Chibbol, one Clove of Garlick, two Heads of Cloves, a few Leaves of Taragon, Thyme and Laurel, a little fweet Bafil; foak it till ready to catch, then add a Glafs of white Wine and good Broth, few Mufhrooms; boil on a flow Fire till the Meat is done, fift it in a Sieve; you may ufe it to what you pleafe, and alfo alter the Tafte by adding chopt Truffles, pounded white Meat of Fowl, pickled Cucumbers, Yolks of Eggs, Lemon, &c.

Sauce à la Morue.

Skate Sauce or Cod.

MAKE a Nofegay of Parfley, Chibbol, two Shallots, two Cloves, a Laurel Leaf, fome Mufhrooms, a Bit of Butter; foak all together on the Fire, add a fmall Spoonful of Flour and Milk or Cream fufficient to boil to the Confiftence of a Sauce; fift it and add to it fome chopt Parfley.

Sauce à la Polonoise.

A Polish Sauce.

SCALD a Clove of Garlick with a little Taragon and Burnet, Charvil, two Leaves of Mint, and chop all together very fine, then boil two Spoonfuls of Confumee and as much white Wine, two Cloves, reduce it to half in boiling; then take out the Cloves and add what you have chopt, with Pepper and Salt; warm without boiling.

Sauce au Foye.

Liver Sauce, or Sauce of Liver.

TAKE Poultry Livers or Game's, chop them very fine with Parsley, Chibbol, two or three Taragon Leafs, two Shallots; soak it with a little Butter till the Livers are done; then pound all together and add some Cullis and Broth, Pepper and Salt, then boil it a Moment with two Glasses of red Wine, Coriander, Cinnamon, and Sugar; reduce it to a Sauce, sift it in a Sieve, and serve it in a Sauce Boat.

Sauces Blanches.

White Sauces.

MELT the Bigness of an Egg of Butter rolled in Flour, a Couple of Anchovies; add some Water, whole Shallots, whole Pepper, a little Vinegar; simmer it awhile and take out the Shallots before you serve it.

Sauce à l'Espagnole.

Spanish Sauce.

GARNISH your Stew-pan with small Slices of Lard, Veal, Ham, one Onion, one Carrot, half a Parsnep; soak it till it begins to take Colour, then add two
large

large Glasses of white Wine, as much Consumee, three Cloves of Garlick, a little Coriander, a Laurel Leaf, three of Taragon, two Heads of Cloves, two Spoonfuls of good Oil, three of Cullis; simmer it till the Meat is done, skim it a Moment before you sift it.

Sauce Robert.

Robert Sauce.

SLICE several Onions and fry them in Butter, turning often till they take Colour, then add a little Cullis and good Broth, Pepper and Salt; let them boil half an Hour and reduce to a Sauce; when ready add Mustard: you may sift it for those that only like the Flavour of Onions.

Sauce à la Moutarde.

Mustard Sauce.

BOIL in Broth two Shallots chopt, coarse Pepper and Salt, mix some Mustard with a little Cullis, a little Vinegar; warm it without boiling.

Sauce à la Carpe.

Carp Sauce.

CUT a Carp in large Bits and put it in a Stew-pan with few Slices of Lard, Ham, Veal, two Onions, one Carrot, half a Parsnep; soak it till it catches a little; then add a Glass of white Wine and good Broth, a little Cullis, a Nosegay of Parsley, Chibbol, a Clove of Garlick, two of Cloves, a Laurel Leaf; simmer for an Hour, skim it well, and sift it in a Sieve.

Sauce à l'Anguille.

Eel Sauce.

CUT the Eels as before and foak them, adding all Sorts of Roots, and three or four Taragon Leafs, inftead of the Nofegay and Laurel; fkim it well and fift it in a Sieve: Sturgeon Sauce is made after the fame Manner: Pike Sauce the fame as the Carp.

Sauce à la Bechamel.

Begamel Sauce.

PUT in a Stew-pan few Slices of Ham, few Mufhrooms, two Shallots, two Cloves, a Laurel Leaf, a Bit of Butter; foak all together till it begins to take Colour; add a little Flour and Milk or Cream; fimmer half an Hour and fift it in a Sieve; you may add fcalded Parfley chopt very fine.

Sauce au Maquereau.

Mackerel Sauce.

SCALD green Goofberries and Fennel, chop the Fennel very fine, a Bit of Butter rolled in Flour, Pepper and Salt; add a little Veal Gravy and reduce it to the Confiftence of a white Sauce.

Sauce Remoulade.

Horfe-radifh or Muftard Sauce.

IF you want it hot, flice two Onions and fry them in Oil, when it begins to colour add a Glafs of white Wine, as much Broth, two Slices of Lemon, firft peeled, two Cloves of Garlick, a Laurel Leaf, Thyme, Bafil, two Cloves; boil a Quarter of an Hour and fift in a Sieve; add a chopt Anchovy and Capers, a Spoonful of of Mustard or Horse-radish reduced to a Marmalade, Pepper and Salt; warm without boiling: this Sauce is made cold with chopt Parsley, Chibbol, Shallots, a Clove of Garlick, Anchovies and Capers, a Spoonful of Mustard or Horse-radish scraped very fine, a Spoonful of Oil, Vinegar, Pepper, and Salt.

Sauce Poivrade.

Sharp Sauce.

TAKE a Bit of Butter with sliced Onions, Bits of Carrots, Parsneps, half a Parsley Root, two Cloves of Garlick, a Laurel Leaf, two Cloves; soak all together till it takes Colour, then add some Cullis, half a Glass of Vinegar and Broth, Salt and coarse Pepper; boil it to the Consistence of Sauces, skim it and sift it with a Sieve.

Sauce au Fenouil.

Another Fennel Sauce.

WARM as much Cullis and Consumet as you have occasion for Sauce, infuse in it some Fennel, and take it out as soon as it has given Taste to the Sauce: add a Lemon-Squeeze when you serve.

Sauce Hachée.

Minced Sauce.

SOAK a Slice of Ham over the Fire; when it catches a little mince it very fine and put it in the same Stew-pan with chopt Mushrooms, Parsley, Chibbol, two Shallots; add a Glass of white Wine, as much Consumee, a little Salt and coarse Pepper; simmer it to a Sauce Consistence, skim it well.

N. B. I shall add from my own Experience, that a pounded Anchovy added to this Sauce, just before using, will add greatly to its Relish.

Sauce au Bain-Marie.

(See Page 2 for Instructions.)

ACcording to what Quantity of Sauce wanted, cut in very thin Slices of Fillet of Veal, Ham, Beef, Carrots, Parsneps, Parsley Roots, Onions, Turnips, Sellery, Leeks, of each an equal Quantity not to overcome each other; put all together in a small Soop-pot upon few Slices of Lard, stop it well and put it on an Ashes Fire to soak some Time; then add a little white Wine, as much Broth; then put your Pot into another to boil for about four Hours; sift this Sauce in a Lawn Sieve to use for what you please.

Sauce au Porc Frais.

Fresh Pork Sauce.

FRY two or three Onions sliced in Oil till it takes Colour, then add Broth, two Spoonfuls of Cullis, chopt Mushrooms, a Clove of Garlick, two of Cloves, a little Vinegar; boil for half an Hour to reduce it to the Consistence of a Sauce; skim it well and sift it.

Sauce à la Nonette.

Nun's Sauce.

TAKE Slices of Veal and Ham, put in a Stew-pan with a Spoonful of Oil, two or three Mushrooms, a Nosegay of Parsley, Chibbol, a Clove of Garlick, two Heads of Cloves, half a Leaf of Laurel, let it catch on the Fire, then add some good Broth, a little Gravy, a Glass of white Wine; simmer it some Time, skim it well and sift it in a Sieve, when ready add to it two or three green Shallots, a Dozen of Pistachio Nuts whole.

Sauce Verte.

Green Sauce.

TAKE Charvil, Parsley, Taragon, Burnet; wash them all well and squeeze the Water out, then pound it very fine; then put it on the Fire with good Consumee, sift it in a Stamine with Expression, and add Butter rolled in Flour, Pepper, and Salt; simmer it without boiling.

Sauce Verte d'une autre Facon.

Another Green Sauce.

SCALD a Handful of Spinage for half an Hour, with Parsley and Tops of green Shallots; then take all out and squeeze it well and pound very fine, put in a Stewpan few Mushrooms, sliced Onions, two Cloves of Garlick, two or three Taragon Leafs, one of Laurel, a little Basil, two Cloves, a little Butter; and two Spoonfuls of Cullis, as much white Wine; boil it a Moment, then add your green Sauce and sift it in a Stamine; add Pepper and Salt, and simmer it without boiling.

Sauce Piquante.

Sharp or Relishing Sauce.

SOAK a good Slice of Veal and Ham, when it catches add a Glass of white Wine, half a Glass of white Vinegar, two of Broth, two Spoonfuls of Oil, two Cloves of Garlick, two Slices of peeled Lemon, four or five Taragon Leafs, one of Laurel, one of Mint, two Cloves, a little Coriander; boil for an Hour on a slow Fire, and reduce it to the Consistence of a Sauce, skim the Fat very clean and sift it in a Sieve; you may add a little Cullis if you would have it thicker.

Sauce au Bleu Celeſte.

A Sky-blue Sauce.

TAKE a ſmall Handful of Crums of Bread ſifted in a Cullender, boil it in Milk until it becomes quite thick; take care to ſtir it, left it ſhould burn; add a little boiled Cream, and ſift it in a Stamine; then boil a Glaſs of white Wine, with a Clove of Garlick; pound very fine ſome Charvil, Parſley, Taragon, and ſift it with the white Wine; add this green with the white Sauce; and add a little Cullis, Pepper and Salt; warm it without boiling.

Sauce au Pontife.

Pontiff Sauce.

SOAK Slices of Veal, Ham, ſliced Onions, Carrots, Parſneps, half a Head of Sallery; let it catch, then add a Glaſs of white Wine, as much good Broth, a Clove of Garlick, four Shallots, one Clove, a little Coriander, two Slices of peeled Lemon; boil on a flow Fire till the Meat is done, ſkim it and ſift it in a Sieve; add a little Cullis, and a ſmall Quantity of fine chopt Parſley, juſt before you uſe it.

Sauce à la Nichon.

The Houſe-wife's Sauce.

TAKE ſome of the former Sauce ſifted without Cullis, add a Bit of Butter rolled in Flour, add chopt Charvil; uſe it when warm.

Sauce au Reverend, Gras ou Maigre.

The Parſon's Sauce.

CHOP Lemon-peel very fine, with two or three pickled Cucumbers, a Bit of good Butter, Salt, and coarſe

coarse Pepper, a little Flour, with two Spoonfuls of Cullis, and make a Liason.

Sauce à la Milanoise.

Milan Sauce.

SLICE two or three Onions, put them in a Stew-pan, with few small Bits of Ham, a Clove of Garlick, two Cloves, a Laurel Leaf, scalded Parsley, two Spoonfuls of Oil; let it catch on the Fire; then put to it a Glass of white Wine, as much Cullis; simmer it some Time, skim it well, and sift it in a Sieve.

Sauce a l'Orange.

Orange Sauce.

SOAK Slices of Veal, Ham, Onions, Roots; let it catch; then add a small Quantity of Broth and Cullis; simmer it on a slow Fire, skim it, and sift it in a Sieve; then add Orange Peel chopt, and squeeze two Oranges, a Bit of Butter, coarse Pepper; warm it without boiling: for Meager, take Fish Broth, a chopt Anchovy, Pepper, and a little Salt, more Butter rolled in Flour, and the same Quantity of Orange Peel and Juices.

Sauce au Canard.

Sauce for Ducks.

MIX Two Spoonfuls of good Cullis with as much Veal Gravy, Pepper, and Salt; squeeze a Lemon or two, and warm it without boiling.

Sauce à l'Echalotte.

Shallot Sauce.

BOIL a Moment five or six Shallots well chopt, in good Veal Gravy, with Pepper and Salt; serve in a Boat.

Une autre Sauce au Percil.

Another Parsley Sauce.

SCALD half a Handful of Parsley, and chop it very fine put it in a small Stew-pan with Butter and Flour, a chopt Anchovy, Pepper, and Salt, a little Vinegar, and Taragon; add a Spoonful of Cullis, as much Gravy of Veal, or Onions; warm it without boiling.

Sauce au Bled Verd.

Green Wheat Sauce.

SIMMER a Crust of Bread in a little Broth, half a Spoonful of Vinegar, a Clove of Garlick; scald a Handful of Green Wheat, and squeeze the Water out very well; pound it, and add the Juice to your Sauce, and sift it all together in a Stamine; make a Liason with some Consumee, Pepper, and Salt.

Sauce à la Reine.

Queen's Sauce.

SIMMER Crums of Bread in good Cullis, until it is quite thick; take it off the Fire; and add three sweet Almonds pounded, two hard Yolks of Eggs, a Breast of Fowl roasted, all pounded very fine; boil some Cream sufficiently for your Sauce, and sift it altogether in a Stamine; add Pepper and Salt, and warm it without boiling.

Sauce d'Acide.

Acid Sauce.

POUND three hard Yolks of Eggs, one Anchovy, with a Pinch of fine Spices and Salt, half a Glass of Vinegar, and Butter rolled in Flour, add a little Veal Gravy, or Onions: if for Meager, make a Liason as for a white Sauce.

Sauce à la Becasse.

Wood-cock Sauce.

TAKE the Bones of roasted Wood-cocks, pound them, and the Livers, put them in a Stew-pan with two Spoonfuls of Cullis, as much red Wine; reduce it to a Sauce Consistence, sift it in a Sieve, when ready add Pepper and Salt, and squeeze one or two Oranges in it.

Sauce au Trufes.

Truffles Sauce.

CHOP three or four Truffles, put them in a Stew-pan with two Spoonfuls of Consumee, two of Gravy, Meager or Meat, a Nosegay of Parsley, Chibbol, half a Clove of Garlick, coarse Pepper and Salt; simmer it to the Consistence of a Sauce, and take out the Nosegay before using.

Sauce Maigre de Plusieurs Facons.

Meager Sauces of different Sorts.

WITH Fish, Broth, Cullis, Gravy, and Consumet, you make Meager Sauces in the same Manner as with Meat.

The ART *of*

Sauce General.

General Sauce.

TO make this Sauce properly, you must infuse all the following Ingredients for four and twenty Hours on Ashes, in an earthen Pot if possible; and that it may be very well stopped, split six Shallots, a Clove of Garlick, two Laurel Leafs, Thyme and Basil in proportion, Truffles, Taragon Leafs, half an Ounce of Mustard Seed bruised, a dozen small Bits of Seville Orange Peel, a quarter of an Ounce of Cloves, as much Mace, half an Ounce of long Pepper, two Ounces of Salt, squeeze a whole Lemon, half a Dozen Glasses of Verjuice, or Vinegar four or five Spoonfuls, a Pint of white Wine; let it rest and sift it very clear, which you keep in Bottle, it will keep a long while, and serve for all Sorts of Meat and Fish; you may also mix it with different Sauces which require a Sharpness; it must be used with Moderation upon the Quantities here given: You may proportion any Quantities.

Sauce au Beure Noir.

Burnt Butter Sauce.

FRY some Butter; when it begins to smoke throw in it Parsley Leaves, or coarse chopt; when it is done add Pepper, Salt, and Vinegar.

Sauce Simple.

Simple Sauce.

TAKE a Bit of Butter rolled in Flour, a little Vinegar, Pepper, and Salt, a Spoonful or two of Water, make a Liason over the Fire; you may add chopt Parsley, Shallots, or an Anchovy.

I shall

I shall take Notice that Oil is recommended in several of these Sauces, but I have rather followed the Author's Direction than my own Inclination, confidering that Oil in England is seldom to be had in Perfection, and that most People by that Means, have a Diflike to have it in their Sauces.

CHAPITRE PREMIER. Du Bœuf.

CHAPTER FIRST. Of Beef.

ALL Sorts of Beef Meat must be chosen of a fine Red, well interlarded with Fat, rather of a Crimson Colour; what Parts are used in Cookery, are the Brains, Palates, Tongue, Suet and Udder, the whole Leg cut in a different Manner, the Marrow, the Rump, Edgebone, Surloin, and the Fillet off the Tail, Ribs and Breast, Flank and Veiny Pieces, &c. The Brains, Palates, and Suet, must be used fresh, also such as is used for Broth, and Gravy, the rest require to be kept some Time, according to the Season; most Pieces of Beef, either boiled or roasted, should be cut across the Grain, as it will always eat tender, and the Head should be stewed to help with a Spoon, and requires a great deal of Care and Attention in cleaning.

Langue de Bœuf au Gros Sel.

Fresh Tongue in a plain way.

LARD a Tongue with large Pieces of Lard, and boil it in the Broth-pot, or in Water with a few Onions, and Roots; when it is done, peel it and serve it with Broth, a little Pepper, and Salt.

Langues de Bœufs en Caisses.

Sham Beefs Tongues.

TAKE a plain boiled Tongue and peel it, and cut it in Slices, simmer over the Fire about a quarter of an Hour, with a little chopt Parsley, Shallots, a Taste of Garlick, a Bit of Butter, Salt, and fine Spices; take it off, and let it cool; mak'd forced Meat with Fillet of Veal, as much Suet, Crums of Bread, Cream, Pepper, Salt, Parsley, Chibbol, three Yolks of Eggs to mix it; garnish the Bottom of the Dish (you intend to serve the Tongue upon) with some of this forced Meat, then the Tongue upon this; cover it over with the Remainder, and smooth it with a Knife dipt in Yolks of Eggs and Crums, in the Form of a Tongue; then bake it in a Dutch Oven, or in the Baking Oven for about three Quarters of an Hour; when it is of a good Colour, take it out and pour the Fat off, clean your Dish, and put upon a clear Sauce made with half Veal Gravy, and good Broth, a little Vinegar, Salt, and Pepper.

Langue de Bœufs à la Remoulade.

Beefs Tongue with a relishing Sauce.

SCALD a fresh Tongue and lard it with large Pieces, boil it in Broth with a little Salt, and a Nosegay as formerly directed; when done peel it, split it not quite into two Pieces; make a Sauce with Parsley, Shallots, Capers, Anchovies, all very fine chopt, a little Vinegar, few Crums of Bread or Raspings, two Spoonfuls of Cullis, as much Broth, a little Salt and coarse Pepper; boil altogether a Moment; then put the Tongue in it to simmer for a Quarter of an Hour; when you serve add a little Mustard.

Langue de Bœuf en Ragout.

Beef Tongue Ragout.

LARD a Tongue as the former, and braze it in a light Braze; mix with Broth a Nosegay of Parsley, Chibbol, Thyme, Laurel, two Heads of Cloves, one of Garlick, Onions and Roots; peel it, split it in two, serve upon it what Ragout you think proper, such as Sweet Breads, Truffles, Mushrooms, small Onions, &c.

Langue de Bœuf Grilleé.

Broiled Beef's Tongue

LARD and braze a Tongue the same as the former, and peel it, cut it in two, and dip it in Oil, and roll it in Bread Crums, broil it slowly, putting a little Oil over it; make a Sauce with chopt Shallots, two Spoonfuls of Broth, as much Veal Gravy, Pepper, and Salt, a little Vinegar or Verjuice; boil it a Moment; pour your Sauce in the Dish and the Tongue upon it.

Langues Fumeés.

Smoaked Tongues.

WHAT Quantity of Tongues you think proper, soak them in Water about three Hours, cut off the Throat end, and wipe them dry with a Cloth before Salting; make a Powder with Laurel Leaves, Thyme, Basil, Coriander, Juniper, Parsley, Shallots, and Cloves, dry them in the Oven to pound them finer, with two Ounces of Salt-patre to one Pound of Salt, mix your Powder with the Salt; have a proper Pan for Tongues and place them very close as they are salted, when all salted cover your Pan very close, and leave it so for eight Days; then take them out and run a String through the small End, put them up in the Chimney until they are quite dried; they will keep a long while, use them either plain boiled or brazed; the Pickle will serve to make pickled Pork.

Langues de Bœuf Foureés.

Smoaked Tongues of another Fashion.

PREPARE the Tongues as the former, have some Beef Guts well cleaned and soaked in Water and sweet Herbs, make a Pickle with boiling Water, a little Salt-petre, great deal of common Salt, Cloves, Mace, Thyme, Laurel, Basil, Juniper, Coriander; boil this Pickle about half an Hour over a slow Fire, let it settle, then sift it in a Sieve, as clear as possible; put the Tongues in the Guts, then in the Pickle, for about twelve Days, take them out and hang them in the Chimney as the former; when drying you burn scented Herbs under them: You use them in the same Manner as the others.

Langue de Bœuf à la Broche.

Beef's Tongue Roasted.

SCALD a Tongue, boil it half in Broth or Water, with Salt and Pepper, two Onions, Carrots, Parsneps, a Nosegay, two Cloves, Garlick, Laurel, and Thyme; when it is boiled enough to peel, take it out, and lard as a Fricandeau, and finish it in Roasting; serve under it a relishing Sauce, or plain.

Langue de Bœuf à la Braise.

Beef's Tongue Brazed.

SCALD a Tongue, and boil it half in your Broth-pot or other, then peel it and lard it through with coarse Pieces, finish it by itself in a small Pot with Broth, Pepper, Salt, Carrots, Parsneps, two Onions,

Slices

Slices of Lard, a Nosegay, Shallots, two Cloves, a Laurel Leaf, Thyme, Basil, few Taragon Leafs, a Glass of white Wine; boil on a slow Fire, put to it what Ragout you please; Calves Tongues, Sheeps, and Pork, are dressed the same way.

Langue de Bœuf en Crepine.

Beef's Tongue in Cowl Veal, or other.

BOIL a Tongue sufficiently to peel as the former, then lard it and split it without separating in two, have some fine sliced Onions, fry them in fresh Hog's Lard; then put to it two or three Spoonfuls of Hog's Blood, about a quarter of a Pound of fresh Lard chopt, few fine Spices, and Salt; simmer it, stirring it continually until the Blood is well mixed; then lay a Cowl in the Bottom of your Dish, and spread upon it part of your Preparation, then the Tongue; then the same as before upon the Tongue, roll it in the Cowl and garnish with Bread Crums, put it in the Oven to bake, and take a good Colour; clean the Dish free from Fat, and serve under it a Sauce made with a little Cullis, Jelly Broth and Lemon.

Langue de Bœuf à la St. Menehoult.

A Brazed Tongue Broiled.

BRAZE a Tongue well larded, when done split it in two without separating, dip it in Yolks of Eggs, and Bread Crums, then in melted Butter and more Crums; then broil it on a slow Fire, basting it sometimes with Butter; serve it with a clear Verjuice Sauce or Mustard in a Sauce Boat.

Langue de Bœuf au Gratin.

N. B. Gratin means every Thing that catches at Bottom.

CUT a brazed Tongue in thin Slices, put in a Stewpan a Bit of Butter, Parsley, Chibbol, Mushrooms, Shallots, half a Clove of Garlick, all well chopt; simmer all on the Fire with a little Cullis, Gravy, and Broth, a little Vinegar, Salt, and coarse Pepper; reduce it to the Consistence of a Sauce; add an Anchovy, and Capers chopt; put half of this Sauce in the Dish intended for Table; place the Tongue properly upon it, soak it until it catches at Bottom; when ready to serve add the rest of your Sauce.

Paté & Tourte de Langue de Bœuf.

Beef's Tongue Pye, with rais'd Puff Paste.

SCALD a Tongue, and boil it in your Pot or plain Water, when almost done peel it and cut it in Slices, make what Paste you please or as it is observed in Pastry Directions; place upon it the Slices with Pepper and Salt, two good Slices of Ham, a Nosegay of Parsley, Chibbol, a Clove of Garlick, three Heads of Cloves, Thyme, Laurel, cover it with Slices of Lard and Butter, bake it in the Oven; when done, take out the Lard and Nosegay, skim the Fat very clean and put in it a Spanish Sauce, or which you think proper.

Langue de Bœuf au Parmesan.

Beef's Tongue and Parmesan Cheese.

BOIL the Tongue as the former, then finish it in a Braze, with a little Salt, peel it and let it cool, and cut it in Slices, put a little Cullis and Parmesan in the Table Dish, and some of the Tongue Slices, then a little more Cullis and Parmesan, let the Cheese be the

last

last Bed, then bake it in a Dutch Oven or the Common; give it a good Colour, and little Sauce remaining.

Cervelle de Bœuf.

Ox's Brains.

OX's Brains are prepared as Calves Brains, which you will find in the Articles of Veal.

Palais de Bœuf à la St. Menoult.

Beef's Palates St. Menoult.

BOIL in Water as many Palates as you please, peel them well, and soak them some time in a St. Menoult, which is thus; put in a Stew-pan a Bit of Butter rolled in Flour, Salt, and Pepper, two Shallots, a Garlick, a Clove, Parsley, a Laurel Leaf, Thyme, with as much Milk as is necessary to simmer your Palates; in about three quarters of an Hour, take them out, and dip them in Yolks of Eggs and Bread Crums, broil them slowly, and serve with a sharp Sauce or Mustard.

Palais de Bœuf à la Poulette.

Fricassee of Palates.

BOIL and peel the Palates as the former, and cut them small, put them in a Stew-pan with a little Butter, a Slice of Ham, Mushrooms, a Nosegay, Shallots, two Cloves, few Taragon Leaves, a Glass of white Wine and Broth, simmer it until the Sauce grows short, take out the Nosegay, add Salt and Pepper, three Yolks of Eggs and Cream, a little chopt Parsley; make a Liason and add a Squeeze of Lemon when ready.

Palais de Bœuf à l'Angloise.

Beef's Palates English Fashion: Or Olive.

BRAZE your Palates and peel them well, split them in two, and spread upon it some good forced Meat made of Veal or roasted Fowl; roll them like an Olive, then dip them in Batter made with Flower and Yolks of Eggs, a Spoonful of Oil, Salt, a Glass of white Wine, which you pour by little and little; make your Batter a little thicker than very thick Cream; fry them of a good Colour.

Palais de Bœuf au petit Lard.

Beef's Palates with pickled Pork.

SLICE some pickled Pork and boil it slowly, take the Fat out, add a little Cullis, and Vinegar, a little Consumee, two or three chopt Shallots, Pepper, brazed Palates cut in large Pieces; warm it without boiling.

Palais de Bœuf au Parmesan.

Beef's Palates and Parmesan. (See Tongue.)

Palais de Bœuf en Fillet.

BRAZE the Palates and cut them small, let them soak an Hour in Lemon Juice, then dry them, and roll them in Batter made of Flour, a Spoonful of Oil, a little Salt and white Wine, and fry them of a fine Colour.

Palais de Bœuf en Timbale.

Beef's Palates in Moulds of any Sorts.

GARNISH your Moulds with Veal, Cowl, and cut the Palates according to the Form of the Moulds; the Palates first brazed make a good forced Meat with Fowl,

Fowl, and the Paring of the Palates; put a Bit of Palates in the Bottom, then forced Meat, and repeat it until the Mould is full, cover it with chopt Truffles, and one Bit of Palate, laſt wrap it in the Cowl, and bake it in the Oven; when done, take them out of the Moulds carefully, and wipe the Fat, and ſerve upon it what Sauce you pleaſe.

Palais de Bœuf à la Brochette.

Beef's Palates broiled on ſmall Scuers.

BOIL three or four Palates in Water, when well peeled and trimmed cut them in four or ſix Pieces, then put in a Stew-pan with Muſhrooms, Shallots, half a Clove of Garlick, Parſley, Chibbol, all finely chopt, Pepper and Salt, a Bit of Butter rolled in Flour, two Spoonfuls of Cullis, a Glaſs of white Wine, boil on a ſlow Fire until the Sauce is quite reduced, then add a little Butter and three Yolks of Eggs, ſimmer it over the Fire to make the Sauce quite thick; then ſerve your Palates as you do Larks rolled in the Sauce and Bread Crums, broil them gently of a fine Colour; you may ſerve them either with or without Sauce, if any, let it be clear Gravy and Verjuice, or Lemon.

Palais de Bœuf en Menus droits.

Beef Palates cut in Fillets or minced.

FRY two or three ſliced Onions in Butter, until half done, then put two or three ſliced Palates plain boiled, add a little Cullis, Gravy and Broth, ſimmer it to reduce the Sauce; ſkim it well and add Pepper, Salt, and Nutmeg, a little Vinegar; when ready to ſerve, add a little Muſtard,

Palais de Bœuf à la Mariette.

Beef Palates in a common Way.

BOIL three Palates in Water for about an Hour, peel them and cut in two length Way; put thin Slices of Ham and pickled Pork between two Palates, and tie them together, finish to boil in Broth with a little Salt, whole Pepper, a Nosegay, two Cloves; serve with Consumet, and a Lemon Squeeze.

Palais de Bœuf à la Provençale.

Beef's Palates Province Fashion.

BRAZE the Palates and cut in small Pieces, put them in a Stew-pan with a Bit of Butter, two Spoonfuls of Oil, Salt, whole Pepper, a little rasped Nutmeg, two chopt Shallots, a Clove of Garlick, five or six Taragon Leafs, Mushrooms, Parsley; simmer it a Quarter of an Hour, then add a little Cullis, a Glass of white Wine, a little Consumee; boil it a Moment, skim the Fat, and add a Lemon Squeeze when ready to serve.

Palais de Bœuf au Parmesan aux Onions.

Beefs Palates with Parmesan and Onions.

BRAZE the Palates and cut each in six, have some small Onions boiled in Broth, which you mix with some Cullis and Consumee, a Bit of Butter, Pepper, and Salt; make a Liason on the Fire, then put half of this Sauce (in the Dish you intent to serve) with rasped Parmesan, then the Palates and small Onions, then the Remainder of the Sauce and Parmesan over it: bake it in an Oven or with a Cover fit for it to take a fine Colour.

Palais de Bœuf au Gratin.

(See the Explanation of Gratin, page 56.)

MAKE a forced Meat with Fat Liver, chopt Truffles fcraped Lard, two Yolks of Eggs, a little Salt; put this in the Bottom of the Difh you intend to ferve; put on a Sand Fire, let it catch, and add the Palates brazed and cut in what Form you pleafe, upon the Gratin and fmall Onions firft boiled, ferve upon it a Sauce *au Pontiffe* or *à l'Efpagnole*, fee Sauce Articles; Veal and Sheeps Palates are dreffed in all the fame different Ways, as Beef's.

Palais de Bœuf à l'Efcalope.

Collop of Beef Palates.

BOIL your Palates in Water, peel and pare them, very well, then flice them to the Breadth of half a Crown, as thin as you can; put in the Stew-pan Slices of Ham, two Spoonfuls of Oil, Parfley, Chibbol, Mufhrooms, Shallots, a Trifle of Garlick, all fine chopt, whole Pepper and Salt; then a Bed of Palates, upon it fweet Herbs chopt, and Palates, and continue till you have done with the Palates; cover it over with thin Slices of Lard, and fimmer it on a flow Fire; when it begins to boil, add a Glafs of white Wine, let it fimmer about an Hour, then fkim the Fat and take out the Lard and Ham; add to it a Spoonful of Cullis, a Lemon Squeeze; ferve with fhort Sauce.

Palais de Bœuf à la Marmotte.

Beef's Palates Country Fafhion.

CUT two or three Palates boiled in Water, cut alfo fome pickled Pork in Slices which you boil to half, then add the Palates with Parfley, Shallots, a Clove of Garlick,

Garlick, chopt together, whole Pepper, a little white Wine; boil all together, when done put the Meat on the Dish you intend to serve, put Crumbs of Bread over it, put in the Oven to take Colour; serve with short Sauce.

Palais de Bœuf à la Ravigotte.

Beef's Palates with a relishing Sauce.

BOIL the Palates in Water, when well peeled cut each in six Pieces, put them in a Stew-pan with a Slice of Ham, a Nosegay of Parsley, Chibbol, a Clove of Garlick, two Heads of Cloves, a Bit of Butter, let it catch a little, then add a Glass of white Wine, as much Cullis, simmer it some Time, skim the Fat, add Pepper and Salt, reduce the Sauce when ready, add sweet Herbs fine chopt, as Taragon, Burnet, Charvil, Cresses, Civet, of each according to their Quality for Strength of Flavour.

Palais de Bœuf de Plusieurs Façons.

Beef's Palates of different Fashions.

WHEN the Palates are boiled in Water and well pared and peeled, cut them to what Form you please, then braze them for half an Hour, take them out and keep them free from Fat, put them in your Dish and add what Sauce you please, rather sharp is best, as these Palates are flat tasted.

Queue de Bœuf au Choux.

Beef's Tail and Cabbage.

CUT a Beef's Tail in several Pieces, scald and boil it in Broth with a Nosegay of Parsley, Shallots, a Laurel Leaf, three Heads of Cloves, when boiled about an Hour put to it a good Savoy, first scalded, a Pound of pickled

pickled Pork cut in Pieces, a little Salt and Pepper; when done take it out of the Braze, squeeze the Fat out; put all in a Turine intermixed, and add Broth and good Cullis sufficient to make it either more or less Liquid.

Queue de Bœuf aux Lentilles.

Beef's Tail and Nantils.

BRAZE the Tail and cut in Pieces, and pickled Pork as before, make a Veal Cullis with Slices of Veal, Ham, Onions, Carrots, Parsneps, Sellery; when it catches add Broth and finish as all other Cullis; boil Nantils either in Broth or Water, make a Porridge which you mix with the Cullis to a thick Consistence, which you serve in a Turine upon the Tail and pickled Pork; they are done the same with all Sorts of Porridge either dry or green.

Queue de Bœuf en Pâté Chaud.

Beef's Rump Pie.

BRAZE two or three Tails to about three Parts, then take them out and cut in Pieces, put a Couple of Slices of Ham in the Bottom of your Pie, then the Rumps; cover it over with Butter and thin Slices of Lard and finish your Pie; bake it in the Oven; when done take out the Lard and Ham, skim the Fat very clean; serve upon it a good Sauce of Sweet Bread, Ragout, Fat, Liver, Truffles or any other.

Queue de Bœuf de Plusieurs Façons.

Beef's Rump of different Fashion.

RUMPS well brazed may be dressed different Ways, you may broil and serve it with a sharp Sauce in a Boat; also as Turine, with all Sorts of Herbs

and

and Roots, as Cucumber, Chesnuts, Truffles, Turnips, Onions, Carrots, Sweet Breads, Coxcombs, &c. &c.

Gras double à la Robert.

Tripes Sauce Robert.

FRY three or four sliced Onions in Butter till they are almost done; boil the Tripes in Water very tender, cut in Pieces, and mix them with the Onions; a little Cullis, a Glass of white Wine, as much Broth, a Nosegay of Parsley, Chibbol, a Laurel Leaf, two Cloves, three or four Taragon Leafs, Pepper and Salt, boil on a slow Fire, skim it well, reduce the Sauce pretty thick and add a little Mustard.

Gras double au Verjus.

Tripes Verjuice Sauce.

BOIL the Tripes very tender, make a Marinade with Oil, Pepper, Salt, Parsley, Shallots chopt very fine, soak the Tripes some Time in this, then roll them in Bread Crums, broil them of a good Colour; serve with a Sauce, half Cullis and half Verjuice.

Gras double de plusieurs Façons.

Tripes of different Fashions.

TRIPES boiled very tender may be cut in different Manner, and dressed with Mushrooms, Parsley, Shallots, a Clove of Garlick, few Taragon Leaves, two Cloves, a Slice of Ham, a Bit of Butter, Thyme and Laurel; let it catch a little, then add a Glass of white Wine and as much Broth, reduce the Sauce and make a Liason with three Yolks of Eggs, Pepper and Salt, Verjuice or Lemon; if you would have it brown, instead of a Liason add Cullis and Gravy, a small Quantity of scalded chopt Parsley.

Rognon

Rognon de Bœuf à la Moutarde.
Beef's Kidney and Mustard Sauce.

FRY sliced Onions in Butter to half, and cut the Kidney in small Pieces; put it together in a Stew-pan with Pepper and Salt, stew it on a slow Fire; the Kidney will furnish Liquid enough, add the Mustard when ready.

Rognons de Bœuf à la Môde.

CUT the Kidneys in small Pieces and clean them very well; also a Pound of pickled Pork cut in Pieces, chop some Parsley, Shallots, a Clove of Garlick, garnish the Bottom of your Stew-pan with Slices of Lard; then Kidney, Pork, and Herbs, then lard again until you have finished; stew it for about three Hours over a slow Fire, or in the Oven; when it is almost done add a good Spoonful of Brandy, serve it in a Turine either hot or cold.

Rognon de Bœuf en Filets.
Kidney Minced.

BRAZE the Kidney very tender and mince it; which you may serve upon stewed Cucumbers, or any other Greens whatever; it must be made pretty relishing.

Rognons de Bœuf en Pâté Chaud.
Hot Kidnies Pie.

CUT the Kidnies in thin Slices, cover the Bottom of your Pie with it, then sweet Herbs chopt, such as Parsley, Thyme, Shallots, Mushrooms, Pepper, Salt, and fine Spices; continue in that Manner, then cover it over with Slices of Lard and finish the Pie; bake it in the Oven, take out the Lard and skim the Fat very clean, make a Sauce with a Glass of white Wine, a good Quantity of Cullis, reduce to the Consistence of a good Sauce, and squeeze a Seville Orange in it when ready.

Rognon de Bœuf à la Bourgeoise.

Kidney Family Way.

CUT a Kidney in two, and put it in a Stew-pan with Parsley, Shallots, a Clove of Garlick, Thyme, Laurel, all chopt very fine, and a Bit of Butter, turn it over the Fire some Time, then roll it in Bread Crums, and broil it, pouring the Sauce over it gently; make the Sauce half Gravy and half Verjuice.

Tetine de Vache au Verjus.

Cow's Udder and Verjuice Sauce.

CUT the Udder in Pieces and put it in a Stew-pan with chopt Parsley, Chibbol, Mushrooms, a Clove of Garlick and Butter, let it catch, then add a Glass of white Wine, Broth, Pepper and Salt, simmer it to a short Sauce, then make a Liason with two Yolks of Eggs and Broth; when ready add a Spoonful of Verjuice or Lemon.

Usage de la Graïsse de Bœuf & Moüelle.

The Way to use Beef's Suet and Marrow.

TO use Suet and Marrow, all the small Skin and Sinews must be taken away very clean (the Way to do it is common to all Kitchen Maids) it serves for most forced Meat, as does Marrow for particular Uses, and extremely good to put in Brazes, as being very nourishing if you would use it instead of Butter, soak it in

Milk-

Milk-warm-Water, turning and pressing it with your Hands to render it soft and squeeze the Water out of it.

Tranches de Bœuf à la Bourgeoise.

Beef Stakes Family Way.

LARD the Stakes here and there with large Pieces, put them in the Pan with chopt Parsley, Shallots, Thyme, Laurel, Salt, whole Pepper, a Glass of white Wine; let it soak two Hours, then simmer it till it is done; serve either hot or cold.

Tranche de Bœuf à la Camargot.

Beef Stakes, by the Name of a famous Dancer.

LARD thick Beef Stakes, half Lard and half Anchovies; put them in a Stew-pan upon Slices of Lard, season it with fine Spices (and no Salt, as the Anchovies will answer) a Nosegay of Parsley, Chibbol, a Clove of Garlick, two Shallots, a Laurel Leaf, Thyme and Basil, a Glass of white Wine, simmer it about four Hours, then sift the Sauce in a Sieve, and add a Bit of Butter rolled in Flour; according to the Quantity of Sauce you want, add Broth and Cullis, a Lemon Squeeze if you like.

Tranches de Bœuf à la Royale.

Beef Stakes, Court Fashion.

LARD a thick Stake with large Bits, and season it with fine Spices, Parsley, Chibbol, a Clove of Garlick, two Shallots, a Laurel Leaf, Thyme, all chopt very fine; put your Beef in the Pan upon thin Slices of Lard, and few sliced Onions, and other sliced Roots, soak over a slow Fire about five or six Hours in its own Gravy, the Pan well covered, upon the latter End, put to it

a Spoon-

a Spoonful of Brandy; it is called à la Mode Beef, when served hot, and à la Royale when cold; sift the Sauce in a Sieve and skim the Fat if you serve it hot, not if cold.

Tranche de Bœuf à la Servante.

Beef Stakes to eat hot or cold, Family Fashion.

CUT the Slices thin, lay a Down of sliced Lard, then of Stakes, fine Herbs, and Spices, and so on till you have done; a Glass of Brandy; stop the Pot very well with Paste to keep the Steam in it, soak five or six Hours on a very slow Fire.

N. B. This is best done in an earthen Vessel, and eats best cold and keeps a long while.

Tranche de Bœuf au Caramel.

Beef Stakes glazed or Fricandeau.

TAKE a Bit of Beef of what Bigness you please, lard it through with large Bits, seasoned with fine Spices, lard the upper Side finely, boil it in Broth, a Glass of white Wine, a Nosegay of Parsley, Shallots, a Clove of Garlick, three Cloves, whole Pepper and a little Salt; when done tender, sift the Sauce in a Sieve, skim the Fat, and reduce the Sauce to a Glaze, with which you glaze the larded Side, and serve it upon what stewed Herbs you please.

Canellons de Bœuf.

Beef Forced Meat in Form of a Pudding.

MINCE a Piece of tender Beef with as much Suet, a Bit of Ham, and small Bits of Lard, two or three Eggs, Parsley, Shallots, Thyme, Laurel, fine Spices, a little Salt, a Glass of Brandy, mix all together, and roll it in the Form of a large Pudding, and round it

thin

thin Slices of Lard, over white Paper, upon the Paper a Paste made of Flour and Water, bake it about two Hours in the Oven, when done take away the Paste and Lard; if you serve them hot add to it a relishing Sauce, they may serve cold for a second Course, if for cold leave the Paste till you are ready.

Andouillettes de Tranches de Bœuf.

Beef Puddings or Sausages.

CUT thin Slices of Beef in Length, put upon it forced Meat made of roasted Fowl, Marrow, Parsley, Shallots, Mushrooms, chopt very fine, and fine Spices, add three Yolks of Eggs to mix it, roll it in the Form of a Pudding; make a little Batter with Oil and Bread Crums, roll them in it, and broil flowly, basting with the Remains of the Oil, serve with it a clear Sauce of Veal Cullis and Verjuice, Vinegar or Lemon.

Bœuf de Desserte à la Sainte Meneboult.

Cold Beef Marinaded.

CUT Slices of cold Roast Beef, and make a Marinade with a little Oil, Parsley, Chibbol, Mushrooms, a Trifle of Garlick, two Shallots, all finely chopt, Pepper and Salt, soak the Beef about half an Hour, make as much of the Marinade keep to it as you can, and deal of Bread Crums; broil on a flow Fire, basting with the remaining Liquid, serve with a clear sharp Sauce.

Bœuf de Desserte à la Bourgeoise.

SLICE three or four Onions, and fry them in Butter; when done, add a Spoonful of Broth, two chopt Shallots, Pepper and Salt, then put Slices of cold Beef in it, boil for a Moment, when ready make a Liason with two or three Yolks of Eggs, and a little Vinegar.

Cold Beef is also very good with cold Sauce made of chopt Parsley, Shallots, Vinegar, Oil, Mustard, and a pounded Anchovy, &c.

Bœuf de Desserte en Papillotte.

Cold Beef broiled in Paper.

SOAK your Slices in a Marinade made of Oil or Butter, Parsley, Shallots, Mushrooms, Pepper and Salt; roll the Pieces in Paper with this Sauce, rub the Paper with Butter, broil on a slow Fire, and serve in the Paper.

Culotte de Bœuf à la Mantouë.

Rump of Beef, Mantoue Fashion.

GARNISH the Bottom of your Pot with Slices of Lard, sliced Onions and Roots, then the Beef upon it, well tied; soak it some time, then add Broth, Pepper and Salt, a Nosegay of Parsley, Chibbol, two Cloves of Garlick, two Laurel Leafs, Thyme, and Basil, four Cloves, and braze on a slow Fire; when half done, put to it small Savoys prepared in this Manner, scald a whole Savoy about half an Hour, then squeeze the Water quite dry, have a good forced Meat made with a Fillet of Veal, Beef Suet, two Eggs, half a Pint of Cream, a little of chopt Shallots, take the Cabbage Leafs one by one, and put some of this forced Meat upon them, then put them together in the Form of a small Cabbage, make as many as you think proper, tie them well all round, and put them in the Braze with the Beef; when done, take them out, and wipe them free from Fat, you serve them in the same Dish with the Beef, and a Sauce made of Cullis, two pounded Anchovies; if you have no Cullis sift some of the Braze, and a Bit of Butter rolled in Flour, add fine chopt Parsley and a Lemon Squeeze or Vinegar.

Culotte

Culotte de Bœuf Fumeé.

Beef's Rump Smoaked.

BONE a Rump of Beef as well as you can without spoiling the Shape, salt it with a Pound of Salt and two Ounces of Saltpetre, put it in a salting Pan in Length, with all Sorts of sweet Herbs, as Parsley, Shallots, Thyme, Laurel, Basil, Winter Savory, half a Handful of Juniper Berries, a little Coriander, two Cloves of Garlick, leave it about a Week in Salt, then hang it in the Chimney, when dried keep it in a dry Place; when you want to use it, boil it in Water without Salt, few Onions, Cloves, a Nosegay of sweet Herbs, a little Nutmeg; let it cool in the Liquor, and serve it cold upon a Napkin, with green Parsley; if you apprehend its being too much salted, soak it some time before boiling.

Culotte a l'Ecarlate sans Salpêtre.

Scarlet Beef without Saltpetre.

BONE a Rump of Beef thoroughly, mix a Pound of Salt with an Ounce of fine Spices, cut about a Pound and a half of Lard thick to lard it with in the Inside, make the Salt and Spices stick to the Lard as much as possible, then rub the Beef with the Remainder, roll it in a Linen Cloth with seven or eight Laurel Leafs, Thyme and Basil in Proportion, about half a Quarter of a Pound of pounded Juniper, put a coarser Cloth round it, and put it in the Ground, about six or seven Days, that will make it red instead of Saltpetre, then you boil it with few Slices of Beef, and Broth without Salt, a Nosegay, Onions, Carrots, let it cool in its Broth, and serve as before.

Culotte de Bœuf à la Gascogne.
Rump of Beef Gascogny Fashion.

SOAK a Rump bon'd, four Days in a Marinade, made of Oil, seven or eight whole Cloves of Garlick, half a Pound of Salt, half an Ounce of fine Spices, Thyme, Laurel and Basil, boil it in the Marinade, a Pint of white Wine, as much Broth, when done wipe the Fat clean off, sift Part of the Broth, and add a little Cullis, reduce to a Sauce pretty thick; the Breast or any Part of the Brisket may be done the same.

Culotte de Bœuf dans son Jus.
Rump of Beef in its own Gravy.

BOIL 'a bon'd Rump of Beef on a very slow Fire and short Liquid about eight or nine Hours, a Nosegay of Parsley, Chibbol, two Laurel Leafs, a Clove of Garlick, two Shallots, Thyme, four Cloves, half a Nutmeg, Pepper and Salt; when it is done sift the Broth, skim the Fat very well, and serve it with it.

Culotte de Bœuf diversifié.
Rump of Beef diversified.

BOIL a Rump of Beef as the preceding, when half done put to it six whole Onions, as many Turnips, Parsneps and Carrots, cut in what Form you please, scald all the Roots before you put them in the Pot, garnish the Beef with the Roots, and mix some Cullis of the Broth for Sauce; another Time do it with Cabbages and Sausages; you may also serve upon it what Ragout you please.

Culotte de Bœuf au Vin de Champagne.

Rump of Beef boiled in white Wine.

MArinade the Beef two Days, first well rubbed with Salt, put it in a Pan with a Pint of Oil, four Cloves of Garlick, fine Spices, two Laurel Leafs, Thyme, Basil, six Cloves; boil it with the Marinade, and a Bottle of white Wine; sift the Broth for Sauce and skim the Fat, add a little Cullis to make it thicker; reduce to a good Consistence.

Culotte de Bœuf à la Royale.

Rump of Beef Court Fashion.

GARNISH your Pot with Slices of Beef, Veal and Ham, then put the Rump boned, with sliced Onions, Carrots, Turnips, Parsneps, few Slices of Lard, Pepper and Salt, soak it about an Hour, then add about a Pint of white Wine, as much Broth, a Nosegay of Parsley, Chibbol, two Cloves of Garlick, four Cloves, half a Nutmeg, simmer it about five or six Hours, take it out and wipe the Fat with a Cloth, serve upon it a Ragout of Sweet Breads, fat Liver, Combs, Mushrooms, Artichoke Bottoms, small Eggs: you'll find the way to make it in the Directions for Ragouts.

Culotte de Bœuf à la Sainte Menehoult.

TIE it well, and boil it to above half in Water and Roots, then braze it in Broth and Salt sufficiently to give Taste, a Nosegay, then put it upon the Dish you intend to serve, make a Batter with three or four Spoonfuls of Cullis, Butter, and six Yolks of Eggs, bathe the Beef with it, and Bread Crumbs, bake it in the Oven.

Aloyau

Aloyau au demy Sel.

Chump of Beef half salted.

KEEP a Chump of Beef in Salt two Days, then roast it, and serve a Sauce made of Gravy, chopt Capers, Anchovies, Shallots and Parsley.

Filets d'Aloyau de toutes Façons.

Fillets of Beef of all Sorts.

CUT a Fillet of Beef out of the Surloin, take out all the Sinews, and lard it thick, put it in a Stew-pan, with a little melted Lard, Parsley, Shallots, Mushrooms, whole Pepper and Salt, simmer it some Time, then put it in a Braze with Slices of Veal, Ham, and Lard, and boil it on a slow Fire, when half done put a Glass of white Wine, when it is done skim the Sauce well from Fat, and sift it, mix a little Cullis, and serve it upon the Fillet; if you would serve it with different Sauces or Ragouts, when it is larded boil it in Broth, a Glass of white Wine, a Nosegay of Parsley, Chibbol, a Clove of Garlick, two Cloves, a Carrot, one Parsnep, small Onions; when it is done, you may serve upon it what Sauce or Ragout you please, you may also lard and dress this Fillet as a Fricandeau: a roasted Fillet may also be dressed, in the same Manner, when cold cut it in thn Slices, and serve it with stewed Cucumbers or any other Garden Stuff, only put the Meat in it a Moment to warm without boiling.

Aloyau au Four.

Surloin baked in the Oven.

ACcording to the Bigness of the Piece, take a deep Pan, garnish the Bottom with a few Slices of Lard, put to it a Nosegay of Parsley, Shallots, a Clove of Garlick,

lick, three Heads of Cloves, Pepper and Salt, soak it half an Hour over the Fire, and put to it a Bottle of Rhenish Wine; when ready to boil cover it well, put it in the Oven six or seven Hours, when done sift the Sauce, clean the Fat off, and serve with the Beef.

Aloyau en Ragout.

Small Surloin Ragout.

BRAZE a Bit of Surloin larded with large Slices, in Broth and a Pint of white Wine, a Nosegay of sweet Herbs, Onions and Roots; when done take it out and serve it with Sweet Bread, Ragout, Mushrooms, or other.

Aloyau à la Dauphine.

Surloin Dauphine Fashion.

TAKE a Surloin thoroughly bon'd, make a Hole in the middle large enough to put in it a Salpicon, viz. Stuffing after this Manner, cut in pretty large Bits Pieces of Ham raw, a Fowl bon'd, two scalded Sweet Breads, a Tongue, all minced together, and chopt Parsley, a Garlick Clove, Mushrooms, Salt and Pepper, rasped Lard, Laurel and Thyme, four Yolks of Eggs; put it in the Beef and secure it well, boil it in a Pot near to its Bigness in a little Broth, a Bottle of white Wine, a large Nosegay, three Cloves, a Laurel Leaf, six Taragon Leafs, three or four Onions, few Roots, finish on a flow Fire; serve upon it a Sauce à l'Espagnole.

Filet d'Aloyau en Crepine.

Fillet of Beef in Cowl.

PARE a Fillet of Beef of all its Sinews, split it Lengthways in different Places, and fill them with a light forced Meat, made of scraped Lard, chopt Mushrooms, Truffles, Shallots, Pepper and Salt, two Yolks of Eggs, the

the Juice of half a Lemon; then roll them in Veal Cowl, tie them to a long Skewer to roast them, bathing with Oil and white Wine; when almost done sweat them a little in a Stew-pan, they will yield their Gravy, then take off the Cowl, and serve the Gravy upon it.

Filet d'Aloyau aux fines Herbes.

Fillet of Beef and sweet Herbs.

LARD a Fillet of Beef with large Pieces, let it catch a little in a Stew-pan with Butter, a Glass of white Wine, as much Broth, Salt, and Pepper, simmer on a flow Fire; when three Parts done, sift all the Liquid, skim the Fat, and add to it a good Bit of Butter rolled in Flour, Parsley chopt, Shallots and Mushrooms, four or five Taragon Leafs; put the Fillet in it to finish, and reduce the Sauce to a good Consistence.

Filet d'Aloyau aux Onions en Crépine.

Fillet of Beef and Onions in Cowl.

SLICE seven or eight Onions, fry them in Butter thoroughly, then add Pepper and Salt, one chopt Anchovy, three Yolks of Eggs, a little Broth; mince a roasted Fillet, and cut the Cowl the Bigness you please, lay a Down of Onions, then Fillet minced, and so on; then roll it, and baste it with Eggs and Bread Crums, bake it in the Oven, serve a good clear Sauce with it.

Filet de Bœuf à l'Intendante.

Fillet of Beef à la Commissary.

MAKE forced Meat with Fowls Liver, rasped Lard, a little Butter, Parsley, Shallots, Mushrooms, three Yolks of Eggs, and fine Spices; cut a Fillet of Beef into two, and flatten it with the Cleaver, lard it through with middling Pieces, then lay the forc'd Meat

upon

upon it, and tie it in a Cloth, boil it in Broth, a Glass of white Wine, a Nosegay of Sweet Herbs, when done serve with it a Ragout of Sweet Bread or Truffles, &c.

Filet de Bœuf aux Anchois.

Fillet of Beef and Anchovies.

SOAK five or six Anchovies in Water about two Hours, and split them, and lard the Fillet with them, intermixed with Lard, boil it on a slow Fire with a little Broth, and a Glass of white Wine, one Clove of Garlick, two of Cloves, a Nosegay; when done sift the Sauce, add a Bit of Butter roll'd in Flour, two Spoonfuls of Cream, few small Capers whole; make a Liason, and serve it upon the Fillet.

Filet de Bœuf a l'Amiral.

Fillet of Beef, Admiral Fashion.

SLICE five or six Onions, and fry them in Butter, then put two Anchovies split in several Pieces, a little rasped Lard, two Yolks of Eggs, a little Salt, and powdered Basil, scald the Fillet of Beef in boiling Water, cut it in different Slices without separating, and between put some of the Stuffing; tie it up in Veal Cowl, and roast it; serve with Cullis, Jelly Broth and Lemon.

Filet de Bœuf Glassé.

Fillet of Beef and Jelly.

MAKE a Jelly with a Knuckle of Veal and Trimmings of Poulteries, boil in Water, skim it well, when done sift the Broth, and put it again on the Fire, with a Glass of white Wine, two Lemon Slices, let it boil, and add two Eggs, Shells and all, reduce it to the Consistence of a Sauce and sift it in a Napkin; lard the Fillet with Lard and Ham, and braze it very tender, let it cool

cool in the Braze; then flice what Quantity you pleafe, and in the Difh you intend; put fome of the Jelly over it a little warm, cool it with Ice or in a very cool Place.

Filets de Bœuf Grillés.

Fillets of Beef Broiled.

CUT Slices of Fillets to what Bignefs you think proper, flatten it with the Cleaver, put upon each Slice a good forced Meat, roll them and tie it with Packthread; put them for about an Hour in a Marinade, made of Oil, Parfley, Chibbol, a Clove of Garlick, two Shallots, a Laurel Leaf, Thyme, Pepper, and Salt; then broil the Fillet flowly and ferve with Cullis Sauce; one Shallot chopt very fine, Pepper, Salt, and the Juice of half a Lemon.

Filet de Bœuf à la Nivernois.

Fillet of Beef Nivernois Sauce.

MAKE a Marinade with Butter and Flour, half a Glafs of Vinegar, two Spoonfuls of Broth, Pepper and Salt, three Cloves, a little Coriander pounded, a Laurel Leaf, Thyme, Bafil, two Garlick Cloves, two fliced Onions, make it Milk-warm, put a larded Fillet in it about five Hours, then take it out and put a Slice of Lard upon the unlarded Side; tie it up in Paper, and roaft it, ferve with it a Sauce à la Nivernoife; fee Page 31.

Filet de Bœuf a l'Italienne.

Fillet of Beef Italian Sauce.

LARD a Fillet of Beef one Side, the other ftuff with chopt Parfley, Shallots, Thyme, Laurel Powder, Mufhrooms, mix it with a little fcraped Lard, Pepper

and

and Salt, tie in Paper, and roast it; garnish the unlarded Side with Bread Crums, and colour it with a Salamander; serve an Italian Sauce, which you will find in Page 31.

Filet de Bœuf à la * Gendarme.

Fillet of Beef Gendarme Fashion.

CUT a Fillet in thin large Slices, and Marinade in Oil, Parsley, Chibbol, a Clove of Garlick, Mushrooms, Salt and Pepper, tie it upon small Skewers rolled in Paper with the Marinade, and roast them; make a Sauce with a little Cullis, a Glass of white Wine, Pepper and Salt, and a few sweet Herbs, first scalded and finely chopt.

Gendarme, Part of the King's Body Guards.

Poitrine de Bœuf à la Monarque.

Brisket of Beef, Monarch Fashion.

BOIL a fine Brisket of Beef in Broth, and a Pint of white Wine, a Nosegay of sweet Herbs, two Cloves of Garlick, four Spice Cloves, Laurel Leaves, Thyme, Shallots, a quarter of a Nutmeg, Pepper and Salt; when done, cut a Hole in the Middle large enough to put a little forced Meat, a Ragout of Pigeons, Sweet Breads, Coxcombs, fat Liver Mushrooms; cover it over with forced Meat, put it awhile in the Oven, and when ready, serve upon it a Sauce pretty thick made with Cullis, Butter, and four Yolks of Eggs.

Poitrine de Bœuf à la St. Menehoult.

Brisket of Beef Broiled, St. Menehoult.

TIE a Brisket with Packthread, boil it to half in the common way, then put it in a Braze with Broth, Pepper and Salt, a Nosegay of Parsley, Shallots, a Clove of Garlick, four Cloves, Thyme, Laurel, Onions, Slices and Roots; finish the Boiling, put upon the Dish and over it a Sauce as the preceeding, then Bread Crums; give it Colour in the Oven, wipe the Dish free of Fat, serve upon it a relishing Sauce.

A Brisket of Beef brazed or boiled in a plain way may be served with any Sauce, Ragout, or stewed Herbs or Roots, such as Conveniency serves.

Tendrons de Bœuf de plusieurs Façons.

Beef Gristle of different Fashions.

CUT Gristles of Beef what Bigness you think proper, scald them a Moment in boiling Water, then braze them with a little Broth, a Glass of white Wine, a Nosegay of Parsley, Chibbol, Laurel Leaves, Thyme, Basil, two Cloves, one of Garlick, whole Pepper and Salt, sliced Onions, and Roots; when done, take the Bottom of the Braze, which you sift in a Sieve, and skim the Fat very clean off, then add to it a Bit of Butter rolled in Flour, a little scalded Charvil finely chopt, add a Lemon Squeeze or a little Vinegar, serve upon the Gristles; when thus brazed, you serve upon it what Ragout you please; also with Cabbage and Sausages, which you braze about an Hour with the Gristles; you may also make them in the Manner of pickled Pork, if you will not smoke them; you may preserve them a long while by simmering them some time in fresh Hog's Lard, then place them close in an Earthen-pan, and pour the Lard upon it enough to cover the Meat; when it is cold cover the Pot, and keep it in a cold Place; you may preserve old Turkeys, Geese, and other Poultries or Game in the same Manner.

Côte ou Carbonade de Bœuf au Four.
A Rib of Beef in the Oven.

TAKE a Rib pretty fleshy, and boil it in a thin Braze, with Broth, a little Salt, few Slices of Onions, and Roots; when it is done, sift the Broth and reduce it to a Glaze, baste the Rib with it all over and let it cool, take a little scraped Lard or Butter, which you mix with chopt Parsley, Shallots, a Trifle of Garlick, Mushrooms, Thyme, Laurel, Basil Powder; put it all upon the Beef and roll it up in Paper, put it in the Oven half an Hour, then take off the Paper, and make a Sauce with Cullis, a little Verjuice or Lemon, and gather all the chopt Herbs which stick to the Paper, and mix with the Sauce, Salt and Pepper.

Côte de Bœuf à la Remoulade.
A Rib of Beef with Mustard or Horse-radish Sauce.

LARD a Rib of Beef with large Pieces, and braze it as the former, when done, take the Fat of the Broth, baste the Meat with it and Bread Crums, broil it slowly, basting it with Butter now and then to keep it from burning; serve it dry with the Sauce in a Boat. See Sauce Remoulade Page 42.

Côte de Bœuf a l'Angloise.
Rib of Beef English Fashion.

FLATTEN a Rib of Beef with the Cleaver, simmer it a few Turns in Hog's Lard, then braze it in the same Lard over a slow Fire, with a Glass of white Wine, as much Broth, all Sorts of Sweet Herbs finely chopt, with Pepper and Salt; when done, skim the Broth, sift it, and make a Liaison with three Yolks of Eggs, and serve it upon the Meat.

Côtes de Bœuf à la Hollandoise.
Ribs of Beef Dutch Fashion.

CUT thin Ribs of Beef, bone them all to a Bit at the thin End, soak them in Butter till they are almost done, let them cool, and take their Gravy, which you mix with forced Meat made of Fillet of Veal, Beef Suet, Charvil, Taragon, Burnet, Garden Cresses, Pepper, Salt, and Nutmeg, three Yolks of Eggs to mix the Farce, wrap up the Beef in the forced Meat, bake it in a *Dutch* Oven, or the baking Oven; take some of the Gravy mixt with Cullis, Verjuice, or Lemon, Pepper and Salt; serve upon the Meat.

Ribs of Beef brazed or plain boiled may be served with all Sorts of Sauces or Ragout, or stewed Garden Roots and Herbs, and Greens broiled like Mutton Chops.

Oreilles de Bœuf.
Beef's Ears.

BEEF's Ears well scalded like Calve's, may be made tender in a strong Braze, full of strong Herbs and Spices, and broiled, served with a Cullis Sauce, or relishing: as they are used but seldom, I shall take no further Notice of their dressing.

CHAPITRE SECOND. Du Veau.
CHAPTER SECOND. Of Veal.

GOOD Veal ought to be very white and fat, I shall not take upon me to give the Direction of cutting up Calves, as the French Author does, as I am very sensible that all Sorts of Meat are cut to greater Advantage in England than in France; and the French Butchers

are

are even so sensible of it, that I have myself known French Butchers come from Paris on Purpose to attend the cutting of Meat at St. James's Market and others, (for Instruction.)

Tête de Veau à la Bourgeoise.

Calve's Head Family Way.

TRIM the Muzzle off near the Eyes without cutting the Tongue; soak it in several Waters to clean it, then scald it in boiling Water, boil it in Water with a few Onions, two or three Cloves, two Shallots, Salt; when done, drain it, open the Skull, serve it quite hot with Vinegar, Pepper, Salt, chopt Parsley in a Boat.

Tête de Veau Farcie.

Calve's Head Stuffed.

TAKE a Calve's Head scalded with the Skin on, bone it, the rest you may boil as the former; make forced Meat, with Fillet of Veal, Beef Suet, Bread Crums, Milk, Parsley, Thyme, Mushrooms, four Yolks of Eggs, Pepper and Salt; put some of this Preparation in the Head, leave room in the Middle to put a Ragout well seasoned, either of Pigeons, Sweet Breads, or other; cover it over with forced Meat, and make the Form of the Head as near as possible; garnish it with Slices of Lard tied in a Cloth; braze it in Broth, white Wine, sweet Herbs; serve upon it a Spanish or Italian Sauce, or which you think best.

Tête de Veau à la Poivrade.

Calve's Head with a sharp Sauce.

TAKE a scalded Head, bone it as far as the Eyes, boil it like the first, and some pickled Pork, which when done you serve in the same Dish; boil half a Glass of Vinegar, as much Broth, chopt Shallots, whole Chibbol; sift it; add coarse Pepper and Salt, serve upon the Head.

Tête de Veau au Verd-galant.

Calve's Head fried with Parsley.

SOAK it twenty-four Hours, scald it in boiling Water, then boil it in Water and a little Vinegar, Roots, Herbs and Spices, as the former; cut it in Pieces, and roll it in Batter made of Oil and white Wine, Salt and Parsley Leaves; bathe the Head in it, and fry of a good Colour; serve crisp.

Tête de Veau en Crépine.

Calve's Head in Cowl.

BONE a scalded Calve's Head, boil the rest as common, and the Tongue which you mince, and a raw Fowl; mix with this, chopt Parsley, Chibbol, Mushrooms, Shallots, Pepper, and Salt; make forced Meat with the Brains, six Yolks of hard Eggs, Bread Crums, and Milk; lay some of this forced Meat upon the Calve's Head, then the Fillets as prepared, then roll it in Cowl, and braze it in white Wine, when done take off the Cowl; serve upon it a Sauce au Pontife as you will find in the Sauce Articles, Page 46.

Tête de Veau à la Sauce au Porc frais.

Calves Head with fresh Pork Sauce.

SCALD and bone a Calve's Head, and boil it in Broth, few Slices of Lard; when done take it out and wipe it clean; serve upon this Sauce as you will find in Page 44.

Tête de Veau à la Sainte Menehoult.

Calve's Head St. Menehoult.

BOIL a Calve's Head as à la Bourgeoise; make a forced Meat with the Brains, and roasted Poultry, scraped Lard, Bread Crums, Milk, Parsley, Mushrooms, three Yolks of Eggs, Pepper, and Salt; stuff it in the room of the Brains, and in the Ears; put upon this a thick Sauce made of Cullis, a Bit of Butter, three Yolks of Eggs, then Crums of Bread; bake it in the Oven of a fine Colour; serve with a relishing Sauce.

Tête de Veau Marinée.

Calve's Head Marinaded.

BOIL a Calve's Head about three Parts, then take the Brains, Ears and Tongues, which marinade with Vinegar, Garlick, Shallots, Parsley, Pepper and Salt; dip it in Batter and fry it; serve with fried Parsley.

Oreilles de Veau Frites.

Calve's Ears Fried.

BRAZE the Ears in a strong Braze to make them tender; dip them in Batter and serve them fried with fried Parsley; you may also stuff them with good forced Meat.

Oreilles de Veau en Menus droits.
Calve's Ears Shreded.

BRAZE the Ears, then cut them in Fillets, (it is the Cutting that gives the Name;) serve with a Sauce Robert as you will find amongst Sauce Articles.

Oreilles de Veau au Gratin.

See the Explanation of Gratin, Page 56. in Beef's Tongue.

THE Ears brazed are done the same Way as all former Directions for Gratin.

Oreilles de Veau au Pontife.
Calve's Ears Pontiff Sauce.

BRAZE the Ears very white and tender, then take them out and wipe them very dry; serve upon a Sauce au Pontife, Page 46.

Oreilles de Veau à la Martine.
Calve's Ears House-wife Fashion.

MAKE a Sauce with a little Jelly Broth, as much white Wine, a Bit of Butter, chopt Parsley, Shallots, Pepper and Salt, boil it to a pretty thick Consistence, when ready squeeze half a Seville Orange and few Bits in it; serve upon brazed Ears.

Panache de Veau.
Calve's Ears broiled.

CUT the Ears in two and boil tender in Broth, a Nosegay of sweet Herbs, Thyme, Laurel, Cloves, a Bit of Butter, when done baste them with Fat and
Bread

Bread Crums; broil of a fine Colour, ſerve with a Sauce à la Nivernoiſe; which you will find, Page 31.

Oreille de Veau au Fromage.

Calve's Ears and Cheeſe.

THE Ears being brazed, ſoak them in melted Butter, Bread Crums and raſped Parmeſan, put them in the Oven to take a good Colour; make a little forced Meat with raſped Cheeſe, Bread Crums, three Yolks of Eggs; lay on the Diſh you intend to ſerve; let it catch a little on a very ſlow Fire, lay the Ears upon it and good clear Cullis for Sauce.

Oreilles de Veau a l'Italienne.

Calves Ears Italian Sauce.

BRAZE the Ears in a ſtrong white Braze with Spices and few Lemon Slices, wipe them dry and ſerve upon the Italian Sauce, which you will find Page 32.

Oreilles de Veau à la Sainte Menehoult.

THE Ears brazed as before, bathe in a good thick Batter and Bread Crums, broil ſlowly, baſting with a little Butter; ſerve with a Sauce Remoulade in a Sauce Boat, which you will find Page 42.

Cervelles de Veau à la Crême.

Calve's Brains Cream Sauce.

SOAK and ſcald the Brains, then boil them in Broth, two Slices of Lemon, ſweet Herbs, a Clove of Garlick, two Spice Cloves, cover with thin Slices of Lard; when done wipe them dry, ſerve upon a Sauce à la Bechamel, as in Page 42.

Cervelles de Veau aux petits Onions.

Calve's Brains and small Onions.

SCALD as many small Onions as you think proper, braze them with the Brains in good Broth, few Slices of Lard, a Glass of white Wine, Pepper and Salt, a Nosegay of sweet Herbs; then drain the Brains and Onions; garnish the Dish with the Onions, serve upon it Sauce Ravigotte or which you please.

Cervelles de Veau aux Ecrevisses.

Calve's Brains and Craw-Fish.

PREPARE the Brains as the former, make a Craw-fish Cullis as in Page 7; boil the Tails in Broth and white Wine; garnish the Dish with the Tails, and serve the Cullis upon the Brains.

Cervelles de Veau au Soleil.

Calve's Brains fried crisp.

CUT the Brains in four Pieces, braze them about half an Hour in white Wine, two Slices of Lemon, Pepper and Salt, Thyme, Laurel, Cloves, Parsley and Shallots, then drain them and soak in Batter made of Flour, a little Oil and white Wine, and fry of a fine Colour; you may equally bathe them in Eggs and Bread Crums to broil. *Soleil*, meaning as bright as the Sun.

Cervelles de Veau à la Gascogne.

Calve's Brains Gascoon Fashion.

MAKE a Sauce with a Bit of Butter, Bread Crums, a Clove of Garlick, Parsley, Chibbol, a Glass of white Wine, as much Broth, Pepper and Salt, reduce to a Sauce Consistence and serve upon brazed Brains.

Cervelles de Veau au Reveil.

Calve's Brains Muſtard Sauce.

THE Brains brazed as the former, make a Batter with Cullis, Butter and Muſtard, bathe the Brains in it, and Bread Crums and Cheeſe; give them Colour in the Oven or with a Salamander, ſerve upon Cullis and Muſtard. The Meaning of *Reveil*, is to quicken the Palate, &c. &c.

Cervelles de Veau à differentes Sauces.

Brains of different Faſhion and Sauces.

BRAINS brazed in Broth and Wine as directed, may be uſed with what Sauce or Ragout moſt convenient, ſuch as fat Liver, Pigeons, Sauſages, Onions, Capers, fried Bread, &c. &c.

Yeux de Veau de differentes Façons.

Calve's Eyes of different Faſhions.

WHEN done like the Brains, you may either fry or broil them; making the ſame Preparation, they may ſerve in Matelots or Turine, or by themſelves with any Sauce.

Langue de Veau.

Calve's Tongue, (ſee Beef's Tongue.)

CALVE's are dreſſed after the ſame Manner, allowing for the Difference of Time in boiling or baking.

Fraiſes de Veau au Naturel.

Calve's Caldron in a plain Way.

SOAK it well and ſcald it, then boil it in Water with a Bit of Butter, Flour, Pepper and Salt, a Noſegay of sweet Herbs, two Cloves, Thyme, Laurel, two Onions; serve it with a sharp Sauce.

Fraise de Veau au Soleil.

Caldron fried of a fine clear Colour.

BOIL it as before, then cut it in Pieces, marinade an Hour or two in Vinegar and Broth, Pepper, and Salt, Cloves, sliced Onions, then drain it, and fry with a good thick Batter of a fine clear Brown.

Fraise de Veau à la Provençale.

Caldron Provençe Fashion.

THE Caldron being boiled as the former, cut it in Fillets, and make a Sauce with Butter, chopt Mushrooms, a little Garlick, a Glass of white Wine, Broth, a little Oil, Pepper and Salt; reduce to a Sauce; put the Caldron in it a Moment and add a good Squeeze of Lemon.

Crepinettes de Fraises de Veau.

Caldron dressed Olive Fashion.

MAKE a light forced Meat and roll it in Cowl as all former Directions, put it in the Oven to take Colour, and serve with a good relishing Sauce.

Baignets de Fraises de Veau.

Caldron fried, small Fritters.

BOIL the same Way then cut it in Pieces, marinade about an Hour in Oil, Butter, Pepper and Salt, chopt Parsley, Shallots; make the Herbs stick to it, dip in Batter and fry very crisp.

Fraises

Fraises de Veau en Crepine.

Caldron in Veal Cowl.

THIS is done with forced Meat as the Crepinettes, only larger Size; serve with it Sauce Italienne.

Tourtes aux Zephirs de Fraise de Veau.

Calve's Caldron Pie.

MAKE a good Puffpaste Pie, bake it by itself, make a Ragout with the Caldron (first well boiled) with Mushrooms, Parsley, Shallots, a Garlick, Cloves, a Glass of white Wine and Cullis; reduce to a good Consistence, then put the Caldron cut in Slices, skim the Fat very clean, add Pepper and Salt, a good Lemon Squeeze, serve in the Pie.

Foye de Veau à la hâte.

Calve's Liver in a hurry.

CUT it in thin Slices, then fry it in Butter with Pepper and Salt, chopt Shallots, when done add a Spoonful of Vinegar.

Foye de Veau à la Rocambole.

Calve's Liver with green Shallots or Chibbol.

CHOP green Shallots and Mushrooms, cut the Liver in thin Slices, put it together in a Stew-pan with a Bit of Butter rolled in Flour, a Glass of white Wine, boil half an Hour, reduce the Sauce; add Pepper, Salt, and Vinegar; if you would have it white, make a Liason of Yolks of Eggs and Cream, Verjuice or Lemon; this is called à la Poulette, when white.

N. B. The Rocambole is much the same relishing Herb as those mentioned, but not so much cultivated in England.

Foye de Veau à la Broche.

Roasted (*la Broche*) the Spit.

LARD the Liver with pretty large Pieces rolled in fine Spices, roast it and serve a Sauce Piquante, viz. relishing, sharp.

Foye de Veau en Hátereaux.

Calve's Liver Haslets.

CUT it in pretty large Pieces, marinade with Butter, Pepper and Salt, sweet Herbs chopt; leave it some Time over a very slow Fire, then roll several Pieces in Veal Cowl with as much Sauce as possible, tie it upon an Hatelet, viz. large Skewer, thin Slices of Lard round, and roast them; serve with it relishing Sauce, as l'Aspic, Nivernoise, or other.

Foye de Veau à la Braise.

Calve's Liver Brazed.

LARD the Liver with large *Lardons*, braze it in a Stew-pan much the same Bigness, with few Slices of Lard, sweet Herbs, Laurel, Onions, Roots, a Jill of white Wine; boil it about an Hour, serve a relishing Sauce, or reduce its own Sauce if not too much salted; skim the Fat, sift it; add a little Butter and Flour, scalded chopt Parsley, Vinegar or Lemon.

Crepinettes de Foye de Veau or *Veau en Crepine*, only differ in Size and are done as all former Directions; which to avoid Repetitions I shall pass over.

Saucisses de Foye de Veau.

Calves Liver Sausages.

THEY are made after the same Manner as Pork's, or other; the Meat used gives the Name.

Rognons de Veau de plusieurs Façons.

Veal Kidney of different Fashions.

MIX sliced Onions and minced Kidney, fry it in Butter, then add a little Broth, a Spoonful of white Wine, Pepper and Salt; and serve with a Liason of three Yolks of Eggs and Cream; if you would have it brown, instead of Eggs and Cream, Cullis Sauce; you may also serve them broiled with a relishing Sauce: roasted Kidnies serve to make Omelets to serve upon toasted Bread, and are very good to mix with most Sorts of forced Meat.

Pieds de Veau de plusieurs Façons.

Calve's Feet of different Fashions.

CALVE's Feet in a plain Way are boiled like the Caldron, and eat with a sharp Sauce; when plain boiled, you make them à la Poulette, viz. a white Fricassee (also en *Menus droits*, viz. cut in small Shreds) also fried, split them in two and take out the large Bones; soak in Marinade, then in Batter to fry or broil.

Pieds de Veau Farcis.

Calve's Feet with Forced Meat.

BONE them quite, and fill them with forced Meat made of whatever you please; tie them in Slices of Lard with Packthread, boil them in Broth and white Wine,

Wine, Sweet Herbs, Cloves, Roots, Onions, boil flowly, and ferve with what Sauce you pleafe.

Pied de Veau au Citron.

Calve's Feet Lemon Sauce.

TAKE Calve's Feet plain boiled, put them in a Stewpan with a little Oil, half a Lemon, fliced and peeled; as much Broth and Cullis as will fimmer on a flow Fire about half an Hour; take them out and wipe them dry; fift the Sauce, fkim it well, add a Bit of Butter and Flour, a little Cullis, a pounded Anchovy, half a Lemon fqueezed.

Ris de Veau de plufieurs Façons.

Sweet Breads of different Fafhions.

SWEET Breads are very ufeful in many Difhes; as in Pies, Ragout, and Fricaffee, and to ufe alone, either fried, roafted or broiled; they muft be foaked in warm Water an Hour or two, then fcalded in boiling Water, about a Quarter of an Hour or more; which the Butchers call Setting, to keep longer.

Ris de Veau à la Ducheffe.

Calve's Sweet Bread à la Dutchefs.

SCALD it, and lard with fine Lard, put in the Middle a little Farce called Salpicon, made with Mufhrooms, Truffles, fat Liver; few it, boil it in good Veal Broth, and reduce the Sauce to a Glaze; ferve with a Wine Sauce, Orange, or others.

Ris de Veau au Pontife.

Sweet Breads Pontiff Sauce.

BRAZE them in the former Manner, wipe them clean from Fat, and serve with Sauce au Pontife; as you will find in the Directions of Sauces, Page 46.

Ris de Veau en Hérisson.

Sweet Breads as Hedge-hogs.

SCALD the Sweet Breads, and lard them with Ham and Truffles cut in small *Lardons*, and fried a short Time in Butter; let the Lardons stick out a little to make the Appearance of Bristle, simmer them in the same Butter with Broth and a Glass of white Wine, very little Salt and Pepper; when done skim and sift the Sauce, add a little Cullis and serve upon them; you may also with any other Sauce: as Sweet Breads are of an insipid Taste of themselves, observe as a general Rule, to serve a sharp relishing Sauce with them, either Cullis Sauce, Fricassee, fried, broiled, called en Hatelet, or Fines Herbes, viz. Sweet Herbs, as they are nothing of themselves; the Sauces being diversified, give the Name: all Cooks take that Licence, as the Dish is rather insipid, call them Sweet Breads à la what you please; the principal, braze them tender and white.

Rissolle à la Choisy.

Fried Forced Meat.

N. B. Rissolles are made of any Sorts of Meat following the same Direction.

BOIL a Bit of Udder in Broth, Parsley, Shallots, Roots, Pepper and Salt, when done let it cool and cut it in thin Slices; put a good Poultry forced Meat, in one or two Bits, roll it in Whites of Eggs, dip them in good Batter, and Bread Crums if you like, fry of a good clear Brown; you may also broil them, bathing with Eggs, Bread Crums, and Butter.

Queuës de Veau aux Choux.

Calve's Tails and Cabbages.

SCALD Calve's Tails and pickled Pork, and scald also a good Savoy, about half an Hour, take it out and press the Water out of it; cut it in Quarters, tie it and braze it all together in Broth, Slices of Lard, Spices and Herbs, as all other Brazes; when done take them out and clean all free from Fat; serve upon it good thick Cullis, if you would have the Cabbage as *Sowrcrout,* add Vinegar.

Queuës de Veau diversifiées.

Calve's Tails of different Fashions.

ALWAYS scald them first; if you would serve them in Fricandeaux, lard them and braze as the former; if without larding, serve them with different Sauces or Ragout, fried or broiled, with any Sharp Sauce in a Boat.

For Brevity's Sake I shall avoid giving a Repetition of *Queuës de Veau* au Gratin, and Farcies, as the Direction is already given in different Places; all those Sorts of insignificant Things are to be brazed in white Brazes, which are called so by putting Slices of Lemon in; as it has the Power of making the brazed Meat very white, at the same Time that it gives it a Sharpness required in all insipid Meat, but very little of it to be used wherein the Braze is to serve for Sauce when well skimmed and sifted.

Amourettes

Amourettes de plusieurs Façons.

Lamb's Fry, and others of different Fashions.

LAMB's Fry must be scalded a Moment, then soaked in Vinegar, Pepper and Salt, Parsley, Shallots; leave it in this Marinade about an Hour, then dip it in a thick Batter and fry it of a good Colour, and fried Parsley with it.

If you would have them Ragout, put them in a light Braze, with small Onions, thin Slices of Lard, sweet Herbs, half a Laurel Leaf, Thyme, a Glass of white Wine, as much Broth, Pepper and Salt; serve what Sauce you think proper, with fried Bread round the Dish.

If you would have them Fricassee, take the Marrow out of the small Bladders (when scalded,) prepare a Cream after this Manner, take a little Flour, and Egg, a Chesnut pounded, rasped Lemon, Sugar and Cream, make small Paper Cases, and put the Fry in them, put them a Moment in the Oven; boil the Cream a Moment before you fill the Bladders with it, and baste them over with Eggs and Cream: you may also make Fries with Guts of Turkey, and of Suckling Pigs, filling the Guts with this Sort of Cream, or in the Manner of white Pudding; boil them in Broth and thin Slices of Lard, and serve with a Sauce à la Reine, Page 48.

Tendrons de Veau au petit Pois.

Veal Gristles and green Peas.

CUT the Gristles of a Breast of Veal in Pieces, scald them; and if you would have them very white, boil them in Broth, few Slices of Lard, half a Lemon sliced, Pepper and Salt, a Nosegay of sweet Herbs;

when done wipe them clean and ferve the Peas ftewed upon; you may alfo when the Meat is half done, take it out of the Braze and put it in a Stew-pan with the Peas, a Bit of Butter, Parfley, a little Winter Savory, a Head of Clove, a Slice of Ham, few Cabbage, Lettuces; add a little Cullis and Flour, reduce the Sauce pretty thick; falt only the Moment you are ready to ferve.

Tendrons de Veau Printaniers.

Veal Griftles Spring Sauce; from the Green Colour.

PREPARE the Griftles as the former, then take them out of the Braze, and put them in a Stew-pan with a good Bit of Butter, Parfley, two Cloves, a Laurel Leaf, few Shallots and Thyme; let them catch a little, then add a Glafs of white Wine, as much Broth, Pepper and Salt; then make a Liafon in this Manner, fcald a Handful of green Wheat about a quarter of an Hour, fqueeze the Water out and pound it to take about a Glafs of Juice, fift the Sauce and mix this Juice with it; reduce to a Sauce.

Tendrons de Veau Frits.

Veal Griftles Fried.

SCALD the Griftles, then boil them in a little Broth, a Glafs of white Wine, a Nofegay of Parfley, green Shallots, Thyme, a Laurel Leaf, two Cloves, one Clove of Garlick, Pepper and Salt; boil on a flow Fire; when done, take out the Nofegay, reduce the Sauce to make it ftick to the Meat; then dip it in Batter, and Bread Crums, fry it of a good Colour; ferve either dry, or with a clear Sauce.

Tendrons de Veau à la Poulette.

Veal Griſtles Fricaſſee.

SCALD them firſt, then put them in a Stew-pan with a Slice of Ham, Muſhrooms, a Bit of Butter, Parſley, Chibbol, two Cloves; let it catch, then add a Glaſs of white Wine and Broth; reduce the Sauce, ſkim it well and make a Liaſon with three Yolks of Eggs and Cream; you may add a Lemon Squeeze.

Tendrons de Veau au Legumes.

Griſtles with any Sorts of Greens.

WHEN well ſcalded, braze them in Broth, and Slices of Lard, few Slices of Lemon, Pepper and Salt, a Noſegay of ſweet Herbs; when done ſlowly, wipe the Fat and ſerve with ſtewed Greens, or what Sauce you pleaſe.

Tendrons de Veau en Fricandeau.

Griſtle or Breaſt of Veal larded Fricandeau.

TAKE off the Skin cleanly, leave the Breaſt whole, ſcald it ſome Time in boiling Water, then lard it and put it in a Stew-pan with few Slices of Veal Fillet, and Ham; a Noſegay of Parſley, Shallots, two Cloves, a little Baſil, Broth and a little Pepper; boil on a ſlow Fire, when done, ſift and ſkim the Sauce, reduce it to a Glaze, and ſpread it upon the larded Side with clean Feathers, then put a little Cullis and Broth to gather the Remains of the Glaze, and ſift it over the Meat; you may ſerve it with ſtewed Greens, either Sorrel, Lettuces, Endives, &c. &c.

Poitrine de Veau a l'Italienne.
Breast of Veal Italian Fashion.

SCALD it as usual, then boil over a stewing Fire with a Pint of white Wine, a good Spoonful of Oil, as much Broth, two Slices of Lemon, Pepper, Salt, a Nosegay of sweet Herbs, two Spice Cloves, one of Garlick, a little Basil; when done wipe the Fat clean off, take the Skin off the Gristles; serve with Italian Sauce, which you will find amongst the Sauces, Vol. I. Page 32.

Poitrine de Veau Frite.
Breast of Veal Fried.

IT is prepared the same Way as the Gristle, only leave the upper Skin; when it is fried with Bread Crums, and served with Parsley, it is commonly called au Basilic; you may equally broil it and serve with a relishing Sauce: See Sauces.

Poitrine de Veau en Surprise.
Breast of Veal Masked, or Wonder, &c.

MAKE a good forced Meat with Fillet of Veal, Beef Suet, Bread, Milk, Chibbol, Mushrooms, all fine chopt, and four Yolks of Eggs; the Breast first brazed, make a Circle round it with the forced Meat, and in the Middle a good Ragout short Sauce; cover it over with the forced Meat, bathe it with Yolks of Eggs, and Bread Crums, bake it in the Oven; when done of a fine Colour, wipe the Fat out of the Dish, and serve a good Sauce upon it.

Observe to trim either Breasts or Necks properly, when dressed whole; this is best judged by the Size of the Dishes.

Oreilles

Oreilles de Veau Farcies à la Quenelles.

Calve's Ears Stuffed.

BRAZE the Ears white, and stuff them with the forced Meat of Quenelles as it is explained for the Quenelles de Poularde, viz. *Fowl*, dip the Ears in thick Batter, to fry. See in Fowl Articles for this Forced Meat.

Poitrine de Veau Marinée.

Breast of Veal Marinaded.

CUT a Breast of Veal in Pieces, boil it in Broth to three Parts; then marinade about an Hour with two Spoonfuls of Vinegar, a little of its own Broth, Pepper and Salt, two Cloves of Garlick, four of Spices, sliced Onions, Thyme, Laurel; then drain it and fry of a good Colour, with Parsley.

Poitrine de Veau Farcie en Ragout.

Breast of Veal stuffed Ragout.

STUFF a Breast of Veal with good forced Meat, between the Skin and Gristle, fasten it well that the Stuffing cannot get out; boil it in Broth, a Glass of white Wine, a Nosegay, Pepper and Salt; when done, wipe it, and serve upon it a good Ragout made of Sweet Breads, Mushrooms, Palates, Coxcomb, Truffles, or other; you will find the Way to make it in the Articles for Ragout: Vol. II. See Ragout Articles.

Poitrine de Veau au Court Bouillon.

Breast of Veal in its own Sauce.

PUT a whole Breast of Veal in a Stew-pan of its own Length, with a little Broth, a good Glass of white Wine, a Nosegay of sweet Herbs, few Mushrooms, few

Coriander tied in a Bag, few sliced Roots, Onions, Pepper and Salt; sift and skim the Sauce and serve it upon the Meat.

Poitrine de Veau au Pontife.

Breast of Veal Pontiff Sauce.

STUFF it as the former, and lard it, tie it up in Paper and roast it; serve with Sauce Pontife: See Sauces, Page 46.

Poitrine de Veau en Crepine.

Breast of Veal in Cowl.

BRAZE it to about half done, then cut the Skin off the Gristly Part, make some small Incision with a Knife wherein to stick some sliced Truffles, or Mushrooms, or both, with pickled Girkins, and Roots of other Colours ready boiled; intermix all properly, throw a little Salt over, and wrap it up in Cowl and Paper; finish it by roasting, then strip it, and serve with what Sauce or Ragout you think proper.

Poitrine de Veau à la Romaine.

Breast of Veal Roman Fashion.

IT is half brazed, and marinaded whole, as the Gristles marinaded; and bathed with Yolks of Eggs, and Bread Crums, to fry or broil of a good Colour; serve dry, or with a Sauce, or fried Parsley.

Cotelettes de Veau à la Mariée

Veal Cutlets Bride Fashion.

CUT a Neck of Veal in Cutlets; when well scalded upon the Fire, put them in a Stew-pan with half a Glass of Oil, two Laurel Leaves, a Slice of Ham, Pepper and Salt; simmer it about half an Hour, then add a Glass of white Wine, as much Cullis, few chopped Truffles,

Truffles, finish on a slow Fire; when done take out the Cutlets, let them drain; take the Ham and Laurel Leaves out of the Sauce, skim it well, and add a Bit of Butter and Flour, with a little scalded chopt Charvil; when ready, a good Lemon Squeeze.

Cotelettes de Veau Grillées.

Veal Cutlets Broiled.

CUT the Cutlets pretty thick, and dip them in good Oil with chopt Parsley, Shallots, Pepper and Salt; make the Herbs stick to it, and Bread Crums or none; broil slowly and serve Cullis and Verjuice, or Lemon, or any clear Sauce, as you shall think proper.

Cotelettes de Veau en Ragout.

Veal Cutlets Ragout.

THEY are brazed, and served in the same Manner as the Breast, with the same Sort of Ragouts, or any you shall think proper: See Ragout, Vol. II.

Cotelettes de Veau en Papillottes.

Veal Cutlets in Paper.

CHOP all Sorts of sweet Herbs, Pepper and Salt, mixt with a little Oil; cover the Cutlets with it, wrap them in Paper, rubbed over with Butter; boil slowly, serve with or without Sauce.

Cotelettes de Veau Marinées.

Veal Cutlets Marinaded.

VEAL Cutlets marinaded are done as all former Directions for Marinade, or as the Breast of Veal marinaded; and served with any Sauce.

Cotelettes de Veau Composées.

Veal Cutlets Composed or Shammed.

TAKE the Remainder of a roasted Neck of Veal, make a forced Meat with it, and Bread Crums, Suet or rasped Lard, sweet Herbs, Mushrooms, four Yolks of Eggs, Pepper and Salt; make this in the Form of Cutlets, in the Middle leave a Cavity to put in it the Remains, or a fresh made Ragout, as Truffles, Coxcomb, Sweet Breads, &c. Stick one Rib to each prepared Cutlet; garnish with Bread Crums, bathed with Eggs; put them in a deep Pan in the Oven to take a good Colour, or fry them; serve with a good relishing or clear Sauce.

Cotelettes de Veau en Fricandeau.

Veal Cutlets Fricandeau, viz. Glazed.

AS this Dish is of such old Practice, every Body the least acquainted with Cookery, knows how to do it, either with Cutlets or Fillet; it is done as all other Directions, and may be served with Ragout or stewed Herbs; Sorrel is the most used, although Endives, Lettuces and Sellery are also very good.

Cotelettes de Veau aux Fines Herbes.

Veal Cutlets and Sweet Herbs.

CHOP all Sorts of sweet Herbs, Mushrooms, a little Winter Savory, Shallots, Pepper and Salt, a Spoonful of Oil or Butter; dip the Veal in it, and reduce the Sauce to make it stick, then bathe with Eggs and Bread Crums; bake in the Oven, add a Glass of white Wine, a little Cullis to the Sauce, skim it well and serve with the Cutlets.

Cotelettes de Veau aux petits Pois.

Veal Cutlets and Green Peas.

THIS is done after the same Manner as the Gristles or whole Breast.

Cotelettes de Veau au Cruchon.

Veal Cutlets in Crust.

CUT your Cutlets properly, and make a Marinade with melted Lard or Butter, Mushrooms, Shallots, half a Clove of Garlick, Pepper and Salt; simmer in this about an Hour, then wrap them in Puff Paste with all the Seasoning; put them in a deep Dish, baste with Yolks of Eggs, make a Hole in the Middle to pour a good clear Sauce in it when ready to serve.

Cotelettes de Veau à la Poële.

Veal Cutlets half Fried.

FRY the Cutlets to about half done in Oil, Butter, or Lard, all Sorts of sweet Herbs finely chopt, Pepper and Salt; then put them in a Stew-pan with few Slices of Veal and Ham, and all their Sauce; cover them with Slices of Lard, simmer on a slow Fire, when almost done add a Glass of white Wine, then sift the Sauce; add some good Cullis, reduce it pretty thick, serve upon the Cutlets.

Cotelettes de Veau à l'Italienne.

Veal Cutlets Italian Sauce. See Breast, Page 100.

Cotelettes de Veau en Crepine.

Veal Cutlets in Cowl. See as before.

Cotelettes de Veau Diverſifiées.

Veal Cutlets of different Manners.

BRAZE Veal Cutlets in a ſlight Braze, thin Slices of Lard, Slices of Lemon peeled, a little Broth, a ſweet Herbs Noſegay, two Cloves, one of Garlick, a little Baſil; when finiſhed white and tender, ſerve with what Sauce you think proper: you may do them with Parmeſan Cheeſe or ſmall Onions, or any thing elſe.

Carré de Veau Glaſſé ou Piqué à la Broche.

Neck of Veal Glazed, Larded or Roaſted.

BONE a Neck of Veal three Parts of the Ribs, if you would glaze it ſcald and ſtew it as Fricandeau; if you would have it roaſted, do not ſcald it, lard it and roaſt in Paper; ſerve with what Sauce you pleaſe.

Carré de Veau à la Servante.

Neck of Veal Stewed.

LARD it with large Pieces, rolled in Pepper and Salt, Shallots, and fine Spices, braze it with Slices of Lard, ſliced Roots, and Onions, a Laurel Leaf, few Drops of Brandy; ſkim and ſift the Sauce, and ſerve upon the Meat.

* All Diſhes under this Denomination are meant as common Dreſſing; *La Servante*, the Maid; which is ſuppoſed not to be a profeſſed Cook; the ſame for thoſe called *au Court-Bouillon* or *Gros Sel*, meaning plain Diſhes.

Carré de Veau à la Poivrade.

Neck of Veal and Sharp Sauce.

MAKE a Marinade with Butter and Flour, which you put on a Sand Fire with ſliced Onions and Roots,

Roots, a little Coriander Seed, one Clove of Garlick, two of Spices, Thyme, Laurel, Basil, Pepper and Salt; put in it a larded Neck of Veal, leave it in it about two Hours, then roast it and serve with a Sauce Poivrade, as you will find in Sauce Articles, Page 43.

Carré de Veau au Monarque.

Neck of Veal Monarch Fashion.

CUT the Fillet of a Neck of Veal, and with it make a good forced Meat with Cows Udder, Lard or Suet, Bread Crums soaked in Milk or Cream, Pepper and Salt, chopt Parsley, Shallots, Mushrooms, four Yolks of Eggs; boil the Remainder of the Neck in the common Pot half an Hour, then take it out, and where you have cut the Meat fill it with this forced Meat, upon this, Slices of Fat, Liver, Truffles; cover it over with forced Meat, bathe it with Yolks of Eggs, Bread Crums, a little Butter over it; put it awhile in the Oven; serve with it a Spanish Sauce or any other as you please.

Carré de Veau en Crepine.

Neck of Veal in Cowl.

IT is done the same as the Cutlets, the Difference only to do it whole.

Carré de Veau en Surprise.

Neck of Veal Stuffed.

IT is brazed and done the same as the Breast, the Meat cut out and stuffed with forced Meat, finished in the Oven, and served with a clear Sauce.

Cuiſſeau de Veau aux Epinards.

Leg or Knuckle of Veal and Spinage.

IT is larded and brazed with all Sorts of Roots and Spices, as uſual; and ſerved upon ſtewed Spinage: it is the Garden Stuff that gives it the Name.

Cuiſſeau de Veau à la Crême.

Leg of Veal white Sauce.

LARD a Leg of Veal with large Lardons, then let it ſoak about twelve Hours in Marinade after this Manner, a Bit of Butter and Flour, about a Quart of Milk, two Lemons ſliced and peeled, ſix Spice Cloves, ſix Shallots, Cloves, three Laurel Leaves, Thyme, Parſley, two Cloves of Garlick, ſix Onions, Pepper and Salt; warm the Marinade and put it in a Pot, much to the Bigneſs of the Veal; wipe it dry before ſpitting, and cover with Slices of Lard, and two or three Sheets of Paper, roaſt it, and ſerve with a Sauce Poivrade, Page 34, or a Cream Sauce, made with a Bit of Butter and Flour, a chopt Anchovy, two green Shallots, brazed and chopt Parſley, grated Nutmeg, Pepper and Salt; as much Cream as neceſſary.

Cuiſſeau de Veau à la Daube.

Leg of Veal Dobed or à la Mode.

IT is brazed with all Sorts of Roots and Spices; reduce the Sauce to a Jelly, and ſerve it with it either hot or cold.

Quartier de Veau au Chevreuil.

Leg of Veal cut Venison Fashion.

IT is larded and marinaded as the former, only adding Vinegar and Coriander, soaked as long and roasted; serve with a Sauce Piquante, viz. relishing.

Quartier de Veau au Caramel.

The Same cut as above, Glazed.

IT is larded and brazed tender, the Sauce skimmed and sifted; reduce the Sauce to a Glaze as Fricandeau; serve with a sharp Sauce or stewed Greens.

Epaule de Veau.

Shoulder of Veal.

IT may be dressed in every Respect and Fashion, as the Leg; I shall only give the different Names, to avoid Repetitions, which are à la Poivrade, à L'Allemande, au Naturel, &c. &c.

Blanquette de Veau.

Roasted Veal with white Sauce.

A Dish well known to all House-wives.

Grenadins de Veau aux Anchois.

Small Fricandeaus Anchovy Sauce.

GRENADINS differ only in Size from what is commonly called Fricandeaux, being cut smaller, larded and brazed white or brown; mix a Glass of white Wine and Cullis with their own Sauce, and add one or two pounded Anchovies; skim and sift the Sauce, or with Greens.

Rissolettes

Riſſolettes de Veau.

Veal Collop.

CUT thin Slices of Fillet of Veal, put them in a Diſh or Stew-pan with Oil or Butter, Pepper and Salt, ſome ſweet Herbs chopt, make forced Meat, let it catch a little; make a Liaſon with Flour and Butter for brown, or Eggs and Cream for white Sauce: you may alſo broil them, and ſerve with Cullis and a good Lemon Squeeze or Vinegar, and ſweet Herbs finely chopped.

Paupiettes de Veau.

Veal Olives.

MAKE a good forced Meat of Poulteries or any other, cut thin Slices of Fillet of Veal, and roll forced Meat in it, to what Bigneſs you think proper; tie them well and boil ſlowly with a Glaſs of white Wine and Cullis, a Noſegay of ſweet Herbs, two Cloves, few Shallots; when done ſkim and ſift the Sauce, to ſerve upon it; if you would have them roaſted, lard the Veal, or cover them with thin Slices of Lard: you may alſo broil them, bathing with Eggs and Bread Crums, ſerve with what Sauce you think proper: you may make Olives of what Sorts of Meat you pleaſe, after the ſame Manner, for Variety's Sake; and ſerve with different Sauces: when roaſted like Haſlets, the French Name is (en Hatereaux) viz. on ſmall Skewers.

Brezolles de Veau.

Veal Brazed, a different Collop.

CUT thin Slices of Fillet of Veal, put two or three Slices of Ham in the Bottom of your Stew-pan, then a Down of Slices of Veal, Pepper and Salt, chopt Parſley,

Parsley, Mushrooms, Shallots, Truffles, a Spoonful of good Oil, Butter or Lard; lay the same three or four Times over, and cover it with Slices of Lard, braze slowly; when done, take the Lard and Ham out of the Sauce, skim and sift it; add a little Cullis, a good Lemon Squeeze, and serve upon the Brezolles.

You may also let them marinade in the Sauce about an Hour before cold, then put them in a Stew-pan singly, and boil or rather fry on a fierce Fire to take Colour, turning of either Side; take them out and put a little Cullis and a Glass of white Wine in the same Stew-pan, serve hot upon the Brezolles.

Poupeton.

Meat-Pudding.

MAKE forced Meat with Veal, Suet, Bread, Milk or Cream, Parsley, Shallots, Mushrooms, Yolks of Eggs, Pepper and Salt; garnish the Bottom of your Stew-pan with Slices of Lard (the Pan to be much of the same Bigness of the Quantity you propose,) put three Parts of your forced Meat round with a Hole in the Middle, to put in it a Ragout of Pigeons or any other; cover it with the Remainder, and bake it in the Oven; when done turn it over gently, wipe the Fat, and cut a small Hole to pour a good Sauce in it made of Cullis, Lemon Juice, &c. cover the Hole again; the Ragout you put in it gives it the Name.

Marbrée.

Marbled, Coloured, &c.

TAKE half a Dozen of Pigs Ears, as many Calves Ears and Feet boned, twelve Palates, Beef or Calves; scald all together for about half an Hour in boiling Water; then braze with thin Broth, two Pound of Ham, a Nosegay of all Sorts of sweet Herbs, six or eight

eight Shallots, four Cloves of Garlick, three Laurel Leaves, Thyme and Basil, six Cloves, half a Nutmeg, Onions, Carrots, and Parsneps; when done, let them cool, and cut all in small Pieces with the Flesh of two roasted Fowls also minced, a Handful of sweet Almonds, as much Pistachio Nuts, green Shallots, mix it altogether in a Stew-pan with a deal of chopt Parsley, a Bottle of white Wine, some melted Hogs-Lard, the Juice of four Lemons, all Sorts of fine Spices; boil all together until the Sauce is quite reduced; let it cool again, then take a Stew-pan the Bigness you would have the Cake; rub it all over with Butter, and garnish it all over with Wafers of different Colours, cut and disposed according to Fancy; then fill it with the Meat well intermixed; take care that the Meat is still warm, put it in a cool Place to settle; when you want to use it, only dip the Stew-pan in warm Water to turn it over in the Dish upon a Napkin; you may also garnish it with Slices of boiled Truffles, Pickles or any Colour you please.

Grenade.

A Grenado.

SCALD four large Craw-fish and Colliflower; garnish the Bottom of your Stew-pan with Slices of Lard, lay the four Craw-fish at the Bottom Star-like, between them some of the Colliflower, and Fillets of Ham, roasted Fowl, and sliced Truffles; bathe it with Eggs to make it stick together, then put a good forced Meat round the Pan of a good Thickness, interlarded with Fillets of Ham and Fowl, leave a Hole in the Middle to put what Ragout you please; cover it over with forced Meat, baked in the Oven, turn it over gently, take off the Slices of Lard, and wipe it with a Linen Cloth; serve with Sauce Pontife.

Grenade en Daube.

Grenado Dobed.

CUT half a Dozen *Grenadins*, viz. small Fricandeaus, and being larded and glazed, as to serve by themselves, cut the Remainder of the Leg of Veal into large Dices; also larded with large Pieces without Form, and a Fowl cut in Pieces, which you boil with the last Veal in Broth, a Pint of white Wine, a Knuckle of Veal, a Nosegay of Parsley, Chibbol, a Clove or two of Garlick, three Heads of Cloves, a Laurel Leaf, Sellery and Thyme, fine Spices; when done, lay the Fricandeaus at the Bottom of your Stew-pan (which you must always proportion to the Bigness of the Dish you propose to make) and thin Slices of Lard under, Bits of Fowl between, then the Bits of Veal, and finish in the same Manner; sift the Broth and pour it over this Preparation, let it cool to a Jelly; you may add a Calve's Foot in the boiling to make the Jelly stronger; when you want to use it, dip the Stew-pan in warm Water and turn it over gently.

N. B. Those cold Dishes will keep a long while, and may be used cold or warm, sliced; the Jelly will serve for Sauce either Way, or adding a little Cullis for hot, or Jelly for cold.

Favorites.

Different Olives.

CUT Slices of Fillet of Veal round, of about the Bigness of the Palm of your Hand without the Paring; make Forced-meat with Remains of roasted Chickens, Suet, Herbs, Eggs and Spices, upon each Slice a little of this Forced-meat and fat Livers sliced, Truffles or Mushrooms; continue to a middling Height, the last to be Veal; then roll them in Cowl, and tie them; put them in a Stew-pan with sliced Ham and Veal, Parsley, Shallots,

lots, two Cloves, one of Garlick, Pepper and Salt, a little Broth, a Glafs of white Wine, boil flowly; when done, take off the Cowl, wipe the Fat cleanly, fkim and fift the Sauce; add a little Cullis, Lemon Juice and chopt Parfley.

Venetienne de Veau.

Broiled Veal Venetian Fafhion; Veal Stakes.

CUT pretty thick Slices of Fillet of Veal, and pretty large; marinade about an Hour in a little Oil, chopt Parfley, Mufhrooms, Shallots, Laurel, Thyme, Bafil, Pepper and Salt; make as much of the Marinade ftick to it as you can, and Bread Crums; broil flowly, bafting with the Remainder; ferve with a Squeeze of Lemon or Seville Orange.

Venetienne au Jambon.

CUT thin Slices of Fillet of Veal, and between two, one Slice of Ham dipt in Eggs, Parfley, Mufhrooms, Shallots, Truffles, a little Pepper; roll them in Slices of Lard, and fimmer gently with a little Broth, a Glafs of white Wine; when done take off the Bacon, fkim and fift the Sauce, add a little Cullis; you may ferve with a relifhing Sauce, or what Sort you pleafe.

Venetienne à la Moële.

Venetian with Marrow.

CUT very thin Slices of Veal, and make Forced-meat with Marrow, Pepper and Salt, chopt Parfley, Shallots, Nutmeg, Bread Crums; put fome of this Forced-meat between two Slices of Veal, as many as will make a Difh, bathe it round with Whites of Eggs to make it ftick, dip them in Butter, and fweet Herbs chopt, and Bread Crums; broil flowly, and ferve with a relifhing Sauce.

Venetienne

Venetienne au Vin de Champagne.

CUT large thin Slices of Veal, between two Slices put Butter, chopt Parsley, Shallots, Mushrooms, Pepper and Salt; braze them about an Hour, then add a Glass of white Wine; finish the brazing, reduce the Sauce, adding a Lemon Squeeze when ready to serve.

Fricandeaux aux Legumes.

Fricandeau with Garden Greens.

AS every Body is acquainted with this Dish, I shall give no further Direction, than what has been done in Veal Cutlets.

Noix de Veau au Pontife.

Knuckle of Veal Pontiff Sauce.

Noix de Veau, Filet, & Rouëlle, mean much the same thing; the first being a pretty large Knuckle, the second a large Fillet, and the third a small one, from the Difference of cutting up the Meat.

CUT long Pieces of Lard, Ham, and pickled Cucumbers, lard the Fillet through and through, tie it with Packthread, and put it in a Stew-pan much of its Bigness, with a little Butter, a Lemon Squeeze; let it catch a little, then add Broth, a Nosegay of sweet Herbs, one Clove of Garlick, two of Spices, a Laurel Leaf; finish it and reduce the Sauce, to glaze it like a Fricandeau, and serve with Sauce Pontiff; Page 46.

Noix de Veau à la Saint Cloud.

The same Saint Cloud Fashion.

THIS is the Fillet of Veal stuffed and roasted, as done in all Families, only Mushrooms and Truffles are recommended in the Stuffing, which are not commonly used, but may be to Advantage, when to be had.

Noix de Veau Glaffée.

Fillet of Veal Glazed.

THIS is done in the fame Manner as the Noix au Pontife; only not larded and ferved with Cullis Sauce, and Lemon Juice.

Rouelle de Veau à la Daube.

Small Fillet of Veal ftewed.

CUT long Pieces of larding Bacon, and feafon them with Pepper and Salt, fine Spices, chopt Parfley, Shallots; lard the Fillet through and through that the Larding may cut with each Slice, put it in a Braze-pan with a little Broth, a Glafs of white Wine, fweet Herbs, two Cloves, Laurel, Thyme, a little Coriander, a Clove of Garlick; when done, reduce the Sauce, fift it and let it cool to a Jelly, and ferve cold with the Veal whole or fliced.

Rouelle de Veau à la Cendre.

A la Cendre means on Afhes or flow Fire, &c.

THIS is done in the fame Manner as the former, only ferved hot with its own Sauce, or what Addition you pleafe.

Andouillettes au Céleri.

Sham Saufages with Sellery

BOIL half a Dozen long Stalks of Sellery, then prefs the Water out, and lay fome good Forced-meat round it; then tie them up in thin Slices of Veal, in the Form of Saufages; boil them in Broth, Herbs and Spices; and ferve with what Sauce you pleafe.

Filets

Filets Mignons.

THESE are the Fillets found under the Kidney of a Loin of Veal all along, larded and glazed; serve with stewed Greens or what Sauce you please.

Filets de Veau à la Conty.
Fillets of Veal Conty Fashion.

CUT out the whole Fillet of a Neck of Veal, strip it of all its Sinews, and cut in several Places to put in it Truffles, Sweet Bread, fat Liver, all sliced; simmer on the Fire with a Bit of Butter, chopt Parsley, Shallots and Mushrooms, then braze it with few Slices of larding Bacon, and Ham, with all the first Seasoning; in about an Hour add a Glass of white Wine; when done take out the Fillet; add two Spoonfuls of Cullis, boil a Moment, skim and sift it; serve upon the Fillet with a little Pepper and Salt, and a Lemon Squeeze.

Timbale à la Romaine.

(The Timbale is a Mould much in the Manner of the Turks Caps, for Blanmangé, &c. &c.)

CUT Slices of Veal very thin, put them in a Stew-pan upon Slices of Lard, bathe them with Whites of Eggs to make them join together; make a good Forced-meat with the Parings, Bread Crums, Cream, Udder, rasped Lard, Parsley, Shallots, Mushrooms, Pepper and Salt, a Couple of Eggs; lay some of this Forced-meat upon the Veal, then a Ragout of Pigeons or any other; and cover it over with the same Forced-meat and Slices of Lard, bake it in the Oven, when done turn it over gently, take off the Lard; serve with what Sauce you please.

Veau à la Folette.

Without Art.

THIS is Slices of Veal marinaded for about an Hour with a little Oil, all Sorts of sweet Herbs; then rolled like Veal Olives with all their Seasoning, roasted, and serve with a sharp Sauce.

Gateau de Mai.

A Spring Cake.

BOIL a Pint of Cream, and Bread Crums, a good Quantity; reduce till it is quite thick, then add pounded Udder, and Suet with fine chopt Parsley, Shallots, Taragon, Burnet, Charvil, Cresses, Pepper and Salt, Nutmeg, six Yolks of Eggs; lay little Parcels of this in a deep Dish, bathe it with Yolks of Eggs and Bread Crums, bake it in the Oven; serve with a sharp Sauce or stewed Greens.

Pain à la Flamande.

A Flemish Loaf.

CUT a Cabbage in four, scald it and press the Water out, then tie it, and braze it with about half a Pound of pickled Pork, half a Dozen Links of Sausages, a Nosegay of Parsley, Shallots, one Clove of Garlick, two of Spices, and Broth; when done enough, take out the Nosegay, and add two Spoonfuls of Cullis; reduce till the Sauce is quite wasted, let it cool; take a Stew-pan which you garnish round with Paste, and put the Ragout in it, cover it over with Paste, and make what Design you please upon it; bake it in the Oven about an Hour, then pour a good Sauce into it.

Crepinettes

Crepinettes de Godiveau.

THE Godiveau is Forced-meat made with Veal, as it is often prepared for Petits Pâtes; which when done, you may use in Cowl rolled, broiled or fried, or baked in the Oven; dip them first in Oil or Butter, with Bread Crums or without; they are best fried, and serve dry.

Gateau de Veau en Crepine.

Veal Cake in Cowl.

MAKE a Forced-meat as the preceding, then cut a Knuckle of Veal in small Pieces like Dices, few Pistachio-Nuts, sweet Almonds, Pepper, Salt, fine Spices, and three Yolks of Eggs; match your Stew-pan the Bigness you would have the Cake, garnish with Slices of Lard upon the Cowl, forced Meat and Meat; cover it over with the Cowl, bake it in the Oven in a moderate Heat; when done, let it cool in the same Pan to serve cold.

Veau à la Villageoise.

Veal Peasant Fashion.

CUT thin large Slices of Veal, season them with Pepper, Salt and fine Spices, Parsley, Shallots; cut also thin Slices of Ham, dip them in Eggs, and lay upon the Veal, wrap the Ham in it, and boil with a Glass of white Wine, as much Broth; when done, skim and sift the Sauce, serve without adding any thing else to it.

Bagatelles de Veau.

Trifles of Veal.

CUT thin large Slices of Veal, feafon them with fine Spices, chopt Truffles or Mufhrooms, Parfley, Shallots, fine Oil, roll them up like a Saufage with all the Seafoning in the Infide; tie them up, fimmer with a Glafs of white Wine, two Spoonfuls of Cullis, fkim and fift the Sauce to ferve upon them.

Filets de Coulis à la Bechamel.

Fillets of Cullis Meat Bechamel.

TO make a Side-difh in a Hurry or inftead of a fpoiled one, pare the Brown off the Cullis Meat, and cut it in fmall Fillets; fimmer a Moment in Bechamel Sauce, as you will find in Sauce Articles: you may alfo ferve it in different relifhing Sauces.

CHAPITRE TROISIEME. Du Mouton.

CHAPTER THIRD. Of Mutton.

La Queuë de Mouton de differentes Façons.

Sheep's Rumps of different Fafhions.

SHEEP's Rumps boiled or brazed, tender, broiled or not, make a very pretty Side-difh; you may ferve with what Sauce you pleafe, fweet Herbs chopt, and Cullis, Mufhrooms, a pounded Anchovy, glazed; alfo with ftewed Cabbages or other Greens.

Langues de Mouton.

Sheep's Tongues.

BOIL them in Water with all Sorts of fweet Herbs; when they are almoft done peel them, and finifh them

in

in a good Braze; and serve with a relishing Sauce, or cut in two, and dip them in Butter or Oil, with chopt Parsley, Shallots, Pepper and Salt, to broil or fry; serve with Sauce Piquante; See Page 45.

Langues de Mouton à la Provençale.

Sheep's Rumps Provence Fashion.

FRY sliced Onions, in Oil; when half done add Flour, chopt Parsley, Mushrooms, a Clove of Garlick, Pepper and Salt, a Glass of white Wine, two Spoonfuls of Cullis; let it boil till the Onions are done, split as many ready boiled Tongues as you please; simmer them a Quarter of an Hour in the Sauce, and serve all together, garnish the Dish with fried Bread.

Langues de Mouton Glacées.

Sheep's Tongues as Fricandeau.

BOIL them to three Parts, peel and let them cool to lard; then finish in a little Broth, a Slice of Ham, sweet Herbs, few fine Spices, skim the Sauce and reduce it to a Glaze, and serve with what Sauce you please: you may also use them without glazing, with a Spoonful of Cullis, and Broth added to their own Sauce, and sifted.

Langue de Mouton à la Royale.

Sheep's Tongue Royal Fashion.

BOIL as the former, then lard through and through, then marinade about an Hour in three or four Spoonfuls of Oil, Pepper and Salt, chopt Parsley, Shallots, Truffles or Mushrooms; finish them with all this Seasoning, between Slices of Lard and a Glass of white Wine; when done skim the Sauce, add a little Cullis to give it Consistence; serve upon the Tongues.

Langues de Mouton aux Onions en Crepine.

Sheep's Tongues with Onions in Cowl.

FRY sliced Onions in Butter; when done add two pounded Anchovies, two Shallots, a little Fennel finely chopt, and Parsley, Pepper and Salt, two Yolks of Eggs raw; put ready boiled Tongues in a Bit of Cowl, and the former Preparation round it, which you roll in the Cowl; bathe with Eggs and Bread Crums, give them Colour in the Oven, and serve with what Sauce you please.

You may also dress them au Gratin, cutting thin Slices and little Forced-meat laid between; basting now and then with Cullis.

Langue de Mouton en Papillottes.

Sheep's Tongues in Paper.

CUT brazed Tongues in two Pieces, and put round it a Forced-meat made of Fowls Livers, or any Sorts of Poultry, with Yolks of hard Eggs, sweet Herbs, a little Suet or Beef Marrow, Pepper and Salt, few fine Spices, pounded together; roll them up in Paper, first rubbed with Oil or Butter; either broil or bake slowly, and serve dry or with a Sauce.

Langue de Mouton au Parmesan.

Sheep's Tongues and Parmesan Cheese.

PUT a little Cullis Sauce and Butter in the Dish you intend to serve, upon this rasped Cheese; split brazed Tongues in two and lay them upon it, then a little more Cullis and Cheese; put it in the Oven, or colour it with a Salamander; serve with short Sauce.

Langues de Mouton en Surprise.

Sheep's Tongues Masked or Shammed.

BOIL Sheep's Tongues to three Parts in Water, peel them and lard through and through, then finish in a flight Braze made of Broth, a Glass of white Wine, a Nosegay of sweet Herbs, two Cloves, few Shallots; when done let them cool, and wrap them up in forced Meat, either (Godiveau) or Poultry, then Cowl over it, which you dip in Eggs, then Bread Crums; put them in your Dish and bake in the Oven; when done, wipe the Fat off very clean, and serve with Acid Sauce: you may also wrap them in thin Slices of Veal, under the Cowl, and simmer them about an Hour with a little Broth, a Glass of white Wine; when done, sift the Sauce, add a little Cullis, a Lemon Squeeze, and serve upon the Tongues: this last is called à la Braise.

Langues de Mouton à la Liaison.

Sheep's Tongues Ragout.

BOIL Tongues in Water, when well peeled cut them in two without separating quite; season them with Pepper and Salt, a little Oil or Butter; broil them of both Sides: make a Sauce after this Manner, a little Butter with chopt Mushrooms, Shallots, two Cloves, a Nosegay of Parsley, simmer this some Time, then add a little Broth, half a Glass of white Wine, Pepper and Salt, a little Flour; reduce the Sauce, take out the Nosegay, and add three Yolks of Eggs with Broth to make the Liason: serve upon the Tongues with a Lemon Squeeze.

Langues de Mouton à la Dauphine.

Sheep's Tongues Dauphin Fashion.

BRAZE the Tongues very tender, then cut them in very thin Slices, and make Forced-meat with Truffles or Mushrooms, fat Livers, Beef Marrow, Pepper and Salt, chopt Parsley, Shallots, mixt with three Yolks of Eggs; cut pretty large Pieces of Veal, intermix this Forced-meat with Tongue Slices; roll it up like a short thick Sausage in the Cowl, which you dip in Eggs, then Bread Crums all over; fry or broil of a fine Colour; serve either dry with fried Parsley, or with Sauce.

Langues de Mouton à la Bourgeoise.

Sheep's Tongues plain Family Fashion.

BOIL in Water, then peel and split in two; marinade awhile in melted Butter, Pepper and Salt, chopt Shallots; broil slowly with Bread Crums, and serve with a Sauce made of a Spoonful of Verjuice or Vinegar, a Bit of Butter, two Spoonfuls of Broth, a little Flour, a little Nutmeg, two chopt Shallots; reduce the Sauce to a good Consistence, and serve under the Tongues.

Langues de Mouton en Tourte.

Sheep's Tongues Pie.

MAKE a good Puffpaste, and lay in the Bottom good Forced-meat, made of roasted Poulteries, Suet or rasped Lard, chopt Parsley, Mushrooms, Pepper and Salt, few fine Spices; upon this, Tongues cut in two; over them, a good Slice of Ham, a little Butter,

ter, a few Slices of larding Bacon; finish the Pie and bake it: when done, take out the Lard and Ham, skim the Fat very clean, add to it what Sauce you please.

Canelons de Langue de Mouton.

Sheep's Tongue Fried in Paste.

Canelon, means a Diminutive of *Canon*, viz. a large Gun; this and all Directions under this Denomination, are prepared after the same Manner; *Canons* and *Canelons* (in the Sense of Cookery) are to each other, as *Crepine* and *Crepinette*.

CUT a Sheep's Tongue in Quarters Length-ways, the Tongue first brazed; put round it a little Forcedmeat well seasoned, then roll it up in Paste very thin, and fry as you do Rissolles; serve dry.

Pieds de Mouton de Différentes Façons.

Sheep's Trotters of Different Fashions.

BOIL them in Water until you can take out the great Bones, then split them to clean properly, then boil them again till they are very tender, and dress them in what Manner you please; either as a Fricassee of Chicken, or Cullis Sauce; taking care to make the Sauce relishing.

Pieds de Mouton à la Belle-vuë.

Sheep's Trotters. See Sauce à la Belle-vuë, Page 39.

THE Trotters brazed very tender with Scraps of Veal, few Bits of Ham, Lard, and Spices, two or three Lemon Slices; take the Leg Bone out, and in the room of it, stick a Bit of fried Bread cut proportionable; serve with this Sauce as above.

Pied de Mouton en Canon.

Sheep's Trotters fried in Paste.

THE Trotters first boiled in Water, then finished in a good tasted Braze, bone them without cutting; then roll them in good Forced-meat, and dip them in thick Batter made of Flour, Oil, white Wine, Pepper and Salt, fry of a good Colour; serve with fried Parsley.

Pieds de Mouton à la Sainte Menehoult.

Sheep's Trotters Fried or Broiled.

WHEN boiled enough to take the great Bone out, put instead of it a Godiveau, Forced-meat, finish them in a good Braze, or in a Sainte Menehoult made with a little Milk, a Bit of Butter and Flour, all Sorts of sweet Herbs, fine chopped; roll them in Bread Crums, broil and serve with a clear sharp Sauce, see Page 45; when brazed very white and tender; you may serve them with Sauce à la Reine, see Page 48; dress them to any Sauce when brazed tender, as the Sauce gives the Name, so call it such as aux Onions, Parmesan, Gratin, &c. &c.

Pieds de Mouton à l'Aspic.

ASPIC means a sharp Sauce or Jelly, wherein is commonly used Elder Vinegar or Taragon Ditto, with chopt Parsley, or Taragon Leaves, Oil, Pepper and Salt, Mustard, Lemon: any Sorts of cold Meat, Poulteries or Game, may be served in Aspic, either hot or cold.

Pieds de Mouton à la Ravigotte.

They are served with the Sauce so called; See Page 38.

I shall pass over any further Directions upon the different Ways of dressing Trotters, also Ears, as very needless; the same with the Kidney, as it may be dressed as Beef's, allowing for Tenderness; Sheep's Rumps are also dressed in all the different Ways, as Calve's Tails, either with Garden Greens or Sauces; Rice or Roots, in Turine with Pinions of Poulteries, or other Meat as Huspot.

Carré de Mouton au Réverend.

Neck of Mutton Larded with Ham and Anchovy.

LARD the Fillet of a Neck of Mutton through and through with Ham and few Anchovies, first rolled in chopt Parsley, Shallots, Thyme, Laurel, Pepper and Salt; then put to braze with few Slices of Lard, some Broth, a Glass of white Wine; braze slowly; when done, skim and sift the Sauce, add a little Cullis to give it a proper Body; and a Lemon Squeeze.

Carré de Mouton en Fricandeau.

IT is done in the same Manner as the Neck of Veal, Larded, Brazed and Glazed, served with Greens or Sauce.

As I have translated an ample Description of the different Ways of dressing a Neck of Veal, I shall avoid repeating any further upon Necks of Mutton, as it may be done the same Way in every Respects, allowing for the Difference of Meat, the Names in the Original are as follows;

Carré de Mouton Sans Façons, viz. Plain.

Carré de Mouton en Crepine, in Cowl.

Carré de Mouton a L'Echalottes, with sweet Herbs.

Carré de Mouton au Jambon.

THIS is brazed, and the few Slices of Ham which serve in the Braze, are cut in Dices and mixt with the Sauce; when well skimmed and sifted, served with the Neck. *Note* that your Braze is appropriated in the Seasoning for Sauce.

Carré de Mouton à la Mode, as Beef Ditto.

Carré de Mouton à la Jardiniere, ou à la Capucine.

So called from the Greens, or the Simplicity of dressing.

THIS is fried Mutton Chops, eat with Garden Greens.

Cotelettes de Mouton Sans Malice.

Mutton Stakes without Art, a plain Way.

Aricot de Mouton aux (Racines) Roots.

THIS is the Harricot of Mutton known to every Body, with Greens and Roots.

Cotelettes de Mouton de Plusieurs Façons.

Mutton Stakes of different Ways; See Veal Cutlets.

Cotelettes de Mouton au Fenouil; Fennel.

THIS is done slowly in Broth, Pepper and Salt; all Sorts of sweet Herbs, adding Fennel to it.

Cotelettes

Cotelettes de Mouton à la (Cendre.)

Mutton Chops Stewed flowly, (Ashes Heat.)

CUT the Chops pretty thick, lard them with Lard and Ham, give them few Turns over the Fire, with a Bit of Butter, chopt Parsley, Shallots, Mushrooms; then put them in a Stew-pan with Slices of Veal at Bottom, seasoned with sweet Herbs, Pepper, and a little Salt and Nutmeg; cover it over with Slices of Lard, stop the Pan very close; let it simmer a long while; when about half done, add a Glass of white Wine, and two Spoonfuls of Cullis; skim and sift the Sauce, and serve upon the Stakes.

Cotelettes de Mouton en (Hérisson.)

Mutton Chops Masqueraded, (Hedge-Hog.)

BRAZE the Stakes in a good seasoned Braze; when about half done, put different Sorts of Roots, cut as for Lardons, long; when done take all out and make small Holes in the Stakes, to lard them with the Roots, which must show pretty long of either Side; serve with a good Cullis Sauce, and relishing Herbs chopped.

Cotelettes de Mouton a l'Amoureux; viz. Lover.

LARD the Stakes; then give them a fry in Butter, with Parsley, a Branch of Winter Savory, then put them in a Stew-pan with small Bits of Ham, sliced Onions, Carrots, Parsneps; which you first give a fry in Oil or Butter; add a Glass of Wine, a little Cullis, skim the Sauce, and serve with all the Roots and Ham.

Cotelettes de Mouton en Crepine.

Mutton Stakes in Cowl. See Veal.

Cotelettes de Mouton en Crepine d'une autre Façon.

Another Way.

THIS is in the same Manner as the Sham Veal Cotelettes: See Veal Cotelettes en Surprise; Page 104.

Cotelettes de Mouton en (Surtout.)

Mutton Stakes Masked; (Frock) Disguised.

CUT Chops in the common Way, and simmer them with a little Broth to three Parts, with a Nosegay of sweet Herbs; reduce the Sauce till no more remains than what will bathe the Stakes, garnish them with Forced-meat round, made of Fillet of Veal, Suet, chopt Parsley, Shallots, Pepper and Salt, Bread Crums, and Cream, pounded all together, and three Yolks of Eggs, bathe with Eggs and Bread Crums, bake in the Oven; serve with Consumée Sauce or Veal Gravy, or Acid Sauce in a Boat.

Cotelettes de Mouton à la Chartreuse.

Mutton Stakes, called after the above, Frier Fashion.

BRAZE Mutton Chops with Slices of Lard, Ham, Broth, and a Nosegay of sweet Herbs, half a Clove of Garlick, two Cloves, half a Laurel Leaf, a little Thyme, two sliced Carrots and Turnips, Pepper and Salt; when done, cut the Turnips and Carrots in what Form you please; then make a Sort of Porridge with Spinage, which you scald, and simmer a Moment in Butter, then pounded and sifted, add the white of an Egg to mix with it: take a Diſh the Bigneſs of that you intend to ſend to Table, and garniſh the Bottom with the ſame Slices of Lard; fix the Cotelettes intermixed with the Roots, and Spinage, Porridge, and ſo keep it warm; when ready turn it over gently upon the Diſh, take off the Bacon; ſerve with a good Conſumée.

Cotelettes de Mouton Frites.

Mutton Stakes Fried.

BOIL Mutton Chops in Broth, a Noſegay of ſweet Herbs; when done ſift the Broth, and reduce it to a Glaze, with which you bathe the Stakes of both Sides when cold, then bathe them with Yolks of Eggs, and Bread Crums; fry a Moment ſharply to give them a good Colour; ſerve with fried Parſley; if you would have them with a Farce (Forced-meat) make it the ſame as the former, and garniſh the Stakes with it before frying.

Cotelettes de Mouton à la Villeroy.

THIS is ſtewed with a great deal of Onions; I don't think it worthy of any further Notice; and alſo the Cotelettes à la *Gaſcogne*, which are brazed with Oil and Garlick in Abundance, as all the Diſhes under the ſame Denomination.

Cotelettes de Mouton à la Servante.

A la Servante means in a common plain Way.

Cotelettes de Mouton a l'Allemande.

L'Allemande, German Faſhion.

THIS deſerves no more Notice than many others, as Oil, Garlick, and a deal of Spices make the whole.

Cotelettes de Mouton à la Dauphine.

CUT the Stakes pretty thick, and lard with half Ham, and half Bacon; fry them with a little Broth, thin Slices of Veal, sweet Herbs; sift the Sauce, and serve upon it.

Bresolles de Mouton.

Mutton Collop.

THIS is the Collop mostly best done in Inns in England, only more common with Veal, but will do equally with the Fillet of a Neck of Mutton; it should not boil in the last Preparation as it will make the Meat hard, and so it will with hashed Mutton or Beef; warm slowly.

Bresolles de Mouton à la (Poële,) Frying-pan.

Mutton Collop another Way.

TAKE a Leg of Mutton long kept, cut the Lean free from any Fat, and cut the Pieces about the Bigness of half an Egg, flatten with the Cleaver, then simmer them a little while in Hog's Lard, chopt Parsley, Shallots, Mushrooms, Pepper and Salt; then put them in a Stew-pan, with few Slices of Veal, a Slice of Ham, and all their Seasoning; cover over with Slices of Lard, simmer about an Hour, then half a Glass of white Wine, a little Broth; when done, take the Mutton out to drain, add a little Cullis to the Sauce, skim it and sift it to serve upon the Bresolles.

Bresolles de Mouton à la Périgord.

THIS is much as the former, only cut very thin, marinaded some time in Oil, sweet Herbs, &c. &c. then brazed in their Seasoning, adding a Glass of white Wine and chopped Truffles, or served with a Ragout of the last.

Bresolles

Bresolles de Mouton aux Concombres.

Mutton Collop with stewed Cucumbers.

THIS is prepared as the former, cut very thin and small, brazed very tender, and mixt with stewed Cucumbers, marinaded some time in Vinegar before stewing; it is needless to use fresh Meat for all those Collops, as part of a Neck or Leg roasted will answer the same, and will be tenderer, if Care is taken not to let it boil, but warm slowly.

Mouton à la Bechamel aux Onions.

SLICE three or four Onions, and fry them slowly in Butter, not to brown them; add some Broth and a little Flour; when almost done, add two or three Spoonfuls of Cream, Pepper and Salt; let it boil to a good Body, then put Fillets of roasted Mutton in it, to warm without boiling: you may add scalded chopt Parsley and a Lemon Squeeze,

Hatereau de Mouton.

Mutton Olive Fried, Brazed or Roasted.

THE Author recommends the Fillets from under the Kidney as the most delicate; cut very thin and fill with good Forced-meat, rolled in it; then you may dress them as you please: serve with a clear Sauce or Cullis, adding a Lemon Squeeze.

Filets de Mouton Marinés.

LARD a Neck of Mutton, and marinade it about two Hours in a little Vinegar, Water, Pepper and Salt,

Salt, sliced Onions, Shallots, Thyme, Laurel, two Cloves, then drain it and roast it; serve with relishing Sauce.

Filets de Mouton à la Coquette.

CUT Pieces of Fillets of Neck of Mutton, the Bigness of a Finger, lard them through and through with Ham and Lard; boil them in Broth, and a Nosegay of sweet Herbs; when done sift the Sauce, reduce it to a Glaze, with which you garnish the Fillets; have good Forced-meat made of Poultry, well seasoned and mixt with Yolks of Eggs; put some of this all round the Fillets, then tie them up in a Slice of Lard, each; bathe with Eggs and Bread Crums; put them in the Oven to take a good Colour: serve with what Sauce you think proper.

Filets de Mouton Glassés aux Concombres.

THIS is done the same as Veal Fricandeaux, larded, brazed and glazed; serve upon stewed Cucumbers, or with any kind of stewed Greens.

Filets de Mouton en Cannellon.

CUT the Fillet of a Neck of Mutton in two, make a Hole in the middle of each with a large Larding-pin; stuff it with rasped Lard, mixt with chopt Shallots, Parsley, Mushrooms, Pepper and Salt; marinade in a little Oil and roast them: serve with what Sauce you please.

Fricandeau de Mouton.

THE only Difference from the former, it is done with the Leg.

Escalopes

Cafcalopes de Mouton au Vin de Champagne.

Mutton Collops and white Wine.

THIS is cut the same as all Collops, brazed with few Slices of Veal, Ham, and Seasoning; adding a Glass of white Wine to the Sauce.

Rouëlles de Mouton aux Onions.

CUT a Leg of Mutton in large Stakes, pretty thick, also several Onions sliced; garnish a Stew-pan with Slices of Lard, upon this the Onions, then the Meat with Pepper and Salt; and continue in the same Manner till you have done; cover the Pan very close, and let it stew slowly, as you would à la Mode Beef; when done skim the Sauce, add a little Cullis.

Poitrine de Mouton de Plusieurs Façons.

Breast of Mutton different Ways.

BREAST of Mutton cut in Pieces, and brazed may be used with all Sorts of Roots or Greens, as Hus-pot, or boiled whole; then broil with sweet Herbs, Seasoning, and serve with a sharp Sauce.

Epaule de Mouton à l'Eau; Water.

Shoulder of Mutton.

PUT a Shoulder of Mutton in a Stew-pan with Broth, a Nosegay of sweet Herbs, two Cloves, Thyme and Laurel, boil slowly; when done, skim and sift the Sauce; reduce it to a Glaze with which you bathe the Shoulder, add two Spoonfuls of Broth in the same Pan, to gather the Remainder of the Glaze; and serve with the Meat.

Epaule de Mouton à la Parme.
Shoulder of Mutton Parma Fashion.

BRAZE a Shoulder of Mutton, and boil some Rice in good fat Broth; when very tender, lay some of the Rice in the Bottom of the Dish, pretty thick, then the Shoulder upon it; mix some dried Currants with the remaining Rice, and cover the Shoulder over with it, then rasped Parmesan Cheese; put it half an Hour in the Oven to take Colour, and serve with a good clear Sauce.

Epaule de Mouton au Four.
Shoulder of Mutton baked in the Oven.

LARD a Shoulder of Mutton seasoned with Pepper and Salt, and sweet Herbs; put it in a Pan of its Bigness, with two sliced Onions, two Cloves, Thyme, Laurel, a little Basil, two Spoonfuls of Water or Broth; when done in the Oven, sift the Sauce, and serve with the Shoulder.

Epaule de Mouton à la Sainte Menehoutt.
Shoulder of Mutton broiled.

LARD or not a Shoulder of Mutton, braze it tender with a good Seasoning, take it out when done; throw Bread Crums over it with chopt sweet Herbs, basting while it broils with little of the Braze Sauce; serve with Cullis, and Verjuice or Vinegar.

Saucissons d'Epaule de Mouton.
Sausages or Colour'd Shoulder.

TAKE up the Skin, and bone the Meat, which cut small with pickled Pork, Ham, a fresh Tongue;

mix

mix all together seasoned with fine Spices, then roll it in the Skin, and truss it into a Bullock's Gut, or tie it with a Roller, boil for about half an Hour, half a Handful of Salt, three Pints of Water, an Ounce of Saltpetre, two Cloves of Garlick, four of Spices, half a Dozen Shallots, Thyme, Laurel, a Sprig of Fennel, half a Handful of Juniper Berries; sift it, and add a Glass of Brandy; let the Meat soak in this two Days, take care to boil it in this Marinade about a Quarter of an Hour, Morning and Evening; then boil it in a Pan much of its Bigness, in Broth and white Wine, Roots and Onions; when done, let it cool in the same Pan; serve cold upon a Napkin or sliced.

Epaule de Mouton à la Bonne Femme.

The good House-wife.

ROAST a Shoulder of Mutton, then mince the under Part without cutting the Skin; put the minced Meat in a Stew-pan, with a little Broth or Cullis, chopt Parsley, Shallots, Mushrooms, Pepper and Salt, bathe the Skin with Butter or Lard, and Bread Crums; and broil it, or colour it in the Oven; serve upon the hashed, also the Blade Bone broiled.

Epaule de Mouton en Timbale.

See Timbale à la Romaine, Page 117.

THIS is prepared with Forced-meat, as the other in Veal Articles; only using the Skin of the Shoulder of Mutton, to wrap it in, tied and brazed.

Epaule de Mouton au Sang, viz. Blood.

TAKE a tender Shoulder of Mutton, make an Incision between Flesh and Skin, into which you stuff Pork Blood with Flee, prepared as you do for Black Pud-

Puddings; adding a little chopt Parsley, Shallots, Pepper and Salt; sew it up, and roast it, covered over with Slices of Lard wrapt in Paper; serve with Sauce au Porc Frais, which you will find, Page 44.

Selle de Mouton à la Sainte Menehoult.

Saddle or Loin of Mutton broiled.

IT is done the same Way as the Shoulder, and it may equally be used like the Neck for Stakes or Harricot.

Selle de Mouton en Canapé, Matted.

TAKE up the Skin of a Saddle of Mutton, scarify the Meat, and in it stick sliced fat Livers, Truffles, fresh Pork, Slices of Onions, Anchovies; cover this all over with a good Forced-meat, made of rasped Lard, Suet or Marrow, Nutmeg, sweet Herbs, Mushrooms, Spices, three Yolks of Eggs, all pounded together; cover it over with the Skin well fastened, braze it (the Skin undermost) with Broth, a Nosegay of sweet Herbs; when done, reduce the Sauce to a Caramel, viz. Glaze; glaze all the upper Side, and serve with Sauce Espagnole, or which you think proper.

Rôt de Bif de Mouton.

WHAT the French call Rôt de Bif de Mouton, is the two hind Quarters cut off together at the first Rib; the Ends of the Legs trussed in each other; it is a large Dish which may be plain roasted, larded or brazed, and served with any Sauce, or stewed Greens or Roots, &c. &c.

Rôt de Bif Glassé, Glazed.

Rôt de Bif à la Garone.

THIS is done with a Stuffing, wherein they put a good deal of Garlick; others call it Gigot à l'Ail, viz. Garlick.

Gigot de Mouton au Chou-Fleur.

Leg of Mutton and Colliflower.

Gigot de Mouton au Vin de Champagne.

SOME of the Meat cut off to mix as Forced-meat, and stuffed into it again; brazed as all other Pieces, adding a Glass of white Wine to the Sauce.

Gigot de Mouton en Filets Farcis.

THIS is done much after the same Manner as the former, only boned all to the End; the Meat made into Forced-meat, tied up in the Skin and roasted or brazed; serve with any Sauce.

Grenadins de Mouton.

Small Fricandeau of Mutton.

THEY are larded and brazed the same as the Veal, and served upon stewed Greens or with Sauce.

Gigot de Mouton à la Mode.

LARD a Leg of Mutton through and through with large Pieces rolled in chopt sweet Herbs, and fine Spices; braze it in a Pan of the same Bigness, with Slices of Lard, Onions and Roots; stop the Steam very close;

when

when done, add a Glass of white Wine, sift the Sauce, to serve with it.

Gigot de Mouton à la Houlan.

IT is done as the former, only adding Brandy instead of Wine.

Gigot de Mouton à la Gascogne.

IT is larded with Garlick scalded, and Anchovies, then roasted.

Gigot de Mouton à l'Italienne.

IT is larded and brazed, served with a Sauce à l'Italienne, see Sauces.

Gigot de Mouton à l'Eau.

SEE Shoulder ditto, it is the same Contradiction, as it is to be glazed the same; but one may call a plain boiled Leg of Mutton, a Gigot à l'Eau, viz. Water.

Gigot de Mouton à l'Espagnole.

Leg of Mutton Spanish Fashion.

BONE it all to the End, then lard through and through with large Pieces, seasoned with Salt and fine Spices; put in a Braze-pan with about a Dozen middling Onions, a Pint of Spanish Wine; cover it with Paper, and put in the Oven; when half done turn it, and put half a Dozen large short Sausages in the Pan, finish baking, turn it over in the Dish; garnish with the Onions, skim and sift the Sauce; squeeze two China Oranges in it, and serve.

Mortadelles de Mouton.

MORTADELLES are a kind of large Saufages, which may be done with any Sort of Meat; it is called by the Kind of Meat ufed, and fmoaked as the German Saufages.

Gigot de Mouton en Venaifon.

LARD it with fine Lard, make a Marinade with half a Pint of Vinegar, a Pint of red Wine, Pepper and Salt, Thyme, Laurel, Cloves, Nutmegs, pounded Coriander, few Slices of peeled Lemon, few Slices of Onions; warm all together, foak the Mutton in it about twelve Hours, then roaft it, ferve with a Poivrade in a Boat; See Sauces, Page 43.

Gigot de Mouton à la Servante; Maid.

LEG of Mutton plain boiled, and ferved with Caper Sauce, or ftewed Turnips, or plain boiled.

Gigot de Mouton à la Modêne.

BONE a Leg of Mutton all-to the End, which you leave very fhort; boil it to three Parts in Water or Broth, then take it out, and cut the upper Part crofsways; into which you ftuff fweet Herbs chopt, feafoned with Pepper and Salt, and few Spices mixt with Butter and Bread Crums; then put in a Stew-pan, with few Spoonfuls of the Broth, a Glafs of white Wine; finifh it, add the Juice of a Seville Orange to the Sauce.

Gigot de Mouton au Militaire.

THIS is in the Nature of à la Mode Beef cut in Pieces, and larded with large Pieces, feafoned

with

with proper Spices, to keep and carry about, as Military Gentleman are often forced to do, which I presume is the reason of its being called au Militaire.

Gigot de Mouton aux Légumes.

PLAIN boiled and served with all Sorts of Roots, either stewed or boiled with the Meat.

Gigot de Mouton au Bacha.

TAKE up the Skin to the End, and lard the Meat all over with scalded Sellery, Taragon, few Anchovies, pickled Cucumbers, Lard and Ham, seasoned with few Spices; fasten the Skin over this, marinade in a little Oil, paper it over to roast; serve with a Sauce Piquante, as you will find in Page 45.

Gigot de Mouton à la St. Geran.

THIS is done in the same Nature as the Shoulder (en Timbale) see Page 137: and Timbale, 117; Veal Articles.

Gigot de Mouton en Salade.

THIS is larded, brazed and kept cold, then garnished over with all Sorts of Herbs fit for Sallet, according to Fancy: and dressed like a Sallet in the Nature of Salmongundy.

CHAPITRE

CHAPITRE QUATRIEME. Du Cochon.

CHAPTER FOURTH. Of Hogs and Pigs.

De la Connoissance & Dissection du Cochon.

How to chuse Hogs Meat, and to cut it up.

HOG's Meat ought to be hard and of a fine blooming Colour, without any bad Smell, occasioned by Heat; that which is soft and pale red is not good; it is easy to know it by small white Spots, which appear in the Flesh: Pigs of six or eight Months are good to make pickled Pork, and to roast; those of a Year or fifteen Months old are better to make Bacon; suckling Pigs should be about three Weeks old, and are to be taken from the Suck for Use; all that is employed for Sausages and Puddings, ought to be used directly, the Guts particularly, as by keeping they are apt to heat, and to burst: the Dissection of the Urne is to be cut close to the Ears quite through, the Neck serves for Haslets; the Ham is always to be cut in thin Slices, mixing Fat and Lean; the wild Boar is cut the same Way as the Hog, and the *Marcassin* (suckling wild Boar) is dressed the same as the suckling Pig.

As it is not the Business of a Cook to cut up Hogs, I shall pass over any further Directions; as every Country has different Ways of cutting up all Sorts of Animals.

Cochon

Cochon de Lait Rôti.

Suckling Pig Roasted.

STICK the Pig in the Throat, as deep as the Heart, that it may bleed well and die sooner, as it makes it easier to scald; when the Water is pretty warm, put the Pig in it, holding it by the hind Legs, when you find the Bristles coming off the Tail by rubbing, take it out and rub it with a little Rosin, then hard with the Hand; when it is well scalded wash it clean, and cut it open while warm: take all out except the Kidneys, truss it with three Skewers, one in the hind Legs, one in the fore, and one in the middle; put in it a Nosegay of Parsley, Shallots, Thyme, Laurel, with Pepper and Salt; wipe it very dry before spitting: cut the Skin a little near the Neck, as much upon the Rump, to hinder it from breaking in the roasting; when it begins to be warm, rub it all over pretty often with Oil, which will make the Skin very crisp; take out the Nosegay when you serve.

Cochon de Lait en Galantine.

Coloured Pig.

AFTER having scalded the Pig as the former, cut off the Head and Feet, and bone it without cutting the Skin, cut some of the Flesh to chop with Beef Suet, Bread Crums, Cream, Salt, fine Spices, five or six Yolks of Eggs, Parsley, Mushrooms, Ham, Bacon, and some of the Pig's Flesh, Truffles, Pistachio Nuts, all chopt together, and well mixt with few sweet Almonds and hard Yolks of Eggs; lay a Down of the Forced-meat, then thin Slices of Ham, and Slices of the Pig's Flesh, so continue till all is used; roll it up in the Skin, and tie it very tight in a Stamine or Roller, with Slices of Lard round it;

boil

boil it in Broth, a Pint of white Wine, a Nosegay of sweet Herbs, two or three Cloves, Thyme, Bay-Leaf; boil on a slow Fire, let it cool in the Braze; serve cold, whole or sliced.

Cochon de Lait au Moine Blanc.

Pig white Monks Fashion.

BONE the Pig thoroughly, except the Head and Feet, take care not to cut the Skin; make a Farce (viz. Forced-meat, I shall use the Word hereafter in common) with Fillet of Veal, Beef, Suet, Bread Crums, and Cream, chopt Parsley, Shallots, Mushrooms, Salt, and fine Spices, mixed with six Yolks of raw Eggs; cut Dices of Ham and Bacon, to mix with the Farce; stuff the Pig with this as if it was whole, tie it well, and cover the Back with thin Slices of Lard, and tie it in a Napkin to boil in Broth and a Pint of white Wine, a Nosegay of Parsley, green Shallots, one Clove of Garlick, two of Spices, Thyme and Laurel, sliced Onions, Carrots and other Roots, Pepper and Salt; when done, if you propose to serve it hot, wipe it clean, and serve with what Sauce you please; if for cold, let it cool in the Braze, then take off the Napkin, and lard; scrape the Fat gently, and serve upon a Napkin with green Parsley round it.

Cochon de Lait au Pere Douillet; (meaning Tender, Delicate, Fribbling, &c. speaking personally.)

Pig in Jelly.

TRUSS a Pig as for roasting, and put it in a Brazepan much of its Length, with Slices of Veal and Beef, four Calve's Feet cut in Pieces, a small Knuckle of Veal, a little Ham, a large Nosegay of Parsley, Shallots, two Cloves of Garlick, a Bay Leaf, Thyme, four Cloves, a Bit of Nutmeg, whole Pepper, a little Salt;

Salt; cover it over with Slices of Lard; boil with a Bottle of white Wine, twice as much Broth; let it boil about an Hour, the Pan well ſtopped; take care it does not boil too faſt as it would crack; when done take it out gently, and put all the reſt in a ſmaller Pan to ſimmer; clean the Brazing-pan, and garniſh the Bottom with fine green Parſley, ſcalded Craw-fiſh, laid in a pretty Manner, then the Pig upon this, Back undermoſt; then ſift the Broth, well ſkimmed; and add Slices of peeled Lemon, the Whites of eight Eggs beat up with the Shells, and boil it till it is quite clear, and ſtrong enough for a Jelly; ſtrain it in a Napkin, and pour it upon the Pig; it ſhould be covered over with it; let it cool; when ready to uſe it, dip the Braze-pan in warm Water, to turn it over upon a Napkin.

Roulades de Cochon de Lait.

Large Olives.

CUT the Head and Feet off, cut the Pig in Quarters, and bone it quite, and put upon each a Farce made of raſped Lard and Bread Crums, three Yolks of Eggs, chopt Parſley, Shallots, Muſhrooms, Pepper and Salt, roll them round, tie them with Packthread, and braze in Broth and a little white Wine; when done, ſkim and ſift the Sauce; add a little Cullis and a Lemon Squeeze, when ready to ſerve.

Cochon de Lait à la Bechamel.

Pig Bechamel Sauce.

TAKE the Remainder of a roaſted Pig, cut in ſmall Pieces, and dreſs it with Bechamel Sauce, as you will find in Sauce Articles; you may alſo ſerve it as a Blanquette, made with Butter, chopt Muſhrooms, a Noſegay of Parſley, Thyme, Shallots, two Cloves,

half

half a Bay Leaf; simmer it some time, then add a Spoonful of Flour, Broth, Pepper and Salt; reduce the Sauce, take out the Nosegay, then put the Fillets in it, making a Liason with two Yolks of Eggs, a little Cream; serve without boiling.

Paupiettes de Cochon de Lait.

Olives of Suckling Pig.

WHEN well boned as the former for Roulades, take part of the Flesh which you chop with Suet, Bread Crums, and Cream; pound all together, and add a Spoonful of Brandy, chopped Parsley and Shallots, Mushrooms, Pepper and Salt; mix with six Yolks of Eggs; roll this Farce in the Skin, cut in small Pieces; and braze in Broth a Glass of white Wine, a few Slices of peeled Lemon; and serve with what Sauce you think proper.

Cochon de Lait en Timbale.

Suckling Pig in Mould.

CUT off the Head and Feet, and bone the rest; cut all the Meat without cutting the Skin, chop the Meat with Truffles, Ham and Bacon; marinade this together in Oil, Pepper and Salt, Parsley, Shallots, finely chopped; put the Skin in a small Stew-pan, and put the Farce in it with all the Seasoning, fasten the Skin round, and cover it over with Slices of Lard; boil in Broth and a Pint of white Wine, Slices of Onions and Roots, a Nosegay of Parsley, Shallots, one Clove of Garlick, three of Spices, Thyme and Laurel; when done, serve with Sauce *Espagnole*, which you will find in Sauce Articles: if you would have it for a cold Dish, season it a little more, and let it cool in the Braze to serve upon a Napkin.

Hure de Cochon en Sanglier.

Hog's Head as Wild Boar.

THE Head cut close to the Shoulder, bone the Neck Part, cut off the Chops, part the Flesh of the Nose as far as the Eyes, cut the Bone off, lard the Inside with Bacon, seasoned with Pepper and Salt, and fine Spices; rub it all over with coarse Salt, half an Ounce of pounded Saltpetre; put it in a Pickle-pan, with half a Handful of Juniper Berries, Thyme, Laurel, Basil, Cloves, half a Handful of Coriander; cover it and let it remain so about eight Days, then tie it well, and wipe it dry; boil it with three Pints of red Wine and Water, Onions, Carrots, a large Nosegay of sweet Herbs, two Cloves of Garlick, six Cloves, half a Nutmeg, Thyme and Laurel, two Pound of Hog's Lard: taste the Braze, when about half done, and add Salt if necessary; when it gives under the Finger it is done; let it cool in the Braze, serve cold: you may garnish it with Bay Leaves, according to Fancy.

Ballon de Cochon.

Made round, the Form of a Foot-ball.

TAKE a Hog's Head, cut off as the former, bone it thoroughly; cut most of the Meat, leaving but little upon the Skin, chop the Meat, season it with Pepper and Salt, fine Spices, chopped Shallots, Parsley; divide the lean Meat from the fat; chop also a Tongue and some Ham, Truffles, Pistachio-Nuts, mix this last together; put the Skin in a large round Stew-pan, then lay a Down of the first Meat prepared, then a Down of Fat again the first and second, then the Tongue; so continue intermixing until it is full; if the Head don't furnish Fat enough, you use fresh Lard instead:

take

take care to put a little Seasoning every Down you lay, fasten it well, and tie it up in a Cloth; boil it with a Bottle of white Wine, a large Nosegay of sweet Herbs, Roots and Spices as the *Hure*; simmer it about eight Hours, let it cool to half in its own Braze, then you may give it what Form you please; lay a Weight upon it to squeeze the Fat out of it, and serve whole or sliced.

Usage du Sang de Cochon & autres.

The Use of Hog's Blood and others.

HOG's Blood is preferable to Calve's and Lamb's, although all serve for the same Use; it is used by itself, and for black Puddings, as it will be explained hereafter; poor People may use it with very little Expence, in boiling sliced Onions, and mixing them with the Blood for a Fry.

Petit Salé.

Pickled Pork.

THE best for Pickling are of about seven or eight Months old, cut the Pieces to what Bigness you please; for fifteen Pound of Meat, a Pound of pounded Salt, rub it well all over; lay the Pieces very close together; it is fit for Use in about a Week: it is very good to boil with all Sorts of Porridge, but for this Purpose, it should be pretty fresh made, as it will give a better Taste.

Echinée à la Poivrade.

Chine of Pork Poivrade Sauce.

SALT it about three Days; then roast it, and serve with it Sauce Poivrade, as you will find in Sauce Articles, Page 43.

Le Lard, comment le Faire.

How to make Bacon for Kitchen Use.

LEAVE as little Lean as possible, upon ten Pound of Meat, use a Pound of pounded Salt, rubbing it very well all over; put the Pieces upon one another, upon Boards in the Cellar, and a Board over it with Weights, leave it so about a Month, then hang it up to dry, the hardest is the best mostly for larding; it is not to be smoked.

Queuës de Cochon de Plusieurs Façons.

Pig's Tails of different Fashions.

BOIL the Tails in Broth, a Clove of Garlick, Pepper, Salt, Laurel and Thyme; when done very tender, serve with what Sauce you please; or broiled, with Sauce Remoulade in a Sauce Boat; also with stewed Cabbages or others.

Pieds de Cochon à la St. Menehoult.

Pig's Feet Brazed and Broiled.

CLEAN the Feet very well, and cut them in two; put a thin Slice of Lard between, and tie the two Pieces together; then simmer them eight Hours with two Glasses of white Wine, one of Brandy, some Hogs Lard, and fine Spices, a Nosegay of Parsley, Shallots, a Clove of Garlick, two of Spices, Thyme and Laurel; when done let them cool in the Braze, untie them, and baste with the Fat of it, and Bread Crums; broil of a fine Colour; serve with or without Sauce.

Oreilles & Panache de Cochon de plusieurs Façons.

Pig's Ears of different Fashions.

RUB them with Salt for three or four Days, a little every Day, and few Laurel Leaves, Thyme, Basil, few pounded Cloves; then boil them in Water alone, or with green or dried Peas; make a *Purée* of the Peas, to serve upon the Ears, or serve them with Sauce Robert: also cut in Fillets called (en Menus droits) either brown Sauce or white Fricassee, broiled or fried.

Boudins de Cochon.

Black Puddings.

TO one Pint of Blood, put two Pound of Lard, half a Pint of Cream, Salt, and fine Spices; boil before half a Dozen of large Onions in fat Broth, with a Nosegay of Parsley, Shallots, Thyme, Laurel, Basil, Pepper and Salt, half a Handful of Coriander tied in a Linnen Cloth; when the Onions are very tender, chop them very fine and mix with the Blood, and fill the Guts not too full; when well tied put them in boiling Water: you will know when they are done with a Pin, if the Fat comes out instead of the Blood.

Boudins de Saint Germain, (a Town near Paris.)

CUT several Onions in Dices, boil them quite tender in the Quantity of Hog's Lard you propose to mix with the Blood; when thoroughly done, let it cool, then mix with the Blood; season it with Salt and fine Spices, and finish as the former.

Boudins Fins.

Fine, delicate, better than the former.

CHOP eight or ten Onions very fine, put them in a Stew-pan, with a Quarter of a Pound of Lard; simmer slowly till they are quite done; take it off the Fire, add half a Pint of Cream, a Pint of Hog's Blood, six Yolks of raw Eggs, two Pound of Lard cut in small Dices, fine Salt and fine Spices, mix it all together very well, and finish as all former Directions.

Boudins Blancs.

White Puddings.

BOIL a Dozen of Onions in fat Broth, with a Nosegay of Parsley, Chibbol, two Shallots, three Cloves, Thyme, Basil, a little Coriander tied in a Bag, Salt and Pepper; boil them till no Liquor remains, mash them very fine, and boil a Handful of Bread Crums in a Pint of Milk, until it becomes to the Consistence of a soft Paste, and mix it with the Onions; pound a Quarter of a Pound of sweet Almonds, and sift them in a Stamine with half a Pint of warm Cream; add eight Yolks of raw Eggs, half a Pound of Lard, cut in small Dices, Breasts of roasted Poultries chopped very fine, Salt and fine Spices; mix it all together, and boil as the former: they require but a short Time, and ought to be pricked with a Pin to hinder them from bursting, they will be the better for being boiled in Milk.

Boudins Blancs Communs.

Common White Puddings.

BOIL Onions as the preceding, according to what Quantity you please; chop them very fine, and mix them with Bread Crums soaked in Cream, and sifted in a Sieve; add half a Pound of Lard cut small, eight raw Yolks of Eggs, Salt and Spices; mix it very well, and boil in boiling Water.

Boudins de Foyes de Merlans.

Puddings of Whitings Livers.

HAVE about two Dozens of Whitings Livers according to their Bigness; wash them very clean, and cut small; give them a fry in Hog's Lard, then let them cool; boil a Couple of sliced Onions in three half Pints of Cream, with one chopped Shallot, Parsley, half a Laurel Leaf, a little Basil; boil until the Cream is reduced to half, then sift it in a Sieve, and add eight or ten Yolks of Eggs, half a Pound of Flee cut in Dices, and the Livers as fried, Salt and fine Spices; don't fill the Guts too much for fear they should burst; boil in boiling Water about a Quarter of an Hour; broil them in Paper Cases as white Puddings.

Boudins de Foyes Gras.

Puddings of Fat Livers.

TO make eight Links of Puddings, take eight fat Livers, which you chop very fine; boil six Onions in fat Broth, a Nosegay of Parsley, Chibbol, half a Clove of Garlick, two of Spices, Thyme, Laurel, Basil, a little Coriander, tied up in a Bag; when thoroughly done, take out the Nosegay, and chop the Onions very fine; add half a Pound of the Lard cut in Dices, half a Pint of Cream, three half Pints of Hog's Blood, Salt and fine Spices, mix it all together, put it over the Fire, just to warm it, stirring it continually for fear the Blood should stick to the Bottom; when it comes to a proper Consistence, finish as all former Directions.

Boudins d'Ecrevisses.
Craw-fish Puddings.

BOIL half a Hundred of Craw-fish, about a Quarter of an Hour, then pick the Tails, which you cut in small Dices, and pound the Shells and Spawns; then simmer them in Butter for about an Hour, then strain them in a Stamine, as to make Craw-fish Butter; boil the Tails and White of Fowl roasted, finely chopped, Bread Crums soaked in Cream, eight raw Yolks of Eggs, few Onions roasted, two fat Livers cut small, half a Pound of Flee cut small, the Craw-fish Butter; add two or three Spoonfuls of good Cullis, Salt, and fine Spices; finish as the fat Liver Puddings.

Boudins de Faisand.
Of Pheasant.

MINCE the Meat of a roasted Pheasant very fine, and chop the Bones very small, and soak them about three Hours in a Pint of Cream; boil half a Dozen of Onions in fat Broth, a Nosegay of Parsley, green Shallots, one Clove of Garlick, two Cloves, Thyme, Laurel, Pepper and Salt; let it boil till the Liquid is quite reduced to a thick Consistence: chop the Onions very fine, and mix them with the Meat, Bread Crums soaked in Cream, sifted; and the Cream wherein you soaked the Bones; add eight Yolks of raw Eggs, three Quarters of a Pound of Lard cut small, Salt, and fine Spices; when well mixed, finish as all former.

Boudins de Lapins.
Of Rabbits.

ROAST a good large Rabbit, or two small ones to three Parts roasted, then chop all the Meat very fine with the

the Liver, and soak the Bones as the last, finish them as the above; Puddings may be made of all Sorts of Poultries or Game.

Cervelats Fumés.

Large Sausages smoaked.

ACCORDING to the Quantity desired, chop fresh Pork, as for common Sausages; season it with fine Spices, and use the largest Guts; fill them very full, and hang them in the Chimney, about three Days, or more if you please; boil them in Broth, a little Salt, Parsley, Shallots, a Clove of Garlick, Thyme, Laurel; let them boil slowly about three Hours, and serve cold.

N. B. Wood Fire is best for all smoaked Meat, and all Sorts of Cervelats are best that come from Germany; they are made equally of all Sorts of Meat, much in the same Manner, as what the French call Mortadelles, and what are commonly called in England Bologna Sausages or Methworth.

Cervelats de Plusieurs Façons.

Of different Sorts.

IF you would have them with Truffles, observe the same Method as the former, only adding chopped Truffles, first fried in Lard, Shallots or Onions, the same; mix it well all together, and finish as the preceding.

Saucisses de Cochon.

Common Pork Sausages.

TAKE fresh Hog's Meat, more fat than lean, chop it well together, season with Salt and fine Spices; do not fill the Guts too full; broil on a slow Fire.

Saucisses

Saucisses en Crepinettes.

In Cowl.

IT is the same Sort of Meat, wrapped in Veal Cowl, which you do to what Bigness you please, and broil slowly; it is equally good, and takes less Time in doing.

Saucisses de Veau en Crepinettes.

Of Veal Meat.

TAKE of Fillet of Veal, according to what Quantity of Sausages you would make; chop it very fine, as much Beef Marrow cut in small Dices, which you mix very well with the Veal, seasoned according to Taste; and broil in Cowl as the above, either Veal or Pork Cowl.

Saucisses aux Trufes.

With Truffles.

IT is the same Preparation as the two former, either Pork or Veal, only mixing chopped Truffles with it.

Saucisses de Plusieurs Façons.

Of different Sorts.

OF whatever Taste you would make your Sausages, always have full as much, or more fat than lean Meat; if you would give them the Taste of Garlick, scald them some Time before you chop them to mix, Parsley the same, and Onions must be fried almost quite done before mixing, and take care, that neither gives too much Flavour.

Saucisses de Champagne.

With Champaign Wine.

CHOP lean Pork Meat rather coarsly, cut the Fat in Dices, seasoned with Salt and fine Spices; then add a Pint of Champaign Wine, mix it well with it, and let it marinade about ten or twelve Hours; then drain the Wine, and make your Sausages, as all former; hang them in the Chimney for two Days, and boil as all others.

Timbale de Boudin.

A Mould so called, filled with black Pudding Preparation.

SLICE seven or eight middling Onions, and fry them in Lard over a slow Fire, until they are quite done; then take them off the Fire, and add chopped Shallots, Parsley, Salt, and fine Spices, eight raw Yolks of Eggs, a Pound of the Flee, three half Pints of Hog's Blood; mix it well all together; garnish the Bottom of your Mould, or Stew-pan with thin Slices of Bacon, upon this a Bit of Cowl, as large as the Pan; fasten it at Top and bake in the Oven of a middling Heat; when you judge it to be done enough, turn it over gently upon the Dish; take off the Bacon, wipe the Fat, and pour over it a Cullis Sauce, with Pepper and Salt.

Saucisses à la Mariniere.

Sailor Fashion.

FRY a Dozen of small Onions in Butter, with a Nosegay of Parsley, Shallots, a Clove of Garlick, Thyme, Laurel, Basil, two Cloves; simmer slowly until the Onions are done, then take out the Nosegay, put

a

a little Flour and a Pint of red Wine; make it boil, and put in it what Quantity of Sausages you please; reduce to the Consistence of a Sauce; a little before serving, skim the Fat clean off, add a pounded Anchovy, few small Capers, a Drop of Vinegar; garnish the Dish with fried Bread.

Saucisses à la Saint Cloud; (St. Cloud, a Place near Paris.)

PUT as many Sausages in a Stew-pan as you think proper, with two Glasses of white Wine, one or two Spoonfuls of Oil, simmer them slowly; when done, drain the Sausages, skim the Fat, add a little Cullis; reduce to the Consistence of a Sauce, and serve upon the Sausages.

Saucisses à la Sainte Menehoult.

Sausages Broiled.

FRY half a Dozen of Onions, sliced in Butter; when done let them cool, and add two chopt Anchovies, Pepper, a little pounded Anniseed, rasped Lard; mix it well together to make a Farce; boil the Sausages about a Quarter of an Hour, with a Glass of white Wine and Broth, then peel the Guts off, and garnish them round with the Forced-meat, and tie them up in Bits of Cowl; dip them in melted Butter, and stew with Bread Crums; put them in the Oven for about half an Hour to take a good Colour, and Time to bake the Cowl: serve upon a Cullis Sauce with a Lemon Squeeze.

Saucisses aux Fines Herbes.

With Sweet Herbs.

GARNISH a Stew-pan with few Slices of Fillet of Veal and Ham, soak it about half an Hour, then put your Sausages in it with two Cloves of Garlick, a Nosegay of Parsley, green Shallots, a little Sprig of Fennel, Thyme, Laurel, two Cloves, chopt Mushrooms and Shallots; add a Glass of white Wine, boil on a slow Fire about half an Hour, take out the Garlick and Nosegay; add a little Cullis, skim the Fat very clean, sift the Sauce in a Sieve, season it with Pepper and Salt; add a Lemon Squeeze, and serve upon the Sausages.

Saucisses au Gratin.

Gratin, catching at Bottom.

BOIL short thick Sausages in a little white Wine, two Cloves, Thyme, Laurel, one Onion sliced, one Clove of Garlick; when done, peel the Guts off, and dip them in Butter mixed with Mustard, then roll them in rasped Parmesan Cheese; have as many Bits of fried Bread, as Sausages, and as long; garnish the Bottom of the Dish you intend to serve upon, with a little Cullis and Bread Crums; put it on Ashes Fire, and mix a little Parmesan with it, then lay a Bit of the fried Bread and a Sausage, and so on till you have done; leave it on the Fire untill it forms a Gratin; colour the Top of the Sausages with the Salamander, and serve upon, a good clear Cullis for Sauce.

Saucisses en Ragout ou Purée.

Sausages as Ragout or with any Sorts of Porridge.

PORK and Veal Sausages may be dressed in many different Ways, being boiled with a Glass of Wine and Broth, a Nosegay of sweet Herbs; you may serve them with what Sauce you think proper, or with stewed Turneps, Cabbages, any other Sorts of Garden Greens; also with Peas Porridge, Lentils; also brazed with Truffles; for the last, put a Glass of white Wine in a small Brazing-pan, then sliced Truffles, then Sausages, and so on: then cover it over with thin Slices of Lard, stop the Pan very close, and simmer on a very slow Fire; when done, add a little Cullis and Consumée, give it a boil to skim the Fat; and serve upon the Sausages and Truffles.

Andouilles de Cochon.

Chitterlings or large Sausages.

ACCORDING to the Length and Bigness you would have them, cut the large Guts in proportion, and when they are very clean, marinade them five or six Hours in a Glass of white Wine, two Cloves of Garlick, Thyme, Laurel, Basil; then cut fresh Pork in Fillets, and of the Flee and fat Gut the same; mix all together, season with a little pounded Anniseed, Salt, and fine Spices, then fill the Guts not too full, for fear they should burst; when well tied at both Ends, put in a Vessel just of their Length; and boil them with half Water and Milk, Salt and Pepper, a Nosegay of Parsley, green Shallots, a Clove of Garlick, three Spice Cloves, Thyme, Laurel, Basil, a little of the Lard; when done, let them cool in their Broth, wipe them well before you broil them; you may also hang them to smoak, they will keep a long Time.

Andouilles

Andouilles de Bœuf.

Beef Chitterlings.

TAKE Beef's Guts well cleaned as the former, and soak them in the same Manner; cut in Fillets, Beef Palates and Tripes, both first boiled to three Parts; also cut in small Pieces, Cow's Udder and pickled Pork; mix all this together, adding sliced Onions, first fried in Lard or Butter, three or four raw Yolks of Eggs, Salt, and fine Spices; then fill the Guts, and boil them in fat Broth, half a Pint of white Wine, a Nosegay as the former, Thyme, Laurel, Basil, sliced Carrots and Parsneps; let them cool in their Liquor; broil them about half an Hour: instead of the Beef's Palates, you may use the Tongue.

Andouilles de Veau.

Chitterlings of Veal.

SCALD a Calve's Caldron and Udder about a Quarter of an Hour, cut it in Fillets with a Pound of pickled Pork; mix it together, and add few chopt Shallots, Salt and fine Spices, three or four Spoonfuls of good Cream, four Yolks of Eggs; finish those as all former.

Andouilles de Rouen, (Rouen a Town in France.)

TAKE Calve's Caldron or Lamb's, cut in small Pieces, and Pork Flee cut equally; season it with a little pounded Anniseed, Salt and fine Spices; boil them in Milk and fat Broth, with a Nosegay of sweet Herbs, few sliced Onions, let them cool in the Liquor of their boiling.

Andouilles à l'Angloise.

English Fashion.

FRY sliced Onions in Butter till they are half done, cut Calve's Ears first boiled, and Lamb's Caldron in small Bits; also some pickled Pork, and fresh Pork Flee and Breast of Fowl; mix all together with the Onions, a few chopped Shallots, a little Parsley, Salt and fine Spices; boil them in fat Broth, half a Pint of white Wine, Thyme, Laurel, Basil, Salt, a Nosegay; finish as all former.

Andouilles de Gibier.

Chitterlings made of Game.

TAKE all the Flesh of a good kept Rabbit, a Calve's Caldron, Pork's Flee, sliced Onions, half fried in Lard or Butter; mix all together, add Salt and fine Spices, chopped Shallots, Nutmeg, Powder of Basil, finish them as all the rest; when you want to use them, dip them in the Fat of their Boiling, to roll them in Bread Crums to broil; you may make the same with any Sorts of Game.

Andouilles à la Béchamel.

White Chitterlings.

SOAK a Slice of Ham over a slow Fire, about a Quarter of an Hour, with a Clove of Garlick, Parsley, green Shallots, Thyme, Bay Leaf, Basil, a Bit of Butter; add half a Pint of Milk; reduce it by boiling to half, then sift it in a Sieve, and put to it a Handful of Bread Crums; simmer it till it becomes quite thick; cut a Calve's Caldron in small Fillets, a Piece of fresh Pork, and some of the Lard, six Yolks of raw Eggs, Salt and fine Spices; boil them in half Milk and Water, a Nosegay, Salt and Pepper; and dress them as all others.

Andouilles de Poisson.

Of Fish.

TAKE Eel's Skin instead of Guts, use what Sorts of Fish you please; cut off all the Flesh, pound the Bones, which you boil in red Wine, two sliced Onions, a Clove of Garlick, Parsley, green Shallots, Thyme, Laurel; boil until it is reduced to half, sift it in a Sieve, and mix the Fish-meat with it, cut in Dices, add six or eight Yolks of raw Eggs, Salt and Spices; cut the Skin the length of five or six Inches, and fill them as other; boil them in Broth and red Wine, a Nosegay of sweet Herbs, Salt and Pepper: let them cool in their Liquor; and serve broiled.

Andouilles à la Flamande.

Flemish Fashion.

TAKE Chitterlings of Veal or Pork, boil them with Savoys cut in Quarters, first scalded and tied; boil all together in good Broth, a Nosegay of Parsley, green Shallots, a Clove of Garlick, Thyme and Laurel, two Cloves, a little Nutmeg, Pepper and Salt; when done, drain the Chitterlings and Cabbages; put them upon the Dish you intend to use, and serve upon it a good Cullis Sauce, rather thick.

Andouillettes de Veau au Parmesan.

Small Chitterlings with Parmesan Cheese.

CHOP some Fillet of Veal coarsly, and as much Hog's Flee cut in Dices, which you mix together;

add chopped Parsley, green Shallots, Pepper and Salt, five Yolks of Eggs, raw; roll up this Forced-meat in thin Slices of Veal, tie them fast with Packthread, and put them in a Stew-pan with thin Slices of Bacon, a Glass of white Wine; when you judge they are done enough, untie them, and sift the Sauce in a Sieve; add a little Cullis to make a Liason, and reduce it till it becomes pretty thick; put half of it in the Dish you intend to use, and rasped Parmesan, then the Chitterlings upon this, and baste them with the Remainder of the Sauce, Parmesan over them; simmer it some Time over a flow Fire, and colour the upper Part with a Salamander or a Brazing-pan Cover: serve with a short Sauce.

Saucissons de Sanglier.

A thick short Sausage made of Wild Boar Meat.

ACCORDING to the Quantity you would make, take the Proportion of one Pound of Meat to half a Pound of Hog's Flee, one Ounce of Salt, Spices in proportion; add a little Saltpetre to redden the Meat, put all together in a Tureen, with a little Muskado Wine; let it marinade about four and twenty Hours, then fill the Guts, and let them soak in a little Wine, with Salt, Shallots, Thyme, Laurel; after some Time soaking hang them in the Chimney, until they are quite dry: when you want to use them, you may braze them about an Hour; most People eat them raw.

N. B. People whose Business is smoaking Meat of any Sorts, know best how to dry those, having proper Places for it.

Saucissons au Brodequin.

Made Square between Boards, racktied.

TAKE four small Boards, a Foot long and three Inches broad, which will serve you to form your Sausages;

Saufages; chop about three Pounds of fresh Pork with a great deal of fat Meat, the Flesh of a long kept Partridge, a Pound of Leg of Mutton, a Pound of Hog's Flee cut in Dices, a Quarter of a Pound of Pistachio-Nuts, half a Pound of Truffles cut in small Bits, five raw Eggs, Salt and fine Spices, mix all well together; put all in a Cowl, which you fasten between the four Boards; boil it with white Wine and Broth, Salt and Pepper, a Nosegay of Sweet Herbs, three Cloves, one of Garlick, green Shallots, Thyme, Laurel, Basil; let it cool in the Liquor, to eat cold.

Façon de faire les Jambons.

How to make Hams.

ACCORDING to the Quantity of Hams you have to make, you make a Brine more or less after this Manner; put in a Tub all Sorts of sweet Herbs, such as Marjorum, Winter Savory, Balm, Thyme, Laurel, Basil, Juniper Berries, a good deal of Salt, and Saltpetre; the liquid half Lees of Wine and half Water: let all those Herbs infuse for two Days, then squeeze them well, and sift the Brine clear, then put your Hams in this to soak about a Fortnight, then drain them, and hang them to dry; to keep them long, rub them some time with Lees of Wine and Vinegar, and throw Ashes over them.

Jambon de Mayence.

Hams Mayence Fashion.

WHEN they are pretty fresh, boil them to half without soaking, then take up the Skin, and roll it in Paper, first butter'd; finish it with roasting, basting now and then with a little Brandy: it will eat very good either hot or cold.

Jambon en Gelée.

Ham in Jelly.

SOAK the Ham to be pretty fresh, and boil it to half in Water, Laurel, Thyme, Basil; when half done put it in a Brazing-pan much of its Bigness, upon Slices of Veal Fillet, and a Knuckle of Veal at Top; boil in two Bottles of white Wine and Broth, two Lemons sliced and peeled, a large Nosegay of Parsley, green Shallots, a Garlick, Cloves, six of Spices, Thyme, Laurel; reduce the Broth until it is fit to make a Jelly, skim it well and sift it; let it cool, and serve with the Ham: this Jelly should be clarified with Whites of Eggs, as most are done, otherwise it will look thick and disagreeable.

Jambon au Naturel.

Ham dressed the common Way.

IF long kept, soak it some Time; if fresh, you need not; pare it round and under, take care no rusty Part is left; tie it up with Packthread, put it in a Brazing-pan much of its Bigness in Water, a Nosegay, few Cloves, Thyme and Laurel Leaves; boil on a slow Fire about five Hours, then add a Glass of Brandy, and a Pint of red Wine; finish boiling in the same Manner; if to serve hot, take up the Skin, and strew it over with Bread Crums, a little Parsley finely chopped, few Bits of Butter, give it Colour in the Oven or with a Salamander; if to keep cold, they will keep better without taking the Skin up.

Jambon Roti.

Ham Roasted.

PARE the Ham as for boiling, it should be much fresher for roasting, so it must soak longer if old; soak it four and twenty Hours with a Bottle of white Wine, and baste it with the Wine while roasting; when done, you may finish it as the former, and skim the Dripping with which it has been basted; reduce it to the Consistence of a Sauce, and serve it with the Ham.

Jambon à la Braise.

Ham Brazed.

PREPARE the Ham for Salt according to your Judgement in regard to soaking; pare it as the former, and put it in a Brazing-pan of its Bigness, with Broth without Salt, a large Nosegay, two Cloves of Garlick, six of Spices, four Bay Leaves, Thyme, Laurel, few sliced Onions, Carrots and Parsneps; when half done, add a Glass of Brandy, a Pint of Wine; when done slowly, take up the Skin: serve with what stewed Greens you think proper, or with a relishing Sauce.

Rôties de Jambon.

Toasted Bread and Ham with Eggs.

TOAST Bits of Bread of what Bigness you please, fry them in Butter of a good Colour; take as many Slices of fresh Ham or soaked; soak them over a slow Fire in Butter till they are done, turning often, then lay them upon the Bread; put a little Cullis in the same Stew-pan; give it a boiling, skim the Fat clear off; add a little Broth and Vinegar; boil a Moment, and

and serve upon the Toast: the Ham is prepared the same, if you would have it with poached Eggs, or any Sorts of stewed Greens.

Filets de Porc Frais.

Fillets of Fresh Pork.

CUT the small Fillets which are found in the Inside of the Loins, they are called Filets Mignons, viz. Favourite; cut these in small Bits, beat them flat with the Handle of a Knife, and marinade them about an Hour in a little Oil, chopt Parsley, green Shallots, Mushrooms, Pepper and Salt; make the Herbs stick to, as much as possible, and strewed over with Bread Crums; broil over a slow Fire, and baste with Oil or Butter; serve under, a clear Sauce of Veal Gravy and Verjuice, or Lemon Squeeze, or any other.

Cotelettes de Porc Frais.

Fresh Pork Stakes.

CUT a Neck of Pork long kept, and pare the Stakes properly; you may dress them in the same Manner, in every Respect, as Veal Cutlets, and in as many different Ways; and serve with any Sorts of stewed Greens or Sauces.

Langues Fourées de Porc.

Pork's Tongs stuffed.

TAKE what Quantity of Tongues you think proper, cut the Throat Part off, and scald them just enough to peel, then salt them with common Salt, and Saltpetre; put them close in a Pan with chopped Parsley, Shallots, Thyme, Laurel, Basil, Coriander, Juniper Berries, a small Quantity of each; lay a Weight upon them

them to keep close; cover the Salting pan close, and let them remain in a cool Place for about ten Days; then take out of the Seasoning to stuff them in Hog's Guts or Beef's, tie them up close and hang them in the Chimney to dry: when you want to use them, boil in half Water and Wine, with a Nosegay of sweet Herbs, few Cloves, and sliced Onions: let them cool in their Liquor.

N. B. The Coal Fire will not give that Flavour to any of those dried Sausages or Cervelats, &c. &c. as we have from Germany or Italy; but whoever would make a Trial here in any Out-houses with Saw-dust and sweet Herbs dried, will come near to the same.

CHAPITRE CINQUIEME. De l'Aigneau.

CHAPTER FIFTH. Of Lamb.

LAMB in England is in all Seasons good, and of great Resource in Cookery, as every Part of it may be used in many different Ways, where Variety of Dishes are required; it ought to be fat and very white; the Fore-quarter is of more Use than the Hind one in the Number of Dishes.

Tête d'Aigneau à la Pluche verte.

Lamb's Head of a pale green Sauce.

CUT the Chops of one or two Lamb's Heads to the Eyes, scald them in hot Water, and give them a Boil in a second; then put in a Stew-pan upon thin Slices of Lard, a little Broth and white Wine, a Nosegay of sweet Herbs, a Clove of Garlick, Salt and whole Pepper; when boiled enough, sift the Broth, reduce it to the Consistence of a Sauce; add a little Butter rolled in Flour, a middling Quantity of fine chopt Parsley: make a Liason, and serve upon the Heads.

Têtes

Têtes d'Aigneau à la Mordienne.

Lamb's Head after the Name of the Inventor.

PREPARE one or two Lamb's Heads as the preceding, well fcalded; then put them in a Stew-pan much of their Bignefs, upon thin Slices of Lard, half a Lemon, fliced and peeled, and Broth; fimmer on a flow Fire, and make a Sauce after this Manner, fimmer a Slice of Ham, two Spoonfuls of Oil, a Nofegay of Parfley, green Shallots, one Clove of Garlick, a little Bafil, two Cloves, - chopt Mufhrooms, Confumee, and a Glafs of white Wine; reduce to the Confiftence of a Sauce; take out the Nofegay, fift and fkim the Sauce, and ferve upon the Head.

Tête d'Aigneau de plufieurs Façons.

Lamb's Head of different Manners.

ALWAYS fcald the Heads very clean firft, then boil them in Broth, with Verjuice-Grapes, if in Seafon, or Lemon Slices, Salt and Pepper, a Nofegay of fweet Herbs, two Cloves, Thyme, Laurel; when done, open the Brains, and ferve with what Sauce you think proper, as Verjuice Sauce which you make with one or two Spoonfuls of Verjuice or Lemon in proportion, a little Cullis, chopt Parfley, a Bit of Butter and Flour, Pepper and Salt, a little Nutmeg: make a Liafon and ferve upon the Heads, or a Spanifh Sauce, Italian, Truffles, or Mufhrooms, any of which you will find in Sauce Articles.

Tête d'Aigneau au Pontife.

The fame another Way.

CHOP fome Mufhrooms, and cut fome fat Livers in Dices, put this in a Stew-pan with a little Cullis, a Glass of white Wine, a Nosegay of sweet Herbs, one chopped Shallot, very little Basil, Pepper and Salt, a Bit of Butter; when this is done, take one or two Heads three Parts boiled; cut the Tongues in Dices, which you mix with the Sauce, and take out the Brains, and instead, put this Ragout which you cover over with the Brains; cut in Slices, baste them over with a little of the Sauce, and Bread Crums, a little melted Butter: give it Colour in the Oven, or with a Salamander; serve under it a Sauce au Pontife, which you will find in Sauce Articles, Page 46.

Tête d'Aigneau à la Condé.

Lamb's Head Condé Fashion.

BRAZE one or two Heads in a white Braze, and serve with a Sauce made with Verjuice, two Yolks of Eggs, scalded Parsley chopped, coarse Pepper, a Pat of Butter, a little Cullis, Salt, Nutmeg; make a Liason without boiling, and serve upon the Brains.

Issu d'Aigneau de plusieurs Façons.

Lamb's Head with all its Appurtenances of different Manners.

ISSU is the Head, Heart and Liver, and Chitterling, which must be all very well scalded in boiling Water several Times; then boil all together in Broth or Water, few Slices of Lard, Pepper and Salt, a Nosegay of sweet Herbs, one Clove of Garlick, two of Spices: you may also put with it, Bits of pickled Pork; when done, put the Head in the middle, and all the rest round cut in Pieces, and the pickled Pork; serve with what Sauce you please: you may also serve this in a plain Way, without Sauce upon it, but a sharp Sauce in a Sauce-boat, made with few chopped Shallots, sliced Onions, Pep-

per

per and Salt, a little Broth and white Vinegar; infuse this about an Hour or two; warm it, and sift it: it may also be dressed as a Chicken Fricassée.

Epaule d'Aigneau à la Dauphine.

Shoulder of Lamb Dauphine Fashion.

BONE one or two Shoulders of Lamb, all to the Handle Bone, chop some Truffles or Mushrooms, and fat Livers which you mix together with scraped Lard, Pepper and Salt, Parsley, Shallots, two Yolks of Eggs; roll this Farce in the Shoulder, and braze them in a Pan much of their Bigness, in a little Broth, few Slices of Lard, a Glass of Wine, a Nosegay of sweet Herbs, Pepper and Salt; when done, serve upon stewed Spinage, or any other Sorts of Garden Greens.

Epaule d'Aigneau à la (Voisine) Neighbour Fashion.

PREPARE one or two Shoulders of Lamb as the former, fill them with Forced-meat of roasted Fowls, Bread Crums soaked in Cream, Calve's Udder, Pepper and Salt, chopt Parsley, Chibbol, (or green Shallots, which is much the same,) mixt with Yolks of Eggs; roll them round and fasten them very well, to hinder the Farce from getting out; lard all the upper Part with middling larding Bits, boil them in good Broth and a Nosegay; when done, sift the Sauce in a Lawn Sieve; reduce it to a Glaze, to put over the upper Part with a light Brush, and serve with what Sauce you please.

Quartier d'Aigneau en Crepine.

Quarter of Lamb in Cowl.

BONE a fore Quarter of Lamb without cutting the Skin, and make a Farce after this Manner; cut

three

three middling Onions in Dices, fry them in Lard; when almost done, add few chopt Shallots, Powder of Basil, Parsley, Salt and fine Spices, a small Quantity; four Yolks of Eggs, two Spoonfuls of Cream, half a Pint of Lamb's Blood, simmer over the Fire without boiling untill it becomes pretty thick; put this Preparation in the Lamb, rolled up in Cowl, and roast it, then baste with Butter, or a thin Batter and Bread Crums; give it Colour in the Oven, serve under it a Sauce au Canard, which you will find in Sauce Articles, Page 47.

Rot de Bif d'Aigneau au Monarque.

(For *Rot de Bif d'Aigneau,* see the Explanation in Mutton Direction, Page 138.)

IT is to be cut the same Way, although unusual in England; I shall follow the Author as near as possible, as it is not deviating from what may be done in all Families, though at present confined to few.

Cut Truffles in Slices, pickled Pork and fat Livers the same, sliced Onions, and Fillets of Anchovies, seasoned with Pepper, Salt and Nutmeg; take up the Skin of the Piece of Lamb cleanly; scarify the Flesh under in several Places, and put the first Preparation in it properly diversified, and cover it all over with a Farce made of six hard Yolks of Eggs, chopt Shallots, Parsley, and scraped Lard, then the Skin over it, fastened well; boil it in Broth, with a Nosegay of sweet Herbs, few Shallots, a Clove of Garlick, two or three of Spices, Pepper and Salt, a Bottle of white Wine, and few Slices of Bacon; when done, take out the Lard and Nosegay: ice the upper Part with a Glaze, made of Veal Cullis, such as you do for Fricandeau, sift Part of the Sauce; add a little Cullis to make a Liason; reduce it pretty thick, and serve under the Meat.

Quartier d'Aigneau aux Fines Herbes.

Quarter of Lamb with Sweet Herbs.

ROLL a Bit of Butter in Flour with few Bread Crums, chopped Parsley, Shallots, a little green Thyme, Salt and Pepper, and a Glass of white Wine, and Broth in proportion; boil a Moment; the Lamb being roasted, take up the Shoulder, and pour this Sauce between, in the same Manner as many People do with Seville Oranges, and Pepper and Salt.

Quartier d'Aigneau à la Reine.

Quarter of Lamb with white Sauce.

TAKE a Fore-quarter of Lamb, roast the Shoulder, and cut the Neck and Breast in Cutlets, which you lard with Truffles, and give few Turns in a Stew-pan with good fresh Lard, Pepper and Salt, chopt Shallots; garnish them with Bread Crums; broil slowly, basting now and then with Lard or Butter: make a Sauce à la Reine, and mince the Shoulder which you mix with the Sauce, pour it in the Dish, the Cutlets upon it or round it as you please.

Quëues d'Aigneau au Soleil, the Sun.

Lamb's Rumps Fried, viz. au Soleil, clear bright Colour.

BOIL the Rumps in Broth, a Glass of Wine, Pepper and Salt, a Nosegay of sweet Herbs, green Shallots, three Cloves, Thyme and Laurel; when done, let them drain, and make a light Batter, made of Flour, a Spoonful of Oil and Salt, and white Wine; fry them of a good Colour, and serve with fried Parsley:

you

you may also put them to any Sauce you please; when brazed in the above Manner, a relishing Sauce is best.

Quartier d'Aigneau en Saucissons.

Quarter of Lamb as thick Sausages or Chitterling.

BONE a Leg of Lamb, and cut above half the Meat out, which you simmer in Butter a little while, mince it with Calve's Udder, scraped Lard, Bread Crums soaked in Cream, chopt Parsley, green Shallots, few Truffles or Mushrooms, Salt and fine Spices; put this Farce in the Remainder of the Leg, and roll it up like a short thick Sausage; tie it up in a Linen Cloth very tight; boil it in Broth, half a Pint of white Wine, a Nosegay, few Onions Slices and Carrots; when done, serve with what Sauce you please, or with any Sorts of stewed Greens, or green Peas, Asparagus, &c.

Carré d'Aigneau (à la Belle-vüe.)

Necks of Lamb well looking, agreeable, &c. &c.

PARE two Necks of Lamb handsomely, and scarify the Fillet which you fill up with chopped Truffles, pickled Cucumbers, Bits of Carrots, Beet-roots, &c. seasoned with Pepper and Salt, fine Spices, a little Powder of Basil; close the Ribs of the Necks close to each other, and cover them over with Slices of Fillet of Veal; tie them up in a fine Linen Cloth, and put them in a Brazing-pan much of their Bigness, with a little Cullis, a Glass of white Wine, a Nosegay, green Shallots, half a Clove of Garlick; simmer over a very slow Fire about four or five Hours; then take off the Cloth and Veal; skim and sift the Sauce, reduce it to a good Consistence fiftence to ferve upon the Meat: you may add a Lemon Squeeze, if the Wine does not make it relishing enough.

Du Chevreau ou Cabrit.

Of Kid.

KID is good to eat when it is but three or four Months old, becaufe its Flesh is delicate and tender; it is not ufed after it has done fuckling; to be good, it ought to be fat and white; it is ufed in the fame Manner as Lambs.

Des Groffes Entrées en Terrine & autre.

Of large, Firft-courfe Difhes, Tureen and others.

Terrines à la Flamande.

Tureen Flemifh Fafhion.

SCALD half a Dozen of Turkey Pinions, four Sheep's Rumps, half a Pound or more of pickled Pork; then tie up each Sort together: fcald alfo a good Savoy, cut in Quarters and tied; put all together in a Pan with good Broth, a Nofegay of fweet Herbs, Parfley, green Shallots, three Cloves, Pepper and Salt; boil flowly; when done, drain the Meat, put it in the Tureen, and ferve a good Cullis Sauce with it.

Terrine à l'Angloife.

Englifh Fafhion.

MAKE a good Lentil Cullis, as it is explained in Cullis Article; and boil a Quarter of a Pound of Rice in good Broth; take Sheep's or Beef's Rumps, well brazed and cut in Pieces, and Bits of pickled Pork,

the

the same, two or three Pigeons cut in Quarters; put in the Bottom of your Tureen some of the Rice, then part of the Meat, then Lentil Cullis, and so continue; the last to be Lentils; fry some Bread Crums, with which you garnish the Top; put it in a soaking Oven for half an Hour: you may use any Sorts of brazed Meat in the same Manner.

Terrine de ce que l'on veut.

Tureen of what you please.

TAKE any Sorts of Butcher's Meat, such as Tongues, Beef's Rumps, Brisket, Sheep's Rumps, or Pieces of Neck and Leg; braze all this with Slices of Lard, a Nosegay of sweet Herbs, one Clove of Garlick, three of Spices, Thyme, Laurel, Pepper and Salt, a little Broth; when the Meat is done, wipe the Fat off, dress it in the Tureen with what Ragout you please, or Cullis Sauce, or other; if you would use their own Broth, take care not to put too much Salt; skim the Fat, sift it, and add a little Cullis.

Terrine de Bécasses.

Of Woodcocks.

GARNISH a Stew-pan with Slices of Fillet of Veal, and Ham; truss the Woodcocks whole, and give them few Turns in Butter, then put them along with the Veal and Ham, covered over with thin Slices of Bacon; add Broth, half a Pint of white Wine, Pepper and Salt, two Onions sliced, and other Roots, a Nosegay of sweet Herbs; when done, put them in the Tureen, free from Fat: serve upon, a good Ragout of Sweet Breads, fat Livers, Mushrooms, &c. &c. you will find the Method to make it in Ragout Articles, Vol. II.

Terrine de Perdrix.

Tureen of Partridges.

YOU may make Partridge Tureen of different Sorts, as with Cabbages, Lentil Cullis, or with Sweet Bread Ragout, as the laft; take what Quantity of Partridges you pleafe, trufs them as for boiling; lard the Breafts of fome to pleafe different Taftes; if you would make it with Cabbages, cut a large one in Quarters, fcald it firft, then put it to boil with the Partridges, or rather to ftew, about half a Pound of pickled Pork, Broth, a Nofegay, Pepper and a little Salt, according as the Pork will admit, two or three Cloves; when done, drain the Partridges and Cabbage; put the Partridges in the Tureen, the Cabbage round or between, the pickled Pork upon; ferve with a good Veal Cullis Sauce; if you would have it with Lentil Cullis, you will find the Way to make it in Cullis Articles.

Terrines de Queuës de Mouton, & Ailerons au Coulis & Ragout de Maron.

Tureen of Sheep's Rumps and Poultry Pinions with Chefnut Cullis and Ragout.

SCALD Six Sheeps Rumps, and as many Pigeons as you pleafe; put the Sheeps Rumps in a fmall Pan upon few Slices of Bacon, a Nofegay, half a Clove of Garlick, two of Spices, a little Thyme and Bafil, half a Bayleaf, a little Broth, a Glafs of white Wine, a little Salt and Pepper, a Slice of Ham, few whole Mufhrooms; boil on a flow Fire; when the Rumps are half done, put the Pigeons to it, let all fimmer gently; take as many Chefnuts as you think proper: roaft them enough to peel both Hufks; take the beft to boil tender in Broth, pound others to make a Cullis, with fome of the Broth of the firſt Preparation; ſift the Cullis in a Stamine, add a little Veal Cullis; put the Rumps in the Bottom of the Tureen, the Fat well wiped off, the Pigeons upon them; then the Cheſnuts whole, and Cullis.

Terrine de Volailles.
Tureen of Poulteries.

TAKE Fowls, Chickens, Turkeys, Pigeons, which you pleaſe, or ſeveral Sorts together, Fowls and Turkeys, cut them in Quarters; Chickens and Pigeons, truſs them whole as for boiling, Legs inſide; lard them with large Pieces of Larding, Bacon and Ham intermixed; braze them in a well ſeaſoned Braze: ſerve with any ſtewed Greens or Roots which you pleaſe, or a Ragout of Sweet Breads: alſo without Ragout or Greens, but any Sorts of Sauce.

Terrine au Monarque.

GARNISH the Bottom of a Brazing-pan with Slices of Fillet of Veal and Ham, upon this a Neck of Mutton larded, pickled Pork, cut in pretty large Bits, two whole Pigeons, truſſed for boiling, ſix Quails, a Couple of Partridges of a good *Fumé*, ſeaſon with Salt, whole Pepper, Powder of Baſil; cover all with Slices of Lard and Veal; put a little Broth, a ſmall Glaſs of Brandy, ſtop the Steam with a Paſte made with Vinegar; ſimmer it on a ſlow Fire, or in the Oven about four or five Hours; make a Ragout with chopped Truffles, Sweet Breads, Cock's Combs, a Bit of Butter, Broth and Cullis; reduce the Sauce pretty thick: the Meat being done, put it in the Tureen, ſift the Broth of it; mix it with the Ragout, take care it is not too ſalted; give it a boil together, and ſerve upon the Meat in the Tureen.

Terrine de Lapreaux.

Tureen of Rabbits.

CUT two Rabbits in large Pieces, lard them through and through with large Pieces of larding Bacon, seasoned with Salt and fine Spices; put them in a Stewpan with a good Slice of Ham, a Bit of Butter, a Nosegay of sweet Herbs, two Cloves, a Laurel Leaf, a little green Basil, half a Clove of Garlick; simmer them a little while in this Manner, then put them in another Stew-pan, upon Slices of Fillet of Veal, with all their first Seasoning; cover it over with thin Slices of Lard, soak it about half an Hour over a slow Fire, then add a Glass of white Wine; when done, put the Rabbits in the Tureen, and add some good Cullis to the liquid of their boiling, give it a boiling together, skim and sift; add a Lemon Squeeze, and serve upon the Meat.

Terrine de Macreuses au Jambon.

Tureen of Wild or Sea Ducks with Ham.

TRUSS them as you do a Fowl for boiling, and make a Farce with the Livers, rasped Lard, Mushrooms, Parsley, green Shallots, raw Yolks of Eggs, Salt and Pepper, with which you stuff the Fowls; braze them four or five Hours with a Pint of white Wine, Slices of Beef and Veal, two Onions, one Carrot, and one Parsnep, a Nosegay of Parsley, green Shallots, one Laurel Leaf, Thyme, three Cloves, Pepper and Salt; for the Sauce, soak few Slices of Ham of the same Bigness, then simmer them on a slow Fire until they are done; then take them out and put in the same Stewpan, some good Cullis, stirring it at bottom, to mix the Glaze which the Ham has made; add a little Vinegar,

then

then put the Slices of Ham in it to warm without boiling and ferve all together upon the Macreufes.

N. B. This Water Fowl is not common in England, but there is a fmall Kind of Duck called Shuffler, which may be dreffed the fame, and any eatable Water Fowl: this is further explained in Wild Fowls Articles. Vol. II.

Terrine de Poiffon.

Tureen of Fifh.

TAKE frefh Water Fifh, which Sort you pleafe, or different Sorts together, if Tenches you muft fcale them before emptying; Pikes and Perches, you leave the Scales until they are done; the Meat will be of a better Colour, and a finer White; if it is *en Gras* ftew them with few Slices of Veal and Ham, a little Broth, a Glafs of white Wine, a Nofegay of fweet Herbs, two Cloves, one of Garlick, Thyme and Laurel, few Slices of Lard, Pepper and Salt; when done, drain them from the Liquor, and put the Fifh in the Tureen; add a little Cullis to their Broth; fkim it and fift it in a Sieve, and ferve upon the Fifh: you add to it what Sorts of Ragout you pleafe: if it is to be Meager, you braze the Fifh as fuch, and ferve with their Sauce, Peas or Lentil Cullis.

Terrine à la Neuvaine.

Tureen as you pleafe, or any how.

USE a Tureen which will bear the Fire, and put in it any Sorts of Butcher's Meat you think proper, or of Game; chop it pretty fmall, and feveral fliced Onions, a little Beef Suet, half a Glafs of Brandy, Salt and Spices; ftop the Steam with a Pafte made of Flour and Vinegar, and ftew it flowly, (as you would à la Mode Beef)

Beef, for about five Hours; then take off the Paste, skim the Fat a little, and serve as it is; it will also eat very well cold: this may equally be done in a Stew-pan.

Terrine de Saumon.

Tureen of fresh Salmon.

GARNISH a Stew-pan with few Slices of Veal and Ham, and put upon it what Quantity of Salmon you please; cover it over with thin Slices of Lard, seasoned with Pepper and Salt, a Nosegay of Parsley, green Shallots, two Cloves, Thyme and Laurel, a Glass of white Wine; soak it over a very slow Fire for about an Hour, then take out the Salmon to put in the Tureen; add a little Cullis to the Sauce, give it a boiling to skim it, and sift it in a Sieve; instead of this Sauce, you may serve a Sweet Bread Ragout or any other; for Meager, serve with a Cullis of Craw-fish and Ragout.

Terrine de Saumon aux Ecrevisses.

With Craw-fish.

TAKE about three Pound of fresh Salmon cut in two or three large Slices; put them in a Brazing-pan, with few Slices of Lard, a Nosegay of sweet Herbs, two Cloves, a small Bit of Nutmeg; the liquid to be half Broth and half white Wine, Salt and Pepper; boil it over a slow Fire about half an Hour, in the same Time prepare about half a hundred of Craw-fish, by scalding them in boiling Water, and boil the Tails in Broth very tender; dry the Carcass, to pound very fine, and add some good Cullis to it, to sift it in a Stamine; let it be pretty thick, mix a little of the Braze with it, first well skimmed, then add the Tails to the Cullis; warm without boiling, to serve in the Tureen upon the Salmon.

Casserole

Casserole au Ris.

TO make a middling First-course Dish; take about half a Pound of Rice, well washed in hot Water several Times; boil it in fat Broth very tender; use what kind of Meat you think proper, brazed very tender, such as Turkeys, Pigeons, or any other Sorts of Poulteries, pickled Pork, Sheep's or Lamb's Rumps, &c. &c. lay a Down of Rice in the Dish you intend to serve at Table, then the Meat upon this, and about an Inch thick of Rice over; rub it over with a Knife dipt in melted Butter or Lard; give it a good brown Colour with a Salamander or in the Oven.

* This *Casserole* is often done in a Stew-pan proportionable to the Dish intended; the different Preparation laid close intermixed, then turned over gently to keep its Form from which it takes its Name, viz. Stew-pan.

Different Hochepot.
Hochpot of different Sorts.

USE what kind of Meat you please, as Brisket of Beef, Mutton Stakes, whole Pigeons, Rabbits cut in Quarters, Veal or any Sorts of Poulteries; boil this in short liquid with some whole Onions, Carrots, Parsneps, Turnips, Sellery, a Nosegay of Parsley, green Shallots, one Clove of Garlick, three of Spices, a Laurel Leaf, Thyme, a little Basil, large thick Sausages, thin Broth or Water; boil a long while over a slow Fire, when done drain the Meat, and place it upon the Dish intermixed with the Roots, sift and skim the Sauce; reduce some of it to a Glaze, if you like; and glaze the Meat with it; then add some Cullis in the same Stew-pan, and Broth sufficient to make Sauce enough, Pepper and Salt; sift it in a Sieve, and serve upon the Meat; if you use Brisket of Beef, let it be half done before you put the Roots to it, which should always be scalded first, as it makes the Broth more palatable.

Salamalec.

A Fancy Dish, or Tureen.

PUT Slices of Beef in the Bottom of a Soop-pot or Brazing-pan, two or three Spoonfuls of Broth, upon this a Neck of Mutton properly prepared, a Couple of Partridges trussed as for boiling, one large Rabbit cut in Quarters, and larded, few thick Sausages, a Bit of Ham, first boiled some Time in Water, few whole Onions, Carrots, Parsneps, a Nosegay of sweet Herbs, Salt and whole Pepper; simmer it on a slow Fire about six Hours; when the Meat is done drain it, and wipe the Fat off clean, and lay it properly, intermixed in the Dish or Tureen you intend to serve; sift the Sauce and skim it very well; add a little chopt Charvil, give it a boiling, and serve upon the Meat.

Financiere.

Meaning a rich expensive Dish.

TAKE a Head of Salmon, pretty long of about five or six Pound, clean it as for boiling; lard the upper Part with fine Lardons, and fill it with a Ragout of Sweet Breads, Truffles or Mushrooms; fasten it so as the Ragout don't get out; put it in a Brazing-pan much of its Bigness, upon thin Slices of Lard and Veal, one or two Slices of Ham, a Nosegay of Parsley and green Shallots, two Cloves, a Bit of Nutmeg, a Laurel Leaf and Thyme, few sliced Onions and Roots; soak this on a slow Fire about an Hour, then put the Salmon to it well tied; add some good Broth, a Pint of white Wine, Pepper and Salt, simmer it about an Hour; while this is doing, boil six small Pigeons, as many small Franceaux, called *Grenadins* larded, and a Dozen of large Craw-fish, as many Truffles peeled; prepare a Glaze with

with Veal and Ham; when it is all done dress the Salmon upon the Dish, and the second Preparation intermixed round it, and glaze the Meat, not the Salmon; for Sauce, mix some good Consumée and Cullis, a Glass of white Wine, a little Pepper and Salt; give it a boil, and serve round the Salmon upon the Meat Part.

Chartreuse.

After the Name of those Friers.

TRUSS a Partridge as for boiling, four Sheep's Rumps scalded, a Couple of Legs of Fowl, braze altogether with few Slices of Lard, a Nosegay of Parsley, green Shallots, Thyme, Laurel, Basil, two Cloves, Pepper and Salt, Broth and a Glass of white Wine: scald Bits of Carrots, Parsneps, Sellery, Turnips cut properly; boil them in good Broth and stewed Spinage; when the Meat is done, sift the Broth, and mix it with the Roots and Spinage; then take a Stew-pan, the Bigness of the Dish you intend to serve upon; lay the Bottom with the Slices of Lard, which were used for the Meat; lay the Partridge in the middle, Breast undermost, then the Sheep's Rumps, and the Legs of Fowls in the Form of Stars, intermixed with the different Roots and Spinage, without Sauce; leave it so some Time on a slow Fire; when you are ready to serve, turn it over gently upon the Dish, and take off the Lard; wipe the Fat off with a clean Rubber, and serve upon them the Sauce of the stewed Greens.

Marbrée.

Marbled, Coloured.

TAKE eight Pig's Ears, as many of Calve's, well scalded, two Pound of Ham, a good large Calve's Tongue, eight Beef Palates; boil this all together with
half

half Wine and half Water, sweet Herbs plenty, four Cloves, Thyme and Laurel, whole Onions, and fine Spices; when done let them cool to chop fine, and put a Bit of Butter in a Stew-pan with few chopped Truffles, green Shallots and chopt Parsley; add a Glass of white Wine, simmer about a Quarter of an Hour, then put the minced Meat in, with Bits of Breast of Fowl roasted, Pistachio-Nuts, and sweet Almonds; cut in four, hard Yolks of Eggs; season it all together with Salt and fine Spices; boil it some time with a Pint of white Wine, until the liquid is quite reduced; then take another Stewpan of the Bigness the *Marbrée* is to be; rub it all over with Butter slightly, only sufficient to stick Wafers of different Colours in what Shape you please; then put the Meat in this very close, with the Juice of two Lemons; put it in a cool Place to cool, Jelly like: when you want to use it, dip the Pan in warm Water, turn it gently over upon a Napkin.

Corbillon.

Intermixed like a Basket.

TAKE Fillets of any Sorts of Game, several Sorts mixed together, small Onions scalded, few Crawfish trimmed, tie all up in thin Slices of Bacon, and boil in good Broth, a Glass of Wine; also seven or eight small Grenadins larded, a Slice of Ham, a Nosegay of Parsley, green Shallots, two Cloves; when the Meat is done, sift the Sauce, and reduce it to a Glaze for the Fricandeaux, lay it intermixed upon the Dish, and serve with a good Sauce as you shall think proper; garnish the Dish round with fried Bread cut properly: this is also often intermixed with all Sorts of stewed Herbs and Roots, in the Form of the *Casserole*, with different Sorts of Meat, Poultry or Game.

Matelotte

Matelotte Royale.

SCALD one Dozen of Cock's Combs, and three Pair of Lamb's Brains, put them in a Stew-pan upon Slices of Lard, and Fillets of Rabbits, larded with Anchovies, Pieces of Eels; alfo larded as the Rabbits, Bits of Carps, Pinions of Fowls or Chickens, a Dozen of large Craw-fifh trimmed, few fmall Onions fcalded, Salt and whole Pepper, half a Lemon fliced, firft peeled; wet it with good Broth, a Glafs of Wine, a Spoonful of Oil, a Nofegay of Parfley, green Shallots, one Clove of Garlick, three of Spices, Thyme and Laurel; when the Meat is done, drain it off the Fat; lay it upon the Difh, well intermixed; garnifh the Difh round with fried Bread, fift and fkim the Sauce; add fome Cullis to thicken it, and Spawns of Craw-fifh; boil it a Moment, and ferve upon the Meat; inftead of this you may ufe a Sauce *à la Carpe*, which you will find in Sauce Articles, Page 41.

Matelottes de ce que l'on veut.

Matlot of what you like.

TAKE fix Sheep's Rumps, half a Pound of pickled Pork, eight Pinions of Fowls, one Dozen of fmall Onions fcalded; put all together in a Stew-pan, between Slices of Lard and Veal, a Nofegay of fweet Herbs, Pepper and Salt, two Cloves, foak it on a flow Fire about half an Hour; then add few Spoonfuls of Broth, a Glafs of white Wine: the Rumps fhould be half boiled, before you put the reft to it; when the Meat is done, drain it, and lay it handfomely on the Difh; fkim and fift the Sauce; add fome Cullis, and a pounded Anchovy, and a Spoonful of whole Capers; ferve upon the Meat; garnifh the Difh with fried Bread, cut in different

rent Forms: you may also use Pig's Tails, and Lamb's, or any Sorts of Meat you think proper.

Prussienne.

Matlot Prussian Fashion.

CUT the Gristles of a Breast of Veal in middling Pieces, scald them with Bits of pickled Pork, braze it together with few Slices of Lard, half a Lemon sliced, without the Peel, a Nosegay as usual, two Cloves, half a Laurel Leaf, Thyme, a little Broth, half a Glass of white Wine; when half done, add a good Chicken cut in four, a good Eel cut in Pieces, Pepper and Salt; when all is done enough, drain it from the Fat, and intermix it upon the Dish; sift and skim the Sauce; add some Cullis and Butter, reduce it to a good Consistence: when ready to serve, add some chopt scalded Parsley, and serve upon the Matlot.

Matelotte au General.

Fit for a General.

TAKE eight large Onions which you scoop Inside, to make room to put a good Forced-meat made of Poultry or Veal; braze them with Slices of Lard, and as many fat Livers, a Nosegay, two or three Cloves, Thyme, Laurel, Basil, Pepper and Salt, and Broth; boil slowly, and prepare a Dozen of Cox's Combs, which you first boil in Broth; then make a Ragout of them, with Consumet, and Cullis, half a Glass of white Wine; simmer it to reduce it to a good Consistence, lay the Onions and Livers, intermixed on your Dish, and serve the Ragout upon the Meat, and garnish the Dish with fried Bread: all those Dishes under the Denomination of Matelotte may equally be served in Tureens.

Matelotte aux Oignons d'Hollande.

With large Dutch or Spanish Onions.

CUT seven or eight Bits of Beef's Rumps, scald them well, and braze in Broth, a Nosegay, two Cloves, Thyme, Laurel, Pepper and Salt; when they are half done, put to it eight large Onions, first scalded; when done, sift the Sauce; add a Glass of red Wine, and some Cullis, and serve it as all former.

Gateau de Viande de ce que l'on veut.

Meat Cake of what Sorts you please.

ACCORDING to the Bigness desired, take of Beef Stakes, of Leg of Mutton, Fillet of Veal, a Hare boned, Beef Suet, raw Ham; chop all together pretty fine, season it with Salt and fine Spices, chopt Parsley, green Shallots, Powder of Basil, one Clove of Garlick, eight Yolks of Eggs, half a Glass of Brandy, two Pound of fresh Bacon, cut in Dices, or less; mix it well all together, then take a Stew-pan, the Bigness of the Cake you intend; garnish it all over with pretty thick Slices of Lard, then your minced Meat; cover it close, put it in the Oven for about four Hours; when it is cold take it out of the Stew-pan, scrape the Lard with a Knife to make it white and even; you may garnish this with all Sorts of Colours, according to Fancy; serve upon a Napkin.

Gateau à l'Espagnole.

Cake Spanish Fashion.

MAKE Forced-meat with about two Pound of Fillet of Veal, a Pound of Beef Suet, chopt Shallots, Parsley,

Parsley, Mushrooms, a small Glass of Brandy, Pepper and Salt, six or eight Yolks of Eggs; garnish a Stew-pan with Slices of Lard, and put this Farce upon it; leave a Hole in the Middle to put a Ragout of Pigeons, finished of a good Taste, cover it over with some of the Farce and Slices of Lard: bake it in the Oven about two Hours, then turn it over gently upon the Dish; take off the Bacon, wipe the Fat off clean, baste it with a little Cullis, mix with two Yolks of Eggs, a little Butter, strew it with Bread Crums; put it a while in the Oven to take Colour: serve upon it a Sauce *à l'Es-pagnole*, which you will find in Sauce Articles; you may use any Sorts of Ragout, well finished, instead of Pigeons.

Composition de Panade pour toutes Sortes de Viandes.

How to make a proper Batter to use with all Sorts of roasting Meat.

MELT some good Butter, and put to it three Eggs with the Whites, well beat up, warm it together, stirring continually; baste any roasting Meat with it and Bread Crums, and so continue to make a Crust of what Thickness you please.

CHAPITRE SIXIEME. *De la Volaille.*

CHAPTER SIXTH. Of Poultery.

Poulets en Fricassé.

Fricassee of Chicken.

CUT a Chicken in Pieces, and throw it in hot Water, as you do it, to scald, also the Liver and Gizzard, and the Legs finged over the Fire, the Claws cut off;

then

then drain all together, and put it in a Stew-pan with a Bit of Butter, few Mushrooms, Artichoke Bottom if you like; first scalded about a Quarter of an Hour in hot Water, a Nosegay of sweet Herbs, one Clove; put it over a good Fire, then add a little Flour, and warm Water, Pepper and Salt; boil it till the Chicken is done, and very little Sauce remaining; when you are ready to serve, make a Liason with two or three Yolks of Eggs, and Cream, a little Nutmeg if approved, a Squeeze of Lemon; such as don't like Cream, mix the Eggs with Broth; a Hen Chicken is preferable to a Cock, as the Meat is tenderer.

Fricaſſée de Poulets à la Fermiere.

Fricaſſée Farmer Fashion or in haste.

KILL one or two Chickens, gut and cut them in Pieces, scald them in hot Water, and without giving time to cool, give it a fry in Butter, few sweet Herbs, two Cloves, Pepper and Salt, then put Flour and boiling Water, and boil till they are done, and the Sauce short; then make a Liason with Yolks of Eggs, Milk or Cream, a little Nutmeg, and Verjuice or Vinegar: this is only to be done in a hurry, and if the Chicken does not cool, it will prove pretty tender.

Differentes Fricaſſées de Poulets.

Chicken Fricaſſée of different Manners.

CUT the Chickens in Pieces, and put them in a Stew-pan with a Bit of Butter, a Nosegay, a little Flour, a Glass of white Wine and Broth, boil till they are done with short Sauce; take out the Nosegay, and make a Liason with Eggs and Broth, a Pinch of chopped Parsley, and a Lemon Squeeze; if you would have it with Mushrooms or fresh Morels, you put the Meat

and

and Mushrooms or Morels together in a Stew-pan with a Bit of Butter and Salt; simmer slowly untill they are done; the Mushrooms or Morels will yield liquid enough: when they are done, add a Bit of Butter and Flour, a little Cream, and warm without boiling: you may also add a Lemon Squeeze.

Poulets à la Giblottes de Plufieurs Façons.

Timbals of Chickens of different Manners.

TRUSS the Chickens as for boiling, then cut them in Quarters, put them in a Stew-pan with Truffles or Morels, a Nosegay of Parsley and green Shallots, half a Clove of Garlick, two of Spices, Thyme and Laurel, a Bit of Butter, Giblet, and Gizzard, and all the Trimmings; simmer all together, then add a little Broth, a Glass of white Wine, a little Flour, and few Spoonfuls of Cullis, Salt and Pepper; finish the boiling, and reduce the Broth to the Confiftence of a Sauce; take out the Nosegay, skim the Fat, and serve very hot: you may also make it with small Onions, you prepare the Chickens the fame; scald the Onions first, then put them in the Stew-pan with the Chickens, a little Butter to simmer some Time, then add Broth, Cullis, and a little white Wine or none; when done, skim the Fat, and add a pounded Anchovy, and few whole small Capers.

Poulets à l'Etuvée.

Chickens stewed or Matlot.

CUT a Carp with Roe in large Pieces, and put it in a Stew-pan with the Roe, a Chicken cut in Pieces, one Dozen of small Onions, scalded, few Mushrooms, a Slice of Ham, a Nosegay of Parsley, Chibbol, Thyme, Laurel, Basil, two Cloves, a Bit of Butter;

simmer

simmer all together on the Fire, then add Broth, a Glafs of Wine, few Spoonfuls of Cullis and Flour, Pepper and Salt; let it boil till the Chicken is done, and the Sauce reduced; then take out the Carp, Nofegay, and Ham, leave the Roe, add a chopt Anchovy, few fmall Capers; place the Chicken upon the Difh, intermixed with Onions and Roes; fkim the Fat off the Sauce: ferve upon the Meat, garnifh the Difh with fried Bread.

Poulets à la Cavaliere.

A la Cavaliere, meaning without Art or Ceremony.

TRUSS the Chickens as for boiling, Legs Infide, flatten the Breaft, marinade them four or five Hours in Oil, Lemon Slices peeled, Sprigs of Parfley, whole green Shallots, one Clove of Garlick, Thyme, Laurel, Bafil, Salt and fine Spices; then tie them up in thin Slices of Lard, and good deal of Paper, with as much of the Marinade as you can; broil them on a flow Fire; when done, take off the Lard and Herbs, which may flick to the Chickens; and ferve with what Sauce you think proper.

Poulets Mignons aux Ecrévisses.

Mignons, a favourite Difh; fmall Chickens with Craw-fifh.

SPLIT two Chickens by the Back, and bone them all to the Legs and Wings; ftuff them with a Farce called *Salpicon* raw cut in fmall Dices, made with Sweet Breads, Mufhrooms, fcraped Lard, chopped Parfley, green Shallots, Powder of Bafil, Salt and Pepper; then give the Chickens their proper Form and few up the Back; tie them up with Slices of Lard, and Bits of Linen or Stamine; boil them in Broth, in a Pan much of their Bigness, a Glass of white Wine, a Nosegay of sweet Herbs; when done, take off the Lard, wipe the Fat off very clean; and serve with a Ragout of Craw-fish Tails and Cullis: you will find the Way to make it in Cullis Articles.

Poulets à la Perle.

Chickens in the Form of Pearl.

CUT two Chickens in two, and bone them all to the Legs; fill each Piece with a *Salpicon* as the former, give each Half, the Form of a Pearl; cut the Leg pretty close to give it a pointed Form; sew them up, and braze them with Slices of Veal, and Lard, a little Broth, and a Glass of white Wine, two Slices of peeled Lemon, a Nosegay, half a Clove of Garlick, two Cloves, a little Thyme and Laurel, Pepper and Salt; when done, sfit the Sauce, and skim it very free from Fat; add a little Cullis to thicken it, reduce to a Sauce, and serve upon the Chickens.

Poulets au Vin de Champagne.

Chickens with White Wine Sauce.

TAKE two good large fat Chickens, and truss them like Fowls, and lard them coarsly; give them a fry in Lard for a Moment, then put them in a Stew-pan with Slices of Veal and Ham, and the melted Lard which you used before; cover them with thin Slices of Bacon, two Slices of peeled Lemon upon the Breast, a Nosegay, two Cloves, Thyme, Laurel, few whole Mushrooms, half a Clove of Garlick, a Glass of white Wine; when done, skim and sift the Sauce, add a little Cullis, and serve upon the Chickens.

Poulets au Pontife.

Chickens Pontiff Sauce.

SCALD and boil eight or ten small Onions to half, then drain them, and put them to marinade with Truffles; cut in Dices two fat Livers, fine Oil, Salt and Pepper, Parsley, Shallots, a little Basil, all finely chopped; take two middling Chickens, which you split, and bone all to the Legs; put the Marinade in them, truss the Legs upon the Breast, and sew them up; give them a fry with a Bit of Butter; tie a Couple of Slices of Lemon upon the Breast, with Slices of Bacon, and roast them: serve with a Sauce au Pontife, which you will find in Sauce Articles, Page 46.

Poulets à la Folette.

Folette, Wanton, Fantask, &c.

CUT Carrots and Parsneps according to Fancy, which boil in Broth, with half a Dozen small Onions; and cut few Truffles and Mushrooms, and a Slice of Ham in Dices; put this last in a Stew-pan, with good Butter, a Nosegay of sweet Herbs, two Cloves, Thyme and Laurel; give it a fry in the Butter, then add Veal Gravy, a Glass of white Wine, and boil slowly; when done, skim the Fat very clean, add a little Cullis, and put to it the first Preparation, half a Handful of Olive stoned, roast two middling Chickens, stuffed with a little Farce, made of their Livers, &c. roll them up in Slices of Lard and Paper: when done, serve the Ragout upon them.

Poulets à la Belle-vūe.

See Sauce à la Belle-vūe, Page 39.

BOIL eight or ten small Onions in Broth to three Parts, then put them in a Stew-pan, with some melted Lard, two Slices of Lemon peeled, Truffles or Mushrooms, fat Livers cut in Dices, Pepper and Salt; simmer this slowly about half an Hour without liquid, then let it cool; bone two good Chickens, and stuff them with the Ragout, wrap them up in Slices of Bacon, with Pepper and Salt, few green Shallots, Sprigs of Parsley, and a double Paper, rubbed over with good Oil or melted Butter; broil them slowly; when done, wipe the Fat, and serve with a Sauce à la Belle-vūe, which you will find in Sauce Articles.

Poulets à la Mariée.

Chickens, Bride Fashion.

BONE two small Chickens, and stuff them with fat Livers minced, and mixed with chopt Parsley, one Shallot, a little Basil, scraped Lard, Pepper and Salt; marinade awhile in good Oil, then wrap them up with thin Slices of Bacon, Veal and Ham, and double Paper; put them in a Stew-pan, upon a very slow Fire; when done, take off all the Slices, and serve with Sauce Nonpareil. See Page 31.

Poulets à l'Italienne.

Chickens Italian Fashion.

TRUSS a Couple of Chickens, as for boiling, lard them with Larding, Bacon and Ham intermixed; give them a fry in Butter, then in a Stew-pan, with
Slices

Slices of Veal, and the Butter you used first, a Nosegay, one Clove of Garlick, two of Spices, Pepper and Salt, covered with Slices of Lard, half a Lemon, sliced, and first peeled; soak it about half an Hour, then add a Glass of white Wine; when done, sift the Sauce, and skim the Fat; add a little Butter, rolled in Flour: reduce to the Consistence of a Sauce, and serve it upon the Chickens.

Poulets à l'Aspic.

See Aspick Sauce, Page 38.

BOIL eight small white Onions to half; serve them whole, and put them in a Stew-pan, with Truffles or Mushrooms cut in Dices, chopt Parsley, Shallots, fat Livers, Thyme, Laurel, a little Powder of Basil, two Spoonfuls of good Oil; simmer this until all is done tender, add Pepper and Salt, then let it cool: split two Chickens, take out the Breast Bone, and stuff them with the Ragout; when well fastened, give them a fry in Oil or Butter, then wrap them up with few Slices of Lard and Paper, and finish them in roasting; and serve with Aspic Sauce, as set forth in Sauce Articles.

Filets de Poulets à la Béchamel Pannée.

Fillets of Chickens Bechamel Sauce with Bread Crums.

CUT the Hind Part of two or three Chickens off, meaning the Legs and Rumps; they will serve you for another Dish; and roast the Breast first, wrapt in Paper, rubbed with Butter; when done, and cold, cut all the Meat in Fillets to put in a Bechamel Sauce, and put it in the Dish you intend to serve at Table; strew Bread Crums over it, basting with a little melted Butter;

ter; give it a Colour in the Oven, or with a Salamander, or a Brazing-pan Cover: you will find Bechamel Sauce in Sauce Articles, Page 42.

Filets Soufflés à la Béchamel.

Fillets Puffed Bechamel Sauce.

PUT a Bit of good Butter in a Stew-pan with a Slice of Ham, two Shallots; cut in few Bits, few Basil Leaves, one sliced Onion; soak all together upon a quick Fire, then add Cream sufficient; boil it till the Sauce is of a good Consistence, and sift it in a Sieve, add Pepper and Salt, then put to it Fillets of roasted Meat, as of Poultry, Rabbits, Partridges, &c. add the Whites of two Eggs, first well beat; mix it well all together, and pour it in the Dish you intend to use for Table; Bread Crums over it, and very small Bits of Butter, close to each other upon the Crums; give it Colour as the former, and serve quite hot.

Fleurons à la Brunette.

Flourish in Form of Petit Paté.

TAKE Petit Paté Moulds or any other, garnish the Inside with very thin Slices of Bacon, then cut Truffles in what kind of Flower you please; lay this upon the Bacon, the upper Part of the Moulds, for a Border; and garnish the lowest with any Sorts of Greens of different Colours, first scalded, and rub it all over with Whites of Eggs, to make them stick, then chop the Parings of the Truffles, with Breast of Fowl roasted, Udder and scraped Lard, half a Shallot, Pepper and Salt, four Yolks of Eggs; fill the Moulds with this, cover them with a thin Slice of Lard, bake in the Oven, the same Heat as for Petit Patés: they will only require about a Quarter of an Hour to bake; when done

done, take off the Lard at the Top, and turn them over gently upon the Cover of a Stew pan, and take the first Slices of Lard off gently for fear of displacing any of the Garnishing, and serve with a good Cullis Sauce, mixed with a little white Wine.

Poulets à la Bricoliere.

This Name is taken from the Way of being trussed, as resembling Part of a Chairman's Strap, or the Harness of a Shaft Horse.

BONE two or three small fat Chickens, all to the Legs, which you truss upon the Breast; give them a few Turns in a Stew-pan, with a little Oil or Butter, and two Slices of peeled Lemon; then put them in another Pan with few Slices of Ham and Veal, the Oil or Butter, and Lemon which you used first; cover them over with Slices of Bacon, a Nosegay, one Clove of Garlick, two Cloves of Spices, Thyme, Laurel, Pepper and Salt; soak all this about a Quarter of an Hour, then add a Glass of white Wine; finish the Brazing, sift and skim the Sauce, add a little Cullis, to make a Liason; and serve upon the Chickens.

Petit Poussins aux Pavies.

Small Chickens, and preserved Nectarines.

TRUSS three very small fat Chickens quite round, and give them a fry in Butter; then wrap them up in Slices of Lard, with few Slices of Lemon upon the Breast, and Paper over it, roast them; take Nectarines, preserved in Vinegar, which you cut in Slices, peel them, and soak in Water awhile, to take out the Taste of Vinegar; mix a little Gravy and Cullis together, and put the Nectarines in it to warm, and serve upon the Chickens; you may also only cut them in Quarters, and simmer a little longer in the Sauce, to make them tender.

Fricaſſée de Poulets à la Bourdois.

Fricaſſee of Chickens; after the Name of the Author *Bourdois.*

CUT two ſmall Chickens as uſual, and put them in a Stew-pan with all the Trimmings, a Slice of Ham, a Noſegay of Parſley, and green Shallots, two Cloves, Thyme, Laurel, few Leaves of Baſil; ſoak all together a Moment, with a Bit of good Butter, then add ſome Broth, a little Flour, a Glaſs of white Wine; boil till the Chickens are done, and the Sauce reduced; then make a Liaſon with two or three Yolks of Eggs beat up with a little Broth, few Drops of Verjuice, or a Lemon Squeeze; pour this upon the Diſh you intend for Table; let it cool, then ſtrew it over with Bread Crums, and ſmall Bits of Butter, cloſe to each other; colour in the Oven, or with a Brazing-pan Cover, or Salamander.

Des Couleurs que l'on ſe ſert à la Cuiſine.

Of Colours uſed in Cookery.

FOR Red, take baked Beet-root pounded, put a little Cullis to it, and ſift it in a Stamine; it muſt be pretty thick; you may make a little thin Paſte of it, which you cut to what Form or Flower you pleaſe, to apply upon any Thing you have a Mind to flouriſh; baſte the Meat with Whites of Eggs firſt, to make it ſtick, then put it in the Oven a Moment, juſt to dry it: *Yellow* is made with Yolks of hard Eggs, pounded, and a little Cullis, and ſifted as the former: *Green* is made with ſcalded and pounded Spinage, and finiſhed as the former; and the ſame of any others: Cochineal and Saffron make alſo very good Colours, and if you

mix

mix a little melted Isinglass with each, it will make the Jelly stronger, and fitter to cut in different Shapes, with which you may garnish any cold Dishes according to Fancy.

Poulets Histories.

Chickens Garnished, embellished, &c.

TRUSS a Couple of large Chickens, as to roast; give them a few Turns over the Fire in a Stew-pan with Butter, and a Lemon Squeeze, to preserve their Whiteness, then take them out, and wipe the Breast very clean; cut a large Onion quite round, and pretty thin, take two or three Rings, which you dip in Whites of Eggs, and apply upon the Breast; and in them lay different Colours, in proper Forms, as your Fancy shall direct, basting the Breast of the Chickens with White of Eggs, to make the Colour stick: for *Red*, use Craw-fish Spawn, or some of the former Colours, or chopped Ham: for *Green*, use green Herbs of a good Flavour, as Ravigotte: for *Yellow*, Yolks of hard Eggs: for *White*, Breast of Poultry minced; then cover this over with thin Slices of Lard, and put them in a Stew-pan to braze, with few Slices of Veal and Ham, and a Nosegay of sweet Herbs, two Cloves, a Bit of Laurel Leaf, a Slice of Lemon peeled, Pepper and Salt, a Glass of white Wine, as much good Broth; cover it over with white Paper; let it braze on a middling Fire about an Hour; when done, take off the Lard gently, add a little Cullis to the Sauce; reduce it to a good Consistence, sift it, and skim the Fat clean off: serve upon the Chickens.

Culottes

Culottes de Poulets aux petits Onions.

(*Culottes* are the Legs and Rumps cut off together.)

WHEN you have occasion to use Breasts of Chickens for Fillets, Forced-meat, or other Use; tie up the Hind Part to what Form you please; give them few Turns on the Fire, with good Butter, then put them in a Stew-pan to braze, with few Slices of Ham and Bacon, a Nosegay, half a Lemon, sliced, and small white Onions, half boiled; cover it over with thin Slices of Lard, add a Glass of white Wine, or a little Broth; braze slowly; when done, sift and skim the Sauce, add two Spoonfuls of Veal Cullis; reduce the Sauce, and serve upon the Meat, with a Lemon Squeeze, if not relishing enough of the Lemon from the Slices.

Poulets aux Ecrevisses.

Chickens with, or as Craw-fish.

BONE two or three middling Chickens, then roll them pointed at the Neck Part, and braze them with Slices of Lard and Ham, two or three Slices of Lemon peeled, two Spoonfuls of good Jelly Broth, a Glass of white Wine, Salt and Pepper, a Nosegay of sweet Herbs, half a Clove of Garlick, and as many large Craw-fish as Chickens, which you braze together; they will only require about an Hour to do, then take them out, and wipe the Fat off; lay them on the Dish you intend for Table, stick the Neck Part in the Tail of a Craw-fish, the Body upon the Chicken, and the Claws on the Side; sift and skim the Sauce, add a little Veal Cullis; reduce it, and serve upon the Chickens.

Poulets

Poulets à la Broche avec Ragoût de Légumes.

Roasted Chickens with stewed Greens.

MAKE a little Forced-meat with the Livers, scraped Lard, chopped Parsley, Shallots, Pepper and Salt; stuff a Couple of Chickens with this, trussed for roasting; lay a Couple of Slices of Lemon on the Breast, and wrapt up with thin Slices of Lard and Paper; roast them and serve upon what Sort of stewed Greens you please, as Spinage, Morels, Mushrooms, Cucumbers, green Peas, Cardoons, small Onions, any Sorts of Roots, Sellery, Olives, &c. you will find the Method to dress each Sort in Articles for Ragout, Vol. II.

Poulets à la Broche à differentes Sauces.

Roasted Chickens with different Sauces.

ROASTED or broiled Chickens may be served with what Sauce you please, as Nonparel, Nivernoise, Italian, Mariniere, Celadon, Coloris, Consumet, Saxe, &c. all the Sauces, which you will find all together, see Sauces.

Poulets à l'Excellence, Excellency.

CUT a Quarter of a Pound of pickled Pork in thin Slices, soak it until it is done to three Parts, then put to it chopped Truffles, fat Livers, Parsley, Shallots, whole Pepper; simmer this together, till all is done enough, with a Glass of white Wine; then add two Yolks of Eggs, to thicken it, and let it cool; take up the Skin of two fat Chickens, and stuff some of this Ragout under, the Rest in the Inside of the Body; truss the Chickens as for roasting, and give them a fry in a

Stew-

Stew-pan with Butter, and a Lemon Squeeze; then wrap them in thin Slices of Lard and Paper, to roast; make a Sauce after this Manner: garnish a small Stew-pan with thin Slices of Bacon, Veal and Ham, Bits of Carrots, Parsneps, two sliced Onions, a Parsley-root, Thyme, Laurel, two Cloves, a little Nutmeg, a Spoonful of Oil, soak it about half an Hour in a Stew-pan, well covered; then add a Glass of white Wine, as much Broth, braze it about an Hour and half on a very slow Fire; sift and skim the Sauce: when you are ready to serve, chop three Shallots scalded, a little Butter and Flour; make a Liason, and serve upon the Chickens.

Poulets à la Jardiniere.

(From the Garden Greens which make the Sauce.)

MAKE a Sauce with few Slices of Veal and Ham, Bits of Carrots, Parsneps, sliced Onions, few Basil Leaves; soak it until it catches a little, then put to it a Glass of white Wine, as much Broth, two Cloves, one of Garlick; boil slowly to reduce to a Sauce, then sift and skim it; add some chopped scalded Charvil, a Bit of Butter and Flour: give a boil, and serve under roasted Chickens.

Poulets à la (Bonne Amie) friendly, easy Way.

Chickens without Art.

CUT off the Wings of four middling Chickens, flatten them with the Handle of a Knife; marinade them with Pepper and Salt, chopped Parsley, green Shallots, Mushrooms, and a little good Oil, then put them in a Stew-pan, separately with the Marinade, on a good brisk Fire, and turn them soon: they will require only about a Quarter of an Hour to do; take the

the Wings out, and lay them on the Dish you intend for Table; add two Spoonfuls of Cullis to the Sauce; skim it well, and when ready, add a good Lemon Squeeze, to serve upon the Meat.

Poulets en Papillottes.

Chickens in Paper.

MAKE a Farce with three hard Yolks of Eggs, two fat Livers, Calve's Udder, Beef Marrow, green Shallots, and Mushrooms, chopped; add two Yolks of raw Eggs to mix it well together, with Pepper and Salt; cut two Chickens, each in four Pieces, and boned; stuff each Piece with some of this Farce, roll them round, and fasten them well, then give them few Turns in a Stew-pan on the Fire, with Lard and Butter; few fine Spices, chopt Mushrooms and Parsley, then cover them with thin Slices of Lard, double Paper; bake them in the Oven; when done, unfold the Paper and Bacon, save as much of the Herbs as you can, to mix with a little Gravy and Cullis, warm together, add a Lemon Squeeze to serve upon the Chickens.

Poulets à la Dauphine.

Chickens Dauphin Fashion.

MAKE a Farce with the Livers, Butter, Nutmeg, Parsley, Shallots, Pepper and Salt, Mushrooms, two Yolks of Eggs; stuff the Chickens with this Farce; when done roasting, put a little Farce under the Wings and Legs, made of Bread Crumbs, Butter, chopt Parsley and Shallots, Pepper and Salt; put the Chickens in a Stew-pan, Breast undermost, with half a Glass of white Wine, two Spoonfuls of Jelly Broth; simmer about a Quarter of an Hour: when ready, add a Lemon Squeeze.

Poulets en Saucissons.

Chickens as large Sausages.

MAKE a Farce with Bread Crums, Cream, Breast of Fowl roasted, Calve's Udder half boiled, a little Tripe or Beef Marrow, few Onions baked in Ashes, chopt Parsley, Shallots, Mushrooms, Salt and fine Spices, a small Spoonful of Brandy, five raw Yolks of Eggs; and add another Farce raw, called *Salpicon*, with a scalded Sweet Bread, few Livers, Mushrooms, a little Salt and Pepper; then split two Chickens at the Back to bone thoroughly: put upon each Part, some of the first Farce, and upon this some of the second, roll them round like Sausages, well tied with Packthread, put them to braze with a Glass of white Wine, as much Broth, few Slices of Lard; when done, let them cool, then put the Remainder of the Farce round the Chickens; wrap them in Cowl, baste them with White of Eggs, dip them in Eggs, and strew with Bread Crums; put them in the Oven, until the Cowl is of a fine brown Colour: for Sauce, sift the Broth in which thy were brazed, add a little Cullis, skim it well; add a Lemon Squeeze, and serve under the Chickens.

Poulets à l'Amiral.

Chickens Admiral Fashion.

MAKE a Farce with the Livers of two Chickens chopped, with Truffles, Parsley, Shallots, scraped Lard, Pepper and Salt; stuff the Chickens with it, and give them a fry in a Stew-pan with Butter; truss them for roasting, wrap them up in Slices of Lard, and few Slices of Lemon upon the Breast, double Paper rubbed with Oil or Butter, and roast them: take some large Oysters,

which

which you scald in their own Liquor, and bearded as for Ragout; rub the Bottom of a Stew-pan with Butter, and lay a Down of sliced Truffles or Mushrooms, with a little Salt and Pepper, chopt Parsley, Shallots, upon this a Bed of Oysters: continue in this Manner, two or three Times over, pouring a little Oil or melted Butter upon them, cover the Stew-pan, and soak it about a Quarter of an Hour on a slow Fire, then drain the Oysters and Truffles, to put upon the Chickens; add a little Cullis to the Sauce; give it a boiling with half a Glass of white Wine; skim the Sauce very clean of Fat; add a Lemon Squeeze, when ready to serve upon the Chickens.

Poulets à la Tartare.

Chickens Tartary Fashion.

TRUSS two Chickens, as for boiling, split them at the Back, and marinade them a while in good Oil, chopped Parsley, Shallots, Mushrooms, a Trifle of Garlick, Salt and Pepper, make as much of the Marinade stick to it as possible, garnish with Bread Crums; broil them on a slow Fire, basting with the Remainder of the Marinade; serve with Sauce Remoulade in a Sauceboat: you will find the Way to make it in Sauce Articles, Page 42.

Poulets entre deux Plats.

Chickens done between two Dishes, viz. stewed slowly.

LARD two small Chickens, half Lard and half Ham, and stuff them with a Farce, made of their Liver, &c. put them between two deep Dishes, with Slices of Bacon, Pepper and Salt, a few pounded Cloves, Bits of Carrots and Parsneps, Slices of Onions, Sprigs of Parsley, fley, two Slices of Lemon peeled, half a Glafs of white Wine; fimmer them on a flow Fire; when done, fift and fkim the Sauce, add a Bit of Butter and Flour, to make a Liafon; and ferve upon the Chickens, which ought to be very white.

Poulets Marinés.

Chickens Marinaded.

CUT one or two Chickens as for Fricaffee, put the Pieces in warm Water, as you cut them; then drain the Water off, then put them for about two Hours in a Marinade, made of Water and Vinegar, Pepper and Salt, Sprigs of Parfley, whole Shallots, Slices of Onions, Lemon, Thyme, Laurel, Cloves; keep the Marinade on hot Afhes, to give it more Tafte, then wipe the Chickens quite clean with a Linen Cloth; dip each Piece in White of Eggs, and floured over; fry them in Oil or Hog's Lard, brifkly, to give them a good Colour, and ferve with fried Parfley.

Poulets à la Sainte Menehoult.

Chickens broiled.

TRUSS one or two Chickens, as for boiling, cut them in halves, and flatten with the Handle of a Knife, lard them, half Ham and Lard; boil them on a flow Fire, in a St. Menehoult, which is done in putting a Spoonful of Flour in a Stew-pan with Milk, fufficient to boil the Chickens, Salt and Pepper, chopped Parfley, Shallots, Thyme, Laurel, Coriander, Bits of Roots, Slices of Onions, a Bit of Butter; when this boils, put the Chickens in it; when done, take them out, and roll them in Bread Crums, give Colour in the Oven, or with a Brazing-pan Cover, or broil them;

ferve

serve with Sauce à la Nivernoise; see Sauce Articles, or any other relishing Sauce, as you shall think proper.

Fricandeaux de Poulets à l'Espagnole.

Spanish Fashion.

BONE two or three middling Chickens thoroughly, stuff them with a Farce, made of fat Livers, scraped Lard, two Yolks of Eggs, Pepper and Salt, one Shallot chopped very fine; sew them up to hinder the Farce from getting out; give them few Turns in a Stew-pan over the Fire with Butter, then wipe them, and lard like a Fricandeau; braze them in good Broth, a Slice of Ham, a Nosegay, a little Basil, two Cloves, half a Clove of Garlick; when done, take them out, sift the Sauce, and reduce it to a Glaze, to put over the larded Part: and serve with a Spanish Sauce, see Sauces, Page 40.

Poulets au Verd-Pré.

(Meadow-green.) See green Sauces, page 45.

MAKE a Farce with the Livers, scraped Lard, chopt Parsley, green Shallots, Pepper and Salt; stuff the Chickens with it; wrap them in Slices of Lard and Paper: roast them, and serve with the above Sauce.

Poulets à la Cardinal.

CUT the Breast Bone out of two fat Chickens, and separate the Skin from the Flesh without breaking it, and stuff them between, with Craw-fish, Butter, a little Pepper and Salt, two Leaves of Basil, one Clove of Shallots finely chopped; sew it up very well; give them few Turns in a Stew-pan over the Fire with Butter,

Butter, then wrap them up in Slices of Bacon and Paper, to roaft; make a Sauce with good Jelly Broth, half a Glafs of white Wine, or a Lemon Squeeze; when ready, add a Bit of Craw-fifh Butter; ferve upon the Chickens.

Matelotte de Poulets à la Broche.

Matlot of Chickens roafted.

SCALD a Dozen of fmall white Onions, which you put in a Stew-pan, with Mufhrooms, a Nofegay of fweet Herbs, green Shallots, Thyme, Laurel, two or three fat Livers, a Bit of good Butter; when fried a little, add half a Glafs of white Wine, Cullis and Broth, Salt and Pepper; put a little Vinegar to it, or fmall Capers whole: ferve under a Couple of roafted Chickens; garnifh the Difh with fried Bread.

Matelotte de Poulets à l'Anguille.

With Eel.

CUT two Chickens, each in Quarters; put them in a Stew-pan, with a good Bit of Butter, a Nofegay of Parfley, Shallots, Thyme, Laurel, one Clove of Garlick, three of Spices, one Dozen of fmall Onions, firft fcalded; foak this awhile, then add a Glafs of white Wine, or more, two or three Spoonfuls of Cullis, Pepper and Salt; when the Chickens are half done, put to them an Eel cut in Pieces, half a Spoonful of whole Capers; when done, take out the Nofegay and Garlick; ferve the reft upon the Chickens, and garnifh round with fried Bread.

Matelottes

Matelotte de Poulets Cuits.

Of roasted Chickens.

CUT roasted Chickens, as for a Fricaffee, and skin them; place the Bits properly on the Dish you intend for Table, and put a little Broth to it to warm; make a Ragout of small Onions, first scalded, then boiled in Broth and Cullis; a Nosegay of Parsley, Shallots, half a Leaf of Laurel, Thyme, two Cloves; when three Parts done, put to it one Dozen of small Craw-fish, a little Salt and Pepper; a little Vinegar, when ready to serve upon the Chickens.

Grenadins de Poulets.

Small Fricandeaux, done after the same Manner as the large ones, stuffed, larded, and glazed.

Poulets aux Trufes.

Chickens with Truffles.

GARNISH the Bottom of a Stew-pan with Slices of Veal and Ham, Truffles sliced or whole, a Nosegay of sweet Herbs, with a little Basil, two Cloves, Pepper and Salt; truss two Chickens as for roasting, and put them in the Stew-pan, covered with Slices of Lard; soak it on a middling Fire about a Quarter of an Hour, then add a Glass of white Wine, and finish on a slow Fire; when done, sift and skim the Sauce, add two Spoonfuls of Cullis, and reduce it to a Sauce Consistence; put the Truffles round the Chickens, and serve the Sauce upon them; Chickens roasted with Truffles, are done with chopping the Livers and Truffles together, mixed with a little Butter; stuff them with it, and serve with a Ragout of Truffles under.

Poulets à la Saint Cloud.

Chickens St. Cloud Fashion.

BONE two Chickens all to the Legs, and stuff them with a Ragout made of small Onions, chopt Truffles or Mushrooms, fat Livers, Anchovies, all cut in Dices, and well boiled with Cullis, pretty thick; sew up the Chickens, and truss them as if they were not boned; give them a Fry in Oil or Butter, and braze them between Slices of Lard, Slices of Lemon, some Cullis; simmer on a slow Fire; when done, sift and skim the Sauce, add a little more Cullis, Pepper and Salt, and serve upon the Chickens: you also serve with what Sauce you think proper; being brazed and stuffed after this Manner.

Poulets à la Liason aux petits Oeufs Composés.

Chickens Liason Sauce, and small Eggs shammed.

CUT two Chickens in Quarters, and braze them with Slices of Lard, a Glass of white Wine, a Nosegay of Parsley, green Shallots, a little Basil, one Clove of Garlick, two Cloves of Spices, a Bit of Butter, Flour, Salt and Pepper, a Slice of Ham, one or two Spoonfuls of Cullis; when done, sift the Sauce, and skim the Fat clean off; add three Yolks of Eggs beat up with some of the Sauce; while the Chickens are brazing make your sham Eggs after this Manner, soak Bread Crums in good Cullis, until it is quite thick; put in a Mortar, with one Clove of Shallots chopped very fine, a Spoonful of Beef Marrow melted, four or five hard Yolks of Eggs; pound this together with Pepper and Salt; then add two raw Yolks of Eggs; mix it well

Flour

all together, make little Balls of it, which you roll in Flour; put them a Moment in boiling Broth, then put them in the Sauce as prepared, and ferve upon the Chickens.

Poulets à la Villageoife.

Chickens Country Fafhion.

CUT out the Breaft-bone of two Chickens, and trufs them as for boiling; give them a Fry in Butter, lard the Breaft with Sprigs of Parfley, the Sides with Lard, and roaft them, bafting with Hog's Lard to keep the Parfley crifp; when they are done, have a Ragout of Cucumber, well tafted; fplit the Breaft and pour it in the Chickens: ferve under a good Cullis Sauce.

Poulets au Gratin.

TAKE Chickens roafted, fuch as have been at Table or others, cut them in Pieces, and put them in a Stew-pan with few Spoonfuls of Cullis, half a Glafs of white Wine, a Bit of Butter, chopped Parfley, Shallots, Mufhrooms, Pepper and Salt; fimmer all together about a Quarter of an Hour; lay the Chickens in the Difh you intend for Table, with half of the Sauce in the Bottom, and Bread Crums or Cruft Parings; fimmer it until it catches at Bottom (which is the Meaning of Gratin); when ready, add the Remainder of the Sauce upon the Chickens.

Poulets en Surtout.

Chickens Mafqueraded.

CUT two Chickens in Quarters, and braze with Slices of Lard, few Slices of Lemon peeled, a little Confumet,

fumet, Pepper and Salt, a Nofegay, and two Cloves; have a large Eel, which you cut in pretty long Pieces; fplit each Bit in two, without feparating quite; take out the Bones, and lard the Outfide with fine Lard: boil it in Veal Cuilis; which, when done, you reduce to a Glaze, to glaze the Eel with; lay the Pieces of Chickens in the Table Difh, and a Piece of Eel upon each: ferve with a Spanifh Sauce, or any other according to Fancy, and Convenience.

Poulets à la Reine.

(See Sauce à la Reine.) Page 48.

TAKE roafted Chickens, which have ferved before; cut all the Flefh from the Breaft, and cut out the Breaft Bone; mince the Meat, and mix it with a Farce made of Bread Crums, Cream, Beef Suet, fcraped Lard, chopt Parfley, Shallots, Pepper and Salt, Nutmeg, and four or five Yolks of Eggs; fill the Chickens with this, as if whole; fmooth it with a Knife dipt in Whites of Eggs, ftrew it over with Bread Crums, and bake in the Oven; ferve with a Sauce à la Reine.

Poulets au Céladon.

(See Sauce au Céladon, Sea-green.) Page 32. or as follows.

SCALD a good Quantity of Parfley, and Garden Crefles, or any other Herbs; fqueeze the Water out, and pound the Herbs very fine; put in a Stew-pan with a good deal of Butter; let it fimmer about half an Hour, then fift it in a Stamine, prefling hard with a Spoon to extract the Green of the Herbs; take Part of this Butter, to make a Farce, with the Livers chopped, Salt and Pepper; ftuff the Chickens with it, and wrap them in Slices of Bacon and Paper to roaft; put two or three Spoonfuls of Cullis in a fmall Stew-pan; boil it a Moment,

ment, and put to it some of the former Butter; add a Lemon Squeeze, when ready to serve upon the Chickens.

Poulets en Caisses.

Chickens in Paper Cases.

Take Chickens roasted, and cut all the white meat in large fillets; marinade them about an hour, with a little oil, parsley, shallots, mushrooms, half a bay-leaf, pepper and salt; make cases of white paper, and put the fillets in it with their marinade; put them in the oven, or under a brazing-pan cover; when done, wipe the fat as much as possible, and a little cullis, and a lemon squeeze.

Poulets au Roumestec.

Roumestec, Cullis made of Fragments.

TAKE a Rabbit long kept, and cut as many Fillets without Bones as you can; marinade these about an Hour in melted Butter or good Oil, chopped Truffles, Mushrooms, Shallots, Parsley, Pepper and Salt, Nutmeg; take out the Breast Bone of two Chickens, without breaking the Skin; fill them up with the Fillets of Rabbits, and the Marinade; sew them up very well, and truss them for roasting; give them a fry in Butter, and roast them, wrapt in Slices of Lard and Paper: for the Sauce, simmer the Carcase of the Rabbit chopped in Pieces, Legs and Pinions of Poulteries; put to it half a Glass of white Wine, three Spoonfuls of good Cullis, well tasted; sift it, and serve upon the Chickens.

Cuisses de Poulets à differentes Sauces & Ragoûts.

Legs of Chickens with different Sauces and Ragouts.

WHEN you have occasion to use the white Meat of Chickens by itself, which is often the Case where a deal of Work is done: the Legs may also serve for a good Dish; braze them with Slices of Lard, and few Slices of Lemon, to keep them white, and serve them with what Ragout or Sauce you think proper.

Poulets à la Duchesse.

CUT some Artichoke, as for to fry, and leave only a few of the tender Leaves; scald them a Moment in boiling Water, then in Broth, with few Slices of Lemon, Pepper and Salt; roast two small fat Chickens, and make a Sauce with chopped Parsley, Shallots, Mushrooms, a Bit of Butter and Flour; then put to it half a Glass of white Wine, two Spoonfuls of rich Jelly Broth, a little Sprig of Fennel, which you only leave to boil a Moment, then take it out; boil the Sauce a Moment, and skim it well: when the Chickens are ready, put them on the Dish, the Artichoke round, and the Sauce over all.

Poulets aux petits Pois.

With green Peas.

CUT one or two Chickens as for a Fricassee, put them in a Stew-pan with a little Broth, a good Bit of Butter, Flour, a Nosegay of Parsley, Shallots, a little Mint; when half done, put a Quart of green Peas in the same Pan, and boil on a slow Fire; add two Spoonfuls of Cullis, a little Salt: let the Sauce be short; take out the Nosegay before you serve: if you would have

have it white, don't put either Cullis or Gravy to it; but put three Yolks of Eggs beat up with Cream: give it a boil, stirring it continually; reduce the liquid as much as possible.

Poulets au Parmesan.

With Parmesan Cheese.

BRAZE a Couple of Chickens, with Slices of Veal and Bacon, a Nosegay of Parsley, Shallots, Thyme, Laurel, a little Basil, two Cloves, half an Onion; soak this some Time; then add half a Glass of white Wine, a little Broth, whole Pepper and Salt, a good Bit of Butter, and a little Cullis; when done, sift and skim the Sauce; put Part of it in the Table Dish with rasped Parmesan, the Chickens upon; baste them with the Remainder of the Sauce, and Parmesan over: put them in the Oven, or under a Brazing-pan Cover, with Fire enough to give them a fine yellow Colour; clean the Border of the Dish, and serve with a short Sauce.

Poulets au Blanc-mangé.

BOIL a Pint of Cream, a little Coriander, a Laurel Leaf; take it off the Fire, and put to it a Handful of sweet Almonds, finely pounded; sift it in a Stamine several Times, then add four or five raw Yolks of Eggs beat up with a little Cream; put it on the Fire, stirring it constantly, for fear the Eggs should turn to Curd: have a Breast of Fowl roasted, minced very fine, and Beef Marrow, seasoned with Pepper, Salt and Nutmeg; mix all together; bone two Chickens, all to the Wings and Legs, and stuff them with said Blanc-mangé; truss them properly, and sew them up very fast; put them a Moment in boiling Water, to scald: braze them with Slices of Lard, some Milk, a Nosegay, two whole Shallots, Pepper and Salt; when done, prick

them

them in three or four Places, to let the Fat out; wipe them with a clean Cloth: serve with a Coulis à la Reine.

Poulets au Verjus.

With Verjuice Grapes or others.

PUT a good Handful of Verjuice Grapes in boiling Water a Moment to scald; then put them in a Stew-pan with two or three Spoonfuls of good Cullis, and Jelly Broth, a good Bit of Butter, Pepper and Salt; serve upon a Couple of Chickens, roasted, and stuffed with their Livers, &c.

Poulets au Sultan.

Chickens, Turkish Fashion.

MAKE a Farce with a Sweet Bread scalded, cut in Dices fat Livers, Mushrooms, scraped Lard, Pepper and Salt, chopt Parsley, Shallots; stuff two boned Chickens with this, braze them with Slices of Bacon, Slices of Lemon, first peeled, Slices of Veal, and one or two small of Ham, a Nosegay, half a Laurel Leaf, two Cloves, a little Broth, half a Glass of white Wine; braze on a slow Fire about an Hour, then sift and skim the Sauce; add a little Veal Cullis, and small Yolks of hard Eggs, or sham ones, as before directed (see Poulets aux Petits Oeufs;) boil it half a Quarter of an Hour, and serve upon the Chickens.

Poulets à la Favorite.

BONE two Chickens thoroughly, and make a good Farce with Breast of Fowl roasted, Beef Suet, or pounded Lard, sweet Herbs finely chopped, Pepper and Salt, Yolks of Eggs, sufficient to mix it well; cut each Chicken in two, and lay some of this Farce upon

upon each half; have an Eel cut in Fillets, which you lay upon the Farce, and cover it over with the Remainder of the Farce; smooth it with a Knife dipt in White of Eggs, then roll them up in Slices of Lard, and Bits of Stamine well tied with Packthread; braze them in Broth, two Glasses of white Wine, a Nosegay of Parsley, green Shallots, a Laurel Leaf, Thyme, half a Clove of Garlick, two of Spices, Pepper and Salt; when they are done, take off the Lard, and wipe the Chickens very clean, squeeze them a little in a Cloth to get the Fat out, and serve with a Sauce after this Manner: put two Slices of Fillet of Veal in a Stew-pan, one Slice of Ham; soak it on a slow Fire about half an Hour; then add two or three Glasses of white Wine, two Spoonfuls of good Cullis; boil it about half an Hour, to reduce to the Consistence of a Sauce; sift it, and skim it very clean; serve upon the Chickens.

Poulets en Salade.

CUT one or two good Lettuces as for Sallad, put it at the Bottom of your Sallad Dish, upon it Fillets of roasted Chickens, intermixed with Anchovies, chopt Capers, and Sallad Herbs properly laid, in the Manner of some Flower, or any Sort of Design.

Poulets Mignons aux Pistaches.

With Pistachio-Nuts.

BONE two small Chickens, all to the Legs and Wings; stuff them with a Farce made of Sweet Breads, chopt Truffles, or Mushrooms, scraped Lard, Pepper and Salt, two raw Yolks of Eggs; truss them as if whole, and sew them up to keep the Farce in; braze them with Slices of Bacon, Slices of Lemon, Slices of Veal, a Nosegay, two Cloves, whole Pepper

and

and Salt, two Spoonfuls of Broth; braze about an Hour on a slow Fire; sift and skim the Sauce, add two Spoonfuls of good Veal Cullis, a Handful of Pistachio-Nuts scalded; boil together few Minutes, wipe the Chickens very clean, and serve the Sauce upon them.

Matelotte des Poulets aux Racines.

Matlot of Chickens with Roots.

CUT a large Chicken in Quarters, and five or six thin Slices of pickled Pork, put it together in a Stewpan, with two or three Spoonfuls of Broth, a little Cullis, a Nosegay, two Cloves; let it simmer slowly, and cut Carrots and Parsneps to what Shape you please, one Dozen of small Onions, which you scald together; then put this in a Stew-pan by itself, with a good Bit of Butter; simmer awhile, then add a little Broth and Cullis; when three Parts done, sift and skim the Sauce of the Chicken, and put it to the Roots: reduce the liquid pretty thick; serve upon the Chicken, the pickled Pork intermixed.

Poulets Glacés.

Chickens Glazed.

TRUSS two Chickens as for boiling, cut them in two, or leave them whole; singe them, then lard as you do Fricandeaux; then braze them with Slices of Veal, one Slice of Ham, three or four whole Mushrooms, a Nosegay of sweet Herbs, half a Clove of Garlick, two of Spices; put a little Broth to it, and simmer slowly; when done, sift the Sauce, and reduce it to a Caramel, to glaze all the Breast Part of the Chickens: put a little more Broth and Cullis in the same Stew-pan, to gather the Remainder of the Glaze, which

which will serve you for Sauce, adding a Lemon Squeeze; you may serve those Chickens with any stewed Greens.

Poulets à la Payſanne.

Chickens Country-wife Faſhion.

BOIL a Handful of Bread Crums in Cream till it is quite thick, then take it off the Fire, and put to it a Quarter of a Pound of Butter, four Yolks of Eggs, Thyme, chopt Parſley, and one Shallot, Pepper and Salt; ſtuff the Chickens with it, and roaſt them wrapt in Slices of Lard and Paper; make a Sauce with a Bit of Butter and Flour, one Anchovy pounded ſmall, Capers whole, Pepper and Salt, a little Vinegar and Broth; make a Liaſon on the Fire, like a white Sauce, and ſerve upon the Chickens.

Poulets en Gelée; appellés Au Pere Douillet.

Chickens in Jelly; called, Au Pere Douillet, viz. a Fribble, Codling, &c.

TRUSS two Chickens as for boiling, ſinge them, and lard them with large Lardons rolled in fine Spices and ſweet Herbs, boil them with a Knuckle of Veal firſt ſcalded, half a Pint of white Wine, two Cloves, a Noſegay of Parſley, Shallots, Thyme, and Laurel, a little Coriander; when the Chickens are done, take them out and let them cool; ſkim the Broth and ſift it, and boil it awhile, put a Lemon ſliced, one raw Egg, and the Shell with it pounded, to clarify the Broth; when it is clear; ſift it in a Napkin, put the Chickens in a Pan much of their Bigneſs, apply upon them Sprigs of green Parſley, and other Colour as you ſhall think proper, bathing the Chickens firſt with White of Eggs to make them ſtick; lay the Chickens Breaſt under-moſt, and pour the

Jelly

Jelly upon them enough that they may be covered; let it cool; when you want to use them, dip the Pan a Moment in warm Water, turn them over gently.

Poulets à l'Indienne. (See Turk Fashion, it is much the same.)

Poulets à la Marmotte. Marmotte a young Wench.

CUT Carrots and Parsneps to what Shape you like, small Onions scalded, boil together in Broth, and cut Mushrooms in Dices, and pickled Cucumbers, put this in a Stew-pan with a Bit of Butter, half a Clove of Garlick, a Nosegay, two Cloves, a little Broth, Pepper and Salt, boil a while on a slow Fire, then add a Spoonful of Cullis, and the Roots; give it a boiling together, and serve with roasted Chickens.

CHAPITRE SEPTIEME. Du Dindon.

CHAPTER SEVENTH. Of Turkey.

Dindon à la Broche à différents Ragoûts.

Roasted Turkey with different Ragouts.

HEN Turkies are mostly preferable to Cocks for Whiteness and Tenderness; the small fleshy ones, are the most esteemed; they ought to be kept as long as the Weather will admit; make a Forced-meat with the Liver chopt, Parsley, Shallots, scraped Lard or Yolks of Eggs, Pepper and Salt; when properly truffed, give it a few Turns over the Fire in a large Stew-pan with Butter, put the Farce where the Craw was taken out; roast it, with Lemon Slices upon the Breast to keep it White, and Slices of Lard and double Paper; serve with what Ragout you think proper, as Mushrooms, Morels, small Onions, or large Spanish ones, Girkins, small

Melons,

Melons, Cucumbers, Truffles, Green Peas, small Garden Beans, Endives, Cardoon, Roots of any Sort, Sellery, Craw-fish, any thing according to Season.

Dindon farci d'Oignons & petit Lard.

Turkey stuffed with Onions and pickled Pork.

SCALD two Dozen of small white Onions, and boil them in Broth, with half a Pound of pickled Pork cut in thin Slices, a Nosegay of Parsley, green Shallots, Thyme, Bay-leaf, two Cloves, whole Pepper and Salt; when done, drain it all, and stuff the Turkey with it; wrap it in Slices of Lard and Paper to roast; make a Sauce with a Bit of Butter, a Slice of Ham, two Shallots, few Mushrooms; soak it awhile, then add two Spoonfuls of Broth, as much Cullis; simmer it about half an Hour, skim it and sift it; when ready, add a small Spoonful of Mustard, a little Pepper and Salt.

Dindon au Pere Douillet.

(See the same Name in Chicken Articles.) Ditto 145.

SINGE a Turkey over the Charcoal, truss it as for boiling, Legs inside; put it in a large Brasing-pan with Slices of Fillet of Veal, a Knuckle, a good Bit of Ham, a few Slices of Beef, a large Nosegay of Parsley, green Shallots, one Laurel Leaf, Thyme, a little Basil, four Cloves, a little Broth, a Pint of white Wine, Salt and Pepper; boil on a slow Fire until the Turkey is done, then take it out, drain it, sift the Broth, and put it on the Fire again, with two raw Eggs and Shells bruised, two or three Slices of peeled Lemon; boil it, stirring often until it becomes clear; sift it in a Napkin or Jelly Cloth, put the Turkey in a Pan much of its Bigness; boil five or six Craw-fish, lay them properly in the Bottom of the Pan intermixed with green Parsley, and other Colour;

put

put the Turkey upon this, Breaſt undermoſt, and pour the Jelly upon it: when you want to uſe it, dip the Pan in warm Water, and turn it over gently upon a Napkin: garniſh the Diſh with Parſley.

Dindon en Galantine.

Turkey Coloured.

CUT a Turkey in two, bone it thoroughly; make a good Farce with Breaſt of roaſted Fowl, and every thing as directed ſeveral Times: lay ſome of it upon each Half pretty thick; then minced Ham, Girkins, Truffles or Muſhrooms, or both; Bacon cut in Dices, hard Yolks of Eggs, White of Fowl, few ſweet Almonds, Piſtachio-Nuts; then cover this with ſome of the Farce; roll up each Half, wrap them up with Slices of Bacon, and Bits of Stamine, or any thing elſe, to keep them faſt: put them in a Brazing-pan much of their Bigneſs, with good Broth, Half a Pint of white Wine, Slices of Veal and Beef, ſweet Herbs, two or three Shallots, one Clove of Garlick, three of Spices, Thyme, Laurel; braze them on a ſlow Fire, about three Hours; let them cool in the Broth, to ſerve cold upon a Napkin, or in Slices: it may equally be done whole.

Dindon à la Daube.

Turkey Dobed.

MAKE a good Salpicon, viz. a Farce with raw Meat as directed before; lard an old Turkey through and through, with large Lardons, rolled in Salt and fine Spices, ſweet Herbs, finely chopped; and mixed all together; put it in a Brazing-pan of its Bigneſs, with Slices of Lard at Bottom, a large Noſegay of ſweet Herbs, four Cloves, one of Garlick, Thyme and Laurel, two or three Onions, two Carrots in Bits, whole Pepper and Salt,

Salt, a Glaſs of Brandy, a Pint of white Wine and Broth; braze ſlowly about ſix or ſeven Hours until the Fleſh gives under the Finger; reduce the Broth, ſkim it and ſift it: let the Turkey cool in the Sauce, to ſerve cold together: it may alſo be uſed hot with the ſame Sauce.

Daube de Dindon Fouré.

Turkey dobed another Way.

BONE an old Turkey thoroughly; lard a middling Fillet of Veal in the ſame Manner, as the Turkey à la Daube: lard alſo the Turkey, and ſtuff it with the Fillet of Veal; finiſh as the former, and uſe it the ſame Way.

Dindon au Court Bouillon.

Turkey in its own Gravy.

TAKE out the Breaſt Bone of a Turkey, and ſtuff it with a Sweet Bread ſcalded; cut in ſmall Bits, Muſhrooms, ſcraped Lard, Pepper and Salt; put the Turkey in a Brazing-pan of its Bigneſs, wrapt up in Slices of Lard, two Spoonfuls of Broth, a Jill of white Wine, a Noſegay, Thyme, Laurel, three Cloves, a little Nutmeg; braze ſlowly, turn it two or three Times; when done, ſkim the Sauce, and ſift it; add a chopt Shallot; reduce the Sauce, and ſerve upon the Turkey.

Dindon Farci de Trufes à l'Eſpagnole.

Turkey ſtuffed with Truffles, Spaniſh Faſhion.

PEEL about a Pound, or a Pound and a half of Truffles, and ſtuff a freſh killed Turkey, with them a little Salt and Pepper, ſcraped Lard, ſew it up cloſe; wrap it up with two or three Sheets of Paper; keep it so three or four Days, that it may take the Flavour of the Truffles; then roast it with Slices of Lard round, and the same Paper: serve with a Spanish Sauce. See Sauce Articles, Page 40.

Dindon en Timbale.

Timbale a Mould made in the Form of a Kettle Drum.

BONE a fat middling Turkey thoroughly, cut it in two at the Back, spread it in a Stew-pan, to fill it with a good *Salpicon* made after this Manner; cut in small Bits, Truffles, Mushrooms, Sweet Bread, always first scalded, fat Livers, Parsley, Shallots, Pepper and Salt; sew it up like a Bag; put few Slices of Lemon upon, wrap it up in a Stamine, giving it the Form of a Kettle Drum (that is, round at Bottom, and flat at Top;) braze it in a Stew-pan of its Bigness, with a little Broth, a Glass of Wine, few Slices of Veal, a Nosegay, three Cloves, half a Clove of Garlick, Thyme, Laurel, Pepper and Salt; when done, skim the Sauce, and sift it; add a little Cullis, reduce it to a good Consistence: and serve upon the Timbale, first well wiped of its Fat.

Dindon à l'Ecarlate.

Turkey Scarlet Colour.

TAKE up the Skin from the Flesh (without breaking it) of a small Turkey, and stuff as much Craw-fish Butter under as possible; stuff the Inside with a Ragout made of the Liver, Mushrooms, Pepper and Salt, done in a good Cullis short Sauce; sew it up, and wrap it with Slices of Lard and Pepper, serve with a Craw-fish Cullis: you will find the Method to make it in Cullis Articles. Method for the Butter in Vol. II.

Dindon à la Mayence.

Turkey Mayence Fashion.

TRUSS a Turkey for roasting, singe it over the Fire; lard all the Breast with Mayence Ham, instead of Lard; cut it with the Grain, otherwise it will break in larding, wrap it up in several Papers, and baste it often with Butter; make a Sauce with a rich Cullis, half a Glass of white Wine, two Spoonfuls of Gravy, Pepper and Salt, two or three Shallots finely chopped.

Dindon à la Poële.

So called for being done with very little Liquid.

TRUSS the Legs Inside, flatten it as much as you can; put in a Stew-pan, with melted Lard, chopt Parsley, Shallots, Mushrooms, a little Garlick; give it few Turns on the Fire, and add the Juice of half a Lemon, to keep it white; then put it in another Stew-pan, with Slices of Veal, one Slice of Ham, also the melted Lard, and every thing as used before, whole Pepper and Salt; cover it over with Slices of Lard; soak it about half an Hour on a slow Fire; then add a Glass of white Wine, a little Broth; finish the Brazing, then skim and sift the Sauce; add a little Cullis to make a Liason, reduced to a good Consistence, and serve upon the Turkey.

Dindon Farci de Marons & Saucisses.

Turkey roasted, stuffed with Sausages and Chesnuts.

ROAST what Quantity of Chesnuts you think proper, sufficiently to peel them, pound a few to make a Farce, with the Liver, chopt Parsley, Shallots, &c. a little Salt and Pepper, a Bit of Butter, then six

Yolks of Eggs; ſtuff the Craw of the Turkey with it, and the Body with the whole Cheſnuts, and a good many ſmall Sauſages, which you fry in Butter to half done; roaſt the Turkey, with Slices of Lard wrapt in Paper: ſerve with a Cheſnut Cullis. See Cullis Articles.

Salmi de Dindon.

Turkey haſhed.

CUT the Remains of a roaſted Turkey properly; put them in a Stew-pan, with a Glaſs of white Wine, chopped Parſley, Shallots, Muſhrooms, Truffles if any, Salt and Pepper, two Spoonfuls of Cullis, a little Broth; boil half an Hour; reduce to a ſhort Sauce; when ready, add a pounded Anchovy, a Squeeze of Lemon, ſkim the Sauce free from Fat, ſerve all together.

Cuiſſes de Dindon à la Provençale; Provence, a County in France.

TAKE two Legs of Turkey roaſted, put them in a Stew-pan with a Glaſs of Wine, as much Broth, Pepper and Salt, a Noſegay of ſweet Herbs, two Cloves, one of Garlick; ſimmer this about an Hour, to reduce the Sauce: make a Ragout with a Sweet Bread, chopped Muſhrooms, Parſley, Shallots, a Bit of Butter, ſoak this a little while; then add a little Broth and Cullis, boil it ſome Time; when ready, add a pounded Anchovy, chopped Capers, a Handful of Olives ſtoned; warm together, without boiling: let your Taſte guide you for Pepper and Salt, and Sharpneſs of the Sauce: it ſhould be reliſhing; ſerve upon the Legs: this is alſo called Cuiſſe Maſquée, viz. Legs maſked.

Ailes & Cuisses de Dindon Glacées.

Wings and Legs of Turkey Glazed.

CUT off the Wings and Legs of a Turkey; if of a large one, the Wings will do for a Dish; cut them pretty large from the Breast, lard them all over, or only one, to please different Palates; braze them with Slices of Veal and Ham, a Nosegay, two Cloves, whole Pepper and Salt, Broth; braze on a slow Fire; when done, skim the Sauce, reduce it to a Glaze, and finish it like Fricandeaux: you may also braze the Legs in the same Manner; and serve them with what stewed Greens, Sauce or Ragout, you shall think proper: the Remainder of the Turkey will serve for Filets à la Bechamel, in Paper Cases, *au Gratin*, for Forced-meat, and many other Purposes, as Occasion shall require.

The above Legs may be dressed à la Sainte Menehoult, or with Sauce Robert; also such as have been roasted before.

Filets de Dindon de plusieurs Façons.

Fillets of Turkey different Ways.

CUT the Remainder of a roasted Turkey in Fillets, all to the Legs; prepare a Sauce with chopt Mushrooms, a Bit of Butter, chopped Parsley, Shallots, half a Clove of Garlick, Broth, Pepper and Salt; boil it some Time, then take out the Nosegay and Garlick; put the Fillets to warm without boiling; add a Liason of two Yolks of Eggs, and Cream; add a Lemon Squeeze, when ready: you may also dress it with Cullis Sauce, or any other.

Cuisses de Dindon en Surprise.

Sham Legs of Turkey.

BONE a Couple of Legs of Turkey, all to the End of the Leg; fill the Inside with a Farce made of Livers, Sweet Breads, Mushrooms, Parsley, Shallots, Pepper and Salt, two Yolks of Eggs, scraped Lard, a little Nutmeg; sew them up; braze them with Slices of Lard and Lemon; such as have served before will do, boiling the Forced-meat in Cullis, first covered with Bread Crums, and done in the Oven: serve with a Spanish Sauce.

Pates de Dindons à la Sainte Meneboult.

Stumps of Turkies, Sainte Menehoult; fried or broil'd.

SINGE ten or twelve Stumps over a Charcoal Fire, pick them very clean, and cut off the Spurs and Claws; braze them in a small Stew-pan with fat Broth, two Glasses of white Wine, a Nosegay, Thyme, Laurel, Nutmeg, one Onion, a Couple of Carrots cut in three or four Pieces, Pepper and Salt; when done, drain them, then dip them in the Fat of their Braze; roll them in Bread Crums, broil them slowly, basting often with Butter; serve with fried Parsley: you may also fry them, being dipt in a good thick Batter; when they are brazed tender, you may put them to what Sauce you please; also in Jelly, with Colours and Taragon Vinegar. Serve cold with the Jelly properly laid.

Du Pigeons.

Of Pigeons.

Fricaſſée de Pigeons à la Poulette.

White Fricaſſee of Pigeons.

SCALD few Pigeons in hot Water, large ones cut in Quarters, middling in Halves, and ſmall ones whole, truſſing the Legs inſide; put them in a Stew-pan, with a good Bit of Butter, a Slice of Ham, chopt Muſhrooms, a Noſegay, Thyme, Bay-leaf, two Cloves; ſoak this a little while, then add a ſmall Quantity of Broth, very little Salt, whole Pepper; ſimmer on a ſlow Fire, reduce the Broth; take out the Ham and Noſegay; make a Liaſon with two Yolks of Eggs and Cream, warm without boiling; add a Lemon Squeeze: if you would garniſh the Pigeons with any thing, ſuch as Sweet Breads, or Artichoke Bottom, ſcald them in boiling Water, before you put them to the Pigeons: you may make the ſame with Cullis, as many People don't like Cream; it is done after the ſame Manner, with Sweet Breads, and Artichoke Bottom, which ſhould be half done, before mixing with the Pigeons, as Sweet Breads require more Time to braze than young Pigeons, which are commonly uſed for this Purpoſe.

Fricaſſée de Pigeons aux petits Pois.

With green Peas.

PREPARE ſmall Pigeons as the former, or cut large ones in two or four, put them in a Stew-pan with a good Bit of Butter, a Slice of Ham, what Quantity of Peas you pleaſe, a Noſegay of Parſley; put to it a little Broth and Gravy; when half done, add a little Cullis, finiſh the boiling, and reduce the Sauce; take out the

Nosegay and Ham: you may put a Trifle of Sugar, Salt and Pepper, according to Taste; you may make it white, only putting Broth to it in the boiling, and finishing with two Yolks of Eggs, beat up with Cream.

Fricassée de Pigeons à la Paysanne.
Country Fashion.

CUT half a Pound of pickled Pork in thin Slices; soak it on the Fire about half an Hour, until it is half done; scald two or three large Pigeons in boiling Water, and cut them in half; put them to the Pork, with a Nosegay of Parsley, Shallots, Thyme, Laurel, two Cloves; soak it a little while, then put Water to it, and whole Pepper; when done, skim and sift the Sauce; add three Yolks of Eggs, and Cream; make a Liason without boiling: when ready, add a little Vinegar.

Pigeons en Surtout, (Pigeons Masqueraded;) see Chickens, ditto.

Pigeons au Soleil, (transparent like the Sun.)

SCALD small Pigeons, leave the Pinions and Legs; split a little at the Back, skewer the Legs to keep pretty close; braze them with few Slices of Lard, Slices of Lemon, a Nosegay, two Cloves, a Slice of Ham, Pepper and Salt, a little Broth; when they are almost done, take them out to drain, and dip them in a good thick Batter made of Flour, two Spoonfuls of good Oil, fine Salt, Cyder, small Beer, or Wine; pour it by little and little, stirring continually to make it of a pretty thick Consistence; fry them in fresh Hog's Lard, or Oil of a fine yellow Colour: serve with fried Parsley.

Pigeons Fourés aux Pistaches.

Stuffed Pigeons and Pistachio-Nuts.

BONE three or four large tame Pigeons, all to the Wings and Legs; stuff them with a *Salpicon* made of Sweet Bread, fat Livers, chopt Mushrooms, Parsley, Shallots, Pepper and Salt; sew them up as if whole, and braze them with Slices of Lard and Veal, a Nosegay, a Glass of white Wine, as much Broth; when done, sift and skim the Sauce, add two Spoonfuls of Cullis, boil a Moment; then add a small Handful of scalded Pistachio, and serve upon the Pigeons.

Pigeons au Court Bouillon.

See Turkey; this is done the same, allowing for the Difference of Time in brazing, &c.

Pigeons à la Sainte Menehoult; this has been repeated so often, that I shall forbear giving any further Direction about it, except any material Reason should require it; as common Sense will guide, for the different Sorts of Meat.

Pigeons Glacés aux Legumes.

Glazed and served with stewed Greens.

THEY are larded and brazed like Fricandeaux, and Chickens as directed; finish the same Way: and serve with such stewed Greens, as the Season affords, or Fancy leads.

Pigeons à la Périgord au Gratin.

PEEL as many whole Truffles as you use small Pigeons, put them in a Stew-pan with a Glass of white Wine, a Slice of Ham, Broth, a Nosegay, two Cloves; simmer

simmer some Time; truss four or five small Pigeons, Legs Inside, and boil them in a little Broth and Flour, few Slices of Lard and Lemon, Pepper and Salt; make this boil before you put the Pigeons in it, stirring it continually; then boil the Pigeons slowly, the Truffles being done; take out the Nosegay and Ham, and put the Pigeons to it; simmer them some time together; make a little Forced-meat with Livers of Poulteries, chopped Mushrooms, Truffles, Parsley, Shallots, mixed with a little scraped Lard, two Yolks of Eggs, Pepper and Salt; put this in the Bottom of the Dish, put it on Ashes Fire to make it catch at Bottom; drain the Fat off, and serve the Pigeon upon it, intermixed with the Truffles.

Pigeons au Cingara, (an old Gascoon Word.)

BRAZE four Pigeons with Slices of Lard and Broth, a Nosegay of sweet Herbs, a little Salt and Pepper; cut four Slices of Ham, which you soak some Time in Water to make it fresh; soak them in a Stew-pan on the Fire, until they are done; then take them out, and put a little Cullis in the same Pan, a little Vinegar, to gather what remains in the Pan; boil it a Moment, put the four Slices of Ham upon Pieces of fried Bread of the same Bigness, and the Pigeons intermixed, the Sauce over all, or only the Ham Slices, upon the Pigeons with the Sauce.

Pigeons à la Broche à differentes Sauces & Ragoûts.

Roasted Pigeons with different Sauces and Ragout.

MAKE a Farce with the Livers, Mushrooms, Parsley, Shallots, scraped Lard, two Yolks of Eggs, Pepper and Salt; stuff the Pigeons with it, and roast them with a Slice of Lard, wrapt in Paper or without; and serve them with what Ragout you shall think proper,

proper, or the moſt convenient: you may alſo braze them, and ſerve with what Sauce or Ragout you pleaſe.

Pigeons au Baſilic.

Baſilic, Baſil Herb.

BRAZE what Pigeons you pleaſe in a common Braze, the Legs truſſed Inſide; make a Farce with Bread Crums ſoaked in Cream, till it is quite thick, Beef Suet ſcalded, a little chopt Baſil, Parſley, green Shallots, Pepper and Salt, mixt with Yolks of Eggs; when the Pigeons are done, drain them, and let them cool, then wrap them all over with ſome of this Farce; bathe them in Eggs, and Bread Crums over; fry them of a good Colour, and fried Parſley with them: you may alſo do this with Pigeons which have ſerved already: alſo without a Farce; cut them in two, dip in thick Batter and Bread Crums; fry the ſame, and fried Parſley with them.

Pigeons en Hochepot à l'Eſpagnole.

Hotchpotch of Pigeons, Spaniſh Faſhion.

TRUSS two or three large Pigeons as for boiling, boil them in a ſmall Soop-pot with Broth, all Sorts of Roots ſcalded, as Carrots, Parſneps, Sellery, one Dozen of ſmall Onions, a Noſegay of Parſley, Shallots, Thyme, one Laurel Leaf, whole Pepper and Salt; boil on a ſlow Fire, ſhort of Liquor; when they are done, put the Pigeons in the middle of the Diſh; take out the Noſegay, and the Roots round, well intermixed: ſerve with a Spaniſh Sauce. See Page 40.

Pigeons

Pigeons en Crépine au Pontife.

Pigeons in Cowl Pontiff Sauce, Page 46.

THEY are done as all other Directions to the same Purpose, stuffed with a good Farce made of Sweet Bread, or Veal Kidney, Herbs, &c. brazed, and served with the above Sauce.

Pigeons aux Ecrevisses.

The same with Craw-fish Cullis.

BOIL the Tails whole in good Broth; you may also add a little Cream to the Craw-fish Cullis, and one or two Yolks of Eggs, to give more Consistence: also dress four middling Pigeons, two larded like Fricandeau; a Couple of Sweat Breads cut in two, and two Pieces larded; you may serve this with stewed Greens, or the usual Sauce; glaze the larded Pieces, and to keep the others white, put a Slice of Lemon, and a Slice of Lard upon each, to keep on it while brazing: Pigeons and Parmesan are done after the same Manner as all other Dishes under the same Direction: also *au Gratin,* only observing that as four Pigeons alone look rather naked in a Dish of First-course, they should be garnished with Sweet Breads, or Artichoke Bottom, or Forced-meat Ball, well tasted and brazed together, Chesnuts or Olives; also whole Craw-fish.

Pigeons en Surprise à la Ravigotte.

Pigeons masked, with Ravigotte Sauce.

TRUSS four or five small Pigeons as for boiling, scald them; and scald also (for about a Quarter of an Hour) as many fine large Cabbage Lettuces; then take them out, and squeeze the Water out of them; make

make a Farce with Whites of roasted Fowl, Beef Suet, scalded Udder, Bread Crums soaked in Cream, chopped Parsley, Shallots, Mushrooms, Pepper and Salt, well mixed with Yolks of Eggs; put some of this Farce round the Pigeons, then put them in the Lettuces, tie them very well with Packthread, and put them in a Stew-pan with some good Broth, a Slice of Ham, a Nosegay of sweet Herbs, two Cloves, Pepper and Salt; when done, drain them, and squeeze them gently to get the Fat out: serve with a Sauce Ravigotte, as you will find in Sauce Articles, Page 38.

Pigeons aux Trufes.

THEY are larded with Truffles and Ham, and brazed with Veal and Ham, few chopped Truffles; their Broth serves for Sauce, adding a little Cullis, and a Lemon Squeeze: also marinade for about an Hour in Oil, and all Sorts of sweet Herbs; then cut in two, or before, dip in good Batter to fry: they may be dressed in all the different Ways of Chickens, allowing for the Time of boiling, roasting, and brazing.

Des Canards, Canetons, Oyes, & Oisons.

Of Ducks and Ducklings, Geese and Goslings

Canard aux petits Pois.

Duck and green Peas.

TRUSS a Duck or two Ducklings, like a Fowl to boil; scald it, and braze it with Slices of Lard, Slices of Lemon, a little Broth, whole Pepper and Salt, a Nosegay, two Cloves, Thyme, and half a Leaf of Laurel; put a Quart of Peas in a Stew-pan, with a Bit of Butter, a Nosegay of Parsley, a little Mint, Broth and Gravy; when done, add a little Cullis, Pepper and Salt, and serve upon the Duck, well drained.

Canetons Roulés.

Duckling Rolled.

MAKE a good Forced-meat with Breaſt of roaſted Poultries as uſual; cut a pretty large Duckling in two, or two ſmall whole; bone them thoroughly, and lay the Farce upon; roll them up, and tie them well with Slices of Lard round; boil them in a little Broth, a Glaſs of white Wine, a Noſegay, two Cloves; when done, ſqueeze the Fat gently out, and wipe them clean; ſerve with what Sauce you pleaſe.

Canetons en Hatereau.

Roaſted on ſmall Skewers called Hatereau.

CUT one or two Ducklings in Quarters, bone them, and fill each Piece with ſuch Forced-meat, as the former, roll them tight, and lard them like Fricandeau; put them on Skewers to roaſt; ſerve with a Sauce made of Jelly Broth, Cullis, half a Glaſs of Wine, a Noſegay, a Slice of Lemon, Pepper and Salt; boil it a little while, ſift it to ſerve under the Duckling: you may dreſs a whole Duck, ſtuffed with the like Forced-meat, and brazed; ſerve with what Sauce you think proper: the Sauce gives it the Name.

Canetons de Roüen à la Broche.

Rouen Duckling roaſted.

IF you would have it for a Firſt-courſe Diſh, give it a few Turns with Butter, in a Stew-pan over the Fire, wrap it up in Paper to roaſt; it muſt not be too much done; ſerve with a good Conſumee Sauce, chopt Shallots, the Juice of an Orange, Pepper and Salt: if for a Second-courſe Diſh, roaſt it without Paper criſp: alſo ſerve with Juice of Seville Orange.

Canetons à l'Italienne.

Italian Fashion.

PUT one or two Ducklings in a Stew-pan, to simmer a little while on a slow Fire, with fine Oil, Parsley, Shallots, Mushrooms, Pepper and Salt; then put them in another upon few Slices of Veal and Ham, and all the first Seasoning; cover them with Slices of Lard, and soak on a very slow Fire; then add a Glass of white Wine and Broth, finish the Brazing; then add some Cullis to the Sauce, and skim the Fat off very clean; sift it in a Sieve, wipe the Duckling clean, drain the Fat out, and serve the Sauce upon; or Sauce Italienne.

Canetons en Fricandeaux.

THEY are larded and brazed as the former, glazed and finished as all other Directions.

Canetons à la Purée Verte.

With green Peas Porridge.

PUT few Slices of Veal and Ham in a Stew-pan, with one sliced Onion, two Carrots cut in Pieces; soak this together on a middling Fire, and put some Broth to it; when it begins to catch like a Cullis, then boil on a slow Fire till the Meat is done; simmer your Quantity of Peas about half an Hour, with a Bit of Butter, green Tops of Shallots, a little Winter Savory and Parsley; when they are done, sift them in a Stamine; and sift the Sauce to mix with the Porridge: you may do the same with dry Peas, putting Spinage Juice to it, to make it green; stuff two Ducklings with scalded Lettuces chopped, White of Fowl and Livers, scraped Lard, Shallots, and Parsley, Pepper and Salt, two Yolks of Eggs; braze as the former, and serve with the green Porridge.

Canard

Canard en Timbale.

(See Veal, Pig, Chickens, &c.)

Canard à la Romaine.

IT is boned, stuffed with a Salpicon Farce, brazed in a common Braze; serve with Cullis Sauce, and Lemon.

Canard à la Nivernoise.

Duck with Sauce Nivernoise.

IT is larded through and through with Lard, the Lardons rolled in sweet Herbs chopped, and fine Spices; then brazed as all other, and the above Sauce with it. See Page 31, for the Sause.

Canard à la Daube.

Duck dobed.

IT is larded as the former, stuffed with Salpicon, Forced-meat; boiled with a Knuckle of Veal, Lemon Slices, Coriander, and every thing necessary to make a Jelly of the Broth, and let the Duck cool in it: you may garnish it with Colours if you please.

Canard aux Navets.

Duck with Turnips.

BRAZE a Duck (larded or not) in Broth, one Onion, Roots, a Nosegay, two Cloves, Thyme, half a Leaf of Laurel, whole Pepper and Salt; cut Turnips to what Shape you please; scald them, and give them a Fry in Butter, then boil them in Veal Gravy and Cullis;

lis; when the Duck is done, skim and sift Part of the Sauce; and add it to the Turnips: reduce it pretty thick, and serve upon the Duck.

Grenadins de Canard à la Royale.

Small Fricandeau of Duck.

IT is boned, cut in Pieces, each filled with a Salpicon Farce raw, larded and brazed with Sweet Breads, Artichoke Bottoms; and finished as all other Fricandeaux, with a Glaze upon: you serve Ducks or Ducklings, brazed with any Sorts of Sauce or Ragout, stewed Roots or Greens, Truffles, Morells, Mushrooms, Chesnuts, all Sorts of Cullis, as most convenient.

Filets de Canard de plusieurs Façons.

Duck hashed of different Ways.

ROAST two Ducks to three Parts done, let them cool, then cut the Breast in thin Slices, and take care to preserve the Gravy; the Legs will serve for another Dish, which you may do by wrapping them in Cowl with a good Farce, and serve with Cullis Sauce, or done in a St. Menehoult: for the Fillets cut Cucumbers, and marinade them about an Hour with a little Vinegar, Salt, one Onion sliced; then take out the Onion, and squeeze the Cucumbers in a Cloth, and put them in a Stew-pan with a Bit of Butter, a Slice of Ham; add a little Broth and Flour, Veal Gravy, and boil slowly; skim it well, take out the Ham, then add the Meat to ditto warm without boiling, and the Gravy: you may also do the same with chopped Truffles, or Mushrooms, or any thing else you think proper, according to Season. A cold roasted Duck will answer much the same end, for this Dish.

Vol. I.   R   *Oyes*

Oyes & Oisons de plusieurs Façons.

Geese and Goslings of different Manners.

TRUSS a green Goose, Legs inside; scald it; and boil it in Broth, a Nosegay of sweet Herbs, Pepper and Salt, one or two sliced Onions, Bits of Carrots, Sellery; serve it with green Peas, or Chesnut Cullis, or Peas Porridge, or Sauce Ravigotte, Sauce a l'Echalotte, or any other; or roast it plain: Goslings the same, or with Forced-meat made of the Livers, Chesnuts, Sausage-meat, Parsley, Shallots, Thyme, Pepper and Salt; simmer all together about a Quarter of an Hour with Butter; then stuff the Goose with it, and roast it crisp.

Cuisses & Aîles d'Oyes, comment les conserver.

How to preserve Legs and Wings of Geese.

ROAST as many Geese as you think proper, to three Parts done; then let them cool; cut off the Wings as large as possible, and the Legs; fix them close in an earthen Pan, with Laurel Leaves between each Piece, few Cloves and Salt, at Discretion; sift the Fat of their roasting, which you mix with Hogs Lard melted, sufficient to cover the Meat, pour it upon hot, and let it cool thoroughly; then cover the Pan with Leather or strong Paper, and keep it in a dry Place; when you want to use them, put them in hot Water to melt the Fat off; and broil or braze a little, or any other Way you please.

Oye à la Daube.

Dobed Goose.

IT is done in the same Manner as a Turkey; an old one is equally proper for this, and for nothing else;

Legs and Wings are also dressed to any Sauce or Ragout, either brazed or broiled in Cowl, with Forcedmeat, or larded as Fricandeaux, with all Sorts of Cullis or Greens: the Feet also done in Jelly as the Stumps of Turkies, fried or broiled, being brazed first.

Des Poulardes & Chapons.

Of Fowls and Capons.

Poularde au gros sel.

Fowl plain boiled.

TRUSS the Legs inside, scald it a Moment; boil it in the Soop-pot or by itself, about an Hour and a Half; it is done when the Leg gives under the Finger, with little pressing; serve with its own Broth, or a little of any other, and Salt over it: it is done the same Way, to garnish any Sorts of Soops.

Poularde au Court Bouillon.

A Fowl in its own Gravy.

TRUSS it as the former, and lard through and through with Lard, Ham and Parsley; put it in a Pan much of its Bigness, with a Bit of Butter, two Slices of Lemon, a Nosegay, Thyme, half a Leaf of Laurel, two Cloves, sliced Onions, Bits of Carrots, Pepper and Salt, a Glass of white Wine, and as much Broth; simmer slowly, skim and sift the Sauce, and serve with it.

Poularde au Reveil.

(Reveil), quick sharp Sauce to the Palate.

PREPARE a Fowl for roasting; make a Farce with the Liver, scraped Lard, two or three Tarragon Leaves, a little Chervil, Burnet, Garden Cresses, Pepper and Salt, two Yolks of Eggs, to mix it; stuff the Fowl with it; wrap it in Slices of Lard, and Paper, to roast; make a Sauce with few of the above Herbs pounded, one Anchovy, few Capers; add a little Cullis, and sift it; then add a little more Cullis, a little Mustard, Pepper and Salt; warm without boiling.

Poulard à la Royale.

Fowl Court Fashion.

STUFF it with a cold Ragout made of Sweet Breads, fat Livers, Mushrooms, done of a good Taste; sew it up, and roast it with Slices of Lard, and Paper; serve with a Ragout of Pistachio-nuts, which you make by putting a Handful in a Stew-pan, with a Bit of Butter, Jelly Broth, a Spoonful of good Cullis, Pepper and Salt; simmer a little while together, and serve.

Poularde à la Servante.

PREPARE a Fowl for roasting, and make a Farce with the Liver, Parsley, Shallot, a Bit of Butter, Pepper and Salt, a little Basil, stuff the Fowl with it; roast it with Slices of Lard wrapt in Paper; when three Parts done, take off the Paper and Lard; baste it all over with Yolks of Eggs, beat up with melted Butter, and Crums of Bread in abundance; finish the Fowl; it must be of a fine yellow Colour: make a Sauce with a Bit of Butter, one chopt Anchovy, few Capers, a little
Flour,

Flour, two Spoonfuls of Broth, Nutmeg, Pepper and Salt: make a Liafon like a white Sauce, ferve under the Fowl.

Poularde au (Duc) from the title Duke.

MAKE a Ragout with Sweet Breads, Mufhrooms; put this in a Stew-pan, with half a Glafs of white Wine, two Spoonfuls of Cullis, as much Broth, a Nofegay, half a Clove of Garlick, few Bafil Leaves, a little Flour, two Cloves; boil it to three Parts, reduce the Sauce thick; take out the Nofegay, let it cool; cut out the Breaft Bone of a good Fowl, lard it like Fricandeaux, and ftuff it with the Ragout; braze it with Broth, few Slices of Lard, a Nofegay of fweet Herbs, two Slices of Lemon; when done, fift the Sauce; reduce it to a Caramel, and glaze the larded Part of the Fowl: ferve under it a Pontiff Sauce, or any other.

Poularde à la Reine.

PUT half a Pint of Cream in a Stew-pan, with a little Coriander-feed, a Laurel Leaf, two of Bafil; boil it a Moment; pound a Handful of fweet Almonds, which you fift in a Stamine with the Cream; then add to it four or five raw Yolks of Eggs, Breaft of roafted Fowl minced, and Marrow, a little Pepper, Salt, and Nutmeg; put your Stew-pan on a flow Fire, ftirring it continually, until the Marrow is melted: bone a Fowl, all to the Legs and Wings, and ftuff it with the above; few it up very clofe, put it a Moment in boiling Water, then braze it with Slices of Lard, at Bottom a little Milk, Salt and Pepper, one large Onion fliced; cover it over with Slices of Lard alfo, and white Paper; braze on a flow Fire; when done, prick it in feveral Places to let the Fat out: ferve with a Coulis à la Reine.

Poularde en Saucisse.

Done in the Form of a large Sausage.

CUT a Fowl in two, bone it thoroughly, flatten the Meat with a Roller; put a middling Quantity of Forced-meat upon each Half, made of Breast of Fowl roasted, Bread Crums soaked in Cream, scraped Lard, Udder, Parsley, Shallots, Salt and fine Spices, mixt with three Yolks of Eggs; tie up each Bit in the Form of a large Sausage; wrapt with Slices of Lard, Bits of Cloth or Stamine; braze it in Broth, a Glass of white Wine, a Nosegay of sweet Herbs, whole Pepper and Salt, sliced Onions and Carrots; when done, squeeze it gently between a Cloth to get the Fat out, after untying the Lard, &c. serve with what Sauce you please.

Poularde Frite.

A Fowl fried.

CUT a Fowl in Quarters; braze it with Slices of Lard, Milk, Coriander, Thyme, Laurel, one Clove of Garlick, a Bit of Butter, Pepper, Salt and Nutmeg, two sliced Onions, Bits of Roots; when done, let it cool in the Braze: take the fattest Part to dip the Fowl in, strew it with Bread Crums; then dip it in Yolks of Eggs, and again Bread Crums, fry in fresh Hog's Lard, crisp, of a fine brown Colour; serve with fried Parsley round.

Poularde en Cingarat.

With Slices of Ham. See Pigeons, ditto.

STUFF a Fowl with a Farce, made of fat Livers, Truffles, Mushrooms, chopped Parsley, Shallots, scraped

scraped Lard, Beef Marrow, Pepper and Salt; give it a fry in a Stew-pan, with Butter for a Moment; have Slices of fried Bread the length of the Fowl, as many thin Slices of Ham as will cover the Fowl; lay the Bread first, then the Ham upon all round tied; then wrap it in a Sheet of Paper, rubbed over with Butter, and roast it; lay a Pan under to save the Gravy, and serve it under the Fowl, with the Ham and Bread Slices.

Poularde à la Sainte Menehoult.

THIS is done in the same Manner as all Sainte Menehoult, first brazed either Whole, in Halves, or Quarters; then dipt in good Batter, strewed with Bread Crums, and finished upon the Gridiron or in the Oven; serve with what Sauce you think proper. Poularde aux Ecrevisses, viz. Craw-fish, is done after the same Manner, as all other Direction under the same Name: the Tails serve to garnish the Dish, a good Craw-fish Cullis with it.

Poularde à la Tartare.

See Chickens ditto, done in the same Manner, except that you may cut the Fowl in Quarters instead of Halves; marinade with the same Preparation, making proper Allowance for Time and Quantities. Proper Attention is the best Guide to all References of one Dish to another, which I do for Brevity's sake.

Poularde au (Point du Jour.)

The Dawn of Day, from the various Colours.

MAKE a well-seasoned Ragout of Truffles, Mushrooms, Craw-fish Tails, fat Livers cut in Pieces; let it cool; cut the Breast Bone out of a good large Fowl, and stuff it with the Ragout; sew it up close, and put

put in a small Brazing or Stew-pan, upon Slices of Fillet of Veal; cover it over with Slices of Lard, a Slice of Ham, whole Pepper and Salt, a Nosegay of sweet Herbs, four whole Truffles, two Sweet Breads cut in Halves; soak this about a Quarter of an Hour, then put to it a Glass of Wine, and a little Broth, and finish it on a slow Fire: make also half a Dozen small Veal Fricandeaux as usual, and glazed the same; make a Gratin in the Dish you intend for Table, with chopt Livers, scraped Lard, chopped Parsley, Shallots, two Yolks of Eggs; simmer it on Ashes until it catches a little at Bottom; put a little Cullis to it, wipe the Fat off of the Fowl, and lay it upon the *Gratin*; the Sweet Breads, Truffles, and Fricandeaux intermixed; you may also mix Craw-fish with it; skim and sift the Braze, add a little Cullis, a Lemon Squeeze, pour over the Fowl and Sweet Breads, and not upon the Fricandeaux, which are glazed.

Poularde aux Trufes.

A Fowl with Truffles.

TRUSS a Fowl for roasting, farce it with its Liver chopt, and Truffles, Pepper and Salt, mixt with a Bit of Butter, and a little scraped Lard; wrap it in Slices of Lard, and Paper over it; cut few Truffles in round large Slices, first peeled; simmer them with a Bit of Butter, a Nosegay of sweet Herbs, half a Garlick Clove, half a Laurel Leaf, one Clove, two Leaves of Basil; then add half a Glass of white Wine, a little Broth and Cullis, Pepper and Salt; reduce it to a good Consistence, skim it well; a Lemon Squeeze when ready to serve.

Fricandeau d'une Poularde.

Fricandeau of a whole Fowl.

CUT a Fowl in two by the Back, and bone thoroughly; make a *Salpicon*, viz. (raw Forced-meat), cut a Sweet Bread in large Dices, few fat Livers, Truffles or Mushrooms, or both, chopped Parsley, Shallots, scraped Lard; mix it with three Yolks of Eggs, Pepper and Salt; put the Fowl in a Pan to make it fit to fill with the Farce, then sew it up, and give it a Fry in Butter for a Moment; then lard it like Fricandeau; braze it in Broth, Slices of Veal, few of Lard; when done, sift and skim the Sauce; reduce it to a Caramel, and glaze the Fowl with it: serve with what Sauce you please.

Poularde Etuvée.

Stewed Fowl.

TRUSS a Fowl for boiling, and put it in a Stew-pan with melted Lard, two Spoonfuls of Oil, chopped Parsley, Shallots, Mushrooms; keep it on a slow Fire in this about a Quarter of an Hour, turning it often; then put it in another Stew-pan, prepared with Slices of Ham and Veal, Pepper and Salt; cover it with thin Slices of Lard, and white Paper, and all the first Seasoning; soak it about a Quarter of an Hour, then add a Glass of white Wine; finish the Brazing on a slow Fire; sift and skim the Braze, add a little Cullis, and a Lemon Squeeze, when ready to serve upon the Fowl well drained of Fat.

A Fowl cut in Fillets is brazed, and finished in the same Manner, or in Fricassee: roasted Fowl will do the same; for the last, to be done without boiling.

Poularde au Song.

Fowl stuffed with black Pudding Preparation.

FRY two fine chopped Onions in Butter, until they are almost done; then add chopped Parsley, Shallots, and a little Coriander-seed pounded, Pepper and Salt, half a Pound of Tripes, or Marrow, four raw Yolks of Eggs, half a Pint of Hog's Blood; thicken it on the Fire without boiling; take out the Breast Bone of a Fowl, and stuff it with this; sew it up, and roast it wrapt in Lard and Paper: serve with Cullis and Consumee Sauce.

Filets de Poularde à la Poulette.

Fillets of Fowl Fricassee.

MAKE a small Ragout, with one Sweet Bread, few small Mushrooms whole; put this in a Stew-pan with one Slice of Ham, a Nosegay of sweet Herbs, one or two Cloves, a Bit of Butter and Broth, Pepper and Salt, one chopped Shallot, Clove; when done, take out the Nosegay and Ham, put the Fillets to it to warm without boiling; make a Liason with two Yolks of Eggs and Cream, a Lemon Squeeze, when ready: observe that this is for such as have been roasted before: you may put those Fillets to any Sauce or Ragout you please; the Sauce gives the Name.

Poularde Glacée.

Fowl Glazed.

THIS is done much in the same Manner, as the Poularde en Fricandeau, only done without stuffing, brazed and glazed the same; serve with its own Sauce, or any other.

Poularde en Crepine.

Done in Cowl.

THIS is cut in two or four Pieces, boned thoroughly, filled with good Forced-meat, rolled up in Cowl, either brazed, or done in the Oven, or under a Brazing-pan Cover, or Dutch Oven; serve with a Sauce Ravigotte, or any relishing Sauce.

Poularde en Galantine.

Fowl in Cake or Marbled.

See Suckling Pig, or any other Dish to the same Direction: it is boned, stuffed, brazed, much in the same Manner; serve either hot or cold.

Poularde à la Silvie.

TRUSS a Fowl as for boiling, cut in two; make a hot Marinade with two Spoonfuls of good Oil, a good Bit of Butter, Pepper and Salt, chopped Shallots, Mushrooms, a little Basil; marinade the Fowl about an Hour in this; then wrap each half in double Paper, with as much of the Marinade as possible; bake it in a Dutch Oven, or under a Brazing-pan Cover, with a slow Fire under and over; when it is done, unfold the Paper; save as much of the Herbs as you can, that stick on the Paper, and the Gravy of the Fowl; mix it with a little Cullis and Broth, boil together a Moment; skim it, and add a Lemon Squeeze, when ready to serve the Fowl.

Poularde à la Financiere.

SPLIT the Back of a good Fowl, and bone the Back only; stuff it with four large Truffles, as many fat Livers, chopped

chopped with Mushrooms, scraped Lard, two Yolks of Eggs, Pepper and Salt; sew it up, put in a small Brazing-pan, with few Slices of Lard without Broth; braze it between two Fires slowly; its own Gravy will serve for Sauce, when well skimmed, adding the Juice of a Seville Orange.

Cuisses de Poularde (Accompagnées) meaning with other Things.

Legs of Fowls garnished.

BRAZE four Legs of Fowls, with one Dozen of small Onions scalded, Broth, few Slices of Lard, a Nosegay, two Cloves, Thyme, Laurel; when half done, add an Eel cut in Pieces, six Craw-fish, half a Glass of white Wine, Pepper and Salt; braze slowly; when all is done, take the Bottom of the Braze, sift and skim it very clean of Fat; add two or three Spoonfuls of Cullis; reduce to a Sauce Consistence; intermix the Fowl and other Things properly on the Dish; the Onions also, and few Bits of fried Bread; pour the Sauce over all, with a Lemon Squeeze.

Filets de Poularde soufflée à la Béchamel.

Fillets of Fowl with a raised Bechamel Sauce.

PUT a good Bit of Butter in a small Stew-pan, with a Slice of Ham, three chopped Shallots, Parsley, half an Onion sliced; soak this awhile together, then add Cream and Flour, boil it together until it is pretty thick; sift it in a Sieve, then put Fillets of roasted Fowl to it, two Whites of Eggs well beat up, Pepper and Salt; beat all together to make it rise; pour it on the Dish you intend for Table; garnish it all over with Bread Crums, and small Bits of Butter, close to each other; give it Colour in the Oven: you dress Fillets of

any

any Sorts of Poulteries, or Game, in the same Manner; also with a Béchamel Sauce and Fillets intermixed with Craw-fish; only observe not to pour the Sauce upon the Craw-fish, as it would spoil the Look of the Dish.

Poularde au Miroir.

Miroir, a Looking-glass, a very clear Jelly.

CUT off the Legs of a Couple of Fowls, and the Rumps, then split the rest at the Back without separating the Breast; roast them wrapt in Slices of Lard and Paper, then let them cool; strip off the Skin, and pare off whatever Spots may be, as they must be very white; lay them Cross-ways on the Dish you intend for Table; put Yolks of Eggs, hard boiled, and Craw-fish, also few green Girkins, all properly disposed, as your Fancy shall direct; then make a good Jelly with Meat, and well clarified with Lemon and Whites of Eggs, and Shell bruized; sift it as all Jelly, and pour it over the Meat, and all belonging: it is a pretty cold Dish. This is also sometimes called *à l'Aspic*; when you mix Taragon Vinegar with Jelly, and few Taragon Leaves with the Meat, and other Herbs called Ravigotte, viz. relishing: any other Sorts of Meat or Fish may also be done the same Way in Jelly, seasoning each according to their Quality and Quantity; also any Sorts of Fruits, &c.

Cuisses de Poularde à l'Eventail.

The Shape of a Fan.

BONE two Legs of Fowl, all to the Stumps; braze them with about a Dozen Pieces of Ham, cut as for larding, a large Piece about three Inches long, a Glass of white Wine, Broth, a Nosegay, two Cloves, half a one of Garlick, half a Laurel Leaf, a little whole Pepper,

Pepper, no Salt; when the Legs are almost done, take them out and the Ham; skim and sift the Sauce; reduce it to a Glaze; for the Legs, let them cool, then make Holes in the Legs to stick the Ham in it, in the Form of Fan-sticks; then dip them in a Batter made of Flour, a Spoonful of Oil, and white Wine, two Whites of Eggs; beat up the Batter of a middling Thickness, fry them in fresh Lard, or Oil of a good brown Colour; serve quite hot: you may do the same with a roasted Fowl, which has served before, cut it in large Pieces: this Dish is also made with Calves Ears brazed, then cut Fan-fashion; ay a good Forced-meat upon, and garnish with Girkins, Beet-Root, and any other Colour; serve upon a good Cullis Sauce.

Cuisses de Poulardes au Quadril.

BRAZE two Legs of Fowl whole, and make a good relishing Ragout, with small round Mushrooms, and Truffles also cut round and small; the Parings of the Truffles will serve to mix with any Sorts of Forced-meat; simmer them with a Bit of Butter and Broth; when done, add few Spoonfuls of Veal Cullis, a Lemon Squeeze; sift half of the Brazing to put to the Ragout; give it a boiling together, skim the Fat very clean off, wipe the Legs very clean; lay them Cross-ways on the Dish, then garnish with the Truffles, and Mushrooms, Quarter-ways, to give it a pretty Look; each must be separated, which gives it the Name of Quadril, by being quartered, different Colour: put no more Sauce, than just to cover the Truffles and Mushrooms. This may be done without Truffles, the Colours being diversified with any Sorts of Garden Stuff, as Carrots, Turnips, &c.

Rissolles

Rissolles à la Béchamel.

A Fry of Poultry with Bechamel Sauce.

CUT the Remainder of a cold Fowl, Turkey, Chicken, or Veal in Dices, like for to mix with Forced-meat; and make a Sauce with a Bit of Butter, a Slice of Ham, Parsley, Shallots, half a Bay-leaf; soak this about a Quarter of an Hour; then add two Spoonfuls of good Jelly Broth, Cream and Flour, a little Salt and Pepper; reduce it to about half, then sift it in a Sieve, and put the Bits of Meat to it, with a raw Yolk of Egg; give it few Boilings together, then let it cool; make a little Puff-paste, very thin, and wrap some of the Ragout in it, as large or small as you shall think proper; pinch them all round like Apple-puffs, then fry them of a good Colour in fresh Hog's Lard.

Poularde en Hochepot.

Hotchpotch of Fowl.

IT is cut in Quarters, brazed, and make a good Ragout with small Onions, and all Sorts of Roots cut differently, pickled Pork, brazed with the Fowl, and all well intermixed on the Dish; serve with a thick Cullis Sauce: you may put to it any other Sorts of Meat, as in all Hotchpotch.

Poularde en Hérisson.

Fowl as a Hedge-hog.

MAKE a Farce to stuff it with its Liver chopped, scraped Lard, Parsley, Shallots, Pepper and Salt; truss it for roasting, then give a few Turns over the Fire in Butter, then lard it with Bits of Ham close, and

Bits of Truffles, to ſtick up pretty far out; roaſt it, baſting often with good Oil: ſerve with Conſumee and Cullis Sauce, and a good Lemon Squeeze.

Poularde au Fumé.

Fumé means the Flavour of Game.

CUT the Meat of a long kept Rabbit in thin Slices; lay them on a Diſh to ſeaſon them with Pepper and Salt, chopped Parſley, Chibbol, Shallots, and a little fine Oil; ſplit a Fowl at the Back, bone it all to the Legs and Wings; ſtuff it with this, then ſew it up, and give it its natural Form; braze it with Slices of Veal and Ham, cover it over with Slices of Bacon; ſoak it ſo about a Quarter of an Hour, then put a Glaſs of white Wine to it, a little Broth, a Noſegay, Pepper and Salt; when done, ſift and ſkim the Sauce, add a little Cullis, and ſerve upon the Fowl.

Poularde en Chipoulate.

A Tureen, or Fowl Matlot.

CUT a Fowl in four, and braze it with Slices of Veal, and Bits of pickled Pork with it, a Dozen of ſmall Onions ſcalded, whole Pepper, a Noſegay, two Cloves, half a Laurel Leaf, Thyme, a little Baſil; ſoak it about a Quarter of an Hour, then put to it few thick ſhort Sauſages; cover it over with Slices of Lard, and ſome good Broth to it, finiſh it on a ſlow Fire; ſift and ſkim the Bottom of the Braze, add a Bit of Butter rolled in Flour; reduce it to a good Conſiſtence; intermix the Fowl, Pork, Sauſages, and Onions, properly on the Diſh: ſerve the Sauce upon all, with a Lemon Squeeze over.

Cuisses de Poularde aux Trufes.

Legs of Fowl and Truffles.

THE Legs are brazed as for any other Dish, and served with a Ragout of Truffles, or Mushrooms; then they will bear the Name of either.

Cuisses de Poularde au Prince.

SOAK few Anchovies, and Bits of fresh Ham cut for larding; when you think they have lost their Salt, drain them; and lard as many Legs of Fowl as will make a good Dish; then marinade them some Time, with a Glass of white Wine, one Lemon cut in Slices, Pepper and Salt; make a Stuffing with Butter, chopped Parsley, Shallots, Capers; put each Leg in a Bit of Puff-paste, and the Marinade mixt with the Stuffing; bake them in a slow Oven; when done, take off the Paste, and serve with a Sauce au Celadon, which you will find how to make, in Sauce Articles, Page 32.

Cuisses de Poulardes à la Gendarme.

Military Fashion.

MARINADE the Legs with Oil, chopped Parsley, Shallots, Mushrooms, Pepper and Salt; then Bread Crums over, to broil on à slow Fire of a good Colour; scald a little Chervil, Taragon, Burnet, Parsley, half a Clove of Garlick, two Shallots; then drain them, to pound them with an Anchovy, few Capers; then mix it with a little Oil and Vinegar, Mustard and Cullis, Pepper and Salt: serve under the Legs, or in a Sauce-boat.

Poires de Poulardes aux Trufes.

Legs of Fowls in the Form of Pears.

BONE three or four Legs of Fowls, all to the Stumps; and stuff each round like a Pear, with a Farce made of fat Livers, scalded Sweet Bread, Truffles, Mushrooms, scraped Lard, Parsley, Shallots, Pepper and Salt, two Yolks of Eggs; sew them up, and braze with Slices of Lard, half a Glass of white Wine, whole Pepper and Salt; when done, serve a Ragout of Truffles with them: you will find how to make it in Ragout Articles, Vol. II.

Cuisses de Poulardes en Gelée.

Legs of Fowls done in Jelly.

THEY are larded with Ham, and Lard intermixed, brazed, and the Jelly done as usual: also Legs au *Consommé*; they are brazed with Veal and Ham, sufficient to make a strong rich Sauce, with all Sorts of Bits of Roots, and proper Spices, few Taragon Leaves; when the Legs are done, sift and skim the Sauce; add a middling Quantity of scalded chopped Parsley, and a Lemon Squeeze.

Culottes de Poulardes à l'Italienne.

WHAT the French call the Culotte, is the two Legs and Rump cut together, and may be dressed in all the different Ways of any other Part, and to all the different Sauces; this is called *Italienne*, as it is recommended to be marinaded in Oil, Herbs and Spices as usual, about an Hour before brazing: Oil ought not to be much used in Cookery in England, as it is seldom to be had so good as the Italians and French can have it, but Butter instead.

Quenelles

Quenelles de Poularde.
Forced-meat Balls.

TAKE the Wings and Breast of a Fowl, scrape the Meat quite fine, pound it in a Mortar with three Yolks of Eggs, chopped Parsley, Shallots, two Leaves of Basil, scraped Lard, Pepper and Salt; when all is well pounded together, put it upon a Dish; boil a Pint of good Broth on a smart Fire; and as it boils, take a Spoonful at a Time of the Forced-meat, and put it to boil in the Broth, and so on till all is done; as they are doing (like poached Eggs) take them out one by one with a Skimmer; sift and skim the Broth; add a little Cullis to thicken it, and serve upon the Quenelles.

Cuisses de Poulardes Bachique, from Bacchus.

BONE few Legs of Fowls thoroughly, and flatten them as much as you can; then lay upon them a Stuffing made of Butter, chopped Parsley, Shallots, few Taragon Leaves, Mushrooms, Bread Crums, two Yolks of Eggs, Pepper and Salt; roll them up, and tie them fast, to braze between Slices of Bacon, half a Pint of red Wine, a little Broth; when done, sift the Sauce; add a little Butter rolled in Flour; make a Liason, and serve upon the Legs.

Ailerons de Poulardes ou Dindons de differentes Façons.
Pinions of Fowls or Turkeys of different Manners.

BRAZE them first in a good seasoned Braze; if you like to keep them white, put Slices of Lemon in the Braze; you may also braze small Onions with it, or any thing else, which you propose to garnish the Dish with; when so done, you may serve them with what Sauce you please: as to those of Turkies, you may lard a few, and finish them like a Fricandeau, with a Caramel, and others left white; also in Jelly, or with a relishing Sauce, en Crepine, au Gratin, in Matlott, in Fricassee, marinaded and fried, &c.

Ailerons Composés.

Shammed Pinions.

YOU must have Moulds made in the Form of Pinions; take the Skin of a Fowl, such as you use for the Broth-pot or other; fill the Skin with a well-seasoned Forced-meat; make it take the Form of the Mould; bake them in the Oven; and serve with what Sauce or Ragout you think proper.

Terrine d'Ailerons aux Marons.

Tureen with Chesnuts.

BRAZE as many Pinions as you think proper, and Bits of pickled Pork with them, and proper Seasoning; serve with a Chesnut Cullis, and few whole ones: you will find how to make it in Cullis Articles: you may also serve them with any other Cullis, or stewed Greens, or small Onions, and Parmesan Cheese; give Colour in the Oven, or with a Salamander, or broiled à la Sainte Menehoult.

Crêtes en Fricassées au Blanc.

Cock's-combs White Fricassee.

SCALD as many Combs as will make a small Dish, and boil them in Broth and Lemon Slices; put a Slice of Ham in a Stew-pan with Mushrooms, a Nosegay, two Cloves, half a Laurel Leaf, Thyme, a good Bit of Butter; soak this awhile; then add some good

Broth,

Broth, a little Flour; sift it, and put the Combs to it; make a Liason with Yolks of Eggs and Cream, Pepper and Salt, and a Lemon Squeeze: you may garnish them with small Forced-meat Balls, or hard Yolks of Eggs, or small Onions: you may also serve them with Sauce Robert, or Sauce Ravigotte, or any other.

Des Foyes gras.

Of fat Livers.

THEY may be kept several Days covered with Fat, to hinder them from turning black; those of Fowls and Capons are the best, as they are not so dry as those of Turkies: fat Livers are of great Utility in Cookery, to garnish different Sorts of Ragout, to mix with Forced-meat, for *petit Patés*, to mix in Pies, and several other Uses, and may be dressed in many different Ways by themselves. I shall not dwell long on the different Ways of dressing fat Livers, as they are much dearer in England than in France; and to make either Pies or other Dishes of fat Livers, would make it very dear to very little Purpose; the Scarcity of, and Season when to get them, render their Uses of very little Signification whatever. They must be brazed with the proper Seasoning, to be served with any Sorts of Sauces or Ragout, half brazed for broiling, or en Crepine, au Gratin; to be sliced, and finished as all former Directions under the same Denomination; also in Tureen, or Matlot, with other Meat; and all Sorts of Roots, or such as have served, may be fried, wrapt up in Forced-meat, served upon Bits of fried Bread; also minced and done in Paper Cases, properly seasoned, moistened with a little Cullis. Although they are recommended often as part of Forced-meat, any others may be used instead, as all depends more on good Taste for Seasoning, than the Quality of the Meat used for any Kind of Farce.

De la Venaison ou Viande Noir, (*Noir*, Black.)

Of Venison, or brown Meat.

WHAT the French call black Meat, under the Name of Venison, (or Viande Noir), is the wild Boar, and the young, called *Marcassin*, the red Deer, its Female the Hind, Bucks, and Does, Fawns, and Kids.

Du Sanglier ou Cochon Sauvage.

Of wild Boars or wild Hogs.

THE Female is more esteemed than the Male, and both are better, when they keep together, and feed upon green Corn; the Meat ought to be kept long before it is used: the best Part of the Boar is the Head; it is mostly served cold; when brazed, the fore Quarter, roasted, larded, served with a sharp Sauce in a Sauce-boat: the hind Quarter dressed as à la Mode Beef, or *Dôbe*; and also prepare it as pickled Pork; any Direction about it is of very little Use in England, as what we see comes from abroad, and seldom any thing else but the Head: the Germans are best acquainted with their different Qualities and Uses, and make those smoked Sausages of wild Boar's Flesh, which are much esteemed, both in England and other Countries.

Sanglier à la Daube.

Leg of a wild Boar dobed.

LARD it thoroughly with large Pieces, seasoned with fine Spices, chopped Garlick, Shallots, Parsley; put it in a Brazing-pan much of its Bigness, with Slices of Bacon, Thyme, Laurel, Basil, sliced Onions,

all

all Sorts of Roots, a large Nosegay of sweet Herbs, Cloves, whole Pepper, Trimmings of any Sorts of Meat; soak it about half an Hour; then add two or three Glasses of Brandy, a Pint of white Wine and Broth; braze slowly for about seven or eight Hours, then let it cool in the Braze; skim the Fat off, to serve the Jelly with the Meat.

Hure de Sanglier à la Braise.

Boar's-head brazed.

SCALD the Head over a Charcoal Fire to clean it, and scrape it well with a Knife; then bone it as far as the Eyes, without cutting the Skin; lard it inside as the Leg, with all the same Seasoning; tie it up in a coarse Cloth, and braze it with all Sorts of Spices, and Roots, one Lemon sliced, three Bottles of red Wine, one of Water; braze it at least six Hours; reduce the Liquid to half: let it cool in the Braze, and serve cold.

Sanglier à la Poivrade.

Roasted, and served with a sharp Sauce.

LARD a Neck as before; roast it, basting with red Wine; serve with it a relishing Sauce, as à la Nivernoise, à la Poivrade, Sauce Piquante, Sauce d'Acide, which you will find in Sauce Articles.

Sanglier en petit Salé.

Pickled.

IT is done in the same Way as Pork, Sanglier à la Mode; it is much the same as à la Daube.

Boudin de Sanglier.

Black Puddings of wild Boar.

THEY are done in the same Manner as those of Pork, *Sausages* to dry; chop six Pound of the Meat, with three of the Flee, or in proportion, six Ounces of Salt, half an Ounce of Pepper, half an Ounce of pounded Mace, half a Pint of sweet Wine; mix it well all together, and put it in a Pan, well covered, for about four and twenty Hours: if you would have them very red, add half an Ounce of Salt-petre, pounded with the rest: then cut a Couple of Hog's Ears in small Fillets, and mix it with the Meat; then fill the Guts, and let them drain about four and twenty Hours; then hang them in the Chimney, until they are quite dry; you will boil them, when you have Occasion, in Broth or Water, with sliced Onions, a Nosegay, and Bits of Roots: serve cold upon a Napkin.

Du Marcassin.

Of the Suckling wild Boar.

WHEN it is quite young, it is roasted whole, the Back larded; leave the Head without cutting it off, and serve with a relishing Sauce in a Boat.

Du Cerf, Biche, Daim, Chevreuil, & Faon.

Of Deer, Hind, Buck, Doe, Kid, and Fawn.

THE Kid which feeds upon Hills is more esteemed, than that which is kept on low Land: the French say, that the Doe is better than the Buck; I presume it is for being so little acquainted with the Quality of either: the red Deer and Hind are only good while young. All these are dressed in the same Manner, as the wild Boar and Marcassin, &c. &c.

Du

Du Gibier en general.

Of Game and wild Fowls.

UNDER this Denomination are comprehended Partridges, Pheasants, Quails, Rails, Land and Water, Larks, Thrushes, Black-birds, Wood-pigeons, Woodcocks, Snipes, Moor-hen, Land and Water Teal, Plovers, Ducks, wild and tame, &c. Hares, Leverets, Rabbits, young and old, &c.

Lapreaux en Cailles.

Rabbits roasted as Quails.

CUT one or two Rabbits in several Pieces; cut out the Back Bone; marinade them about an Hour with a little Oil, chopped Parsley, Shallots, Mushrooms, Pepper and Salt; then wrap each Piece in a Vine Leaf, and a thin Slice of Bacon, with as much of the Marinade as you can; roast them; when almost done, strip them to take Colour; serve with what Sauce you think proper, when so marinaded: you may also do them in Cowl, in the Oven, or broiled slowly.

Lapreaux au Pontife.

Rabbits, Pontiff Sauce.

CUT the Fillets of two large Rabbits of middling Sizes, and marinade them as before, for an Hour or two; then tie them up with all the Marinade, in Slices of Lard and Paper; roast them as you do Pork Astlets; then put them in the above Sauce, well finished; warm all together without boiling. Young Rabbits are sometimes trussed like Partridges, and also as Chickens to roast, &c.

Lapreaux

Lapreaux à l'Escalope.

Rabbit Collop.

CUT the Fillets of one or two Rabbits in thin Slices, and put them in a Stew-pan upon a Slice of Ham, few Slices of Veal, a little Butter or Oil, Pepper and Salt, chopped Parsley, Shallots, Mushrooms, then few thin Slices of Bacon for covering; soak this on a slow Fire, about a Quarter of an Hour, then add a Glass of white Wine; finish the Brazing; take out the Fillets, drain the Fat off; sift the Braze, add a little Cullis, skim it very clean: you may add a Lemon Squeeze, if the Wine does not make the Sauce sharp enough; serve upon the Fillets; when so brazed, you may put them to what Sauce you please, or in white or brown Fricassee, or Gratin, &c. &c.

Lapreaux en Galantine.

In Cake or Marbled.

THIS is done as all other Sorts of Meat under the same Denomination, thorougly boned; stuffed with a good raw Forced-meat, and brazed to eat cold. Rabbits may be dressed in every Respect as Chickens. I shall only give the different Names for the Satisfaction of the Reader; as by it it will easily appear, that a Repetition of every Articles in the Dressing would only be tedious without Improvement.

Lapreaux aux Pois. With green Peas.

Roulades de Lapreaux. Rolled like a large Sausage with Stuffing.

Lapreaux en Papillottes. Broiled in Paper.

Lapreaux Marinés. Marinaded to fry.

Lapreaux en Fricassée. Fricassée white or brown.

Cuisses de Lapreaux à la Dauphine. Legs of Rabbits, as all others under this name.

Filets de Lapreaux en Surprise. Sham Fillets made of Veal and Farce.

Lapreaux en Ragout de plusieurs Façons. Ragout of different Manners.

Lapreaux à la Broche aux fines Herbes. Roasted, stuffed with sweet Herbs.

Lapreaux à la Provençale. See any Direction under this Name.

Lapreaux en Timbale. See as above.

Lapreaux en Grenadins. Small Fricandeaux.

Lapreaux en Matelottes.

Filets de Lapreaux Mêlés. Fillets mixt with any thing else.

Filets de Lapreaux au Jambon. Brazed and intermixed with Bits of Ham.

Lapreaux en Achis. Hashed with other Sorts of Meat.

Lapreaux

Lapreaux en (Racourci), Shortened; truffed the fame, as is moftly done in England for boiling, and boiled in Broth; ferved in the fame Manner.

Filets de Lapreaux Grillés. Fillets broiled.

Lapreaux en Crepine. Rabbits in Cowl.

Lapreaux au Monarque. With faid Sauce.

Lapreaux en Salade. Salmagundy.

Terrine de Lapin à la Purée, & petit Lard. Tureen of Rabbit and pickled Pork with any Sorts of Porridge.

Terrine de Lapin à la Payfanne. Tureen Country Fafhion.

Lapin en Gelée. In Jelly.

Lapin en Paupiettes. Olives of Rabbits.

As an ample Direction has been given in Chicken Articles under all thofe Names, follow the fame for Rabbits; the Meat requires much the fame Seafoning, and the fame Time of finifhing.

Liévre en Terrine à la Daube.

Tureen of Hare Dobed.

CUT an old Hare in fix Pieces, bone it thoroughly, and lard each Piece with Lard, feafoned with fine Spices, Thyme and Laurel Powder, chopped Parfley, Shallots, one Clove of Garlick; braze it in a fmall Pan with Slices of Lard, and all the Bones, and as much of the Blood as you can fave; a Quarter of a Pound of good Butter, a Glafs of Brandy; ftop the Pan well, and let it fimmer on a flow Fire, or in the Oven for about four or five Hours; then take out the Bones, and put
the

the Hare in the Tureen, each Piece close, and the Slices of Bacon upon it; sift the Sauce, pour it in the Tureen; let it cool; before using, it ought to be like a Pie.

Lièvre au Sang.

Hare with its own Blood.

SAVE the Blood of an old Hare, and cut it in Pieces to lard; put it in a Stew-pan with its Liver, a good Bit of Butter, a Nosegay, Mushrooms, three Cloves, Thyme, Laurel, a Slice of Ham; soak it a while; then put to it two or three Glasses of red Wine, and Broth, a little Flour; when the Liver is done, take it out, and pound it; sift it in a Sieve, with the Blood and some of the Sauce; reduce the rest quite thick with boiling, add Pepper and Salt; take the Hare out, sift the Sauce; add as much to the Blood as is required, and serve together.

Roulades de Lièvre.

Coloured Hare.

BONE a large Hare thoroughly, and lard it all over with thick Lardons, seasoned as for all other Dobe; put a good Farce in it, or braze it without; roll it up, and tie it well; braze it with Slices of Veal, half a Pint of white Wine, as much Broth, and covered over with Slices of Bacon: you may also put such Meat, and other Seasoning to make a Jelly of the Braze after: and serve cold with it, either whole or sliced.

Filets de Levreaux à l'Escalope. Collop of Leveret; see Rabbit Collop.

Gateau de Lièvre.

Hare Cake.

CHOP all the Meat of a Hare, and of a Rabbit, half a Leg of Mutton, two Pound of Fillet of Veal, or fresh Pork, two Pound of Beef Suet; season all this together with Pepper and Salt, fine Spices pounded, chopped Parsley, Shallots, a Quarter of a Pound of Pistachio-Nuts peeled, about a Pound of raw Ham cut in Dices, half a Pound of Truffles or Mushrooms, also cut in Dices, six Yolks of Eggs to mix it, one Glass of good Brandy; garnish a Stew-pan all round with Slices of Lard, and put all your Preparation in it close, and cover it all over with Slices of Lard, rather thick; stop the Pan all round with a coarse Paste, and bake it about four Hours; let it cool in the same Pan, then turn it over gently; scrape the Lard quite off, or leave a little of it to garnish it with any Sorts of Colour, or to make it more even, and to give it a better Form; cover it over with Hog's Lard or Butter, in order to garnish it with different Colours according as your Taste shall direct.

Cotelettes de Levreau.

Cutlets of Leveret.

CUT the Fillets pretty large, and take out as many Ribs as you make Cutlets, which you cut in the Form of, stick one Rib in each; lay them in the Dish you intend for Table (if Plate); put a little Broth to it, and all Sorts of sweet Herbs chopped, Mushrooms, Pepper and Salt, a Bit of Butter; simmer between two Dishes,

Dishes, slowly turning, two or three Times; and reduce the Liquid quite; when done, serve with a rich Cullis Sauce; or make a Sauce with the Bones, and a little Cullis, and proper Seasoning, which will be better: A roasted Hare, or the Remains, may also be done in the same Manner, cutting the Meat in Fillets, and making a Sauce with the Bones bruized, a little Broth, Cullis; and made relishing with one chopped Shallot, few Taragon Leaves, a little Butter rolled in Flour, and a Lemon Squeeze or Verjuice.

Lièvre en Civet.

Hare stewed.

CUT a Hare in Pieces, scald it in boiling Water; you may lard some of the Pieces if you please; then put it in a Stew-pan with a Pint of Water; let it simmer some Time; then if the Hare is large, add a Bottle of red Wine, one or two Dozen of small Onions scalded, few whole Mushrooms, whole Pepper, three Cloves, Salt, few Bits of fresh Ham, or of such as has been boiled; let it simmer a good while, until the Liquid is reduced to half; then add a good Bit of Butter rolled in Flour: make the Sauce pretty thick; serve with fried Bread round the Dish.

Levreau au Chevreuil.

Leveret, Kid Fashion.

SINGE a good large Leveret over a Charcoal Fire, then lard it, and marinade it three or four Hours, in a warm Marinade, made of Water, Vinegar, Butter, Flour, Pepper and Salt, chopped Parsley, Shallots, Thyme, Laurel, Basil, sliced Onions, Lemon-peel, Cloves; then roast it, basting with some of the Marinade; sift the Remainder, add a little Cullis, and serve it in a Sauce-boat.

Lièvre à la Polonoise.

Hare Polish Fashion.

SAVE the Blood, and cut the Hare in large Pieces; lard it coarsely, and give it few Turns on the Fire, with a Bit of Butter rolled in Flour, a Nosegay, two Cloves, Thyme and Laurel, half a Clove of Garlick, Pepper and Salt; then put a Pint of red Wine to it, a little Broth, a Spoonful of Vinegar; when it is almost done, add the Blood and Liver pounded; boil it together a Moment; when ready, add half a Spoonful of small Capers whole, scalded Olives stoned; serve all together.

Lièvre en Haricot.

MAKE a brown Sauce with Butter and Flour; cut a Hare in Pieces, and give it a Fry in this; then add half a Pint of white Wine, a Spoonful of Vinegar, a little Broth, a Nosegay of Parsley, Shallots, one Clove of Garlick, two of Spices, Thyme and Laurel, a little Veal Gravy, whole Pepper and Salt; when half done, put scalded Turnips to it cut properly; fry Bits of Bread in Butter, to garnish the Dish: when the Hare is done, take out the Nosegay, and as much of the Spices as you can; skim it well, and serve the Hare covered with the Turnips.

Levreaux en Crepine, & Gratin.

THIS is done after the same Manner as all such Directions boned; the Meat filled with a good Forced-meat, and done in the Oven; serve with a relishing Sauce for either.

Filets de Levreau aux Legumes.

Fillets of Hare with stewed Greens.

CUT the Remainder of a roasted Hare in Fillets; warm it upon the Dish you intend for Table, with a little Broth, a few Drops of Vinegar and Salt; warm without boiling; when ready to serve, pour the Sauce out, and serve the Hare with a Ragout of Cucumbers, Endives, Sellery, or any other.

Boudins de Levreaux.

Black Puddings made of Hare or Leveret.

THEY are prepared like all other Sorts of Puddings, with the Blood of the Hare, or may be done with Hog's Guts, and any other Guts besides; as those of Hare would be very apt to burst in the cleaning: Turkies or Lamb's will do equally.

Filets de Levreaux aux Anchois.

Fillets with Anchovies.

CUT out the Fillets of one or two Leverets whole; lard them with Fillets of Anchovies, soaked in Water some Time; simmer between two Dishes for about half an Hour, with Butter enough, a little Pepper, half a Dozen of fine chopped Shallots; then put the Fillets upon the Table Dish; put a little Cullis in the first, one large Spoonful of Verjuice, a Bit of Butter rolled in Flour; keep it on the Fire until it becomes pretty thick, and serve upon the Fillets: the Remainder of the Leverets will serve for either a Civet or a Pie, or to make a *Coulis au Fumé*; to serve with any Sorts of Game.

Levreaux à la Minute.
Quick in a Moment.

LIGHT a good Stove while you are drawing the Leveret, and cut it in middling Pieces; boil the Liver, and put all together in a Stew-pan, with a good Bit of Butter, Pepper and Salt, chopped Parsley, Shallots, Mushrooms, half a Clove of Garlick; cover it well, turn it in about eight Minutes; it will only require about a Quarter of an Hour to do, if the Leveret has been properly kept; then dress the Meat upon the Table Dish; put a little Broth and Vinegar to the Sauce, to gather the Seasoning, and serve upon the Hare; the Sauce ought to be pretty thick.

Des Ramereaux.
Of Wood-pigeons.

THE Wood-pigeons perch upon Trees, contrary to other Kinds; the Flesh is very good, although dry: young ones are distinguished by the Shortness of their Claws, as they grow longer with Age; they are commonly eat roasted, but may be dressed in all the different Ways of other Pigeons.

Ramereaux à l'Allemande.
German Fashion.

LARD them through and through, and boil them with scalded Savoys, half a Pound of pickled Pork, Broth, two Cloves, a little Nutmeg, whole Pepper and Salt; when done enough, drain them of the Fat, and squeeze the Cabbage to get it out; intermix each Sort on the Dish; serve with a rich Cullis Sauce, with Butter in it.

Ramereaux

Ramereaux aux Fenouil.

With Fennel Sauce.

SCALD few Sprigs of Fennel; chop some of it to mix with the Livers, a Bit of Butter, two Yolks of Eggs, Pepper and Salt; stuff the Pigeons with it; roast them wrapt in Slices of Bacon, and Paper; and mix some chopped Fennel with some Cullis, a Bit of Butter, half a Lemon Squeeze, and serve upon the Pigeons.

Bécasses, Bécassines, & Bécaux à la Broche à différentes Sauces.

Wood-cocks, Snipes of both Kinds, roasted with different Sauces.

WHAT the French call the *Bécaux* is what is commonly called a *Jack Snipe* in England, and is more esteemed by them than it is here: they allow, that being roasted is the best Way to eat them; but for the sake of Variations required in large Tables, give several other Methods of dressing them. Each Kind is dressed in the same Manner: split either Woodcocks or Snipes at the Back, take all the Inside, to mix with a little scraped Lard, chopped Parsley, Shallots, Pepper and Salt; stuff them with it, and sew them up; roast them wrapt in Slices of Lard, and Paper; and serve with what Sauce or Ragout you please.

Salmie de Bécasses.

TAKE ready roasted Wood-cocks; cut the Legs and Wings in two, and the Breast; pound the Bones and the Inside, and boil them with a little red Wine, three or four chopped Shallots, Pepper and Salt; reduce the Liquor to half; then sift it in a Sieve; mix a little Cullis, and a Bit of Butter with it; also few Bread Crums to thicken it: put the Wood-cocks or Snipes in it; warm without boiling; garnish the Dish round with fried Bread.

Salmie de Bécasses à la Sainte Menehoult.

WITH a cold Salmie, such as the above, will do equally for a good Dish; put it in the Table Dish; garnish the Dish round, with a Farce made of the Remains of roasted Poultries, Bread Crums soaked in Cream, Beef Marrow, chopped Parsley, Shallots, Pepper and Salt, mixt with two Yolks of Eggs; cover it also thinly all over with the same; basted over with Eggs and Bread Crums, few Drops of melted Butter over all; give it a good Colour in the Oven, or with a Salamander, keeping the Dish a Moment on an Ashes Fire.

Bécassines à la Duchesse.

SPLIT six Snipes at the Back; take all the Inside out, to make a Farce with two pounded Anchovies, half a Spoonful of Capers, Parsley, Shallots, Mushrooms, all chopped very fine; mix it with a good Bit of Butter, a little scraped Bacon, two Yolks of Eggs, Pepper and Salt; stuff them with it; sew them up close, and braze with few Slices of Veal, one of Ham; cover it with thin Slices of Lard; add a good Glass of red Wine, one or two Spoonfuls of good Cullis; when done, sift and skim the Sauce, which ought to be pretty thick, which may be done with a little Butter and Flour.

Bécaux à la Perigord.

THIS is done much in the same Manner, as the last, stuffed; only Truffles chopped in the Forced-meat, which give the Name of *Perigord*, as all other Dishes under the same Denomination; Perigord being a Province in France, where Truffles are very good, and in great abundance: you may either roast or braze them, and serve with a Ragout of Truffles, as directed in Ragout Articles. Those *Perigord* Dishes are not very fit for England, where Truffles are so very dear, and so different in Flavour to foreign ones. It is much the same with *Italian* Dishes, where Oil is in the Composition; but, as very good Butter is to be had in England, at all Times of the Year, it may very well supply the want of good Oil in Cookery: also those Dishes under the Denomination of *à la Provence*, ought to be done with Caution, as the principal Flavour is Garlick, only relished in that Country.

Bécaux au Salmie de Provence.

Snipes Salmie, Provence Fashion.

TAKE out the Inside of roasted Snipes, cut off the Heads, and pound them with two or three Cloves of Garlick, first scalded, then a little Cullis to it, and sift it in a Stamine; squeeze one Orange or two in it, Pepper and Salt; cut the Snipes in Fillets, and warm all together without boiling: garnish the Dish with fried Bread.

Filets de Bécasses au Jus de Canard.

Fillets of Wood-cocks with Duck Gravy.

MINCE the Meat of two or three roasted Wood-cocks, and roast one or two old Ducks; when the

Ducks are half done, put a proper Dish under, and give them new Cuts to let the Gravy out; then put the Fillets in it, and the Juice of a Seville Orange, with Pepper and Salt; warm without boiling.

Bécasses & Bécassines aux Trufes, & aux Olives.

Wood-cocks and Snipes with Truffles and Olive Ragout.

THEY are brazed in the same Manner as all others, with as many large Truffles as Birds, intermixed together on the Dish, and served with a Truffles Cullis, or Ragout, the same with Olives; also with Cullis of Wood-cocks, to take the Inside and the Trimmings pounded, and boiled in good Cullis, a Glass of white Wine, few Mushrooms, and all proper Seasoning; the Birds brazed, and a Sweet Bread with it; serve the Cullis upon, which ought to be pretty thick.

Des Alouettes.

Of Larks.

To make Ragout, put them in a stew-pan with a bit of Butter, some Mushrooms, a Nosegay, a Slice of Ham, a scalded Sweet Bread cut in Pieces; simmer this a Moment; then add a little Broth, a Glass of Wine, Pepper and Salt; reduce the Sauce; when almost done, add a little Cullis, take out the Nosegay and Ham: if you would have them stewed, you [ ] prepare them at first in the same manner, but without Sweet Bread; instead of it, put small Onions, first [ ]; when three Parts are done, add a little Cullis, a Bit of Butter rolled in Flour, half a Spoonful of Verjuice, or a Lemon Squeeze: you may also mix with it Cabbage Lettuces, boiled in good Broth, or serve with any Sorts of stewed Greens or Cullis.

Alouettes en Cerises.

Larks in the Form of Cherries.

BONE the Larks thoroughly, and roll the Meat in the Form of Cherries; ſtick one Leg in each; braze them with proper Seaſoning; when done, add a little Cullis and Gravy; put the Cherries on the Diſh for Table, the Legs upwards; ſift and ſkim the Sauce; ſqueeze an Orange into it, and ſerve upon the Meat.

Des Pluviers, Vaneaux, et Grives.

Of Plovers, Lapwings, and Thruſhes.

THESE different Kinds of Birds are commonly eat roaſted, but may alſo be dreſſed in many different Ways. I ſhall obſerve in regard to Thruſhes, that they are much more valued in France than in England, and for a very good Reaſon, as they feed moſtly upon Grapes, which gives them a very agreeable Flavour; and it is only thoſe which are eſteemed: the common Wood-thruſhes are the ſame as in England.

Pluvier à la Perigord.

Plover with Truffles.

THEY are brazed with Veal, Ham, and Truffles, and all other proper Seaſoning, a Glaſs of Wine and Broth; ſift and ſkim the Braze; add a good Lemon Squeeze, when ready to ſerve: you may alſo roaſt them ſtuffed in the ſame Manner as Wood-cocks; ſerve with any Sorts of Ragout; alſo *au Gratin*, making a Forced-meat with the Livers, &c. as all other under the ſame Denomination; braze the Plovers, put them upon the Gratin, ſerve with a very good Cullis Sauce.

It is needless to say much about Thrushes; however, they may be dressed in all the different Ways of Pigeons; a good Sauce will make any thing relishing, and palatable for Change's sake.

Cailles à la Flamande.

Quails Flemish Fashion.

TRUSS six Quails, as for boiling; put them in a small Pot with a scalded Savoy, cut in Quarters and tied, half a Pound of pickled Pork; boil this together about half an Hour, then take them out, and drain the Water from the Cabbage; untie it, and put all together in a Stew-pan with some good Broth, Pepper and Salt, two Cloves, a Nosegay; when all is well brazed, dress it on the Dish intermixed; serve a good Cullis and Butter Sauce upon; few Drops of Vinegar to it: you may also braze as many Quails as you think proper, with as many Craw-fish and Truffles; the Braze sifted and skimmed, adding a little Cullis; and a Lemon Squeeze will serve for Sauce: this is called *Accompagnées*.

Cailles au Laurier.

Quails with Laurel.

STUFF the Quails with a Farce made of their Livers, scraped Lard, chopped Parsley, Shallots, Pepper and Salt, one Laurel Leaf, chopped very fine; roast them wrapt in Slices of Lard, and Paper over it; put a Slice of Ham in a small Stew-pan; simmer it some Time; when it begins to stick to the Pan, put a Glass of white Wine, a little Cullis, half a Clove of Garlick; reduce it to a good Consistence; sift it, and add a Lemon Squeeze; when ready, put the Quails, each upon a Laurel Leaf: serve the Sauce upon the Birds.

Cailles en Ragoût, ditto en Matelotte, au Gratin, &c.

THEY are all done in the same Manner as Chickens, and may be dressed in all the different Ways of any other Birds. As they are neither very good, nor plentiful in England, I shall pass over any further Direction about Quails.

Des Perdreaux & Perdrix.

Of Partridges young and old.

Perdreaux à la Broche à differents Sauces & Ragoûts.

Roasted Partridges with different Sauces and Ragout.

MAKE a litte Farce with the Livers, scraped Lard, Shallots, Parsley, Mushrooms, Pepper and Salt; stuff the Partridges with it; give them a Fry in Butter, then wrap them in Slices of Bacon, and Paper to roast: serve with what Sauce or Ragout you please.

Perdreaux à la Madelaine.

TRUSS three Partridges for roasting; put the three Livers in one of them, and roast them to three Parts; then take them off to cut in Pieces, as for a Salmie; take out the Livers to chop with Truffles, few Shallots, a Spoonful of Oil, a Glass of white Wine, Pepper and Salt; simmer all together about a Quarter of an Hour; add a Lemon Squeeze; such as have served may do equally for this.

Perdreaux Grillés aux fines Herbes.

Broiled with sweet Herbs.

TRUSS the Legs inside, and split them at the Back; then put them to marinade for about an Hour, with a little Oil, Pepper and Salt, and all Sorts of Seasoning-herbs chopped; then roll them up in Paper, and all the Herbs; broil slowly; and gather all the chopped Herbs, to mix with a good Cullis, and a Lemon Squeeze.

Perdreaux à la Provençale, au Pontife.

(See any Direction under the same Name.)

Perdreaux au Consommé.

With rich Cullis Sauce.

TRUSS the Legs inside; put them in a small Stew-pan, between Slices of Bacon and Veal, both under and over, one Slice of Ham, a Nosegay, two Cloves, Bits of Carrots, Slices of Onions; braze on a slow Fire, without putting any Liquid to it; when they are done, sift the Braze in a Sieve; skim it well, and serve upon the Birds.

Perdreaux à la Perigord.

STUFFED with Truffles chopped, and all other Requisites, as often directed; brazed with few whole Truffles, a Glass of Wine, and all other proper Seasoning; the Braze serves for Sauce, sifted and well skimmed, a Lemon Squeeze, or Truffles Cullis, *Salmie*; done with roasted Partridges, just warm in Broth, a little Butter, chopped Herbs, Pepper and Salt, as all other.

Perdreaux à la Dauphine.

BONE the Birds thoroughly, and fill each with a Farce made of Truffles, Mushrooms, Sweet Breads, chopped Parsley, Shallots, Pepper and Salt, all mixt with scraped Lard; truss them as if they were whole, and give them few Turns on the Fire, with a little Butter in a Stew-pan; then lard the Breast Part all over; braze them with Slices of Veal and Ham, some Broth, a Nosegay, two Cloves; when done, reduce the Sauce to a Glaze, as for Fricandeau: serve a good Sauce under the Birds.

Partridges filled with a good Farce, may be served with any Sorts of Sauces or Ragout; *Perdreaux au Citron*, with Lemon Sauce; *Perdreaux Glacés*, larded, brazed, and glazed, like Fricandeaux; *Perdreaux à la Polonoise*, Polish Fashion, brazed in the common Way, except they put a Glass of Brandy to it, and Orange Juice. *Achis de Perdreaux au Gratin:* this Hash is done with cold roasted Partridges, the Gratin made as usual. *Au Fumet*; cut the Meat off, and pound the Bones, to mix with Cullis; sift it, add proper Seasoning; warm all together without boiling. *Pardrix à la Braze aux Choux*, brazed with Cabbages, (Savoys are the best for brazing,) a Bit of pickled Pork, with a good Cullis Sauce. Such as would have them in the Nature of *Sowrcrout*, stew the Cabbage very tender, and pretty high of Spices; add as much Vinegar as will give it a tartish Taste: this last is commonly served in a Tureen, then it is so called. Old Partridges are very good for brazing, and may be served with any Ragout, stewed Greens, and all Kinds of *Purée:* the Remains of roasted Partridges may also be used for Petit Pates; also Woodcocks, or any other Land Birds, or to mix with any

Sorts of Forced-meat, or for a Dish minced very fine; warm in good Cullis; garnishing the Dish with fried Bread.

Perdrix à la Villeroi, (from the title.)

BOIL a Dozen of small Onions in Broth, and a Bit of Butter, Pepper and Salt; reduce the Sauce, that the Onions may take a brown Colour; bone two or three Partridges, and fill them with the Onions, then truss them as whole; give them a Fry in a Stew-pan with a little Oil, Parsley, Shallots, Mushrooms; then put all together to braze with Slices of Bacon and Veal, a Glass of white Wine and Broth; braze slowly for about four or five Hours; sift and skim the Sauce, add a little Cullis: serve short Sauce, and pretty thick.

Perdrix en Aspic.

Aspic, a sharp relishing Sauce.

CHOP all Sorts of Herbs called *Ravigotte,* as Parsley, Shallots, Taragon, Burnet, Civet, Garden Cresses; mix all this together with Oil, Mustard, Taragon Vinegar, a pounded Anchovy, a little Basil, one Clove of Garlick, Pepper and Salt: if you would serve the Partridges whole, serve the Sauce cold in a Sauce Boat; if for hot, cut the Bird as for a Salmie; warm it in a little Broth, then put it to the Sauce; warm together without boiling: you may also mix it in the same Manner, cold: it will be better cold, if put together about an Hour or two.

Perdreaux à la Mandui.

After the Name of the Maker.

TRUSS Partridges as for boiling; lard them with Ham, and Lard, and Anchovies, through and through; braze them with Slices of Lard, a Nosegay, Pepper, and very little Salt or none; the Saltness of the Ham must guide you in that; a Glass of Wine: when done, sift the Bottom of the Sauce, add some Cullis; skim it well; serve upon the Birds. *Perdreaux à la Jardiniere:* this is brazed, and served with stewed Greens of what kind you please.

Achis à la Turque.

Hash Turkish Fashion.

TAKE what Sorts of Game you please, ready roasted, such as has been at Table; mince the Meat, pound the Bones, and boil them with a little Broth and Cullis, and proper Seasoning, then sift it; put the Meat to it, and boil Roes of Carps in Wine, a Nosegay, Pepper and Salt; or use such as have been dressed in Matelotte, or otherwise: pour the Hash upon the Dish, the Roes upon the Hash, and poched Eggs round.

Perdrix à la Daube Sicilienne.

Partridges dobed Sicily Fashion.

TRUSS the Birds as for boiling; lard them, half Lard and half Anchovies; seasoned with fine Spices without Salt; put them in a Brazing-pan, with a Knuckle of Veal, a Quarter of a Pound of Butter, two Glasses of Brandy, some Broth, sufficient to cover all, a Nosegay of all Sorts of sweet Herbs, three Cloves, two of Garlick, two whole Onions; braze on a slow Fire, five or six Hours; then take the Birds out to put in the Table Tureen; sift the Broth in a Sieve, without skimming; if too much, reduce it by boiling: pour it in the Tureen, stir it now and then; when it begins to turn to Jelly, mix the Butter with it, as it will shew like Marble by that Means.

End of the First Volume.

THE ART OF MODERN COOKERY DISPLAYED.

VOL. II.

THE ART OF MODERN COOKERY DISPLAYED.

Translated from the FRENCH.

CHAPITRE HUITIEME.
CHAPTER EIGHTH.

Des Ragoûts & Rissolles.

Of Ragouts, Collops or Fries.

Ragoût de Salpiquon. Forced-meat Ragout.

IT is a Mixture of several Sorts of Meat cut in Dices, such as Sweet-breads, fat Livers, Ham, Truffles, Mushrooms; which you put all together in a Stewpan, with a good Bit of Butter, a Nosegay of Sweet-herbs, two Cloves, two or three Shallots; soak it some time; then add Veal-cullis, Broth, Pepper and Salt; simmer it till the Meat is done, and the Sauce much reduced; skim it well: you may serve this by itself, or with any Sorts of brazed Meat; many more things may be added to this Ragout, as Beef-palates, Artichoke-bottoms, Cock's-combs, Lamb's-stones, small Eggs, &c. &c. taking care to boil the hardest sufficiently, before it is mixed together: Breaſt of roaſted Poultries, and Girkins chopped together, to be in it only long enough to warm without boiling.

Ragoût de Salpiquon, a Farcir.

Prepared for Stuffing any thing.

THIS Salpicon, for a Farce, is uſed for brazing Pieces, either Butcher's-meat or Poultries; make the ſame Preparation as the firſt, which you mix raw with Yolks of Eggs, ſcraped Lard, chopped Parſley, Shallots, Muſhrooms, Pepper and Salt; and ſtuff what you propoſe with it, only of large brazing Pieces.

Ragoût de Salpiquon a (L'arlequine), viz. various Colours.

SOAK a good Slice of Ham on the Fire, until it is almoſt done; then cut it in ſmall Dices, alſo one boiled Carrot, one Truffle, few Muſhrooms cut the ſame; put all together in a Stew-pan, with a Bit of Butter, a Glaſs of white Wine, a little Gravy and Cullis; ſimmer this a little while; then add chopped Breaſts of roaſted Poultries, Girkins, ſcalded Parſley, two Anchovies, half ſoaked, a little Pepper, Salt if neceſſary, a Lemon-ſqueeze: ſerve with what kind of Meat you pleaſe.

Ragoût de Foyes gras. Of fat Livers.

CUT off the Gall, and ſcald them in hot Water; then ſoak them about a Quarter of an Hour, with a Slice of Ham, a Bit of Butter, a Noſegay, Muſhrooms, half a Clove of Garlick, two Leaves of Baſil; add Broth and Cullis; ſimmer on a ſlow Fire; ſkim the Fat pretty often, reduce the Sauce rather thick; take out the Noſegay and Ham; add a Lemon-ſqueeze, Pepper, (and Salt, if the Ham does not make it Salt enough);

enough); if you would use this Ragout with any large Pieces of First-course Dish, you may add small Onions, Sweet-breads, Crawfish-tails, Roes of Carps: it will do equally to serve alone with the last Addition.

Ragoût de Crêtes. Of Cock's-combs.

SCALD the Combs in hot Water; then boil them in Broth, and two Slices of Lemon; prepare few chopped Mushrooms, with a Bit of Butter, a Nosegay, a little Broth and Cullis; simmer this on a slow Fire until it is done; take out the Nosegay; skim the Sauce, and reduce it pretty thick, then put the Combs to it; season it with Pepper and Salt, a Lemon Squeeze: if you would have them with a white Sauce, make a Liason with Yolks of Eggs and Cream, without Gravy or Cullis.

Ragoût de Jambon. Of Ham.

CUT five or six Slices of fresh Ham of equal Bigness; if of an old Ham, soak the Slices; then simmer them on a slow Fire until they are done; take them out, and put in the Stew-pan half a Spoonful of Vinegar, Gravy and Cullis; reduce it to the Consistence of a Sauce; then put the Slices to it to warm without boiling: serve this upon any Sorts of Meat which you please to garnish, (*masquer*, to hide); if you would use this by itself as a Second-course Dish, serve the Slices of Ham upon Slices of Bread of the same Bigness, fried in Butter, and the Sauce over them.

Ragoût de petits Oeufs & Rognons de Coq.

Ragout of small Eggs and Cock's-kidneys.

N. B. What is here meant by small Eggs, are those taken out of Pullets with Eggs in the Spring.

SOAK a Slice of Ham a Moment; then add a Bit of Butter to it, chopped Mushrooms, Parsley, Shallots,

lots, two Cloves, half a Glass of white Wine, Gravy and Cullis; let this boil about half an Hour; scald the Eggs and Kidneys in warm Water; peel the skin off the Eggs, and drain them very well; take the Nosegay and Ham out of the Ragout, and put these last in the Sauce, Pepper and Salt; the Sauce to be reduced pretty thick: if you would have it white, make a Liason with Yolks of Eggs and Cream, without Cullis or Gravy, only a little Broth to simmer it at first.

Ragoût de Ris de Veau. Of Calves Sweet-breads.

SCALD two or three Sweet-breads, cut each in three or four Pieces; put them in a Stew-pan with Mushrooms, Butter, a Nosegay of Sweet-herbs; soak this together a Moment, then add Broth, Gravy and Cullis; simmer on a slow Fire; skim it well, reduce the Sauce; season it with Pepper and Salt; a Lemon-squeeze, when ready to serve: if you would have it white, follow the former Direction.

Ragoût Mêlés de Trufes & d'Huîtres.

Ragout of Truffles and Oysters.

SCALD two or three Dozen of Oysters in their Liquor, beard them, have some chopped Parsley, Shallots, Mushrooms; which Part of it you put in a Stew-pan, first rubbed with Butter, then a Down of chopped Truffles, and Oysters upon, few Drops of Oil over, then over again with the chopped Herbs, Truffles and Oysters; simmer together about a Quarter of an Hour, the Stew-pan well stopped; then take out the Truffles and Oysters, and put half a Glass of white Wine, a little Cullis and Gravy, Pepper and Salt; boil the Sauce some time to give it a good Consistence; then put the Truffles and Oysters to the Sauce, to warm without boiling: serve for a Second-course Dish, or to garnish any first Course, called *Entrée* Dish.

Ragoûts

Ragoûts à l'Angloife. English Fashion.

CUT a good Bit of Ham in Dices, one Carrot, one Parfnep the fame, fmall whole Mufhrooms; put this together in a Stew-pan, with a Bit of Butter, a Nofegay of Parfley, green Shallots, two Cloves, Thyme, Laurel; foak it fome time on the Fire; then add a Glafs of Wine, Broth and Cullis; reduce the Sauce to a Liafon; take out the Nofegay; and put to it a fmall Handful of fcalded Piftachio-nuts, one Dozen of fmall round Onions, firft boiled in Broth; boil all together a Moment; add proper Seafoning of Pepper and Salt; if needful a Lemon-fqueeze: ferve for (Entremets, viz. Second-courfe Difh) or to (*masquer*) garnifh any other of firft Courfe.

Ragoût d'Ecreviffes. Of Craw-fifh.

MAKE a fmall Quantity of Cullis, with a Slice of Ham, a Slice of Veal, Bits of Carrots, fliced Onions, a Nofegay of Parfley, green Shallots, one Bay-leaf, two Cloves; foak it fome time until it catches at Bottom; then put what Quantity of Broth you think proper; fimmer it about an Hour, then fift it: pound the Shells of half a hundred of Craw-fifh, and ufe the Cullis to ftrain in a Stamine; boil the Tails in fome of this Cullis; let it be pretty thick: you may put this Ragout to the fame Ufe as the former: if you would have it Meager, ufe Fifh for the Cullis inftead of Ham and Veal.

Ragoût de Laitances. Of Carp Roes.

SOAK Slices of Ham and Veal, about half an Hour, on a flow Fire; then put a good Bit of Butter to it, Mufhrooms, two Cloves, a Nofegay of Sweet-herbs, a little Bafil, a Glafs of white Wine, a little Veal-gravy and Cullis; boil it until the Veal is done; fkim it, and take out the Veal and Ham: scald the Roes in hot Water, and put them to this Cullis, to boil about a Quarter of an Hour; skim it well; it ought to be as thick as very good Cream; season it with Pepper and Salt, a Lemon-squeeze, when ready; and make the same Use of it as directed before: you may make it in Meager, observing the last Direction for the Cullis, or with a white Liason.

Ragoût de Moules. Of Mussels.

THE first Care is to wash them very clean, to get the Sand all off of the Shells; then drain them well, and put them on a good Fire without Water, to make them open; take them out of the Shells with care, one by one; take out what little Crabs you may find, as Mussels are seldom without; keep their Water, and soak a Slice of Ham on the Fire, with few Mushrooms, a Nosegay of Sweet-herbs; then put some of the Water, and some Cullis; reduce it to a good Consistence; sift it in a Sieve, and put the Mussels to it to warm with boiling, and a little scalded Parsley chopped: you may also dress them with Fish-cullis, or a white Sauce.

Ragoût d'Huitres de plusieurs Façons.

Of Oysters of different Manners.

SCALD three or four Dozen of large Oysters in their own Liquor; if you would have them bearded, you must have more Oysters; sift the Liquid in a Lawn-sieve, put the Oysters by; chop few Mushrooms, Truffles, Parsley, green Shallots; put all in a Stewpan with a Bit of Butter, a little Cullis, and some of the Oyster-liquor, a Glass of white Wine; reduce the Sauce; then put the Oysters to it, to warm without boiling; a Lemon-squeeze when ready: you may also serve them in a plainer Way, by making the Sauce with

a Bit

a Bit of Butter rolled in Flour, a little Cullis, some of the Liquor, or with a white Sauce, and chopped Parsley as a Fricassée.

N. B. Although a particular Cullis is directed for each Ragout, it is not absolutely necessary, as a good Cullis is one of the principal Articles in Cookery; it is always made, where made Dishes are wanted, and may serve for all those Ragouts, with a little Attention to what is dressing; as some Sorts of Things require to be made more relishing than others: the Addition of Sweet-herbs called *Ravigotte*, Lemon, or Verjuice, is sufficient to make the Difference of Taste to each Particular; the professed Cook knows it, so will the Learner with a little Attention.

Ragoût de Morilles. Of Morels.

THEY must be washed in several Waters with great Care, as the Sand is very apt to stick to them; when well cleaned and drained, put them in a Stew-pan with a Bit of Butter, a Nosegay, some Gravy and Cullis; when done, take out the Nosegay, put Salt and Pepper; you may also dress them as a Fricassée; garnish the Dish with fried Bread, cut in different Shapes, for the better Look of the Dish.

Ragoût de Champignons. Of Mushrooms.

PEEL the Mushrooms, and cut each in two; soak a Slice of Ham, then put the Mushrooms to it, and a Bit of Butter, a Nosegay of Sweet-herbs, two Cloves; add Cullis and Gravy; simmer this together about an Hour, the Sauce to be reduced thick; take out the Ham and Nosegay; skim it well, add a Lemon-squeeze, Pepper and Salt, when ready: this is prepared to serve with Meat; but if you would have them alone, put neither Cullis nor Gravy, but make a Liason with Yolks of Eggs and Cream: serve them in a Bit, or several Bits of Bread fried, cut in some pretty Shape, or only small Bits round the Dish.

The French have another Sort which they call *Mouſſe-rons*, which is much like the Champignons; they are dreſſed much in the ſame Way, when freſh; and alſo dried, reduced to Powder, to mix with other Spices, to ſeaſon the Larding-bacon for large brazing Pieces; they are not plenty in England; they have much the ſame Flavour as all Spices, when reduced to Powder.

Ragoût de Concombres. Of Cucumbers.

PEEL the Cucumbers, and cut each in four; if pretty large, marinade with two Spoonfuls of Vinegar, one Onion, ſtuck with a Clove or two, and Salt; ſtir them now and then; when they have thrown their Water, ſqueeze them between a Cloth, and ſoak them on the Fire with a Bit of Ham, a Bit of Butter, till they begin to take colour; then put a little Broth and Gravy; ſimmer it till the Liquid is much reduced; take out the Ham, add a little Cullis: ſerve with what Kind of Meat you pleaſe, or alone, or with poached Eggs; when they are done for Sauce, cut them in ſmaller Pieces, and thinner, and follow the reſt of the Direction.

Ragoût de Pois. Of green Peas.

THEY ought to be young, and very freſh ſhelled; put them in a Stew-pan with a Bit of Butter, a Noſegay of Parſley, a ſmall Sprig of Winter-ſavory, one Clove, a little Veal-gravy; ſimmer on a flow Fire, and ſhort Sauce; when ready, add a little Cullis, and fine Salt: ſerve with what Meat you pleaſe, or alone: to ſtew Peas in a plain Way, only put a Bit of Butter, a little Flour, one or two Cabbage-lettuces, which will produce Liquid ſufficient, to ſtew the Peas without Broth or Water; and ſerve the Lettuces with them, or without.

Ragoût de Verjus. Of Verjuice-grapes, or others.

SCALD Verjuice-grapes, or others, a Moment, and stone them; beat up two Yolks of Eggs, with a Spoonful of liquid Verjuice, a little Flour, a little Broth, a Bit of Butter, chopped Parsley, Pepper and Salt; boil this a Moment, then put the Grapes in it; stir it with a Spoon on the Fire, to warm without boiling; you serve this with what kind of Meat you think proper.

Ragoût de Trufes. Of Truffles.

CUT the Truffles in pretty thick Slices, and boil them with a Glass of Wine and Broth, a Nosegay; when done, take the Nosegay out; add some good Cullis, Pepper and Salt; reduce to a good Consistence; serve with what you please: if you would have it for a Dish of itself, mix some Mushrooms with it, and garnish the Dish with fried Bread.

Ragoût d'Asperges en petits Pois.

Asparagus as green Peas.

CUT small Asparagus like green Peas; the best Method is to break them off first, then tie them in small Bunches to cut; boil them to half in Water, then drain them, and finish with Butter, a little Broth, a Nosegay, one or two Cloves, a Sprig of Savory; when done, take out the Nosegay, Cloves, and Savory; make a Liason with two Yolks of Eggs, a little Flour, and Broth: this, if you design it, to garnish a First-course Dish; if for alone, in the second Service, make the Liason with Cream, a little Salt, and a little Sugar.

Ragoût de petits Oignons. Of small round Onions.

SCALD what Quantity of small Onions you think proper; braze them very tender in Broth, a Slice of Bacon, a Nosegay of Sweet-herbs, and Salt; then drain them, and give them a few Boilings in a good Cullis, to garnish any Kind of Meat.

Ragoût de Racines. Of Roots.

CUT Carrots and Parsneps, the length of a Finger, and much the same Bigness; boil them to half in Water, then put them in a Stew-pan with small Bits of Ham, chopped Parsley and Shallots, Pepper and Salt, a Glass of Wine and Broth; let them stew slowly, until the Sauce is reduced pretty thick, a Squeeze of Lemon, when ready to serve: for Meager, instead of Ham, use Mushrooms, and make a Liason with Yolks of Eggs, beat up with Meager-broth: Sellery is done much the same, only cut smaller, if they serve in a Boat for Sauce; boil them tender in the Broth-pot, or in Water; then cut them to what length you please: serve with a good Cullis, or white Sauce.

Ragoût de Navets. Of Turnips.

CUT them to what Form you please; boil them a Moment in Water, then finish them in Broth and Cullis, Pepper and Salt; if you like to have them look of a brown Colour, fry them in Butter first, after they are scalded; this is all to garnish other Things: the Dish is commonly called by the Name of the Ragout.

Ragoût de Chicorée.

Of Endives or any Sorts of Lettuces.

SCALD them a good while, to get the bitterish Taste out; then boil them in Broth; when done, drain
them

them well, and put them to stew in good Cullis, with a whole Onion stuck with a Clove, few Drops of Vinegar, Pepper and Salt; after stewing a little while, take out the Onion, and serve under what Kind of Meat you please: if you would have it for Meager, boil them in Fish-broth, and thicken the Sauce with Yolks of Eggs, beat up with Broth or Cream.

Ragoût d'Ozeille. Of Sorrel.

BOIL it to half in Water, with few Lettuces, a little Charvil, then chop all together; put it in a Stewpan with few chopped Mushrooms, few green Shallots, a Slice of Ham, a little Broth and Cullis, Pepper and Salt; let it simmer a good while; take out the Ham, reduce the Sauce quite thick, and serve with what Sort of Meat you please: this is mostly done to serve with Fricandeau; if the Sorrel is too sharp, you may mix Spinages with it, or a Bit of Sugar to take off the Sharpness: few People use Charvil with it, as the Flavour is too strong for many, although very agreeable when used with Moderation.

Ragoût d'Epinars. Of Spinages.

DONE in much the same Manner as the former, either to garnish any Thing, or served alone, with fried Bread, or poached Eggs. *Pourpier*, viz. Pursley is very little used in England, but may be dressed in the same Manner as the former, and is very good in a mixed Sallad, in small Quantity.

Ragoût de Cardons d'Espagne.
Of Spanish Cardoons.

CHUSE the whitest, thick and sound; cut them the Length of a Finger; scald them in boiling Water, to peel off the hard Part all round; if pretty large, cut them

them in Quarters, or in halves; braze them with Broth, Beef-suet, a Bit of Butter, rolled in Flour; cover them over with Slices of Bacon; when done, drain them, and wipe clean with a Linen-cloth, then put them in a well-seasoned Cullis; simmer them on a slow Fire, until they have taken the Taste of the Cullis, and reduced to a middling thick Consistence; add a little Nutmeg, a Lemon-squeeze; make the Sauce pretty relishing; serve alone, or to garnish any Thing.

Ragoût de Pistaches. Of Pistachio-nuts.

SCALD a Handful of Pistachio-nuts, as you do Almonds, and warm in a good strong Cullis, without boiling; serve as a Ragout to garnish any Dish you please; Ragout de *Cornichons*, viz. Girkins; cut the large ones in Quarters, the small whole; soak them some time, to take the Vinegar out, and finish as the former: *Olives* the same, only stoned.

Ragoût de Cerneaux. Of green Walnuts.

SCALD them in boiling Water some time, with a Bit of Butter, two Slices of Lemon and Salt; drain them, and put them in a Sauce made of good Cullis, a Bit of Butter, Pepper, Salt, Nutmeg, and a Lemon-squeeze, when ready to serve.

Ragoût de Choux. Of Cabbage.

SCALD one Cabbage, cut in Quarters; Savoys are best; drain the Water quite out, tie them with Pack-thread; braze in a good Braze; serve with a good thick Cullis-sauce, pretty high of Pepper. (Choux-fleurs) Colliflower done in the same Manner.

Ragoût d'Haricots verd. Of Kidney-beans.

IF pretty large, cut them length-ways; if young, only break them in two; boil them in Water, then put them

them in a Stew-pan with a Slice of Ham, a Nosegay, two Cloves, one of Shallots, a little Gravy and Cullis; reduce the Sauce thick; take out the Ham and Nosegay, use them as all the rest: you may also dress them with a white Sauce, to serve alone; a Lemon-squeeze, when ready to serve.

Rissolles à la Béchamel. White Collops.

THE Meaning of Rissolles, is fried brown, and comprehends all Kinds of Meat cut in thin Slices for Collops; Forced-meat-balls fried, either to serve alone, or to mix with any thing else: to fry a little Flour and Butter, to give a brown Colour to any Sauce, is called a *Rissollet*, viz. a browning; but as there is different Ways in this as in many other Dishes, it is necessary to give some particular Direction about it: soak a Slice of Ham, with a Bit of Butter, chopped Parsley, Shallots, half a Laurel-leaf; simmer this on a slow Fire, about a Quarter of an Hour; then put to it a good Spoonful of Cullis, as much Cream, a little Flour, a little Pepper; reduce it quite thick, then sift it in a Sieve; cut the Breasts of roasted Poultry in small Bits; put it in the Sauce with one Yolk of Egg, give it few Boilings together; cut Bits of thin Paste to what Form you please; put this Ragout between two Pieces, pinch it all round to secure the Sauce, and fry them of a fine brown Colour.

Rissolles à la Choisy.

This, as many others, is either after the Name of a Nobleman, Count Choisy, or the Inventor.

BOIL Calves-udder very tender, in the common Pot, and let it cool; then cut a thin Slice, and one of Bacon upon each other; lay a fine relishing Forced-meat upon

upon this, and roll it up; dip them in a Batter-paste made of Flour, Salt, a little Oil, and white Wine, and fry as the former: you may serve a little Sauce under.

Rissolles de Palais de Bœuf. Of Beef-palates.

CUT one or two brazed Palates, the Bigness of half a Crown; have Bits of Puff-paste, as for those *à la Béchamel*; lay a little Farce upon the Paste, then the Palates and Farce again, roll it up and fry as the former; observe that your Forced-meat is made with Meat, either roasted or boiled before; any Remnant of roasted Fowls, or Chickens, or Veal, will do, properly seasoned.

Rissolles de Gibier. Of Game.

MINCE the Remainder of any roasted Pieces of Game, and chop the Bones; put them in a Stew-pan with a Glass of Wine, a Nosegay of Sweet-herbs, one or two Shallots, a little Cullis; simmer it some time, then sift it, and put it on the Fire again, to bring it to a thick Sauce; then put the Minced-meat in it, with a raw Yolk of Egg whipt, Pepper and Salt; then let it cool, and finish as those à la Béchamel.

Rissolles de differentes Farces.

Of different Forced-meat.

MAKE a Farce with any Sorts of boiled or roasted Meat, as Poultries, fat Livers, Lamb, Veal, Game, &c. &c. chop it very fine with Udder, a little Suet, Parsley, Shallots, Mushrooms, Truffles, any other Sweet-herbs, Pepper and Salt; mix with Yolks of Eggs; make little Balls, or finish in Paste as directed.

Rissolles

Rissolles à la Présidente.

From President the Husband.

MINCE a Veal-kidney roasted, with a little of its own Fat, a little rasped Parmesan Cheese, Pepper and Salt; mix with Yolks of Eggs; cut Bits of Bread, to what Shape you please, and lay as much of the Farce upon each Piece as you can; smooth it with a Knife dipt in Whites of Eggs; strew Bread-crums over; bake a little while in the Oven, or with a brazing Pan-cover.

Rissolles à la Provençale.

MAKE a Farce with roasted Poultry, scraped Lard, three chopped Anchovies, few chopped Capers, Pepper and Salt, two or three Shallots, a little Basil-powder; mix it with four or five Yolks of Eggs, and finish as the former.

DU ROTI, & DE LA FACON DE LE PREPARER.

OF ROAST, AND HOW TO PREPARE EACH KIND.

ALTHOUGH it seems very easy to roast any Kind of Meat, nevertheless there is a certain Point of roasting very necessary to observe, according to the Quality of the Meat, to serve it with its proper Flavour and Goodness; large Pieces are only to be judged by the Time, or feeling under the Finger, and are very forward, when they begin to burst into small smoking Bladders: a little Use and proper Attention guide the Time exact to take it up. I will give an Explanation, how to prepare Poultry and Game: as each Season furnishes some things different, it will not be unnecessary to give a few Examples of what we can give for Roast, and of the Choice of each Season in the Year. So far the Author. As a Translator, I found it necessary to be particularly acquainted with the English Productions of this Kind, as is already mentioned in my Apology. Although this is already given with other Productions in the First Volume, I shall here lay down each Article, wherein seasonable Roast may be more readily found out.

Du Printems. Of the Spring.

PRODUCTION of Poultries according to the London Market. In the Spring, Ducklings scalded, green Geese, Turkey-polts, wild Pigeons, tame Pigeons, Squob ditto, Quails, wild Stop-rabbits, Guinea Fowls, Pea-fowls, Capons, Pullards, Pullets with Eggs, Spring Fowls, Chickens.

N. B. Wild Ducks, Teals, Widgeons, Easterlings, Dun-birds, Bustards, Wood-cocks, going out of Season: Other Articles to be had of the Poulterers; Dish of Combs, fat Livers, Knots of Eggs, Turkey Pinions, Leverets, Plovers Eggs, Rabbits.

De l'Eté. Of Summer.

DRY pulled Geese, dry pulled Ducks, wild Rabbits, Wheat-ears, wild Pigeons, Fowls, dry pulled Turkeys, tame Pigeons, large Fowls, middling Fowls, Chickens, Guinea Fowls and Chickens, Quails, Leverets; Giblets to be had of the Poulterers.

De l'Automne. Of Autumn.

GEESE in Perfection, tame Ducks the same, Moorhen, large Fowls, and middling ditto, Chickens, Quails, Hares, Pheasants, Partridges, Wood-cocks, Snipes, Larks, Wood-pigeons, Land and Water Reals.

N. B.

N. B. Wild Ducks, Teals, Widgeons, Dun-birds, coming into Seafon; Giblets alfo to be had.

De l'Hyver. Of Winter.

LARGE Cock Turkies, Hen Turkies, large wild Rabbits, ditto Ducks, (dry pulled Geefe and Ducks, but moft out of Seafon), Larks, Snipes, Wood-cocks, Plovers, Buftards, Capons, Pullards, middling Fowls, Chickens, Quails, Pheafants, Partridges, Hares: altho' few of thofe Articles do not abfolutely agree with the Game-act, they neverthelefs are in Seafon (not to be found at Market, Pheafants, Partridges, and Hares) at prefent.

De la Preparation de toutes Sortes de Rotis.

Of the Preparation of all Sorts of Roaft.

POULTRIES ought to be kept without Food five or fix Hours before killing; pluck it directly after, and draw the Guts, then hang it up in a cool Place; keep it as long as the Weather will permit, it will be tenderer and better tafted; when you prepare it for Ufe, begin to draw by the Gizzard, by thrufting one Finger round, to loofen the Infide, to come out eafily; large Pullards are opened at the Side, and leffer ones at the End, as is ufual in England; finge it over the Fire all round, and wipe it clean with a Cloth; then trufs it properly, either for Boiling or Brazing, which is the fame, or for Roafting, which is different. All Sorts of Roaft fhould be done with a Fire as equal, during the Roafting, as it is poffible to keep it, and of a fine pale brown Colour, except it is to be ferved with any Sorts of Ragout; then obferve feveral Directions in Fowl Articles, Volume Firft: the fat Livers which you draw, roll them up in their Fat, if you have no immediate Occafion for their Ufe.

Wild Pigeons are ufed quite frefh out of the Neft; when they are plucked and drawn, cut off the Pinions, Neck and Claws; roll them up in Vine-leaves, and a Slice of Bacon quite round; when they are almoft done, ftrew Bread-crums over them; give them a good brown Colour; ferve either with or without Sauce. *Tame Pigeons*; gut them as foon as killed, and take out the Craw, and keep them fome time before ufing. *Wood Pigeons* are done the fame. Alfo *Thrufhes*, and *Moorgame*, and alfo *Turkey Polts* are prepared in the fame Manner, as Fowls and Chickens. *Lamb* ought to be kept fome time, and roafted flowly, as all fuckling Meat ought to be; the Fore-quarter is the moft efteemed, and of greater Ufe for Variety in Cookery.

Des Oifeaux de Riviere. Of Frefh-water Fowls.

WILD and tame Ducks, Teals, &c. &c. all thofe Kind of Fowls, when well plucked and drawn, trufs the Legs undermoft, roaft them without any thing: they require but a fhort Time to be done; as they ought to be full of their own Gravy, which will wafte if too much roafted.

Des Oifeaux que l'on fert avec des Rôties deffous.

Of the Kind of Birds, which are ferved with a Toaft under.

OF *Larks*, they ought to be fat and frefh killed; you may lard them or barded, and roaft them with Toaft under, or roaft them wrapped in Vine-leaves, and a Slice of Bacon, ftrewed with Bread-crums, and ferve with the fame: alfo *Quails* are done in the fame Manner: and *Reals*, *Wood-cocks*, and *Snipes*; trufs the Legs undermoft, the Bills ferve for a Skewer; lard the Breaft-part if agreeable, and roaft them without drawing, with toafted Bread under; Wheat-ears, when in full Seafon,

may

may be called the *Ortolans* of England, and are dressed in the same Manner as Larks. *Partridges* are drawn like Chickens, and ought to be spared in the Basting, as too much of it will waste the Flavour; singe them over a Charcoal-fire before roasting, larded or barded. The same Observation is necessary in basting Hares and Rabbits, and all Game of high Flavour. It is to be observed, that the Female of Poultry and Game is in general more delicate than the Male, and ought to be kept as long as possible, for the sake of Tenderness and Flavour.

Du Poisson d'Eau douce, & de Mer.

Of fresh and Sea Water Fish.

THE Direction of Fish-broth, Gravy, Sauces, Soops and Cullis, are to be found at the End of the said Direction for Meat, at the Beginning of the First Volume.

Des Glaces & Braises Maigres.

Of Meager Glazes and Brazes.

FOR a Braze, according to the Largeness of the Piece, put a middling Quantity of Butter in a Brazing-pan, white Wine, Roots, Broth, a Nosegay of Parsley, Chibbol, Thyme, Laurel, Basil, Pepper and Salt, Onions sliced, Bits of Carrots, Parsneps, Sellery; regulate one Quantity by the other: all Fish-brazes are done after this Manner. For *Glazes*, put some Fish-broth in a Stew-pan, with Fish-bones, and all Sorts of Fragments well washed; boil this a good while, with a Nosegay of Sweet-herbs, Bits of Roots; then sift it in a Lawn-sieve; and reduce it to a *Caramel*, to glaze any Sorts of Fish.

Farce de Poisson. Fish Forced-meat.

BOIL Bread-crums in Cream or Milk, until it is quite thick; let it cool; chop any Sort of Fish very fine, with Parsley, Shallots, Pepper and Salt, few Spices; mix it with the Cream and Bread; and pound it all together with a Bit of good Butter Mushrooms, and Yolks of Eggs: it will serve to stuff any Kind of Fish, or to make *Rissolles*, as before directed.

Farce maigre sans Poisson. Farce without Fish.

CHOP some Sorrel, and put it in a Stew-pan, with a Bit of Butter, Cream, and Bread-crums; boil it till it is reduced quite thick; let it cool, then pound it in a Mortar, with chopped Parsley, Shallots, Mushrooms, hard Yolks of Eggs, Pepper and Salt, Nutmeg, a Bit of Butter; mix it with few raw Yolks of Eggs, and use it to what you please.

DU POISSON. OF FISH.

Carpe au Court-bouillon, & au bleu.

Stewed Carp, blue Sauce.

WHEN the Carp is gutted, and well washed, lay it on a Dish, and pour a Glass or two of boiling Vinegar upon it, to turn it blue; tie it up in a Linen-cloth, to put in a Brazing-pan, with a good Bit of Butter, red Wine, according to the Bigness of the Fish, one third Part of Water, Slices of Onions, Bits of Carrots, Parsley, Shallots, Cloves, Slices of Lemons, Thyme, Laurel, Pepper and Salt; the Broth ought to be pretty high seasoned; sift the Sauce, and serve some upon the Fish, and some in a Sauce-boat, or, as some, without Sauce upon a Napkin; garnish with green Parsley, Sauces in Boats.

Carpe à la Bourgogne. With red Wine.

MAKE a little Stuffing with Butter, chopped Parsley, Shallots, Pepper and Salt; stuff the Carp with it; put it in a Fish-kettle, much of its Bigness, with two or three Spoonfuls of Broth, one Bottle of Burgundy, or Port Wine, a Nosegay of Sweet-herbs, two sliced Onions, Bits of Carrots, Parsley-roots, whole Pepper, Salt and Nutmeg; boil it over a smart Fire; when done, drain the Carp; sift the Sauce without skimming; reduce it rather thick, and serve upon the Fish, with fried Bread round it.

Carpe à la Financiere.

Financier, a Manager of the King's or public Money, and mostly rich and expensive.

HAVE a large Carp, which you clean very properly; open it on the Side to gut it, and be very careful not to break the Gall; skin it thinly of the whole Side, and lard it finely; make a Ragout sufficient to fill it, with Sweet-breads, Truffles, Mushrooms, fat Livers; boil this together properly seasoned, with two Glasses of white Wine, a Bit of Butter, Gravy and Cullis; when it is reduced to the Consistence of a thick Ragout; let it cool, and stuff the Carp with it, and sew it up fast; braze it with Slices of Ham and Veal, covered over with Slices of Lard, Slices of Onions, Bits of Roots, one Clove of Garlick, a large Nosegay of Parsley, green Shallots, two or three Cloves, Thyme, Laurel; soak it some time on a slow Fire; then put Wine, and Broth, equal Quantity, sufficient to cover the whole, Pepper and Salt; braze it slowly; when done, drain the Carp; glaze the larded Side, with a good Veal-glaze; then lay it on the Dish you intend for Table; garnish it round with what you please, as Craw-fish, Truffles,

Truffles, large Cock's-combs, small Partridges, Whites of Fowls, or Pigeons glazed; serve with a Spanish Sauce, which you will pour upon the Pieces, that are not glazed, or some of its own Sauce, properly reduced and seasoned.

Carpe farcie à la Gendarme. Military Fashion.

CLEAN and chop a good Handful of Sorrel; and stew it with Butter, Bread-crums, Parsley, Shallots, and Cream; let it be thick; when done, mix three hard Yolks of Eggs chopped, and three raw, Pepper and Salt; stuff a Carp with it, and sew it up close, and marinade it about an Hour or two, in Oil, Salt, whole Pepper, Shallots, Parsley, one Clove of Garlick, few Leaves of Basil, Thyme and Laurel; then broil it, basting with the Marinade; and make a Sauce with chopped Mushrooms, and Butter; simmer this about a Quarter of an Hour; then add a little Flour, chopped Capers, Shallots, Parsley, two or three Anchovies, Butter and Broth, sufficient to make Sauce enough; boil all together a little while; when ready, add a little Vinegar, or a good Lemon-squeeze; serve under the Fish.

Carpe grilleé à la Farce.

Carp stuffed and broiled.

SEE Ragout *de Farce d'Ozeille.* Prepare such, to stuff the Carp with part of it, when properly cleaned; make the Remainder rather more liquid with Cream and Broth, to serve under the Carp, when well broiled, first marinaded with a little Oil, chopped Parsley, Shallots, Thyme, Laurel, Pepper and Salt; baste with the Marinade and Butter, while broiling.

Carpe frite. Fried Carp.

SPLIT a Carp at the Back, flatten the Back-bone, or cut it out; marinade it about two Hours, with a Glass of Vinegar, and Water, Parsley, whole Shallots, one Clove of Garlick, two of Spices, Thyme, Laurel, whole Pepper and Salt; then drain it, and flour it over; fry on a smart Fire, and serve with fried Parsley round it.

Carpe à l'Etuvée. Stewed.

MAKE a *Rissollet* (viz. brown Butter and Flour) with Flour and Butter; then half Wine and Water sufficient, according to the Bigness of the Fish, which you cut in large Pieces, to put in the Rissollet, with small Onions, half boiled, a Nosegay of Sweet-herbs, two or three Cloves, Mushrooms, Pepper and Salt, Thyme and Laurel; stew on a middling Fire, until the Liquid is reduced pretty thick; take out the Nosegay, and Laurel-leaf; add one or two chopped Anchovies, whole Capers; garnish the Dish with fried Bread.

Etuveé de Carpe à la Chartreuse.

Chartreux, an Order of Friars, who eat no Meat, and are famous for dressing Fish and Greens.

SAVE the Blood of a large Carp, and well cleaned and gutted; wash the Inside with red Wine, which you also keep; garnish the Bottom of a stewing Fish-kettle, with Bits of Carrots, Parsneps, Slices of Onions, one Clove of Garlick, two large Cloves of Shallots; each stuck with a Clove, Sprigs of Parsley; put the Carp upon this, with Salt and whole Pepper; the Blood and Wine sufficiently, a good Bit of Butter, two or three Spoonfuls of Water; stew it on a middling Fire;

Fire; when the Fish is done, sift the Liquor; reduce it to the Consistence of a Sauce; add another Bit of Butter, mixed with chopped Anchovies, Capers, and Flour; make a Liaison pretty thick, and serve upon the Fish.

Carpe en Matelotte

CUT a Carp in large Pieces, and any other Kind of fresh Water-fish, as Pikes, Eels, Tenches, &c. &c. put it all together in a Stew-pan; and make a *Rissollet*, with Butter and Flour, half Broth, and half red Wine; add one Dozen of small Onions scalded, some whole Mushrooms, a Nosegay of Sweet-herbs; boil this together, until the Onions are almost done; then put it to the Fish with Pepper and Salt, two Cloves, a little Nutmeg; boil it on a smart Fire, it will only require about half an Hour; let the Sauce be much reduced; take out the Nosegay; add one or two chopped Anchovies; garnish the Dish with fried Bread.

Carpe en Matelotte à la Mariniere.

(*Mariniere* from *Marains*, Seafaring Men.)

BOIL some small Onions to three Parts, and put them in a Pan or Pot, with a Carp cut in large Pieces, and other Sorts of Fish the same, without being washed, after gutting; keep the Blood, which add to the Fish, with as much red Wine as covers the whole, a Bit of Butter, a good Bit of Lemon-peel, two Laurel-leaves, Pepper and Salt; boil on a smart Fire; stir it some Time, for fear it should catch at Bottom; when done, take out the Lemon-peel; turn it over upon the Dish, *sans Façon*.

Carpe à la Jacobine.

An Order of Friars, called *Jacobin*.

PUT a Dozen or more of small Onions scalded, in a Stew-pan, with half a Dozen of Truffles sliced, a Nosegay of Sweet-herbs, a Bit of Butter; simmer this on the Fire until it catches a little; then put a Pint of white Wine, and boil on a slow Fire about half an Hour; then put a Carp to it cut in large Bits, some Broth, Pepper and Salt; reduce the Sauce; when ready to serve, make a Liason, with three Yolks of Eggs, and Cream, and a good Lemon-squeeze.

Carpe aux finis Herbes. With Sweet-herbs.

CUT a Carp as before; put it in a Stew-pan, with chopped Parsley, green Shallots, Mushrooms, a little Taragon, a Trifle of Garlick, a little Powder of Basil, a good Bit of Butter rolled in Flour, a Spoonful of Oil, a Pint of white Wine, Pepper and Salt, two or three Spoonfuls of Onion-gravy; boil on a smart Fire, and reduce the Sauce thick.

Carpe farcie. Stuffed.

WHEN the Carp is well cleaned and trimmed, take up the Skin from the Flesh, which you will do easily, by beginning at the Belly, running the Finger betwixt to the Head, where the Skin must hold, the same at the Tail; chop some of the Flesh to mix with Bread-crums, chopped Mushrooms, Parsley, Shallots, a Bit of Butter, a little Basil: you may also mix the Meat of other Kind of Fish; season with Pepper and Salt; make it malleable with four or five Yolks of Eggs; cut out all the large Bones, and stuff the Carp with this Farce, and sew it up; put it upon a Dish,

buttered

buttered at Bottom, and baste all over with Butter; strew it with Bread-crums, and bake it in the Oven; take care to baste it now and then, with a little Butter, to hinder it from taking too much Colour: serve with what Sauce you please, or with a Ragout of Roes, which you will find in Ragout Articles in this Volume, Page 293.

Carpe à la Dauphine.

MAKE a good Ragout of Sweet-breads, fat Livers and Truffles; let it be pretty thick; open a Carp on one Side, and stuff it with this Ragout, and sew it up; lay it on the Side that has not been opened, upon Slices of Veal and Ham, whole Pepper, very little Salt, a good Bit of Butter; cover it over with thin Slices of Lard, a Nosegay of all Sorts of Sweet-herbs; soak it about a Quarter of an Hour; then put a Bottle of Champaign; finish the Boiling slowly; sift the Sauce, and skim it very clean; add some Cullis, reduce it to a good Consistence, and serve upon the Fish.

Carpe au Monarque. Monarch.

GUT a Carp on the Side, and fill it with a Ragout of small Onions, well tasted; sew it up, and take up the Skin of the other Side; lard it all over like a Fricandeau; boil it with white Wine and Broth, a Nosegay, Pepper, Salt and Cloves; when done, drain it, and glaze the larded Side with a Veal-glaze; serve upon a Ragout of Sweet-breads, Cock's-combs, small Eggs, fat Livers, and the Roes.

Carpe à la Polonoise. Polish Fashion.

CUT a Carp in large Pieces, also the Head in two; put it in a Stew-pan, with a Bit of Butter, Slices of Onions, Bits of Carrots, Parsley, green Shallots, Thyme, Laurel, whole Pepper and Salt; soak it a little

tle while; then add a Pint of Beer, a good Glass of Brandy; when done, sift the Sauce; add a Bit of Butter, rolled in Flour, the Juice of a Seville-orange; reduce the Sauce pretty thick, serve upon the Fish.

Carpe à la Broche. Roasted.

STUFF a Carp, with a Farce made of Butter, Bread-crums, fine Spices, Capers, Anchovies, Parsley, green Shallots, all finely chopped; lard it with Fillets of fresh Anchovies; or soaked to take the Salt out; tie it to a Skewer, to tie it then to the Spit; cover it over with two or three Doubles of Paper, well buttered; baste it with white Wine, boiled with some Butter, two Laurel-leaves, and one Clove of Garlick; serve with what Sauce or Ragout you think proper.

Carpe en Hachis. Hashed.

CUT small Carps in small Bits, and put them in a Stew-pan, with a Bit of Butter, chopped Parsley, Shallots, Pepper, Salt and Nutmeg, half a Pint of white Wine, few Spoonfuls of Onions-gravy, a little Flour; boil slowly, reduce the Sauce; garnish the Dish round with fried Bread.

Carpe en Redingotte, (a Great-coat) masked.

STUFF a Carp with chopped Parsley, green Shallots, Pepper and Salt, mixed with Butter; boil it in Broth, and half white Wine, Bits of Roots, Onions sliced, a Nosegay, two or three Cloves, Salt and Pepper; cut a large Eel in three Pieces; open it at the Belly, and cut out the Bones; lard it like a Fricandeau; and boil it also in Broth and white Wine, few Slices of Ham and Veal, whole Mushrooms; boil on a smart Fire; when the Eel is done, sift the Sauce, and reduce it to a

Caramel,

Caramel, with which you glaze the Eel; cover the Carp with it, and serve with what Sauce or Ragout you please, either of Meat or stewed Greens.

Carpe en Ecuſſon. In the Form of a Scutcheon.

CLEAN two or three small Carps, and take up the Skin; cut some of the Meat in small long Fillets, and make a Farce with some of the Meat, Roes, Bread-crums soaked in Cream, chopped Parsley, Shallots, Pepper and Salt, mixed with few Yolks of Eggs, a little Butter; cut Bits of Bread, the Bigness of a Crown-piece, or in what Shape you please; lay some of the Farce upon each Piece, the Tail of a Craw-fish in the Middle, the Fillets of Carp round, intermixed with Fillets of Truffles; cover this with more Farce; make them either high or flat, according to the Quantity; cut the Skins in Bits to cover the upper Part of each Scutcheon; bake it in a moderate Oven; serve with a Sauce made of the Trimmings of the Carps, white Wine and Cullis.

Carpe au Prince.

From the Richness of the Preparation.

STUFF a Carp with a good ready-made Ragout; sew it up, and take up the Skin of one Side; lard it as a Fricandeau; boil it few Minutes in white Wine, then take it out to drain; garnish the Bottom of a Dish, with a Farce made of fat Livers of roasted Poultries, scraped Lard, and proper Seasoning, Bread-crums, all mixed with Yolks of Eggs; lay the Carp upon this; cover the larded Side with Slices of Bacon, and bake it in the Oven; when done, drain the Fat off; glaze the larded Side, with a Glaze made of Veal and Ham; serve with a Spanish Sauce, or any other, and a good Lemon-squeeze.

Filets de Carpes de plusieurs façons.

Carp Fillets of different manners.

CUT the Fillets of what Bigness you think proper; and make a Sauce with the Trimmings, and the Head, which you soak together some Time, with a Bit of Butter, Shallots, Parsley, two Cloves, Mushrooms, a little Fennel, a Glass of white Wine and Broth; let it simmer a good while, then sift it, and put the Fillets to it, to simmer sometime; reduce the Sauce pretty thick; add Pepper and Salt, and a Lemon-squeeze, when ready to serve; another way is to boil the Fillets in white Wine and Broth, a Nosegay, Salt, and whole Pepper; when they are done, drain them, and serve upon a Ragout of stewed Greens, as Sorrel, Lettuces, Cucumbers, &c.

Du Brochet. Of Pike.

PIKES catched in Rivers and clear Water, are preferable in Goodness to those in Ponds, the Meat is sweeter and firmer; the large ones may be kept some time dead, they will be tenderer; it is not esteemed in England nor much any where else, where Sea-water-Fish is plentiful, although it bear its own Merit in inland Countries.

Brochet à la Poulette. Pike white Fricassee.

WHEN the Pike is properly cleaned, cut it in large Bits, and put them in a Stew-pan with Butter, some Mushrooms, one Dozen of small Onions half boiled, a Nosegay of Parsley, green Shallots, two Cloves, Thyme, Laurel; soak this together some Time; then add a Pint of white Wine and Broth, Salt and whole Pepper; boil it on a smart Fire, reduce the Sauce, take out the Nosegay; make a Liason with Cream and Eggs as usual, a little Nutmeg and a Lemon-squeeze, if the Wine does not make it tart enough.

Brochet frit. Fried.

CUT it in Pieces, and let it marinade about two Hours in a little Vinegar and Water, Pepper and Salt, Parsley, Shallots, Onions sliced; then wipe it dry; roll it in Batter to fry of a fine Colour; serve upon a Ragout of the Roes, or any other Meager Ragout, or with fried Parsley.

Brochet à l'Italienne à la Broche.

Roasted Italian Fashion.

STUFF a good large Pike with a Farce made of Poultry, Cow's Udder, Bread-crums soaked in Cream, scraped Lard, chopped Parsley, Shallots, Mushrooms, Pepper and Salt, mixed with a few Yolks of Eggs; lard it on one Side, and wrap it up in Paper, well buttered; tie it to the Spit without running it through; serve with an Italian Sauce, which you will find in Sauce Articles, Vol. I. p. 32.

Brochet en Dauphin.

In the form of the Dolphin Fish.

WHEN the Fish is gutted and scalded, make a few Incisions on the Back and Sides; rub it over with Salt and coarse Pepper; then marinade it in Oil, Parsley, Shallots, one Clove of Garlick, two Laurel-leaves; tie it on a Skewer in the form of a Dolphin; bake it in the Oven, basting now and then with some of the Marinade; when done, drain it off, and serve with what Sauce you please.

Brochet à la Mariée. Bride-fashion.

CUT a Pike in several Pieces; bone them and flatten as much as you can; have a good Farce, which you roll round the Fish, and tied in Bits of Cloth, and braze

it

it in white Wine, a Bit of Butter and Broth, Bits of Roots, a Nosegay, Pepper and Salt; when done, strip each Bit, and serve with what Sauce you think proper: a relishing sharp Sauce will prove best.

Brochet au gros Sel. In a plain Way.

WHEN it is well cleaned, rub it over with Salt about two Hours, before you propose to boil it; then wash the unmelted Salt off, and boil it in Water, with Parsley-roots, half a Clove of Garlick chopped; serve with Anchovy-sauce.

Brochet à la Broche en Gras & en Maigre.

Roasted Pike with Meat-sauce or Meager.

IF for *Gras*, stuff it with a good Farce, and lard one Side with Bacon, and one Side with Anchovies, and few Bits of pickled Cucumbers through and through: for *Maigre*, stuff it with a Farce made of Fish; and lard it with Eels instead of Bacon, the other Side the same with Anchovies; roll it up in double Paper, well buttered, and Parsley, Shallots, two Cloves, Thyme, Laurel, all whole, under the Paper; tie it well with two or three Skewers to the Spit, and baste it with Butter boiled with white Wine; when it is done, take off the Paper to give it a good Colour: serve with what Sauce you think proper.

Brochet à la Simone. Country-wife Fashion.

CUT a Pike in Pieces; marinade it in Vinegar, Pepper and Salt; cut Turnips to what Shape you please, and fry them in Butter and Flour, to give them a brown Colour; then add a little Broth, a Nosegay of Sweet-herbs, a Laurel-leaf, one Clove; then put the

Fish to it, and a little more Butter; when done, thicken the Sauce with Flour; add Pepper and Salt, a little Vinegar: garnish the Dish with fried Bread.

Brochet en Grenadins. As small Fricandeau.

CUT a large Pike in middling Pieces; skin it; take out the Back-bone, and lard it; braze it with thin Slices of Veal and Ham, whole Mushrooms, a Nosegay of Sweet-herbs, some Broth, half a Pint of white Wine, two Spoonfuls of Oil; simmer it slowly until the Fish is done; then take the Grenadins out, and sift the Braze; reduce it to a *Caramel* to glaze them with; serve upon any Sort of stewed Greens, or what Sauce you think proper.

Brochet en Etuvée. Stewed as Matlotte.

MAKE a *Rissollet*, with Butter and Flour, a Pint of red Wine, a Nosegay, two or three Cloves, Thyme and Laurel, one Dozen of small Onions, half boiled, first Pepper and Salt, then the Pike cut in Pieces; simmer it till the Fish is done; take out the Nosegay, add a good Bit of Butter; when ready to serve, add half a Spoonful of Capers, one or two chopped Anchovies; garnish the Dish with fried Bread, and serve the Sauce over all: you may also put Artichoke-bottoms, Mushrooms, Carp-roes, pickled Girkins, or any thing else, as Conveniency offers.

Brochet au Vin de Champagne. With white Wine.

GUT the Pike without scaling it, and stuff it with a Farce made of Butter, chopped Parsley, green Shallots, one Clove of Garlick, Thyme, Laurel, Basil, Salt, and fine Spices; put it in a Kettle much of its Bigness, and Wine sufficient to cover it, two or three large Lemons cut in Slices, first peeled; boil it some time;

time; set Fire to the Wine with Paper, let it burn till the Fish is done; then sift the Sauce; reduce it to a good Consistence, to serve upon the Pike.

Brochet à la Provençale.

LARD it through and through, with Eel and Anchovies; braze in a Kettle much of its Bigness, Broth, a little Cullis and white Wine, Slices of Onions, Bits of Roots, Sweet-herbs, a good Bit of Butter, Pepper and Salt; serve with Craw-fish Cullis, or any Sauce or Ragout you please.

Brochet à la Duchesse.

LARD it half Lard and half Ham; braze with thin Slices of Veal, few Bits of Ham; cover it over with Slices of Bacon, Bits of Roots round it, a large Nosegay, two Cloves of Garlick, three or four of Spices; soak it on a flow Fire about half an Hour; then add a Bottle of white Wine and Broth; boil it until the Pike is done; take it out, and strew it with Breadcrumbs, and small Bits of Butter very close; put it in the Oven to take a good brown Colour; skim and sift the Braze; add a little Cullis, and serve under the Fish.

Brochet Moitié au bleu. Moitié frit; half stewed and half fried.

CUT a good large Pike in two; stew the Head-part as you do Carp with red Wide; split the other Part in two, and marinade it some time in Vinegar and Water, Pepper and Salt, two Cloves, sliced Onions, Shallots; then wipe it clean, and flour it to fry; serve upon the same Dish, with a little of the Sauce upon the stewed Part, and fried Parsley for the other: you may serve the Remainder of the Sauce in a Sauce-boat.

Brochet à l'Allemande.   German Fashion.

KEEP the Pike killed a day or two, then clean it whole, and put it in a Fish-kettle, with two Bottles of red Wine, or in proportion more or less, according to the Bigness, a large Nosegay of Sweet-herbs, Pepper and Salt, three or four Cloves, two Laurel-leaves, Thyme, a little Basil; boil it some time; then set Fire to the Wine, with a Bit of Paper; let it burn until it is reduced to about a Pint of Liquid; then take out the Nosegay, and put a Bit of Butter, about the Bigness of an Egg, which you stir to incorporate it with the Wine; and continue to add Butter in this Manner, until the Sauce is well mixed and pretty thick; serve quick and hot, for fear the Sauce should turn to Oil.

Brochet à l'Espagnole.   Spanish Fashion.

GUT a Pike by the Gills, without opening the Belly; and when it is well cleaned, lard it all round, half Bacon and half Ham; stuff it with a Farce made of roasted Poultry, Beef-marrow, and Seasoning as usual, two or three Glasses of white Wine, and Yolks of Eggs to mix it; roast it wrapped in Slices of Lard and Paper, and baste it with Butter and white Wine boiled together; when done, serve a Spanish Sauce under it: you will find how to make it in Sauce-articles, Page 32.

Brochet à l'Arlequine.   Of various Colours.

CUT a pretty large Pike in four or six Pieces, and lard each with Lard, Ham, Girkins, and Truffles through and through; put them in a Stew-pan, with a Pint of white Wine, a Nosegay, two Cloves, whole Pepper, some good Broth; boil on a smart Fire to reduce the Liquor quite; serve with a Ragout à l'Arlequine: see Ragout-articles, Page 290.

De l'Anguille. Of Eels.

THE best are those catched in running Waters, and ought to be used as fresh as possible; they are prepared many different Ways, and also very useful to lard other Kind of Fishes.

Anguille en Fricassée de Poulets.

As Chicken Fricassée.

ACCORDING to the Bigness, to one or two Eels, skin them and cut in Pieces; put them in a Stew-pan, with a good Bit of Butter, some Mushrooms, a Nosegay of Sweet-herbs, two Cloves; simmer this some time, then put to it half a Pint of white Wine, some Broth, Pepper and Salt; boil on a smart Fire, reduce the Sauce; take out the Nosegay; make a Liason, with two or three Yolks of Eggs and Cream: observe as a general Rule, that the Liason must not boil; add a Lemon-squeeze, when ready to serve.

Anguille à la Nivernoise.

From the Sauce, Vol. I. Page 31.

WHEN it is skinned and well trimmed, cut it in Bits of about two or three Inches in Length; marinade it in Oil, chopped Parsley, Shallots, Mushrooms, Pepper and Salt; make as much of the Marinade stick to it as possible; strew it with Bread-crums; broil it on a slow Fire, basting with the Remainder of the Marinade; when done of a fine Colour, serve with a Sauce à la Nivernoise.

Anguille à la Broche diversifiée; roasted, to different Sauces.

CUT a large Eel as the former, and marinade it with Oil and Lemon-juice, Pepper and Salt, two Cloves, two or three whole Shallots, Thyme, and Laurel; let it marinade about two Hours, then tie each Bit to a Skewer; wrap it up in Paper well buttered; squeeze the Herbs of the Marinade, and baste it with the Liquor, and a little melted Butter added to it; serve with what Sauce or Ragout you think proper.

Anguille glacée. Eel glazed, or as Fricandeau.

CUT a large Eel in Pieces of what Length you think proper; lard it, either of one Side or both; if you lard both Sides, take out the Back-bone; if of one, leave it; then braze it with thin Slices of Veal, and few small Bits of Ham, a Nosegay of Sweet-herbs, two Glasses of white Wine, and some good Broth; simmer it as all other Brazes, (it requires but a short time); when it is done, take out the Eel, and reduce the Braze to a Glaze, to rub over the larded Part; and put a little Broth and Cullis in the same Pan, to gather the Remainder of the Glaze; give it a Boil or two; sift it; add a Lemon-squeeze, and serve under the Eel: it may also be served with any Sauces, or stewed Greens of any Sorts according to the Season.

Anguille à la Chartreuse.

From an Order of Friars so called.

SIMMER a good Handful of Bread-crums in a Pint of white Wine, until the Liquid is quite reduced; then let it cool; make a Farce with this, and Flesh of a Carp minced, a Bit of Butter, Parsley, Shallots, and Mushrooms chopped very fine, Pepper and Salt, and mixed with Yolks of Eggs; lay some of this Farce on the Dish you intend for Table; upon this Slices of Eel, again some Forced-meat and Eel, and so continue, and finish by the Farce uppermost; smooth it over with a Knife dipt often in Whites of Eggs; strew it pretty thick

thick with Bread-crums, and Parmesan Cheese rasped; bake it in a moderate-heated Oven, or under a Dutch Oven-cover; when it is done, drain off the Butter, and serve under a good clear Cullis-sauce, with a Lemon-squeeze.

Anguille à la Sainte Menehoult.

MAKE a Batter with a Bit of Butter, a Spoonful of Flour and Milk, a Laurel-leaf, Pepper and Salt, Shallots, Slices of Onions, Bits of Carrots and Parsneps; put it on the Fire to boil; then put the Eel in it, cut in middling Pieces; boil it slowly; when done, drain, and dip it in Eggs beat up, and strew it with Crums; dip it again in the boiling, and Bread-crums again; broil it of a fine Colour; serve with Sauce *Remoulade*, in a Sauce-boat.

Anguille au Brodequin. Racktied.

CUT an Eel in Pieces, the length of three Inches; marinade it in Oil, Pepper and Salt, Parsley, Shallots, Thyme, Laurel, all whole; cut Pieces of Bread-crums pretty thick, and the Length of the Pieces of Eel, four to each; fry the Bread in Butter; lay Fillets of Anchovies upon the Bread, and tie a Bit of Eel between four Pieces; finishing all in the same Manner; roll them up in Paper well buttered; roast them, basting with the Marinade; and serve with what Sauce you think proper.

Façon de conserver les Anguilles, ou autres Poissons.

How to preserve Eels, or any Kind of Fishes.

ACCORDING to the Quantity, boil a Pint of Wine, or more, with the Proportion of a Quarter of a Pound of Sugar, and a Quarter of a Pound of Salt, for a Bottle of Wine; let it cool, and trim the Fish as for present Use; fry it (in Oil, and few Laurel-leaves) to three Parts; when it is almost cold, put it in an earthen Pot; pour the Wine upon it, and the Oil used for frying, with the Laurel-leaves; when it is quite cold, cover the Pot with Leather or strong Paper; tie it fast; it will keep a long while, if kept in a cool Place.

Anguille frite. Fried Eel.

CUT an Eel in Pieces, and score it with a Knife of both Sides; cut out the Back-bone; put it to marinade about an Hour, in Vinegar, Parsley, Shallots, Slices of Onions, two or three Cloves; then drain it, and fry it of a good Colour: serve with fried Parsley, or a relishing Sauce in a Boat.

Anguille à l'Etuvée. Stewed or Matlotte.

MAKE a brown Sauce with Butter and Flour, called *à Roux* or *Rissollet*; when this is of a good Colour, put a Pint of white Wine, a little Broth and Cullis, one Dozen of small Onions scalded, some Mushrooms, a Nosegay of Sweet-herbs, two Cloves, Salt and whole Pepper; boil this until the Onions are almost done; then put the Eel to it, cut as the former; boil on a smart Fire; reduce the Sauce; when ready, add a pounded Anchovy, fine Capers whole; and garnish the Dish with fried Bread.

Anguille à la Choisi.

CUT a large Eel in two or three Pieces; take out the Bone, and flatten it pretty much; make a Ragout with sliced Onions fried in Butter, chopped Truffles, Mushrooms, fat Livers, Shallots, Parsley, Pepper and Salt, a Glass of white Wine; boil it until the Sauce is quite reduced; let it cool; then mix it with scraped Lard, two or three Yolks of Eggs; put some of this

Ragout

Ragout upon each Bit of Eel; roll them up tied in Cowl; wrap them up in buttered Paper, to roast; when done, take off the Paper; baste one Side with Eggs beat up, and Bread-crums; give it a good Colour with a Salamander, this Side uppermost: serve with a Sauce-pontiff, or Spanish, or a relishing Sauce.

Anguille en Canapé.

Matted, or any other Kind of Fish.

CUT an Eel in Pieces, the Length of two or three Inches; cut the Back-bone out for Use; cut some of the Meat in small Dices, with Mushrooms, and Carp-roes if any; a little Butter, chopped Parsley, Shallots, Pepper and Salt, and a finer Farce, with some of the Meat and Bread-crums, soaked in Cream, Parsley, Mushrooms, chopped very fine, Pepper and Salt, mixed with two or three Yolks of Eggs; cut Pieces of Bread-crums, the same Length of the Pieces of Bone, and about two Inches wide; lay a Down of the last Farce upon each Piece, then the Back-bone, and some of the Salpicon, or first Forced-meat upon it, then some of the fine Farce again; smooth it over with a Knife dipped in Eggs; strew it with Crums and small Bits of Butter; bake it in a middling Oven, or under a brazing Pan-cover: serve with what Sauce you please.

Andouillettes d'Anguilles.

Sausages or Chitterlings of Eels.

THE Meat is prepared as the last, only put in ano-ther Form; cut Bits of Veal, Cowl, the Length and Breadth you please; and lay the Pieces of Back-bone in the Farce; roll them up tied, in the Form of Sausages; broil them slowly in Paper well buttered; when they are done of a fine brown Colour, wipe the Fat off with a clean Cloth, and serve with any Sauce.

Anguille

Anguille à la Napolitaine. Naples Fashion.

SPLIT an Eel its whole Length; cut the Back-bone out, and flatten it with the Handle of a Knife; cut it in Pieces of about three Inches long; make a Farce with some of the Meat, few hard Yolks of Eggs, a little Butter, chopped Parsley, and green Shallots, Pepper and Salt, all mixed with two or three raw Yolks of Eggs; lay this Farce upon the Bits of Eels, and roll them up, tied with Pack-thread; simmer them in a Stew-pan for about half an Hour, with the Juice of a Lemon, a Bit of Butter, Pepper and Salt; then let them cool; take off the Pack-thread; dip them in a good Batter-paste, to fry of a good Colour; and serve with fried Parsley.

Anguille à l'Aspic. With a sharp Sauce.

CUT an Eel in small Pieces; marinade it about an Hour, in melted Butter, chopped Parsley, Shallots, Mushrooms, Pepper and Salt; let the Butter cool, and mix all together, with two Yolks of Eggs; spit the Eel on a small Skewer, with all the Marinade like Pork-haslets; strew it well with Bread-crums; broil on a slow Fire, basting with good Oil or Butter; serve with Aspic-sauce, either in the Dish, or in a Sauce-boat: see Sauce Articles, Page 38.

De la Lamproie. Of Lampreys.

THIS Fish is seldom to be had fresh in London, and but in few Parts of England, which makes it almost unnecessary to give any Instructions about it. For the sake of those who may meet with this Fish fresh out of the Water, I shall give few Receipts, as one Method of dressing any Kind of Aliments may very properly be made useful for others. Lampreys are best in the

Spring;

Spring; it resembles a good deal an Eel in Colour, thicker and shorter in Size; they ought be fat, and the Male is preferable in Goodness.

Etuvée de Lamproi. Stewed Lamprey.

SAVE the Blood, and give it a Scald in hot Water; cut the Head off, and cut the Fish in three or four Pieces; make a *Roux*, with Butter and Flour, and half white Wine and Broth; put to it one Dozen of small Onions scalded, a Nosegay of all Sorts of Sweet-herbs, whole Pepper and Salt; boil this until the Onions are almost done; then put the Fish in it, and stew gently; when done, add the Blood, two or three green Shallots bruised, a little Vinegar; warm it without boiling; take out the Nosegay, when ready to serve.

Lamproi grillé à la Remoulade. From the Sauce, Page 42.

CUT it in three Pieces, and boil it in white or red Wine, a Bit of Butter, whole Pepper and Salt, Slices of Onions, Parsley, Bits of Carrots, Parsneps, Thyme, Laurel and Cloves; when it is almost done, drain it; rub it over with Butter and Bread-crums; broil it slowly, basting with Oil or Butter; serve it dry, and a Sauce Remoulade in a Sauce-boat: see Sauces, Page 42.

Lamproi à l'Italienne. Italian Fashion.

CHOP a couple of Onions very fine; and put in a Stew-pan with a Bit of Butter, one or two Spoonfuls of Oil, a Nosegay of Sweet-herbs, two Cloves of Spices, and two of Garlick; the Blood, and the Fish cut in small Pieces; add a Pint of red Wine, and boil all together on a smart Fire, until the Liquor is much reduced; take out the Nosegay; when ready, add a good Lemon-squeeze, or Seville-orange.

Lamproi à la Burgogne.

With Burgundy or any other red Wine.

SCALD the Lamprey in hot Water, cut it in middling Pieces; put it in a Stew-pan, with a Bit of Butter, chopped Mushrooms, a little Flour, a Pint of red Wine, a Lemon sliced and peeled, a little Cinnamon, a good Bit of Sugar, whole Pepper and Salt; boil it smartly to reduce the Sauce; just before you are ready, add the Blood, and warm without boiling; take out the Slices of Lemon and Cinnamon; garnish the Dish with fried Bread.

De la Perche. Of Perches.

PERCHES out of Rivers or clear running Water are best; those of Marshy Pools or muddy Ponds are apt to have a muddy Taste; it is a very good and wholesome Fresh-water Fish, when pretty large and fat.

Perche au Beurre. Perches with Butter Sauce.

TRIM off the Gills, and half of the Roe by the Gills, to hinder them from bursting; tie up the Head with Pack-thread, and boil them with half white Wine and half Water, a good Bit of Butter, Slices of Onions, Bits of Carrots and Parsley, two Cloves, two Slices of Lemon, Pepper and Salt; when done, drain and scale it, make a Sauce with good Butter, a little Flour, some good Broth, Pepper and Salt, a good Lemon-squeeze: serve upon the Fish.

Perche à la Tartare. Tartary fashion.

SCALE some middling Perches, cut them in two, flatten them a little with the Handle of a Knife; marinade them about an Hour in Oil, chopped Parsley, Shallots, Mushrooms, Powder of Basil; let as much of the Herbs stick to it as possible, and Bread-crums over; broil them
slowly,

flowly, bafting them with the Marinade; ferve with a Sauce made of Cullis, a Bit of Butter, Pepper and Salt; a Lemon-fqueeze.

Perches à differentes Sauces & Ragoûts.

BOIL Perches in Broth and Wine, or braze them with a few Slices of Bacon and Veal; when done, fcale them, and ferve with a Craw-fifh Ragout upon it, or Carp-Roes, Sweet-breads or any other: you may alfo ferve them upon a Napkin, with what Sauce you think proper, in a Sauce-boat.

Perches à la Sainte Menehoult, are done after the fame Manner as all fuch Directions, and fo may all kind of Fifhes either of Frefh or Salt-Water.

Perches à l'Angloife. Englifh fafhion.

BOIL fome Water with a good deal of Parfley, few green Shallots, two or three Cloves, one Onion fliced, Thyme, Laurel, a fmall Handful of Salt; boil this half an Hour, then fift it clean, and fcale the Perches and boil them in this Water; make a Sauce with Butter and Flour, a little Vinegar, chopped Capers and Anchovies, two Yolks of hard Eggs chopped very fine, a few fpoonfuls of Broth, Pepper and Salt, a little Nutmeg make a Liafon pretty thick, and ferve upon the Fifh, when well drained of the Water.

Mattelotte de Perche à l'Eau. (L'Eau, Water.)

MAKE a *Roux*, (as formerly explained), with Butter and Flour; then put Water to it, Parfley-roots, Carrots, Parfneps, Slices of Onions, two or three Cloves, a Laurel-leaf; boil this about half an Hour, and fift it in a Sieve; put to this what Quantity of Perches you think proper, well cleaned and fcaled; one Eel cut in Pieces, or any other fort of Frefh-water Fifh; a Glafs of Brandy, Salt; boil on a fmart Fire, reduce the Liquor;

when

when almoſt done, put ſome Parſley coarſely chopped: you may add a little Butter if neceſſary.

Perches au Vin de Champagne. With white Wine.

TAKE out the Gills and half the Roe, boil them (without ſcaling) in a Pint of white Wine and ſome good Broth, a Noſegay of Sweet-herbs, two or three Cloves, whole Pepper and Salt, two Spoonfuls of good Oil; when done, take them out to ſcale; boil and reduce the Sauce, take out the Noſegay: add ſome Butter rolled in Flour, a little chopped ſcalded Parſley, a Lemon-ſqueeze, when ready to ſerve.

Perches frites. Fried.

CLEAN and ſcale them, and ſlit the Sides in ſeveral Places; marinade them about an Hour, in the Juice of a Lemon, Pepper and Salt, Sprigs of Parſley, one whole Clove of Garlick, a Laurel-leaf; then drain, and roll them in Flour, to fry of a good brown Colour; ſerve with fried Parſley.

Des Tenches. Of Tenches.

Tenches à la Poulette. As a Chicken-fricaſſée.

SCALD the Tenches in boiling Water a Moment; then take them out to clean; cut the Heads off, and cut them in middling Pieces; waſh in freſh Water, twice at leaſt; fry ſome Muſhrooms in Butter; then add one or two Spoonfuls of white Wine, a little Broth; put the Fiſh to it, and boil ſmartly; reduce the Sauce; put Pepper and Salt; when done, make a Liaſon of three Yolks of Eggs, with Cream or Broth, a little Nutmeg, a little fine chopped Parſley; warm without boiling; add a Lemon-ſqueeze, or a little Vinegar, when ready to ſerve.

Tenche au Pontife. With Pontiff-sauce.

SCALD two Tenches as the former, and split them at the Back; take out all the Bones, and slice off the Meat almost to the Skin; mince the Meat, to make a Farce with Bread-crums, soaked in white Wine, scraped Lard, Udder, chopped Parsley, Shallots, Mushrooms, Pepper and Salt, Yolks of Eggs; fill the Tenches with this Farce, and sew them up to look as whole; bathe them in melted Lard, and strew with Bread-crums; bake them in the Oven in a Dish, with Slices of Lard at Bottom; when done of a fine Colour, wipe the Fat off, and serve a Sauce-pontiff under: see Sauce-articles, Page 46.

Tenches en Ragouts.

PUT a Slice of Ham in a Stew-pan, with a scalded Sweet-bread, cut in four, a Bit of Butter, some Mushrooms, scalded Cock's-combs, a Nosegay of Sweet-herbs, two Cloves, a little Basil; simmer this some time; then add two Glasses of white Wine and Broth, a little Cullis, Pepper and Salt; when this is half done, put the Tenches to it, cut in middling Pieces: they require but a short Time; then skim the Sauce; take out the Nosegay and Ham; add a good Lemon-squeeze, when ready to serve: you may also dress them as a Fricassée, with small Onions, a white Liason of Yolks of Eggs and Cream, one or two pounded Anchovies; garnish the Dish with Bits of Bread, without being fried: this last is called *à la Vestale*, viz. white, un-spotted, &c. &c.

Tenches à la Bonne-femme.

The good House-wife's Fashion.

CLEAN and scale, then scald them in warm Water; then put them in a Stew-pan, with a good Bit of Butter, chopped Parsley, green Shallots, Mushrooms, a Glass of white Wine; simmer them slowly, and turn them now and then; add Pepper and Salt, a Bit of Butter rolled in Flour, to make the Sauce pretty thick; when ready, put a little Verjuice or Vinegar.

Tenches à la Ravigotte. See *Tenches au Pontife.*

THIS is done in the same Manner, only the Difference of the Sauce: See Sauce-articles for Ravigotte; observe that this must be hot.

Tenches au Monarque. Monarch.

SPLIT them at the Back, and cut some of the Meat to chop with Parsley, Shallots, Mushrooms, Bread-crums soaked in Milk, a Bit of Butter, two or three Yolks of Eggs, and proper Seasoning; stuff them with this, and sew them up; fry of a pale Colour, in fresh Hog's-lard, and serve them upon a Ragout made of Artichoke-bottoms, cut in Quarters, few Mushrooms, a good Bit of Butter, a Nosegay of Sweet-herbs, two Shallots, two Cloves; soak it some Time, then add a Glass of Wine and Broth, Pepper and Salt; when half done, put some of the Roes to it, either of Tenches or Carps first scalded, Craw-fish Tails; finish the Ragout pretty thick, and a Lemon-squeeze, when ready to serve.

Tenches de plusieurs Façons. Of different Manners.

SCALD them in boiling Water, and gut them by the Gills; mix a little chopped Parsley and Shallots, Pepper and Salt, with some Butter; stuff the Fishes with it; then put them to marinade about an Hour in Oil, with Pepper and Salt, Parsley, Shallots, one Clove of Garlick, Thyme, Laurel, Basil, all whole; then broil the Tenches, and squeeze the Seasoning of the Marinade, and baste them with the Liquid; serve them with

what

what Sauce you think proper: you may ferve them for a Difh of Roaft; when they are pretty large, then you do not fcale them. Another Way; when they are fcaled, and properly cleaned, ftew them in white Wine, a Bit of Butter, Bits of Roots, Slices of Onions, a Nofegay, Cloves, Thyme, Laurel, Pepper and Salt, and a little Water; when they are done, drain them out of the Braze, and ferve with what Sauce you pleafe.

Tenches à l'Italienne. Italian Fafhion.

SCALD them in boiling Water, and clean them properly; cut off the Heads and Tails; put them in a Stew-pan with a Spoonful of good Oil, two Glaffes of white Wine, a little Broth, Pepper and Salt, one Clove of Garlick bruized, chopped Parfley, Shallots, Mufhrooms, two Slices of Lemon peeled; fimmer flowly; when almoft done, take out the Lemon; fkim it clean; then finifh it on a fmarter Fire, to reduce the Sauce rather thick.

De la Truite. Of Trouts.

THE Salmon-trout, whofe Flefh is reddifh, is an excellent Fifh, and far preferable to the white in Goodnefs; they are prepared both after the fame Manner.

Truite aux fines Herbes. With Sweet-herbs.

SCALE it, and gut it by the Gills; ftuff it with chopped Parfley, Shallots, Pepper and Salt, and Butter, well mixed together; marinade it in Oil, Mufhrooms, Parfley, Shallots, whole Pepper and Salt, a fmall Bit of Garlick, all chopped very fine; roll it up in double Paper well buttered, and as much of the Marinade as poffible; broil it on a flow Fire, or in a middling hot Oven; boil two or three Spoonfuls of good Cullis, as much Fifh-broth, and two Glaffes of white

Wine; reduce this to the Consistence of a Sauce; the Trout being done, unfold the Paper, and scrape all the Herbs off, to mix with the Sauce; and serve upon the Fish: observe to add Seasoning, if the Cullis is not enough.

Truite à l'Allemande. German Fashion.

PREPARE a Trout with a little Farce as the former; then put it in a Brazing-pan much of its Bigness, with Bits of Carrots, one Onion stuck with two or three Cloves; put two thirds of white Wine, and one of red, sufficient to cover it above an Inch over; put it on a smart Fire; when it boils, set Fire to the Wine, and let it burn until it goes out of itself, or that it is reduced sufficiently to leave only Sauce enough; take out the Carrots and Onion; add a good Bit of Butter, which you stir in the Sauce as it melts, to mix it well, and serve upon the Fish.

Truite au Bleu. Of a fine blue Colour.

IT is not to be scaled, only gutted by the Gills, and well washed; lay it on a Dish, and pour two Glasses of boiling Vinegar upon it, according to the Bigness of the Fish, more or less; wrap it up in a Linen-cloth, and put it in a long Pan, with a good Bit of Butter, Slices of Onions, Bits of Carrots, one Clove of Garlick, two of Spices, Parsley, Shallots, Thyme, Laurel, Basil, Pepper and Salt, a Pint of red Wine, and some Broth; boil on a middling Fire; when done, take it off the Fire, and keep it warm in the Liquor some time, before you are ready to serve, that it may take more Taste of the Seasoning; then drain it, and serve dry upon a Napkin, with green Parsley round; you may serve a Sauce in a Sauce-boat, or in the Dish without a Napkin.

Truites à la Chartreuse.
An Order of Friars so called.

SCALE and clean the Fish very well; cut each Trout in three or four Pieces; boil them in Broth, Pepper and Salt, few Slices of Lemon; make a Sauce with a Bit of Butter rolled in fine Bread-crums, fine chopped Parsley, green Shallots, Mushrooms, a little Basil, Pepper and Salt, a Glass of white Wine, as much Fish-broth; put the Fish upon the Table-dish; squeeze a Seville-orange over it, and the Sauce upon; strew fine Bread-crums over.

Truite à la Perigord. With Truffles.

SCALE and gut a good large Trout by the Gills; stuff it with a Farce made with Butter, chopped Truffles, Pepper and Salt; braze it with thin Slices of Veal, Ham and Bacon, a little Wine and Broth, a Nosegay of Sweet-herbs, whole Pepper; cut few Truffles in Slices, and stew them with some of the Braze-liquor, and some good Cullis; reduce it to the Consistence of a Sauce; drain the Trout out of the Braze, and serve the Ragout of Truffles upon it.

Truite glacée. Glazed as a Fricandeau.

SCALE it, and gut it at the Gills; stuff it with a Ragout of Sweet-bread, fat Livers, Mushrooms, Truffles, and well seasoned, and as thick as possible; lard the Trout of one Side; and braze it with Slices of Lard, white Wine and Broth, a Nosegay of Sweet-herbs, whole Pepper and Salt; when it is done, drain it; and glaze the larded Side, with a Glaze made of Veal-cullis; and serve with what Sauce or Ragout you please.

Filets de Truites de differentes Façons.

Fillets of different Manners.

SCALE and clean a Trout of a middling Size; cut the Flesh in Bits of what Bigness you think proper; marinade for about half an Hour, with the Juice of a Lemon, Pepper and Salt, or with a common Marinade; then wipe it, and flour it to fry crisp: serve with any Sauce, or Ragout, or dry with fried Parsley.

Truite au Four. Done in the Oven.

WHEN properly scaled and cleaned, stuff it with a good Bit of Butter mixed with all Sorts of Sweetherbs finely chopped, Pepper and Salt; marinade it about an Hour, in Oil, a little Vinegar, Pepper and Salt, chopped Mushrooms, green Shallots, Parsley, one Clove of Garlick; make as much of the Marinade stick to it as possible, and strew it with Bread crums, and baste it over gently with the Remainder of the Marinade; put it on the Dish you intend for Table; bake it in a moderate-heated Oven, smart enough to give it a good Colour: serve without any other Sauce, than a good Lemon-squeeze.

Filets de Truites aux Vin de Champagne.

With white Wine.

CUT the Fillets of equal Bigness, all pretty large; lay them separately in a Stew-pan, with a good Bit of Butter, two or three Glasses of white Wine, (Champaign will give it a better Flavour, if to be had), a little Flour, Pepper and Salt, few Truffles sliced, or Mushrooms, chopped Parsley, two Cloves, Shallots, two Spoonfuls of good Broth; boil on a smart Fire, it will be done in about a Quarter of an Hour; reduce the

the Sauce pretty thick, which you may do, by adding a proper Quantity of Floor; garnish the Dish round with fried Bread.

Du Barbillon, Goujon, & Grenouilles.

Of the Barbel-fish, Gudgeon, and Frogs.

Du Barbillon. Of the Barbel-fish.

WHEN it is scaled, gutted, and well washed, boil it in the same Manner as all other Kind of Fishes; when so plain boiled, serve it with Capers or Anchovy Sauce, or any other: you may also stew as a Carp, or broil it, after having being marinaded, in Oil, Pepper and Salt, and chopped Sweet-herbs, for about half an Hour: the best Method is to broil it in Paper, with Sweet-herbs chopped very fine, and Butter. This Fish is neither common nor esteemed in England.

Des Grenouilles. Of Frogs.

I Hope I shall not offend the puny Stomach of any of my Readers, in taking notice of a Dish, which is so much reflected upon (*by the Vulgar*) in England, in Prejudice to Foreigners: but as it has found Place in the Cookery of a Nation, so much imitated in this Respect, as well as in many others, and in Justice to my undertaking as a Translator; I shall only say, that the Kind of Frogs here meant, are those found in the Spring in Spawning-time; also in some Parts, those found in Corn-fields in Harvest-time: it is only the Legs cut off at the Rump, which are used, after they are skinned and scalded in boiling Water; they are dressed as Chicken Fricassée, or marinaded and fried, as all other Fritures, and might pass as such, as well as the Rabbits *en Poulets*, often used in very polite Company.

Des Goujons. Of Gudgeons.

Matelottes de Goujons.

SCALE them, and when properly cleaned, lay them on the Dish you intend for Table, with a little Butter under and over, and chopped Sweet-herbs, such as Parsley, a little green Basil, Shallots, Mushrooms, Pepper and Salt, a couple of Glasses of white Wine; boil on a smart Fire; reduce the Sauce; when ready to serve, wipe your Dish clean, and squeeze half a Lemon over the Gudgeons: you may also marinade them a little while, then wipe them dry to fry.

As it is a Fish of no Consequence, it is needless to take any further Notice of it.

Du Saumon. Of Salmon.

Saumon au Court Bouillon. In its own Sauce.

TAKE a Bit of Salmon of any Bigness, without being scaled; tie it up in a Cloth or with Pack-thread; put it in a Vessel much of its Bigness, a good Bit of Butter, Meager-broth, and half red Wine, Salt and whole Pepper, a Nosegay of Parsley, Thyme, Laurel, two or three Cloves, Bits of Carrots, sliced Onions; when done, drain it, and serve it upon a Napkin, and the Sauces in Boats.

Saumon aux Ecrevisses en Gras & en Maigre.

Salmon with Craw-fish, Gras or Meager.

FOR Meager, scale the Salmon, and boil it after the same Manner as the last, and serve a good Craw-fish Ragout upon it. *En Gras*, braze it with Slices of Veal and Ham; cover it over with thin Slices of Bacon; put a Nosegay of all Sorts of Sweet-herbs, Cloves, Pepper and Salt, Bits of Roots, one or two Onions sliced; soak it a
little

little while on the Fire; then add half Broth, and half Wine, sufficiently, according to the Largeness of the Fish; when done, drain it out of the Braze, and serve it with a Craw-fish Ragout, such as you will find at the Beginning of this Volume, Page 393.

Saumon accompagné, viz. garnished with other Things.

TAKE a strong Joul of a Salmon, or a whole one; gut it by the Gills, and stuff it with a good Bit of Butter, mixed with a little Pepper and Salt, chopped Parsley, Shallots, Mushrooms; wrap it round in thin Slices of Bacon, and tied in a Napkin; put it in a brazing-pan, upon Slices of Veal and Ham; soak it over the Fire about half an Hour, without putting any Liquid; then put half Broth and white Wine, Bits of Roots, and sliced Onions, a Nosegay of all Sorts of Sweet-herbs; when it is done, drain it, and dress it upon the Table-dish, and garnish it round with Craw-fish, boiled in good Cullis, and white Wine, Pinions of Turkeys glazed; and upon the Salmon, a good Farce called a *Salpicon*, well finished: see Page 289, for *Salpicon*.

Saumon aux fines Herbes. With Sweet-herbs.

CHOP some Parsley, Shallots, Mushrooms, a little green Basil, Pepper and Salt; mix all this together with good Butter; lay some of it pretty thick in the Bottom of the Dish you intend for Table; put one or two thin Slices of Salmon upon it, and the same upon the Salmon; strew it over with Bread-crums, and small Bits of Butter; put it on a slow Fire, covered over with a Brazing-cover, to hold Fire on it; when it is done, drain the Butter out of the Dish: serve with a clear Italian Sauce; see Sauces, Page 32.

Saumon en Fricandeaux.

LARD the Salmon as all other Fricandeau, and braze it upon Slices of Veal and Ham, a Nosegay of Sweet-herbs, two or three Cloves, Bits of Roots, and one Onion sliced; let it soak a little while; then add some white Wine, a little Broth, whole Pepper and Salt; when done, take it out gently, and glaze the larded Side, with a Caramel made of Veal-cullis; serve upon it a good Italian Sauce, or Sauce-pontiff, or any other: see Sauce-articles, Page 32. and 46. for Pontiff.

Saumon à la Bonne-femme.
The good House-wife's Fashion.

MARINADE a few thin Slices of Salmon in Oil, whole Pepper and Salt; then broil them, basting with the Marinade; then put them on the Table-dish, with a good Bit of Butter, two or three Spoonfuls of Broth, chopped Parsley, Shallots, Mushrooms; simmer it about a Quarter of an Hour; when ready to serve, add a good Lemon-squeeze; such as has served before, may do again, being cut properly and prepared according to this last Direction, as done in the Dish.

Saumon frit. Fried Salmon.

CUT the Salmon in Slices of what Bigness you think proper; put them in a Milk-warm Marinade, made of a Bit of Butter melted, one or two Spoonfuls of Vinegar, and a little Water and Flour, Pepper and Salt, Bits of Roots and Slices of Onions, Parsley, Shallots, Thyme, Laurel, Cloves; let it remain about an Hour, then drain and flour them to fry; serve with fried Parsley, you may also, when marinaded after this Manner, broil, basting with the Liquid of the Marinade, and a few sweet Herbs finely chopped, strewed over: serve with

Caper-

Caper-sauce, or Sauce à la Carpe. See Sauce Articles, p. 41.

Filets de Saumon à l'Italienne.

CUT the Salmon in smaller Slices than the former, and marinade them after the same Manner, with Parsley, Shallots, Mushrooms, a little Basil, all chopped very fine, about a Quarter of an Hour before you are to be ready; lay each Piece on a Silver Dish separately, or in a Stew-pan in the same Manner; put the Marinade to it, and boil it over a smart Fire a Moment, and turn them; it is best to do them in a Stew-pan, as when they are done, lay the Fillets on the Table-dish, add a little Cullis to the Sauce, reduce it pretty thick; add a Lemon-squeeze if necessary, and serve upon the Fillets.

Saumon en batelet. As Haslets.

CUT the Pieces of a middling Bigness, and season them with fine Herbs chopped, and mixed with Butter and a raw Yolk of an Egg, Pepper and Salt; skewer them like Haslets, with all the Seasoning, and strewed with Bread-crums; either broil or roast them, basting with some good Oil or Butter; when they are done of a fine Colour, serve dry with a Sauce in a Boat, such as Sauce Remoulade, Ravigotte, or any other.

Hure de Saumon à differentes Sauces & Ragoûts.

Joul of Salmon with different Sauces or Ragouts.

SCALE and clean the Salmon very well; braze it with Slices of Lard, Ham and Veal, white Wine and Broth, a Nosegay of Sweet-herbs, two or three Cloves, whole Pepper and Salt; if for Meager, braze it with half Fish-broth and white Wine, a good Quantity of Butter, Trimmings of any Sort of Fish well cleaned, Bits of Roots and Onions, all Sorts of Sweet-herbs, as the first when done; drain it out of the Braze, and serve upon it what Sauce or Ragout you think proper, either way.

Darde

Darde de Saumon à la Choisi.

Darde means a large Slice, speaking of Fish (cut lengthways.)

LARD a large Slice of Salmon through and through with larding Bacon and Ham; give it a few turns on the Fire in melted Lard, chopped Parsley, Shallots, Truffles, Pepper and Salt; then put it in a Stew-pan, upon thin Slices of Veal; cover it over with thin Slices of Lard, and all the Seasoning; soak it a while on a slow Fire; add two or three Glasses of white Wine, and finish still on a slow Fire; then sift and skim the Braze; add some good Cullis to it and Crawfish Spawn; reduce it to the Substance of a thick Sauce; add a Lemon-squeeze when ready to serve.

Caisses de Saumon fumé. Cases of smoked Salmon.

CUT your Slices very thin, and let them be soaked in Water or Milk (which last is best) about half an Hour or more, according to the Saltness of the Fish; make small Paper-cases, or one large; drain and wipe the Salmon, and roll each Piece in melted Butter, chopped Mushrooms, Parsley and Shallots, a little green Basil if you please; put them in the Paper, a little fine Breadcrums over, a few Drops of good Oil; broil a Moment over a slow Fire: you serve with a Lemon or Orange Squeeze.

Saumon Salé à la Hollandoise.
Dried Salmon Dutch Fashion.

SOAK the Salmon according to your own Judgment, and boil it a Moment in Water; then drain it, and pull it in Fleaks; make a Sauce with a good Bit of Butter, rolled in Flour, a little coarse Pepper, one Clove of Garlick bruised, some fine chopped Parsley and some good Cream; make a Liason pretty thick, and put the Salmon to it; give it a few turns on the Fire, then pour

pour it on the Table-dish; strew it with Bread-crums, and small Bits of Butter close to each other; give it a Colour in the Oven, or with a Salamander.

Salade de Saumon Salé & autres Façons.

Sallad of dried Salmon, and other Manners.

IF you would use a large Piece, it must be soaked in different Waters, two or three Days, handling it as gently as possible; then boil it a few Minutes in Water, on a smart Fire; drain it, and let it cool; when it is to be used, garnish the Dish round the Salmon with all Sorts of Sallading; or if you would serve it hot, make a good Butter and Anchovy Sauce, or Capers, or Sweet-herbs: serve in a Sauce-boat.

De l'Esturgeon. Of Sturgeon.

Esturgeon au Court-Bouillon.

BOIL the Sturgeon as is customary under this Direction of Court-Bouillon, viz. just as much Liquid as will do between boiling and stewing; put to this some Broth, Butter, a little Vinegar and white Wine, all Sorts of Sweet-herbs, Bits of Carrots, Slices of Onions, whole Pepper and Salt, according to the Bigness of the Fish, if a whole one; when properly cleaned, stuff it with all Sorts of Sweet-herbs chopped, Pepper and Salt, all mixed with good Butter; serve upon a Napkin garnished with green Parsley; serve what Sauces you think proper in Boats, such as Anchovies, Capers, or relishing Ravigotte, &c. &c.

Esturgeon à differentes Sauces en Gras et en Maigre.

Sturgeon with different Sauces, Gras or Meager.

FOR Meager, lard it with Anchovies, and braze it in white Wine, a good Bit of Butter, some Fish-broth, or any Meager-broth; all Sorts of Sweet-herbs, two

Cloves,

Cloves, Pepper and Salt. For *Gras*, lard it with Ham and larding Bacon, and braze it with Slices of Veal and Lard, white Wine and good Broth, the same Seasoning; and serve with what Sauce you think proper.

Esturgeon à la Broche en Gras & en Maigre.

Sturgeon roasted, Gras or Meager.

LARD the Sturgeon with Lard and Ham: for Meager, with Eel and Anchovies; prepare a Liquid for basting it after this Manner; put a good Bit of Butter in a Sauce-pan, with chopped Parsley, green Shallots, one Clove of Garlick, Thyme, Laurel, Basil, a few Glasses of white Wine; boil this together about a Quarter of an Hour; while the Sturgeon is roasting as all other kind of Roast, baste it with it when done; serve it with acid Sauce, Gras or Meager, or with any Ragout you shall think proper. See Acid Sauce, p. 49.

Esturgeon à la Mayence.

LARD the Sturgeon with fresh Westphalia Ham, fat and lean, cut together; wrap it up in Paper, and roast it as the former; baste it with Butter, and make a Sauce after this Manner: soak one or two Slices of Veal and Ham on the Fire, some time, with Bits of Carrots, Parsley-roots, Slices of Onions, two Shallots, two Cloves; when it begins to catch at Bottom, put a Pint of white Wine to it, a few Spoonfuls of good Cullis, whole Pepper, a little Salt; simmer it about an Hour; reduce it to the Consistence of a pretty thick Sauce; skim it and sift it; add a good Lemon-squeeze, and serve upon the Sturgeon.

N. B. This is called *à la Mayence*, for being larded with Westphalia Ham, which are called in France *Jambon de Mayence*, and so of others.

Esturgeon à la Bonne-femme. The good House-wife.

MARINADE a thin Slice of Sturgeon in Oil, and all Sorts of Sweet-herbs chopped, coarse Pepper and Salt; broil it on a Gridiron to three Parts; then put it on the Table-dish, with a Glass of white Wine, chopped Parsley, Chibbol, Mushrooms, a good Bit of Butter; simmer it about half an Hour; when ready to serve, add a good Lemon-squeeze all over, and sift fine Bread-crums over it.

Esturgeon grillé. Broiled.

MARINADE thin Slices of Sturgeon in Oil, chopped Mushrooms, Parsley, Shallots, a little Basil, coarse Pepper and Salt; let it marinade about an Hour; then roll each Piece in Bread-crums, and broil slowly, basting with the Remainder of the Marinade; serve with a clear sharp Sauce under: you may also serve them without Sauce, only a Squeeze of Lemon on each Piece.

Esturgeon à la Sainte Meneboult en Gras & en Maigre.

TAKE a thick Slice of Sturgeon. For *Gras*, lard it through and through with larding Bacon, seasoned with Pepper and Salt, and fine Spices, as for *Dôbe* formerly directed; braze it with Slices of Lard, Bits of Roots, Slices of Onions, a moderate Quantity; a Nosegay of Sweet-herbs; put Liquid sufficient to hinder it from burning, half white Wine and half Milk, whole Pepper and Salt. For *Meager*, lard it with Anchovies well soaked, or do it without larding; braze it with white Wine and Milk, a good nourishing Quantity of Butter, and all the above Seasoning; when done, skim the Fat off the Braze; and beat it up with two or three Yolks of Eggs; thicken it on the Fire a little while; then bathe the Sturgeon with it, and strew it with Bread-crums; baste it with a little melted Butter, and put it in the Oven to take a good Colour, or under a Brazing-pan-cover, or with a Salamander;

lamander; serve with Sauce (Remoulade) in a Sauce-boat See Sauce Articles, p. 42.

Esturgeon à l'Angloise. English Fashion.

PUT the Fish in a Kettle, much of its Bigness, and Water sufficient to cover it, one fourth of Vinegar to the whole Quantity of Water, Salt, and a little whole Pepper, one Onion cut in two, Bits of Carrots and Parsley-roots; when boiled sufficiently, serve with Caper and Butter Sauce, or Anchovies, or any other as you shall think proper for Fish.

Esturgeon à la Provençale.

LARD it half Lard and half Anchovies; braze it with Slices of Veal, one Slice of Ham, a Nosegay of Sweet-herbs, one Clove of Garlick, two or three Shallots, three Cloves, a little Basil, whole Pepper; cover it over with thin Slices of Lard; let it soak on the Fire about half an Hour; then add a Pint of white Wine, or more according to Reason and Judgment; finish the Brazing; then skim the Braze, and sift it; add some good Cullis; reduce it to the Consistence of a Sauce; add a Lemon-squeeze, and serve the Sauce upon the Fish.

Esturgeon à la hâte. Sturgeon in haste.

CUT thin Slices of Sturgeon, of what Length you think proper; put them in a Stew-pan with a good Bit of Butter, and give them a few turns over the Fire, turning them once or twice; it will require but a short Time to do it; when you take them out, season them with Pepper and Salt; put to the Butter in the Stew-pan first used, two or three Glasses of red Wine, two Spoonfuls of Cullis, chopped Parsley, green Shallots; boil this a few Minutes on a smart Fire; add proper Seasoning, and put the Slices in it to warm together without boiling; add some chopped Capers, and garnish the Dish with fried Bread.

Grena-

Grenadins d'Esturgeon. Small Fricandeau of Sturgeon.

CUT the Sturgeon in small Fricandeau, and lard the same; braze them with a few Slices of Veal, one Slice of Ham, a Nosegay of Sweet-herbs, the Liquid, half white Wine and half Broth; braze on a slow Fire; when done, sift the Braze, skim it, and reduce it to a *Caramel*, to glaze the larded Side of the Grenadins; serve with what Sauce you think proper, as Sauce *au Vin de Champagne, a l'Espagnole, au Pontife*, &c. &c. You may equally prepare a large Slice in the same Manner, or a whole Sturgeon; it must be skinned: small Sturgeon are often dressed whole, in all the different ways herein mentioned; adding the Seasoning with Judgment and Taste, which are the best Guide in Cookery.

Esturgeon à la Cendre. On Ashes, or brazed very slowly.

LARD a good Bit of Sturgeon, half Lard and half Ham; give it a Fry a few Minutes in Butter, with fine chopped Parsley, green Shallots, two Cloves of Garlick, two of Spices, a small Sprig of Fennel, a little coarse Pepper; then put a few thin Slices of Veal under the Fish in the same Pan; cover it over with thin Slices of Lard, and white Paper upon it; let it stew on a very slow or Ashes Fire, both under and over; add a Glass or two of white Wine; when done, take out the Fish; add a few Spoonfuls of Cullis; sift and skim the Braze; very free from Fat, give it a boiling; add a Lemon-squeeze, if necessary, to make the Sauce pretty relishing.

Du Turbot & Turbotin. Of large and small Turbots.

LARGE and small Turbots are prepared each in the same Manner; chuse them for the best, of a fine Grain, lively white Colour, fat, and free of any Bruises or Spots of any Sorts; Brills may be dressed in the same different Manners, as the Turbotins, viz. small Turbots.

Turbot au Court Bouillon.
Meant as plain boiled as others.

MAKE a Brine after this Manner; boil two Quarts of Water, more or lefs, (according to the Size of the Fifh), with Bits of Carrots, Parfneps, Parfley-roots, one Onion fliced, two Shallots, Thyme, Laurel, a little Bafil, a good deal of Salt; boil all together about an Hour, then lift it; boil the Turbot in this Brine, and as much Milk, and a Bit of Butter; fimmer it on a flow Fire, Time fufficient; take care to have a Fifh-plate under, to take it out without breaking it; drain it well; ferve upon a Napkin, and what Sauces you think proper in Sauce-boats; you may alfo ferve it with any Sorts of Ragouts; as of Craw-fifh, Carp-roes, Cock's-comb; wipe it very dry with a clean Napkin, and put the Ragout in the Difh under the Fifh.

Turbotins aux fines Herbs.   With Sweet-herbs.

GUT and wafh the fmall Turbots very clean, then marinade them about an Hour in Oil, the Juice of a Lemon, chopped Parfley, Shallots, Mufhrooms, Powder of Bafil, Salt and coarfe Pepper; then lay them on the Difh you intend for Table, with all their Seafoning; ftrew Bread-crums over, and a little melted Butter upon it; bake them of a fine brown Colour in the Oven; if the Sauce is not fharp enough, add a Lemon-fqueeze, when ready to ferve; you may ferve any other Sauce with it in a Boat: you may alfo broil them, when marinaded after this Manner.

Filets de Turbot de différentes Façons.

TAKE the Remainder of a plain boiled Turbot, which has been ufed already; cut it properly in fmall Slices, and put them juft to warm in a good Sauce,

Sauce, such as Béchamel, Sauce à la Reine, à la Morue, Craw-fish Cullis, or any other: in all large Tables, where a great Number of Dishes are wanted, this and many other small Dishes will serve as well as fresh ones, with very little Cost.

Turbotin à la Sainte Meneboult.

Small Turbot broiled.

BOIL it to half in Water, and a little white Wine, a good Bit of Butter, and other proper Seasoning; then drain it; skim the Butter of the Boiling, and mix it with a little Cullis, and Yolks of Eggs; give it few Boilings on the Fire to thicken it, and dip the Turbot in it; then put it on the Dish you intend for Table; strew it with Bread-crums, few Drops of Butter upon it; give it a good Colour in the Oven, or with a Salamander: serve with a relishing Sauce.

Turbotins au Parmesan.

Small Turbots with Parmesan Cheese.

WHEN they are properly cleaned, put them to marinade about an Hour, in melted Butter, chopped Parsley, Shallots, coarse Pepper and Salt; then put in the Dish (you intend for Table) some of the Marinade, and two or three Spoonfuls of Cullis, a little Bread-crums, with as much grated Parmesan Cheese: lay the Fish or Fishes upon this, and do the same over as under; bake in the Oven; let the Sauce be much reduced; wipe the Dish clean, and serve without any other Sauce.

Turbot au Pontife. With Pontiff-sauce.

USE a Pan or Fish-kettle, much of the Size of the Fish, with a Fish-plate in it; and garnish the Pan with thin Slices of Veal and Ham, Bits of Carrots, and other Roots, few Slices of Onions, whole Pepper, one Clove of Garlick; foak it on a flow Fire about half an Hour; then add a Bottle of white Wine, as much Broth; braze on a flow Fire, until the Meat is thoroughly done; then fift this Cullis in a Sieve, and put the Turbot in it, to fimmer on a flow Fire, until it is done; then drain it very well, and ferve it with Sauce-pontiff: fee Page 46.

Turbot Glacée. Glazed.

WHEN the Turbot is properly cleaned and trimmed, Fins and Tail; lard it as a Fricandeau, either all over one Side, or Quarter-ways, as other Pieces are often done to give them a better Look; boil it flowly in the fame Preparation as the former; when done, glaze the larded Part, with a Glaze made of Veal-gravy or Cullis: few Feathers tied together, are very proper to ufe for glazing any tender Pieces: ferve with Spanifh fauce under, or any other.

Turbot au (Citron, Lemon.)

RUB a Brazing-kettle or Pan with a good deal of Butter, and put in it fliced Onions, Parfley, few Shallots, Thyme, Laurel, Bafil, Pepper and Salt; lay the Fifh upon this, and the fame Seafoning upon it, with a couple of Lemons fliced, firft peeled, and a good deal of Butter; bake it in a middling-heated Oven; when it is done, fcrape off all the Seafoning, and drain it very clean from the Liquid: difh it on the Table-difh, and ferve Sauce à la Garonne upon it; fee Sauce-articles, Page 35.

Turbot à la Financiere. See Carp under the fame Name.

MAKE the fame Preparation as for Cullis, with Slices of Veal and Ham, Bits of all Sort of Roots, fliced Onions, a large Nofegay of Sweet-herbs, one
Clove

Clove of Garlick, four of Spices, Thyme, Laurel, Basil; let it soak on a slow Fire, until it is ready to catch at Bottom; then put about a Pint of good Broth to it, and let it simmer about two Hours; then add a Bottle of white Wine, and let it boil half an Hour longer; then sift it in a Sieve; put this Cullis in the Kettle you intend to boil the Fish, and put a Fish-plate in it, under the Turbot; let it boil very slowly until it is done, then drain it very well; take part of the Cullis to make a Ragout with Sweet-breads, Cock's-combs, fat Livers, Truffles or Mushrooms; reduce it pretty thick; add such proper Seasoning, as will make it highly finished, and serve upon the Turbot: the Remainder of this Cullis will serve for any other Fish-dishes.

Turbot à la Hollandoise. Dutch Fashion.

PUT two Glasses of white Wine in a Sauce-pan, and two Spoonfuls of Oil, Sprigs of Parsley, Chibbol, Thyme, Laurel, Basil, one Clove of Garlick, all whole, Pepper and Salt; boil this together about half an Hour, or more; then put the Turbot in a Baking-dish, and pour all the first Preparation upon it; cover it with another Dish, and simmer it between two slow Fires; when it is done enough, pour out all the Seasoning, and put the Fish on the Dish you intend for Table; make a Sauce with some good *Consommé*, a good Bit of Butter rolled in Flour, a little fine chopped Parsley scalded; make a Liason on the Fire, and serve upon it.

Des Carlets, Plies, & Halibotte.

Of Flounders, Plaice, and Hallibut.

THE Hallibut is a large flat Fish, much resembling Turbots, but nothing in Comparison so good Eating; it may be dressed in all the different Ways of Turbots: Plaice may equally be dressed the same, at least what is commonly called in England Dutch Plaice, as they are much larger, and very good when quite fresh and firm, and not spent by long keeping, which may soon be distinguished by the Hardness of the fleshy Part, and watery Streaks, which appear through the Skin, after long keeping. The *Carlets*, viz. Flounders, are esteemed by most People better Fish than the Plaice, and ought to be chosen with the same Observation; it is distinguished from the Plaice, by having less Spots, smaller, and more of a yellow Cast; it is a general Observation in flat Fishes, as Turbots, Hallibuts, Flounders, Soals, Plaice, that if the middle Bone appear any thing black, the Fish was not fresh; I believe it is not an absolute Decision, and will appear as such to those who will be at the Trouble of Observation: I shall only observe in regard to these flat Fishes, that the middle Size of every Sort generally proves the best Eating.

Carlets au Citron. Flounders Lemon-sauce.

WHEN the Flounders are gutted, and properly cleaned, score them on the Back, in three or four Places; then put them to marinade, in Oil, Sprigs of Parsley, two or three whole Shallots, one Laurel-leaf, whole Pepper and Salt; broil them, basting with the Marinade; when done, put them on the Table-dish, and pour upon it a Sauce made with few Spoonfuls of Cullis, a Bit of Butter, the Juice of a Lemon, and three or four Slices peeled: Plaice may be dressed in the same Manner as this, and all the different Ways of small Turbots.

De la Sole. Of Soals.

Soles au Suprême, viz. excelling, &c.

WHEN properly cleaned, put them in a Stew-pan, with two or three Glasses of white Wine, two
Spoons

Spoonfuls of good rich *Confommé*, two Slices of Lemon, a Nofegay of Sweet-herbs, two or three green Shallots, two Cloves, whole Pepper and Salt; braze them flowly; when done, fift part of the Braze, which mix with few Spoonfuls of Cullis; fkim very free from Fat; reduce it to a proper Confiftence; add a Lemon-fqueeze if neceffary, and ferve upon the Soals.

Soles au Pontife. With Pontiff-fauce.

BRAZE the Soals, with a good Bit of Butter, two Glaffes of white Wine, as much good Broth, one Clove of Garlick, two of Spices, Sprigs of Parfley, green Shallots, whole Pepper and Salt, two Slices of Lemon firft peeled; when done, drain them, and ferve with Pontiff-fauce: fee Sauce-articles, Page 46.

Soles de plufieurs Façons. Of different Ways.

WHEN fcaled, and properly cleaned, you may fry them whole, or cut each in four Fillets; dip them in clear Batter, and fry in frefh Hog's-lard, or Oil; if to broil, make an Opening at the Back, and ftuff in it fome chopped Parfley, Shallots, Mufhrooms, properly feafoned with Pepper and Salt, and mixed together with Butter and Bread-crums, a trifle of Bafil; then marinade them in Oil about half an Hour; and broil flowly, bafting with Oil or Butter: ferve with *Sauce Achéee,* or Capers, or Anchovies, in a Sauce-boat.

Soles aux fines Herbes. With Sweet-herbs.

TAKE Soals, which have been either plain boiled or fried; if fried ones, take up the Skin, cut each in four or eight Pieces, properly trimmed; prepare a Sauce with a Glafs of white Wine, two or three Spoonfuls of Cullis, a Bit of Butter, fine chopped Parfley, Chibbol,

Mushrooms, a trifle of Garlick, the same of Basil; boil this together about half an Hour; then put the Fillets of Soals to it; simmer about a Quarter of an Hour; add Pepper and Salt, and a good Lemon-squeeze.

Soles au Four. Baked in the Oven.

SPLIT them on the Back, after they are properly cleaned, and stuff in it the same Preparation as for broiling; see before; rub the Table-dish with a pretty deal of Butter; and lay the Soals upon it; and melt a Bit of Butter, to mix with two Yolks of Eggs, and Sweet-herbs chopped, Pepper and Salt; mix this well together, and rub it upon the Soals with a Brush; lay it on pretty thick; then strew Bread-crums over, and put the Dish in the Oven; when they are done of a good brown Colour, drain the Butter out, and serve with a good relishing Cullis-sauce.

Soles en Hatereaux. Olives, either fried or roasted.

SPLIT small Soals, either in two or four; make a Farce with some of the Flesh, or of any Kind of Fish; mix it with Bread-crums, soaked in Milk, a Bit of Butter, chopped Sweet-herbs as usual, Pepper and Salt, few Yolks of Eggs, well worked together; lay some of this Farce upon each Piece, and roll them up tight; braze them in good Broth, a little white Wine, and good Seasoning; when done, drain and dip them in a Batter, made of Flour, a little Oil, and white Wine; fry them, and serve with fried Parsley: you may also serve them with a good Cullis-sauce.

Soles en Fricandeaux.

TAKE good fresh thick Soals; take up the Skin of the white Side, and lard them with fine *Lardons*; soak some Slices of Veal and Ham on the Fire, with Bits of Roots, Onions, half a Clove of Garlick, half a

Laurel-

Laurel-leaf; when it is ready to catch, add two Glasses of white Wine, as much good Broth, or rather more, few whole Mushrooms; let it simmer until the Meat is done; then fift it, and put it in another Stew-pan, with the Soals, the larded Side undermost; when done, take the Fish gently out; and reduce the Sauce to a Caramel, to glaze the larded Side: serve with a clear relishing Sauce.

Filets de Soles à la Béchamel.

HAVE a Sauce Béchamel ready, and use and prepare the Fillets of Soals, in the same Manner, as those aux fines Herbes; such as have served before, will do equally; just simmer them a Moment in the Sauce, to warm without boiling.

Filets de Soles au Verjus. Verjuice-sauce.

TAKE up the Fillets as the preceding; rub the Table-dish with Butter, and lay the Fillets upon, a little Cullis, two or three Spoonfuls of Verjuice, (where Verjuice is not to be had, put Vinegar to give it a proportionable Sowrness), Pepper and Salt, Sweet-herbs, chopped very fine; simmer it about half an Hour, and serve quite hot: you may also serve those Sorts of Fillets with any Sorts of stewed Greens, as Sorrel, Endives, Sellery, and others; warm the Fillets in a little Broth, and serve upon the Ragout: Soals à la Sainte Menehoult, à la Braze, are done in the same Manner as all former Directions: it is needless to crowd too many Repetitions, having done so pretty much already.

De l'Alose. Shad-fish.

THIS Fish is not common in England, at least in the London Markets; but however, where-ever it is to be had, it may be dressed in all the different Ways of Salmon, or any other Kind.

De la Vive. Of the Fish called Weaver.

THIS Fish is not esteemed in England, nor is it very common; the Scarcity may probably be a Reason for its not being in Repute amongst good Fishes, as so few People ever eat it: the French Author gives it the following Character.

La Vive is one of the most excellent of Sea-fishes, (giving it the feminine Gender); she has sharp Points at the Ears, and on the Back, which prove venomous to such as are pricked by it; whenever this happen take out the Liver, and bruise it, to apply to the Wound, or Salt and Onions mixed together; or apply Spirits of Wine, as another Remedy: I shall pass over any particular Direction about this Fish, for the same Reason as I have observed before; only giving the Names, by which the French distinguish the different Ways of dressing it, which may be referred to former Directions.

Vives de différentes Façons. See Soals of different Ways.

Vives à la Cardinal. See Soals au Pontiff.

Vives à la Royale. See Soals au Suprême, excelling.

Matelottes de Vive à la Provençale. Broiled and served with Sauce à la Perigord; see Sauce aux Trufes, Page 49.

Vives à la Saint Cloud. Brazed and served with a good Cuilis-sauce.

Vives glacées. Glazed. See Soals glazed.

Vives à la Broche. Roasted.

Vives aux fines Herbes. See Soals, ditto.

Vives à la Duchesse. See Turbot à la Financiere.

Vives farcie à differentes Sauces. See broiled Soals.

Vives à la Poulette. As Chicken-fricassée; see Soals à la Bechamel.

Vives à la Provençale. See Sturgeon, ditto.

Vives à l'Allemande. See Trouts, ditto.

Des Merlans, & Surmulets.

Of Whitings and Mullets.

IF to fry, skin them, and in gutting, leave the Livers; for plain Boil, leave the Skin, and serve with Anchovies-sauce, or Capers; they must be fried in very hot Friture, and serve with fried Parsley round: you may also broil them in Paper, with all Sorts of Sweetherbs, finely chopped, basting with Butter; also rub the Paper with Butter first, and cut off the Heads and Tails: you may also marinade them as other Fish: marinade either to broil, roast, or fry, or braze to put in Jelly, or serve cold with Sauce-ravigotte: Mullets are dressed in every Respect the same Way as Whitings, being much of the same Bigness, and require much an equal space of Time in the different Manner to finish them; the red Mullet is the only one esteemed; the gray being a coarse indifferent tasted Fish.

Merlans à la Sauce à la Morue.

See the Sauce, p. 39.

MAKE a Brine with Salt and Water, Sprigs of Parsley, whole Shallots, Chibbol, Bits of Roots and Onions; boil all together about half an Hour; then sift it, and boil the Whitings in it, adding one third Part of Milk; when done, drain them; make a Sauce with a
good

good Bit of Butter, a little Flour, two whole green Shallots, Pepper and Salt; put Cream sufficient to make the Sauce pretty thick; take out the Shallots; and serve upon the Fish.

Merlans en batereaux.

See Soals under this Direction.

Quenelles de Merlans. Quenelles, little Forced-meat Balls.

TAKE either small or large Whitings; bone them as clear as possible; scrape the Flesh, and pound it in a Mortar; boil some Bread-crums in Cream, until the Liquid is quite soaked; put this in the Mortar, and a good Bit of Butter, a little chopped Parsley, Chibbol, half a Shallot, Salt and Pepper, three or four Yolks of Eggs, and the Whites of them well beat up; mix it well together; have a Stew-pan of Broth on a strong Fire; and when it boils hard, add a Glass of white Wine to it; take a small Quantity of this Farce at once, and throw it in the Broth, and so on till you have done; take Care to turn them about; they require but a few Minutes; take them out one by one according as you threw them in; put them on a Sieve to drain: serve with a good Cullis Sauce, relished with Lemon-juice.

Merlans à la Moutarde. With Mustard-sauce.

Merlans au Pontife. With Pontife-sauce.

Filets de Merlans à differentes Sauces. See Fillets of Soals.

Merlans à la Servante. Common plain Manner.

SKIN them, and cut the Heads off; then simmer them between two Ashes-fire; the under Dish well rubbed with Butter, and all Sorts of fine chopped Sweet-herbs,

herbs, strewed upon them; turn them once or twice; and when you put them on the Table-dish, pour the Sauce over, with all the Sweet-herbs.

Eperlans à la Sainte Meneboult. Smelts broiled.

TRIM off the Gills, and wash them clean; put them in a Stew-pan with a good Bit of Butter, chopped Sweet-herbs, Pepper and Salt; give them a few turns in this; then take them out, and add one or two Yolks of Eggs, to the Butter; mix it well together; dip the Smelts in it; strew Bread-crums over, and fry or broil them gently; serve with melted Butter, and Verjuice, or a Lemon-squeeze, without any thing else, or a relishing Sauce in a Sauce-boat, or dry with fried Parsley.

Eperlans en Surtout. Masked.

MAKE a good Fish Forced-meat; and put Part of it on the Dish you intend for Table; put the Smelts upon this, and the Farce to cover them singly in their own Form, Bread-crums upon the Farce, and small Bits of Butter, close to each other: bake them in the Oven; and serve with a Sauce au Vin de *Champagne,* or a clear relishing Cullis-sauce.

Eperlans au Fenouil. Smelts with Fennel-sauce.

MAKE a Sauce with a couple of Sprigs of Fennel, two Cloves, one of Garlick, which you scald together a Moment in boiling Water; put two Glasses of white Wine in a Sauce-pan, and a few Spoonfuls of Cullis, a good Bit of Butter; boil this together a little while; then put the Fennel and Garlick pounded; warm it together, and serve under fried Smelts.

Matelottes, ou Eperlans aux fines Herbes.

LAY them on the Table-dish, and all Sorts of fine chopped Sweet-herbs, one Spoonful of Oil, Pepper and

and Salt, a Glass of Wine; cover them; and let them simmer on a slow Fire, until they are near catching at Bottom, meaning till the Liquid is quite reduced; then drain the Oil out, and serve with Sauce *Achée*. See page 43.

Du Maquereaux. Of Mackerels.

Maqueraux à la Maître d'Hôtel; the Clerk of the Kitchen.

CLEAN them by the Gills; and with the Point of a Knife, or any thing else, take out a small Gut which you will find in the middle of the Belly-part, it is very easy to come at; split them along the Back to the Bone, and make a little Stuffing with chopped Parsley, green Shallots, Pepper and Salt, mixed with Butter; put this in the Belly, and broil them slowly; you will find that they are done enough when the Flesh looks white to the Bone: serve with a good Lemon-squeeze, or burnt Butter, with a few Drops of Vinegar; also with Caper and Anchovy Sauce.

Maqueraux aux fines Herbes.

With Sweet-herbs.

CUT part of the Heads and Tails off, and split them as the former; put them to marinade about an Hour in melted Butter, Pepper and Salt, fine chopped Parsley, Shallots, a little Basil; put two or three Slices of Veal, one of Ham, in a Stew-pan; let it soak a while, then put half a Pint of white Wine, and some Broth to it; boil it till the Veal is almost done; put the Mackerels to boil in this, with all the Seasoning; sift the Sauce, and skim it very well; add two or three Spoonfuls of good Cullis, and some of the Herbs chopped; boil this a Moment, and serve upon the Fish.

Maqueraux à la Flamande. Flemish Fashion.

STUFF them in the same Manner as à la Maitre d'Hôtel; wrap them up in Paper, well buttered; broil them slowly, basting now and then with melted Butter; you may also roast them; being prepared after this Manner, serve with Verjuice-sauce, or any other you think proper.

Maqueraux au Court-Bouillon.

MAKE it with half a Pint of white Wine, some weak Broth, Sweet-herbs, Bits of Roots, Slices of Onions, Pepper and Salt; boil this together about half an Hour; then boil the Fish in it, and serve with a Sauce made of Butter, a little Flour, some scalded chopped Fennel, one Shallot chopped very fine, a little of the boiling Liquid, and a Lemon-squeeze, when ready.

Maqueraux à l'Italienne. Italian Fashion.

MAKE a Sauce with two Spoonfuls of Broth, a good Bit of Butter, half a Clove of Garlick, two Spoonfuls of good Oil, chopped Parsley, Pepper and Salt, the Juice of half a Lemon; warm it without boiling, stirring it continually; serve this Sauce with broiled Mackerels.

Maqueraux en Fricandeaux.

SKIN one Side, and lard it as a Fricandeau; prepare a slight Braze, with a few Slices of Veal, one Slice of Ham, half Broth and half white Wine; simmer this together till the Veal is almost done; then put the Fish to it; let it simmer on a slow Fire; add a few whole Mushrooms; a Nosegay of Sweet-herbs; when done, sift the Braze, reduce Part of it to a Caramel; glaze the larded Side with it; add a Bit of Butter to the Remainder, and proper Seasoning; reduce it to a good Consistence, and serve under the Fish.

Maqueraux frit. Fried Mackerels.

CUT eight Fillets of each Mackerel; marinade them about half an Hour, with the Juice of a Lemon or more, Pepper and Salt; then wipe them dry, and dip them in Wine-batter; fry crisp; and serve with fried Parsley.

Maqueraux à la Nivernoise.

BOIL them in the same Manner as those *au Court-Bouillon*, and serve with Sauce *à la Nivernoise*. See Sauces, p. 31.

Filets de Maquereaux au jus d'Orange.

Orange-sauce.

SPLIT each Mackerel in two; cut out the Bones as clean as possible; then make four large Fillets of each, and boil them a Moment in white Wine; prepare some fine chopped Parsley, green Shallots, Mushrooms, Pepper and Salt, a little Nutmeg; rub the Bottom of the Dish (intended for the Table) with Butter, and some of the Seasoning upon it; then lay the Fillets upon, and more Seasoning over them; add two Spoonfuls of good Cullis; simmer it on a slow Fire, about a Quarter of an Hour: when ready to serve, squeeze a Seville Orange or two upon.

Caisses de Maquereaux aux Trufes.

Broiled in Paper-cases, with a Truffles Farce.

CHOP two or three Truffles very fine, Parsley, Shallots, Pepper and Salt; mix it with Butter, and stuff the Mackerel with it; wrap them in Vine-leaves, and thin Slices of Bacon; put them in Paper-cases, well buttered, one double Sheet of Paper, dipped in Oil, under the Case;

broil

broil them on a gentle Fire, turning several Times while broiling; when done, pour the Fat out: take off the Bacon; serve with a good Lemon-squeeze.

Maquereaux aux Ecrevisses.

With Craw-fish Sauce.

MAKE a Craw-fish Cullis, and chop the Tails to mix with chopped Parsley, Shallots, Pepper, Salt and Butter; stuff the Fish with it; wrap them up in buttered Paper, and broil as the former; when done, take off the Paper; serve the Craw-fish Cullis upon the Fish.

Maquereaux en Cailles; as Quails.

CUT one or two Mackerels, each in three Pieces; give them a few turns on the Fire with Butter, chopped Parsley, Shallots, Mushrooms, Pepper and Salt; wrap up each Bit in Vine-leaves and a Slice of Bacon, with some of the Seasoning; lay them separately on a Baking-dish, and pour the Remainder of the Seasoning in it, if any; bake them in the Oven; when almost done, strew Bread-crums over; put it back to take Colour; and serve all together with Sauce *au Vin de Champagne*, meaning Wine mixed with the Sauce.

Des Harengs & Sardines.

Of Herrings and Pilchards.

WE have three Sorts of Herrings; first the fresh, which is the best; they ought to be very fresh, firm, and the Flesh very white: the pickled Herrings; the Dutch is the best, and the dried commonly called red Herrings: the Pilchard resembles much the Anchovy, and is very good when very fresh.

Harengs frais à la Moutarde.

Fresh Herrings, Mustard-sauce.

THEY must be scaled, gutted, and well washed, and dried with a Cloth; melt some Butter with chopped Parsley, Shallots, Pepper and Salt in it; dip the Herrings in it; then roll them in Bread-crums to broil, and serve upon a Sauce made of melted Butter, a little Flour, a few Drops of Vinegar, a little Broth; when ready to serve, mix Mustard with according to Direction.

Harengs frais marinés. See Maquereaux frit.

Harengs frais Sauce au Capers.

Fresh Herrings with Caper-sauce.

MARINADE them in Oil and Sprigs of Sweet-herbs; broil them, basting with the Marinade; and serve with Caper-sauce.

Harengs frais au Fenouil. With Fennel-sauce.

SPLIT them at the Back to the Bone, and marinade them about half an Hour in melted Butter, Pepper and Salt, a few Sprigs of Fennel; broil them as the former, basting with the Marinade; serve with Sauce Ravigotte, or Sauce au pauvre homme, or as above said.

Harengs frais à la Sainte Meneboult.

MAKE a Sainte Menehoult with melted Butter; a little Flour and some Milk, all Sorts of chopped Sweet-herbs, Bits of Roots, Slices of Onions, Pepper and Salt; boil this about half an Hour; then put the Herrings to boil in it; when they are almost done, take them out, and skim the Fat off the Liquor; dip the Herrings in it, roll them in Bread-crums, broil a Moment; serve with Sauce *Remoulade*, in a Sauce-boat.

Harengs frais aux fines Herbes. See Mackerels.

Harengs frais en Matelotte.

MAKE a *Roux* with Butter and Flour; when of a fine brown, put some Broth and white Wine to it, a Nosegay of all Sorts of Sweet-herbs, one dozen of small Onions, scalded, a few Mushrooms; boil this about half an Hour; cut the Heads and Tails off of the Herrings, and put them to boil in this; add Pepper and Salt; boil on a smart Fire, reduce the Sauce; when ready to serve, add a chopped Anchovy, whole small Capers; garnish the Dish round with fried Bread.

Sardines grillée. Pilchard broiled.

SCALE and gut them without washing, marinade them as the Herrings, broil them, and serve with the same Sauces.

Harengs sors & salés à la Sainte Menehoult.

Dried and pickled Herrings broiled.

SOAK them first in Water, then in Milk; cut the Heads and Tails, and skin them; broil after the same Manner as the fresh ones, under this Denomination; observe, that they do not require so long to be done; a Lemon-squeeze upon when ready to serve; when they are well soaked, they may be dressed in all the different Ways of fresh Herrings: the Dutch often eat them with stewed greens, and the French with Eggs dressed in different Manners.

Rouget aux Capre. Roaches Caper-sauce.

THIS is but an indifferent Fish; it may help where there is a Scarcity of other Kinds, and may be dressed in all the different Ways of Tenches.

DU CABILIOT, DE LA MORUE, ET MERLUCHE.

THESE three are all the same Fish, only the Difference of Preparation; the *Cabiliot* is the fresh Cod, the *Morue* the Baril, the *Merluche* is the dried, soaked: the French Author says, that the best they have is that which they get from Newfoundland; they have also some from Holland, which is of a very fine white, but is apt to be tough; the *Cabiliot* is the large Cod; they call the Codling *Morue* fresh, viz. small Cod.

Merluche à differentes Sauces.

Dried Cod, or Stock-fish to different Sauces.

BEAT it well first, with a wooden Billet, upon a wooden Block; then soak it in Water, with green Wood-ashes, about twenty-four Hours, changing both two or three times; then wash it in several Waters to get the Ashes out, and boil it in Water until you find it grow tender; take it out, and drain it, and break in Fleaks; make a Sauce with Butter and Flour, one Clove of Garlick pounded, Sweet-herbs, chopped very fine; add Cream sufficient to make a good Liason; put the *Merluche* to warm in it, without boiling; add one or two Spoonfuls of good Oil, a good Lemon-squeeze; stir it constantly, till the Oil is well incorporated with the rest, and serve quite hot; this may be served in a Puff-paste Crust, then it is called *Paté de Merluche*; also with *Ravigotte*, or Aspic-Sauce, or any other according to Taste and Fancy; it also eats very good cold, as Sallad, with Oil, Vinegar, and chopped Sweet-herbs.

Hure de Cabiliot aux Huitres.

Cod's Head, Oyster-sauce.

SCALD the Oysters in their own Liquor, drain them to trim the Beards off; put the Liquid in a Saucepan with a good Bit of Butter rolled in Flour, a Glass of white

white Wine, Pepper and Salt, Nutmeg; reduce it to the Confiftence of a good *Liafon*; add a Couple of pounded Anchovies, and the Oyfters; warm together without boiling; ferve this with a Cod's-head plain boiled and well drained, fome of the Sauce upon it, and the Remainder in a Sauce-boat.

Morûe fraiche aux fines Herbes.

Codling, with Sweet-herbs.

CUT a fmall Cod in fix or eight Pieces; bone it as clean as poffible; marinade it in melted Butter, and Lemon-juice, all Sorts of Sweet-herbs chopped; then lay it on the Table-difh with all the Marinade, both under and over; ftrew Bread-crums over, and fmall Bits of Butter, or Drops of melted, clofe to each other; bake it in the Oven; it will require but a fhort Time.

Morûe ou Merluche à la Flamande.

Flemifh Fafhion.

SOAK it according to Judgment; the older it is the more it requires; boil in plain Water in abundance, then drain it; and ferve either in large Bits or in Fleaks, with Butter, Nutmeg, and hard chopped Eggs.

Morûe à la Capucine; an Order of Mendicant Friars.

PUT a good Bit of Butter in a Stew or Sauce Pan, with two Cloves of Garlick, ftuck with each a Spice-clove, chopped Mufhrooms, Sweet-herbs; fry this a Moment together; then add about a Pint of Cream according to the Quantity of Fifh; boil it about a Quarter of an Hour; then fift it in a Sieve; put the *Morue* in it with a Bit of Butter, a little fcalded chopped Parfley; fimmer it a Moment to make a Liafon, and ferve directly; you may also put Mushrooms, chopped Girkins and Anchovies to it; the Girkins and Anchovies to be put only when you are just ready to serve.

Morûe à la Jardiniere.

CUT Carrots, Parsneps, Parsley-roots, to what Shape you please; boil them in Broth with Pepper and Salt; then put them in a Stew-pan, with a good Bit of Butter, and boiled *Merluche* in Fleaks; add a little Cream and Mustard, when ready to serve.

N. B. This is called *à la Jardiniere* by being dressed with Garden-stuff, and so all others under the same Name.

Morûe à la Maitre d'Hotel. See Mackerels ditto.

PUT ready boiled *Morue* upon the Dish you intend to serve, with a good Bit of Butter, chopped Sweet-herbs, Pepper and Nutmeg, the Juice of a Lemon; warm it upon the same Dish, and stir it in the Sauce as you serve it.

Morûe à la Moutarde.

BOIL it to three Parts, then drain it, and put it to marinade in Oil and Lemon juice, Sprigs of Sweet-herbs, whole Pepper; then drain, and dip it in Whites of Eggs beat up; roll it in Flour, and fry of a good Colour: serve with Mustard-sauce. See Sauce Articles, p. 41.

Morûe au beurre noir. With burnt Butter.

WARM it in the Dish you intend for Table, with a little Broth and Vinegar, some coarse Pepper; fry some burnt Butter to pour upon; serve quite hot; observe, that this is done with ready boiled *Morûe*; serve with fried Parsley.

Morue à la Crême; this is the Béchamel Sauce; it is only to put the Fish in it to warm, without boiling; also the same with *Morue aux Verjus de Grains*: scald Verjuice-grapes, and put them a Moment in a Sauce made of Butter and Cream; put the *Morue* in Fleaks to warm in it.

De la Raie. Of Scate.

THE French reckon the Thornback Scate the best; they have the smooth which they call *Turbotée*, meaning nearer to the Turbot kind; and *la Raie Ange*, which I take to be what is called Maids in England. Observing that Scate mostly eats tough when dressed very fresh, the Author says, that in Sea-ports where it is to be had quite fresh, they put a Piece of broken Glass-bottle in the Water with the Fish to boil, and that it makes it eat tenderer; it is an easy Experiment. Sea-port Towns are the only Places to do it.

Raie a differentes Sauces. Scate to different Sauces.

THE different Sorts are prepared in the same Manner. Gut and wash it well, boil it in Water, a little Vinegar, Slices of Onions, Sweet-herbs; when it is half done, put the Liver to boil with it; when done, serve the Fish and the Liver upon, with Caper and Anchovy, or Ravigotte or Sauce Achée.

N. B. Notwithstanding this Direction of boiling the Liver with the other Part of the Fish, it is better to boil all Fish-livers apart, as it certainly spoils the Whiteness of the Fish if boiled together.

Raie au beurre noir. With burnt Butter.

BOIL it as the preceding; season it with Pepper and Salt, and fry some Butter until it is quite black, and still in the Frying-pan; put Vinegar to it at discretion, and Parsley; serve quite hot upon the Fish.

Raie marinée. Scate marinaded.

CUT it in Pieces of what Bigness you think proper; put it to marinade about two or three Hours in a Milk-warm Brine made of Butter, Water and Vinegar, Pepper and Salt, all Sorts of Sweet-herbs, coarsely chopped, one Clove of Garlick, Slices of Onions, Bits of Roots, two Cloves; then drain it well, and flour it to fry; serve dry, or with what Sauce you think proper in a Sauce-boat.

Raie grillée. Broiled.

PREPARE the Pieces as the former, and boil in Milk and Butter, all Sorts of Sweet-herbs, chopped, and proper Seasoning; when done, dip each Piece in melted Butter, roll them in Bread-crums; broil of a good Colour; serve with Mustard, or Sauce *Remoulade*, under the Fish, or in a Sauce-boat.

Raie aux fines Herbes à la Jacobine. Friars so called.

MAKE a Sauce with chopped Parsley, Shallots, a little Basil and Taragon, Capers, Anchovies, coarse Pepper and Salt; boil this in Butter and Flour, and a Spoonful of Water; when the Herbs are done enough, serve upon plain boiled Scate.

Raie en Matelote au Parmesan.

As Matlot and Parmesan Cheese.

PREPARE it as directed for broiling; and boil it in the same Seasoning; make a Ragout of whole Onions, with a very thick Sauce; put a good Quantity of Butter to it; put some of this Ragout in the Dish you intend for Table, and a little rasped Parmesan Cheese over it; lay the Pieces of Scate upon this, and Onions and Bits of fried Bread, between each; put a Spoonful of Mustard in the Remainder of the Sauce, and
two

two Yolks of Eggs; mix it well together; pour this all over the Fish; and strew Bread-crums and Parmesan all over; put it a Moment in the Oven, or give it Colour with a Salamander.

Raie au Vin de Champagne. Wine-sauce.

PREPARE the Scate as directed for marinaded, and fry it; make a Sauce with a Bit of the Liver bruised; boil it a Moment with two Glasses of white Wine, one or two Spoonfuls of Cullis, chopped Parsley, green Shallots, Pepper, Salt and Nutmeg; add a good Bit of Butter; make a Liason, and serve upon the Fish: Raie *à la Burgogne* is done after the same Manner, only red Wine instead of white, and the Fish plain boiled.

N. B. I have passed over several Kinds of Fishes, which are not found upon the English Coast; as it is in Fish as in Fowls, every Country has some particular Sorts of these Kinds, and others, &c. I am also very sensible, that many People will call absurd, so many different Directions for dressing Fish; as few other Methods are adopted in England, besides boiling, frying, and broiling, and much the same Sauces with all. I presume this Book was done upon the Principles of cooking in Paris, where they have not Sea-fish so fresh, and are obliged to dress it in many different Ways, for so many Fast-days as they have in the Year, when no Meat is used, and a Number of Dishes required. My greatest Motive, in regard to giving a Translation of many of these Receipts, was rather to give Informations than Improvements; however, they are not all void of Merit; and I believe, there are few Books of such a Number of Receipts for any Kind of Instructions, but what are (in Part) equally fulsome with this.

DE LA PATISSERIE. OF PASTRY.

FOR a common Crust to send abroad, or to keep long, according to the Bigness of the Pie you intend, make the Paste with common Flour, a little Butter, Salt and warm Water: this Crust is not proposed for eating, but to keep the Inside properly.

Pâte brisée.   Puff-paste.

PASTE made for raised Crust is done with less Butter, and firmer, and is done with warm Water; let it rest some Time, then raise it upon Paper for Puff-paste; use about a Pound of Butter to a Quarter of a Pound of fine Flour, and some Salt, and cold Water to work it.

Pâte feuilletée.   Rich Puff-paste.

MIX some fine Flour with cold Water, Salt, one or two Eggs; the Paste ought to be as soft as the Butter it is made with; in Winter soften the Butter, with squeezing it in your Hands; in Summer, ice it; put Butter according to Judgment, to make it very rich, and work it with a Rolling-pin several times, folding it in three or four Folds each Time: use it to any Kind of Pies, or small Cakes.

N. B. The Meaning of *Feuilletée*, is when the Crust breaks short in thin Leaves or Scales, after it is baked, occasioned by the Richness of it.

Pâte feuilletée à l'Huile.   The same with Oil.

TO one Pound of Flour, make a hole in the Middle upon the Table; put Salt, one Egg, half a Spoonful of Oil, and cold Water, only sufficient to keep it pretty firm; mix it with the Hands, then let it rest a while; work it very thin with the Rolling-pin, and rub it with as much Oil as it will take; strew a little Flour under, to hinder it from sticking to the Table, or Roller: finish it as the former.

Pâte à la Graisse de Bœuf.   Paste with Beef-suet.

CUT some Beef-suet in small Dices, and melt it with a little Water; sift it in a Sieve into some fresh Water; when it is cold, take it out, and work it with your
Hands

Hands to press the Water out; pound it in a Mortar, putting now and then a little Oil to it, until it is come to the Consistence of Butter: use this Preparation for any Sorts of Paste, either raised Crust, or as the former.

Pâte à Demi-feuilletage. Not so rich; *demi*, half.

MAKE a Puff-paste with cold Water, as the first Direction for Paste; put a Quarter of a Pound of Butter to the same Quantity of Paste, and give it five or six Turns with the Rolling-pin, as all others.

Pâte à Baignets. Friture-Paste, or Batter.

PREPARE it with fine Flour, Salt, a little Oil, Beer or white Wine, few Whites of Eggs, beat up; it must not be very thick, nor very thin, but to drop out of the Spoon, about as big as a Nutmeg at once; fry in Oil, or Hog's-lard.

Pâte Croquante. Paste for Crokants.

MIX as much Flour as Sugar, with some Orange-flower Water, Whites of Eggs; do not put too many, as this Paste must be kept firm.

Pâte à la Royale. Royal Paste.

BOIL half a Pint of Water a Moment, with a little Sugar, a Quarter of a Pound of Butter, a little fine rasped Lemon-peel, a little Salt; put Flour to it, little and little, to mix it well, and pretty thick; turn and stir it continually on the Fire, until it quits the Pan; take it off, and while it is warm, put Eggs to it, one by one; mix it well, and put Eggs, until it is come to the Consistence of a Paste *Feuilletée*, and stick to the Fingers.

Pâte

Pâte à la Reine. Queen-paste.

IT is done after the same Manner as the last, except you are to use Cream, instead of Water; it will have a richer Taste, but will not be so light.

Pâte à l'Espagnole. Paste Spanish Fashion.

MAKE a hole in the Middle of the Flour; put Salt to it, and half Butter, and half fresh Hog's-lard; mix it with warm Water; make it pretty firm, and let it rest; cut it in several Pieces, and roll each as thin as possible, and rub each Leaf with melted Hog's-lard; put all the Pieces one upon another; roll them together; let it cool; cut it with a Knife, to put to what Use you please.

Pâte à Canellon.

A particular Paste, to bake or fry any thing in it.

MELT a little Butter, in a Glass of Water, and some fine rasped Lemon-peel, and an Egg; mix half as much Powder-sugar as Flour; mix it, and work it with the above Liquid; put Flour enough to keep it firm.

Pâte au Ris. Rice-paste.

WORK some Flour with a couple of Eggs, and a little Water; let it rest; have some Rice boiled very tender, in good rich Broth; when it is cold, pound it in a Mortar with the ready prepared Paste, and a little Butter, until it is properly mixed: it will serve for any Sorts of Cakes, as all other Paste.

Pâte au Beurre d'Ecrevisses.

With Craw-fish Butter.

UPON a Pound of Flour, put a Quarter of a Pound of this Butter, one Egg, a little Water and Salt, and work it as all other Paste.

Pâte au Sucre. Sugar-paste.

FOR a Pound of Flour, put a Quarter of a Pound of Sugar, and as much Butter, a little Salt, Water, and one Egg; this Paste may serve for any Second-course Dish.

Pâte au Fromage. Cheese-paste.

MAKE a Paste with a Cream-cheese, and Flour, a little Butter, three or four Eggs, both Yolks and Whites, and some good Cream; you must judge for the Quantity of Flour, according to the Quantity of Cheese, and the Consistence you would have the Paste; this may be put to the same Use as the former; this Cheese must be understood, as a ready-made or Curds Cheese, as hereafter directed.

Pâte à la Duchesse.

WORK about half a Pound of Flour, with three Eggs, a Quarter of a Pound of Sugar, a little Salt, and some good Spanish Sweet-wine, as much as is necessary, to keep the Paste pretty firm: this Paste may serve for a Number of Second-course Dishes, being used with any Sorts of Cream, or Sweet-meats, or Sugar, froughted, fried, or baked.

Pâte d'Amande. Almond-paste.

ACCORDING to the Quantity of Paste wanted, scald and peel Sweet-almonds, and few bitter amongst them;

them; pound them in a Mortar, putting a little Whites of Eggs, now and then, to hinder them from oiling; then put them on a middling Fire, with two thirds of Sugar, to one of Almonds; put the Sugar only as it mixes with it, and so on, till the whole Quantity is performed by degrees, and the Paste does not stick to the Pan, nor Fingers; put it to what Use you please; turn it to any Sorts of Shape; very little Heat will dry it; flatten it with the Rolling-pin, as all other Paste; if too soft, add a little Flour and Sugar; if too hard, few Drops of the same Wine as above.

Pâte à Echaudée. Shoudy-paste.

THIS must be calculated according to the Quantity of Shoudies wanted, upon one Pound and a half of Flour; take one sixth, viz. one Quarter of a Pound, to make a *Leaven* with warm Water, and fresh Yeast; knead this well together, and keep it in a warm Place, or before the Fire, about an Hour, or rather less; then put the Flour on the Pastry-table; make a Hole in the Middle, and put about half an Ounce of Salt, about three Quarters of a Pound of Butter, one Dozen of Eggs; work this well together; then pat it a little with the Hands; and put the *Leaven* in small Quantities all over; and mix it very well together; then roll up the Paste, and wrap it up in a Linen-cloth, with a little Flour strewed all about it; keep it in a cool Place, till the next Day: when you propose making the Shoudies, cut the Paste in small Pieces; throw them in hot Water for few Minutes, without boiling; take them out as they rise, on the Water; put them into fresh Water a Moment; then drain them very well, and put them in a middling Oven; they require but a very short Time to be done; this may be done (if in a Hurry), as soon as the *Ferment* is raised, and the Paste prepared, without keeping it from one Day to another, nor using the hot
Water;

Water; they will be lighter after this Manner; but if the dough is well raised, and not too hard, they may be made very good in an Hour's time, after the same Manner: those called *Echaudée au Sel*, and those *au Beurre*, are done after the same Manner, except to those *au Sel*, viz. Salt, you put no Butter; and to those *au Beurre*, you put no Eggs.

Pâte à Brioche.

Brioche, a Cake twisted like a Turk's Cap.

UPON a Quarter of a Pound of Flour, take one third Part to make a *Leaven*, with about half an Ounce, or about a Spoonful of Yeast, and a little warm Water; keep it in a warm Place about half an Hour, wrapped in a Cloth; then mix the Remainder of the Flour, with about eight Eggs, half a Pound of Butter, some Salt; work it well together; then add the first Preparation: also knead it together very well; roll it up, and wrap it in a Cloth; let it rest four or five Hours before using: this Paste is also proper for thin Wafers.

Pâte de Flan, Dariole, & de ce que l'on veut.

Paste proper for large and small Custards.

MAKE the Paste pretty hard, with a little Butter and Flour, a little Salt, and warm Water; this is commonly baked in Moulds; rub the Moulds with a little Butter, then the Paste, and in it the Custard-cream: the *Flans* is the largest, and the Cream covered over with some of the Paste: the *Dariole* is a small Mould so called; prepare this as the first, only you do not cover the Cream, but let it rise as it will; this requires but a very short Time to bake; a Dutch Oven is the best for it.

Pâté à la Flamande. Flemish Fashion.

BOIL half a Pint of Milk, with half a Quarter of a Pound of Butter; add Flour to it, and thicken it as *Pâte Royale*,; put no Eggs to it; work it with the Rolling-pin as all other Paste; flatten it to the Thickness of half a Crown; cut it to what form you please with a Paste-cutter; fry it, and strew powdered Sugar over, which you glaze with a Salamander, holding it hot a Moment over.

DE PATE. OF PIES.

Pâté de Bœuf. Beef-pie.

BEEF Pies are made of any Part, but the Rump is the best, and most generally used: bone it thoroughly, and lard it through and through with large *Lardons*, properly seasoned with all Sorts of Spices, and all Sorts of Sweet-herbs finely chopped; braze it with Slices of Lard, a large Nosegay of Sweet-herbs, whole Onions, all Sorts of Roots, a good Quantity of Butter, a Glass or two of Brandy; simmer it about four or five Hours, until it is quite tender; then let it cool; raise a good Paste, or make a Pie with Puff-paste; put the Beef in it, with the Slices of Lard upon, and a little of the Braze-liquid, without being skimmed; add a good Bit of Butter to nourish it well; cover the Pie, and garnish it with Bits of Paste cut according to Fancy; baste it with Eggs beat up, and put it in a middling-heated Oven: if it is to be served hot, take out the Lard, and skim the Fat very clean off; and add such Sauce or Ragout as you think proper: if it is to be served cold, for second Course, let it cool as it comes out of the Oven, or you may even add some melted Butter and fresh Hog's-lard: observe that all Pies designed to be served cold ought to be more seasoned, than for eating hot, as the Flavour of Spices and other Seasonings are stronger while hot.

Pâté de Veau. Veal-pie.

ACCORDING to the Bigness of the Pie intended, cut a Fillet of Veal, and lard it after the same Manner as directed for Beef; season it again over and under; before you put it in a raised Pie, put a few thin Slices of Lard under the Meat and over, a good Quantity of Butter; finish the Pie in regard to form and garnishing, according to Fancy; bake it three or four Hours; when it is almost done, put a Glass of Brandy to it; let it cool thoroughly before using.

Pâté de Mouton melé. Mutton-pie mixed.

CUT part of a Leg of Mutton, and chop it with other Sorts of Meat, such as Hare, an old Rabbit, Fillet of Veal, Bits of fresh Pork, old Partridges, or any kind of Meat as is most convenient; put a Quarter or half a Pound of Beef-suet, chopped Ham, scraped Lard, chopped Truffles, Pistachio-nuts, four or five hard Yolks of Eggs, all Sorts of Spices and Sweet-herbs, two Glasses of Brandy; put it in a raised Crust-pie; bake it in a soaking Oven about five or six Hours; let it be cold before using: this is in much the same Nature as the *Gâteau de Lievre* in Volume I. only this is done in Paste, so it is called Pie.

Pâté de Cochon de Lait. Of Suckling Pig.

BONE a Suckling Pig thoroughly, and lard the Legs and Shoulders in the same Manner as the Veal, with all Sorts of Spices and Sweet-herbs finely chopped; put it in raised Crust-pie of its own Length, and some of the same Seasoning under and over as you used for the larding, and some pounded scraped Bacon, well mixed with Butter, about half and half; cover it over with Slices of Bacon; garnish the Pie with cut Paste as Fancy leads you; bake it about three or four Hours; when it is almost done, put a Glass of Brandy to it; let it be quite cold before using.

Pâté de Jambon. Ham-Pie.

BONE the Ham thoroughly; trim it properly; in the trimming, take particular Care to cut off all rusty yellow, fat or lean, till you come quite to the wholesome looking Flesh; soak it according to Judgment; if an old Ham, soak it at least from one Day to another; if fresh, about seven or eight Hours will do; then braze it upon Slices of Beef, a Pound of pounded Bacon, a Pound of Hog's-lard, a Pound of Butter, whole Pepper, a large Nosegay of all Sorts of Sweet-herbs, and all Sorts of Roots; braze it to three Parts done; then let it cool, and put it in a good thick raised Paste, with all the Braze, except the Slices of Beef, and a Nosegay; put a good large Glass of Brandy to it; bake it about an Hour, and let it cool before using; but if it is to be served hot, skim it very clean; and serve with a good relishing Cullis-sauce, without Salt.

Pâté de Venaison. Venison-pie, or Pasty.

USE Haunch, or the Neck of Bucks or Does, or wild Boars, Marcassin, viz. young Boar or Kid; lard it as directed for Beef: all these Kind of Meat must be high of Spices for hot; and more so for cold; but as most of these Pies are kept cold, though used hot, Judgment and Taste must regulate the Seasoning.

Pâté de Poulardes, Dindons, & autres Volailles.

Pies of all Kinds of Poultries, and wild Fowls.

THEY are all done after the same Manner, observing the Age and Bigness of the different Kinds. A large Fowl or Turkey; bone it, or only cut out the Breast-bone; stuff them with a good *Salpicon*, or singly without any thing; but the same Seasoning as all other fresh Meat; put Slices of Veal, with the same Seasoning, in the Bottom of the Pie to feed the principal Meat; lay it upon this, and cover it over with Slices of Lard, and some Butter, and bake it as all other Pies.

Pâté d'Amiens en Pâté fine. Fine Paste.

Amien, a Town in Picardy famous for Pies.

MAKE a Paste with about half a Pound of Flour, and a Pound of Butter, Salt and warm Water; let it rest about two Hours before using; truss a couple of fine Ducks, as for boiling; singe them very well on a Charcoal-fire; then lard them with larding Bacon, rolled in Pepper and Salt; Powder of Laurel, Thyme, Basil, a little Nutmeg, Cloves, Cinnamon, Coriander; make a pretty thick raised Pie, and cover the Ducks in it, with Slices of Lard, and a good deal of good Butter; then finish the Pie, and bake it about three Hours in a middling Oven, not to take too much Colour; then let it cool some time; when it is half cold, put three or four Spoonfuls of *Restaurant*, viz. rich Jelly-broth, a Quarter of a Pound of Butter, one Spoonful of good Brandy, boil this a Moment together; when it is poured in it, shake it well, or turn it upside down, to disperse it properly all over.

Pâté d'Amiens en Pâté bise.

The same in common Paste.

PREPARE and season the Ducks in the same Manner as the former; make a common raised Pie, and put in it Hog's-lard and Butter; cover the Ducks in it, with Slices of Lard; finish the Pie; when half done, add a little Brandy; finish the Baking, and let it cool: it is very proper also, in both of these Pies, to braze the

Ducks to about half, with proper Seasoning, before they are put in the Pie; they will always be tenderer. In regard to the Appellation of this last Paste, *bis* means brown, as the French call brown Bread, *Pain bis*.

Pâté de Perdrix. Partridge-pie.

TRUSS the Partridges, Legs inside; and make a little Farce with their Livers, scraped Lard, Sweet-herbs, and proper Seasoning; flatten the Breast-bone; parboil them in Butter about half an Hour, then put them in the Pie, upon Slices of Fillet of Veal, well seasoned; finish it as all others; when done, if for hot, skim it well, and serve with a rich relishing Sauce; if for cold, put some good Jelly-broth in it, before it is quite cold.

Pâté à la Choisi.

BONE as many Partridges as convenient; and stew the Bones with a little Broth and Gravy; take as many fat Livers as Partridges, and lard them with Truffles and soaked Anchovies; pound the Bones, and sift the Liquor, which you mix with the Partridge-livers chopped, and Truffles, scraped Lard, Pepper and Salt; stuff the Partridges with this last; put them in the Pie with the Livers between, and few whole Truffles, some good Butter, Slices of Lard over all; bake it as usual; add a little Brandy, when it is almost baked enough: this is meant for cold.

Pâté de pluviers, Becasses, & Becassines.

Plovers, Wood-cocks, and Snipes Pie.

GUT them, and throw the Gizzards away; pound the Guts, and make a Farce with them, with Sweet-herbs chopped, and proper Seasoning, chopped Truffles;

fles; mix it with scraped Lard, and Butter, or Butter alone; lard the Birds; stuff them with this Farce, and finish as all others.

Pâté de Pigeons, Ortolans, Cailles, Alouette, &c. &c.

Pigeon-pie, Quails, and all Sorts of small Birds, fit for eating.

FOR Pigeons, make a Farce with their Livers chopped with Sweet-herbs, mixed with Butter and proper Seasoning: *Quails*, gut them, and lard them: *Larks*, mix the Gut with Lard or Butter, Sweet-herbs; stuff them with it: any other the same Way; put few Slices of Veal and Ham; each Bird wrapped in a Slice of Lard, one Laurel-leaf, a little Butter; finish in the same Manner as other Pies.

Pâté de (Périgueux.) A Town in Perigord famous for those Pies, commonly called *Périgord* Pies.

MAKE a Farce with the Partridge-livers, and Livers of Poultries, a good deal of chopped Truffles, and Sweet-herbs, scraped Lard, and Seasoning in Moderation; truss the Partridges, with the Legs inside; stuff them with some of this Farce, and lay some of it in the Bottom of the Pie; singe them pretty much on a Charcoal-fire, and lard them with *Lardons*, rolled in mixed Spices; then lay the Birds in the Pie, upon the Farce, and whole Truffles betwixt; a little more Seasoning over all, and Butter, and scraped Lard, pounded together; cover it over with Slices of Lard; finish the Pie according to Fancy, with cut Paste; bake it in the Oven, about four or five Hours: observe the Direction already given, if it is to serve hot or cold.

Pâté de Liévres & de Lapins.

Of Hares and Rabbits.

IN all Kind of Game, if you bone it, pound and stew the Bones, with Broth and Cullis, for this makes a better Sauce for it, than any other; if even for a Ragout, for a Pie, mix what Farce you put in it, with this Cullis; lard them, and finish as usual.

Pâté de Faisand. Of Pheasant.

LEAVE it whole, and make a Farce with the Liver chopped and Truffles, scraped Lard or Butter, a little Pepper and Salt; lard it as usual, and put scraped Lard and Butter mixed round in the Pie, Slices of Lard upon; finish as all others.

Pâté d'Esturgeon. Sturgeon-pie.

PIES may be made of all Sorts of Sea and fresh Water Fish, following the same Method in all the different Kinds. I shall only speak of such as are most in Use; Sturgeon for *Pâté maigre*, lard it with Eel, seasoned with fine Spices, and chopped Sweet-herbs: for *Gras*, lard it with Lard, and the same Seasoning; and put a sufficient Quantity of Butter in the Pie, according to the Quantity of Fish; finish as all other Pies.

Pâté de Macreuse. A wild Fowl.

THIS is a Water-fowl, not common in England; it resembles a small Kind of Ducks, which mostly come to London out of Lincolnshire: the Market-people call them Shuffler. The Macreuse is a larger Bird, and of cold Blood, for which it is reckoned of the Fish-kind; and the most rigid Papist will eat it in Lent, or any other Fasting-day: it is trussed like a Duck for a Pie, or for any thing elfe, larded with Anchovies, feafoned with Pepper, Salt, and Sweet-herbs, a good Quantity of Butter in the Pie; and finifhed as all others.

Pâté de Truite. Of Trouts, a cold Difh.

CLEAN it properly; cut the Head off, and the Tail; lard it through and through, with Anchovies and Truffles, feafoned as ufual; ftuff it with chopped Truffles, and Sweet-herbs, mixed with Butter; put the Fifh in a raifed Pie, and a good deal of Butter upon; bake it about two Hours. Note, that thofe Fifh-pies are equally made with Meat, and much better than Meager.

Pâté de Soles. Of Soals.

MIX five or fix pounded Anchovies, with a Pound of Butter, or more, half a Pound of chopped Truffles, a little Powder of Bafil; take up each Soal in four large Fillets; marinade them about two Hours, in Lemon-juice; then drain them; and lay a good Down of the firft Preparation in the Pie, then fome of the Fifh; fo continue, the Butter to be the laft; finifh the Pie; and bake it about two Hours.

Pâté de Saumon. Of Salmon.

LARD it with Eel and Anchovies, foaked and feafoned with fine Spices, and all Sorts of Sweet-herbs, finely chopped; put Butter under, and over, with fome of the fame Seafoning. Eels, Pikes, or any other Kind of Fifhes, may be dreffed in Pies after the fame Manner, either for *Gras* or Meager: make all Pies of this Sort pretty relifhing with Lemon.

DES TOURTES, PATES CHAUDS & PETITES PATISSERIE.

Of Pastry for First-course, and small for Second, hot or cold.

A Puff-paste Crust Pie, is called a *Tourte*, and raised Crust Pie is called a *Pâté*: the following Dishes are mostly to be done in Puff-paste, for the First-course, and *petits Pâtés* the same.

Tourtes d'Ailerons. Of Pinions of Poultries.

SCALD them in boiling Water, to clean very well; then stew them to about three Parts, with good Broth, and Cullis, a Slice of Ham, all Sorts of Sweet-herbs, chopped or whole, Mushrooms, a Nosegay, some good Butter, and Slices of Lard over; prepare the Puff-paste in the Baking-dish; put all together in it, with the Slices of Lard on the Top; cover it with Paste; put a Border round it as you shall think proper; wet it round with Water, to make the Paste stick together; bake it in a gentle Oven; when it is done, cut the Top off properly; and take out the Lard and Nosegay; skim the Fat very clean, and add what Sauce or Ragout you please.

Tourtes de Becasses. Of Wood-cocks.

CUT each Wood-cock in four, and pound the Inside, to mix with scraped Lard, Sweet-herbs chopped, and proper Seasoning; put this Farce in the Bottom of the Pie, and the Meat upon it, some Butter, and Slices of Lard; and finish it with a good relishing Cullis-sauce, when baked, and the Lard taken out.

Tourte aux Cailleteaux. Of young Quails.

TRUSS the Quails as a Chicken for boiling, Legs inside; and make a Farce with the Livers, scraped

Lard, and chopped Sweet-herbs, and other Seasoning; lay this in the Bottom of the Pie, and put the Birds in a Stew-pan, with a good Bit of Butter, four or five large Craw-fish trimmed; fry all together about a Quarter of an Hour, then intermix them in the Pie; season it as the Pinions; bake slowly, about an Hour or more; serve what Sauce you think proper in it.

Tourte de Filets de Levrauts.
Of Fillets of Leverets.

CUT the Flesh in Pieces of what Bigness you think proper; rub each Piece over with scraped Lard, Pepper and Salt; put a little Butter upon the Paste, and the Meat upon it, and more Butter, a Nosegay of Sweet-herbs, one Slice of Ham, Slices of Lard over; finish the Pie as usual; when properly baked, take out the Lard, Ham, and Nosegay; boil the Bones with Broth and Cullis, (as before directed, in Game-articles), to make a good relishing Sauce; finish it as all other.

Tourte de Foies gras. Of fat Livers.

GARNISH the Bottom of the Pie with pounded Lard; put the Livers, properly seasoned, upon it, and Butter over, a Nosegay of Sweet-herbs, one Slice of Ham, few of larding Bacon; bake it as usual; when done, take out the Lard, Ham, and Nosegay; skim the Fat off very clean, and serve a good tasted Cock's-combs Ragout in it.

Tourtes de Langues de Bœuf, Veau, & Mouton.
Puff-paste Pies of Beef, Veal, and Sheep's Tongues.

THEY are all prepared after the same Manner, allowing for Tenderness in the Baking. Whatever

Tongues you use, scald and peel them very clean; lard them through and through; braze to three Parts, with good Seasoning, then let them cool; cut them in what Pieces or Shape you please, or leave them whole; make a good seasoned Farce for the Bottom of the Pie; finish as all the rest; and serve a good relishing Sauce in it.

Tourte de Lapreaux. Of Rabbits.

CUT it in Pieces, and scald it a Quarter of an Hour, in boiling Water; or you may do it without scalding, it will taste more of Game; make a Farce with the Livers, with Lard, and good Seasoning; make the same Use of it as the former; make a Sauce with the Heads and Trimmings of the Rabbits, by stewing with a little white Wine, Cullis, and good Seasoning; sift it, to pour in the Pie

Tourte de Pigeons. Of Pigeons.

SINGE your Pigeons a Moment, and truss them, Legs inside; put some Butter or pounded Lard in the Bottom of the Pie, and the Pigeons upon; finish the Baking as usual; when done, skim the Fat very clean off, and a good relishing Ragout in it, made of Sweet-breads, fat Livers, Mushrooms, Cock's-combs, and hard Yolks of Eggs; if the Pigeons are pretty old, give them a Fry in Butter, before you put them in the Pie.

Tourte de Perdreaux. Of young Partridges.

TRUSS them as the Pigeons, and stuff them with a Farce, made of their Livers, chopped Truffles, or Mushrooms; mix with Lard or Butter, and pretty high Seasoning; when finished as usual, serve a Ragout of Truffles or Mushrooms in it, or any other: if the Partridges are pretty old, they ought to be stewed whole some time.

N. B.

N. B. As these Tourtes, or Puff-paste Pies, may appear, at the first Sight, to be only a Recapitulation of the Pâtés, only made in different Crust; please to observe, that, as the *Tourtes* are to be served hot, the Seasoning is not so high, and that the different Kinds used are to be young; except that old Game, or Poultries, are used for *Pâté*, viz. raised Crust Pies.

Tourte de Godiveaux. A raw Forced-meat.

I Have already given an Explanation of this, under the same Appellation: As it is now to be used by itself, I shall still give a further Explanation, to impress the true Meaning of it: it is made of any Sorts of raw Meat, or several Sorts mixed together; either to stuff any large Brazing-pieces, or to use by itself: this last, make it with Fillet of Veal chopped, with Calf's-udder scalded, raw Breast of Poultries, Beef-suet, Sweet-herbs, Pepper, Salt, and Nutmeg, two or three raw Eggs; when well pounded, and seasoned, make it into Balls, or in the Form of Sausages; put this in the Pie, and add (if you think proper) Artichoke-bottoms, Mushrooms, Truffles, Sweet-breads, &c. &c. some Butter; finish as all the rest.

Tourte de Tendrons de Veau. Of Veal-gristle.

CUT the Gristle of a Breast of Veal in middling Pieces; scald them in boiling Water some time; put some scraped Lard and Butter in the Bottom of the *Tourte*, and the Veal upon, seasoned with Pepper and Salt, whole Mushrooms, a few Slices of Ham, two Slices of peeled Lemon, a Nosegay of Sweet-herbs, Slices of Lard over it; bake it about an Hour; when done, take out the Lard, Ham, Nosegay, and Mushrooms, or leave the last; skim it very clean; pour a Cullis *à la Reine*, or Sauce *à la Crême* on it; if you would have it brown Sauce, make a good relishing Cullis.

Tourte de Saucisse accompagnée.

Of Sausages garnished with other things.

SCALD large Sausages in boiling Water, cut each in two, and skin them; put a Farce of what you think proper in the Bottom of the Pie, and the Sausages upon it; about a dozen of small Onions half-boiled, fat Livers or others, a few Truffles or Mushrooms, cut in Dices; a little Seasoning, some good Butter, a Nosegay of Sweet-herbs, all covered over with Slices of Lard; finish it in the usual Manner; when done, take out the Lard and Nosegay; skim the Fat, and serve with Spanish Sauce or any other in the Pie.

Tourte à la Condé.

Condé, the Title of one of the Princes of the Blood.

SCALD some small Onions as the former, and Sausages the same way as the last; boil a Piece of pickled Pork, about half done, and cut it in thin Slices; put a Farce in the Bottom of the Pie, made of chopped Livers of Poultries, scraped Lard, and light Seasoning; put upon this a small Chicken, cut in Quarters, or Pinions of any Poultries scalded properly; upon this, the Sausages, pickled Pork, and Onions, intermixed with a little more Seasoning, some good Butter, and Slices of Lard at the Top; when well baked and the Fat skimmed off, make a Sauce with good rich Consommée, a Bit of Butter rolled in Flour, a little scalded chopped Parsley, and a good Lemon-squeeze; when ready to serve, pour this in the Pie.

Tourte de Lasaques. A Dumpling Paste-pie.

MAKE a Puff-paste with Flour, Eggs, Butter, Salt and cold Water; when it is well worked, let it rest some time; then roll half of it in very thin Sheets, and cut it in small Pieces; have some boiling Water, and boil this Paste in it, with a little Salt; let it boil a few Minutes;

Minutes; take care to separate them in the boiling; then put them into fresh Water a Moment, and drain it out; make a Pie with the Remainder of the Paste, and Butter and Parmesan Cheese at Bottom; then a Down of the scalded Paste, and one of Truffles, or Mushrooms, mixed with Butter or pounded Lard; then more Paste, and so on till all is laid one over the other; finish by the Butter and Cheese; cover it over with Paste as all others; bake it slowly about an Hour and a half, and serve without any thing else.

Tourte de Viandes blanches. Of white Meats.

TAKE Chickens, Fowls, Turkey-polts, Ducklings, or any other Sorts; singe them, cut in Quarters; make a seasoned Forced-meat to put under and over in the Pie; when done as usual, serve what Sauce or Ragout you think proper in it.

Tourte de Filets de Mouton à la Robert.
Of Fillets of Mutton with Onions.

MAKE a *Godiveau* Farce as for the Tourte under that Name; and cut the Fillet of a Neck of Mutton in thin Slices, and a few Onions in the same Manner; put some of the *Godiveaux* in the Bottom of the Pie; then some of the Mutton, and Slices of Onions upon it, with a little Pepper and Salt; continue in the same Manner till all is laid; then some Butter and thin Slices of Lard over it; finish the Pie; bake it about an Hour and a half, or more, according to its Bigness; when done, take out the Lard; skim it very well; add a Cullis-sauce, with a little Mustard well mixed with it; shake the Pie to disperse it every where.

Tourte en Puits. Puit, a Well or Wells.

TAKE six or eight large Onions; make a good hollow Inside, without cutting through; scald them in boiling Water a Moment, then drain them; make a Farce with scalded Sweet-breads, Mushrooms, Truffles,

scraped

scraped Lard, Pepper, Salt, chopped Shallots and Parsley, two Yolks of raw Eggs: fill the Onions with this Farce, and some of it in the Bottom of the Pie; put the Onions upon, and some good Butter; finish the Pie as usual; bake it about two Hours in a middling Oven; serve with a good Sauce, or a Sweet-bread Ragout in it.

Tourte de Cannetons au Vin de Champagne.

Of Ducklings.

SCALD a couple of Ducklings, and clean them properly; cut each in Quarters; put them in a Pie upon a good Farce, two Slices of peeled Lemon upon, to keep them white; season as other Poultries; mix two Glasses of white Wine, with some good Cullis; boil it some time together to reduce it to a good Sauce-consistence: serve this Sauce in the Pie.

Tourte au Zephir.

MAKE a Paste as directed in *Pâte feuilleté* in Paste Articles; roll a couple of Sheets with the Rolling-pin, much the same Thickness; put these one upon another in the Baking-pan; pinch them together as if the Meat was in it; baste it with Eggs and bake it; when it is baked enough, cut it round; and if the Paste is well made, the Inside is puffed up, and to be taken out easily; take out all this Pudding Crust or Dough, and serve a Ragout of any Sorts in it, or minced Meat the same: also Fish of any kind, and to any Sauce.

Tourte de Lapin au Zephir.

Of Rabbit. See the following Explanation.

CUT a Rabbit in Pieces as for a Fricassée; put it in a Stew-pan with a good Bit of Butter, Mushrooms, a Nosegay of Sweet-herbs; when it is half done, add two
Glasses

Glasses of white Wine, some Cullis, and a scalded Sweet-bread; season it of a good relishing Taste; serve this Ragout in the same Sorts of Pie as the last.

Tourte de Macaroni au Zephir.

SCALD the Macaroni, and boil it in good Broth, and Hog's-lard; when it is tender and thick, put some Parmesan Cheese to it, and serve it in the same Sort of *Tourte*, with some good Veal-cullis in it.

N. B. This is called Zephir by that doughy Paste being taken out, meaning gutted, as is the Caldron and Chitterlings of a Calf, &c. when gutted, it is called Zephir, viz. Entrails. See the Explanation under Veal Articles, p. 91.

Tourte d'Oeufs. Of Eggs.

MIX some chopped Sweet-herbs, with a good Bit of Butter, Pepper and Salt, Nutmeg; put it in the Bottom of the Paste made after the Direction of *Demi-feuilletage*, and what Quantity of hard Eggs you please, cut in Quarters, and some raw beat up as for an Omelet, some good Butter; finish the Pie as usual; you may add a Caper-sauce when ready, or Cream-sauce.

Tourte de Soles. Of Soals.

USE the same kind of Paste as the former, and put a good Farce in the Bottom: if *Meager*, make it with Fish and good Seasoning; if *Gras*, make it with Breast of roasted Poultries; boil the Soals a Moment; then take up four large Fillets of each, lay them upon the Farce, a little Pepper and Salt, and Butter; when done, add what Sauce you please: Mackerels done after the same Manner.

Tourte de Moules & d'Huitres. Of Oysters and Mussels.

BOIL the Oysters in their own Liquor, and beard them; then mix them with Butter, Pepper, Nutmeg, Shallots and Parsley; serve with Sauce *à la Bechamel*: Mussels are done the same, when well picked one by one; you may also serve either with Sauce au Verjus. See p. 37.

Tourte de Cabilliot. Of Cod, &c. &c.

CUT it in middling Pieces, and fry it in Butter a Moment, with a Nosegay of Sweet-herbs; then put it into a Bechamel-sauce, or Anchovies or Crawfish Cullis; warm it without boiling; serve it in the *Tourte aux Zephir*. *Tourte de Morüe* is done after the same Manner, without Salt; the Remainder of plain boiled Cod or any other Fish will do for those Pies, only warming it in what Sauce you please, and serve it in Pie-crust, made after the Zephir Direction.

Tourtes d'Esturgeons, Tourte d'Anguilles, de Brochet & Carpes.

TURBOT, *Merlans*, Whitings, *Eperlans*, Smelts, Perches, are all done after the same Manner; you may either prepare each in a Stew-pan as a Ragout or Fricassée, or bake it in a less rich Paste, and serve the Sauce or Ragout you think proper in it.

Des petits Pâtés de Godiveaux.

MAKE a Farce as directed for *Pâté de Godiveaux*, only chop it rather finer, and Paste as the Feuilletage, viz. rich Puff-paste; cut it to the Bigness of the Pates Moulds rubbed with Butter, and fill them with this Farce, and cover them with the same Paste; bake these in a middling-heated Oven about three Quarters of an Hour; when ready to ferve, put a little warm Cullis with a Lemon-fqueeze to it.

Petit Pâté en Sauciffes.

In the form of Saufages.

MAKE a Farce as the preceding, and wrap it up in Puff-pafte in the form of fhort thick Saufages, and cut fome of the Pafte length-ways; roll it in the form of a fmall Rope to twift round it according to Fancy, and finifh it as the former; thefe Differences are proper upon a large Table, where two Difhes of the fame Preparation are ferved, and fhows the Ingenuity of the Workman.

Petits Pâtés à la Reine.

Queen Pates from the Sauce ditto.

USE the Sort of Pafte as for the two former; rub the Moulds with Butter, before you put the Pafte in it; bake them in a pretty quick Oven to make the Pafte rife the better: if you fear their taking too much Colour, put a Sheet of Paper over, minced Breaft of roafted Poultries, Chickens, Fowls or Turkey, Hare, Partridges, or any thing elfe; make this relifhing with Cream or Cullis accordingly, if you would have them white or brown, and pour it in the Pates when you are juft ready to ferve; when the *Farce* is prepared with Cullis, it is commonly baked in the Cruft, either of Veal, Mutton, or Beef, minced; pour the Cullis after they are baked; and this laft is called *Petits Pâtés au Jus,* viz. Gravy or Cullis: both are the Effence of Meat: *Petits Pâtés à la Bechamel* are much the fame as *à la Reine*; they are called after the Name of the Sauces, which only differ in very little Alteration. See Sauces, p. 42. and 48. for *à la Reine* and *Bechamel.*

Petits Pâtés au Pontife.

From the Sauce, p. 30. and 46. Numbers of other Denominations.

MAKE a raised Paste, and prepare a little Farce with Breast of roasted Poultries, or Remainder of Sweet-breads, chopped Sweet-herbs, and proper Seasoning; put this in the Bottom of the Pâtes and fat Livers, and sliced Truffles upon it, with a little scraped Lard, and the same Farce upon it; bake these Sorts of Pâtes a pretty good while; when done, make a little Hole at the Top, to pour a Sauce *au Pontife* in it; you may make *Petits Pâtes dressé*, viz. raised Crust, with any Sorts of Meat, either minced or cut in thin Slices; it is the Sauce you put to it that gives them the Name. In regard to Mushrooms, Truffles, Morels, Asparagus, or any kind of Greens you may make Pâtes of; then they are called by the Substance, and not the Sauce you add to it; for it is mostly either with Cream or Cullis, with proper Seasoning according as the Quality of the Thing used requires.

I shall give no further Direction, but the different Names by which *Pâtes* are served; hoping the former Explanation sufficient, without crowding more Repetitions; but as People unacquainted with the Names, and anxious to know whether any thing particular is meant, more than has been given already; and to make all familiar with Bills of Fare, as great Merit is often put upon their not being understood; they are as follows.

Petits Pâtés de ce que l'on veut. Of what you please.

Petit Pâtés à la Choisy. With Sweet-bread, &c.

Petits Pates à la Perigord. With a Farce mixed with Truffles.

Petits Pâtes à la Neſſe. With Udders, &c. minced.

Petits Pâtes à la Mincelle. With minced Meat of any kind.

Petits Pâtes de Gibier. With any Sorts of Game.

Petits Pâtes de Poiſſon. With any kind of Fiſh.

Petits Pâtes de Poiſſon aux Ecreviſſes. With Crawfiſh, Butter, or Cullis.

Petits Pâtes de Poiſſon à la Crême. With Bechamel or Cream Sauce.

Petits Pâtes d'Oeufs. With Eggs.

Petits Pâtes de Foies & Laitance. With Livers and Roes.

Whoever has over-run this Book will know how to ſeaſon each Article of which thoſe Petits Pâtes are compoſed.

DES TOURTES & AUTRES PATISSERIES D'ENTREMETS.

Of Tarts and other Second-courſe Paſtry.

Fruits in Paſtry are equally called Tourtes as thoſe before with Meat.

Tourte de Ceriſes froide. Cold Cherry Tart.

MAKE a Compote, viz. ſtewed, of ſtoned Cherries, with half as much Sugar as for preſerving; they may alſo be prepared without being ſtoned; put this in a rich Puff-paſte, and Bits of Paſte upon; cut and laid according to Fancy; it requires no longer Time to bake, than is neceſſary for the Paſte to be done of a good Colour: this and other Sorts are alſo done in Paſte as directed for *Demi-feuilletage*; then the Fruit is put in raw, and Sugar according to Judgment; raiſe a proper Border

Border according to the Bigness of the Baking-dish; and bake it longer than the first Direction: this last is used either hot or cold.

Tourte de Framboise. Of Rasberries.

SIMMER the Rasberries a Moment in a Syrup; then let them cool, and finish the Tart as the first Direction for Cherries.

Tourte de Fraises à la Glace.

Of Strawberries and iced Cream.

MAKE an Almond-paste as directed in Page 407. put it in a Baking-dish, and raise a Border as to any other Sorts of Paste; it requires but a short Time to bake, and very little Heat: just before you are ready to serve, put Ice-cream in it not very hard, and the Strawberries upon; this Ice-cream is made with a Pint of good Cream, and Sugar sufficient to make it pretty sweet, a little Orange-flower Water, two Yolks of Eggs; put it on the Fire till it is ready to boil; stir it to mix the Eggs very well; when it is cold, put it in a Mould to ice, as shall be explained in Ice Cream Articles; you may also boil Pistachio-nuts in this Cream, and sift it before icing.

Tourte d'Abricots. Of Apricocks.

CUT each in two, and break the Stones to get the Kernels; if the Fruit is not ripe enough, boil them a little while in Water; then drain them very well, and put them in the Paste with Sugar according to Judgment, a few Bits of preserved Lemon, and half a Kernel upon each Piece; cover it with the same Sort of Paste, and strew a little Powder-sugar over it to give it a Glaze, which it will take in baking.

Tourte

Tourte de Franchipane.

Italian, after Frangipani, a proper Name.

MIX three Eggs with a Pint of Cream, two or three Spoonfuls of Flour, a proper Quantity of Sugar; boil this together about half an Hour, stirring it continually; then add some Almond-biscuits, called Macaroni-drops, bruised to Powder, a little Lemon-peel minced very fine, a Bit of Butter, two Yolks of Eggs, a little of the Orange-flower dried and pounded, or a few Drops of Orange-flower Water: use the best Sort of Paste, viz. *au Feuilletage* or *Zephir*; put the Cream in it, a few Bars of Paste over, laid according to Fancy, or cut Flowers; sugar it over to give a Glaze: serve cold.

Tourte à la Moële. Of Marrow.

TAKE a Cream as the preceding; instead of Butter use Beef-marrow melted and sifted in a Sieve, four Whites of Eggs well froughted; put no Cover of any Sort upon it, only a good high Border round; when it is baked, strew some Powder-sugar over, and glaze it with the Salamander.

Tourte d'Amande. Of Almonds.

IT is done as the Italian Franchipane, putting a good many pounded sweet Almonds in the Cream, and a few bitter ones with it.

Tourte de Verjus. Of Verjuice-grapes or any others.

STONE the Grapes, and scald them a Moment in boiling Water; then drain them very well, and simmer a little while in a rich Syrup; when this is cold, put it in the Paste without covering: glaze the Border of the Tart with Sugar.

Tourte de Muscat. Of Muscado, or sweet Grapes.

IT is done much after the same Manner, as the Verjuice, excepting that the Sweet-grapes are not scalded, nor so much Sugar or Syrup put to it.

Tourte de Pistache. Of Pistachio-nuts.

MIX Flour of Rice with three or four Yolks of Eggs, Orange-flower dried and chopped, Cream, and Sugar; boil it about half an Hour, stirring continually; then take it off, and add a Quarter of a Pound of pounded Pistachio-nuts, and a Bit of preserved Citron; finish it as usual: if you would have it iced, make as directed for Strawberries, putting the Nuts pounded upon the iced Cream.

N. B. Although the Flower of the Orange-tree is here recommended, and in several other Directions; as it is not so common in England, few Drops of the Water will equally answer the same End.

Tourte à la Chantilli.

Chantilli, a small Town near Paris.

PUT a little Orange-flower Water, in three Pints of Cream; frought it like Whites of Eggs; take the Frought as it is raised; when finished, put a little rasped Lemon-peel, and Sugar-powder, at Discretion; ice it a little, and serve in an Almond-crust.

Tourte de Pommes. Of Apples.

PEEL the Apples; clean out the Kernels, and boil to a Marmalade, with few Drops of Water, a sufficient Quantity of Sugar, and a little Cinnamon, a Lemon-squeeze; you may also put a Bit of the Rind; when done, take out the Lemon-peel, and Cinnamon; use the *Pâte de Feuilletage*; cover it with the same, and glaze it with Sugar.

Tourte de Poires. Of Pears.

PEEL the Pears, and cut them in Quarters; take out the Kernels; and if they are large, and pretty green, boil

boil them to half in Water; then simmer them some Time, in a good rich Syrup; bake them in the Tart, made of Pâte à Demi-feuilletage: see Paste-articles.

Tourte de Prunes. Of Plums.

THE large Kinds used for Tarts, must be split in two; put a good Quantity of Sugar, both under and over: use the same Paste as the last, with the Top-crust the same, and glaze it to give it a better Look on the Table; in regard to glazing any Sorts of Tarts, it is no further necessary than agreeable, as many People like the Crust, without its being glazed.

Tourtes d'Epinards. Of Spinages.

SCALD the Spinages in boiling Water, and drain them very well to chop; then stew them in Butter and Cream, with a little Salt, and Sugar, few small Bits of dried Comfit-citron, and few Drops of Orange-flower Water; use either the finest Puff-paste, or the second.

Tourtes de Groseilles vertes. Of green Goosberries.

YOU may either use them whole, or make a Marmalade of them, with a good Syrup: this last is recommended as the best Method; for by this Means you can judge easily how sweet they are, and ought to be, to please; for the Marmalade, they ought to be stoned, when they are pretty large.

Tourte de Chocolat, & Tourte de Caffé.

Of Chocolate, and Coffée.

MIX a little Flour and Cream, with a proportionable Quantity of Chocolate, a Bit of Sugar, three Eggs; boil it about half an Hour, stirring continually, for fear it should catch at Bottom ; put it in the Paste, and Whites of Eggs, beat up, froughted, upon it; glaze it with Sugar: that of Coffee is done after the same Manner; boiling one or two Dishes of good clear Coffee, with the Cream, instead of the Chocolate; finish it after the usual Manner, without Top-crust.

Tourte à la Paysanne.

Common, or Country-fashion.

TAKE a fresh Cream-cheese, made the Day before, or only made five or six Hours; mix a Bit of Butter, and few Eggs with a little Salt; make the Paste pretty thick, and the Top the same; bake it, without glazing the Top-crust, or Border.

Tourte de Trufes à la Glace. Of Truffles iced.

SOAK few Truffles in warm Water; then clean them very well with a Brush; and boil them in a Pint of Cream, a Quarter of a Pound of Sugar; boil it till the Cream is reduced to half; take out the Truffles, to pound very fine, then mix them with the Cream; ice it, and serve with Almo d Paste Crust.

Tourte d'Entremets de ce que l'on veut.

Second-course Pastry of any Kind of Fruits or Jelly.

THESE Toûrtes may be made with any Kind of preserved Fruits, such as have been at Table, or such as lose their Colour or Goodness. Observe to cover all preserved Fruits with Paste cut in Flowers, or any different Shape, as it hinders it from turning black in the Oven; those made with fresh or raw Fruits, it is not necessary, unless by Choice: *Tourtes* made of Jelly; bake the Crust first, and let it cool; then put

the

the Jelly upon it, if of different Sorts; it will look the better, as is done in *Croquante*.

Petites Jaloufii.

From a blind Window or Grate, where cloiftered Nuns, or Spanifh Wives are fpoken to, &c.

ROLL the Pafte pretty thick, cut in fmall fquare Pieces; make three or four Holes, or rather finking; rub them over with Yolks of Eggs, or glaze them with Sugar; when done, fill each Hole with different Kinds of Sweet-meats or Jelly: obferve that thofe little *Patifferies* are to be done with the beft Puff-pafte.

Tartelettes à la Crême. Cuftard in Pafte.

MAKE a Cream as directed for the Franchipane; let it cool, and prepare the Pafte in Moulds, as for Petit Pâtes; put fome of this Cream in it, few Bits of Pafte, crofs-ways at Top; bake about half an Hour; glaze them with Sugar.

Tartelette à la Bonne; this is done in Petit Pate-pan, as the former; bake the Pafte, then fill them with Sweet-meats, or preferved Fruits of any Kind, or a cold Marmalade, well prepared.

Tartelettes de Maffepains. Tartlets of Sugar-pafte.

TURN fome Almond-pafte in different Shapes and Sizes; bake it a Moment in a very flow Oven; when it is cold, fill each with what Sorts of Jelly or Sweet-meats you think proper; you alfo fill this Pafte with the fame Sort of Cream, as directed for the Tourte *à la Chantilli*; then they are called by that Name: all *Tartelettes*, viz. fmall Tarts, may be made with all the different Sorts of Creams, as directed for Tarts; the Difference is only by way of Variety, on the Table:

also all Creams, as directed here, without Fruits, as Coffee, Chocolate, &c. may be served upon a Dish singly, or with only a low Paste Border round, which gives it a better Look on the Table.

Riſſolles d'Entremets de ce que l'on veut.

Fritures for Second-courſe of any Kind.

ROLL ſome of the ſecond-beſt Paſte *Demi-feuilletage* very thin; put in it what Cream, or Sweet-meat, or Marmalade you think proper; roll them up in what Form you pleaſe, and in different Shapes, and fry them in very hot Friture; glaze them with a little Sugar-powder, and the Salamander.

Soufflets. A raiſed Puff-cake.

MAKE the richeſt Puff-paſte; roll it pretty thick, and four or five Pieces, or more, all of the ſame Bigneſs; lay one Piece in a deep Baking-diſh; upon it ſome good prepared Cream, or Sweet-meat, then another Piece of Paſte, then ſome more Cream, or Marmalade, and ſo on, as many as you pleaſe; the Paſte to be the laſt, in which make a little Hole, which you fill with Sweet-meat, or Jelly, when it is well baked: this muſt be done in a pretty hot Oven, to raiſe the Paſte properly: this is done alſo, by baking the Paſte firſt upon a Baking-plate, and putting the Cream, Jelly, or Sweet-meat, when it is cold, and finiſhed after the ſame Form.

Croquantes à la d'Eſtrées; either by that Nobleman's Name, or the Inventor.

USE the beſt Puff-paſte; roll it pretty thin, and cut it in different Shapes, as Fancy leads; bake it, and dreſs each Piece upon the Diſh, in a handſome Manner; rub them with a little Sugar-caramel, to make them stick as you place them; then put some Currant-jelly all over the Top, and make what Flower or Design you please, with Nompareil of different Colours, round it.

N. B. The Nompareil is a small Sugar-seed, which is sold at the Confectioners; it serves to garnish Frames for Desserts, and any Sorts of Pastry, being first rubbed over with Whites of Eggs, to make it stick; intermix the Colour, according to Ingenuity.

Croquante en Caramel. Burnt Sugar Crokant.

IF you have no Mould made for the Purpose, take a round Stew-pan, according to the Bigness you desire the Croquante to be; rub the Outside with Butter or Oil; warm it a little in the Inside, then rub it very clean; when it is cold, rub it again all over, with a little Butter or Oil, and keep it in a cool Place; boil about a Pound of Sugar, with two Spoonfuls of Water, on a smart Fire; skim it well; then do not stir it any more, till it begins to rope, which you will find drawing it up with a Knife, Fork, or Skewer; if it ropes as it cools, then drop it directly on the prepared Pan, according to your Fancy; do not make it too heavy and thick; it ought to be clear and transparent; when it is cold, put the Pan a Moment over an Ashes-fire; watch the Moment that the Oil or Butter is warm, to take it off, with both Hands, from the lower Part: observe that the Dish you intend to serve it upon, be ready prepared, and put it upon it directly, for it is a great Chance but you break it, if you handle it more than once; and the same Attention for all Croquantes, either of Sugar or Paste: Croquantes made a Day or two before using, they must be kept in a warm Place, otherwise they will tumble to Pieces.

Croquante de Pâte d'Amandes. Of Almond-paste.

PREPARE the Pan upon which you propose to make it as the former; make the Paste pretty supple, and
easy

easy for handling; roll it pretty thin, and cut it in Flowers, or Birds, and so on, as you please; and place it accordingly: you must observe, that each Piece sticks to one another, by Kopes and Twist, or otherwise; put it a Moment in a very moderate Oven, or it will do at a good Distance from the Fire, turning it round several Times; then take it off as the former; if any Part stick to the Pan, or breaks, join it with Sugar Carameled; you may serve it in its natural Colour, or glaze it with a white froughted Glaze, made of fine sifted Sugar, beat up with Whites of Eggs, and a little Lemon-juice; beat it up with a wooden Spoon, in an earthen Vessel, or China, until it is very white; use a light Brush or Feathers, to spread it about the *Croquante*; then you may also garnish it with Nompareils; make the Bottom of the same Paste, or any other Sorts; lay cross Bar Divisions, according to Fancy, to intermix Sweet-meats, Jelly, preserved Fruits, &c. &c.

Nœuds d'Epées. Sword-knots.

MAKE a second-best Paste, viz. *Demi-feuilletage*, and roll it very thin; cut it in Thongs like Ribands, some with a Knife, and some with a dented Paste-cutter, to make the Scollop; fold them like a Sword-knot; baste the Paste with Eggs, where it should join together; bake them on a Baking-plate; and when ready to serve, garnish with Currant-jelly, Apricock-marmalade, froughted Cream, or any thing else.

Massepains de Fleurs.

Sugar or Almond Paste, cut in Flowers.

CUT Almond-paste in Flowers, and in any Form, according to Taste and Invention; bake it a Moment in a slow Oven; this Paste will keep good from one

Week

Week to another, if kept in a warm or very dry Place; when you want to use it, put different Sorts of Jelly or Marmalade upon it.

Paniers de Vendange.

Small Baskets; they are called *de Vendage,* after the Baskets used to gather the Grapes. *Vendanger,* to vintage.

MAKE Baskets upon proper Moulds, prepared as directed for *Croquantes*; it is recommended to be done with Almond-paste, as being the most delicate; but may be made with all Sorts of firm Paste, for the Almond-paste is extremely short, and consequently apt to break; cut the Paste in long narrow Tape; make it either flat or twisted; after the Baskets are done, join the Handles with Sugar *Caramel*; give them what Colour you please, with a Pencil, with the different Colours used in Cookery, and what Fruits or Sweet-meats you please in it.

Petites Rossettes. Small Knots.

THIS is done after the same Manner, as the Sword-knots, only lesser, as a Tartlet is to a Tart; and garnished with different Sorts of Jelly, or Marmalade, &c. &c.

Petites Corbeilles de Massepains à la Glace.

Small Buckets of Sugar-paste, with Ice-cream.

MAKE small Buckets of this Paste in small Moulds, like Petit Pates; and make Baskets of common Paste, large enough to put the Buckets in it; join the Ears and Handles, with *Caramel* Sugar, after they are baked; make Covers for the Buckets of the same Paste; fill them with iced Cream, of any Sorts; and cover them,

them, and serve them in the Baskets: you may form this Paste to what Form you please, and colour it according to what you propose to represent; one's own Imagination in this is the best Rule; it may be made in the Form of Fruits, Snuff-boxes, or any thing else; and it may be served for Second-course Dishes, in its natural Colour, or for Dessert painted; these small Dishes, although of no Consequence of themselves, shew the Ingenuity and Delight the Workman takes in his Business, as those Things require a good deal of Time and Care.

Gâteaux à la Madeleine. Common small Cakes.

TO a Pound of Flour, put a Pound of Butter, eight Eggs, Yolks and Whites, three Quarters of a Pound of Sugar-powder, a Glass of Water, a little Lemon-peel, chopped very fine, dried Orange-flowers; work it well together; then cut it in Pieces, of what Bigness you please, to bake, and glaze them with Sugar.

Gateaux à la Neige.

Whipt Cream, like Snow.

MAKE small Cakes in the Form of Pâtes, with a good Paste; when they are baked, take off the Top, and take out as much of the Inside as you can, without breaking; fill them with good whipt Cream, and put the Covers on to serve.

Gâteaux de Niauffles. The Place most in repute for this Sort.

MAKE a good Puff-paste; roll it pretty thick, and cut in Lozenges, about the Bigness of the Palm of your Hand; brush it over with Yolk of Eggs, beat up, and strew Macaroni Drops Powder over them, with a little Powder of Orange-flowers, and Lemon-peel chopped very fine; stick Bits of scalded Sweet-almonds

in

in the Paste, pointed upwards; cover them with Paper in the Oven, to keep them of a palish Colour.

Gateau de Bourneville. The Name for the same Reason as before.

WORK about half a Pound of Flour, with five or six Eggs whole, some fine chopped Lemon-peel, few Drops of Orange-flower Water, a Spoonful of plain Water, a little Salt; then let it rest about an Hour; you will put about as much Butter as Paste; after work it well together; bake it in a Mould or Hoop; garnish it as you shall think proper, with Sugar or Nompareils, or Colours.

Biscuit de Turin, ou Gateau de Savoy. Savoy Cake.

TAKE an equal Weight of Eggs and Sugar; separate the Yolks and Whites; put the Sugar to the Yolks, with some Lemon-peel finely chopped, Powder of Orange-flowers, or a Spoonful of the Water; beat up this very well together, and also the Whites; which you mix with the Yolks, stirring continually, and half as much Weight of Flour, as you used of Eggs; pour it in the Vessel you intend to bake it in, well rubbed with Butter; bake it in a soaking Oven, about an Hour and a half; if it is of a good Colour, you may serve it without garnishing; and if not, as it may be too brown, or too pale, glaze it with a white Sugar-glaze, as directed in Almond-paste Croquante, or with any other Colours, as directed in the last.

Bonnet de Turquie à la Glace.

Turk's Cap, with Ice-cream.

MAKE a clear Paste, or Batter as the former; and butter the Mould, so called, to pour it in, to bake; when it is cold, cut off the Top gently, and a

good

good deal of the Inside; which dry in the Oven, till it can be reduced to Powder or Crums; boil a Pint of Cream and Sugar, according to Judgment; reduce it to half, and add the Crums in it; mix it well, to ice it to a certain Degree, that you may put it in the Cap, and cover it over with the Top to hide the Cream: you may masquerade the Outside as you think proper, or serve it plain, if of a good Colour.

Bonnet de Turquie en Surprise.

Sham Turk's Cap.

RUB the Cap-mould with Butter as the former, and bake a pretty thick Almond-paste in it; be careful how you take it out; garnish the Outside between the Ribs, with Jelly of different Colours, and the same Sort of Paste at Bottom, with different preserved Fruits.

Gateaux en Turbans.

THIS is the same Composition as the first Turk's Cap, only baked in small Moulds, ribbed or twisted in the same Manner as the large ones, and served in their natural Colour: *Bonnet aux Pistachés* the same, only adding what Quantities of pounded Pistachio-nuts you think proper, when you are mixing the other Ingredients.

Biscotins. Small Biscuits.

MAKE a Paste with a Quarter of a Pound of Flour, three Spoonfuls of fine Sugar-powder, as much Sweet-meat Marmalade; add Whites of Eggs, to work it pretty soft; with this Paste-form small Biscuits, to what Size and Shape you please.

Gateaux

Gâteaux en Feuillage. Feuillage, a rich Puff-paste, that scales off in small Leaves.

THIS is the finest Paste cut in Lozenges, or any other Form, baked singly, then served, five or six Pieces, one upon another, in the Form of a Sugar-loaf, with a Sugar-glaze.

Gâteau à la Polonoise. Polish Fashion Cake.

MIX a Handful of Flour with a Pint of good Cream, half a Pound of Beef-suet, melted and sifted, a Quarter of a Pound of Sugar-powder, half a Pound of Raisins stoned and chopped, dried Flowers of Orange, a Glass of Brandy, a little Coriander and Salt; bake it as all other Cakes, about an Hour, and glaze or garnish it.

Gâteaux au Sultan.

THIS is the same Preparation as the *Pâte à la Royale*, only mixing Lemon-peel finely chopped, dried Orange-flowers; when the Cake is ready for the Oven, strew the Top with Pistachio-nuts, mixed with Sugar and Whites of Eggs.

Gâteaux d'Amandes. Almond-cake.

TAKE half a Pound of Flour, half a Pound of pounded sweet Almonds, and five or six bitter with it, half a Pound of Sugar, six Eggs, and work it well all together; form it into a Cake; bake it on a sheet of Paper, well buttered; when cold, glaze it with a white Sugar-glaze: another Method for the same Sorts of Cakes; bake it in a Mould, or Baking-hoop; pound a Pound of sweet Almonds very fine, and one Dozen of bitter ditto, putting a little Whites of Eggs, to hinder them

them from turning to Oil; then put to it half a Pound of fine Sugar-powder by Degrees, two whole Eggs, Lemon-peel, finely chopped or rasped; when this is properly mixed, add eight Eggs, the Yolks and Whites first beat up separately; stir it, and mix it all properly; and pour it in the Mould, to bake about an Hour: serve it in its natural Colour.

Gâteaux à la Bechamel.

BOIL a Pint of Cream with few pounded sweet Almonds, and a little Coriander-seed; then sift it; use it to about a Pound of Flour, three Eggs, and about as much Butter, as it makes of Paste; finish it like all other Paste; and make Cakes with it, to what Shape and Bigness you please.

Gâteaux de Compiegne.

So called after the Place, as Banbury Cakes, &c.

MAKE a Mould with strong Paper, in the Form of a Muff; butter it well inside; fill it with a Paste, as directed for *Pâte à Brioche*; wherein you mix a little rasped Lemon-peel; when baked, take off the Paper; rub it all over with melted Sugar, or Whites of Eggs, and garnish it with Nompareils.

Gâteaux au Ris. Rice-cake.

TAKE what Quantity of Rice you think proper; boil it in good Broth, and some Hog's-lard; when it is cold, mix it with as much Flour as Rice, a good deal of Butter, some Eggs, and Salt; make a good Puff-paste of it; and make hot Cakes of what Shape and Bigness you please with it; rub them over with Eggs, before baking, to give them a good Colour.

Gâteaux de Pistache. Of Pistachio-nuts.

THIS is done after the same Manner, as the Almond-cake; only using the said Nuts instead of Almonds.

Gâteaux de Verjus. Of Verjuice-grapes preserved.

USE such Moulds as you do for Petit Pâtes, with the second-best Puff-paste; fill them with preserved Verjuice-grapes, or any other; cover them with the same Paste; solder them, wetting the Borders with Water, and pinching all round: you may make these Sorts of Cakes, with all Sorts of preserved Fruits; glaze them with Sugar, or serve in their natural Colour.

Gâteaux à la Dauphine.

USE the same Paste as directed by the Name of Pâte Royal; the Form gives them the Name, by being twisted in the Shape of the Fish so called, *Dauphin*.

Ramequins. Cheese-cakes.

TAKE good Parmesan-cheese, or Gruyere, viz. Swiss Cheese; you may also mix Cheshire with it; melt it in a Stew-pan, with a Bit of Butter, one or two Spoonfuls of Water; then add as much Flour, as will make it pretty thick, and quit the Sides of the Pan; put it in another Pan, and put Eggs to it, one by one; mixing well with a wooden Spoon, until it becomes pretty light and clear; add one or two pounded Anchovies, and a little Pepper; bake them singly upon a Baking-plate, or in Paper-cases of what Shape you please; they require but a short Time in a soft Oven; and serve quite hot.

Ramequins, (*Vole-au-vent*).

Light to fly with the Wind.

MAKE the Paste as the former; only put the Yolks of Eggs, and beat up the Whites alone; which, when properly froughted, add to the Paste, and mix it all together very well; use the finest Puff-paste, rolled very thin, and wrap a little of the Ramequin Preparation in the Paste; pinch them round; bake them about a Quarter of an Hour; serve quite hot.

Ramequin à la Touloufe. A City in France.

THIS is the same Preparation as the former; only baked upon toasted Bread, or without toasting; cut into what Shape you like.

Timbales.

A Mould so called, for being in the Shape of a Kettle-drum.

IT is only the Form of it which makes the Difference between these and the *Gateaux au Verjus*, just mentioned; as they are filled with preserved Fruits, or Sweet-meat, after they are baked, covered over, and glazed with Sugar-glaze.

Petits Choux. A small Sort of Choudee.

USE the Paste as directed in *Pâte Royale*, with a little rasped Lemon-peel, Orange-flowers, few Macaroni-drops bruised; drop it with a Spoon upon a Baking-plate, in a small Quantity, a little Sugar-powder over; bake in a soft Oven.

Biscuit au Clinquant.
Beautified with Tinsel. Tinsel Cake.

MAKE the same Preparations as directed for *Biscuit de Turin*, Page 411; make three or four large Paper-cases, a Sheet to each; rub them well with Butter, and pour the above Composition in it; bake in a soft Oven; take the Cakes out of the Papers, while hot, and cut one to the Largeness of the Bottom of the Dish you intend for Table; the rest must be cut lesser and lesser, to finish in the Form of a Sugar-loaf, and hollow in the middle; solder each Piece with Sugar Caramel; and when it is finished, pour some Caramel Sugar round it, as if tied with Pack-thread: you will find how to prepare the Sugar in Page 407, under the Direction of *Croquante au Caramel*.

Talmouses. Cheese-cakes of a different kind from Ramequin.

BOIL a Bit of Butter in a little Water and a little Salt; thicken it with as much Flour as it will take, stirring it on the Fire constantly until it become quite a Paste; then mix the Eggs with it one by one, to make it almost as liquid as a thick Batter; and mix some good Cream-cheese with it; bake it in good Puff-paste, coloured with Yolks of Eggs: serve hot or cold.

Talmouses de Saint Denis.

MIX a Spoonful of Flour with a fresh Cream-cheese well drained, commonly called Curds, a little Salt, a proper Quantity of Eggs, and finish as the former. *St. Denis*, the Place famous for these Cakes.

Flancs. A large Custard.

CUT a Bit of good Paste pretty thick to the Size of the Dish you intend for Table, and a pretty Border round it about an Inch high or more; or if for small Custard, in proportion; and fill it to about half with the same Compofition as the laft Cheefe-cakes; you may alfo fill it with Cream firft boiled with Sugar, Cinnamon, Coriander-feed, and ftrained; then a few Yolks of Eggs beat, and added to it, and baked in the fame Manner as the Cheefe-cakes.

Darioles. A Mould fo called.

MAKE the Pafte pretty thin; rub the Moulds with Butter infide, and prepare thefe as *Petits Pâtés*; when the Pafte is half baked, drop a Spoonful of the forementioned Preparation in them, or prepare it after this Manner; beat up a little Flour with three or four Eggs, a little Salt, Milk, and Sugar; it muft be about the Confiftence of a thick Batter: the fame may be done in raifed Pafte without Moulds; then they are called *Darioles à Pâté.*

Feuillantine. A Cream-cake.

THESE are made to any Size all after the fame Manner; ufe the *Pâte de Feuilletage* for it, which you put in a Mould or Pan of what Bignefs is moft convenient, or a good raifed Cruft without Mould; put in it whatever Cream you think proper; cover it like a Pie, and garnifh it according to Fancy.

Echaudés au Sel. Dumpling-pafte.

MAKE a Pafte with Flour, Milk, and Salt and Yeaft; let it reft fome time in a warm Place to foment; then cut the Pafte in Bits of what Bignefs you think proper, and boil them a good while; let them cool; then cut each in two, and foak them in Milk, Sugar, and Lemon-peel about an Hour; drain and flour them to fry; alfo dip them in Oil or melted Butter to broil, bafting with the fame as they were dipped in. *Brioches* made with the Pafte under that Denomination, may be dreffed after the fame Manner.

Puits d'Amour.   From Moulds to cut Paste so called.

THIS is a Diminutive of the Tinsel Biscuit, as these Moulds are commonly made five or six, each lesser than the other, to finish by the smallest; they are made with the best Puff-paste, and baked singly, served one upon another, with Jelly betwixt, or none; the Moulds are to be had by that Name at all Braziers and Tin Shops in London.

Gobelets à la Moëlle.   Marrow-tumblers.

MAKE a Cream as directed for *Tourte à la Moëlle*, Page 401; rub the Moulds with Butter inside; they ought to be plain, and about an Inch and a half deep, but may be done with others; put about a good Spoonful of the Cream in each, and bake in the Oven; you may serve them plain, or garnished with Nompareils.

Différents entremets de Biscuits.

Different second or last Course Dishes of Biscuit Paste.

WITH the Composition of the *Biscuit de Turin*, (see page 411), you may make what kind of small Pastry you please; it is the Form and Moulds which gives the Name; some you glaze with Sugar, some masqueraded with Colours or Nompareils, and baked of a fine Colour, are mostly served in, without any Alterations.

Genoises.   Olive-fritures.

MAKE a thin Puff-paste cut in small Bits, and in each put a little prepared Cream as under the Direction of *Franchipane* boiled, and mix a few Pistachio-nuts bruised in it; wet the Borders with Water or Yolks of Eggs, to pinch them close; fry of a good Colour; you may also glaze them brown or white; these are also done with Apples, Marmalade, or any other, either baked or fried.

Canellons. In the form of a Cane or small Gun.

MAKE a pretty hard dried Paste with a little melted Butter, a Spoonful or two of Water, some rasped Lemon-peel, one Egg, about a Quarter of a Pound of Flour and half as much Sugar; roll it very thin; make a little Cane of Card-paper; butter it well outside, and wrap it in some of the Paste cut for that purpose; bake it a few Minutes; then take the Paper or Cane out, and fill the Paste with Currant-jelly or any other.

DES ENTREMETS DE CREME, LEGUMES, & AUTRES EN GRAS & EN MAIGRE.

OF LAST COURSE DISHES, OF CREAMS, GARDENINGS, AND OTHERS, GRAS OR MEAGER.

Crême Legere. Light Cream.

BOIL a Pint of Cream until it is reduced to half, with a Quarter of a Pound of Sugar; then take it off the Fire; put a few bruised Macaroni-drops in it, Lemon-peel, finely chopped, six Whites of Eggs well beat up; put the Table-dish on an Ash-fire; pour the Cream in it; cover it with a brazing-pan Cover with a little Fire upon it; serve it hot: if it does not take Colour enough in this Manner, colour it with a Salamander; it ought to be a fine brown, and not too much done, but to shake like a Jelly.

Crême au Chapelet. From the Border made in the Form of Beads.

BOIL a Pint of Cream; reduce it to half, and in it Lemon-peel, Cinnamon, Coriander-seed and Sugar, the Skin of a Fowl's Gizzard, chopped; strain it in a Stamine; prepare a Border for the Dish, with some pounded Chocolate, a Spoonful of melted Gum-dragon, thick and sifted through a Cloth; put fine Sugar to it until it becomes

comes a hard Paste; then roll Bits of it in Beads, and put them to dry; garnish the Dish round with it; the Cream being finished as the former, only left white; the Beads are joined together with Carameled Sugar in the Form of Crosses or any other, and made to stand up round the Cream.

Crême en Quadrille.
Four Squares, or Partition of four Colours.

MAKE a Bit of hard Paste with Flour, one Yolk of an Egg, and half of the White; make a Border with Part of it, and four Partitions in the Dish of what Shape you please; rub the Bottom with Yolks of Eggs to make the Paste stick; bake it a Moment; then boil a Pint of Cream, reduce it to three Parts, and fine Sugar in it; mix Part of it with some ready-boiled Chocolate, which you put in one Partition; also one Part mixed with Caramel Sugar, and put it in the Partition over-against the first: add four Yolks of Eggs to the Remainder to fill the two others, and strew Nompareils upon one.

Crême à la Croix de Malthe. Malta Cross.

FORM a Malta Cross with the same Sort of Paste as the former upon the Dish intended for Table, and bake it as the last; put a white Cream in the middle, and some mixed with Coffee round it; bake it between two Ashes-fires; which is also called *Bain-Marie*, for Creams.

Crême à la Sultane.

BOIL and reduce a Pint of Cream to three Parts, with Sugar, Lemon-peel; when it is half cold, add a little Flour, six Yolks of Eggs; sift it in a Sieve, and pour it on the Table-dish to bake like the last, without colouring; when half done, put some Orange-flour, preserved, upon it, as to appear when it is done: these Orange-flowers are dried and prepared like burnt Almonds: Almonds after this Manner may serve to garnish this Cream; they are both called after the same Name, viz. *Pralinée*.

Crême à l'Abbesse. The Lady Abbess of a Convent.

Nuns Cream.

BOIL a Pint of Cream with Cinnamon, Coriander-seed, Lemon-peel and Sugar; reduce it to three Parts; then mix six Yolks of Eggs with it, and sift it in a Sieve; then add burnt Orange-flowers, dried preserved Citron, a few Macaroni-biscuits bruised, a Bit of Chocolate pounded; and finish it as the former, between two slow Fires.

Crême à la Mariée. Bride-cream.

BEAT up six Yolks of Eggs, and two of the Whites, with a Spoonful of Flour, Lemon-peel, chopped very fine, a little Orange-flowers, Chocolate and Macaroni as the last, half a Pint of Cream, a good Quantity of Sugar according to Taste; boil it on the Fire about a Quarter of an Hour; then pour it on the Dish; colour the Top with a hot Shovel.

Crême frite. Fried Cream.

BOIL a Pint of Cream with Sugar, Lemon-peel, Coriander-seed, Cinnamon; reduce it to half; then mix six Yolks of Eggs beat up, and sift it in a Sieve; bake as all others, only rather more when it is cold; cut it in small square Pieces, or in any other Shape; flour them to fry, and serve with a Sugar-glaze; which is done easily by strewing a little Sugar-powder over, and a hot Shovel.

Autre

Autre Crême frite. Another fried Cream.

BEAT up three Spoonfuls of Flour with six whole Eggs, half a Pint of Cream, Macaroni-biscuits bruised, Citron-chips, Orange-flowers, and Sugar; boil all together, stirring continually; when it is boiled quite thick, drop it upon a Dish, floured in the Bottom, about a Spoonful separately, and flour it again over; let it cool, and fry it as the last; you may glaze some, and serve some without glazing.

Crême de Chocolat.

BOIL a Quarter of a Pound bruised, with three Half-pints of Cream, Sugar in Proportion as the Chocolate requires; reduce it by boiling to about one Pint; add six Yolks of Eggs beat up, and mix it very well; bake it between two Fires as other Creams, without Border.

Crême de Caffé.

MIX three Cups of good Coffee, with one Pint of Cream, Sugar according to Taste; boil it together; reduce it about one third: observe that the Coffee must be done as if it was for drinking alone, and settled very clear, before you mix it with the Cream; finish this as the last.

Crême d'Herbages de ce que l'on veut.

With Garden-herbs of what kind you please.

BOIL three Half-pints of Cream to one Pint, and Sugar sufficient; a few Minutes before you take it off the Fire, put what Herbs you think proper to be in it, just long enough to give it the Taste of whatever it is, as Tea, Anise-seed, Charvil, Taragon, Sellery, Parsley, &c. &c. add a Spoonful of Flour, six Yolks of Eggs; mix it well

well together; fift it in a Sieve upon the Table-difh; finifh it as the laft; it is called by the Name of Herbs or Seeds.

Crême Veloutée. Veloutée, velveted, foft, rich, requiring no Addition.

THIS is the fame Cream as directed in the fecond Cream *au Chapelet*; only it is ferved in the Table-difh alone, without any Border or garnifhing, and kept very white in the baking between Afhes-fire.

Crême Brûlée. Burnt Cream.

BEAT up a Spoonful of Flour with fix Yolks of Eggs and four of the Whites, Orange-flowers, Citron, Macaroni-drops, all finely chopped, three Half-pints of Cream, fome Sugar; boil it about half an Hour on a flow Fire, ftirring conftantly; when it is reduced about one third Part, and pretty thick, pour it on the Table-difh; make a Caramel with Sugar and Water; when it is of a fine Cinnamon Colour, pour it gently round, and over Part of the Cream; you may alfo brown it with a hot Salamander or Shovel, and keep it a while like the reft on a very flow Heat.

Crême de Vermicel ou de Ris.

With Vermicelly or Rice.

BOIL fome Vermicelly or Rice in Milk, until it is to a Marmalade; let it cool, and mix it very well with a Pint of Cream, Macaroni-drops, Orange-flowers, Lemon-peel, all chopped very fine, a little pounded Cinnamon, five whole Eggs well beat up, Sugar-powder according to Tafte; pour it on the Table-difh; bake it as ufual, or in a foft Oven.

Crême

Crême à la (*Strasbourg.*) A City in (Alsatia,) or the Inventor's Name.

BOIL a Pint of Cream and Sugar; reduce it to about half; put the Skin of a Gizzard chopped in it, a Moment before you take it off the Fire; put the Dish on a very slow Fire a little while; then sift the Cream in it, when it has been a little while between two Fires, as usual; ice it on the same Dish without stirring it.

Crême à la Dauphine.

BEAT up six Yolks of Eggs, and a Spoonful of Flour, Sugar, Orange-flowers, Citron, Macaroni Drops, a Pint of Cream; boil it about half an Hour, stirring continually; add a little Cream, if it become too thick in the boiling; when it is almost cold, put the Whites of four Eggs beat up to it; and pour Part of the Cream in the Dish, then Slices of Spunge-biscuits, or any other Sorts, then Cream, and so on; finish by the Cream; bake it in the Oven, and glaze it, as already directed for Cream-glazing.

Crême au Gratin.

BEAT up half a Dozen of Eggs, and a Spoonful of Flour, chopped preserved Citron, Macaroni, and Orange-flowers, *Pralinées,* a Pint of Cream and Sugar; put the Dish on a pretty smart Fire, and pour the Cream in it, by little and little, to catch at Bottom without burning; it only requires proper Attention, to make a very palatable Cream; when done, glaze the Top with a little Sugar, and a hot Shovel or Salamander.

Crême au Caramel.

BOIL a Pint of Cream, with Lemon-peel, and Coriander-seed; strain it, and make a *Caramel,* as directed

rected for *Croquante au Caramel*; when it is of a good Colour, mix it with the Cream, and give it a Boiling; then add five or six Yolks of Eggs, beat up with a Spoonful of Flour; boil all together a Moment; and finish it as most usual, between two slow Fires.

Crême Meringuée. Whites of Eggs froughted, called a *Meringue*: also a Syringe made on Purpose to squirt a thick Cream to fry.

BEAT up six Yolks of Eggs, one Spoonful of Flour, preserved Citron, Orange-flowers the same, Macaroni-drops, all finely chopped, a Pint of Cream and Sugar; boil it together slowly about half an Hour, then put it on the Table-dish; smooth it even with a Knife; frought up the Whites with a little Sugar; put the Frought as it is whipped upon the Cream; finish it Sugar-loaf Fashion: it will stand so, if the Eggs are well beat up; strew a little fine Powder-sugar over it, and bake it in a mild Oven, as for Biscuits.

Autre Crême meringuée.

With the Syringe, viz. squirted Cream.

BEAT up the same Quantity of Eggs, with a Spoonful of Flour or two; boil half a Pint of Cream, with Cinnamon, Coriander-seeds, one Bay-leaf; put the Eggs to it, to boil and thicken a Moment; it must be pretty thick, which you may do by adding Flour and Sugar, according to Discretion; warm some frying Hog's-lard, ready to fry; and squirt the Cream in it, to fry of a fine Colour.

Crême soufflée. Raised or Puff Cream.

PREPARE a Cream, as the first *Meringuée*; boil it in the same Manner; then add six Yolks of Eggs beat up, and mix all together with a little more Cream;

put

put it on the Table-dish; bake it in a middling Oven; it will raise pretty high; and to keep it so, leave it in the Oven, till you are ready to serve, as it will sink, if it is let to cool.

Crême à la Reine. Queen's Cream.

BOIL a Pint of Cream to half reduced, with fine Sugar, Orange-flower Water; when half cold, mix it with six Whites of Eggs well beat up; bake it between two very moderate Fires, and to remain in its natural Colour.

Crême d'Oeufs à l'Eau. Eggs and Water Cream.

BOIL a Pint of Water to about half, slowly, with Cinnamon in it, Coriander-seeds, Lemon-peel, Orange-flower Water, a small Quantity of Sugar, and preserved Citron; let it cool a while, then mix six Yolks of Eggs, a Spoonful of Flour, well beat up together; sift it in a Sieve; bake it between two slow Fires; and colour it brown, with a little powdered Sugar, and a hot Salamander.

Crême au Blanc-Mangé.

POUND a Quarter of a Pound of sweet Almonds, and the Breast of a roasted Fowl; add six Yolks of Eggs, and few Spoonfuls of good Cullis, a little Water, boiled with Coriander, and a little Sugar; strain it in a sifting Cloth, several Times, rubbing with a wooden Spoon; bake it as the former

Crême d'Ecrevisses. Craw-fish Cream.

BOIL a Pint of Cream, and fine Sugar; reduce it to about half; pound the Carcases of eight or more Craw-fish, and put this Cream to it, and the Skin of a

Fowl's

Fowl's Gizzard, for about a Quarter of an Hour; then sift it as the last; and finish it after the same Manner: you may serve it in its natural Coolness, or ice it.

Crême Bachique; or Bacchus, from Bacchanal's Feast, kept in Honour of the God of Wine, as the Receipt shows.

BOIL three Half-pints of sweet Wine, about a Quarter of an Hour, and a little Sugar; when half cold, add it to one Dozen of Yolks of Eggs, well beat up; bake it as usual, and ice it after.

Crême à la Bourgogne. Burgundy Cream.

BOIL a Pint of Milk, with a Bit of Lemon-peel, Orange-flower Water, a Bit of Sugar; and boil a Quarter of a Pound of Rice in a little Water, till it is tender, and become thick; then add the Milk to it, by little and little, until all is boiled quite thick; sift it in a Stamine as a Cullis; and mix it well with six or eight Whites of Eggs, well beat up; put it in the Table-dish; and bake it in a mild Oven, or with a Brazing-pan Cover; when ready to serve, glaze it with a little Sugar strewed over it, and the Salamander, or a hot Shovel, to catch slightly upon the Sugar.

Crême de Ris au Bouillon.

Rice-cream boiled in Broth.

BOIL about a Quarter of a Pound of Rice in Broth, until it is boiled very tender, and pretty thick; put a couple of bitter Almonds pounded; when half boiled, a little Coriander, and some good Cullis; boil all together some time, then strain it in a Stamine, and finish it as usual; serve hot: also a Rice-cream is made to serve cold, with Rice-flour, Cream, Lemon-peel, Sugar;

gar; boil it some time; sift as the first, and finish it in the same Manner, as all cold Cream; and most Creams ought to be served cold, as it is a Dish that is commonly eat at the latter Part of the *Repast*; if it is served hot, then it is neither one nor the other.

Crême à la Duchesse. See Cream *à la Sultane.*

IT is prepared the same on the first Part, only glazed with whipt Whites of Eggs, and Sugar, when ready to serve, and coloured with a hot Shovel, instead of being garnished, with Orange-flowers preserved, or burnt, as what is called burnt Almonds.

Crême à la Nourrice.

Nurse-fashion, or Nurse-cream.

BEAT up six Yolks of Eggs, and two Whites, with a Spoonful of Flour, a Pint of Cream, Sugar, Citron, Orange-flowers, Macaroni-drops, as before directed; boil this together, stirring continually; when it is grown pretty thick, pour it on the Dish for Table; and simmer it a good while on a slow Fire, sufficient to make it catch a little, and colour the Top with a hot Shovel.

Baignets Italiens. Fritures Italian Fashion.

BOIL a Quarter of a Pound of Rice, very tender in Milk; when it is pretty thick, put a little Salt, some fine Sugar, Orange-flower preserved, and green chopped Lemon-peel, a Handful of Flour, three whole Eggs; mix it all very well; and add some Currants, or Couple of good Apples, peeled and cut in small Bits; butter a Sheet of Paper; and put this Preparation upon singly, with a Spoon, each about the Bigness of a large Nutmeg; put this Sheet of Paper into hot Friture;

ture; when the *Baignets* quit the Paper, take them out, and continue frying, till they are of a good Colour; take them out, to drain upon a Sieve; and strew a little Sugar-powder upon; and serve them as hot as possible.

Baignets à l'Angloise. English Fashion.

BEAT up six whole Eggs, with a good Handful of Flour, Salt, fine Sugar, green Lemon-peel chopped, Orange-flower Water, Macaroni-drops bruised, half a Pint of good rich Cream; rub the Inside of a Stewpan with Butter; and boil this Preparation slowly, between two Fires, without stirring it; when it is simmered thick enough, turn it over upon a Dish, and let it cool to harden it; when you mean to use it, cut it in small Pieces, and fry it of a good Colour: finish as the last.

Baignets en Surtout. Masked. *Surtout,* a Covering or Frock.

MAKE a good Cream as directed for *Franchipane* or Marrow; it must be pretty thick; when it is cold, roll it in small Balls, and dip in a good thick Wine-batter, to fry; glaze them with Sugar, and a hot Shovel: serve quite hot.

Baignets d'Amandes. Of Almonds.

POUND half a Pound of sweet Almonds, and six or eight bitter ones, Orange-flowers, chopped Lemon-peel, Sugar in Proportion, a Handful of Flour, two or three Whites of Eggs; pound all together some Time, few Drops of Water, or more Whites of Eggs, to make it of a proper Suppleness, to roll it in little Balls; roll them in Flour, to fry as Force-meat Bullets; strew a little fine Sugar-powder upon, when ready to serve.

Baignets soufflés de Pâte.   Raised Paste Fritures.

MAKE a Paste as directed in *Pâte Royale*, Page 375; mix preserved Citron, Orange flowers chopped fine, and Macaroni-drops, as usual; spread it upon a Dish, with a little Flour under and over; cut it, to roll in Bullets, the Bigness of a Nutmeg; fry in a middling hot Fritures, on a slow Fire, as they require a longer Time to raise, than a lighter Composition; fry of a good brown Colour; drain them as usual: serve quite hot, with rasped Sugar over.

Baignets de Pain à Chanter.   Wafer-baignets.

CUT two pretty large Pieces of Wafer; wet them a little to hinder from breaking; lay a little Sweet-meat, or a good ready-boiled Cream, between two Bits; wet the Border round, to pinch it together; dip each gently in a frying Batter, pretty thick; fry as usual of a good Colour, about a Dozen for a Dish: serve with Sugar as the last.

Baignets de Blanc-mangé.

MIX a Quarter of a Pound of Rice-flour, with a couple of Eggs, some fine Sugar, a little Salt, a Pint of Cream; simmer it on a slow Fire, about an Hour, stirring it often for fear it should burn at Bottom; when it is quite thick, add pounded Breast of Fowl, Orange-flowers, Macaroni-drops, fine chopped Citron; flatten like a Paste with Flour; let it cool; and cut it in what Shape you please to fry; finish with rasped Sugar as usual, or glazed.

Baignets de Pommes en Piédesteaux.
Apple-fritures on Pedestals.

CUT ten or twelve good baking Apples in two, or leave them whole if small ones; peel them, and take out the Pippins with a Gorer; marinade them three or four Hours in Brandy, Sugar, Orange-flower Water, Lemon-peel; drain and flour them to fry, in a very hot Friture, and glaze them with Sugar, and a hot Salamander, or Shovel: the Pedestals are made with Bits of Puff-paste, baked, cut with *Puits-damour-moulds*; raise them properly upon each other, intermixed as you think proper.

Baignets de Pommes en surprise.

Masked, &c. &c.

CUT eight large Apples in two; hollow each Piece inside; marinade them as the last; when ready to fry, fill the Hollow with Sweet-meat, or Jelly; wrap each Piece in a thin Paste; dip them in a good Batter, to fry of a fine brown Colour; powder with Sugar, and glaze some for Variety.

Baignets à la Mariée. Bride-fritures.

PEEL and gore the Apples; and cut each in four or five round Slices; marinade them as the former; and dip them in a good Batter made of Cream, Sugar, Flour, Wine, and Yolks of Eggs; powder with Sugar, or glaze them according to all others.

Baignets de Pêches & d'Abricots.

Of Peaches and Apricocks.

THEY are peeled and marinaded like the Apples; you may either wrap them in a very thin Paste, and dip in Batter, or only flour them to fry; serve very hot with rasped Sugar.

Baignets à la Crême. Cream-fritures.

BOIL half a Pint of Cream, with a little Salt and Sugar, the Bigness of an Egg of Butter; put as much Flour to it as the Cream can soak; make it

pretty

pretty dry, by keeping it on the Fire; then work it with a couple of Eggs; roll it pretty thick; cut it in Lozenges to fry, and glaze them with Sugar.

Baignets de Fraises. Of Strawberries.

MAKE a Paste with Flour, a Spoonful of fine Oil, chopped Lemon-peel, half Whites of Eggs beat up, and half white Wine sufficient to make it pretty soft, just fit to drop with a Spoon; mix some large Strawberries with it; and drop the Bigness of a Nutmeg in the hot Friture, as many as you propose to make; be careful to take them out, in the same Manner as they are draining, and glaze them with Sugar.

Baignets de Sureau, & de Vigne.

Of Elder-flowers, and Vine-leaves.

THOSE of Elder-flowers are made while in Bloom, in breaking off, small tender Branches also of Vine, in breaking the Tops in small Bunches; both to be marinaded as the Apples, on Pedestals; when drained, dip them in good thick Batter to fry; and serve with rasped Sugar, as most usual.

Baignets à l'Espagnole.

Spanish Fashion, or Orange-fritures.

TAKE one or two preserved Oranges, which you cut in as many Pieces as you think proper; make a good thick Batter, with sweet Wine, and finish these as all others: the same may by done with Lemon, Bergamotte, or any other Fruits.

Baignets de Ramequins.

MAKE a Paste as directed for Ramequins, Page 415. flatten it pretty much, and put it to cool upon a

Pewter-dish, with a little Flour under and over; when you are ready to fry, cut in small Pieces; roll it about the Bigness of a Nutmeg; fry of a good Colour: serve very hot, with rasped Sugar over.

Baignets à la Dauphine.

MAKE a Paste rather supple, with an equal Quantity of Flour and Sugar, Macaroni-drops bruised, preserved Orange-flowers, Lemon-peel, all chopped very fine; mix it with Whites of Eggs, until it is to what Consistence required, which is to be just hard enough to bear working with a Rolling-pin; roll it in Sheets, about the Thickness of half a Crown; let it cool to harden; then cut it in what Shape and Form you please, with Moulds of any Sorts of Flowers; fry this as usual, and glaze with Sugar.

Baignets à la Fermiere.
Farmer, or House-wife Fashion.

MIX some well-drained fresh Cream-cheese, with Salt, two Spoonfuls of Flour, and few Eggs, a small Quantity of Sugar; when this is all properly worked together, butter a Sheet of Paper, and drop it upon separately; put the Paper with the Cream in hot Fritures; when they loosen from the Paper, take it out, and continue frying briskly of a good Colour; serve with rasped Sugar over.

Baignets à la Nonnette. Nuns Fritures.

THIS is done with *Pâte Royale*, see Page 375. flour it, to make it of a proper Consistence; and cut it in what Shape you please to fry; and finish as usual.

Baignets en Caisses. In Paper-cases.

MAKE the same Preparation, as those au Blanc-mangé, all to the Meat-part, which is not to be; prepare

pare one Dozen or more of small Paper-cases in different Shapes; rub the Inside with Butter, and fry in a very hot Friture; when done, take them out of the Paper, and glaze that Part that was in the Paper, with Sugar, and a Salamander, or dip them in carameled Sugar.

Baignets de plusieurs Façons. Of different Sorts.

MIX a fresh Cream-cheese with five or six Eggs, some Salt and Sugar, a Pint of Cream and Flour, sufficiently to make it pretty substantial; boil it, stirring continually; when become quite thick, spread it upon a Dish; flour it first, and over it; let it cool; cut it to what Shape you like; you may mix Almonds, Citron, Orange-flowers, Pistachio-nuts, or any Thing else; whatever of these you mix with it, gives the Name.

Baignets Mignons are made of a Cream Veloutée, baked pretty hard, cut in Pieces, rolled in Flour, and fried; glaze them with Sugar, and a hot Shovel.

Rôtie (Toast) *à la Minime.*

An Order of Friars so called.

CUT pretty large Pieces of Bread-crums, and fry them in Oil; put them in the Table-dish, when properly drained; and mix chopped Parsley, Shallots, Capers, Pepper, and a pounded Anchovy, with some good Oil; pour this over the Toast; and garnish round with Fillets of Anchovies soaked.

Rôtie à la Genoise. Italian Toast.

LARD a French Roll with half Ham and half Anchovies; then cut it in Toasts, and a thin Slice of Bacon; dip each in a good thick Batter, made mostly with Eggs; fry slowly, and drain them very well with a Linen-cloth; serve a Ravigotte-sauce under: see Sauce Ravigotte, Page 38.

Rôtie à l'Infante.

Spanish Fashion; from *Infanta*, Spanish Princess.

MAKE the same Preparation, as directed for *Crême à la Moëlle*, Page 401. make an Almond-paste, which you prepare as a Toast; raise a little Border; bake them; and when cold, pour some of this Cream in it, as high as the Borders; brush it over with Whites of Eggs, beat up with Sugar; and colour them with a hot Shovel.

Rôties au Mortier.

Pounded in a Mortar; pounded Toast.

HAVE a Bit of rich Paste, which you put in a Mortar, with a Veal-kidney roasted, a little of the Fat, Salt and Sugar, two or three bitter Almond-biscuits, or the Almonds alone, Orange-flowers, Lemon-peel, and a little preserved Citron; pound all this together, and add four Whites of Eggs, beat up, to mix it; put this upon Bread-crums, cut as Toasts; bake in the Oven.

Rôties de Bretagne. Brittany Toast.

CHOP all Sorts of Sallading-herbs, and mix them with Salt, Pepper and Butter, a Lemon-squeeze; serve this upon toasted Bread.

Rôties de Foies gras. Fat Liver Toast.

MAKE a Farce, finely chopped, with Bread soaked in Cream, Truffles, one or two fat Livers, Marrow, Parsley, Shallots, Pepper and Salt, all well mixed with Eggs; spread it upon Pieces of Bread, cut in Toasts; Bread, and Farce, much of an equal Thickness;

smooth

smooth it over with a Knife, dipped in Yolks of Eggs; strew Bread-crums over; fry them: serve a little clear Sauce under.

Rôties de Rognons de Veau. Veal-kidney Toast.

MINCE a roasted Kidney, with half of its Fat; season it with Pepper and Salt, chopped Shallots, Parsley, a little green sweet Basil; mix it together with Yolks of Eggs; lay it upon Pieces of Bread as the former, or cut the Bread in what Shape you think proper; finish them with Eggs, and Bread-crums; put them in a Baking-dish, upon thin Slices of Lard, to bake in the Oven; when done, drain the Fat off, and wipe the Bread with a Linen-cloth; serve with a little Gravy under.

Rôties au Jambon. Ham-toast.

CUT as many thin Slices of Ham, as you propose making Toasts; it must be soaked some Time, excepting it should be quite fresh; soak the Slices of Ham, in a Stew-pan, over a slow Fire; turn them once or twice, it requires but a short Time to do; take the Ham out, and fry the Bread in the Fat; you may add a little Butter; put them on the Table-dish, and the Slices of Ham upon; keep it warm; add a little Cullis, in the same Pan, a little Vinegar, and Pepper; boil it a Moment, stirring with a Spoon: serve this Sauce upon the Toast: you may make the same with fresh Bacon, also pickled Pork, which is to be dipped in Batter, and fried: serve upon fried Bread, with a little Sauce under.

Rôties de Foies de Raies, & autres.

Of Scate Livers, and others.

MINCE the Livers of any Sorts of Fish, also Parsley, Shallots, Capers, Pepper and Salt; simmer it on the Fire some Time, with a good Bit of Butter; then let it cool; fry some Bread in Butter, cut in different Shapes; lay this Preparation upon, and Cross-barred over with Fillets of Anchovies; baste with melted Butter, and Bread-crums; bake in a mild Oven, about half an Hour, on a Baking-plate; and serve with a little melted Butter, and a good Lemon-squeeze.

Rôties à l'Allemande. German Fashion.

THE Remainder of a Ragout of Salpicon will do for this as well as to make a fresh one; chop it finer than for a Ragout, and mix a little chopped Parsley and Shallots with it, and two Yolks of Eggs; reduce it very thick on the Fire; when it is cold, put it upon toasted Bread, cut to what Form you please; stick Bits of hard Yolks in it, and rub it over with raw, beat up; garnish with Bread-crums; fry in a very hot Friture, or bake in the Oven: serve a little Cullis-sauce under, with a good Lemon-squeeze, see Page 289. for Salpicon.

Rôties de Légumes. Of Garden-greens, &c.

MAKE a Ragout of Spinages, or any other; season it as if for the Table, without Toast; when it is cold, mix it well with few Yolks of Eggs; and finish after the same Manner, with Eggs and Bread-crums; fry or bake.

Rôties en Rochers.

Rock, to look like Biscuits so called.

MAKE a Cream as directed for *Franchipane*, Page 401. when it is cold, mix it with four Yolks of Eggs, and beat the Whites to frought; spread the Cream upon Pieces of fried Bread, cut in different Shapes;

Shapes; mix some Sugar with the Whites; and put the Frought upon indifferently, a little rasped Sugar over; bake in a soft Oven; serve dry, hot or cold.

Rôties soufflées.
Puffed or raised. *Soufflées*, blown.

POUND a Breast of a roasted Fowl, with some Beef-marrow, Parmesan-cheese, five Yolks of Eggs, and the Whites whipped to Frought; prepare it upon Pieces of Bread, cut like Toasts, and fried in Butter; rub them over with Yolks and Whites of Eggs; and garnish with Bread-crums and Parmesan-cheese mixed; bake in the Oven, and serve a good relishing Cullis-Sauce under; you may make a Toast with Truffles, Mushrooms, or any thing else.

Pommes en Farbalat. Apples festooned.

PEEL some fine golden Pippins, or any other good stewing Apples; gore them whole, and stew them to three Parts with Sugar, and a little Water; make the Syrup pretty rich, to clog to the Apples; wrap them round with a thin Paste; cut with a Paste-cutter, which are mostly scolloped; and make Knots or Flowers with the same Paste, to put on the Top of the Apples; rasp some Sugar over, and bake a Moment in the Oven.

Pommes en Colimaçon. In the Shape of Snails.

MAKE a Marmalade of Apples, as directed for Tarts of the same; make a thin Paste, in which put some of this Marmalade, and give the Shape of Snails, or any other, and accordingly they are called; brush them over with Whites of Eggs, froughted with Sugar; give a good Colour in the Oven; although this is directly Apple-puffs, as Variety of Shapes for the same Thing is agreeable, according as you would have them, they must be directed by Names.

Pommes en surprise, unexpected. Masked Apples.

PREPARE the Apples as directed for *Farbalat*; only make a larger Gore in the Middle; let them cool to fill with what Sort of Sweet-meats you please; wrap them in thin Paste, and garnish with small Flowers, or any thing else cut according to Fancy; rasp some Sugar over, and bake them in a soft Oven.

Pommes farcies. Stuffed Apples.

GORE them as the last, and fill them with a good Franchipane-cream; brush the Outside with Whites of Eggs to make as much Sugar-powder stick to as possible; bake them in a mild Oven upon the Dish you intend for Table; serve either cold or hot.

Pommes glacées. In Jelly, or glazed.

PEEL them and leave the Tails; gore at the opposite Side, not quite through; boil them with Half a Pint of red Wine, some Sugar, a Spoonful of Brandy; observe that this is calculated for about a dozen, and so in Proportion; simmer them slowly, that they may not break; when almost done enough, take them out, and reduce the Syrup to a *Caramel*, and put the Apples to rub them all over with it; you may serve them so, or wrapped in a thin Paste, and finished as directed for *Farbalat*, glazed with a white Glaze, as directed in *Croquante*.

Pommes au Chocolat, *Pommes à la Crême* of any Sorts, are finished after the same Manner, either glazed or not.

Pommes au Gratin à la Crême; when boiled as the last, put some prepared Cream in the Table-dish, on a slow Fire, to catch a little at Bottom; the Apples upon, and more Cream over; keep the Dish some time between two slow Fires.

Pain

Pain de Jambon à la Mayence.

Ham-roll, or cold Loaf.

CUT thin Slices of ready boiled or roasted Westphalia Ham, and make a little Farce with some of the Fat, and chopped Sweet-herbs; have such kind of Paste as is made for French Rolls; beat a Bit of it flat with the Hand according to the Bigness required; put some of the Farce upon a few thin Slices of Ham; then Paste; continue two or three Times over, finishing with the Paste, which you form as a small Loaf that nothing else may appear; bake it upon a Baking-plate in a middling Oven; serve cold; these kinds of Loaves are mostly used on a Journey, as being very convenient to carry about.

Pain en Surprise.

THIS Name has been explained in several Places: take a French Roll well crusted, and take out all the Crums; dry the Crust in the Oven, and glaze it all over with white Glaze; and put it again a Moment in the Oven to dry it; when it is cold, fill it with *Blancmangé*; when it is pretty thick, put it on the Table-dish in a cool Place, or upon Salt or Ice, till the *Blancmangé* is quite firm: this is done either with one large Roll, or three or four small ones.

Pain de Morilles & de Champignons.

Morels or Mushroom Loaf.

CUT a Slice of Bread round the Loaf, about an Inch thick; sink it about half, leaving a pretty thick Border; pare it properly in Scollop, or in any other Shape, to give it a handsome Look; fry it in Butter, and serve a good Ragout of Mushrooms or Morels in it; you may also serve Asparagus, Pease, or stewed Spinage in the same Manner; the two first are also served upon a flat Toast, or fried Bread, or half a Roll dried in the Oven, and put in the Middle of the Dish: some Bakers in London make little hollow Rolls fit for the Purpose, which they call Oyster-rolls, as being often used to serve Oyster-ragout in.

Pain à l'Espagnole.

Spanish, from being dipped in Spanish Wine.

TAKE out all the Crums of five or six small Rolls, and fill them with a ready-prepared Cream, and cover the Holes with the Bits cut off, to make them appear as if whole; soak them in sweet Spanish Wine a little while, then flour them to fry and glaze.

Pain à la Crême.

TAKE a good large round Roll rasped, and the Crums taken out as the last, and soak it a little while in Milk, Sugar, and Lemon; then drain, and fill it with *Franchipane* Cream, and stop it up as the last; put a little Cream in the Bottom of the Table-dish, the Roll upon, and pretty thick of Cream all over, and Sugar-powder; bake it in a pretty hot Oven, to give it a fine brown Colour.

Pain à la Duchesse.

POUND half a Pound of sweet Almonds scalded, half a Quarter of a Pound of *Pistaches*, as much dried preserved Citron-chips, half a Pound of Sugar; when all is finely pounded together, mix it with six Eggs, or more if required; beat up the Whites; butter the Dish you intend for Table; and put this Composition upon it, in the Form of a small Loaf; bake it in a mild Oven, and glaze it white; or rub it over with Whites of Eggs, and

garnish

Modern Cookery *Displayed.*

garnish it, with Colours or Nompareils, *Macaroni:* an *Italian Paste*; the French Author names in what Street the best is sold in Paris; but I shall not take upon me to be so affirmative for London, but only say, that it is very apt to be musty, and very easily found out by smelling, and so of all Italian Paste in general; it is to be boiled in good Broth; when it is very tender and thick, mix some Parmesan-cheese with it, or *Gruyere*; put it on the Table-dish, and colour it in the Oven, or with a Salamander. The *Lazagne* mentioned in Page 25. was through Mistake inserted as flat Macaroni; it is made more in the Form of Corn; but all Italian Paste is much of the same Composition.

Fondues en Caisses.

Melted Cheese in Paper-cases.

FOR one dozen of little Paper-cases of about an Inch square, melt or toast a Quarter of a Pound of Swiss-cheese, half as much Parmesan, some good Cream-cheese in Proportion, to answer to the French *Fromage de Brie*; then mix it in a Mortar with four or five Eggs, one after another, fill the Cases with it, and bake a Moment in a soft Oven, that is hot enough to give them a good Gold Colour: Here follows a *Pouding à l'Angloise*; but as I find that a Kitchen-maid of six Weeks Practice can make a better, I shall take no further Notice of it.

Gaufres à la Flamande. Flemish Gawfers.

QUANTITY for one dozen according to the Flemish Gawfer-irons; mix a Pound of Flour with a Pint of Cream, and a little Yeast, a little Salt, a Pound of melted Butter; keep it in a warm Place about half an Hour or more; if it is not liquid enough to pour easy with a large Spoon, add more Cream; warm the Iron, and rub it with Butter tied in a Cloth, or a Bit of fresh Bacon, and

pour

pour a Spoonful of this Batter in it; bake them of a good brown Colour, turning the Iron once or twice; serve hot, they are also served in hot Cream and Sugar.

Laitances de Carpes à la Hollandoise.

Carps Roes, Dutch fashion.

BOIL a dozen of small white Onions scalded in Half a Pint of white Wine, a Nosegay of Sweet-herbs, a good Bit of Butter, Pepper and Salt; when three parts done, put scalded Carps Roes in it; finish the boiling; they require no longer than time enough to finish the Onions very tender; reduce the Sauce pretty thick; put the Roes in the Middle of the Dish, the Onions round; mix a little Spinage-juice with the Sauce, to give it a pale green Colour, or a strong Green if you think proper; serve the Sauce upon the Onions only, or in the Bottom of the Dish, and the rest upon it; garnish it round with fried Bread: Carps Roes are also dressed as a Chicken Fricassée with Mushrooms, a little chopped Parsley, and white Liason-sauce.

Laitances de Carpes à la Bellevûe.

Agreeable, well-looking.

SCALD the Roes in warm Water, and prepare a Stew-pan with thin Slices of Lard, one Slice of Ham, upon this a scalded Sweet-bread, a Nosegay of Sweet-herbs, Onions, cut in Hoops pretty thick, a Glass of white Wine, whole Pepper, and a little Salt, (or none if the Ham is not very fresh); when the Sweet-bread is almost brazed enough, put the Roes to it, a little Broth, about two dozen of Crawfish-tails picked; simmer together about a Quarter of an Hour; then put the Sweet-bread in the Middle of the Dish; put two or three of the Onion-rings upon it, which you baste with Whites of Eggs to make them

them stick better; fill them with Crawfish-spawn, boiled a Moment in a good Cullis, and the Roes and Crawfish-tails round separately; add some good rich Cullis to the Sauce; make it pretty thick; sift it in a Sieve, and pour it upon the Roes only.

Laitances de Carpes à l'Angloise.   English fashion.

BOIL scalded Roes, about a Quarter of an Hour, in some good Jelly-broth; season with Pepper and Salt; when ready to serve, add a Bit of Butter rolled in Flour; simmer it a Moment without boiling; add a Lemon-squeeze, the Sauce to be of a middling Consistence, neither very thick, not clear or thin; *à la Bechamel* done with Bechamel-sauce; scald them first, and simmer them a while in it.

Laitances de Carpes frites.   Carps Roes fried.

SCALD them as usual; and when they are well drained, marinade about an Hour with Lemon-juice, and a little Salt; drain and flour them to fry in a very hot Friture, to give them a good brown Colour: drain upon a Sieve or with a Cloth; squeeze an Orange over, and garnish with fried Parsley.

Timbals d'Anchois.   From the Moulds so called.

RUB the Moulds with a little Butter inside, and garnish them all over with Fillets of Anchovies, soaked; intermix them handsomely with Fillets of Breast of Fowl, roasted; fill them with light well-seasoned Farce; bake in the Oven; turn them over in the Dish; serve a little Cullis-sauce under.

Anchois au Basilic.   Anchovies with Basil.

WASH them very clean, and split each in two; take the Bone out, and soak them about an Hour in a little white Wine, a few Leaves of sweet Basil; then

drain

drain them, and dip in Batter made of Eggs and Wine; ſtrew Bread-crums over; fry a Moment; ſerve with fried Parſley; when ſoaked in this Manner, they are alſo wrapped in thin Paſte, giving what Form you pleaſe when fried.

Anchois au Parmeſan. With Parmeſan-cheeſe.

SOAK the Anchovies very well, each ſplitted in four Fillets; fry ſome Bread, cut in the ſame Manner, and put a little Cullis in the Table-diſh, with chopped Parſley, Shallots, and raſped Parmeſan; the Bits of fried Bread upon, laid with Taſte; then the Anchovies upon; pour a few Drops of Cullis over and a Lemon-ſqueeze; cover it over with Bread-crums and Parmeſan; give it a good Colour in the Oven.

Oreilles de Liévres & de Lapins de pluſieurs façons.

Hares and Rabbits Ears, to different Sauces.

SCALD them well as thoſe of Lambs, and braze tender in a light Braze, with a Glaſs of Wine, one or two Slices of Lemon; when they are very tender, put them to what Sauce you pleaſe; or fry, dipped in a good thick Batter: the Sauce ought to be pretty reliſhing.

Grêlée de Viande. Meat-jelly.

ACCORDING to the Quantity wanted, uſe Knuckle of Veal, a Cock-fowl, or half a one, Water ſufficient; ſkim it very well, and boil it until the Meat is quite done; ſift it in a Sieve, and ſkim the Fat clean off; let it reſt to ſettle; then pour the clear in a Stew-pan, and boil it with Lemon-peel and Juice according to Diſcretion, a little Salt and Sugar, three or four Eggs, the Whites beat up and the Shells pounded; ſtir it continually, until it grows clear, and reduced enough to turn to Jelly; dip a Napkin in warm Water to take out any Smell it might have; ſtrain it, and tie it on a Jelly-ſtand; ſtrain the Jelly ly several Times through, keeping it in a warm Place while it is straining; and pour it in the Moulds or Glasses before it is cold. *Pied de Veau*, Calves-feet Jelly, is made after the same Manner, mixing what Quality and Quantity of Wine you please with it.

Gêlée de Blanc-mangé.

MAKE a Meat-jelly as the former, as far as mixing the Eggs, which you do not do; when you think it is reduced enough for a Jelly, put some pounded sweet Almonds, mixed with Cream, and strain through a Napkin several Times like a Cullis; while it is warm, rub it hard with a Spoon in sifting, to make it taste of the Almonds, and ought to be very white; pour it in what Mould you please to cool upon Salt or Ice; it should not be too substantial. *Blanc-mangé* is also made with Almond-milk, Cream, and Ising-glass, to make it take to a Jelly; the Ising-glass should be used with Moderation, as it is apt to give a bad Taste to whatever it is used with.

CONTINUATION DE PETITS PLATS D'ENTREMETS.

Small Last-course Dishes continued.

Huitres grillées. Broiled Oysters.

MELT a little Butter with chopped Parsley, Shallots, a little Powder of Basil, coarse Pepper; put a little of this in each Oyster, and rolled in Bread-crums; broil quickly; they may be broiled singly, or in their Shells with this Seasoning; colour the Top with a hot Salamander; they are also broiled with Bread-crums mixed with Yolks of Eggs, a little Pepper and Butter, and done in the Shells.

Huitres frites. Fried Oysters.

MARINADE some large Oysters with Vinegar, chopped Sweet-herbs, Pepper; drain them, to dip in a thick Batter to fry; serve with fried Parsley.

Huitres en Ragout.

SCALD them in their own Liquor, without boiling; then drain them, and prepare a Sauce with some good Broth or Cullis, a good Bit of Butter, some Pepper, chopped Parsley, a Spoonful of good Oil; simmer the Oysters a little while in it; make the Sauce pretty thick; add a Lemon-squeeze, when ready to serve; they are also dressed like a Chicken-fricassee, or with Bechamel-sauce in Rolls.

Huitres sautées. Jumped, or done in a hurry.

TO eat them hot done quickly, without any other Preparation, put them on a Gridiron upon a smart Fire, and hold a hot Salamander over, which will make them open very soon; serve quite hot; or if you have a hot Oven, put them in it, which will do the same with less Trouble.

Huitres à l'Espagnole. Spanish Fashion, or Sauce.

MAKE a little Farce to make a Gratin in the Bottom of the Table-dish, with a few chopped Oysters, Parsley, one Clove of Garlick, a Bit of Butter and Pepper; put scalded Oysters upon this; pour a little Sauce over, made of a little Cullis, chopped Mushrooms, a Bit of Butter and chopped Capers, one pounded Anchovy; cover it over with Bread-crums, keep the Dish on a slow Fire, and a Brazing-pan Cover over it, with Fire on; when ready, serve a little Spanish Sauce upon it.

Huitres à l'Etuvée. Stewed Oysters.

SCALD three or four Dozens of Oysters in their Liquor a Moment; then strain the Water in a Napkin, for fear it should be sandy; put it in a Stew-pan, with two or three Spoonfuls of good Cullis, coarse Pepper, chopped Parsley, green Shallots, a Glass of white Wine; boil it, and

and reduce it pretty thick; put the Oysters in it to warm, without boiling; garnish the Dish round with fried Bread.

Huitres en Coquilles. Scollop Oysters.

THIS has been observed already. *Hatelet d'Huitres*; scald the Oysters as usual, without boiling; drain them well, and give them a few turns in a Stew-pan on the Fire, with a good Bit of Butter, chopped Parsley, Shallots, Pepper, a few Yolks of Eggs; then skewer them with as much of the Sauce as possible, Bread-crums over; broil a little while: serve without Sauce.

Huitres en Surtout.

THIS is done in the same Manner as the *Coquilles*, only with a Farce made of Fish and good Seasoning; you may also make a Farce with chopping the Oysters, and mixing with Bread-crums, soaked in Cream, Shallots, Parsley, Mushrooms, a few Yolks of Eggs, Pepper and a little Salt; fill the Collops with it; put Bread-crums and Parmesan-cheese upon, and bake in the Oven, about a Quarter of an Hour. *Moules*, Mussels, are dressed in all the different Ways of Oysters.

Ecrevisses au Court-bouillon. Crawfish plain boiled.

BOIL them with half Wine and Water, or Vinegar instead of Wine, and Salt, some sweet Herbs, half an Onion or a whole one according to the Quantity; and if you would give them a particular Taste, keep them in Milk and Parsley, about ten Hours alive; then boil as usual; and you may also put a Spoonful of Aniseed in the Liquor while they are boiling; this last is the Dutch Fashion, and it gives them a very agreeable Taste, when used with Taste and Moderation; trim the small Claws or Fins, and lay them on the Table-dish with *Address*.

Ecrevisses à la Poulette, ou à la Bechamel.

Craw-fish Fricassée, or Bechamel-sauce.

WHEN boiled as the former, pick the Tails without separating from the Bodies; trim the Fins off, and cut half of the large Claws off also; dress them as a Chicken-fricassée with Mushrooms, &c. being prepared in the same Manner; they are also warm in Bechamel-sauce, without boiling; put a little chopped Parsley to it.

Ecrevisses farcies.   Stuffed Craw-fish.

BOIL some large Craw-fish as usual; strip off the Body-shells and the Fins under the Tails; make a little Farce with the Remainder of a well-tasted Ragout; the *Salpicon* is the best; fill them as large as if the Shells were on; rub this Farce over with Yolks of Eggs, and Bread-crums upon, and fry them; you may also bake them in the Oven; then use the Whites of Eggs to brush them over with; a very mild Oven will do, or a Brazing-pan Cover as usual, a good Lemon-squeeze under when you are ready to serve.

Ecrevisses à la Flamande.   Flemish Fashion.

BOIL them in Beer with a good Quantity of Butter, a Nosegay of Sweet-herbs, coarse Pepper and Salt; boil on a smart Fire; serve in the Liquor with Sprigs of Parsley, taken out of the Nosegay.

Ecrevisses à l'Italienne,

ARE boiled with all Sorts of Seasoning, two Spoonfuls of Oil, two Glasses of white Wine, the Juice of a Lemon, half a Clove of Garlick, Mushrooms, just Water sufficient to make liquid enough; this is calculated for a Quarter of a hundred, and serve in

their

their Sauce. *Ecreviſſes à l'Intendante*; put ſome large Craw-fiſh in a Stew-pan, with a good Bit of Butter, the Juice of a good Lemon, chopped Truffles, Muſhrooms, Parſley, Shallots, Pepper and Salt; ſimmer them on a ſlow Fire till they are done; let them cool; thicken the Sauce with Flour and Yolks of Eggs ſufficiently to be like a Farce; when it is cold, wrap the Craw-fiſh in it each ſeparately; lay them on the Table-diſh; ſtrew with Bread-crums, and give them a good Colour in the Oven; add a good Lemon-ſqueeze upon, when you ſerve.

Ecreviſſes aux Trufes. With Truffles.

BOIL the Craw-fiſh ſimply with Water, Salt and Vinegar; when they are cold, pick the Tails, and pound the Bodies to make a Cullis, as directed for Craw-fiſh Cullis; put a few Truffles in a Stew-pan, cut in large Slices, a good Quantity of Butter accordingly, a Noſegay of Sweet-herbs, a few Spoonfuls of *Conſommée*; when the Truffles are almoſt done, put the Tails to ſimmer in it ſome time, till the Sauce is much reduced; a little Pepper and Salt; take out the Noſegay; add the Cullis juſt long enough to warm together before you ſerve.

Ecreviſſes à la Sainte Menehoult.

THEY are ſtewed like thoſe *à l'Intendante*, and dipped in Batter; garniſh with a good deal of Bread-crums by baſting with melted Butter, while broiling, and throwing more Bread-crums over; ſerve a little Gravy and Lemon-ſauce under.

Ecreviſſe au Pontife. Boil them in Water, half a Lemon ſliced, Sweet-herbs; when they are done, trim the ſmall Claws off, cut off the Tips of the largeſt, and pick the Tails without ſeparating from the Bodies; put them to warm in Pontiff-ſauce, and dreſs properly on the Diſh.

Ecrevisses en Surtout. Boil them as the preceding, and make a Farce with roasted Breast of Poultries or Livers, a little scraped Lard, Bread-crums, three or four Yolks of Eggs, Pepper and Salt, chopped Mushrooms, Shallots, Parsley; pound this very well all together; put some of it in the Bottom of the Table-dish, the Craw-fish upon, and more Farce over; baste lightly with Yolks of Eggs, and Bread-crums upon; give it a good Colour in the Oven; serve with a clear Sauce and a Lemon-squeeze.

Ecrevisses aux fines Herbes.

Crawfish stewed with Sweet-herbs.

PUT a couple of small Slices of Fillet of Veal in a Stew-pan to soak on the Fire, with one Slice of Ham, a good Bit of Butter, chopped Sweet-herbs of all Sorts, a Glass or two of white Wine; boil slowly like a Cullis; when the Meat is half done, put live Craw-fish in, enough for a middling Dish; trim the Fins off first; add Pepper and Salt; when they are done, take out the Veal and Ham; add a little Cullis; skim the Sauce; add a Lemon-squeeze: serve upon the Craw-fish.

Ecrevisses à la Broche.

TRIM them as the last, and put them in a Stew-pan with a Bit of Butter, a Glass of Wine, Sweet-herbs chopped, two or three Slices of Lemon; simmer on a slow Fire till they are dead; then drain them, and stuff a little Farce in the Bodies; tie them to a small Skewer or Spit to roast; baste with the Liquid of the boiling, with a Dish under to save it; sift it to serve under the Crawfish.

Ecrevisses à la Hâte. Quickly done.

PUT three or four Spoonfuls of good Cullis in a pretty large Stew-pan with a Glass of white Wine, all Sorts of of Seasoning; cut seven or eight large Craw-fish in two, and put in the Stew-pan, over a smart Fire; stir them well to catch the Taste of the Seasoning; a few Minutes will do; add a good Lemon-squeeze, when ready to serve.

Ecrevisses au Monarque.

BOIL the Craw-fish in the most simple Manner; take out the Inside of the Bodies, which you fill with a Farce made of Carp-roe, mixed with chopped Sweetherbs, Butter, Pepper and Salt; cover it with Fishfarce, also properly seasoned; rub it over with melted Butter, mixed with Yolks of Eggs; and strew Breadcrumbs over; bake about half an Hour in the Oven; make a Sauce with two Spoonfuls of Veal-gravy, as much Jelly-broth, the Tails cut in Dices, a Bit of Butter, Pepper and Salt, *Ravigotte* Herbs, chopped very fine; boil it a Moment, and serve under the first Preparation: they are also done without the Shells, by sticking the Claws in the Carp-roe, and Farce, and finishing after the same Manner.

Fromage d'Ecrevisses.   Craw-fish Cheese.

POUND about three Dozen of small Craw-fish alive; when pounded thoroughly, add one Dozen of Eggs, the Juice of a good Lemon, Salt in moderation, a Pint of Cream; strain it several Times through a sifting Cloth, rubbing hard with a Spoon, as for Pease-porridge, or any other; then put it on the Fire, turning continually, until the Curd is formed, and drain it like a Cheese; when done, put it on a Dish; flour it under and over; cut it in Pieces to fry; serve with *Salpicon* Sauce, or Craw-fish Cullis. *Ecrevisses à la Condé*; boil a Spoonful of Oil, two Glasses of Wine, and two Spoonfuls of Cullis together, with a Laurel-leaf, two or three Slices of Onions, and the same of Lemon peeled, two Cloves, a little Basil, Parsley and Shallots, Pepper and Salt; reduce it to a Sauce-confiftence; fift it in a Sieve; cut the Craw-fifh in two alive, being properly trimmed; boil them a Moment, and ferve with a little Sauce under.

BEURRE D'ECREVISSES. CRAW-FISH BUTTER.

BOIL about half a Hundred of middling Craw-fifh in plain Water; trim off the Tails, and put the Carcafes to dry in the Oven, or in any other Manner; then pound them very fine; put this in a Stew-pan, with a Pound of good Butter, about half an Hour on the Fire, ftirring continually; when the Butter is melted, to give it a good red Colour, fift it in a Stamine, like a Cullis; pour it upon frefh cold Water to cool; keep it in a Pot for Ufe; the Tails will ferve for a Ragout of itfelf, or to mix with any other; alfo to make a Sallad with Fillets of Anchovies, fried Bread, and fmall Sallading-herbs chopped. *Ecreviffes de Mer*, Sea Craw-fifh; *Houmars*, Lobfters; *Crabes*, Crabs; are all dreffed after the different Manners of Craw-fifh, allowing Time and Quantities of Seafoning.

OMELETTES. OF OMELETS.

BEAT up what Quantity of Eggs you think proper, with a little Salt, and a little Water; melt fome good Butter in Proportion to the Quantity of Eggs, viz. about a Quarter of a Pound for eight Eggs; pour them in the Frying-pan, ftirring continually, over a clear Fire, till the Omelet is formed, and of a fine Gold-colour; put the Difh upon it, to turn it over, and ferve hot: this is the moft common and moft natural Way. They are alfo made with any Sorts of chopped Sweet-herbs, as Burnet, Taragon, Charvil, green Shallots, &c. &c. and are called by the Name of what is put to it; alfo with ftewed Greens, or minced Meat Ragout, as Livers, Kidneys, and others, provided it is minced very fine, and properly feafoned.

Omelette

Omelette à la Gendarme. Military.

MAKE a little Ragout of stewed Sorrel, with a little Parmesan-cheese rasped, and mixed with Bread-crums; make two Omelettes, as the first, and put this Ragout between; garnish the Dish round the Omelettes, with fried Bread, standing up like a Paste-border; which you may do, by dipping the Edge of each Bit in Whites of Eggs, to make them stick; pour a little melted Butter over it, and strew Bread-crums and Parmesan-cheese as before; give Colour in the Oven, or with a hot Shovel.

Omelette au Basilic en Baignets. With sweet Basil.

MAKE two or three thin Omelets, with a little sweet Basil chopped; cut them to roll like Olives, or to what Bigness you think proper; when they are cold, dip them in good Batter to fry, or wrapped in Paste; serve with fried Parsley.

Omelette soufflée. Raised, &c. &c.

PUT eight or ten Yolks of Eggs in a good Bechamel-sauce, mixed very well; beat up the Whites to frought, to put to it, in a deep Pan, and some good Butter; make it raise by keeping it over a smart Fire; serve as soon as possible, as it will fall by keeping any Time after it is done enough.

Omelette à la Farce.

With a Ragout of stewed Greens.

THIS is explained already; *Omelettes de Rognons de Veau,* Veal-kidney; *Omelette au Jambon,* with Bits of ready-boiled Ham in it, or upon; or a Sauce made with a Slice of Ham, poured upon, and a Slice minced in the Sauce.

Omelette à la Crême de Ris.

With Cream, and Rice-flour.

MIX two Spoonfuls of Rice-flour, with three Eggs, a little Salt, a Quarter of a Pound of fine Sugar, a Quarter of a Pound of good Butter, a Pint of very good Cream; boil this together, until it grows as thick as the *Franchipane* Cream; when it is almost cold, add a little chopped Lemon-peel, preserved Citron, Orange-flowers, Macaroni-drops, in Powder, eight or ten Eggs, the Whites well beat up; garnish the Inside of a deep round Pan, with a Sheet of Paper, well buttered of both Sides; bake it in the Oven; turn it over upon the Dish; glaze it with a Sugar-glaze.

Omelette aux Amandes.

THIS is done after the same Manner as the last, by mixing with pounded sweet Almonds, and a little Beef-marrow melted and sifted; make it either as the last, or in petty Patès-pan, or any other Sorts of Moulds.

Omelettes à la Servante, meaning Country-Fashion, done with chopped Parsley, Shallots, Sorrel, Pepper and Salt; fried Bread upon, and rolled round.

A la Sainte Meneboult, done after the same Manner, as that *à la Gendarme*, except that you put a ready-made Fish-farce between, and finish as the last-mentioned; you may also serve Omelette with any Sorts of Cullis upon: that of Craw-fish is rather preferable; then it is called *Masquée*, masked, &c. &c.

Omelettes d'Anchois, ou de Harengs Sorets.

With Anchovies, or red Herrings.

EITHER of these must be well soaked, and well stripped of the Bones, cut in small Fillets; mix with the

the Eggs, a couple of Spoonfuls of Cream, a little sweet Basil-powder, coarse Pepper, Nutmeg, Bits of Butter; bake it as usual, not too stiff, but Marrow-like.

Omelette aux Onions.

FRY two or three sliced Onions in Butter, till they are quite done; and add two Yolks of Eggs, and a little chopped Parsley; make two small Omelets, without Salt; put the Onions upon, and few Fillets of Anchovies; roll them Length-ways, and have some Pieces of Bread, cut like Toast, and fried in Butter; cut the Omelets according to the Largness and Length of the Bread, upon which you lay them; pour a little melted Butter over, and strewed with Bread-crums, and rasped Parmesan-cheese; give them a good Colour in the Oven, or with a Salamander; serve what Sauce you please under.

Omelette à la Dauphine.

MAKE a couple of thin Omelets; spread them upon a Dish, and garnish with Pistachio-cream, Cherries, and Apricock-marmalade; roll them up, to cut to the Bigness of any little Almond-paste, done in any Sorts of Moulds, or any other Pastry; glaze them with a little Sugar, and a hot Shovel.

Omelette à la Crême.

BOIL a Pint of Cream, with the Crums of a French Roll, chopped Parsley, green Shallots, a little Pepper and Salt; boil it till it is quite thick, then add five or six Eggs, or more, to make the Omelet as usual; only observe, that it requires a longer Time to do.

Omelette en Hatereaux; this is done thin, with chopped Sweet-herbs, and Oil instead of Butter, Pepper and Salt;
serve

serve with Bits of fried Bread, garnished with Fillets of Anchovies, betwixt two Bits of Omelets; cut to what Bigness you think proper.

Omelette à la Fermiere; see ditto *à la Servante*.

Omelette au Foie, with minced Livers of Poultries, or Game; first seasoned, and prepared as for Ragout; either mixed with the Eggs, or served between two, or folded in one Omelet.

Omelette au Sang, with Blood, mixed with the Eggs, either of Poultries or Lamb's-blood, a Bit of Butter and Seasoning.

Omelette au Parmesan. With Parmesan-cheese.

BEAT up about a Dozen of Eggs, and mix a couple of Spoonfuls of rasped Parmesan-cheese, some Pepper, and no Salt, as the Cheese will make it salt enough; make four Omelets of this Quantity pretty thin; spread some Parmesan-cheese over each; roll them up, and lay them on the Table-dish; pour a little melted Butter over, and a little more Cheese; put the Dish in the Oven, about a Quarter of an Hour, to take Colour.

Oeufs brouillés, viz. mashed, instead of being in Omelettes, are done with the same Seasoning, or Minced-meat as Omelets.

Oeufs en Neige. Snow-balls of Eggs.

BOIL about three Half-pints of Cream, with a little Lemon-peel rasped, few Drops of Orange-flower Water, a little Salt, a Quarter of a Pound of Sugar; reduce it to half in boiling; break about eight Eggs; separate the Yolks from the Whites, which last beat up to Frougth; put this in the Cream by Spoonfuls, while it is boiling, and keep them separated like poached

ed Eggs, and turn them about the same; take them out to drain, according as they are done; lay them upon the Table-dish, one over another, and mix the Yolks with the Cream, keeping on the Fire without boiling, only long enough to give it the Consistence, as is done to a Liason for a Fricassée; sift it in a Sieve, and serve upon the Whites.

Oeufs à la Dauphine.

BOIL a Pint of Cream, with a Quarter of a Pound of Sugar, a little rasped Lemon-peel, a Bit of Cinnamon; sift it, when you find that the Cinnamon prevails enough; and put it to boil again, to boil five or six Spoonfuls of Whites of Eggs, as the last, and drain them the same; when the Cream is half cold, beat up six or eight Yolks with it; pour it on the Table-dish; bake it between two slow Fires; frought up the Remainder of the Whites, which you put upon the Cream, raised in the middle; powder it with Sugar; and keep it a little while under a Brazing-pan Cover, or in a mild Oven; when ready to serve, put the Snow-balls round it; and garnish with Nompareils, as you shall think proper.

Oeufs au Caffé. Coffee-eggs, or with Coffee.

MAKE some good strong Coffee; let it rest to clear as usual, and sweeten it with Sugar according to Discretion; beat up six Yolks of Eggs, with about four Cups of Coffee, and sift it; pour this in little Moulds, in the Form of Eggs, or of any other; do not fill them quite; and bake in a mild Oven, or a Dutch one, or with a Brazing-pan; cover between two Fires; they are made after this Manner, in the Shape of any Fruits, or Birds, if you have proper Moulds for it, either of Copper or China, &c. &c.

Oeufs à l'Eau au Caramel.

Eggs with Water Caramel.

BOIL a Quarter of a Pound of Sugar, with a Glass of Water, until it is come to a pretty-brown Colour; then add a Pint of Water; and boil about half an Hour, adding some Cinnamon, Coriander, Lemon-peel; when this is half cold, mix six Yolks of Eggs beat up with it; sift it in a Sieve; pour it on the Dish you intend for Table, or in Moulds, or Cups, as the last; and bake in the same Manner, as *au Bain-Marie.*

Oeufs brouillés à la Provençale.

Mashed Eggs, Provençale Fashion.

DONE with pounded Anchovies, and mixed with a Spoonful of Cullis, half as much of the Whites as Yolks of Eggs; mash on the Fire to three Parts; then put them on the Dish, and a little rasped Parmesan over; bake a Moment in the Oven.

Oeufs à la Bagnolet. This is the common poached Eggs, served with a Vinaigrette, viz. sharpish Sauce, and minced ready-boiled Ham strewed upon the Eggs.

Oeufs à la Robert, done with Onions fried in Butter, and Mustard to it, as a Sauce Robert.

Oeufs à la Mouillette, boiled in the Shells, or prepared after this Manner, to serve in the Shells; break them at one End, and only use the Yolks, which you beat up a little while, with a little Cream, and Salt, Pepper if agreeable; and put it back into the Shells, to serve hot, either in Stands, or a Paste with Holes, prepared for that Purpose; serve with Bits of Bread fried in Butter; they are called the *Mouillette,* viz. to wet, or dip in.

Oeuf au Gratin au Parmesan.

MAKE a little Farce of what you think proper, with a little Cullis and Butter; put it in the Bottom of the Dish, on a slow Fire; break the Eggs upon it, as for poached; strew rasped Parmesan-cheese over; give them Colour with a hot Shovel; the Yolks must remain as tender as poached Eggs; they are also done au Gratin, viz. catching upon a Silver-dish, without any Farce under, only a little Butter, Pepper and Salt, and coloured after the same Manner; it is customary enough to pour a little burnt Butter and Vinegar upon, when they are done without Cheese, either whole or beat up.

Oeufs au (Prevôt), as Sheriff, or Judge-Advocate, &c. &c.

HAVE a little Salpicon-farce or Ragout ready prepared, made with pickled Pork, Mushrooms, Onions, and proper Seasoning; rub the Table-dish with some fresh Hog's-lard; and break the Eggs upon it, whole as the last, Pepper and Salt; bake on a slow Fire; and pour a little melted Lard upon, as they are doing; when done pretty hard, pour the Fat out of the Dish, a good Lemon-squeeze upon the Eggs, and the Ragout upon, to hide them.

Oeufs à l'Etuvée. Stewed.

BREAK the Eggs in hot Friture, as is done in hot Water for poached; turn them about with a Skimmer, to make them round; and fry of a fine brown Colour; have some Carp-roes and Onions, stewed together, and properly seasoned; put the Eggs in the Middle of the Dish, and the Ragout round, pouring the Sauce equally upon the Eggs; garnish the Dish round with fried Bread: the Eggs being fried so, are also

also served with fried Bacon, and fried Parsley, a sharp Sauce under; and called *Oeufs au Lard*, viz. Bacon and Eggs; the same if done in a Frying-pan, with a Bit of Bacon under each Egg, as is done upon all Occasions every where.

Oeufs à la Coque, in the Shells; see *Oeufs à la Mouillette*: you also make sham Eggs, by filling the Shells with any Sorts of Cream, ready prepared.

Des Oeufs frits, & des Oeufs pochés, à ce que l'on veut.

Of fried and poached Eggs, to any Sauce or Ragout.

EGGS for poaching ought to be very fresh, or they will never look well; put some Vinegar, and a little Salt in the Water, and break the Eggs in it while it boils hard; boil the Eggs but a Moment; turn them about with a Skimmer; leave them a little while in the Water, after it is taken off the Fire; and cover the Pan; pare them properly, as you take them out; dip them again in the hot Water, and drain upon a Cloth; serve upon any Sort of stewed Greens; Sorrel, or Spinages are the most in use; but may be done with Endives, or any Kind of Lettuces; also served upon a Ragout of Minced-meat of any Sorts, or with a little Cullis-sauce, with a little Vinegar, or a Lemon-squeeze; fried Eggs are used to the same Purpose, either fried round in Hog's-lard Friture, or with Butter in a Frying-pan.

Oeufs à la Tripe ou à la Crême. Eggs Fricassée.

PUT a good Bit of Butter in a Stew-pan with chopped Parsley, Shallots, Mushrooms, Pepper and Salt; when the Seasoning is done enough, put Cream to it according to the Quantity of Eggs intended, which are first

hard

hard boiled, and each cut in six or eight Fillets; put the Eggs to it with a little Flour to thicken the Sauce, which ought to be very short.

Oeufs en Fillets à la Moutarde.

THE first Preparation is done with Onions instead of Sweet-herbs, and Onion-gravy instead of Cream, with a Glass of white Wine, Pepper and Salt, finished as the last; add Mustard sufficiently, when ready to serve: this is also done by cutting an Omelet in Fillets as is commonly done with Pigs Ears, and put into the Sauce just long enough to warm without boiling.

Oeufs à la Tripe aux petit Pois. With stewed Pease.

Oeufs à la Tripe au Concombres. With stewed Cucumbers.

Oeufs farcis au Concombres.
Stuffed with a Cucumber-ragout.

CUT the hard Eggs in two, without breaking the Whites; pound the Yolks with Bread-crums, soaked in Cream; a little Butter, chopped Parsley, Shallots, Mushrooms, Pepper and Salt; mix it well with raw Yolks, and fill the Whites with it; smooth with a Knife dipt in Yolks, and Bread-crums over, a few Drops of melted Butter; bake in the Oven a little while, and hot enough to give them a good Colour; serve upon stewed Cucumbers. Hard Eggs are mixed with any kind of Pickles or Preserves, as Girkins, small Melons, Peaches, Nectarins, &c. cut the Fruit in the same Manner as the Eggs, and scald them a little while in hot Water to take the Strength of the Vinegar and Salt out.

Oeuf à la Farce. Hard boiled.

THE Eggs cut, each in four, to garnish stewed Greens, as is done with poached Eggs; it is commonly called a Farce, for being done with as little Sauce as poſſible.

Oeufs au Miroir, meaning as clear as a Looking-glaſs; this has been explained in *Oeufs au Gratin*, in the laſt Direction of that Article.

Oeufs au Beurre noir, fried in burnt Butter; which is prepared before the Eggs are broken in it, and the Top coloured with a hot Shovel, a little Vinegar added to the Butter for Sauce.

Oeufs à la Ducheſſe; boil ſome Cream and Sugar, few Drops of Orange flower Water, a Bit of Lemon-peel; poach the Eggs in it; and reduce the Cream for Sauce, to ſerve upon.

Oeufs au Lait, with Milk; beat up a Spoonful of Flour with three whole Eggs (meaning Yolks and Whites), a little Salt and Sugar, raſped Lemon-peel, Orange-flower Water, and a little Milk; put the Table-diſh upon a moderate Stove; rub the Bottom with Butter; pour the Preparation upon, when it is pretty hot; leave it on the Fire few Minutes; colour the Top with a hot Shovel.

Oeufs à la Flamande. Flemiſh Faſhion.

BRAZE ſome Cabbage-lettuces tied, and well ſeaſoned; when done, drain, and put them whole on the Diſh ſeparately; cut Eggs in two, to put a half upon each Lettuce; the Yolks ſhould not be boiled very hard, but juſt like Marrow; ſerve a little Cullis and Butter-ſauce upon. *Oeufs à la Payſanne*; this is the Country-faſhion of ſpreading Eggs upon Slices of Bread, very common in Flanders amongſt poor People, to give their Children, as Bread and Butter in England; the Eggs being boiled betwixt hard and ſoft.

Oeufs

Oeufs à la Môde.

SIMMER a Handful of Bread-crums, in good fat Broth; when it is quite thick without Liquid remaining, take it off the Fire; chop a good Slice of Bacon, ready boiled, to mix with it; and add a Spoonful of à la Mode Beef Sauce, not too high seasoned, one Dozen and a half of Yolks of Eggs beat up, and six of the Whites also, and a little pounded Coriander, Pepper and Salt, if the Sauce does not give it Taste enough; mix it all together very well; garnish a round deep Stewpan, with Slices of Lard all round, and put the Preparation in it; bake it in the Oven; when done, turn it over gently, and take off the Bacon; wipe the Fat with a Cloth; pour a brown Glaze over it, and let it cool before using.

Oeufs glacés. Glazed.

BOIL a little Broth in the Dish you intend for the Table, and break the Eggs in it, as those for poached, a little Pepper and Salt over; keep them but a Moment so, the Yolks should not be hard; take them off the Fire, and boil few raw Yolks and Cream beat up together, until it is pretty thick; pour this upon the Eggs, and rasped Parmesan over, with few small Bits of Butter; glaze it with a hot Salamander.

Oeufs au Pere Simon.

Father Simon, or Gaffar any thing.

MAKE a Sauce with chopped Parsley, Shallots, Pepper and Salt, a little Ginger-powder, a good Bit of Butter, rolled in Flour, a Spoonful of white Wine, as much good Cullis; boil this a Moment; add a good Squeeze of Seville Orange; serve this Sauce upon poached Eggs.

Oeufs au Coulis de Légumes.

With a Cullis or Garden-stuff Porridge.

MAKE a Porridge of green Pease, or of Lentils, properly seasoned; leave few whole ones in it, to show what it is; serve poached Eggs upon.

Oeufs en Caisses, in Paper-cases. Mix some chopped Sweet-herbs, with a Bit of Butter, Pepper and Salt; put a little of this in the Bottom of each Paper-case; break an Egg in each Case upon the Farce, and some more upon; strew Bread-crums over; broil over a gentle Fire; and colour the Top with a hot Shovel; they must be as soft as if boiled in the Shells.

Oeufs à la Vestale.

Virgin, from being white, unsoiled, &c. &c.

BOIL half a Pint of Cream, and as much Milk, with a Bit of Lemon-peel, a Pinch of Coriander-seed, and Sugar; reduce it to half; when it is almost cold, mix some sweet pounded Almonds with it, and two or three bitter ones, five or six Yolks of Eggs; sift it in the Table-dish; and bake it between two slow Fires, as a Cream.

Oeufs au Salmi. Boil half a Dozen of bruised Shallots, with a Glass full of white Wine, for about five or six Minutes; and mix this Liquid with pounded roasted Livers of Hares, Rabbits, or any other Kind of Game, to give it the Taste of, (for which this Dish is called Salmi); add six Yolks of Eggs, beat up with a little Gravy, and one or two Spoonfuls of well-seasoned Cullis; strain it through a Stamine, and bake it *au Bain-Marie*.

Oeufs à la Crême. Soak the Crums of a French Roll in good Cream, till it is quite soaked; put Sugar, Macaroni-drops, preserved Orange-flowers, rasped Lemon-peel, a little Salt, eight Eggs, whipt up together; butter a Sheet of white Paper of both Sides, which you put in a Pan; pour the Composition in it; bake it in the Oven; when done, take off the Paper; garnish it with Nompareils, like a Cake.

Oeufs aux Epinars. With Spinages.

SCALD a Handful of Spinages in boiling Water; drain them to pound in a Mortar; add a Pint of Cream, when well pounded, to make the Cream of a fine Pea-green; put a little Salt, six or eight Yolks of Eggs, Orange-flower preserved, Macaroni-drops, rasped Lemon-peel; sift it in a Stamine with Expression; pour it on the Table-dish; keep it a good while on a middling Fire, to catch a little at the Bottom without burning; glaze it with Sugar-powder, and colour it with a hot Shovel: all these Dishes ought to be done on Plate-dishes.

Oeufs meringués. Beat up the Whites of four Eggs, and eight Yolks, with two Spoonfuls of Water, some Salt and Sugar, the Juice of one Lemon; fry this as mashed Eggs; put it on the Table-dish, and the remaining four Whites, whipped up with Sugar, upon the other; bake it in a Dutch Oven, or with a high Cover, fitted for those Purposes. I shall again repeat, that it is the Whites of Eggs froughted, that gives the Name *Meringue.*

Oeufs à la bonne Amie, in a friendly easy Way. Beat up six Yolks of Eggs, and four Whites, with a Spoonful of Rice-flour, half a Pint of Cream, a little Salt, rasped Lemon-peel, Orange-flowers, Macaroni-drops; boil it in a Stew-pan slowly, about half an Hour, stirring continually; glaze it with Sugar as usual of a brown Colour.

Oeufs au Naturel. Mix a Spoonful of Flour, with eight or ten Eggs, Pepper and Salt, and Nutmeg, a Quarter of a Pound of melted Butter; sift it in a Stamine; rub the Table-dish with Butter, and bake on a slow Fire, with the Salamander or hot Shovel.

Oeufs à l'Eau. With Water.

BOIL five or six Spoonfuls of Water, with Lemon-peel, Coriander-seed, and Sugar; when it tastes enough of the Seasoning, let it cool, and beat up six or eight Yolks of Eggs with it; strain it through a Stamine; finish this as the last.

Oeufs en surprise au Basilic.

Sham Eggs, with Basil.

CUT hard-boiled Eggs in two; take out the Yolks, and instead, fill the Whites with a good ready-prepared *Salpicon* Farce, or Ragout, (the Farce is the most proper by its being minced finer); join the two Halves together; solder them with Yolks, as if whole; dip them in Yolks beat up, with Salt and Pepper, chopped green Basil; fry them in Hog's-lard Friture, or Oil; serve with fried Parsley.

Oeufs au Point-du-jour

The Dawn of Day, taken from the Colour of.

CUT a Quarter of a Pound of Ham in Dices; and simmer it with a little Bit of Butter, till it is done; roll well-poached Eggs in pretty thick Batter, made of Flour, Wine, Salt, and a little Oil; then the Bits of Ham strewed upon; fry them in Hog's-lard; and serve with fried Parsley.

Oeufs

Oeufs en Crépine, a ce que l'ont veut.

Eggs in Cowl to what you please; and above thirty Ways abridged.

CUT Bits of Cowl, large enough to wrap a poached Egg with, a little ready prepared Farce, of any Kind, minced Meat, or stewed Greens, or Onions fried in Butter, as for Sauce Robert; roll them up; dip in Yolks of Eggs; bake in the Oven, about a Quarter of an Hour, in a Baking-dish; and serve with what Sauce you please: the most used is Cullis-sauce, made pretty relishing or sharp, with Lemon-juice.

Oeufs au Zéphir, puffed or raised. Separate the Whites and Yolks of eight Eggs carefully, without breaking the Yolks; frought up the Whites, and one of the Yolks in a Spoonful of it, well wrapped in it; and so on, as many as you propose; slide them gently off, in a hot Friture, one after another; serve with much the same Sauce, as the last.

Oeufs au Président. Dip well-drained poached Eggs in Yolks beat up; and strew Parmesan rasped over, and Bread-crums; fry a Moment in very hot Friture: serve with fried Parsley.

Having already dwelt longer upon Egg-articles than can be pleasing and instructive, I shall only take such Notice of the Remainder of Receipts as will give a general Idea of them; as these Varieties are more properly calculated for Popish Countries, where a great Number of Meager Dishes are necessary: At the same Time, I shall give the Names, that none may be deceived by a pompous Names, upon a Bill of Fare, and very frivolous in the Execution.

Oeufs au Céladon. Sea-green.

POACHED in Water, made green with pounded Spinages.

Oeufs au Verd-pré. Pale or Meadow-green Sauce.

Oeufs à la Charmante; mashed with a little Sugar-caramel and Cream, called *Charmante*, viz. handsome, from the different Colour given by the Caramel and Cream.

Oeufs à la Nonette, from Nuns. See *Oeufs au Lait.*

Oeufs au Vin de Champagne, beat up with a Glass of white Wine, or done with Onion-ragout, with Wine in it; the Eggs boiled hard, cut in Quarter, and warm in it.

Oeufs en Poupeton à la Crême. Poupeton from *Poupetoniere*; a Stew-pan so called, for being made round and deeper than usual. See *Oeufs à la Crême*; done as a Cake; the Difference is only the Addition of Onions, done in Butter first.

Oeufs en Capote, a Great-coat; hide or masqueraded with the Whites froughted, with chopped sweet Herbs, much as those *au Miroir.*

Oeufs accompagnés, viz. garnished with something else, done upon the Table-dish, Bits of fried Bread and Bacon betwixt each Egg.

Oeufs à la Princesse, beat up with Orange-flower, Macaroni-drops, and few chopped Pistachio-nuts, Cinnamon; and finished like a Cream.

Oeufs à la Coquette; the Yolks of poached Eggs, beat up with Cream and Orange-flowers, &c. &c. finished like a Cream, and put into the Whites again.

Oeufs

Oeufs au Trufes; the Yolks taken out, and mixed with Truffles as a Ragout, and served in the Shells, or in the Whites, hard boiled.

Oeufs à la Suisse; beat up with rasped, or melted Swiss Cheese, sweet Herbs, and other Seasoning; finished like an Omelet or Brouillés.

Oeufs en Puits, scooped as a Well; make a Gratin, with a well-seasoned Farce, pretty thick; sink as many Holes as you propose serving poached Eggs in.

Oeufs à la Celestine, an Order of Nuns, so called; a Fricassée of hard Eggs, with all Sorts of Seasoning; garnished round as the Cream *au Chapelet*, and a thin Omelet upon the Fricassée as a Cover.

Oeufs en Canelons, hard boiled, cut long-ways; wrapt in Paste; dipped in Batter, and fried of a brown Colour.

Oeufs à la Moëlle, hard Eggs pounded with Marrow and Seasoning, made into small Bullets, wrapped in thin Paste to fry.

Oeufs au Fromage, with Cheese; done upon the Table-dish, as those *au Miroir*, with rasped Cheese under and over; coloured with a hot Shovel.

Oeufs à l'Ail, Garlick; a Cullis-sauce, with sweet Herbs, and a pretty strong Taste of Garlick, to serve upon poached Eggs.

Oeufs à la Folette, Fantask, &c. &c. See *Oeufs meringues*; the Yolks put upon a thick Ragout of Sorrel, done with Cream; and finished as above.

Oeufs en Ragout, hard boiled, cut in Quarters, and just warmed in Mushroom-ragout, Cock's-combs, Sweet-breads, or other.

Oeufs à l'Estragon, the Yolks boiled; taken out to mix as a Farce, with chopped Taragon, and other Seasoning, and put in the Whites to fry.

Oeufs à la Ravigotte, poached Eggs, with Ravigotte-sauce. See Sauces.

Oeufs aux fines Herbes; a Farce made with Butter, and all Sorts of seasoning Herbs; the Eggs done upon, between two Fires, or in the Oven.

Oeufs à la Béchamel Fricassée, or boiled hard, warmed in the Sauce.

Oeufs à la Sauce de Merluche, hard boiled, and warmed in this Sauce.

Oeufs à la Piemontoise, from Piemont, a Province in France; done upon a Gratin, made of Cheese and Butter, Bits of Bread, Yolks and Whites beat up together, with proper Seasoning; finish as usual.

Oeufs à la Poële, a Frying-pan; boiled hard; cut in Quarters, and tosted up with a little Butter, Lard, chopped sweet Herbs; served with Cullis-sauce.

Oeufs farcis, boiled hard; the Yolks taken out, to make a Farce with Butter, and Seasoning, a little Cream, put into the Whites, soldered with Yolks to fry.

Oeufs au Macarons, done like a Cream, with Macaroni-drops bruised. Orange-flowers preserved, Sugar and Cream.

Oeufs au Jus, poached, and served with Gravy-sauce.

Oeufs à l'Ecarlate, reddened with Spawns of Craw-fish or Lobsters; and sifted like a Cream; finish the same; garnish the Dish with the Tails.

Oeufs à la Grand-mere, Grand-mother; beat up with a little Gravy and Cullis; fift in a Stamine; finifh like a Cream, a little Gravy upon.

Oeufs à l'Espagnole, done as the laft, all to a Bit of Partridge, and one Shallot pounded; and fifted as the former; finifhed the fame.

Oeufs de plufieurs Façons au Gobelet, in Cups, as Cuftard, to different Odours and Taftes.

Oeufs au Plat en Ragout, done in the Table-difh, with Afparagus, Peafe-ragout, or any other Sorts of Gardening.

Oeufs en petit Timbale diverfifies, prepared as for the Poupeton, only done in fmaller Moulds; ferve with what Sauce you pleafe.

Oeufs au Verjus, with Verjuice-fauce; the Difh garnifhed round with Verjuice, or other Grapes, fcalded a Moment.

Oeufs en Piédefteaux, Pedeftal. See *Oeufs à la Coqué*, Page 461.

Oeufs en Salade, mixed with any Sorts of Sallading, when hard boiled, or by themfelves, with only chopped fweet Herbs; dreffed as a Sallad.

Oeufs au Gratin de Piftache, poached in Sugar-fyrup; and ferved upon a Gratin made of Cream, Bread-crumbs, and chopped Piftachio-nuts, few hard Yolks.

Oeufs à la Sauce d'Ofeille, one or two Spoonfuls of Sorrel-juice, to make a Sauce with Butter, two raw Yolks, Pepper and Salt, to ferve upon poached Eggs.

Oeufs en Fricaffée de Poulets; the fame Sauce and Seafoning, as is done for Chicken-fricaffée, made pretty thick, to ferve upon poached Eggs.

Façon de faire le petits Oeufs pour garnir.

How to make small Eggs or little Bullets for garnishing.

POUND six hard Yolks of Eggs with two raw; when well mixed, you may add a little Pepper and Salt, according to what Use they are intended for; roll this in little Bullets like Marbles, some larger, some lesser, to imitate the Groups found in Pullets; roll them in Flour, to make them more or less hard; they serve to garnish Pies or Ragouts of any Sorts.

Bouillie. Pap or thick Milk.

MIX a little Flour by degrees in Milk, and half Cream, if agreeable, a little Salt and Sugar; simmer a long while on a slow Fire, stirring continually; when it is almost done, put the Dish you intend to serve it in, on the Fire, and few Spoonfuls of the Bouillie in it, to catch a little at Bottom as a Gratin; pour the Remainder upon it; serve it in its natural Colour, or colour it with a hot Shovel like a Cream,

Du Ris, & Greuau au Lait.

Rice, Milk and Gruel.

WASH the Rice several Times in warm Water; then boil it in a little Water, till it bursts; then pour boiled Milk upon, by little and little, as it thickens; keep it on a slow Fire, about two Hours or more; put a little Salt and Sugar to it: you may also boil a Bit of Cinnamon in the Milk, or a Bit of Lemon-peel, or both; the Gruel is only boiled in Milk or Water some Time; let it settle; clear it off, to drink as a cooling Liquor, as Barley-water, &c.

Ris au Caramel. Glazed with Sugar-caramel.

BOIL some Rice in Milk very tender, and pretty thick; mix it with preserved Orange-flowers, rasped Lemon-peel, a little Salt; make a brown Caramel with Sugar, and a little Water; pour a little of it in the Bottom of the Table-dish, the Rice upon, and some Caramel; pour it handsomely round and over.

Ris soufflé; when the Rice is prepared as the last, all to the Caramel, put it in the Dish, five or six froughted Whites of Eggs upon, raised as high as possible; put it in a pretty smart Oven, and keep it in, or in any warm Place, till you are ready to serve: it is also called *Meringué.*

Des petits Pois. Of green or young Pease.

Petits Pois dans leur Suc.

Green-pease in their own Juice.

THEY ought to be used as soon as shelled, as they are very apt to decay, both in Colour and Suction, by being exposed to the Air; put them in a Stew-pan, with few Hearts of Cabbage-lettuces, a Nosegay of Parsley and Chibbol, a Sprig of Winter-savory, one Clove, a little Salt, a good Bit of Butter; cover them, and stew on a slow Fire, stirring now and then, for fear of burning at Bottom; when done, add a Bit of Butter rolled in Flour; make a Liason short Sauce; take out the Nosegay; serve the Lettuces in it.

Petits Pois au Lard.

With Bacon, or pickled Pork.

CUT about a Quarter of a Pound of fresh Bacon, or pickled Pork, in thin Slices; soak it on the Fire in a Stew-pan, until it is almost done; then put about a Quart of Peafe to it, a good Bit of Butter, a Nofegay of Parfley, as in the firſt, a Spoonful or two of hot Water; fimmer on a flow Fire; reduce the Sauce; take out the Nofegay, before ferving all together.

Petits Pois à l'Angloife. Engliſh Faſhion.

PUT the Peafe in a Stew-pan, well ſtopped, on a flow Fire, without any Liquid or Seafoning; fimmer them in this Manner, until they are quite done; then add a good Bit of Butter, rolled in Flour, a little Salt, and a little Surgar; ſtir them about, to make the Liafon.

Petits Pois à la Crême.

Stewed Peafe, or Fricaffée.

PUT the Peafe in a Stew-pan, with a Bit of Butter, a Nofegay of Parfley, a little Winter-favory, one or two Spoonfuls of warm Water; fimmer on a flow Fire a long while; when they are almoſt done, add few Spoonfuls of good Cream; take out the Nofegay; finiſh them very tender; add a little Salt, a Bit of Butter rolled in Flour, fufficiently to make the Sauce quite thick: ſerve quite hot.

Pois Sans Parchemin, or *Pois (goulus)* greedy.

THIS is a Kind of Peafe which are eat in the Shells, as they have not that Kind of tough Skin common to other Peafe; boil them in Water about a Quarter of an Hour; drain them upon a Sieve, and toffed up about as long in a Stew-pan, with Butter, a Nofegay of Parfley, a little Salt and Water; take out the Nofegay; add a Liafon of Yolks of Eggs and Cream, a little Sugar: ſerve in the Shells.

Pois secs. Of dried Pease.

BOIL them to a Mash in Water; they serve for Porridge, for Soops, or thick Cullis, to put to any Use, either with Meat or Poultry, Game or Fish, in Meager-dishes.

Féves de Marais à la Crême.
Garden-beans, Cream-sauce.

SCALD the large ones, to peel the Husks; the young ones are dressed with it; boil them in Water, about a Quarter of an Hour; drain, and put them in a Stew-pan, with a Nosegay of Parsley, Chibbol, a little Savory, a good Bit of Butter, Salt, chopped Parsley, a good Pinch of Flour, a little Broth. *Gras* or *Meager*; take out the Nosegay; add a Liason of Yolks of Eggs and Cream, when just ready to serve.

Haricots verds. Green Kidney-beans.

WHEN they are properly picked, if pretty large, cut them in Fillets; if quite young, only break in two; boil in plain Water, a Bit of Butter, and a little Salt; when done tender, and drained, stew them with a Bit of Butter, chopped Parsley, green Tops of *Rocambole*, or Chive, Pepper and Salt, few Spoonfuls of good Broth; reduce the Sauce; add a Liason as the former, with the Addition of few Drops of Verjuice.

Haricots verds en Salade.
Green Kidney-beans Sallad.

BOIL them as the preceding; when they are well drained, mix all Sorts of small Sallading with them, one or two chopped Shallots with it; season it as any other Kind of Sallad.

Haricots verds au Coulis.

With Cullis-sauce, or as a Ragout.

BOIL the green Beans as the former, and drain the same; put them in a Stew-pan, with a good Bit of Butter, a Slice of Ham, a Nosegay of Parsley, Chibbol, one or two green Shallots, Broth and Cullis; simmer about half an Hour; then take out the Nosegay; reduce the Sauce; when ready to serve, add Pepper and Salt if necessary, (as the Ham may salt it enough, which you also take out), and a Lemon-squeeze.

Haricots verds frits. Fried.

THESE ought to be pretty large, picked without breaking or cutting; boil them a Moment in Water; then braze them with thin Slices of Lard, a Nosegay of sweet Herbs, Broth, and whole Pepper; when done, wipe them dry with a Cloth, to dip in frying Batter pretty thick; and fry of a fine Gold Colour.

Haricots verds à la Flamande. Flemish Fashion.

WHEN they are boiled tender in plain Water, put them to soak some Time in good Broth, to take the Taste, with Pepper and Salt; drain them; and serve with a thick Sauce, made of Butter rolled in Flour, one or two Shallots chopped very fine, a little Cream, and few Drops of Vinegar.

Haricots verds aux Capres; the Beginning is done as the former; then tossed up with Cullis-gravy, a Bit of Butter rolled in Flour, sweet Herbs, and chopped Capers; the Sauce reduced very thick; which may be done, with adding Flour at Discretion.

Haricots verds pour confire & fécher.

How to keep dried or preserved green Kidney-beans.

PICK them as usual; they ought to be gathered in a good growing Weather, to be very tender; boil them a Moment in Water, and drain them very well: those you propose to dry, tie them with Thread, to dry in the Sun, or upon Sieves, or any thing else, in the Oven, when the Bread is taken out; and keep them in a dry Place; when you want to use them, soak in warm Water, till they become swelled and tender: those that you would pickle or preserve, put them in a Brine made of three Parts of Water, to one of Vinegar, a good deal of Salt, several Cloves; make Brine enough to cover them over; pour some Oil in good Quantity upon, which will always keep the Air from it; tie a Bladder or Leather over: by this Means, any body may have green Kidney-beans at all Seasons of the Year: use the same Method as with the dried, when you want to dress them.

Haricots blancs à la Poulette.

White Kidney or Roman Beans Fricassée.

I Believe, they do not grow in England to that Perfection, as do those brought over from Holland or Flanders, being much larger, tenderer, and better tasted; they are sold in several Places in London: fresh ones are boiled in Water, and drained; then simmered with a good Bit of Butter, Pepper and Salt, chopped Parsley, Chibbol; when ready to serve, add a Liason of Yolks of Eggs, Cream, a little Nutmeg, few Drops of Verjuice or Vinegar: dried ones should be soaked in warm Water several Hours, before they are boiled for Use, and boiled slowly; otherwise they are apt to crack and mash; drain them, to finish as first directed; a little Mustard added, becomes the Taste very well, or finished with Gravy and Cullis, and proper Seasoning; then they are called *en Ragout*.

Haricots blancs en Salade. The same as a Sallad.

PUT ready-boiled Beans in a Stew-pan, with a proper Quantity of Oil and Vinegar, Pepper and Salt, chopped Parsley, Shallots; toss this up together warm; garnish the Dish with fried Bread: they are also served cold, as a Sallad, a pounded Anchovy in the Seasoning.

Haricots blancs à la Maître d'Hotel. Take ready-boiled and drained Beans; give them a few Boilings, with a good Bit of Butter, chopped Parsley, Shallots, Salt and Pepper; when ready, a Spoonful of Verjuice, or Vinegar: also done with burnt Butter, Mustard, Salt and Vinegar, poured upon, or tossed in it, while warm.

Haricots blancs à l'Oignon. With Onions.

MAKE a *Roux* with Butter and Flour; put the Quantity of sliced Onions in it, which you stew in, adding a proper Quantity of Butter; when they are done, put the ready-boiled Beans to it, with Salt and Pepper, a little Vinegar; reduce the Sauce quite thick; add Mustard if you like.

Lentilles Fricassées. Fricassée of Lentils.

THIS is meant to be done with fresh Lentils; but the best coming from abroad, cannot be had fresh; but may be soaked like dried white Beans. Although this Seed is cultivated in several Parts of England, I hope I shall not be thought partial, by the Notice already taken; and without Prejudice to several Shop-keepers, and Corn-chandlers, who, for the sake of a

little

little more Gain, will impofe fome of Englifh Growth for Foreign; which are moftly fold at the Italian Shops, much larger, and of better Colour and Tafte; prepare fliced Onions, as in the laft for Beans, and put the Lentils ready boiled and drained to it, Broth and Butter, Pepper and Salt, a Sprig of Savory, which you take out before you ferve; reduce the Sauce of a good Confiftence; add a little Vinegar, when juft ready: they are done in *Ragout* the fame as the white Beans, with Cullis, Gravy, and proper Seafoning; it is moftly the Colour that diftinguifhes between the Name of Ragout or Fricaffée; the firft made brown with Cullis, the laft white, with Cream, &c. &c.

Choux Brocolis. Brocoli, white or green.

THE ftringy Rind ought to be well picked, to leave only the Stem or Heart, and the Head-tops; boil them in plain Water, and a little Salt; drain, and lay them properly on the Table-difh; and ferve what Sauce you pleafe upon, as white Sauce, or Cullis, or Verjuice, &c.

Choux Rave. It is of Italian Growth, called in common Turnip Cabbage.

PEEL it as Turnips, and braze it tender; cut in Pieces of what Bignefs you think proper: ferve with a white Sauce, or a good Cullis-fauce, as the common Cabbages; being of a flat Tafte of itfelf, either of the Sauces muft be pretty relifhing.

Choux Rouge. Red Cabbages.

THEY are moftly ftewed to eat with Ham, Bacon, or fmoked Saufages, or without any thing of Meat; they are very ftrong Eating, but fhould be fcalded firft, then ftewed with Butter, Pepper, Salt and

Cloves, and Vinegar, added to it just before serving; they are reckoned wholesome, to make Broth with Veal, for Consumptions; and also to pickle, as Girkins, &c. &c.

Choux farcis. Cabbage stuffed. The Savoy Kind is the best.

CUT off the Outside Leaves to the Heart, and scald them in boiling Water, about half an Hour; squeeze the Water out; take up the Leaves, one by one; and wrap some good ready-made Farce in each, three or four Leaves, to tie them round, as many as you want for a Dish; braze them in a light Braze properly seasoned, with Pepper and Salt, Cloves, a little Nutmeg, except there is some in the Farce; when thoroughly done, drain them with a Linen-cloth; and serve a good relishing rich Sauce upon: you may also cut each Half in two; and garnish any Kind of brazed Meat with it.

Choux à la Flamande. Cabbages Flemish Fashion.

CUT a good large Cabbage in Quarters; scald it in boiling Water some Time; drain it very well, by squeezing; cut the Stem quite out of each Quarter, and chop it pretty fine; put it in a Stew-pan, with one or two Slices of Ham, some Butter, and a little fresh Hog's-lard melted; simmer it, till it is quite mashed, stirring it often; put some good Consommée, Pepper and Salt, if necessary; the Sauce must be very thick, like a very strong *Liason*; toast a Bit of Bread, as for a buttered Toast; put it in the Table-dish; pour the Ragout upon; and garnish round with fried or stewed Sausages.

Choux à la Saint Cloud; either the Name of the Place, or the Inventor.

MINCE half a Pound of Fillet of Veal, and as much of Ham; season this with Pepper and Salt, chopped Parsley,

Parsley, Shallots, a little melted Lard; have a scalded Cabbage, as before, whole; stuff this Farce between every two or three Leaves, with all the Seasoning; tie it up round, like the Cabbage, before boiling; and braze it with Slices of Lard, some good Broth, a Glass of white Wine; when done, wipe the Fat off; and serve a Spanish Sauce upon: see Page 40.

Choux à la Marechal.

Field-general of an Army, &c. &c.

CUT about a Pound of pickled Pork in middling Pieces, and a large hard Savoy in Quarters; scald both together, about a Quarter of an Hour; squeeze the Cabbage; cut out the Stem; tie it up in Quarters; braze it in good Broth, a Nosegay of Sweet-herbs, a Sprig of Fennel, two or three Cloves, as many whole Shallots, a Spoonful of Oil, whole Pepper, a little Salt; when done, sift it; skim Part of the Liquid; and add few Spoonfuls of Cullis to it; reduce it to a good Consistence; put the Cabbage well wiped upon the Table-dish, the Pork upon, and the Sauce over all: Cabbages, brazed after this Manner, are used either for a Dish alone, with a good Jelly-broth Sauce; or to garnish any Kind of Meat, either Butchery, Poultry, or Game.

Choux à la Lyonnoise.

From Lyon, a City in France.

THE Cabbage is prepared as the last, either whole, or cut in Quarters; then stuffed with Bits of Sausages, and stewed Chesnuts; brazed, and served with a good Cullis-sauce, or Chesnut-cullis: this being a Country abounding with good Chesnuts, they are often used with many other Things.

Des Oignons, Ail, Perfil, Ciboules, Echalottes, & Rocamboles.

Of Onions, Garlick, Parſley, Chibbol, Shallots, and Rocamboles.

THEIR Utility in Cookery is known enough in the Firſt Volume, and Part of the Second. Onions are ſtill in full Uſe. Garlick is much diſcarded, either by its too predominant Flavour, or the Imprudence or Careleſſneſs of the Workman, as has already been obſerved in Vol. I. Shallot is ſo well known, and ſo much uſed, that it ſtill anſwers for itſelf. Chibbol, or Chive, may be called a *Diminutive* of Shallots, either green or dried, the Flavour being much leſs. Rocambole is much the ſame as Chibbol: it is moſtly uſed green, either in Sallad or in made Diſhes, the green Tops cut as Parſley or Garden-creſſes, &c. and grows again the ſame. Its *Affinity* to the two laſt-mentioned has been my only Reaſon for not taking Notice of it, in every Receipt where it is directed as Part of the Compoſition. I am uncertain whether this may be the Reaſon why it is not more cultivated in England. Parſley, for its great and general Uſe, is known to the meaneſt Capacity; it ought to be uſed freſh gathered, as it is apt to foment in keeping: the Root is as uſeful in Broth, as the Green is in Sauces.

Oignons à l'Italienne. Italian Faſhion.

TAKE ſome good large Onions; when properly picked, ſcoop them Inſide as much as poſſible; and fill them with a good raw Farce; and braze them with few Slices of Lard and Ham, a little Broth, Pepper and Salt; when done, drain them very well; ſerve Italian Sauce upon: ſee Page 32. Onions are alſo uſed as Sallad, either brazed or baked in the Oven; the ſmall ones are

are mostly brazed, the large baked; dressed like any other Sallad, with red Beet-roots: the common English Onions are rather too strong for this Use; Spanish or Dutch are better.

Oignons aux Oeufs de Carpes.

Stewed with Carp-roes.

MAKE a *Rissollet* with Butter and Flour; when of a fine brown, add some Onion-gravy; put large scalded Onions in it, some Mushrooms, a Nosegay of Parsley, Chibbol, Thyme, Laurel, Basil, a few Cloves; when they are almost done, put the Carp-roes to it; braze a little while longer; take out the Nosegay; reduce the Sauce; when ready to serve, add some chopped Capers, one or two Anchovies; garnish the Dish with fried Bread.

Des Navets, Ravioles, Raves, Poireaux, Carotes, & Panais.

Of Turnips, Turnip-radishes, common Radishes, Leeks, Carrots, and Parsneps.

LARGE Turnips, Carrots, Parsneps, and Leeks, serve to boil in Broth, to give it a proper Flavour; and to garnish many Sorts of Dishes. *Ravioles* are the small round Radishes; they are commonly eat raw, as Sallad, as well as the common long Radishes.

Navets en Cardons. Turnips as Cardoons.

TAKE some long Turnips, commonly called French Turnips; cut each in Quarters length-ways, in the Shape of Cardoons: you may give them the true Resemblance, by cutting Ribs as in Cardoons; braze them in the same Manner, and serve with the same Kind of relishing Sauce; this Sort of Turnips are also very good to stew in their own Juice, with a Bit of Butter,

Pepper and Salt; the Turnips cut in Fillets, or boiled whole, and served with any Sauce, either white or brown.

Ravioles & Raves de plusieurs Façons.

Radishes different ways.

THE first may be used hot, as a Last-course Dish; peel them as Turnips, or only scraping like Carrots; boil in plain Water to three Parts, then drain and finish the Boiling in good *Consommée*; keep on a slow Fire a good while, that they may take the Taste thoroughly; season with Pepper and Salt; when ready to serve, add a Bit of Butter rolled in Flour; make a Liason pretty thick; or instead of Butter, add some good Cullis. *Other Method*; when three Parts boiled in Water, finish them in Sugar-syrup, and dip them in Wine Batter to fry: the second Sort is dressed after the same Manner.

Des Carotes, Panais, Racines de Percil, de plusieurs Façons.

Carrots, Parsneps, and Parsley-roots, of different Fashions.

FOR Ragout of Roots, see Page 298. they are also used as a Dish; when boiled tender in the Broth-pot, cut them to what Shape you please; have a good Sauce ready, either white or brown; put the Roots to soak in it some time; simmer a Moment, before you are ready to serve. Parsley-roots must be very well scalded first, and thoroughly boiled, on account of their strong Flavour.

Poireaux & Celleris. Leeks and Sellery.

SEE Ragout of Sellery in Ragout-articles; it is also used as Sallad, when fine, white, and tender, also to put in Broth;

Broth; it ought to be used in Moderation, on account of its strong Perfume: it is also used as a Last-course Dish; when boiled in the common Broth-pot, to about three Parts, take it out to drain; and marinade it with a little Vinegar, Pepper and Salt, Cloves; then drain it again upon a Linen-cloth; dip in white Batter to fry; they ought to be tied in a Bunch, when put into the Pot for this Use. Leeks are also good to put in Broth; and when three Parts done, stuff the Heart with a good ready-prepared Farce, and fry as the Sellery.

Epinars à la Crême.

Spinage with Cream.

SCALD the Spinages in boiling Water a few Minutes; drain, and give them a few Chops with a Knife; put them in a Stew-pan, with a good Bit of Butter and Salt, a little Nutmeg; simmer a good while on a slow Fire; add some Cream, only sufficient to keep a good strong Liason; garnish with fried Bread, properly cut.

Epinars en Tabatieres. In Snuff-boxes.

CUT Bits of stale Bread, pretty thick; and give them the Form of Snuff-boxes of any Shape; scoop the Inside without breaking through, and leaving a Border of a proper Thickness; fry them of a good brown Colour, in Butter, Oil, or Hog's-lard; drain as all Fritures; fill them with a well-seasoned Spinage-ragout: serve with or without a Cover; the Trimmings will serve to make Bread-crums. *A l'Angloise;* when properly washed and drained, put them in a Stew-pan on a slow Fire, until they are quite done; drain their own Water out, and put a good Bit of Butter rolled in Flour, Salt, and a little rasped Nutmeg; toss them up, to make a Liason of the Flour and Butter; garnish with fried Bread.

Epinars à la bonne Femme.

The good House-wife.

WHEN well picked and washed, put them in a Stew-pan, with a good Bit of Butter, a Nosegay of Parsley, few Shallots, one Clove, Salt and coarse Pepper; simmer on a slow Fire, stirring now and then; let the Sauce be much reduced; when ready, add a Bit of Sugar, a Bit of Butter rolled in Flour; finish as the last.

A la Provençale, done the same Way, only using Garlick instead of Shallots, and Oil instead of Butter. I have already observed in Part, that all Dishes under this Denomination, are very much *characterized* with Oil and Garlick; the People of the Country being very fond of both.

Epinars au Bouillon, stewed in good Cullis, when scalded and drained.

A la St. Claud, scalded and drained as usual; then stewed with a little Butter, a Slice of Ham, a Nosegay of Parsley, Chibbol, one Shallot; simmer a while; then take out the Nosegay and Ham; add a little Cullis and Cream, and proper Seasoning; reduce the Sauce to a good strong Liason.

Du Pourpier. Of Purslain.

TIE it in Bunches to boil in the Broth-pot; it serves to garnish Herb-soops: it is also dressed stewed like Spinages, or preserved as Pickles; also cut to what Length you please, dipped in Omelet-batter to fry; and sugared over like Baignet-fritures; also marinaded in Brandy, dipped in Wine-batter; and fried the same.

Des Cardes de plusieurs Façons.

Cardoons of different Manners.

CUT them to what Length you think proper; and pick the stringy Part very clean off the Heart; you may do them whole, but it is most common and proper to cut them in Quarters, or Halves at least; boil them in Water, a little Butter rolled in Flour, a Slice of peeled Lemon; to keep them white, put them in a good white or brown Sauce to soak, being first drained from the Boiling; use a Bit of Butter; also with Cullis-sauce, and proper Seasoning; add a Lemon-squeeze when ready: if you would finish them with Parmesan-cheese, as is often done, boil in the same Manner; put a little Cullis in the Table-dish, as many Bits of fried Bread as Cardoons, properly laid upon the Bread, a little Sauce over, and stewed with rasped Parmesan-cheese; give it a good Colour in the Oven; the same must be much reduced; if you do not put too much of it, the Bread and Cheese will soak it.

De l'Oseille, Laitues, & Chicorées.

Of Sorrel, Lettuces of different Sorts, and Endives.

THEY are stewed as Ragout, as set forth in Ragout-articles; Lettuces and Endives are used mostly as Sallad, or boiled in the Broth-pot, tied, and taken out to garnish Soups: the Stock of Roman Lettuces or Gofs may be dressed after the Manner of Cardoons, being well scalded in boiling Water, and brazed.

Laitues de plusieurs Façons.

Different Ways of dressing Lettuces.

SCALD them whole in boiling Water for a few Minutes; drain the Water out, and cut out a little of the Heart, and instead thereof, put a well-seasoned Farce; wrap it up up in the Leaves, and tie them with Packthread; braze them in a light-feafoned Braze; when done, and well drained, place them upon the Table-difh, and pour a good Chicken-fricaffée Sauce upon, or a good Veal-cullis Sauce: you may alfo let them cool, while boiled tender, and dip in Egg-batter, and Bread-crums over to fry.

Choux-fleurs. Colliflowers.

PUT the Colliflowers in frefh Water as they are picked, and boil in Water or Broth, a Bit of Butter and Salt; Spring-water is beft to keep them white; take them off the Fire before they are quite done; leave them in the Water a while, to finifh; then drain them very well, and place properly on the Table-difh; ferve a Meager-fauce upon, made of Butter, Cream, Pepper and Salt, a little Nutmeg if agreeable; if you fimmer them a while in the Sauce, they will have more Tafte, but will not look fo well; follow the fame Method with brown or Cullis Sauce.

Choux-fleurs à la Reine.

Colliflower, Queen's-fauce.

MAKE this Sauce with a Bit of Ham, cut in fmall Dices, Bits of Fillet of Veal the fame, a little Butter, chopped Parfley, Shallots, one Clove of Garlick; foak this a while on the Fire; then add few Spoonfuls of good Jelly-broth, half a Pint of Cream; reduce it to a good Liafon; fift it in a Sieve; pour Part of it in the Table-difh, then a Colliflower, boiled as the preceeding, the Remainder of the Sauce over; garnifh with Bread-crums, and few Drops or Bits of Butter upon; colour it in the Oven; they are done with Cullis and Parmefan-cheefe, after the fame Manner, and called *au Parmefan.*

Choux-fleurs en Baignets, as Fritures, boiled in the same Manner; dipped in good Wine-batter, and fried of a fine Gold-colour.

Choux-fleur au Jus. With Gravy.

BOIL a Colliflower as the former; put it in a Stew-pan much of its Bigness, laid close, the Stalks upwards; pour some good Gravy upon it, and let it infuse some Time on an Ashes-fire; then close it properly on the Table-dish, the Bloom upwards; and do not put the Gravy to it; but a good Cullis-sauce, thickened with Butter and Flour, Pepper and Salt, according as the Cullis requires.

En Ragout; boil a Colliflower in good Broth, and a good Bit of Butter and Salt; when done, drain it; lay it properly on the Dish, and serve a small well-tasted Ragout upon, as Sweet-bread, fat Livers, Mushrooms, &c. &c.

Concombres à la Poulette.

Cucumbers Fricassée, or white Sauce.

CUT them in large Dices; scald them in boiling Water a few Minutes; drain, and put them in a Stew-pan, with Butter, chopped Parsley, Shallots, Pepper and Salt; add a little Broth; simmer some time; reduce the Liquid; and add a Liason of two or three Yolks of Eggs, beat up with a little Verjuice or Vinegar, Butter rolled in Flour; Bits put in at different Times, rasped Nutmeg: the Sauce ought to be pretty sharp.

Concombres farcis. Stuffed Cucumbers.

PEEL, and take the Middle out with an Apple-gorer, or any thing else; scald them as the last; fill them with a well-seasoned Farce, made of ready-dressed Meat, and proper Seasoning: for Meager with Fish-farce, tie them

them up with Packthread; braze in a light Braze: they serve to garnish made Dishes, or alone, with a good Colour-sauce upon.

Au Basilic; green Basil, chopped with the Farce; brazed in the same Manner; when cold, dipped in Egg-batter to fry, or finished in the Table-dish, with Bread-crums and Parmesan-cheese, as the Colliflower.

A la Reine. See Colliflower ditto; and pursue the same Method for Cucumbers.

Melons, comment les confire.

How to preserve Melons for Cookery.

BOIL the Proportion of two Parts of Water to one of Vinegar, Salt, and Cloves proportionable; the smallest Melons are the best; wipe them all over with a Cloth, and put them in a Pot; pour the Brine boiling upon; keep it on an Ashes-fire till the next Day; and do the same over again several Times, till they are of a fine Green, then let them cool, and stop the Pot very close; keep it in a cool Place, to use for Ragout or Sallad; soak them some time in warm Water before using.

Melons en Baignets. Melon-friture.

MELONS are served raw, when ripe; the French use Melons as little Dishes, in the first Course; also Radishes, Oysters, &c. and are removed with the Soop with made Dishes: if you would make a Last-course Dish, called *Entrement* the first, *Hors d'Oeuvre*, cut a Melon in large Dices; marinade with a little Brandy, and Sugar, about half an Hour; drain it well, to dip in good thick Batter; fry as all other Fritures; serve with rasped Sugar over, as usual.

Des Chervis, Salsifix, & Taupinambours.

Of Skirret, Salsifix or white Beet-root, and Potatoes.

SKIRRETS are scraped as Carrots, boiled in Water, a little Butter and Salt; they require only about a Quarter of an Hour's boiling; drain them to fry, being first dipped in pretty thick Wine-batter; the Salsifix is much harder, and requires a longer Time; boil in the same Manner; serve with relishing Sauce like Cardoons. Potatoes are boiled in Water, then peeled, cut in Slices, and just warm in white Liason-sauce, or pounded, and baked to a Gratin upon the Table-dish; seasoned with Pepper and Salt, Butter and Cream.

DES FINES HERBES. Of Sweet-herbs.

WHAT go under the Denomination of Sweet-herbs in Cookery, are Parsley, Chibbol, Garlick, Rocambole, Shallots, Winter-savory, Fennel, Thyme, Laurel, or Bay-leaf, sweet Basil. Under the Name of *Ravigotte*, are Taragon, Charvil, Burnet, Garden-cresses, Civet, green Mustard; there are other Sweet-herbs, which are not called Ravigotte, although they are often used together, as Mint, Borage, Water-cress, Rosemary, Marigold, Marjoram.

Du Houblon. Of Hops.

THE Spring is the only Season to eat it; it is first to be boiled in Water, then served in the same Manner as Asparagus.

Des Artichauts.

Of Artichokes, dried or preserved.

FOLLOW the same Method, as is done for dried and preserved Kidney-beans, see Page 479. only observe, that they must be boiled enough, to take the Hearts, or

Hay out; those that you preserve in Brine, trim the Leaves, as is commonly done, when served fresh; and those to dry, strip all the Leaves off; scald them in hot Water, when you propose to use them, as is said for the Beans.

Artichauts à la Sauce blanche. With white Sauce.

TRIM the Points of the Leaves with a Pair of Scissors, or a sharp Knife; boil them in Water and Salt, and a Bit of Butter; drain and take the Choak out; serve a white Sauce in it, made of Butter and a little Flour, Pepper and Salt, few Drops of Verjuice or Vinegar, or Lemon-juice.

En Feuillage, meaning with the Leaves; scald them first in boiling Water a few Minutes; then boil in Broth, a Nosegay of Sweet-herbs, few Slices of Lard under, two or three Cloves; drain, and take the Choak out as the first; pour a Cullis-sauce in it, mixed with Butter, Pepper and Salt, and a Lemon-squeeze.

Artichauts frits. Fried Artichokes.

TAKE young Artichokes, and cut them in Quarters or more Pieces, according to the Bigness; trim the Bottoms, both In and Outside, leaving only three or four of the tenderest Leaves; put them in fresh Water some Time, after they are picked; and drained, to marinade about have an Hour in Batter, made of Yolks of Eggs, Flour and Salt; fry crisp in a very hot Friture; serve fried Parsley for garnishing: another Method is to braze them, being trimmed after this Manner, and dipt in good thick Wine-batter to fry.

Artichauts à la Glace, ou en Crysteaux. From Looking-glass, or cut Glasses.

BRAZE the Bottoms of Artichokes very tender, in a well-seasoned Braze; lay them on the Table-dish;
and

and pour a good clear Jelly over, sufficient to cover them; let it cool; this first is called *à la Glace ou au Miroir*; otherwise let the Jelly cool first, and cut it in little rocky Pieces, to put upon and round the Artichoke-bottoms: this last is called *en Chrysteaux*, from its transparent Clearness, as cut Glasses.

Artichauts à la Barigoult.

From the Inventor's Name, &c.

TRIM the Artichokes properly; boil them in plain Water, till you can take the Choaks out; drain them very well; have a Sauce prepared, with two Yolks of Eggs, beat up with a Spoonful of Oil, chopped Parsley, Shallots, Basil, Mushrooms, Chibbol, Pepper and Salt; put the Artichokes in a Stew-pan, with few thin Slices of Lard under, a little Broth; and pour this Sauce in them; braze on a slow Fire, both under and upon the Pan-cover; when done, pour a little Sauce in the Dish, made of Cullis, Butter, a Lemon-squeeze, and some of it in the Artichokes. *A la Crême*, white Liason-sauce: make a Sauce with Bits of Fillets of Veal and Ham, Parsley, Shallots, two Cloves, a little Butter, and few whole Mushrooms; soak it some time, then add a little Broth; simmer it about an Hour, and sift in a Sieve; make a Liason of two or three Yolks of Eggs and Cream, a Lemon-squeeze when ready, Pepper and Salt; pour this upon the Artichoke-bottoms, trimmed and brazed very tender.

Artichauts au Prévôt.

PREPARE some sliced Onions, in Butter, as for Sauce Robert; and when done, add two pounded Anchovies, and Pepper, a Liason of Yolks of Eggs and Cream; put this in brazed Artichoke-bottoms; cover it over, half Bread-crums and rasped Parmesan-cheese; put it in the Oven, upon the Table-dish, to take Colour; serve dry.

A l'Italienne; cut each in four, and trim them as for frying; braze with Slices of Lard, Veal and Ham, a Spoonful of Oil, one or two Cloves of Garlick, whole Pepper and Salt; finish on a slow Fire; when done, sift the Sauce; mix Part of it with some Cullis, a Glass of white Wine; boil it together a Moment; skim it well; and serve in the Dish, with the Artichokes, Leaves upwards.

A la Marinière; from *Marins*, Sailors or Seafaring-men.

THIS is much as the last, in regard to Seasoning, only boiled in plain Water; cut and trimmed in the same Manner; then tossed up with the same Seasoning; chopped, and not sifted.

Aux fines Herbes. This has been repeated often; it is prepared as usual; the Artichokes first boiled, and trimmed as usual; the Sauce poured in, and put in the Oven to soak, and crisp the Tops of the Leaves.

Au Vin de Champagne; brazed with the Leaves on prepared as the last, and Wine-sauce poured in them.

Artichauts aux Trufes. With Truffles-farce.

PREPARE a Farce with chopped Truffles, and Sweet-herbs, a little Butter, and proper Seasoning; put it in ready-boiled Artichoke-bottoms; simmer them some time, in two or three Spoonfuls of Cullis, a Glass of white Wine, a Nosegay of Sweet-herbs; when done, take out the Nosegay; add a good Lemon-squeeze: they are also stewed with Truffles sliced, and the same Seasoning, one or two Spoonfuls of Oil; the Sauce well skimmed before serving, intermixed together.

A la Poile, in the Pan, tossed up; Bottoms of Artichokes boiled to three Parts; cut in Quarters, and tossed up up with Butter, few Spoonfuls of Cullis, a Glafs of white Wine, chopped Parfley, Shallots, Fennel, Mufhrooms, Pepper and Salt; fimmer a good while, to reduce the Sauce; a Lemon-fqueeze or Vinegar, fufficient to fharpen the Sauce, when ready to ferve.

Artichauts à la Brie.

TRIM the Artichokes handfomely, both under, the Leaves cut pretty fhort; boil them in Water, until the Choak quits, and take it out; drain, and fill them with a good ready-prepared Farce, or whatever you think proper; make it even with the Leaves, and glaze them with Yolks of Eggs, and Bread-crums over; put them on a Baking-difh, upon Slices of Lard, or Butter under, Pepper and Salt, a Glafs of white Wine, a Nofegay of Sweet-herbs, in the Middle; bake about half an Hour in the Oven; drain the Fat out: ferve what Sauce you pleafe under.

Artichauts à la Saint Cloud. This Name explained before.

PREPARE, and boil them as the laft, or in a Braze to three Parts, then drain, and let them cool; have as many fmall Pigeons, ftewed and well feafoned, as Artichokes, which are each ftuffed with a Pigeon; dip them in good frying Pafte, or thick Batter, made of Eggs and Flour, a Spoonful of Oil, a little Salt; fry in a very hot Friture, and Plenty of it.

Another Method, called after the fame Name of *Saint Cloud*; the Artichokes being prepared, and filled with the fame Sorts of Ragout, or any other; put a little Farce all over the Ragout and Leaves, and Breadcrums, and Drops or Bits of Butter upon; put them in a Baking-difh, with thin Slices of Lard, and Fillet of Veal; bake in a middling Oven of a good Colour; when ready to ferve, drain the Fat, and lay them on the

Table-dish; make a little Hole in the Middle, to pour some Spanish Sauce in it, and serve in the Dish; stick a Cock's-comb, or any thing cut in the same Shape, in the Hole at Top.

Artichauts au Pere Bernard.

Father or Gaffar Bernard, &c.

CUT each Artichoke in two; trim In and Outside properly; braze them to three Parts done; take them out to drain; flour and fry; serve with fried Parsley.

A la Gendarmes, half boiled, then broiled, with Sweet-herbs in it, mixed with Oil, Butter; and Verjuice-sauce, poured in, when done.

A la St. Menehoult; the Bottoms only being boiled, and filled with a good Farce; finished as all Directions under this Denomination.

Artichauts à la Pompadour. This is exactly as directed before for *à la Glace, ou au Miroir*. Bottoms of Artichokes brazed very tender, in a good rich Braze, and a fine clear Jelly, poured upon, in the Table-dish; and iced for *à la Glace*.

A la Hollandoise. Dutch-Fashion Bottoms of Artichokes, brazed as the last; and simmered in a Stew-pan, with a good Bit of Butter rolled in Flour, some good Broth, Pepper and Salt, a Nosegay; when ready to serve, take out the Nosegay; reduce the Sauce to a good Consistence; add some scalded chopped Parsley, and Lemon-squeeze.

Artichauts en Accolade.

Glued or soldered together.

HAVE eight or ten Artichoke-bottoms, brazed whole, and properly trimmed; put a little ready-prepared *Salpicon* Farce between two of them, and so on, as many as you please; rub the Borders with Yolks of Eggs, which make the *Accolade* soldering; dip them in Eggs, beat up as for Omelets, then Bread-crums over; fry of a fine Gold-colour.

En Baignets; each Bottom ready boiled or brazed; cut in Quarters, and dipt in good think Wine-batter, to serve as Fritures, with fried Parsley.

En Salade; Bottoms of Artichokes, brazed whole, and cold; garnish them with Fillets of Anchovies soaked, small Capers, small Sallad round; seasoned as a Sallad, with Salt, Pepper, Oil and Vinegar.

Au Parmesan; brazed first, and finished as usual, under this Denomination, with some good Cullis in the Dish, and Bread-crums, and Parmesan-cheese; coloured in the Oven.

A la Bechamel. Bottoms brazed and warmed in Begamel Sauce.

Artichaut à la Mayence.

With Westphalia Ham-sauce or Slices.

CUT as many thin Slices of Ham, as you propose of Artichoke-bottoms, which are brazed as usual; soak the Ham over a slow Fire, until it is done; put the Slices separately on the Table-dish, and the Bottoms of Choaks upon; put a little Cullis in the Pan, to gather the Flavour and Sauce of the Ham; add a Spoonful of Jelly-broth, a little Butter rolled in Flour, a little Pepper and Vinegar; simmer the Sauce to thicken it; and serve upon the Bottoms of the Artichokes.

Au Bacha; make a Sauce with Butter, chopped Parsley, Shallots, Chibbol, Mushrooms, a little Broth; simmer some time, till the Seasoning is done; beat up three

three Yolks of Eggs, with some chopped Charvil, Verjuice, Pepper, Salt, and Nutmeg grated; reduce it to a thick Consistence: serve upon brazed Bottoms of Artichokes.

Des Trufes. Of Truffles.

THE French Author says, they are brought to Paris from the hot Provinces, particularly from *Perigord, Gascogne, Limosin, Agenois,* and other Parts of the South of France. It is well known to all Travellers, and many others, that the Flavour of foreign Truffles is far superior to those found in England; atributed to the Coldness of the Climate. I believe Hampshire produces the most; also Windsor-park, and several other Counties in England, as Sussex, &c. They are imported from abroad, and sold at a very high Price in most Italian Shops; but their Flavour is much wasted, and very little superior to those found in England, if any at all, as they grow in the Ground without any outward Appearance. The Author says, that, as Pigs are very fond of them, and have often been the Occasion of discovering where they grow; the same Observation might be useful in England, with a little more Attention.

Trufes au Court-bouillon.

This is commonly meant for plain boiled.

SOAK the Truffles a while in warm Water, to clean with a Brush with care; when done in this Manner, boil them in half Wine and Water, Pepper and Salt, a Nosegay of Sweet-herbs, Bits of Roots, Slices of Onions; serve hot in a Napkin; the middling Sorts are boiled enough in about a Quarter of an Hour.

Trufes au Vin de Champagne; clean them as the former, and boil in this Wine, with a little Salt; serve the same in a Napkin.

A la

A la Maréchal; when cleaned as ufual, feafon them with Salt and coarfe Pepper, wrapt up in Paper; put them in a Skillet or Iron-pot, without Liquor; bury the Pot in warm Afhes, about an Hour or more, and ferve hot in a Napkin; they are alfo baked in Afhes, without a Pot, but wrapped in feveral Papers; wet the laft, and bake them about an Hour; brufh them clean, if the Paper fhould burn.

Trufes en Puits. Truffles gored and ftuffed.

CLEAN them as firft directed; gore, or fcoop the Infide without fplitting; chop what you take out, with fat Livers, Beef-marrow, Pepper and Salt, Parfley, Shallots; mix it with Yolks of Eggs beat up; ftuff the Truffles with this Farce, and cover the Holes with the firft Bits cut off; braze them with Slices of Veal, Ham, and Lard, a Glafs of white Wine, a Nofegay of Sweetherbs; when done, add two Spoonfuls of good Cullis; take the Truffles out; fimmer the Sauce fome time, with the Addition of the Cullis; fkim it very well; fift it; reduce it to a good Confiftence; add a Lemonfqueeze.

Trufes à la Poële. See Artichokes, ditto.

TRUFFLES boiled or baked will do for this Purpofe, fuch as have been ferved at Table; peel them whole, or cut in thick Slices; make a good Cullis-fauce, with chopped Sweet-herbs, and proper Seafoning; put the Truffles in it, to fimmer on the Fire fome time; brazed Truffles in Purpofe are alfo directed to be dreffed the fame Way; Plenty is neceffary to abufe their much better Flavour, with all this Seafoning.

Trufes en Tymbale; wrapped in Pafte, Pepper and Salt; and baked as *petit Patés aux fines Herbes* alfo.

Trufes aux Croutons; Truffles in Slices, and ftewed in Oil-cullis, and all Sorts of Sweet-herbs, feafoning with

with a Glass of white Wine; finish as all Ragout; garnished round with Bits of fried Bread, which gives it the Name, being called *Croutons*.

Trufes en Crustade, viz. in Crust; make a second-best Paste, called *Demi-feuilletage*, see Paste-articles; prepare it as for a Pie, and put Truffles in it, with a little Salt; cover them up with the same Paste as any other; bake about three Quarters of an Hour in a middling heated Oven: serve in the Pie.

Asperges en Batons, Sticks.

Asparagus plain boiled.

THEY are to be scraped, and boiled in Water and Salt, pretty crisp; drain them; and serve with a white Sauce, a Cullis, mixed with Butter, also with Oil, a little Vinegar, Pepper and Salt.

En petit Pois; as green Pease, either plain or Fricassée, and in all the different Ways of green Pease.

Asperges confites; preserved for Kitchen-use; boil as much Vinegar as Water, according to the Quantity of Asparagus intended, Slices of Lemon, Salt and Cloves; trim the Grass as for ready Use; scald them a Moment in Salt and Water; then put them in a Pot, and pour the Brine upon; the next Day, boil the Brine again; and when it is almost cold, pour it upon the Grass; let it cool, and pour some Oil upon, as directed for Kidneybeans; keep the Pot in a dry Place, and stop it with Bladder or Leather; soak them a while in hot Water, before using hereafter.

Des Morilles, Mousserons, & Champignons.

MORELS are much of the same Nature as the Mushrooms; they grow in shady Places, and are only to be had in the Spring; they require a deal of Attention,

tention, to clean them properly, being very fandy. By the Defcription given by the Author of *Moufferons* and *Champignons*, it feems, that one Nation or the other is miftaken in the Appellation, as I apprehend, that Mufhrooms is literally tranflated from Moufferons. He fays that *Moufferons* are found in fhady moffy Places, fmaller than the Champignons, reddifh Outfide, and white undermoft; calls it alfo a Species of *Champignons*, of an excellent Flavour and Tafte: I have already taken Notice of its Ufes. The beft Champignons are thofe that grow on hot Beds; they ought to be very white and firm, and ufed very frefh; they are of very great Utility in Cookery, and to add to their Merit, are to be had almoft all the Year.

Morilles à la Provençale.

WASH them in feveral Waters warm, and pour them from one Pan to another, to beat the Sand out; when well drained, put them in a Stew-pan, with a good Quantity of Butter, a Spoonful of Oil, coarfe Pepper and Salt, chopped Parfley, Shallots; fimmer on a flow Fire, till they are done: ferve upon a Piece of Bread, cut as a Toaft, and fried in Butter.

Morilles au Prince.

TAKE large Morels; and when properly cleaned, ftuff them with a Farce, made of roafted Poultry, and Seafoning as ufual, for this Farce; braze them with few Slices of Veal, Ham and Lard, a Nofegay of Sweetherbs; when done tender, take them out; wipe the Fat off, and keep warm; add a little Confommée to the Sauce; boil together a Moment; fkim, and fift it in a Sieve; add a Lemon-fqueeze: ferve upon the Morels.

Morilles à la Créme, with Liafon-fauce, as all under the fame Denomination; firft brazed in Butter, and Seafoning;

soning; when done, the Liason of Eggs and Cream added to it.

Morilles au Lard. With Bacon.

CUT about a Quarter of a Pound of middling Bacon; soak it in a Stew-pan on the Fire, till it is done; have large Morels well washed, which you cut in two, and give them few Turns in the same Pan, taking the Bacon out, and putting a little Butter to the Fat; then take them out, to marinade some Time in Oil, melted Butter, chopped Parsley, Shallots, coarse Pepper and Salt; roll them in Bread-crums; and skewer them on small Skewers, to broil slowly, basting with the Remainder of the Marinade, and the Fat of the Bacon and Butter, in which they were tossed; put the Slices of Bacon singly on the Table-dish, and the Morels upon: serve in this Manner without Sauce.

Mousserons ou Champignons de plusieurs Façons.

Champignons or Mushrooms, different Ways, being both dressed alike.

WHEN they are properly cleaned and washed, put them in a Stew-pan, with a Spoonful of Oil, a good Bit of Butter, two or three Spoonfuls of Cullis, half a Glass of white Wine, chopped Parsley, Shallots, Pepper and Salt; garnish the Dish with fried Bread: also *à la Crême*, first done in Butter, then Cream added sufficiently; a Nosegay of Sweet-herbs, a little Salt; reduce the Sauce pretty thick; when ready to serve, make a Liason with Yolks of Eggs, and more Cream if necessary; take out the Nosegay; serve upon Bread fried in Butter, or such Pieces as directed for *Epinars en Tabatieres.*

Champignons en Canellons.
Mushrooms fried in Paste.

CHOP some Mushrooms in Dices, and put them in a Stew-pan, with chopped Parsley, Shallots, Chibbol, a good

good Quantity of Butter; let it brown a little; then add some Broth, Pepper and Salt; simmer till the Mushrooms are done, and the Sauce much reduced; beat up three Yolks of Eggs with Cream, to make a Liason pretty strong, and a Lemon-squeeze; let it cool, and prepare some good Puff-paste, rolled pretty thin, and cut in Pieces, longer than wide, to roll the Ragout in it, in the Form of a short thick Sausage; wet the Borders with Water, to make the Paste stick together; fry of a good brown Colour: serve without Sauce or Garnishing.

Champignons à la St. Meneboult.

Broiled Mushrooms.

CLEAN some large Mushrooms whole; chop one or two with Parsley, Shallots, Chibbol; give this a Fry in Butter, with Pepper and Salt, or Oil instead of Butter; put this Farce upon the Inside of the Mushrooms; strew Bread-crums over with few Drops of Butter or Oil; broil, or bake in the Oven.

En Salade; cut some Mushrooms in Dices, and simmer them some time in Oil, and one or two peeled Lemon-slices; then drain, and let them cool; use a Salladdish; put the Mushrooms in the Middle; garnish round, with chopped Parsley, Shallots, Pepper and Salt; and prepared like a Sallad, with Oil and Vinegar.

Champignons au Pere Douillet.

See *Cochon de Lait* ditto, Page 145.

CLEAN the Mushrooms whole, only cut half of the Stalk off; braze them slowly, with a little Oil, two Glasses of white Wine, a Nosegay of Parsley, Shallots, two Cloves, half a Clove of Garlick; simmer them long enough, to reduce the Sauce pretty much; take out the Nosegay; serve, and garnish round with fried Bread.

A l'Etuvée, stewed; put the Mushrooms whole in a Stew-pan, with a Nosegay of Sweet-herbs, one Clove of Garlick, two of Spices, a Laurel-leaf, a little Basil, two or three Spoonfuls of Oil; simmer this some time; then add a Glass of white Wine, one or two Spoonfuls of Jelly-broth, chopped Parsley, Shallots, Pepper and Salt; skim the Sauce very well; let it reduce on the Fire; take out the Nosegay; garnish the Dish with fried Bread.

A very savoury Powder is made of Mushrooms, Truffles, and Morels, dried in the Sun, or in the Oven; pounded equal in Quantity; sift it, and keep it well stopped in a dry Place: it serves to season, and mix with other Spices. For *Dôbe*, and any large brazed Pieces, season the Bacon with it for Larding; also in Forced-meat, and large Pies, or any thing else.

DE L'OFFICE.

OF CONFECTIONARY.

THE Names or Appellations by which the different Degrees of refining Sugar are distinguished, seem (as far as I am able to judge) to have no other Meaning to this Application, than their being adopted by Custom in the French Language. As I am unable to translate them *literally* to their true Sense and proper Meaning, and being very willing to explain them to the utmost of my Power, as it is a very necessary Part of Knowledge, to such as are employed in the Preparation of Sweet-meats; I shall still retain the French Appellations, with an Explanation of their Meaning, and distinguish each by *first, second, &c. &c. Degrees* of refining. The different Terms used in the French Language will soon become familiar, as well as great Numbers in Cookery are already. I am unacquainted with the Terms

used

used by English Confectioners; they are, in every Nation, very secret in regard to the Preparations of Sugar. The Reason is very natural. To avoid any Reflection of Ungenerosity, I have not applied to any body in the Course of the whole Translation; but shall continue in my first and firm Resolution, to finish it according to the Original, upon the Plan already mentioned in the Translator's Apology, with such Explanation as my small Capacity enables me to give.

Des différentes Cuissons de Sucre.

Of the different Degrees of preparing Sugar.

CUISSONS means the Preparations of Eatables, in all the different Manners by Fire, either boiling, roasting, &c. &c. In this Case I shall use the Word *refining*, after the first, which is clarifying. We have different Ways of refining Sugar after it is clarified; each appropriated to different Purposes, according to what Use it is proposed; they follow according to their Degrees of refining; they are distinguished by the following Names. The first is called *petit Lissé*, second *grand Lissé*, third and fourth *Le petit & grand Perlé*, fifth and sixth *Le petit & grande Queue de Cochon*, seventh *Le soufflé*, eighth and ninth *La petite & grande Plume*, tenth and eleventh *Le petit & gros Boulet*, twelfth *Le Cassé*, thirteenth *Le Caramel*. It is to be observed, that it is with fine Sugar.

De la Façon de clarifier le Sucre.

The Method to clarify Sugar.

PROPORTION for three Pounds of Sugar; put a Pint of Water in a Skillet, with half the White of an Egg in it; beat it up with a Whisk, to frought the White of the Egg; put it on the Fire with the Sugar; make it boil, and as it rises, put a little Water to it; so continue,

nue, till the Scum begins to turn blackish; then take it off the Fire and let it settle; the Scum rises of itself; take it off with a Skimmer, and put the Kettle on the Fire again; continue to boil it as it rises; throw a little Water as before, and skim it continually, it will cease to rise; when it is done, to clear it properly, sift it in a wet Napkin; regulate the Quantity of Water and Egg by this Rule, for more or less.

Premiere Cuisson du Sucre, qui est le petit Lissé.

First Degree of refining Sugar, called small *Lissé*, sleeked.

PUT the clarified Sugar on the Fire, to boil gently; you will know when it is to this first *Degree*, by dipping one Finger in it, and join it to another, by opening; if it draws to a small Thread, and in breaking, returns to each Finger in the Nature of a Drop, it is done.

Le grand Lissé, second Degree; it is boiled a little more, and the Thread extends further before it breaks, and is proved after the first Manner.

Le petit Perlé, third Degree; it is still boiled a little more, until it does not break, by extending the Fingers half as much as is possible to do; one Pound of Sugar is sufficient to make a Trial of all the different Degrees.

Cuissons au grand Perlé, à la petite, & la grande Queue de Cochon, au soufflé, & à la petite Plume.

Third, fourth, fifth, sixth, seventh, and eighth Degrees of refining. *Perlé*, from Pearl, large and small, small and large Pig's tails puffed or blowed; *Plume*, Feather.

THE grand Perlé is boiled a little longer than the small, and is known to be to the Degree wanted, by not breaking, by all the Extension that can be made
with

with the Fingers; and also when it forms in small Pearls in the Boiling, round and raised; by which I presume it takes its Name, in boiling this last a little longer, it comes to the fifth Degree, *petite Queue de Cochon*; it is known, by taking up some of the Sugar with a Skimmer, and drop it into the boiling Sugar again; if it forms a slanting Streak on the Surface, this is the little Pig's-tail. The sixth Degree is *la grande Queue de Cochon*, which directed as follows by a little more Boiling; and tried in the same Manner as the last, forms a larger Pig's-tail: After a little more boiling comes the seventh Degree, *au souffle*, blowed; which is known by dipping a Skimmer in it; give it a Shake, and blow through it directly; if it blows to small Sparks of Sugar, or Kinds of small Bladders, it is to the proposed Qualification. The eighth comes with a little more Boiling, *La petite Plume*, small Feathers, which is known by the same Trial; the Difference only is, that the Sparks or Bladders are to be larger, and of a stronger Substance.

La grande Plume. A large Feather, ninth Degree.

IT is known by the former Method, by still more boiling, and the Proof stronger; or the surest is by dipping a Skimmer in it, and give it a strong Turn-over Shake of the Hand; if it turns to large Sparks, which clog together in the Rising, it is done to this Degree.

Le petit Boulet.

A small Ball or Bullet, tenth Degree.

IT is done by a little more Boiling, and proved by dipping two Fingers in cold Water, and directly into the Sugar, and into cold Water again; what sticks to your Fingers, ought to roll up like a Bit of Paste, hard enough to roll in small Bullets, and to remain pretty supple, when cold. Eleventh Degree, *Le gros Boulet*, large Bullet;

Bullet; this is proved by the last Method, which by a little more Boiling makes the Bullet harder, when cold, as it ought to be. *Le Cassé*, broken; by continuing to boil the Sugar, it is known by the same Method, as in the two last; the only Difference is, that the Bullet which is made of this, ought to crumble between the Fingers, being first dipped in cold Water; twelfth Degree.

Le Caramel. Burnt Sugar, thirteenth Degree.

THE refining is little different from the last; to make it pretty clear, squeeze some Lemon in it, while it is boiling; there is also a deep Colour Caramel, of which the Uses shall be mentioned; it is made with only a little Water, with the Sugar boiling it, without stirring to raise any Scum, until it is to the Colour required; and take it off the Fire for present Use, to all the different Degrees of Preparation; if missed at first, add a little Water to refresh the Sugar, and boil it over again, untill it comes to the Qualification required.

DE PATES DE TOUTES SORTES DE FRUITS.

PASTE OF ALL SORTS OF FRUITS.

Pâte de Cerices. Cherry-paste.

STONE two Pounds of fine ripe Cherries; boil them some time, and sift through a Sieve with Expression; take all the sifted in a Skillet; put it on the Fire some time, to bring to a drier Substance; then mix with a Pound of Sugar, prepared to the ninth Degree, *grande Plume*, and stir it continually with a wooden *Spatula*, viz. a flat Spoon; the Paste ought to be of a fine red Colour, and pretty substantial; put it directly to what Use you propose:

propose: this is mostly done in Moulds of different Sizes and Shapes; these Moulds are like Hoops without Tops or Bottoms; put them on a Baking-plate to dry *à l'Etuve*, an artificial Stove, or Hot-house, in which Place all Sugar-paste and Sweet-meats ought to be kept: where there is no artificial Stove (which are rather scarce in England), those Pastes may be dried in a very mild Oven, or in any moderate Heat, and always kept in a very dry Place.

Pâte de Groseille. Of Goosberries and Currants.

GOOSBERRY-paste is made much after the same Manner; upon two Pounds put about a Glass of Water; boil them a little while, and sift them as the Cherries; put it on the Fire again, to reduce the Juice to a soft Paste-consistence, stirring continually; when it is come to a pretty thick Substance, put a Pound of Sugar, prepared as the last; and finish it in the same Manner. It is also done after the following, viz. when the Goosberries are sifted upon about three Half-pints of Juice, put a Pound of Sugar-powder, and boil together, until it throws large Sugar-sparks, in blowing through a Skimmer, dipt in the Boiling; then take it off the Fire, to mould it; and garnish as the first.

Pâte de Framboise, of Rasberries. This Paste is done in the same Manner, as the last Direction for Goosberries, with raw Sugar in Powder.

Pâtes d'Amandes vertes, & Abricots verds.

Paste of green Almonds, and green Apricocks.

THEY are both made after the same Manner; begin by taking the Down off, which is done by making a Lye, with five or six Handfuls of green Wood-ashes, sifted and boiled, till the Water is quite sleek, and smooth to the Fingers; put the Almonds in it, or

Apricocks; let them soak, till the Down comes off easily; stir the Ashes pretty often, to hinder it from settling at Bottom; take the Pot off the Fire, to clean the Fruits one after another, and throw in fresh Water as they are doing; then boil them in fresh Water, tender enough to sift as usual; and boil the Juice till it comes to a good Consistence, stirring continually, for fear it should burn; weigh the Quantity, and put as much Sugar, *au Cassé*, twelfth Degree; and mix it very well together off the Fire; use it in Moulds directly, and dry as usual.

Pâte de Violettes. Violet-paste.

UPON a Pound of Sugar prepared to the ninth Degree, *grande Plume*, mix a Quarter of a Pound of Violet, pounded very fine, and mixed by little and little; finish as usual.

Pâte d'Abricots murs. Paste of ripe Apricocks.

PEEL and stone two Pounds of ripe Apricocks; soak them pretty dry on the Fire, and mash them very fine; put a Pound of Sugar prepared *à la grande Plume*, ninth Degree; stir it well together on the Fire, till the Paste quits the Spoon; finish it directly in the Moulds; and dry it rather hotter than the former Paste: it is done also, by putting as much Weight of raw Powder-sugar, when the Fruit is soaked some time pretty dry, and stirring continually, till it is come to a good Consistence on the Fire; finish as the last.

Pâte de Pêches. Peach-paste.

PEEL and stone the Peaches, and cut them in Dices; refine half as much Sugar-weight as Peaches, to the ninth Degree; then boil together, to bring it to a Paste, and put it in Moulds directly, to dry in the Stove. *Pâte de Prunes*, of Plums; boil them with a little Water to a

Marmalade, and sift in a Sieve; put the Juice on the Fire again, to dry it to a Paste; always take care to stir it continually; put as much Sugar, boiled *au Cassé*, twelfth Degree, as the Paste weighed, mixed well together on a slow Fire, and finish this as usual.

Pâte de Raisin Muscat. Paste Muscadine-grapes.

GRAIN the Grapes, and boil a Moment with a little Water, and the Kettle covered; then sift as usual, and put on the Fire again, to bring it to a strong Marmalade; weigh as much raw Sugar as the Weight of the Fruit, which you refine to the ninth Degree, *la grande Plume*; mix it well together on a very slow Fire, and put it to what Form or Mould you please directly to dry.

Pâte de Verjuis. Of Verjuice-grapes.

THIS is done much after the same Manner as the last, only that it is well bruised in the Pan, before it is put to boil; then sifted, and reduced as usual; mixed with as much Weight of Sugar, prepared as the last; and finish the same: this is often done, with mixing Apples with the Grapes, peeled and cut in Pieces, about half as much as Grapes; reduced to a Marmalade; sifted, and dried to a Paste-consistence; then add as much Weight of Sugar, *à la grande Plume*, as the Paste; and finish as the Muscadine.

Pâte de Coings. Quince-paste.

BOIL ripe Quinces in Water, till they are quite tender; drain and sift them as usual; reduce the Marmalade (on the Fire) to a Paste-consistence, stirring continually, according to the Quantity of Quince-marmalade; refine a Pound of Sugar, *à la petit Plume*, eighth Degree, to three Quarters of Quinces; mix them together on a very slow Fire without boiling; put it to what Form you please directly, and dry as usual. *Pâte de Corrings rouge*, red Paste: To make the Paste of a fine red, bake the Quinces in the Oven a long while; then peel and sift them in a strong Hair-sieve, with strong Expression; dry the Marmalade over a slow Fire a little while, to about half the Consistence of a Paste; then to redden it the more, keep it a good while on a slow Ashes-fire, stirring some time; and to add to this Redness, put a little steeped Cochineal; and reduce, on a slow Fire, to a thick Paste; that is, when it lozens from the Pan; put as much Sugar as Marmalade or Paste, *à la petit Plume*, eighth Degree; soak it a little while on the Fire, and let it cool, just enough to work it well with the Hands; and finish directly as usual.

Pâte de Marons. Chesnut-paste.

BOIL the Chesnuts to Marmalade in Water; and sift them as all others, or pounded and sifted in a Stamine with a little Water; upon the Proportion of three Quarters of Chesnut-marmalade, put a Quarter of a Pound of any other Fruit-marmalade to it; put as much Weight of Sugar, *à la grande Plume*, ninth Degree, and work it well together, to finish as usual.

Pâte de Citrons. Lemon or Citron Paste.

CUT off the hard Knobs at both Ends; gore them, as is done with Apples, through and through; boil them in Water, till they are tender; take them out, and put into cold Water a Moment; drain by pressing in a Linen-cloth, to get the Water out; then pound and sift them; upon a Quarter of a Pound of Marmalade, put half a Pound of Sugar, *à la grande Plume*, ninth Degree; simmer it a while together, to mix, stirring continually; and finish as all others.

Pâte de Pommes.   Of Apples.

PEEL what Quantity of golden Pippins you think proper; cut them in Halves or Quarters; and boil to a Marmalade, with a little Water; sift, and reduce it (on a slow Fire) to a Paste-consistence; put as much Sugar, ninth Degree, as Marmalade; work it very well; and finish in Moulds as all others.

Observation sur les Pâtes des Fruits.

Observation on Fruit-pastes.

OF all the different Kinds heretofore mentioned, out of Fruit-season, use Marmalade of any Sorts, mixed with Sugar refined to the ninth Degree, *grande Plume*, viz. large Feather; simmer it a little while together on the Fire, and put it in Moulds, in the same Manner, to dry in a very moderate Heat; turn it over now and then, to dry equally of both Sides. Paste of any other Kind of Fruits may be made after this Manner; observing the Quantity of Sugar, according to the Sharpness of the Fruits: they serve to garnish Frames in Desserts, or for Plates intermixed.

DES PATES DE PASTILLAGES.

OF PASTIL-PASTES.

Pâte de Pastillage de Chocolat.

Pastil-paste of Chocolate.

IT is done by melting half an Ounce of Gum-dragon in a little Water, till it is quite dissolved and thick; sift it through a Linen-cloth; pound it in a Mortar with a Quarter-part of a White of Egg, a Chocolate-cake bruised, half a Pound of fine Sugar-powder, mixing by little and little; and put either more or less Sugar, according as the Paste is malleable; it must be pretty firm; form it into what Flowers or Designs you please, as Shells, Lozenges, any Kind of Corns or Beans, &c. &c.

Pastillage de Réglisse. Licorice-pastils.

SCRAPE and bruise a Quarter of a Pound of Licorice-root; boil it in a little Water, till it is much reduced; let it settle, and pour the clear off, in which dissolve half an Ounce of Gum-dragon; when thoroughly melted, sift it in a Linen-bag with Expression; and mix Sugar with it, till it is brought to the Consistence of a Paste; and finish in the same Manner as the last, in small Cakes, Flowers, or Lozenges, &c.

Pastillage de Violettes. Violet-pastils.

BOIL a Glass of Water; take it off the Fire, and pour it upon half a Quarter of a Pound of picked Violets; let it infuse about three Quarters of an Hour; sift it as the last; and dissolve half an Ounce of Gumdragon in it; and finish with Powder-sugar as the last: when out of Season, for fresh Violets use preserved, either in conserved or pulverised, *in Powder*; and mix it with Gum-dragon melted in Water and Sugar as the first: this may be had all the Year, by drying Violets in the Season, and reducing to Powder; it ought to be kept close stopped in a very dry Place.

Pastillage de Fleurs d'Orange. Of Orange-flowers.

CHOP and pound very fine, a good Pinch of Orange-flowers; if you have no green ones, use preserved; and pound them the same with Gum-dragon, dissolved in a Glass of Water, and a Glass of Orange-flower Water; add as much Sugar as is necessary, to bring it to a supple Paste-consistence; finish as usual.

De

De Citrons, of Lemons. Rasp the Rind of a Lemon slightly, and infuse in a Glass of Water, with half an Ounce of Gum-dragon to dissolve; sift it in a Cloth with Expression; and finish it with mixing Sugar in a Mortar, till it is brought to a proper Paste-substance; dry in the Stove as usual.

Pastillage de Caffé. Coffee-pastils.

UPON half an Ounce of Gum-dragon, dissolved in a Glass of Water, put an Ounce of Coffee-powder; sift in a fine Lawn-sieve; mix it in a Mortar, with as much Sugar-powder as is necessary, to give it its proper Consistence; and finish as all others.

Pastillage de Canelle. Of Cinnamon.

UPON half an Ounce of Gum-dragon, dissolved as before, and sifted in a Cloth, put a small Tea-spoonful of sifted Flour of Cinnamon Sugar-powder; and finish as usual.

De Girofle, of Cloves; upon half an Ounce of Gum-dragon, dissolved as before, and sifted, put six Cloves, pounded very fine; finish the same.

Pastillage d'Epine-vinette. Barberry-pastil.

DISSOLVE half an Ounce of Gum-dragon, in a Glass of Water, or a little more, as it must be pretty thick; strain in a Cloth or Bag as usual; put it in a Mortar, with a Spoonful of Barberry-marmalade; mix it very well; and add as much Sugar-powder as is necessary, to bring it to a malleable Paste; you may add a little dissolved Cochineal, to give it a deeper red; and finish as all others.

The ART *of*

DES SABLES D'OFFICE ET DES COULEURS.

OF THE SANDS AND COLOURS USED IN CONFECTIONARY.

AS the Sands are made with the Colours used in Confectionary, I shall here give their Explanation; they may be used upon several other Occasions, as Necessity requires, or Fancy leads.

De la Couleur rouge.

Of red Colour. how to make it.

BOIL an Ounce of Cochineal in half a Pint of Water, for about five Minutes; then add half an Ounce of Cream of Tartar, half an Ounce of pounded Allum; boil on a slow Fire about as long again: it is known to be done, by dipping a Pen or a small wooden Skewer in it, and write with it on white Paper; it ought to write like Ink, and keep its Colour the same; when done to this Mark, take it off the Fire; and put half a Quarter of a Pound of Sugar; let it settle, and pour the clear off, to keep in a Bottle well stopped.

De la Couleur bleue. Of bleu Colour.

THIS Colour is only made for present Use; put as much warm Water in a Plate, as Colour required; rub an *Indigo* Stone in it, until the Colour is come to what Degree of Colour is wanted, either pale or deep Blue.

De la Coleur jaune. Of the yellow Colour.

IT is done after the same Manner, by rubbing a Plate and a little Water, with a Bit of *Gum-gutta*, Gamboge:

boge: it is also done better with yellow Lye; take the Heart of the Flower, and infuse it in Milk-warm Water; preserve it in a Bottle well stopped; also the Flowers dried and pulverised as the Violets, and kept for this Use.

De la Couleur verte. Of green Colour.

TRIM the Leaves of Spinages, and boil them a Moment in Water; then drain them very well to pound; and sift the Juice in a Sieve for Use; of these Differences, you may make any Alteration in Imitation of Painters, by mixing to what Shade you please. Taste and Fancy are the only Guide for this last.

Maniere de faire les Sables.

How to make the Sands.

CLARIFY some Sugar, as directed in Sugar-articles; and put what Quantity you please on the Fire, with a sufficient Quantity of what Colour you propose to make the Sand; boil it, till it comes to the ninth Degree of refining, viz. *La grande Plume*; then take it off the Fire, and work it constantly, till it returns to Sugar again; and sift it in a Sieve, into Sand: mix the different Colours in this Manner: this Sand serves to prepare any Sorts of Flowers or Designs, upon Dessert Glass-frames; you may also make Sands, with old Sugar-preserve, by pounding and sifting in a Sieve.

DES CANDI.

OF CANDIED SUGAR.

CANDIED are different Sugar-works, which serve for garnishing Dessert-frames; they are made of many different Kinds, with any Sorts of Fruits, and are all made much alike.

Candi

Candi de Fleurs d'Orange.

Orange-flower candied.

BOIL some Sugar to the seventh Degree, viz. *soufflé*; put some Orange-flowers to it; and take it off the Fire, for about a Quarter of an Hour, while the Flowers throw their Juice; as it refreshes the Sugar, put it on the Fire again, to bring it to the same Degree; let it cool to half, and put in the Moulds; dry it in the Stove of a moderate Heat; kept as equal as possible; It is known to be candied, by thrusting a small Skewer in each Corner of each Mould, to the Bottom; the Top must be sparkling like a Diamond; put the Moulds upon one Side, to drain a good while before you take it out, and turn it over upon white Paper, to be always kept in a dry place.

Candi de Canelle. Candied Cinnamon.

SOAK some Cinnamon-bark in Water, about four and twenty Hours; cut it in Pieces of what Length you please; and boil it a Moment in Sugar, prepared *au grand Lissé*, second Degree; drain it, and dry it in the Stove, upon Rails, till it comes to a proper Substance, to put in candied Moulds; garnish with Sugar, *au soufflé*, seventh Degree; when it is half cold, put it to dry, as the Orange-flower candied.

Candi de Jonquilles. Of Jonquils.

FILL the Moulds with Sugar *à la grande Plume*, ninth Degree; when it is half cold, press Jonquil-flowers in it, with a little Skewer, and dry it in the Stove as the preceding.

Sucre candi en Pierre. Rock candied Sugar.

SOME is made without any thing but the Sugar, to give it the Taste of Orange-flowers; boil three

Pounds

Pounds of Sugar, (or the same Proportion), to the twelfth Degree, *au Caſſé*; put a Pound of Orange-flowers; give it two or three Boilings together, covered; take it off the Fire; and smother it with a double Napkin, till the Sugar is half cold; take out the Orange-flowers with a Skimmer; give the Sugar a Boiling, and sift it in a Linen-cloth wetted; it is much refreshed by the Juice of the Orange, and must be boiled again, to the ninth Degree, *grande Plume*; pour it in an earthen Jar, and keep it a long while in the Stove to dry; the Pot must be broken, to come at it; and Sugar is broke in Pieces, like Bits of Stone, or Rocks, when wanted for Use.

Candi de Violettes.   Of Violets.

IT is done as the Jonquils. *Candi de Boutons de Fleur d'Orange*; pick the Knobs of Orange-flowers before they open; make a Preserve in Sugar, and dry in the Stove; fill the candied Moulds with Sugar *à la grande Plume*; thrust the Preserve in it, when it is half cold, and dry as usual: Candied may be made with all Sorts of dried preserved Fruits, after the same Manner; when these Candied lose their Colours, or crumble by being kept in a damp Place, dry them in the Oven, and being pounded, may serve for Sands.

DES CLAREQUETS.
OF CLEAR TRANSPARENT PASTE.

Clarequets de Pommes.   Clear Apple-paste.

PEEL some golden Pippins; take care to leave no Sorts of Spots; slice the Flesh thin, and wash it in several Waters, to clear it of all Kinds of Spots, which might be made with the Fingers in peeling; boil in a little Water slowly, (the Pot or Pan covered), until the Liquid

Liquid becomes clammy to the Fingers; sift it in a wetted Napkin, and measure it, to refine as much clarified Sugar, to the twelfth Degree, *au Caſſé*, as of the Decoction; which you pour to the Sugar, by little and little, as it refreshes the Sugar; boil a Moment, and take it off the Fire, to skim it; give it two or three more Boilings: it is known to be proper to put in Cups, called *Clarequets*, or Glaſſes, by taking ſome with a Silver-ſpoon; if it falls out, by turning it over, extending a little like pretty firm Jelly, it is done.

Clarequets de Verjus. Of Verjuice-juices.

MIX a Spoonful of Apple-marmalade, with a Glaſs of Water, and a Glaſs of Verjuice Grape Juice, moſt ripe; boil a Pound of Sugar, *au Caſſé*, twelfth Degree; add the Mixture ſlowly, ſtirring without boiling; put it in the Moulds, to cool to Jelly or Jam.

Clarequets de Coings. Of Quinces.

PEEL them free of all Blemiſhes, and ſlice them in thin Slices; boil them to a Marmalade, with a little Water; ſift in a wetted Napkin to get the Juice out, as the Apples keep it warm; upon half a Pint of this Decoction, put half a Pint of clarified Sugar refined, *au Caſſé*, twelfth Degree; boil together a Moment; ſkim it very well, and put it in the *Clarequets* Moulds; prove the Qualification by the ſame Method, as the Apple tranſparent Paſte; if you would have either this or any other of a certain Redneſs, put Cochineal in proportion.

Clarequets de Poires. Clear Pear-paſte.

PEEL and cut them as the laſt; and make a Decoction in the ſame Manner, adding Bits of Lemon-peel; the Quantity of Water according to Judgment, which ought to be only sufficient to hinder it from burning; reduce to a Marmalade; finish as the last, either natural, or improved in Redness, with Cochineal.

Clarequets de Prunes. Of Plums.

BOIL the Plums in a little Water, to a Marmalade; sift in a Napkin, to get the Juice; boil the same Quantity of clarified Sugar, *au Caffé*, twelfth Degree; mix it gently together on a very slow Heat, and finish as the preceding. The Sharpness of the Fruits employed, ought to be considered with Judgment, in this and every other Kind, to regulate the Proportion of Sugar accordingly.

Clarequets de Fleur d'Orange. Of Orange-flowers.

MAKE a Decoction of golden Pippins, as set forth heretofore; sift it upon half a Pint of the Apple-decoction; put a good Spoonful of Orange-flower Marmalade, which you mix together in boiling a Moment; sift it in a wetted Linen-cloth; mix it with as much clarified Sugar, boiled *au Caffé*, as of Juices; and finish as the Apple-paste.

De Groseilles, of Goosberries; bruise the Goosberries raw; boil a Moment, and sift in a Sieve, then in a coarse Stamine, upon half a Pint of this Juice; mix it with one Pound of Sugar, *au Caffé*; and finish it as that of Pears.

Clarequets de Violettes. Violet clear Paste.

PICK the Violets very free from any stained Leaves; put them in a deep Pot or Tureen; pour a little boiling Water over; put a Plate or proper Cover upon the Violets, to keep them down; let it stand in a warm Place till the next Day, then strain in a Linen-cloth with Expression; mix some thick Apple-marmalade with this

Decoction; and keep it on a flow Heat some time, stirring now and then, with a Silver-spoon; refine as much clarified Sugar, *au Caffé*, as the Quantity of the first Preparation; mix it gently together, stirring continually with the *Spatule*; skim in the first Boiling; finish this as that of Apples in proper Moulds, and dry in the Stove the same moderately.

Clarequets de Muscat. Of Muscadine-grapes.

BOIL about a Pound of Muscadine-grapes, with a Glass of Water, the same with two common baking Apples, peeled, and boiled to a Marmalade; sift together first in a Sieve, then in a Linen-cloth; refine a Pound of Sugar, *au Caffé*, twelfth Degree; and pour the Liquid gently in it, stirring continually over a flow Fire; it is come to its Perfection, when it quits the Spoon, being turned over like Jelly; dry it in the Stove as all other: all the said transparent Pastes are cut for Use, to what Size is agreeable and convenient, and so on of other Kinds of Fruits.

DES CONSERVES.

OF DRIED CONSERVES.

FOR all Sorts of Conserves, prepare the Sugar after the ninth Degree, according to the Quantity wanted; they are all made much after the same Manner: the only Difference is in the Quantity of Fruits proposed; few, who are not done with the Sugar prepared to this Degree, shall be observed: Conserves are made with all Sorts of Sweet-meats Marmalade; use which you please; sift it in a Sieve; and soak it pretty dry over a flow Fire; use about half a Pound of the Sugar prepared as set forth, to a Quarter of a Pound of Sweet-meats Marmalade; take the Sugar off the Fire to work

it

it well together; warm it a Moment, and pour it in Paper-cases made for that Purpose: when it is cooled, cut it in Cakes of what Bigness you please.

Conserve de Fleurs d'Orange.

Of Orange-flower Water.

HALF a Pound of clarified Sugar being prepared to the ninth Degree, take it off the Fire, and pour a small Spoonful of Orange-flower Water in it; mix it well together, or any Quantity to the same Proportion; pour it in the Paper as the last.

Conserve de Safran. Saffron-conserve.

THE Sugar being prepared as before, have a little Saffron-powder, soaked in Water; and only pour a small Quantity, just sufficient to colour the Sugar of a pale Saffron-colour.

Conserve verte, green; it is done by mixing some green Colour, as set forth in Confectionary, with the Sugar being prepared as the last *à la grande Plume*, viz. large Feather, ninth Degree.

Of *Cinnamon*, done in the same Manner as the Saffron; the Cinnamon-powder being soaked in clarified Sugar warm.

Conserve de Pistache, of Pistachio-nuts; upon half a Pound of Sugar as usual, in foresaid Conserves, put an Ounce of dried, pounded, and sifted Pistachio-nuts.

Conserve d'Avelines. Conserves of Filberds.

UPON half a Pound of Sugar, put an Ounce of Filberds, cut in as small Fillets as possible; scald the Kernels first, as is done to blanch Almonds, to get the Skin off; finish as all others.

Conserve d'Amandes au Jus de Citron.

Almond-conserves, with Lemon-juice.

FOR half a Pound of Sugar, prepared as usual, pound two Ounces of sweet Almonds very fine, squeezing half a Lemon in it by Degrees; mix it with the Sugar, only when it begins to whiten.

Conserve de Cédre, of Cedar; prepare half a Pound of Sugar as usual; put about an Ounce of rasped Cedar to it; mix it; when the Sugar is half cold, add a little Lemon-squeeze; mix it well with the *Spatule*, and pour it in the Paper as all others.

Conserve d'Oranges douces, Bigarades, & Citrons.

Conserve of China and Seville Oranges, and Lemons.

THEY are all made after the same Manner; rasp the Rind of half an Orange or Lemon very fine; boil it with half a Pound of raw Sugar, without skimming, till it is boiled to the eighth Degree, *petite Plume*; take it off the Fire; and when half cold, stir it a little round the Pan with a Spoon; pour it in Moulds, when it begins to thicken.

Conserve blanche de Citron.

White Lemon-conserve.

THIS is made differently as follows; boil a Pound of the finest Sugar to the eighth Degree; take it off the Fire, and squeeze the Juice of a Lemon in it, at different Times, stirring continually; it will whiten the Sugar as white as Milk, if properly done; take care not to drop any of the Seeds in it; work it well together, and pour it in the Moulds, when it is mixed of an equal Substance, which you will prove by pouring some with a Spoon, as any other Jelly.

Conserve de Muscat.
Conserve of Muscadine-grapes.

GRAIN a Pound of ripe Muscadine-grapes; boil it a Moment, and sift it through a Sieve; reduce it on the Fire to a Quarter-part of what was sifted; put it to a Pound of Sugar prepared *au Cassé*, twelfth Degree; let it cool a little; then work it well together, until it begins to grow white; then finish it in the Moulds.

Conserve de Grenade. Of Pomegranate.

TAKE a good large ripe Pomegranate of a fine Colour; feed it one after another; then squeeze it in a Linen-cloth, to get the Juice, which you boil, and reduce to half; put it to a Pound of Sugar, refined to the ninth Degree; when it is half cold, work it well together, and dress it in the Moulds as usual.

Conserve de Guimauve. Of Marsh-mallows.

IT is done with the Roots newly gathered; scrape about half a Pound of it; cut it in Pieces, to boil in Water, until it crumbles between the Fingers; sift it in a Sieve as other Marmalade; soak it pretty dry on the Fire, and mix it with half a Pound of Sugar prepared *au Cassé*, twelfth Degree; and work it well together, till it begins to whiten, and grows to small shiny Sparks.

Conserve de Verjus, of Verjuice-grapes; it is done with ripe Grapes, after the same Manner as the Muscadine, only a little more Sugar, to the same Proportion of Juices; any other Grapes will do equally as Verjuice.

Conserve d'Abricots. Of Apricocks.

PEEL some ripe Apricocks, and slice them to boil to a Marmalade, with a Drop of Water; reduce it pretty thick on the Fire; mix a Quarter of a Pound of the

Marmalade to a Pound of Sugar *à la grande Plume*; work it well together, when it begins to cool.

Conserves de Pêche & de Pavie, Peaches and Nectarines; are done after the same Manner as the Apricocks.

Conserve de Cérises. Of Cherries.

STONE them, and boil a Moment; sift in a Sieve; and reduce the Juice on a slow Fire, till it comes to a pretty thick Marmalade, the Proportion of a Quarter of a Pound to a Pound of Sugar, prepared as the former.

De Framboises, of Rasberries. Bruise a Pound of Rasberries, with a Quarter of a Pound of red Currants; sift in a Sieve with Expression; reduce it on the Fire to about one third Part; it is the Proportion for a Pound of Sugar, prepared *à la grande Plume*, ninth Degree, which you mix very well together, when it cools; and finish as all others.

Conserve de Groseilles. Of red Currants.

GRAIN them free of any Branches; boil a Moment to sift in a Sieve; let the Juice settle a little, and pour the clear off: it will serve to make Ices or Jelly; sift the Remainder again with Expression; and reduce it on the Fire one third Part; about a Quarter of a Pound is the Proportion of a Pound of Sugar *au Caffé*; work it well together, till it is almost cold, and begins to form into small Sparks; put in Paper-moulds as usual, and to dry in the Stove.

Of *Chocolate*; work an Ounce of Chocolate in Powder, to half a Pound of Sugar, *grande Plume*; half an Ounce of Coffee, to half a Pound of Sugar of the Preparation to both; take the Sugar off the Fire, when it

is

is refined to this Degree; when half cold, work the Powder with it; and finish in Paper-cases, as all other Conserves.

DES COMPOTES DE POMMES ET DE POIRES.

COMPOTES, OR STEWED APPLES AND PEARS.

IF you would have it of a fine white, peel some fine golden Pippins, cut them in two, and cut out the Hearts; put in cold Water as you prepare them; then boil them with a little Water, a Quarter of a Pound of raw Sugar, few Slices of Lemon; boil on a slow Fire; when they are done very tender, take them out gently, to put in the *Compotier*; sift the Syrup through a Sieve; reduce it to the second Degree, *grand Lissé*; and serve upon the Apples: observe that this Quantity is meant for a small Quantity; for more, proportion the Sugar according to Taste for Sweetness, and the Lemon the same; cut a little off the Rind of the Lemon, to mix with the Compote.

Compôte Bourgeoise.

Common Family-way.

CUT the Apples in the Rind, being rubbed very clean; take out the Hearts; prick each Piece in several Places with the Point of a Knife; boil with a little Water and Sugar; it is done when the Apples are tender; this will do for present Use, but will not keep any time, unless the Syrup is reduced to a stronger Consistence.

Compôte de Gelée blanche. Compote of white Jelly.

CUT six or eight golden Pippins in Slices; boil in a little Water to a Marmalade; sift it in a Sieve, and mix it with a Pound of clarified Sugar; put six or eight golden Pippins, whole, peeled and gored properly; boil all together, till the Apples are done tender; take them out gently, to put in the *Compotier*, or what Kind of Dish you please; sift the Syrup again through a Sieve; reduce it on the Fire, till it quits the Spoon like a strong Jelly; let it cool on a Plate, to slide it upon the Apples, which may be done by warming the Plate a Moment.

Compôte à la Cloche.

Bell or Cap Fashion, Black Caps.

CUT the Apples in two, without peeling; cut out the Hearts, or cut it out at one End, without parting the Apple; put them on a Baking-plate, with Sugar-powder under and over, a little Water; bake in the Oven, or with a Brazing-pan Cover upon a slow Stove: they are also done after this Manner, with Bits of Cinnamon, and Lemon-rind stuck in the Apples, and red or white Wine in the Dish, instead of Water, and more Sugar, to correct the Sharpness of the Wine.

Compôte de Pommes farcie. Stuffed Apples.

IT is done as the white Compote, if you chuse to stuff them with the same Marmalade; otherwise boil Apples pretty much gored, with a little Water, Sugar clarified, Bits of Lemon-peel; when done tender, stuff the Apples with Apricock-marmalade, or any other Sort; sift and reduce the Syrup to a Jelly; let it cool on a Plate; just warm it, when you want to garnish the Apples with it.

Compôtes grillées. Broiled or fried.

SUCH Compotes as have been served, or begin to lose their Colour and Goodness, to make them serviceable still, put the Fruits in a Frying-pan, with a little of the Syrup; colour them of both Sides; take them out, and add a little raw Sugar to the Syrup, which you reduce to a Caramel; and masquerade the Fruits with either, by pouring it over, or by rolling the Fruits in: serve on a Plate or Compotier.

Compôte de Pommes en Gelée rouge. Red Jelly.

IT is done as the white, by mixing Cochineal with the Marmalade, sufficient to give it a proper Redness, according to Fancy: you may quarter it in the Plate, with white, while it is cooling, by having some white; pour it, when it is almost cold, by which it will not mix; or do it separately.

Compôte d'autres Pommes.

Of other Sorts of Apples.

THE different Sorts of Apples fit for Compotes, are done after the same Manner as the golden Pippins; only they are not to be peeled, not having the same Substance; they mostly all turn to a Marmalade in the Boiling.

Compôte de Poires d'Eté, d'Automne, & d'Hyver.

Compotes of Summer Pears, Autumn, and Winter.

THEY are all made much after the same Manner: the small ones are done whole, gored; the large ones are cut in Halves or Quarters: boil them in Water, till they give under the Finger, by pressing gently; put them into cold Water, and peel properly; scrape the Tails, and put them into fresh Water again; drain, and simmer them in clarified Sugar; skim it well, then on a smarter Fire, till they are thoroughly done: if the Syrup is not strong enough, take out the Pears, and reduce it on the Fire; if you would have it white, put some Lemon-juice with the Sugar, while clarifying; put the Pears in a Tureen, or any proper Vessel; pour the Syrup upon; cover it over with Paper-till used.

Compôte de Poires à cuire.

Compote of baking Apples.

SUCH Pears as are not fit to eat raw, are prepared as the Cap-apples, commonly called Black Caps; first fry them with a little Sugar in a Frying-pan, till the Rind can be rubbed off in washing the Pears in Water; cut them in two, to boil them in Water and Sugar, a little Cinnamon; or baked in the Oven as directed for Apples; if for a Compote, put few Bits of Lemon-rind in the Syrup; and reduce it to what Consistence you think proper.

Compôte rouge. Red Pear-compote.

IT is done with the same Sorts of Pears; if you would have them remain whole, do not peel them; otherwise do, and cut them in Quarters; cut out the Hearts; bake them a long while in a little Water, Sugar, a Bit of Cinnamon, few Cloves, and a Glass or more of red Wine; stop the Pot very well with a Paste to keep the Steam in; simmer it till the Syrup is quite reduced.

DES COMPOTES DE COIGNS, DE PECHES, ET ABRICOTS.

COMPOTES OF QUINCES, PEACHES, AND APRICOCKS.

Compôtes de Coigns.   Of Quinces.

BOIL them in Water, till they feel tender under the Preſſure of the Finger; put them in freſh Water, to cut them in Halves or Quarters; cut out the Hearts, and peel them; finiſh them in clarified Sugar, as all other Compotes.

Compôte de Coigns en Gelée vermeille.

A lively Colour Jelly.

PEEL them raw, and cut them in Quarters; ſtew them in Sugar, a little Water; ſimmer ſlowly; ſkim it often; then ſtop the Pan very cloſe, which will give them a pretty Redneſs; when done very tender, reduce the Syrup to the Conſiſtence of a Jelly; cool it on a Plate as ſet forth in Apple-articles; and uſe it in the ſame Manner upon the Quinces, in an open Compotier: a Compote is alſo made of baked Quinces; wrap them in ſeveral Papers; wet the laſt; bury them in warm Aſhes, till they are tender; then peel and cut them in Quarters; trim as uſual; and finiſh them very tender in clarified Sugar; ſkim it very well in the Boiling: ſerve hot or cold.

Compôte d'Abricots vertes.   Of green Apricocks.

RUB them with Salt, to take off the Down, or in a Lye, as directed for Apricock-paſte, page 511. then cut them in two, and boil till they are tender under the Finger; take them off the Fire; and leave them in the Water some time covered, to bring them back to their proper green; drain and boil a little while in clarified Sugar, half a Pound to a Pound of Fruits; let them soak three or four Hours in the Syrup, to take the Sugar; put it on the Fire again, to reduce it to a proper Consistence.

Compôte d'Amandes vertes. Of green Almonds.

THIS is done after the same Manner, while they are tender, much in the same State, as the Walnuts for pickling; if you make it for keeping, the Syrup must be stronger, and give them a few Boilings before using; this Compote is also made in Winter with such as are preserved; boil them a Moment in their Syrup and a little Water; the dried preserved, boil them a little while, with a little Water and raw Sugar.

Compôte d'Abricots mûrs. Of ripe Apricocks.

PEEL them, and cut in Halves; break the Stones, and peel the Kernels; put them in the Pan, with a little Water and Sugar; regulate the Quantities according to the Ripeness of the Fruits; boil accordingly like any other Compote; take it off the Fire; skim it with Bits of Paper; put a Bit of Kernel upon each Half; if to keep any time, reduce the Syrup pretty strong: they are also dressed *à la Cloche*, as black Cap, when pretty large, and almost ripe, taking out the Stones, and baking in the same Manner, either whole or in Halves.

Compôte de Pêches. Of Peaches.

CUT them in Halves, and if pretty ripe, peel them by tearing the Rind off; if not, boil them a Moment in Water, till you can peel them in this Manner; and finish stewing in clarified Sugar: they are also served in Compotier when ripe, being peeled and cut in Halves; ſtrew ſome Powder-ſugar over, or a light Syrup; the ſame with thoſe preſerved in Brandy, or *à la Cloche*, as the laſt.

Compôte grillée de Pêche. Roaſted or broiled Peaches.

THIS is made differently; ſuch as are not quite ripe may be roaſted before the Fire like Apples, ſerved with Powder-ſugar over, or a light Syrup under; others are fried in a Frying-pan over a ſmart Fire, till the Rind can be rubbed off, by waſhing in Water; then boil them whole in Sugar and Water: alſo boiling Peaches in Water till the Rind can be torn off; drain them, and prepare ſome Sugar *au Caramel*; roll the Peaches in it gently until they are done; put them in the *Compotier*; add a little Water in the Pan to gather the remaining Sugar; pour it upon the Peaches; this is moſtly done with October Peaches.

DES COMPOTES DE VERJUS, DE MUSCAT, DE PRUNES & MARONS.

Compotes of Verjuice and Muſcadine-grapes, Plums and Cheſnuts.

De Verjus & Muſcat.

THIS is done when it is almoſt ripe; grain it, and put it in Water ready to boil; take it off as ſoon as it changes Colour, and put a little cold Water to refreſh it; let it cool in this Water, it will bring it to its firſt natural Green; upon a Pound of Grape, boil half a Pound of Sugar with a little Water; when the Sugar is properly melted, put the Raiſins in it, drained; boil it a Moment together; take it off the Fire; take off the Scum with Bits of Paper; put the Verjuice in the *Compotier*;

potier; reduce the Syrup to what Confiftence you think proper to pour upon the Grapes: when the Grapes are out of Seafon, boil fome of the Liquid preferved; warm it in fome of the Syrup, and a little Water; ferve in the fame Manner. Mufcadine is made after the fame Manner; after boiling a Moment and drained, boil it a Moment in Sugar prepared, *Petite Plume* eighth Degree, Half a Pound of Sugar to one of Fruits.

Compôte de Prunes. Of Plums.

THERE are but few Sorts of Plums in England that will bear boiling. Green Gages are in the firft perfection for this Purpofe, and muft not be thoroughly ripe for it, nor any others; alfo the Mirabel Plum, and few others moftly of foreign Appellation: boil them in raw Sugar, and a little Water, a little while, according to their Ripenefs; fkim it when cooling with Bits of Paper; reduce the Syrup according as you propofe to keep them; if for prefent Ufe, it is fufficient to make a good palatable Syrup; ferve hot or cold; the beft Method for preferving is to prick them in feveral Places, and fcald them in boiling Water until they rife on the Surface; then take them off the Fire, and let them cool in the fame Water; cover the Pan, and put on a flow Fire, which will bring them back to their proper Colour; then drain them into cold Water, and boil them a Moment in Sugar *au petit Liffé*, firft Degree; leave them in the Sugar till the next Day, boil a little more; when prepared after this Manner, they will keep a long while. Such Sorts of Plums as will not bear boiling without breaking to a Marmalade, are only to be prepared for prefent Ufe, and are foon done; fcald them a Moment in boiling Water; then boiled in Sugar and a little Water, and fkimmed in the fame Manner.

Compôte de Marons. Of Chefnuts.

PRICK the Chefnuts in feveral Places with the Point of a Knife, to hinder them from cracking and flying out;

out; broil them in Aſhes, and take off the Huſks; ſimmer them ſome time in clarified Sugar; add a Seville Orange-ſqueeze; when taken off the Fire, ſqueeze them a little before boiling in the Sugar, by which Means they will take the Sugar better; it muſt be done gently, for fear they ſhould crumble; let them be in the Syrup a Day or two, or more, before uſing for Table.

DES COMPOTES D'ORANGES & CITRONS.

COMPOTES OF ORANGES AND LEMONS.

Compôte d'Oranges douces.

Of Sweet or China Oranges.

THEY are ſerved as Compotes, without any other Preparation than peeling; ſlice them, and ſerve with a cold light Syrup or Powder-ſugar over; you may alſo ſerve them whole, peeled or not; prick them with a Knife in ſeveral Places, and ſtuff as much Sugar in every one as they will admit; the Lemon is ſerved after the ſame Manner; Sugar in proportion to its Sharpneſs.

Compôte de Zeſtes. Of Bits of Rinds of the ſame.

THEY are made with the Rinds of China or Seville Oranges; the firſt called *Orange douce*, the ſecond *Bigarade*; and Lemons in the ſame Manner; peel them pretty thin, and ſoak in Water ſome time, and boil them in freſh Water till they are tender, which is to be known when they give between the Fingers; then pour them in cold Water a Moment, then drain; boil a little while in clarified Sugar; take them off the Fire; let them ſoak in the Sugar ſome Hours, and boil again to bring the Syrup to a proper Conſiſtence.

Compôte de Tailladins.

Cut in Pieces, Quarters more or less.

CUT Lemons in Quarters, and cut out all the fleshy Part to the thick Rind; boil them after the same Manner: for these Sorts of Compotes, clarify as much Weight of Sugar as Fruits; both Sorts of Oranges and Lemons are done after this Manner, either whole, Halves or Quarters: observe to soak them a long while in several Waters before boiling, which draws the Bitterness of the Rinds out, and makes them much tenderer.

DES COMPOTES DE CERISES, GROSEILLES, FRAMBOISES, & FRAISES.

COMPOTES OF CHERRIES, GOOSBERRIES, RASBERRIES, AND STRAWBERRIES.

Compote de Cerises. Of Cherries.

CUT the Tails to about half; if they are very ripe, they require only a Quarter of a Pound of clarified Sugar to each Pound of Cherries; if not, they require more; boil the Sugar to a Syrup; put the Cherries to simmer a little while in it; take it off the Fire; skim it with Paper; dress them in the Compotier, the Tails upwards; this is meant for present Use: such as are to be kept, the Syrup ought to be refined more, and still they require to be boiled a Moment, pretty often: *Morellas* require more Sugar, and are almost the only Cherries fit for Preserves in England, both in Sugar and Brandy, or dried either with Sugar, or without.

Compôte de Groseilles.

Of Goosberries, meant for ripe ones.

PREPARE the Sugar to the eighth Degree, *Petite Plume*; put the Goosberries in it to boil a Moment; let them cool before you skim them; if for present Use, serve in this Manner; if for keeping, refine the Sugar still more by boiling: this is also done with red Currants, which are called the same, only distinguished by the Colour, viz. red, and may be done without being grained, that is, in Branches, boiled and served in the same Manner; only require rather more Sugar, and never used until they are ripe for this Purpose.

Compôte de Groseilles vertes. Of green Goosberries.

GIVE them a little Cut on one Side to squeeze out the Seeds, and put them in hot Water to scald, until they rise at the Top; then put some cold Water to it, and a little Salt, to bring them to their natural Green; simmer them a while in clarified Sugar, and let them rest in it some time to imbibe the Sugar; take them out with a Skimmer to put in the Compotier; reduce the Syrup to a good Consistence to pour upon the Fruits out of the Season of having green ones, warm preserved in their own Syrup and a little Water, and serve hot or cold; these will not keep after being kept any time and warmed again; if exposed to the Air any time, they lose their Colour, and so do most of other Fruits.

Compôte de Framboises. Of Rasberries.

PREPARE the Sugar *à la grande Plume*, ninth Degree; take it off the Fire to put the Rasberries to it; stir the Pan gently to mix them in the Sugar without bruizing; let them take Sugar about a Quarter of an Hour, and give them a Boiling before using; this Fruit being of a very strong Flavour of itself, it is commonly mixed

ed with red Currants or some other Sorts. *Compôte de Fraises*, Strawberries, is done after the same Manner, mostly the Fruit without Mixture.

DES GATEAUX. OF CAKES.

FOR all the following Flour-cakes, make a Paper-case to what Bigness you think proper; have always some Whites of Eggs ready beat up, with Powder-sugar, to rub the Paper round, and to mix with the Cake, to make it as light as you think proper; it must be pretty thick of Sugar.

Gâteau de Fleurs d'Orange. Of green Orange-flowers.

TO Half a Pound of the Bloom well picked, prepare two Pounds of Sugar, *grande Plume*, ninth Degree, and put the Flowers in it to yield their Juices; this refreshes the Sugar greatly, and must be boiled again to the same Degree; take it off the Fire, to work it well with a flat wooden Spoon; put it again on the Fire an Instant; as soon as it begins to rise, put the Whites of Eggs and Sugar beat up together; mix it all well directly and pour it in the Paper-mould; hold the Bottom of the Pan over at a certain Distance, to make it rise by the Heat; bake in a very mild Oven. *De Fleur d'Orange Pralinée*, Orange Flowers dried preserved; half a Pound of these to a Pound and a half of Sugar prepared as the first, and finish it after the same Manner; this Cake may be done also with a proportionable Quantity of Orange-flower Water.

Gâteaux de Violettes & de Jasmins.

Of Violets and Jessamines.

THEY are made after the same Manner, the only Difference is in the Quantity of Sugar; one Pound and a half of Sugar prepared as the former to half a Pound of picked Violets or Jessamines.

Gâteaux

Gâteaux grillés. Put a little Powder-sugar in the Pan without Water; give it a broiled Taste; then add a little Water and Sugar to boil to the former Degree, two Pound of Sugar to half a Pound of Orange-flowers; finish this as the former.

DES GRILLAGES. OF BROILINGS.

This is what is commonly called burnt Almonds, &c.

Grillage de Bigarade. Of Seville Orange-chips.

THIS is made with the Rind of Oranges or Lemons, when the Juices are used for other Purposes; cut the Rinds in thin small Fillets; boil them a little while in Water; drain and put them in Sugar prepared to the ninth Degree, *grande Plume*; stir them well in the Sugar till they take a good Colour; drop them on a Baking plate like Macaroni-drops, the Plate first rubbed with Oil; strew a little Powder-sugar over; dry in the Stove; the Proportion is half as much more Sugar then Peels.

Grillage de Citrons. Of Lemons.

CUT or scrape the Rind very thin; do not boil this in Water as the last, but put it raw in the Sugar prepared as the last, two Parts of Sugar to one of Lemon-peel; put a good Lemon-squeeze before you finish on the Baking-plate.

Grillage d'Amandes. Of Almonds.

SCALD the Almonds in warm Water to peel them; cut them in Halves or Quarters, or they may be done whole; put them in the Pan with as much Weight of Sugar, and a little Water; boil them, stirring about till they crackle; continue stirring to make them take the Sugar and turn to a good broiled Colour; spread them on a Baking-plate slightly rubbed over with Oil, and dry in a slow Heat; for the sake of Variety, you may also

spread

spread Nompareils of different Colours on the Baking-plate, and strew some more over, or give them a Toss in a Pan in any Colour; finish the same.

Grillage de Pistache. Of Pistachio-nuts.

PREPARE them scalded as the sweet Almonds; mix them with as many Almonds; the same Method to be followed in the broiling; when they are ready for the Baking-plate, strew them with Nompareils, mixed with a little Aniseed, dried preserved Citron, chopped very fine, and the same over; dry these in the former way.

Grillage d'Avelines. Of Filberds. They are done in the same Manner as the Almonds from the Beginning to the End, and so may any Sorts of Seeds or Kernels.

DES GAUFRES, CORNETS, & AUTRES PATES.

Of Gaufers, Wafers, and other Pastes.

What is here meant by *Cornets*, Horn, is the thin Dutch Wafers twisted like a Horn.

Des Gaufres. Of Gaufers.

THE most in fashion are those made with Cream; mix as much fine Powder-sugar, as fine Flour, a little Orange-flower Water; put this in a proper Vessel, and pour some good Cream to it by little and little, stirring it very well with a Spoon to hinder it from mixing in Lumps; put as much Cream as will make the Paste or Batter pour pretty thick out of the Spoon: this is also made with Spanish or sweet Wine; mix as much Weight of Sugar-powder and Flour as before, and work it with one or two new-laid Eggs, and sweet Wine, sufficient to make the Batter of the same Consistence as the first: they are also done with Butter for this Purpose; use the Flour and Sugar as usual, and a little rasped Lemon-peel, a few Drops of Orange-flower Water, and mix it as the others by Degrees, with very good Butter melted in

a little

a little Milk until it comes to the same Consistence as others ; the Paste being prepared after this Manner, of either kind, warm the Gaufer-iron on both Sides, and rub it over with some Butter tied in a Linen-bag, or a Bit of Virgin-wax ; put a Spoonful of the Batter, and bake over a smart Fire, turning the Iron once or twice, until the Gaufer is done on both Sides of a fine brown Colour ; if you would have them twisted, put them upon a Mould ready at hand for that Purpose; put it up directly as you take it out, and press it to the Shape of whatever Form you please, and so continue always; keep them in a warm Place.

Gaufres au Caffé. With Coffee.

TO a common Table Spoonful of grounded Coffee, put a Quarter of a Pound of Sugar-powder, a Quarter of a Pound of fine Flour ; mix it well with good thick Cream as the preceding ; you may also put a little Salt to either. *Des Cornets*; they are done with the same Preparation as the first or second, only a little more Liquid ; as soon as you take them out of the Iron, twist them to what Shape you please ; they will remain so in cooling.

Des Gimbelettes. Of Jumbals or Buns.

PUT half a Pound of Flour on the Table ; make a Hole in the Middle, to put six Ounces of fine Sugar-powder, a small Glassful of Orange-flower Water, as much Brandy ; work this to a malleable Paste ; add a little Water, if the Liquid already used is not sufficient ; form the Jumbals to what Shape you please ; put them in Water ready to boil ; stir them about as they rise on the Surface ; take them out with a Skimmer, and drain on a Sieve ; bake them in the Oven with a moderate Heat ; when done of a fine Colour, take them out, and glaze the Tops with Feathers dipped in the clear Liquid of Whites of Eggs beat up ; this Water is found under the Frought, after settling a little, that will dry with the Heat of the Buns.

Pâte de Vin d'Espagne. Spanish Wine Paste.

TO make a Paste fit to make any Sorts of Designs or Flowers in Moulds, work a little fine Flour with some Orange-flower Water, one, two, or more new-laid Eggs according to the Quantity proposed, Butter accordingly, and Spanish Wine only sufficient to keep the Paste pretty firm; form it to what Form you please, or in Moulds; bake to three Parts in a mild Oven; take them out to glaze with hot Sugar prepared *grande Plume*; put them again in the Oven to finish the Baking and Colouring.

Pâte pour des petits Ronds.

Paste for small Hoops or Rings, &c.

BEAT up some Whites of Eggs with Sugar-powder, a little Orange-flower Water; soak it on the Fire till it comes pretty dry; form the Rings to what Bigness you think proper, or in Lumps, as Macaroni-drops, or any other Forms; lay them upon white Paper, and bake in a very moderate Heat; make them of what Colour you think proper by colouring the Paste.

DES MOUSSELINES & MERINGUES.

Coloured Pastry diversified.

This is what is commonly called Rock Sweet-meat.

TO make this, first prepare different Colours as directed for Colours, p. 518. dissolve an Ounce of Gum-dragon in the Colours, and sift it in a Cloth with Expression; pound it in a Mortar with Sugar sufficient to bring it to the Consistence of a supple Paste; form this Paste in what Manner you please, in the Form of Fruits, or Rocks, Pyramids, or any other; join them with Caramel Sugar; dry in the Stove, or in any moderate Heat:

Des Meringues. Whites of Eggs Batter.

THIS is done with Whites of Eggs well beat up, and as much Sugar as will make it to the Confiftence of a thick Batter; put a little rafped Lemon-peel in it; drop it in fmall Drops upon white Paper; ftrew Powder-fugar over; bake in a very moderate Heat; when done, glue two Drops together with Caramel-fugar, and put a Bit of Sweet-meat betwixt: this is made of what fize is moft agreeable.

DES MASSEPINS & MACARONS.

Sweet Pafte of different Fafhions.

Maſſepins, eatable or Sugar Pafte.

TO make the firft; fee Almond-pafte, Page 511. Roll it about the Thicknefs of a Half-crown, and cut to what Size you think proper, either to bake fingly on Paper, or in Moulds of any Shapes.

Maſſepins en Laqs d'Amour. Lover's Knot. Roll the Pafte pretty thin; cut it lengthways with a Pafte-cutter, like a Riband; twift it like a Lover's Knot; join it with Yolks of Eggs beat up where it ought to join; bafte it over with Whites of Eggs and Sugar beat together; you may alfo beautify it with any Colours, either liquid or Nompareils. *A la Dauphine*; cut it much as the former, and twift in Rings or what Defigns you think proper; dip it in Cherry-marmalade, beat up with Whites of Eggs; ftrew Sugar-powder over each Parcel upon the Paper, and ftick a preferved Cherry in each, or any other Fruit; bake in a moderate Heat. *Au Verjus*; work the Pafte in the Form of fmall Cups or Bafkets; when dried, put one or two Verjuice-grapes preferved in Syrup; the fame of any other liquid Sweet-meats.

Maſſepins à la Reine.

CUT Bits of this Pafte the Bignefs of Shillings or larger; make a little Hollow in the Middle, to contain a little

little Marmalade of any kind; cover it over the same, wetting the Borders with Yolks of Eggs to make it stick together; bake as usual; when done, glaze it with a white Glaze. See *Glace Royal* in Paste Articles. *A la Saint Cloud*; roll the Paste about half an Inch thick; cut it in the Form of Buttons; put them on white Paper and a Brazing-pan covered over with a little Fire; when done of one Side, dip the undermost Side in Marmalade beat up with Whites of Eggs, Sugar-powder over; this Side to be uppermost to finish baking in the same Manner. *Au Chocolat*; make a Paste as directed for Chocolate, Page 515. add some pounded Chocolate beat up with Whites of Eggs; work it together, and form it in what Flowers or Shapes you please. *Massepins au Pistache* done after the same Manner with Pistachio-nuts, pounded and mixed as the last. *Au Canelle*, with Cinnamon; Cinnamon-powder beat up with Orange-flower Water, and mixed with the Almond-paste. *A la Fleur d'Orange*, with dried preserved Orange-flowers pounded.

Massepins vole au Vent. Meaning very light to fly in the Air.

THIS is done by pounding as much Weight of Sugar as sweet Almonds together, the Sugar prepared *à la grande Plume*, ninth Degree; put the Almonds to it over a slow Fire, to work them with the Sugar until it quits the Pan by Driness; when cold, pound it with a little rasped Lemon-peel, a little raw Sugar, and a few Whites of Eggs; dress it upon Paper of what Form and Bigness you please; bake in a very moderate Heat.

Massepins de Cerises. Of Cherries.

BRUISE half a Pound of fine ripe Cherries; sift in a Sieve, and put the Marmalade to a Pound of sweet Almonds pounded and a Pound of Sugar; work it on the Fire till it is quite dry; let it cool, and pound it in a Mortar with three or four Whites of Eggs, a little raw Sugar; finish as the last.

De

De Framboises, of Rasberries; done the same, only the Rasberries put to the Sugar and Almonds without sifting.

De Fraises, of Strawberries; done as the last; glaze some with some of their Marmalade for Variety.

Des Macarons. Commonly called Macaroni-drops. Pound some sweet Almonds very fine, and a few bitter ones with them; put a few Drops of Orange-flower Water while pounding, for fear they should turn oily, and Powder-sugar; when done, mix them with as much Weight of Sugar, and some Whites of Eggs beat up, four to each Pound of Almonds and Sugar; when this is all well worked together, drop it on white Paper in small Nuts, and bake in a soft Oven; they require but a short Time; when done of a fine Colour, you may glaze some with white Glaze or any other Colour; they are more useful without glazing, as they make a Part in many Pastes, and in most Creams.

Macarons en Canellon.

Longways, Macaroni-biscuits.

POUND half a Pound of sweet Almonds, with a little Whites of Eggs instead of Orange-flower Water; mix to half a Pound of raw Sugar-powder, two Ounces of Rice-flour, four Whites of Eggs beat up as usual; dress them on white Paper in the Form of Sausages; bake in a soft Oven, and glaze with what you think proper, or not glazed.

Macarons au Liquide. With Cream or Marmalade.

THEY are prepared as the first, except the bitter Almonds; when dressing upon the Paper, make a small Cavity in the Middle, to put a little Marmalade or good thick Cream in it; cover the Hole with the same Paste, and finish as usual.

DES BISCUITS.
OF BISCUITS.

TAKE care the Eggs are new-laid, or as fresh as possible; put eight Eggs in a Scale, and as much Weight of Sugar against; take out the Sugar, and put the Weight of four Eggs of Flour; if you would have them very light, only put Flour to the Weight of three Eggs; take out three of the Yolks, and put three other Whites instead; put the Yolks by themselves, in a Tureen, with some rasped Lemon-peel, and the Sugar; beat it up a long while together; then add the Whites, also well beat up, then the Flour, by little and little, to mix it very well; then pour this Preparation in Paper-cases, of what Forms and Bigness you please; strew some fine Sugar-powder over to glaze them; and bake in a very moderate Oven.

Biscuit à la Cuillere. Spoon-biscuits.

THE former Composition serves for these; they are only to differ in the Shapes; take a small Spoonful of it, and spread it longways upon the Paper, a little Powder-sugar over; bake as the last: you may also mix dried preserved Orange-flowers, chopped very fine, which you mix with the rasped Lemon in the Composition.

Biscuit de Fruits confits. Of preserved Fruits.

TAKE dried preserved Fruits, such as Apricocks, Verjuice-grapes, Plums, Oranges, a little Orange-flower Marmalade; pound it together, and sift it in a Sieve; then mix it with Yolks of new-laid Eggs, and fine Powder-sugar, till it is come to a supple Paste, not too liquid; bake them on Paper as the last.

Biscuit à la fleur d'Orange.

Orange-flower Biscuits.

MIX up three Spoonfuls of Orange-flower Marmalade, six Yolks of new-laid Eggs, rasped green Lemon; add twelve Whites of Eggs well beat up, a Quarter of a Pound of fine Flour; when all is properly mixed together, bake in Paper-cases; when done, glaze them with a white Glaze.

A la Duchesse. They are done with Rice-flour, sifted as fine as possible; dried Orange-flower, preserved and chopped very fine; rasped Lemon-peel; a Quarter of a Pound of Flour to one Pound of Sugar, six Yolks, and twelve Whites of Eggs, well beat up; finish as the last: you may also mix any Sorts of dried Fruits; mix with a little of their Marmalade, and the same Quantities of each different Article.

Biscuits d'Amandes. Almond-biscuits.

POUND a Quarter of a Pound of sweet Almonds, dropping a little of Whites of Eggs in pounding, to hinder the Almonds from turning to Oil; put three Quarters of a Pound of fine Sugar, mixing with Whites of Eggs beat up, till it comes to a good malleable Paste; bake it on Paper, made in what Form your Fancy leads; bake in the Oven, or under a Brazing-cover, with a little Fire over; when done the uppermost Side, glaze the under Side with a white Glaze; and finish with the glazed Side uppermost.

Biscuits de Chocolat.

POUND about a Quarter of a Pound of Chocolate, which you mix with four Yolks of Eggs, and half a Pound of fine Powder-sugar; add eight Whites beat up, a Quarter of a Pound of Flour; pour them on the Paper with a Spoon, of what Length or Bigness you please.

please. Another Method with Chocolate; make a Paste with much the same Quantity of Chocolate, six Whites of Eggs, and Sugar sufficient, to make the Paste pretty firm; dress it in Flowers, Designs, or Moulds, according to Imagination and Fancy; bake as the Biscuits.

Biscuits à la Glace. Iced Biscuits.

MAKE a Composition as directed for *Biscuits de Turin*, Page 411. which you bake in large Biscuit-moulds; when cold, take up the upper Part handsomely without breaking it, and use the Inside-crums as directed in *Bonnet de Turquie à la Glace.* See the next Direction to the first Reference; the Ice being ready, put the Biscuits in Paper-moulds, and serve directly.

Biscuit de Pistachie. Pistachio-nuts Biscuits.

THEY are done in the same Manner, as those of Almonds; also of Avelines, viz. Filberts.

DES OUVRAGES D'AMANDES, ET DE PISTACHES.

OF THE DIFFERENT PREPARATIONS OF ALMONDS AND PISTACHIO-NUTS.

Amandes à la Prâline.

Dried, preserved, or burnt Almonds.

THEY are done with sweet Almonds, without scalding; rub them well in a Cloth, to clean them properly; put them in a Frying-pan, with as much Weight of Sugar, and a little Water; keep them on the Fire, stirring continually, until they crackle, and fly about, and the Sugar begin to colour; stir them about gently,

gently, to gather the Sugar; and leave them in the Pan to dry, about two Hours in the Stove, or any moderate Heat.

Amandes à la Prâline rouge. Red Colour.

PREPARE them as the first, until they have taken the Sugar, and ready to take off the Fire; put the Almonds upon a Sieve, with the Dish under; take the Sugar that drops, and put it in the same Pan, and a little fresh; refine it, till it comes to the twelfth Degree, viz. *au Caffé*; then put some Chocineal-colour sufficient to colour the Almonds; put the Almonds into it; give them a few Turns over the Fire in the Sugar; and finish as the first.

Amandes soufflés. Blowed or raised.

SCALD few Almonds, and pound them to about Half, as fine as for Biscuits; and beat this Powder with Lemon-juice, Whites of Eggs, and Powder-sugar; drop this Composition on Paper, the Bigness of Almonds; dry in the Stove, or a mild Oven.

Another Fashion of preparing sham Almonds, is, when scalded, to cut them in small Fillets; and mix them with rasped Lemon-peel, Whites of Eggs, and Sugar sufficient, to make a pretty firm Paste, that you may roll it in the Shape of Almonds; finish as the last, either the first or last: they ought to be picked from the Paper, while warm.

Amandes masquées; warm the Almonds while peeling, and while warm, dip them one by one in Sugar *au grand Perlé*, fourth Degree, and strew them with Nompareils of different Colours; dry them as usual.

Prâlines blanches. Sugar-almonds, white.

SCALD and peel the Almonds, and put them in the Pan, with the Sugar prepared *au grand Boulet*, eleventh

venth Degree; boil them a Moment in it, and take them off the Fire, before the Sugar changes its Colour; ſtir continually, as long as the Sugar ſticks to; if it cools too ſoon, put on the Fire again, and roll the Almonds in it as before.

Tourons, ſo called for being made like round Drops; chop the Almonds after they are ſcalded; put them on the Fire, with a little Sugar, and raſped Lemon-peel; then let them cool, to mix with more raw Sugar, and Whites of Eggs, until it comes to a pretty firm Paſte; make little round Bullets like Macaroni-drops, and dry in the Stove as uſual: you may alſo mix few bitter Almonds with the ſweet in the Chopping: this is commonly called Ratafia Drops.

Amandes à l'Angloiſe. Engliſh Faſhion.

MIX half Almonds and Filberds ſcalded; chop half of the whole very fine, the other half only each in two or three Slices; put the whole in double of the Weight of Sugar, prepared *à la grande Plume*, and ſome Lemon-peel raſped; ſtir the Almonds very well in the Sugar, taking it off the Fire; add one or two Whites of Eggs; pour it in a Paper large enough to contain the whole; cut it for Uſe as you think proper, when baked as uſual.

Piſtache au Caramel.

SCALD them, and wipe very dry; you cut each in Quarters, and ſtrew them on a Plate; rubbed over with Oil, and pour a Caramel over; turn them over, and do the ſame over again upon the other Side. Another Manner, is to pound Piſtachio-nuts; put it on the Fire, with half as much Weight of Sugar; ſtir it about, and keep it on a ſoaking Fire, till it quits the Finger for Drineſs; cut it in ſmall Bits, to form Piſtachio-nuts, Almonds,

Almonds, or any thing else; if in Shape of Fruits, stick a Bit of Wood to resemble the Tail; and dip each in Sugar-caramel; dry the Fruit upon Hurdles.

DES MARMELADES.

OF MARMALADES.

Marmalade de Pommes & de Poires.

Of Apples and Pears.

PEEL golden Pippins, and cut them in thin Slices; boil with a little Water very tender; sift in a Sieve, and put the Marmalade on the Fire, to reduce the liquid Part; then put it to as much Weight of Sugar *à la grande Plume*, on a slow Fire, to simmer a little while, stirring continually, to incorporate it with the Sugar; pour it in the Pot, and let it cool very well, before covering. That of Pears is done the same.

Marmalade d'Orange. Orange-marmalade.

THIS is mostly made with China-oranges; cut each in Quarters, and squeeze the Juice out; cut off the hard Parts at both Ends; boil in Water until they are quite tender; squeeze them, to get the Water out, and pound them in the Mortar to a Marmalade, to sift; mix it with as much Weight of raw Sugar, and boil till it turns to a Syrup; the Proportions are for keeping, two Pounds of Sugar to one Pound of Marmalade.

Of *Plums*; stone them, and boil a Moment with a little Water; sift as the former; soak the Marmalade a little while on the Fire; then mix it with as much Sugar *au Cassé*, twelfth Degree; and finish as the former.

Marmelade d'Abricots.   Apricock-marmalade.

PEEL and ftone them; pound the Kernels feparate; and boil the Apricocks on a clear Fire, with a little Water, and three Quarters of a Pound, or a Pound of Sugar, to each Pound of Fruits; (this is to be judged according to their Ripenefs); bruife them in the boiling with a wooden Spoon; boil until it fticks to the Fingers pretty hard, by joining two together; then take it off the Fire, to put it in Pots; put the Kernels to it a Moment before. It is alfo done, by boiling the Apricocks to a Marmalade alone; and mix it with as much Weight of Sugar *au Caffé*; boil a Moment, to mix together; and finifh as the firft.

Marmelade de Fleur d'Orange.

Orange-flower Marmalade.

WHEN properly picked, fcald them a Moment; then put them in Water, which has been warmed with a little Allum in it; boil fome other Water, with a good Lemon-fqueeze in it, and boil the Flowers in it a few Minutes, that is as long as they feel tender; fift them of this Water, and put into frefh, with a Lemon-fqueeze alfo; then drain them in a Napkin to pound; and mix with Sugar, prepared *au petit Liffé*, firft Degree, after Clarification; pour them gently to mix the better, without boiling; the Proportion is five Pound of Sugar to two of Orange-marmalade; finifh as ufual.

Marmelade de Cerifes.   Cherry-marmalade.

TRIM the Tails, and ftone them; and boil with the Proportion of half a Pound of Sugar, *grande Plume*, to a Pound of Cherries; boil till it comes to a good Confiftence.

De

De Framboises, Rasberries; bruise, and sift them through a Sieve; reduce to half on the Fire; then mix with half a Pound of Sugar, as the last, to a Pound of Fruits.

De Groseilles, of Goosberries; boil a Moment, or only scalded in boiling Water; sift, and finish by the same Proportion as the Rasberries.

De Violettes, of Violets; pick them very well, and pounded quite to Juice; mix with Sugar, prepared as before; the Proportion is five Pound of Sugar to one of Violets.

Marmelade d'Amande & d'Abricots verts.

Of green Almonds and Apricocks.

RUB the Down off, and boil either in Water, very tender; sift as usual; and reduce about half on the Fire; mix it with as much Weight of Sugar *au Cassé,* without boiling; and finish as all other.

De Coigns, of Quinces; sift as most others; and mix to the Proportion of five Pound of Sugar, to four of Quinces; if you would have it red, mix Cochineal with it.

DES GELEES. OF JELLIES.

Gelée de Pommes. Jelly of Apples.

PEEL and slice golden Pippins, according to what Quantity of Jelly is required; boil with a little Water, a Lemon sliced; when boiled to a Marmalade, sift the Juice through a pretty fine Sieve; the Proportion is about a Pint of this Juice to a Pound of Sugar, prepared *au gros Boulet,* eleventh Degree; simmer it together on a slow Fire, till it quits the Spoon clean, by dropping it out of it; then it is fit to put in Pots or Glasses.

Glasses. Other Sorts of Apples also serve for Jelly, done in a different Manner; peel any Kind of sharp Apples, and cut in Slices as the last; wash them in several Waters; then boil in a good deal of Water, the Pot covered, until the Water is much reduced, and becomes gluish; strain it in a thin Linen-cloth; measure the Decoction; and refine as much clarified Sugar to the twelfth Degree, viz. *au Caffé*, and pour the Juice in it gently; boil a Moment, then take it off the Fire to skim it; then boil it again, till it comes to the Consistence as the last; prove it in the same Manner.

Gelée rouge de Pommes, the same red; it is done as the first, only putting a sufficient Quantity of Cochineal-colour, while mixing.

Gelée de Muscat. Muscadine-grapes Jelly.

BOIL ripe Grapes a Moment in Water, just enough to burst; then sift in a fine Sieve, or as the last; mix the Juice with Sugar, prepared *grande Plume*, ninth Degree; a Pound of Sugar to half a Pint of Grape-decoction; and reduced to the same Consistence as the last. Of Verjuice-grapes or others, follow the same Method; only proportioning the Quantity of Sugar to the Sharpness of the Fruits employed.

Gelée de Grenades. Of Pomegranate.

MAKE a Marmalade with the Pomegranate; and sift it in a Sieve; then put the Seeds pounded to the Marmalade; and boil a Moment; and sift it again through a Sieve; the Proportion of a Pound of Sugar *au grand Boulet*, to half a Pint of the Marmalade; and finish as the preceding.

D'Epine Vinette, of Barberries. Boil this on a smart Fire, with a little Water; and sift it as usual; reduce a Pound of clarified Sugar, *au Caffé*, to each Half-pint of Juice; mix it together gently; boil a Moment; take it off

off the Fire to skim it; put it on a slow Fire again till it is finished to the Consistence of others; prove it by the same Method.

Gelée de Cerises. Of Cherries.

THEY must be thoroughly ripe; bruise and sift in a Sieve; let it settle a little; then pour the clear off; mix according to the same Proportion as the last, and finish the same.

De Groseilles, of Goosberries. *De Framboises,* of Rasberries. They are done after the same Method as the Cherries except that you mix half as much red Currants with the Rasberries.

Gelée de Groseilles d'une autre Façon.

Another Method of making Currant-jelly

The French distinguish all Sorts of Groseilles only by the Colour, as red or black, &c.

WEIGH seven Pound of red Currants without being picked; boil with a Glass of Water, and sift in a Sieve; weigh the gross Substance that does not sift; if there remains half a Pound, there ought to be near five Pound of Juice; put this Juice in a Pan, with as many Pounds of pounded Sugar, which you pour in it by little and little; or to keep it pretty tartish, put only five Pound; boil, stirring continually; when it has boiled a Moment, take it off the Fire to skim it and boil a little while longer; let it rest in the Pan, and skim again very clean.

Gelée de Coigns. Quince-jelly.

CUT them in Pieces, and boil with half a Pint of Water to one Pound of Quinces; cover the Pan, and let them stew to a Marmalade to sift as usual; prepare the Sugar *à la grande Plume,* the Proportion of one Pound to half a Pint of the Decoction; boil till it is reduced to the same Consistence as all others; to make it red, simmer it a long while, while the Mixture is made; and you may add a little Cochineal to give it a better red.

Gelée de Groseilles vertes. Of green Gooseberries.

PUT them into hot Water, and keep on a slow Fire till they rise on the Surface of the Water; then take them off the Fire, and pour a little cold Water in the Pan to cool it, and to bring them to their proper Green; put a little Vinegar and Salt to it, in about half an Hour after drain them off this Water into cold a Moment; drain again off this second, and mix with as much Weight of Sugar, *au Perlé*, third Degree; boil a little while till the Sugar is again to the same Degree; take care to skim it, and sift it through a Sieve to put it in Pots or Glasses.

N. B. It is to be observed, that as these Jellies are directed to be done much in the same Nature as the Marmalades, that the Difference must be observed in sifting the different Sorts of Fruits, not to force the gross fleshy Particles, rather only the Juices, which make the Jellies clearer, and ought for that Purpose to be strained in Linen Cloths, rather than any kind of Sieves.

DES CONFITURES AU LIQUIDE.

OF LIQUID SWEETMEATS.

Confiture d'Abricots. Liquid Apricock Sweetmeats.

THEY ought to be used when they are almost ripe; peel them and split only sufficiently to get the Stones out; boil them in Water, till they feel tender under the Pressure of the Finger; then take them out to drain; put them into as much Weight of Sugar, *grande Plume*, ninth Degree; boil a Moment; take them off the Fire, and let them be in the Sugar till the next Day; take them out, and boil the Sugar two or three Minutes; put the Fruits in it again, and boil a Moment together the next Day to finish.

Confiture d'Abricots d'une autre Façon.

The same Fruits of another Manner.

IF they are ripe, you do not scald them, after they are peeled and stoned; boil them a Moment in as much Weight of Sugar, *à la grande Plume,* ninth Degree; let them rest in the Sugar about three Hours; then boil again slowly; skim as clean as possible; when they yield no more Scum, take them off the Fire; let all rest till the next Day; take the Fruits out gently, and boil the Sugar, *au grande Perlè*; pour it upon the Apricocks to cool before they are potted.

D'Abricots verts, of green Apricocks. Prepare them with Lye as directed for Paste, Page 511. being very well cleaned, prick them in several Places; put them on a slow Fire with a little Water, Vinegar and Salt; they are only to simmer gently; when pretty tender, cool the first Water with some cold, and leave them some time in it, the Pan covered, which will bring them to their proper Green; an Hour or two after drain them from the first Water into cold, and leave them an Hour or two in it; melt some Sugar with a little Water, and put the Fruits in it till next Day; when you take them out, and boil the Sugar a few Minutes, to put upon the Fruits; continue in this Manner for two or three Days; put Sugar sufficiently, that the Syrup may cover the Fruits; the last Time boil them in the Sugar a Moment; let them cool before covering the Pots or Glasses. Liquid, preserved, green Almonds are done in the same Manner as the last for Apricocks.

Confiture de Groseilles. Of Goosberries or Currants.

USE them either grained or in Grapes, and put them in Sugar prepared *au Cassé*; stir them in it without boiling, holding the Pan by the Handle just rolling about for a few Minutes. Goosberries, and red or black Currants, are prepared after the same Manner, also Rasberries.

Confiture de Cerises.   Of liquid Cherries.

THE Proportion of Sugar prepared *à la grande Plume*, is three Quarters of a Pound to one Pound of Cherries, which ought, as all Fruits for this Purpose, to be quite ripe; cut the Tails about half; put them in the Sugar, and simmer about five Minutes, the Pan covered; let the whole rest together till the next Day; add a Quarter of a Pound of Sugar for each Pound of Cherries, prepared as the first, a little Decoction of red Currants; simmer together till the Syrup is quite rich and gluish. *Another Way* is, to strip the Tails, and stone them; boil two or three Minutes in Sugar prepared as before; half a Pound of Sugar to one of Cherries; let it rest till the next Day; drain out the Cherries, and boil the Sugar again to the aforesaid Degree; put the Fruits to it again to simmer a little while; let it cool before potting. The same called *Framboises*, with Rasberries; the Cherries are prepared as the first, and a Quarter of a Pound of Rasberries sifted to each Pound of Cherries, to give a stronger Flavour.

Confiture de Mûres.   Of Mulberries.

REFINE three Quarters of a Pound of Sugar, *au grand Perlé*, to one Pound of Mulberries; simmer them a Moment in the Sugar, and stir them about in the same Manner as directed for Goosberries; leave them in the Sugar till the next Day, when you must boil the Sugar again to the same Degree; then put the Fruits in it, and they are ready for potting. Of *Violets*; prepare the Sugar *au petit Lissé*, first Degree, after clarifying; put the Violets in it till the next Day, and boil together a few Minutes till they are done.

De Fleurs di Orange, of Orange-flowers; prepare them as for Marmalade as far as the pounding; when properly drained, put them in Milk-warm clarified Sugar, one Pound to a Quarter of Flowers; boil them a few Minutes for three Days succeffively before potting.

Confiture de Pêches ou Pavis.

Of Peaches or Nectarines.

THEY ought to be almoft ripe; peel and cut them in Halves; fimmer them in boiling Water till they rife on the Surface, which you drain accordingly; then boil in clarified Sugar till they have done fcumming; leave them in this Sugar till the next Day; drain them out, and boil the Sugar *au grand Liffé*, fecond Degree, and put the Fruits in it to boil a Moment, the fame over again the next Day; let Sugar and Fruits incorporate together two Days before potting, and keep the Pan in a warm Place; the Proportion is half and half of Fruits and Sugar.

Confiture d'Epine vinette. Of Barberries.

THEY ought to be quite ripe; boil them a few Minutes in Sugar prepared *grande Plume*, a Pound and a Quarter to one Pound of Fruits; let them reft two or three Hours in the Sugar; then boil it again to bring it to a good Syrup-confiftence.

Confiture de Verjus. Of Verjuice-grapes.

USE it when full grown, and not ripe; cut a little opening on one Side to feed it; put it into boiling Water a Moment; as foon as it turns its Colour, take it out, and add fome cold Water to it; leave it in this Manner till it turns green again; then drain it very well to boil in clarified Sugar a Moment, one Pound of Sugar to each Pound of Grapes; let them take Sugar in two thirds of the Sugar till the next Day; drain the Grapes out, to boil the Sugar with the remaining Part; boil a Moment covered up, and pour it upon the Fruits, the same over again next Day; boil the Sugar to the third Degree, *grand Lisse*; then put the Grapes to it, and boil a Moment together till the Sugar is refined to the next Degree; then it is fit for keeping.

Confiture de Coigns. Of liquid Quinces.

USE them when ripe, and boil in Water till they feel tender; drain and cool them in cold Water, to peel and cut in Quarters; cut out the Hearts, and drain them very dry; boil them slowly in as much Weight of Sugar as Fruits, prepared *au grand Lissé*, second Degree; take the Pan off the Fire to skim it; Simmer till you find they are quite tender; then take them out of the Sugar gently to boil it by itself to the fourth Degree, *grand Perlé*; put the Quinces in it while it is still warm, and put them in Pots for keeping: if you would have them red, put a proper Quantity of Cochineal with the Sugar in the last Boiling, and finish the same.

De Raisin Muscat, of Muscadine-grapes. This is done as the Verjuice-grapes, either grained or in small Bunches; only the Difference of a little less Sugar.

Confitures d'Orange, Citron, Cedras, Bergamottes, & Bigarades.

Liquid Sweetmeats of China and Seville Oranges, Citron, Lemon, and Bergamotte Pears

THESE are all made after the same Manner; cut the Rind in Designs of what Flowers or Form you please; cut a small Opening at the Tail-end; soak them in cold Water a good while; then boil in Water till they prove tender by pricking with a large Pin; cool them in cold Water, and get the Hearts out with a small Spoon; boil them

them in clarified Sugar sufficiently to the Fruits to swim in it; let them rest in the Sugar about four and twenty Hours; then boil again a few Minutes; the next Day boil the Sugar alone, and pour it upon the Fruits to rest a couple of Days; repeat the last over again, boiling the Syrup alone; rest altogether for three Days; then boil the Sugar, *au grand Perlé*, and put the Fruits in it to simmer a few Minutes; observe that you must add a little more Sugar every Boiling; pot them singly, the Hole upwards to pour the Syrup in it, and must be quite covered with it; let them cool before covering the Pots. Small green Lemons or Oranges are preserved in the same Manner, following the same Method as directed for green Apricocks, only require more Boiling to be tender; then follow this last to finish them in the Sugar; they are scarce for this Purpose in England.

Confiture de grosses Noix. Of Walnuts.

TAKE them at the same Growth as for pickling, that is, before they are hard shelled; peel them, and soak in Water a long while, changing the Water often; in a Day or two boil in Water till a Pin will get through easily; then drain them, and pour some hot clarified Sugar upon sufficiently to cover the whole Quantity; boil the Sugar again the next Day, to pour it hot upon as the first Time; continue two Days longer in the same Manner the fourth Time; prepare the Sugar *au grand Perlé*, third Degree, and simmer the Fruits in it a few Minutes; put them all together, or as many as you please, in a Pot to swim in the Syrup, which must be strong, and boiled over again now and then. Filberds are prepared after the same Manner, being employed while a Pin can be pricked through as to the Walnuts.

Confiture de Prunes. Of Plums.

THEY must be employed before they are quite ripe, and the Tails left to all Fruits which are preserved with the Stones in; prick them with a Pin, and simmer a Moment in boiling Water; then drain very well and boil them a Moment in Sugar prepared *à la grande Plume*, ninth Degree; skim it well, and let all rest together a couple of Days; then boil the Syrup to the fourth Degree, *grand Perlé*; adding a little more raw to it; boil the Plums in it a few Minutes; the Proportion is a Pound of Sugar to each Pound of Fruit. For *green Gages*, follow the same Method to keep them green as given for green Apricocks and Almonds.

DES CONFITURES AU SEC.

Of dried Sweet-meats.

ALL kinds of dried Sweet-meats are mostly done with Liquids, and are all made much after the same Manner; after they have being used several Times, or lose their Colour by any other Means, they will always serve to dry; take green Apricocks or Almonds out of the Syrup of Liquids; roll them in Sugar; dry upon a Sieve in the Oven. *Strawberries, Rasberries*, &c are done the same.

Confiture de Cerises au Sec en Bouquets, &c. &c.

Dried preserved Cherries in Nosegays or Bunches, &c.

USE the liquid ones with the Tails on, which you tie several together, and dry them in the Oven without being rolled in Sugar, or only one with the Tail on; and stone four or six others, which you apply upon the first, with the Syrup, so as to appear as an only one; strew a little Powder-sugar over, and dry as the first. Liquid Orange-flowers are done by putting the Pot in boiling Water to melt the Syrup clearer; drain the Flowers, and powder with Sugar to dry. Apricocks, Almonds, Pears, Apples, Peaches, Nectarines, Bergamotte, Lemon, and Citron, and so on of all the aforesaid Liquids preserved, are all done the same.

Confiture de Prunes, & Pommes tapées.

Of Plums, and dried or baked Apples.

THESE are made of another Manner; any Kind of Plums, provided they quit the Stone like Apricocks; cut them of one Side, to stone them; clarify half a Pound of Sugar for each Pound of Plums; and simmer together on a slow Fire a little while; then let them rest in the Sugar till the next Day; boil the Sugar *au Perlé*; simmer the Fruits in it a little while, the Pan covered; leave them in it till the next Day; then drain them out to dry as usual.

Les Pommes, Apples. Any good baking Apples will do the same Use, the clearest, and free of any Spots; prick them pretty deep with a pointed Knife, in several Places; put them in a moderate Oven, upon a Baking-plate; when they are half done, squeeze them pretty flat with the Hands; strew them with Powder-sugar of both Sides; and put them again in a soaking Oven, and Sugar over again; keep them in a dry Place constantly for Use.

Confiture d'Abricots tapés; they are done after the same Manner as the Plums, only break the Stone, and put the Kernels in the Fruits, before they are ready to be dried.

DES SIROPS.

SYRUP D'ORGEAT AND OTHERS.

POUND sweet Almonds and a few bitter ones very fine; put half a Pint of Water to each Pound, and a Quarter-part of the four greater cold Seeds, also pounded; let the Almonds infuse on the Water (Milk-warm) about four Hours; then sift several times through a Napkin with Expression; prepare two Pounds of Sugar

gar *au Caſſé*, to each Half-pint of the Almond-decoction; mix it together without boiling; and add a little Orange-flower Water; keep it some time in a moderate Heat; then bottle it cold.

Sirop de Citrons, of Lemons; it is only made for present Use; upon half a Pound of Sugar *au Liſſé*, squeeze half a good Lemon in it, and boil it a Moment, to bring it to the third Degree, *petit Perlé*.

Sirop de Pommes, of Apples; boil the Apples with a little Water to a Marmalade; sift it in a Napkin, and mix it; half a Pint of Juice to two Pound of Sugar, prepared *grande Plume*; it refreshes the Sugar greatly, as most others; and boil it together to the fourth Degree, *grand Perlé*.

Of *Quinces*; use them thoroughly ripe; peel them, and pound to a Marmalade; sift as the last; and mix it with Sugar *au Caſſé*, which is also called *Caſſonade*; finish it as that of Apples; the Proportion, a Pound of Sugar to half a Pint of Decoction.

Of *Verjuice*; it is done the same as the last; only double Sugar, to the same Quantity of Juice.

Sirop de Capillaire. Maiden-hair Syrup.

THIS Plant is said to grow in Cornwall; but the most that is used in England, comes from abroad; the French Author says that the best comes from *Canada*; the Proportion is one Ounce of the dried Leaves, infused in half a Pint boiling Water; keep it on an Ashes-fire, from one Day to another; sift it in a Napkin; and mix it to a Pound and a Quarter of Sugar *au Caſſé*; and keep it in a warm Place some time, then bottle it: observe the same Proportion for a greater Quantity.

Sirop

Sirop de Mûres. Mulberry-syrup, and others.

BOIL them a Moment, with a little Water; and sift through a Sieve; let it settle, and pour the clear off; prepare the Sugar *au Caſſé,* one Pound for each Half-pint of the Juice; mix it together, and keep it on a very moderate Heat, about five or six Hours, or as long as the Sugar is to the fourth Degree, *grand Perlé.* Syrup of Pears is made after the same Manner, as that of Apples: also that of *Apricocks*; pound the Kernels very fine, to mix with the Syrup.

De Ceriſes, of Cherries; they must be very ripe; strip the Tails and Stones; follow the same Method as the Mulberries.

De Graſeilles, of Goosberries, or Currants; bruise them, with a Quarter-part of the whole of Cherries; sift in a Cloth; and mix it with Sugar prepared *grande Plume,* ninth Degree, one Pound to half a Pint of Juice; simmer together, till the Sugar is *au Perlé.*

Sirop Violat, of Violet-colour; infuse a Quarter of a Pound of Violets, to half a Pint of boiling Water; cover the Pot or Pan till the next Day; put a small Weight upon the Flowers, to sink them under Water; then sift in a Napkin; mix this Decoction, half a Pint to two Pounds of Sugar *au Caſſé*; and simmer some time together on a slow Fire; finish it as the *Capillaire.*

Autre Sirop de ce que l'on veut. Syrups of whatever you please.

THE remaining Syrups of any Fruits, of which you have dried *, simmer it a little while, adding a little clarified Sugar, according to Discretion; bottle it for use as the former: it is readily seen, that Syrups may be made of any Kind of Fruits, Seeds, or Plants, by fol-

---

* This is meant of those liquid preserved, spoiled by long keeping, or any otherwise damaged.

following the same Method, as is here laid down; only observing to regulate the Quantities of Sugar, to the Sharpness and Flavours of each Kind.

DES FRUITS A L'EAU-DE-VIE,

OF BRANDY-FRUITS.

Pêche à la l'Eau-de-Vie. Peaches in Brandy.

WIPE the Down off very clean, and the Fruits almost ripe; prepare as many Half-pounds of Sugar (as Pounds of Fruits) *au Perlé*; and put the Peaches whole in it, to boil a Moment together; being cold, put them in Bottles; mix half a Pint of the Syrup, to three Half-pints of Brandy, which you pour upon the Peaches, and stop the Bottles very well, to preserve them clear; if you would have the Peaches peeled, use them before they are quite so ripe as the first; boil them in Water, until you can pull the Rind off with the Fingers; and put them in cold Water, as soon as done, one after another; being drained, boil a Moment in the same Proportion of clarified Sugar, as directed at first; skim it, and let all rest together till the next Day; then drain the Fruits out, and boil the Sugar few Minutes; pour it again upon the Fruits till the next Day; then bottle the Peaches, and mix the Syrup with as much Brandy, to pour upon the Fruits; observe that in this, and all other preserved Fruits, they must swim in it; this last Method is not so proper for long keeping, as the first: observe the same Rule for Apricocks or Nectarines.

Poires à l'Eau-de-Vie.

Pears preserved in Brandy.

THE best for this Purpose, are the Rousset-pears; take them almost ripe; prick them here and there,

and

and boiled in Water, till they feel pretty tender; then peel, and put them in cold Water, as the last Peaches, and a good Lemon-squeeze in it; clarify half as much Weight of Sugar as Pears, and boil them in it slowly few Minutes; being well skimmed leave them in the Sugar, till the next Day, the same oven again; then the third Day; simmer Fruit and Sugar together a Moment; when cold, put them in Pots or Bottles; the Syrup must be boiled in *grand Perlé*, fourth Degree; put it on a slow fire; and add as much Brandy, which you mix well together without boiling, let it cool, to pour upon the Pears.

Prunes à l'Eau-de-Vie. **Plums in Brandy.**
PREPARE them as the *Prunes au Liquide*, only that you do not put above three Quarters of a Pound of Sugar, to each Pound of Plums, being drained and cold, put them in Bottles; boil the sugar *au gros Boulet*, eleventh Degree, and as much Brandy, being well mixt together; pour it upon the Fruits, when half cold.

Noix, Walnuts; use them in the same Growth, as set forth for *Consiture*, see Page 563. and prepare them in the same Manner; the only Difference is, that you only use half a Pound of Sugar to the same Proportion of Walnuts, and as much Brandy, which being well incorporated together with the Sugar *au Perlé*, pour upon the Fruits, when it is almost cold.

Cerises à l'Eau-de-Vie. **Cherries in Brandy.**
BRUISE few cherries, Mulberries, and Raspberries sufficiently, to get half a Pint of clear Juice; mix it with a Pint of Brandy, a Pound of Sugar, or rather more; let it dissolve very well; bottle some fine ripe Cherries, as free from Spots as possible; cut the Tails about half off; pour the first Preparation upon, regu-

late

late your Quantities accordingly, as the Liquid must cover the Cherries. In Winter; these Cherries, serve to glaze with Caramel, or white Glaze.

Amondes vertes & Abricots verts a l'Eau-de-Vie
Green Almonds and green Apricocks in Brandy.

PREPARE them in the same Manner as the Liquids, only the Difference of less Sugar, that is, half a Pound of Sugar to each Pound of Fruit, and as much Brandy as Syrup; and warm together a good while on a slow Fire, to incorporate them in the Syrup; let them cool before bottling, as usual.

Oranges douces a l'Eau-de-Vie
Sweet or China Oranges.

PREPARE them as the Liquids; boil them in Water, till you can run a Pin in it easily; these are not to be gutted, only cut a little Hole quite through the Rind, at the Tail-end; boil them a Moment in clarified Sugar; let it rest till the next Day; then boil the Sugar again, and pour it hot upon the Oranges; the same over again the next Day, with the Oranges in it; put as much Brandy as Syrup; warm it together without boiling; pur it upon the Fruits, when cold; the Orange must swim in it, as all other Fruits.

DES MOUSSES.
OF FROUGHTED OR WHIPPED CREAMS

THIS is often served iced abroad, and so may be made two or three Hours before it is wanted for Table; for that Purpose they have a Tin Mould, made large enough to contain as many Glasses, Cups, or thin silver Tumblers, as will ice a Quantity sufficient for a Dish; it has commonly two Plates, the Bottom solid; the next bored in small Holes, to let the melted Ice run off, and Rings in it, to hold the Glaſſes, and Ice under pounded with Salt, and the ſame upon the Cover, when the whipt Cream is in it.

Mouſſe à la Crême. Whipt Cream.

UPON the Proportion of a Quart of very good Cream, put few Drops of Bergamotte-water, or of Cedar, a little Orange-flower Water, about half a Pound of Sugar; when it is diſſolved, whip the Cream to a Frought, and take it up with a Skimmer; drain it upon a Sieve a Moment; if for icing, let it ſettle a good while, before you put it in the Cups or Glaſſes; continue in this Manner to the End, and uſe what drops in the Diſh under the Sieve, to make it frought better; put one or two Whites of Eggs: any Kinds of prepared Waters may be done with this Cream, as well as thoſe ſaid before, according to Taſte and Fancy.

Mouſſe de Caffé.

UPON three Half-pints of Cream, put two Diſhes of ſtrong Coffee cleared; add four Yolks of new-laid Eggs beat up, half a Pound of Sugar, about as much more Cream; and finiſh as the firſt.

De Chocolat; it is done after the ſame Manner, diſſolving a proper Quantity of Chocolate in Cream, and the ſame Quantities of Eggs and Sugar.

De Safran, of Saffron; it is made as the firſt, without Yolks of Eggs, only one or two of the Whites, to make it frought better; and inſtead of any of the Waters mentioned, infuſe a little Saffron on a ſlow Fire in ſome of the Cream, juſt enough to give it the Taſte without prevaling too much; ſift it in a Sieve, and add it to the Cream and Sugar.

DES GLACES. OF ICES.

ALL Kinds of Ices are finished in the same Manner; the Cream or Mixture being prepared, put it in the Icing-pot, which ought to be twice or three times as large as the Contents in it; the best Sorts are those made of Pewter; put them in a proper Tub, and pounded Ice with Salt sufficient, to bury the Pots in it, stirring continually with a flat Pewter-spoon, till it begins to freeze; work the Ice so in freezing, that it may not be in harder Flakes in one Part than another; only put them in the proper Moulds, a little while before serving: observe that they are not iced too hard at first, before they are to be changed into the Moulds to go to Table: if you find any difficulty to get them out, just dip the Moulds in hot Water, and turn them over with a Stroke of the Hand.

Glace à la Crème. Cream-ice.

BOIL a Pint or more Cream, with six or eight sweet Almonds scalded and bruised; when you take it off the Fire, put half a Pound of Sugar, or such Proportion as you please; thin Bits of Lemon-peel, a little Orange-flower Water; let it rest about half an Hour; sift it, and pour it in the Icing-pot.

Glace de Caffé; make three Dishes of strong Coffee; pour it off very clear, to mix with three Half-pints of Cream, or the same Proportion for more or less, and three Quarters of a Pound of Sugar; boil it a Moment together, and ice it when cold.

De Chocolat; dissolve the Chocolate in a little Water on a slow Fire; when properly done, mix it with a Pint of Cream, and three Yolks of new-laid Eggs, and about half a Pound of Sugar.

Glace

Glace de Fruits, Fruit-ices; *de Cerises*, of Cherries, &c. &c.

BRUISE about two Pounds of Cherries, with a Pint of Water; sift in a Sieve with Expression, and put Sugar sufficient to give it a proper Sweetness: all Kinds of Ices are made in Winter or Summer, with the Juices or Marmalades, as well as with raw Fruits. Taste is the best Direction for the different Mixtures.

Framboises, Rasberries; it is done in the same Manner as the last.

Groseilles, Gosberries or Currants; boil two Pounds of red Currants a Moment, with a Quarter of a Pound of Rasberries; sift in a Sieve, putting a Pint of Water to it, then the Sugar, which must be very well dissolved before icing.

Des Fraises, of Strawberries; it is done after the same Manner as the last; some mix a Quarter of a Pound of red Currants, to each Pound of Strawberries, as is mostly done with Rasberries, Sugar according to Taste: these ought not to be very sweet, as the Tartness of these Fruits is relishing to most People.

Glace de Violettes, de Jasmin, & de Fleurs d'Orange.

Ices of Violets, Jessamines, and Orange-flowers.

POUND a Handful of Violets, and pour about a Pint of hot Water upon; let them infuse about an Hour; put about half a Pound of Sugar; when it is properly dissolved, sift through a Napkin. The Jessamine is done after the same Manner, to make the Liquid taste more of the different Flowers; pour it several times from one Pan into another before sifting; the same with the Orange-flowers; those different Infusions are also mixed with Cream, instead of Water.

De Verjus; half a Pint of the Juice to three Half-pints of Water, and a Pound of Sugar.

Glace de Citron, Lemon-ice; *de Grenade*, Pomegranate.

INFUSE the Rind of four or five Lemons, peeled very thin, with the Juices, and three Half-pints of Water, three Quarters of a Pound of Sugar; sift through a Napkin; bruise the Seeds of three or four Pomegranates; and infuse with hot Water as the Lemon-rinds; and finish the same.

Glace de Bigarades, & d'Oranges douces.

Of China and Seville Oranges.

THEY are made in the same Manner as that of Lemon; only observing that the Seville-oranges require a little more Sugar than the China ones, either with the Juice or Marmalade.

Glace de Canelle. Cinnamon-ice.

INFUSE a proper Quantity of Cinnamon, about an Hour, in hot Water, and boil it a Moment; and put half a Pound of fine Sugar to a Pint of Water; sift through a Sieve; finish as others.

Glace de Roses & Jonquilles.

Of Roses and Jonquils.

THEY are both done after the same Manner as that of Violets, and so of any other Herbs or Flowers, which you think proper to make Ices of, either with Water or Cream.

Glace

Glace de Pavis, de Pêches, & d'Abricots.

Ices of Nectarines, Peaches and Apricocks.

USE the Marmalade or Jelly as directed, or in the Season; cut seven or eight of either when quite ripe; bruise them, and sift with a Pint of Water, the Nectarines must be boiled in the Water, to fit them for sifting; put a sufficient Quantity of Sugar to the sifted Juice: the Peaches and Apricocks need not be boiled, if they are thoroughly ripe, only stoned and bruised.

Glace de Coriandre, d'Anis, & de Génievre.

Ices of Coriander-seeds, Anise, and Juniper-berries.

BRUISE an Ounce of Coriander-seeds, and infuse it about an Hour in a Pint of warm Water, half a Pound of Sugar, and sift it through a Napkin: Aniseeds done the same; Taste must direct, when the Water has got a sufficient Flavour of the different Infusions: that of Juniper-berries is done also by Infusion, or by boiling a Moment about a Handful of the Berries, with a Pint of Water, half a Pound of Sugar, a Bit of Cinnamon; then sifted as usual, either through a fine Sieve, or a thin Napkin or Cloth.

DES FRUITS GLACÉS.

OF ICED FRUITS.

FOR this Purpose you must have Moulds, made in the Form of the different Shapes of the Fruits proposed; accordingly, make Marmalades of the different Sorts of Fruits, as directed Page 553: ice in the same Manner as the former Ices; when iced, work them with the Spoon, till the Ice is in Marmalade, to put in the Fruit-moulds; shut them close, and wrap in Paper to ice them again as before; the Pail or Bucket in which the Fruits are to be iced, should be bored, that the Water may run off as the Ice melts; when ready to serve, have the proper Colour of the Fruits ready, which you colour with a Pencil, to imitate the natural; the best Method is to have a natural one, or one properly painted for Pattern. See the different Colours used in Confectionary, as directed how to be made; Page 518.

DES FROMAGES GLACÉS.

ICED CHEESES.

Fromage à la Crême glacé. Iced Cream-cheese.

BOIL a Pint of good Cream; then put half a Pound of Sugar to it, about a Dozen of sweet Almonds pounded, a little of preserved Orange flowers, or Orange flower Water, rasped Lemon-peel; boil toegther few Minutes; when you take it off the Fire, add five Yolks of Eggs beat up, and stir it continually, till they are well mixed with the Cream; sift it in a Sieve, and put it in the Icing pot; when it is pretty much iced, work it well, to put it in Cheese-moulds; ise it again, and serve as the ices: it is also done with Coffee and Chocolate, in the same Manner as the Ices, only that each is thickened with four or five Yolks of Eggs, as directed in the first, and moulded like a Cheese, which gives it the Name.

Fromage de Marmelade glacé.

Of Marmalade of any Sorts.

THEY are made after the same Manner; when the Cream and Eggs are well mixed, add a sifficient Quantity of what Marmalade you please, to give it a proper Taste of the Fruits desired.

De Pistache, of Pistachio-nuts; boil a Pint of Cream few Minutes, with half a Pound of Sugar, a Spoonful of Orange-flower Water; take it off the Fire, to mix five Yolks of new-laid Eggs with it, done over a slow Fire without boiling; and pound about a Quarter of a Pound of scalded Pistachio-nuts, which are to be infused in the Cream about half an Hour, being kept warm; then sift through a Sieve, and finish as all former.

Fromage à la Chantilly glacé.

From the Name of the Place where made.

IT is at first prepared as the first directed, and put to Ice in Moulds; beat up a Pint of good Cream to froughs, with rasped Lemon-peel, half a Pound of pounded Sugar, a Spoonful of Orange-flower Water; serve the Frought upon the Cheese, raised as high as possible: you may also ice the Frought a little, or serve without icing.

Fromage de Beurre glacé. As iced Butter.

BOIL a Pint of good Cream a few Minutes, with rasped Lemon-peel, a good Spoonful of Orange-flower Water; when taken off the Fire, put one Dozen of Yolks of Eggs well beat up, and mix together without boiling; sift through a Sieve, and put into an Icing-pot to freeze, working it like Ices; ice it in such a Manner, that you may take it with a Spoon, to serve like Pats of Butter stamped, and Bits of clean Ice between, to appear as Crystals.

DES EAUX RAFAICHISSANTES SANS ETRE A LA GLACE.

OF COOLING LIQUORS, WITHOUT ICING.

Eau rafraîchissante d'Orgeat.   Orgeat Water.

PROPORTION for a Quart; pound about a Quarter of a Pound of sweet Almonds scalded, a few bitter ones, and about two Ounces of the four cold Seeds, either greater or lesser; take care to put a little Water to it while pounding, for fear the Almonds should turn to Oil; then put it in a Bowl, with about a Quart of Water to this Proportion, and about two Ounces of fine Sugar; let it rest about an Hour, then sift through a Stamine with Expression: you may add a little Milk, to give it a better white Colour.

De Pistache; it is done after the same Manner; only that you do not put Milk to it, but a Lemon-squeeze instead; and proportion the Sugar, to make it of a proper Sweetness; Orange-flower Water to both, if agreeable.

Eau rafraîchissante de Fenouil, & de Cerfeuil.

Cooling Waters of Fennel, and of Charvil.

THESE are done simply, by steeping some of either in hot Water, till it has the Taste of the Herbs sufficiently; add what Quantity of Sugar you think proper; and keep it in a cool Place a good while before using: the same is done with any other Kind of Herbs, and in general, with all Sorts of Fruits used in Confectionary, and

and with the Syrups of Liquid-preserves, mixing some of the Liquor with Water and Sugar, just sufficient to make it palatable, and may be iced or not.

Lemonade.

PROPORTION for a Gallon; weigh a Pound of Sugar in Lumps, and wash eight good Lemons; rub the Rinds of two slightly upon the Sugar, or one Seville-orange, instead of a Lemon, according as it is desired; squeeze the eight Lemons, and put few Bits of cut Rind squeezed, to steep in it some time; then sift it in a Lawn-sieve; less Sugar at first is rather better, as more can be added, by proportioning the Sweetness to good Taste: and may also be done with less Lemons; but then it is apt to taste very watery.

Lait de Pistache, & d'Amande.

Almond and Pistachio Milk.

THEY are both done in the same Manner; scald them, and pound with a little Milk to it, then much with the same Proportion as for the Orgeat; steep either in boiled Milk and Cream, a little Orange-flower Water, and Sugar; sift it several times through a Stamine, or Napkin: it is used either hot or cold.

Pâte d'Orgeat. Orgeat-paste.

POUND the Almonds as directed for Orgeat, with a little Orange-flower Water; and when it is very fine, work it with as much Weight of pounded Sugar; it will keep a long while; and by this Means you may have Orgeat ready much sooner, by dissolving about an Ounce of this Paste, in the Proportion of a Half-pint of Water: and sift it for Use.

DES FROMAGES A LA CRÊME.

OF FRESH CREAM-CHEESE.

Fromage à la Crême Bourgeoise.

A plain Family-way.

WARM three Half-pints of Cream, with one Half-pint of Milk, or according to the same Proportion; and put a little Rennet to it; keep it covered in a warm Place, till it is curdled; have a proper Mould with Holes, either of China or any other; put the Curds in it, to drain about an Hour or less; serve with a good plain Cream, and pounded Sugar over it.

A la Crême fouettée, with whipt Cream; put a good Pinch of Gum-dragon Powder in a Quart of Cream; whip it till it is quite thick, with fine rasped Lemon-peel; pour it in a Cloth-strainer, or a Piece of Muslin; drain it so in a Basket, and serve with pounded Sugar strewed over it.

Fromage à la Crême de Marmelade.

BOIL a Pint of Cream; and mix few Spoonfuls of any Sorts of Marmalade, and a little dried, preserved Lemon, chopped very fine; when it is but just Milk-warm, put some Rennet to turn it, and serve as the first.

Aux Oeufs, with Eggs; boil three Parts Cream and one of Milk, a Spoonful of Orange-flower Water, a Bit of dried Lemon-peel, a Quarter of a Pound of Sugar to a Quart; let it boil, to reduce to three Parts; then take it off the Fire; and add four Yolks of Eggs beat up; make a Liason over the Fire without boiling; sift it in a Sieve; finish it with Rennet as the last; serve either with or without Cream.

A la Salbotiere; it is the Name of Icing-pots. Ice some good Cream in the Salbotiere, with rasped Lemon, and stir it at first with a Whisk, until it is quite thick; and serve in a Compotier with Sugar over it: you may also ice it quite hard, and then cut it in Pieces to serve; then it is called *en Filets*.

DES CRESMES D'OFFICE.

Of Creams as Part of Confectionary.

Crême fouettée. Whipt Cream.

THIS has already been mentioned; the only Difference is, that the Cream with Orange-flower Water, rasped Lemon-peel, with a proper Quantity of Sugar, is drained in a fine Cloth, and served in the Compotier instead of Cups or Glasses; you may either put one or two Whites of Eggs to make it frought better, or Gum-dragon Powder; drain it well, and raise it as high as you can in the Compotier; and stick Bits of Lemon-peel in it, as is done sometimes with Almonds in *Blanc-mangé*.

Crême au Blanc d'Oeufs.

With Whites of Eggs.

BOIL a Pint of Cream with a little Sugar and Orange-flower Water; when it is taken off the Fire, put three Whites of Eggs beat up; stir it on a slow Fire some Time to thicken it without boiling; serve in a Compotier. All Sorts of Cream are made much after the same Manner, and have all been observed already; it is the Quality of the different Mixtures that gives the Names.

DES RATAFIATS, OF SWEET DRAMS OR CORDIALS.

Ratafiat de Noyaux. Of Kernels.

POUND about a Quarter of a Pound of Apricock-kernels without being scalded or peeled, a small Handful of Coriander-seed, about half an Ounce of Cinnamon; put this in a proper Vessel, and pour about half a Gallon of Brandy upon it with a Pound and a half of clarified Sugar, or more according to the same Proportion; stop the Vessel very well; let it infuse about a Month in the Sun, or a warm Place; then strain it through a Sieve, and after through a Funnel, in which put some Cotton that it may filtrate clear; or strain it two or three Times over in this Manner; the more the better, and fresh Cotton every Time.

Ratafiat de Citron. Of Lemon-peel.

RASP the outward yellow Rind of seven or eight Lemons, or peel it off very thin not to come to the white; infuse this in three Quarts of Brandy for about three Weeks; then add three Quarters of a Pound of clarified Sugar to each Quart of Brandy; let it infuse about a Fortnight longer; then strain as directed in the first; this is much better for being kept long: the Vessel in which the Infusion is done, ought to be kept in a moderate Heat, while infusing.

Ratafiat de Genièvre. Of Juniper-berries.

THE Proportion for a Gallon, is to infuse about a Pint of fresh Juniper-berries, or about half a Pound, which is much the same, two Ounces of dried preserved Orange-flowers, three Pound of Sugar clarified; let it infuse about a Month or six Weeks in a moderate Heat, and filtrate as the former; this is better the second Year than the first, and may be kept Numbers of Years, in which it still improves.

Ratifiat de Muscat, &c.

Of Muscadine-grapes and others.

USE it when ripe; bruise it to strain the Juice; and you may mix it with a moderate Quantity of pounded Kernels as the first, a little Coriander and Cinnamon upon, three Pints of Grape-juice, and as much Brandy; put a Pound of clarified Sugar; ten or twelve Days will do to infuse it without Kernels or Seeds, otherwise it requires a longer Time; finish this as usual. *De Coigns*, of Quinces; use them when thoroughly ripe and mellow; free from Blemishes; rasp the Rind off, and keep the Fruits together a Day or two in an earthen Pan; then squeeze the Juice out; strain it through a Cloth; boil it a Moment with half a Pound of Sugar to each Half-pint of Juice; then taking it off the Fire, add as many Pints of Brandy, the Rind of a middling Lemon peeled very thin, and a little Cinnamon; let it infuse about a Month; then sift as usual.

Ratafiat d'Anis. Of Aniseeds and Apricocks.

BOIL half a Pound of Aniseeds, about a Quarter of an Hour, in a Pint of Water; let it cool together, and pour it in the Vessel, with four Quarts of Brandy, or a less Proportion of the whole, three Pounds of clarified Sugar; let it infuse about three Weeks, and strain it as usual. *D'Abricots*, of Apricocks; use them while thoroughly ripe; peel and cut them in Pieces to boil in white Wine, about a Pint to four Dozen; sift in a Sieve like a Marmalade; mix it with as much Brandy; put it in a proper Vessel with the Kernels bruised, a Quarter of a Pound of Sugar to each Pint of Liquor, infuse about three Weeks, and filtrate as the first.

Ratafiat de Noix: Of Walnuts.

THIS is mostly made with fresh ripe Walnuts; when properly peeled and cleaned, split about two dozen of Nuts with the Shells for the Proportion of three Quarts of Brandy; infuse about a Month in a cool Place, stirring the Vessel now and then; then strain the Brandy off, and put it in the Vessel again, with a little Cinnamon, Coriander, two or three Cloves, two Pounds of clarified Sugar; infuse this as long again; then strain it as usual; it is the better for being long kept.

Ratafiat de Fleur d'Orange.

CLARIFY the Proportion of two Pounds of Sugar to one Pound of Orange-flowers, which you simmer a few Minutes in the Sugar, the Pan covered; take it off the Fire to put two Quarts of Brandy; let it rest six or eight Hours, and strain it; you may then preserve the Flowers dried for any other Use; otherwise infuse the Flowers in a less Quantity in the Brandy, and strain them through a Cloth pretty hard to filtrate with the Liquor: this is also made with mixing a Pint of Orange-flower Water with a Quart of Brandy, three Quarters of a Pound of Sugar, Coriander and Cinnamon infused some Time.

Ratafiat de Cerises: Of Cherries, &c.

UPON the Proportion of three Pounds of ripe Cherries, put a Pound of Rasberries, which you bruise together, and sift through a Sieve the next Day, to mix with as much Brandy, and a Pound of Sugar for each Quart of Liquor; you may also put the Stones and Kernels pounded in the Vessel to infuse in a warm Place about six Weeks; then strain it as usual. That of Mulberries, Currants, &c. is made after the same Manner.

Du Caffé. Of Coffee.

THE best is that which comes from Turkey, and is known by its superior good Flavour to others; it is light, and the Beans of a middling Bigness, the Colour tending much to grey, and ought to be roasted fresh for Use: the French mostly roast it in flat earthen Pans, stirring continually till it is of a fine brown and high Flavour; then smothered in Paper or a Linen Cloth; and what is roasted in particular ought to be kept in a warm Place; boil the Water first, and according to the Quantity of Cups wanted, put for each a Table-spoonful of grounded Coffee or more; and as it rises in boiling, pour a little Water upon it; many People do not clear it off to serve, and by that means it preserves its Flavour better; and to make it clear directly, have a pair of red-hot Tongs, and burn a Bit of Sugar in the Pot that will clear and settle it directly: if you would have it with Cream or Milk, you must make it much stronger than with Water, and should be strained through a Cloth; Coffee is also made by putting it in the Pot without Water, and on the Fire a Moment till it throws a great Smoke; then the Water poured upon it, and boiled a Moment. *Caffé au Lait*, viz. with Milk, is very much *à la mode* in France.

DU CHOCOLAT.

OF CHOCOLATE.

SIMMER the Chocolate on a slow Fire about the Proportion of two Ounces to each Cup; stir it about a good deal with a Chocolate-mill; when it is properly dissolved and thickened, add a Yolk of Eggs beat up to the Proportion of four Cups, or the Whites equally beat up, and the first Frought thrown away; mix it first with a little of the Chocolate to add it to the whole, and mill it very

very well to incorporate it together; this will make it of a proper Consistence, and frought better; it is better to be made the Day before, or Days; if you keep it ready-made any Time, boil it a Moment every other Day; sweeten it according to Taste.

N.B. The French Author says, Dissolve and boil one *Tablette*, viz. a Cake or Lozenge, to each Cup. It is to be observed, that their Chocolate is made into small Cakes, which contain about twelve to a Pound, and is sweetened in the making, which is commonly called Dutch Chocolate in England.

DES OUVRAGES DES DIVERSES FAÇONS.

OF VARIOUS SORTS OF WORKS.

Des Amandes vertes. Of green Almonds.

TAKE green Almonds preserved in Brandy; being drained, dip them one after another in Sugar prepared *au Cassé*, twelfth Degree; and roll them in white *Nompareils*, or of any other Colour, or several Colours mixed together; and dry them in the Stove, or in a soft Oven: they are also done after this Manner; cut them in two or four Pieces, and put them on a Baking-plate rubbed over with Oil, and pour some hot Sugar caramelled over, and turn them to do the same over again; keep in a very dry Place.

Des Fraises. Of Strawberries.

LEAVE a Bit of the Tails, and dip them in Whites of Eggs beat up; then roll them in Sugar-powder; lay them separately on Paper; and dry in a moderate Heat. This is the Manner in which all kinds of *Dragées*, Sugar-fruits, are made either white or of different Colours; also all Sorts of Almonds and Seeds, and may be made as large as you please by repeating the same as they dry.

Des Fraises au Caramel. The same another Way.

DIp them in caramelled Sugar, and lay them upon drying Plates, rubbed over with a little Oil, to dry; or dip them in Sugar prepared *au Cassé*, and roll them directly in Nompareils, either of one single Colour or several intermixed; and follow the same Rule for all those kinds of Fruits, as Grapes, Mulberries, Cherries, Kernels, Filberds, and small Nuts and Seeds, &c.

Des Marons. Of Chesnuts, &c.

ROAST them slowly not to colour them too much; husk them very clean; and follow the former Method, either with white Glaze or brown, which is the Caramel, either whole or cut to what Shape you please. *Orange douce*, sweet Oranges; are done, being cut in Quarters, and dipt in white Glaze or Caramel; stick a Bit of Skewer to each Bit of Orange, and thrust them in a Hurdle to keep the Fruits from touching any thing. Lemons or Seville Oranges may be done the same; observe that either must be peeled. Pears, Apples, and Plums are also done after this Manner; Hops or any kinds of Fruits, Flowers, or Leaves.

Des Diablotens.

From Diable, small or young Devils.

THIS is made with Chocolate pounded, and made malleable with some good Oil into a hard Paste; roll Bits of it in the Hand in the Form of Nuts, Olives, Pistachio, or any others, either round or flat; stick Bits of sugared Cinnamon here and there, and strew them with Nompareils of different Colours; you may also put a Kernel in each of the different kinds of Fruits proposed to imitate; dry these in the same Manner as all sugared Fruits.

Des Cerise en Surtout. Coated Cherries.

USE such as are preserved liquid; of four or six Cherries, let them be done with a Tail; drain and split them properly to stone them and apply upon the one with the Tail of the fleshly Side; round them properly in the Form of a good large Cherry; roll them in fine Sugar-powder, and dry in the Sieve as usual.

F I N I S.